Handbook of Research on Transforming Government, Nonprofits, and Healthcare in a Post-Pandemic Era

Joanne E. Howard
Illinois Institute of Technology, USA

IGI Global
PUBLISHER of TIMELY KNOWLEDGE

A volume in the Advances in Public Policy and Administration (APPA) Book Series

Published in the United States of America by
IGI Global
Information Science Reference (an imprint of IGI Global)
701 E. Chocolate Avenue
Hershey PA, USA 17033
Tel: 717-533-8845
Fax: 717-533-8661
E-mail: cust@igi-global.com
Web site: http://www.igi-global.com

Library of Congress Cataloging-in-Publication Data

Names: Howard, Joanne E., 1954- editor.
Title: Handbook of research on transforming government, nonprofits, and healthcare in a post-pandemic era / Joanne Howard, editor.
Description: Hershey PA : Information Science Reference, [2023] | Includes bibliographical references and index. | Summary: "This book researches how government and the nonprofit sector (including healthcare, education, and social service organizations) can utilize best practices, greater collaboration, and joint venturing to survive post-pandemic"-- Provided by publisher.
Identifiers: LCCN 2022013975 (print) | LCCN 2022013976 (ebook) | ISBN 9781668423141 (hardcover) | ISBN 9781668423165 (ebook)
Subjects: LCSH: Public administration--United States. | Nonprofit organizations--United States--Management. | Health services administration--United States. | School management and organization--United States. | COVID-19 Pandemic, 2020---Social aspects--United States.
Classification: LCC JK421 .T84 2022 (print) | LCC JK421 (ebook) | DDC 351.73--dc23/eng/20220511
LC record available at https://lccn.loc.gov/2022013975
LC ebook record available at https://lccn.loc.gov/2022013976

This book is published in the IGI Global book series Advances in Public Policy and Administration (APPA) (ISSN: 2475-6644; eISSN: 2475-6652)

British Cataloguing in Publication Data
A Cataloguing in Publication record for this book is available from the British Library.

All work contributed to this book is new, previously-unpublished material. The views expressed in this book are those of the authors, but not necessarily of the publisher.

For electronic access to this publication, please contact: eresources@igi-global.com.

Advances in Public Policy and Administration (APPA) Book Series

ISSN:2475-6644
EISSN:2475-6652

Mission

Proper management of the public sphere is necessary in order to maintain order in modern society. Research developments in the field of public policy and administration can assist in uncovering the latest tools, practices, and methodologies for governing societies around the world.

The **Advances in Public Policy and Administration (APPA) Book Series** aims to publish scholarly publications focused on topics pertaining to the governance of the public domain. APPA's focus on timely topics relating to government, public funding, politics, public safety, policy, and law enforcement is particularly relevant to academicians, government officials, and upper-level students seeking the most up-to-date research in their field.

Coverage

- Government
- Law Enforcement
- Political Economy
- Politics
- Public Administration
- Public Funding
- Public Policy
- Resource Allocation
- Urban Planning

IGI Global is currently accepting manuscripts for publication within this series. To submit a proposal for a volume in this series, please contact our Acquisition Editors at Acquisitions@igi-global.com or visit: http://www.igi-global.com/publish/.

The Advances in Public Policy and Administration (APPA) Book Series (ISSN 2475-6644) is published by IGI Global, 701 E. Chocolate Avenue, Hershey, PA 17033-1240, USA, www.igi-global.com. This series is composed of titles available for purchase individually; each title is edited to be contextually exclusive from any other title within the series. For pricing and ordering information please visit http://www.igi-global.com/book-series/advances-public-policy-administration/97862. Postmaster: Send all address changes to above address.

Titles in this Series

For a list of additional titles in this series, please visit: http://www.igi-global.com/book-series/advances-public-policy-administration/97862

Maintaining International Relations Through Digital Public Diplomacy Policies and Discourses
Türker Elitaş (Hatay Mustafa Kemal University, Turkey)
Information Science Reference • © 2023 • 270pp • H/C (ISBN: 9781668458228) • US $240.00

Minding the Gap Between Restorative Justice, Therapeutic Jurisprudence, and Global Indigenous Wisdom
Marta Vides Saade (Ramapo College of New Jersey, USA) and Debarati Halder (Parul Institute of Law, Parul University, India)
Information Science Reference • © 2023 • 260pp • H/C (ISBN: 9781668441121) • US $215.00

Societal Transformations and Resilience in Times of Crisis
Ghazala Shoukat (University of Sindh, Jamshoro, Pakistan) and Muhammad Nawaz Tunio (Mohammad Ali Jinnah University, Karachi, Pakistan)
Information Science Reference • © 2023 • 252pp • H/C (ISBN: 9781668453261) • US $215.00

African Policy Innovation and the Political Economy of Public-Private Policy Partnerships
Fred Olayele (Sprott School of Business, Carleton University, Canada)
Information Science Reference • © 2022 • 297pp • H/C (ISBN: 9781799873839) • US $215.00

Interdisciplinary Approaches to the Future of Africa and Policy Development
Icarbord Tshabangu (Leeds Trinity University, UK)
Information Science Reference • © 2022 • 375pp • H/C (ISBN: 9781799887713) • US $215.00

Direct Democracy Practices at the Local Level
Christophe Emmanuel Premat (Stockholm University, Sweden)
Information Science Reference • © 2022 • 325pp • H/C (ISBN: 9781799873044) • US $215.00

Handbook of Research on Interdisciplinary Studies on Healthcare, Culture, and the Environment
Mika Markus Merviö (Kibi International University, Japan)
Information Science Reference • © 2022 • 365pp • H/C (ISBN: 9781799889960) • US $270.00

Challenges and Barriers to the European Union Expansion to the Balkan Region
Bruno Ferreira Costa (University of Beira Interior, Portugal)
Information Science Reference • © 2022 • 372pp • H/C (ISBN: 9781799890553) • US $215.00

IGI Global
PUBLISHER of TIMELY KNOWLEDGE

701 East Chocolate Avenue, Hershey, PA 17033, USA
Tel: 717-533-8845 x100 • Fax: 717-533-8661
E-Mail: cust@igi-global.com • www.igi-global.com

Editorial Advisory Board

List of Contributors

Table of Contents

Detailed Table of Contents

used is the reflective analytical based on the literature review and empirical study. It is concluded that these institutional transformations of participatory governance have been sourced and evolved into a governance structure to govern the behaviors of the communities, organizations, leaderships, and members.

This chapter addresses public administration in the context of the government as an employer. In doing so, the relationship between a public employer and its employees is at issue. To understand public sector labor relations requires a basic understanding of legal principles that govern a public employer's rights and obligations to its employees. While this chapter does not, and cannot, address every aspect of labor management relations in the public sector, it provides an overview of the most important aspects of this relationship and how government can successfully function as an employer.

Anchor organizations are typically, but not exclusively, not-for-profit organizations that are based in a city or town and are unlikely to move because their mission is intrinsically bound up in that area. The author has worked for non-profit-organizations embedded in residential communities. The communities may benefit from their relationship with the non-profit. Some non-profits and communities have a beneficial relationship. The author will review a nonprofit that has aligned its core functions to improve the socioeconomic conditions of the community where it is based. The analysis will be with Centers for New Horizons, a 52-year-old nonprofit located in the Bronzeville section of Chicago.

The National Association of Health Services Executives and Deloitte Consulting administered a survey to assess the status of diversity, equity, and inclusion in March 2021 following social unrest in the United States. One-hundred and five NAHSE members responded to the topics on personal experience working in healthcare, organizational priorities and strategies in DEI, and opportunities in career advancement. A follow-up webinar in February 2022 with 211 participants explored compliance, accountability, and sustainability of diversity, equity, and inclusion initiatives. Sixty-seven percent stated there was no measurement in determining achievement of DEI goals. One-third of respondents stated there was no accountability if DEI goals were not achieved. The good news was that 53% of respondents thought the DEI initiatives developed at their organization would be sustained.

In Summer 2020, prior to the U.S. November 2020 elections, the "NAHSE Political Leadership in the United States" survey was administered to 2,000 members with a 12.6% response rate to assess member views on the Presidential candidates. The purpose of the survey was to assess healthcare concerns of the membership, which would help frame the organization's public policy agenda. Of the respondents, 98% stated they would definitely vote with 80% very confident or confident that their votes would be counted. Approximately 65% of respondents plan to vote in person on the day of the election or through early voting opportunities, and 35% intend to vote via mail or absentee ballot, with 1% stating they do not plan to vote. The top five issues the membership recommended to be addressed by the new President of the United States are (1) COVID-19, (2) criminal justice/police brutality, (3) race relations/police brutality, (4) jobs/economic insecurity, and (5) economy.

The National Association of Health Services Executives issued a national survey to determine how its membership was responding to COVID-19 at its initial outbreak. Of the 201 respondents, 84% stated they were employed full-time; 4% were students; 4% were retired; and 4% were consultants, entrepreneurs, or working outside of the healthcare industry. More than half (53.5%) were employed by a hospital or hospital system, 12% worked at a university or academic institution, 9% were employed by consulting firms, with the remaining 14% employed in a variety of settings. Fifty-nine percent of respondents indicated they were always or usually working remotely, 13% worked remotely sometimes, and approximately 28% indicated that they rarely worked remotely. The survey results revealed COVID-19 had changed the way

current intervention strategies and frameworks and offers recommendations for how these systems may be improved to better support nurses. Numerous instruments have been developed in an attempt to study compassion fatigue. One of the most widely used of these instruments is the professional quality of life (ProQOL) scale. Using the ProQOL scale as a foundation, the author conducted an anonymous survey of nurses (n = 91) employed at a major university-affiliated hospital in Chicago. The author also conducted two longer individual interviews with nurses who are employed at this hospital. The pandemic has profoundly harmed nurses and triggered a cascading stream of consequences. The pandemic has increased the prevalence of both compassion fatigue and moral injury. Nurses are chronically overworked and lack critical resources and support from hospital management.

Section 3
Community and Education

Chapter 15
Perspectives on Building Racial Equity in Science, Technology, Engineering, Math, and Health Science Education and Workforce Systems 274
Rukiya Curvey Johnson, Rush University Medical Center, USA
Natalia Gallegos, Rush University Medical Center, USA
Angela Freeman, Rush University Medical Center, USA

Persistent and deeply entrenched systemic racism too often contributes to the lack of Black and Latinx people from low-income communities ascending and succeeding at the highest levels of STEM and healthcare careers. The authors examine the relationships between equity-centered innovations in K-12 STEM education, persistence, and attainment. The authors identify community-specific constructs with potential to engage partners and increase collective capacity for more Black and Latinx youth. They focus on how to structure social-emotional health into STEM and health science learning models, occupational identity development, and specific work-based learning strategies for students. Data and infrastructure are considered, and approaches to program design are discussed from a methodological point of view. This analysis considers these elements through its case study of the rush education and career hub (REACH), a pipeline and workforce intermediary. REACH is distinct for its position within Rush University Medical Center, an anchor institution on Chicago's west side.

Chapter 16
Motherhood: Parent-Child Separation 292
Sandy Orozco, Illinois Institute of Technology, USA

The incarceration of women and the impact on children, families, caregivers, and the prisoner in terms of motherhood and parenting has become an increasingly prominent area of interest within the criminal justice system. The number of women in state and federal prisons has dramatically increased; however, gender-responsive policies and practices that address incarcerated women's needs and circumstances have been limited. These findings give rise to concern regarding the number of women in jail or prison who are mothers of minor children. This paper investigates the differences between inmate mothers' and fathers' reported incarceration rates and examines the associations between early mother-child separation behaviors and children's outcomes. The impact of COVID-19 will also be included to address the ongoing harms to the lives of female prisoners. Based on these findings and other studies, prisons and jails need to develop a comprehensive strategy to fully address the needs of incarcerated mothers and reduce the harmful impact of incarceration on their children.

The Education Trust singled out New Jersey as a state that has made real progress in terms of funding. In 1997, the state had a funding gap of $787 per student in cost-adjusted dollars. By 2002, the gap had been erased, and the state had a $566 positive difference for low-income students. Starting in 1998, spurred partly by the state's long running Abbott v. Burke school funding lawsuit, the state implemented a series of new funding programs designed to help low-income students. This chapter details the progress.

This chapter provides a comparative analysis of the Dutch versus American primary public education systems within the framework of Donald Moore's Five Essential Supports. In addition, it analyzes and explores the importance of professional capacity/quality and its connection to standardized test scores on the TIMSS, PIRLS, and PISA. It starts with an overview of the state of the American public education system and moves into a comparative analysis in two separate parts: (1) within the macro, meso, and micro levels and (2) within the Five Essential Supports. Special focus is given to the professional capacity/quality of pre-service teacher training programs to better understand the interconnectedness of this support within the framework and its effects on test outcomes. By analyzing test score data, the authors explore if and how improved practicum teacher-training may improve standardized test scores and explore ways in which policy can change to improve teacher-training at the university level.

The primary purpose of this qualitative review was to examine the benefits of the Sigma Beta Club mentoring program on the educational experiences of African American male participants and to explore the perceptions and challenges mentors incurred while working with young men of color in the Sigma Beta Club mentoring program. The secondary purpose was to provide understanding regarding the utilization of SCT by the Sigma Beta Club mentoring program. The effects of systemic racism and discrimination have resulted in African American young men developing a distrust for lawmakers and their agents. A reconnection and an establishment of trust needs to take place.

Black, racialized minorities, and Indigenous leaders (BrmI) in higher education are part of an elite group of educators. Less than 5% of full professors are Black and Hispanic, and it is typically from this pool that academic leaders (e.g., Provost, Dean) are selected. This research aims to understand one potential reason for lack of ascension into positions of power for academic leaders of color: the cost of that

Preface

The opportunity to write this book came by invitation from IGI Global as I had made contributions to other IGI publications. Several current and former students had approached me about their need to publish prior to making application to doctoral programs. To assist them, the idea of the book was hatched. The plan for the book came as Covid-19 began to be a constant in many of our lives around the globe hence the opportunity to include a United States and international perspective of how government, education, healthcare, and various community groups would be impacted. Despite the pandemic, we persevered.

In addition to my current and former students, I solicited the views of several of my colleagues in the healthcare, education, and community space to develop an outline for the book. IGI graciously solicited for scholars from the international community which provided contributions that would appeal to a wider public.

It is a pleasure to have the opportunity to sustain the relevance and impact of IGI Publications. The chapters present the most current research, theory, and practice in the fields of government, healthcare, education, and community organizations. Throughout the chapters, we focused our attention on the challenges that confront all government and nonprofit leaders regarding accountability, transparency, and the increased pressure to demonstrate outcome and results during a time of an international health crisis.

This book arrives at an interesting time in the development of the nonprofit sector, government, healthcare, and for enhancing community. Our book goes to press when the world is still recovering from Covid-19, seeing it morph into another strand, and now, dealing with Monkeypox. The world continues to deal with the economic fallout from the pandemic. The challenges and threats that have convulsed many governments and organizations, still offer opportunities and hope.

The intended audience for this volume includes members of the academic and social services communities. For practitioners and scholars interested in management practices, relevant to and applicable throughout government and any nonprofit organization. We trust that the book is of value to all who practice nonprofit leadership or management, as well as those who aspire to do so.

The volume is organized into three parts. The chapters in Part I examine government in all its multiplicities: finance, public safety, air traffic, labor relations, and government transformation. Part II reviews healthcare through the lens of management, diversity/equity and inclusion, and the burnout from the pandemic. Part III reviews the cost of labor and the communities labor serves through the lens of community and education.

Finally, in the Conclusion, I discuss the ways that each of the sectors may develop and change by offering a few observations as a consultant to the three sections. I share thoughts about the various ways that nonprofit leaders and managers can address the myriad conflicting and complicating forces that continue to batter these sectors.

Government (Chapters 1–8)

The Deloitte "Insights" from March 24, 2022 (deloitte.com) reports on the most transformative trends in government today, grouped under three themes:

1. Building resilience: Focus on long-term resiliency to future shocks
2. Connected for greater value: Overhaul and integrate structures, systems, and data-sharing to drive greater impact
3. Government for all people: Make programs and services truly equitable and inclusive.

The first two chapters by Calia and Wang focus on lessons learned regarding fiscal policy. They both indicate how government funding and policy have changed since the pandemic. Mack looks at policing and how policing occurs. Dominguez and White examine transportation systems and infrastructure, and how rail and air transportation systems could be enhanced to better serve the population. Vargas-Hernandez looks holistically at reforming organizations, while Hensel and Howard both look at organizations through the lens of public servants and their impacts on communities. All public sector organizations look decidedly different post-pandemic.

Healthcare (Chapters 9–14)

This section looks at healthcare through the prism of COVID and its impact on a professional organization's members who are employed in the healthcare sector through three survey instruments addressing the member perspectives on diversity, equity, and inclusion, COVID, and the U.S. presidential election of 2020.

From the surveys, the section moves to a Chicago-based academic medical center to discuss how it implemented its diversity leadership through programming in student community service, disability leadership, business diversity, women's leadership, and LGBTQ programming. The section moves to a discussion of the Portuguese perspective on burnout due to COVID and concludes with a chapter on nursing dissatisfaction in response to COVID at another academic medical center.

What this section attempted to do is bring DEI and COVID to the individual level and frame the challenges that healthcare management, nurses, and allied health employees feel at the ground level.

NAHSE and DEI

The National Association of Health Services Executives and Deloitte Consulting administered a survey to assess the status of diversity, equity, and inclusion in March 2021 following social unrest in the United States. One-hundred and five NAHSE members responded to the topics on personal experience working in health care, organizational priorities and strategies in DE&I, and opportunities in career advancement.

Two out of three respondents agreed that their management and leaders encourage them to continue with their professional growth and development. Four in five respondents reported their organization had active DE&I committees or were launching initiatives. Sixty-one percent of these organizations had funding directed toward these initiatives/committees. Two in three respondents felt that all employees have not been fairly treated regardless of differences in background. Three in four respondents did not believe that everyone in their organization has the same general ability to get promoted regardless of gender, race, ethnicity, disability, sexual orientation, socioeconomic backgrounds, or other factors.

A follow-up webinar in February 2022 with 211 participants explored compliance, accountability, and sustainability of diversity, equity, and inclusion initiatives. Sixty-seven percent stated there was no measurement in determining achievement of DEI goals. One-third of respondents stated there was no accountability if DEI goals were not achieved. The good news was that 53% of respondents thought the DEI initiatives developed at their organization would be sustained.

COVID and the Presidential Elections

The year 2020 brought on seismic disruptions in the United States brought on by the murder of unarmed African Americans with the deaths of Ahmaud Arbery, Breonna Taylor, and George Floyd. On top of these deaths was an outpouring of outrage with marches and demands for better interaction between police and communities of color. These street protests occurred during the onset of an international pandemic and U.S. presidential elections.

The National Association of Health Services Executives issued a national survey to determine how its membership was responding to COVID-19 at its initial outbreak. Of the 201 respondents, 84% stated they were employed full-time; 4% were students; 4% were retired; and 4% were consultants, entrepreneurs, or working outside of the health care industry. More than half (53.5%) were employed by a hospital or hospital system; 12% worked at a university or academic institution; 9% were employed by consulting firms; with the remaining 14% employed in a variety of settings. Fifty-nine percent of respondents indicated they were always or usually working remotely; 13% worked remotely sometimes; approximately 28% indicated that they rarely worked remotely. The survey results revealed COVID had changed the way individuals interfaced at their work environment based on the nature of the work conducted and the age of the respondents and if they had school-age children at home.

In 2005 and 2018, the member priorities focused on health disparities related to access, insurance reimbursement, and workforce recruitment and retention. After the COVID-19 pandemic, public health issues related to criminal justice, racism, economic insecurity, and the economy were center stage. The focus went from medical delivery issues around hospitals/facilities to macro-level issues that involved communities and broader existential threats to populations. Since the majority (60%) of the NAHSE membership has been employed in hospital/health systems, the health care priorities have been influenced by the needs of the institution where they were employed. With COVID-19, the social unrest related to the deaths of unarmed Blacks, and the upcoming Presidential elections, the members focus transcended a facility focus to that affecting a broader scope of issues that would indirectly affect a hospital/health system.

The political landscape did change. Joseph R. Biden and Kamala Harris were elected President and Vice-President, respectively, of the United States. Prior to their inauguration on January 6, 2021, former President Trump instigated an insurrection to overturn the election results. Nonetheless, the inauguration went forward on January 20, 2021 and the Biden/Harris Administration identified its priorities as COVID-19, Climate, Racial Equity, Economy, Healthcare, Immigration, and Restoring America's Global Standing (The White House, 2021). The NAHSE members 2021 top 5 priorities mirror the White House's priorities. The medical delivery and public health sectors have long been viewed as two separate systems in the U.S. and perhaps under a new administration, the focus can be on the better integration of these sectors.

Rush University Medical Center and DEI

The diversity and inclusion initiatives at a Chicago academic medical center are reviewed in the context of its activities over 15 years. The team of leaders discuss how the diversity initiatives were introduced and the strengths, weaknesses, opportunities, and threats of pursuing diversity, equity, and inclusion as staff move in and out of the organization. Five employee resource groups and initiatives that serve as the backbone of the DEI initiatives are discussed including Rush Community Service Initiatives Program, Americans with Disabilities, Business Diversity, Women's Leadership, and LGBTQ programming.

Burnout Syndrome in Health Professionals in Portuguese Public Hospitals During the Pandemic Context

The chapter addresses burnout from a Portuguese perspective with the corresponding emotional exhaustion, depersonalization, and decrease in professional fulfillment. The chapter reviews the physical outcomes on the individual including anxiety, depression, and post-traumatic stress brought on by managing patients with COVID. The literature review and figures used to describe the burnout syndrome are excellent.

Underappreciated and Undervalued: Nurse Dissatisfaction and the COVID-19 Pandemic

The chapter focused on the patients' primary care giver – the nurse. The article incorporates survey results of nurses to educate the reader on how nurses are intellectually processing the COVID pandemic and their resulting compassion fatigue. The variability between nursing units and how nurses are reacting to their employer and understanding their frustration. With the use of excellent graphics and appendices, the nursing staff gives voice to employer responsibility; changes to be implemented; what it is like to work as a nurse; and how the pandemic has changed their perspective of nursing.

These chapters were developed in the second year of COVID when the NAHSE survey participants, Rush DEI leadership, Portuguese public hospital staff, and academic medical center nurses were tiring of the pandemic. It will be interesting to address the issues of diversity, equity, and inclusion, presidential elections, nursing, and allied health burnout once there is distance from COVID.

Community and Education (Chapters 15–21)

During this unprecedented time, non-profits, academic institutions and community-based organizations are responding to the COVID-19 pandemic with hope, resiliency, and innovation. To identify and explore the shared concerns of practitioners, researchers, and policy experts in the fields of education and community development, the preceding chapters in this section present the best available knowledge on approaches to effectively enhance education at the global, national, and local levels of society.

This section can be viewed in two distinct ways. First, it is accessible to those new to the intersecting worlds of education, community and public engagement. Achieving a high standard of education necessitates a multi-sectoral approach since it is a complicated and varied process. This approach is crucial to success and overall growth. The development of methods and policies that make ensuring everyone has access to a high-quality education the duty of society as a whole requires the collaboration of many stakeholders, including educational institutions, instructors, professors, researchers and community members. One of the key characteristics of this section is that it does not follow a textbook format where the chapters must be read in the specified order in order to be comprehended. According to your areas of interest, you may really start from any chapter.

The second group of readers will be represented by professionals from the education sector, academia, and government agencies, as well as non-profits, community-based organizations and advocacy groups. We hope that the knowledge and information provided will serve as a wake-up call for the general public, organizations, business leaders, researchers, and practitioners, coming to the realization that education systems must consider how to emerge stronger from crisis, with a renewed sense of accountability among all stakeholders, a better understanding of the need to close the opportunity gap, and a sense of urgency regarding the need to ensure that all have an equal opportunity to receive a quality education.

The Community and Education section comprises seven chapters.

Chapter 15 examines the relationships between equity-centered innovations in K-12 STEM education, persistence, and attainment. The authors identify community-specific constructs with potential to engage partners and increase collective capacity for more Black and Latinx youth. Chapter 16 explores focuses on the specific constraints faced by those affected by parent-child separation. Chapter 17 considers school finance reform via analysis of The Abbott v. Burke Case. Abbott v. Burke litigation launched one of our nation's most ambitious and far-reaching efforts to improve public education for poor children and children of color. Written by an expert in the field of international education, Chapter 18 examines the key themes of this evolving field. Chapter 19 considers social learning theory and social cognitive theory as frameworks benefitting education and social well-being of African American males. The research of Chapter 20 aims to understand one potential reason for lack of ascension into positions of power for academic leaders of color: the cost of that success. Through the lens of stigma and discrimination, the author hypothesize that academic BrmI leaders consider the interpersonal and intrapersonal time-based cost of their career success to be greater than their White counterparts. Finally, Chapter 21, offers a call for educational democracy in ushering a new age of progressive educators.

Acknowledgment

This manuscript was professionally edited and formatted by George Rumsey (MA, English, University of Chicago, and president, Computer Resource Center Inc.). I wish to thank the contributors, faculty and staff at Illinois Institute of Technology, and Roosevelt University for decades of collegial support and friendship.

The students who took my courses were great contributors.

This book is dedicated to Phillip Richard Donaldson. Today, tomorrow, forever.

Section 1
Government

Chapter 1
Countercyclical Fiscal Policy During the COVID-19 Pandemic:
Federal Stimulus Funding for State and Local Governments

Roland Calia
Illinois Institute of Technology, USA

ABSTRACT

The COVID-19 pandemic has posed a monumental economic and fiscal challenge to state and local governments. Their ability to use fiscal policies to address these challenges is limited due to structural and capacity issues. Only the federal government has the resources and capacity to implement meaningful countercyclical fiscal policies to mitigate the severe economic and fiscal disruption in the states caused by the pandemic. This chapter presents data on the amount of direct financial assistance provided to state and local governments through the CARES Act of 2020, Coronavirus Relief Fund, and the American Rescue Plan Act of 2021 and describes how the State of Illinois, Cook County, and the City of Chicago are utilizing those funds.

INTRODUCTION

The COVID-19 pandemic has posed a monumental economic and fiscal challenge to American federal, state and local governments. The impact on revenues has been particularly acute for state and local governments. Their ability to use fiscal policies to address these challenges is quite limited due to structural and capacity issues. Only the federal government has the resources and capacity to implement meaningful countercyclical fiscal policies to mitigate severe economic and fiscal disruption in the states caused by the pandemic.

DOI: 10.4018/978-1-6684-2314-1.ch001

Since the inception of the pandemic, the federal government has embarked on a massive countercyclical fiscal policy program that has provided billions of dollars in funding to individuals, schools, universities, nonprofit organizations and businesses. Much of this funding has been provided directly to state and local governments.

The primary purpose of this chapter is to present data on the amount of direct financial assistance provided to state and local governments through the CARES Act of 2020 Coronavirus Relief Fund and the American Rescue Plan Act of 2021 and to describe how the State of Illinois, Cook County and the City of Chicago are utilizing those funds. To provide a framework for those discussions, this chapter provides a brief review of the monetary and fiscal policies that the federal government uses to stabilize the economy in times of serious disruption and examines the limitations that states face in implementing fiscal policies in times of economic distress.

A Brief Overview of Monetary vs. Fiscal Policy

Governments seek to stabilize the economy, mitigate unemployment, control inflation and improve economic opportunity by means of monetary and fiscal policies.

Monetary policy is conducted by the Federal Reserve Bank of the United States. It involves manipulating the money supply and setting the terms under which credit may be provided (Mikesell, 2018, p. 17).

Monetary policy can be either expansionary or contractionary. As an independent government agency, the Federal Reserve Bank can work quickly to stabilize the economy. It does not have to work through political approvals by the executive and legislative branches.

Expansionary monetary policy is designed to increase the money supply, injecting liquidity into the economy. The Federal Reserve Bank implements monetary policy by reducing interest rates on the premise that the ability to borrow funds at lower rates will spur increased business investment and consumer spending. Another tool is the use of quantitative easing, which involves the Bank purchasing long-term securities in order to increase the money supply and encourage both lending and investment (Investopedia, 2021).

Implementing expansionary monetary policy is made complex by the fact that the Federal Reserve Bank has a dual mandate: to maintain stable prices and to achieve maximum sustainable employment. The Fed has adopted a 2% target for inflation as the goal for price stability (Federal Reserve Bank of Chicago, 2020). The Bank does not have a definitive target for maximum employment; rather it seeks to implement policies that can lead to the lowest unemployment rate that is consistent with its inflation goal (Stone, 2017). The Bank estimated this rate to be 4.1 percent recently (Federal Reserve Bank of Chicago, 2020) (Federal Reserve Bank of Chicago, 2021).

Contractionary monetary policy is designed to slow the rate of growth in the money supply or decrease it in order to combat high rates of inflation. This is achieved by the Federal Reserve Bank increasing interest rates. This type of action can trigger a recession (Investopedia, 2021).

Fiscal Policy

Fiscal Policy involves changing tax burden and/or levels of spending to influence aggregate demand in the economy. It is primarily based on the economic theories of John Maynard Keynes, who argued that these types of policies could stabilize the business cycle in times of economic stress. The federal government as well as state and local governments develop and implement fiscal policy on a regular basis.

When there is an economic downturn, government spending on programs such as infrastructure or healthcare directly helps increase demand in the economy. The increase in government spending functions as a stimulus, compensating for the decrease in private sector spending.

Reducing taxes indirectly influences demand by letting taxpayers keep more of their income, which they in turn can spend in the economy. It also allows businesses to have additional funds to maintain or expand operations.

The impact of fiscal policy can be relatively slow because: (1) it requires government action, such as legislative approval, and (2) once the policy is approved, it takes time for implementation to occur.

There are several potential downsides to fiscal policy solutions that employ increased spending or tax cuts. They can generate large budget deficits which may be difficult to stabilize in the long-term. Rapid increases in public spending can trigger inflation. For example, in late 2021 a combination of events, including the rapid increase in government spending, goods shortages caused by large increases in consumer demand and supply chain issues leading to shortages caused inflation to rise to 6.8% year over year, the highest level since 1982 (Tapper, 2021). Government spending may also crowd out private investment. Finally, once stimulus programs are operational, it may be extremely difficult politically to reduce or rescind them (Investopedia, 2021).

Procyclical Versus Countercyclical Fiscal Policies

Fiscal policy can be either procyclical or countercyclical.

Procyclical fiscal policy is expansionary in good economic times and contractionary in economic downturns. In short, it is directly correlated with changes in business cycles. During an economic expansion, governments may increase spending and cut taxes. This can boost economic performance but also dramatically increase budget deficits. In a recession, a cash-strapped government would take the opposite action, cutting spending and increasing taxes, which could make the impact of the recession worse by reducing government services when residents need them most or harm businesses and individuals by requiring more in taxes when they have less in revenue and income (Alesina, Campante, & Tabellini, 2008, pp. 1-2).

Countercyclical fiscal policy moves in the opposite direction of the business cycle. In boom times, government spending would decrease or be diverted into budgetary reserves, and taxes would be increased in an effort to achieve budgetary balance. In recessionary times, government would pursue stimulus programs that increase spending and cut taxes in order to increase demand, prevent reductions in public services and stabilize employment (Baldacci, Gupta, & Mulas-Granados, 2012, p. 3). The federal response to the COVID 19 pandemic is an example of countercyclical fiscal policy.

During the COVID-19 pandemic, the federal government has embarked on a massive and historic effort to stabilize the economy. Three major pieces of legislations were approved by Congress, providing over $4.8 trillion in assistance to individuals, schools, universities, nonprofit organizations and businesses through a variety of programs.

Countercyclical Fiscal Policies in the States: Structural Impediment and Limited Options

The following discussion outlines the limitation states face in implementing countercyclical fiscal policies and the primary tool they do use, which is spending reserve funds.

The states are limited in what they can do to address a significant fiscal crisis or recession. These limitations include:

- Balanced budget requirements;
- Borrowing limitations; and
- Insufficient revenue capacity to deal with serious economic disruptions.

The federal government, in contrast, does not in theory have to deal with these limits. It is able to respond to economic downturns by using countercyclical fiscal policy tools such as deficit spending using borrowed funds, though in practice the federal government's response is limited by political considerations.

Balanced Budget Requirements

Most state constitutions and/or statutes include balanced budget requirements. However, there is no uniformity regarding the meaning of a "balanced budget" requirement. Some states have very explicit requirements as to what constitutes a balanced budget while others do not, and the state's political culture is important to whether the limits are reinforced. The National Conference of State Legislatures (NCSL) has identified three distinct elements of balanced budget requirements. The exhibit below shows the results of that survey:

1. 44 states require that the governor's proposed budget must be balanced;
2. 41 states require the enacted budget must be balanced; and
3. 38 states require that no deficit can be carried forward from one fiscal year into the next (National Conference of State Legislatures, 2010, pp. 1-2).

The NCSL study counted Illinois' Constitution as requiring both a gubernatorial balanced budget and an enacted balanced budget. However, Illinois is one of only 12 states that does allow a deficit to be carried forward to the next fiscal year.

Borrowing Limitations

Most states have constitutional and/or statutory limitations on the issuance of new debt or debt service. These restrictions may limit the dollar amount of debt that can be issued, cap the issuance of debt to a certain percentage of revenues, limit the use of debt, prohibit the use of debt for operations or detail the method of debt repayment. In some states, voter approval is required for new debt. States may circumvent debt limits by issuing other forms of debt such as revenue or taxable debt or by creating public authorities or other dependent governments authorized to issue debt.

Three states place limits on debt service, fifteen place caps on authorized debt and another 25 limit the issuance of authorized debt and debt service payments. Only seven states have no constitutional or statutory limits on debt issuance (Reuben & Randall, 2017). Illinois is one of the fifteen states with limits on authorized debt.

The bond markets also place limits on how much states can borrow. If a state attempts to borrow in excess of its financial capacity, its debt issuances will likely face costly credit downgrades and it may not be able to identify willing purchasers.

Figure 1. Characteristics of state balanced budget requirments

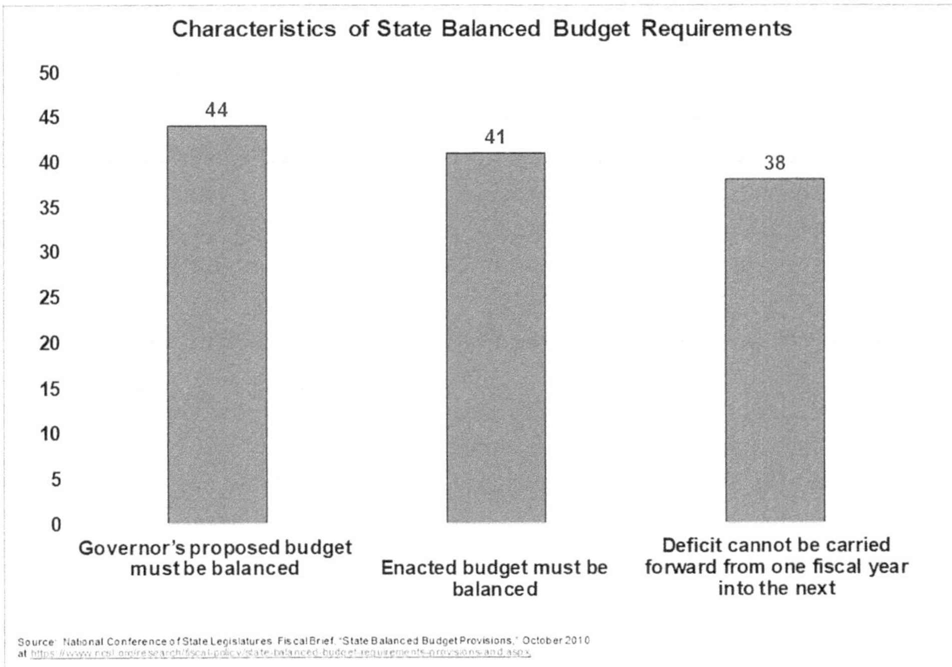

Figure 2. Debt limitations in the US

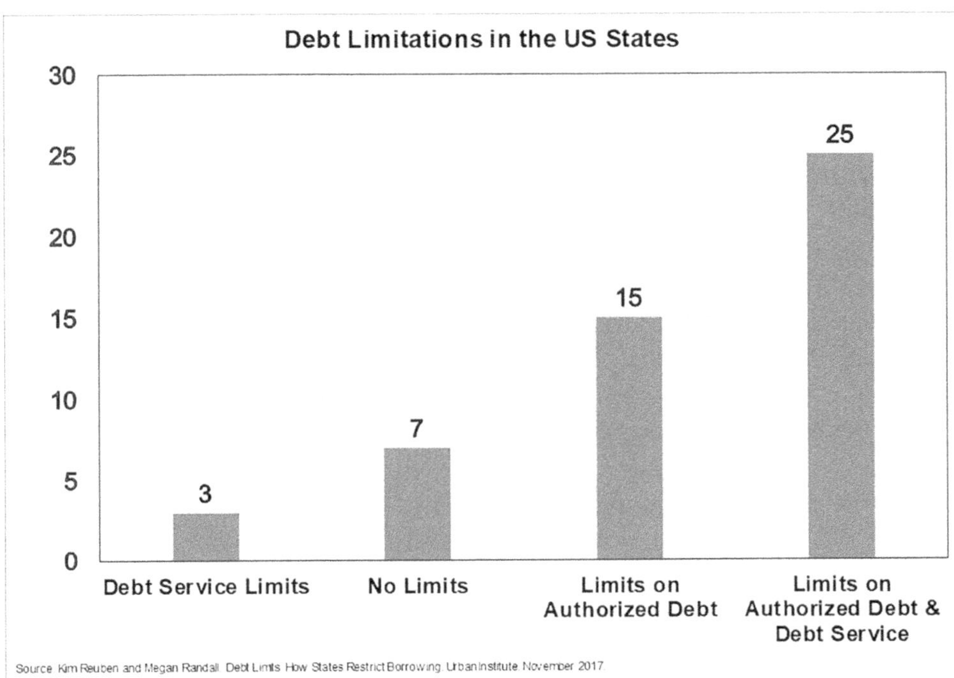

In sum, because of these legal and market limitations, states are not able to borrow funds for operations to the same degree as the federal government. They generally cannot rely on deficit spending to stimulate the economy (Hou & Moynihan, 2008, p. 141).

It is important to note that the practice in some states such as Illinois of creating a bill backlog by pushing off the payment of bills into the next fiscal year is not the same as deficit spending; it is simply a tool to make it appear as if the fiscal year budget is balanced (Civic Federation, 2019). Funds are not being spent, but rather payment is being delayed and can be considered borrowing from vendors. In a recent report from the State Comptroller's Office, the State's bill backlog was estimated at $4.4 billion. While this has declined considerably over the past few years, it remains high (Illinois Comptroller, n.d.).

Insufficient Revenue Capacity to Deal With Major Economic Disruptions

In periods of economic disruption such as recessions or the current coronavirus pandemic, states face severe revenue shocks as tax and fee receipts plummet.

The states' response to revenue shocks is constrained because they are only authorized by statutory or constitutional provisions to utilize a limited number and amount of taxes and fees. Many types of revenue heavily relied upon by states such as income and sales taxes are economically sensitive, which means that they fluctuate in response to upswings and downswings in the economy. In an economic downturn, these types of revenues will fall as individuals reduce consumption and workers lose their jobs. Finally, states are also limited in how much revenue they can raise by tax capacity, which is the ability of residents and businesses to pay taxes. In an economic downturn, that capacity is severely strained.

States may attempt to mitigate revenue shocks with an austerity-based regime of raising taxes and/or cutting spending in an effort to balance the budget. However, these are forms of procyclical action at a time when countercyclical action is likely needed. In addition, deep cuts in spending can have an extremely negative impact on delivering core public services in a time of the greatest need (Hou & Moynihan, 2008, p. 141).

It is important to note that the states in the aggregate ended calendar year 2020 with only $1.7 billion less than they reported in 2019, if federal stimulus funding is not counted, according to a report by the Tax Foundation. This is a 0.2% year over year decline. For most states overall revenues increased in 2020 because of revenue stability or increases as well as federal assistance. The revenue growth continued in some states in 2021; the State of Illinois released a FY2022 General Funds revenue forecast on May 12, 2021 that updated its numbers to increase General Funds revenue projections by $792 million over its original March 2021 projection. Despite this, a number of state and local governments, especially those with economies dependent on tourism or the energy sector, have struggled with fiscal difficulties during the pandemic (Walczak, 2021).

Spending Reserves Is the Major Countercyclical Fiscal Policy Tool States Use

States tend to rely on fiscal reserves, often called "Rainy Day" funds, as the primary tool they use to cushion revenue shocks in economic downturns and avoid steep budget cuts or tax and fee increases. Reserves can be structured as General Fund balances or Budget Stabilization funds. General Fund balances are discretionary funds that can be used at any time while Budget Stabilization Funds are reserved for use only in emergencies (Hou & Moynihan, 2008, p. 141). Research suggests that $100 in reserves can reduce unplanned budget cuts by $5 or $6 and it can reduce tax hikes by $12 to $18 (Hou & Moynihan, 2008, p. 141). However, many states have little or no reserve funding.

Fiscal reserves are a useful fiscal tool. However, when an economic downturn is severe, they are woefully inadequate to meet those challenges. The National Association of State Budget Officers reports that in fiscal year 2020, state Rainy Day funds totaled $69.6 billion. This amount was 8.4% of all state expenditures (National Association of State Budget Officers, Fall 2019, p. 67). State rainy day funds dropped overall by approximately $1.3 billion as states drew on these funds to help deal with the effects of the pandemic. However, a combination of federal stimulus funding and better than originally anticipated tax collections allowed most states to avoid using their rainy day funds in fiscal year 2021 and reserves rose to $126.5 billion, the highest amount in two decades (Pew Foundation, 2021).

While individual states may have enough in their reserve to weather a moderate recession, it is clear that no state can effectively deal on its own with impact of the economic and revenue shocks that a major crisis like the coronavirus epidemic.

Illinois does not maintain a functional rainy day fund, even though a law was enacted in 2004 to build such a fund. The law established a goal of maintaining 5% of General Funds revenues in an existing account called the Budget Stabilization Fund (Illinois General Assembly, 2004). The fund was created to help reduce the need for future tax increases or short-term borrowing, maintain high credit ratings and address budgetary shortfalls. However, the fund has never received significant resources, in large part because annual revenue projections have not met the threshold requirement to trigger deposits into the fund (Institute for Illinois' Fiscal Stability, 2019). As part of a stopgap spending plan passed in June 2016 during the State of Illinois' budget impasse, the Fund's entire balance was appropriated to pay for State operations in FY2017 and it was subsequently folded into General Funds.

The CARES Act

The Coronavirus Aid, Relief, and Economic Security (CARES) Act was enacted by the U.S. Congress and signed into law by President Trump on March 27, 2020. The legislation was a $2.0 trillion package of benefits that provided direct assistance to individuals, aid to businesses, tax incentives, an extension of unemployment benefits, aid to health care providers and support for state and local governments (U.S. Congress, 2020).

A key component of the CARES Act was $150 billion in direct support for state, local, territorial, and tribal governments through the Coronavirus Relief Fund. Approximately 93% of that amount, or $139.0 billion was earmarked for state and local governments. The remaining $11 billion was reserved for tribal governments, the District of Columbia and the U.S. territories (Center on Budget and Policy Priorities, 2020). The allocation was based on population, with states guaranteed to receive at least $1.25 billion. CARES Act funding was earmarked to cover new COVID-19 related expenses incurred between March 1 and December 30, 2020 (Civic Federation, 2020).

The following chart shows the distribution of CARES Act funds per state, including original state and local share allocations. Approximately 21%, or $29.1 billion, was allocated to local governments and the remaining 79%, or $109.9 billion, was distributed to state governments.

Figure 3. Estimated Cares Act fundng by amount

ESTIMATED CARES ACT FUNDING BY AMOUNT ($000s)							
	State Share	Local Share	Total		State Share	Local Share	Total
Alabama	$ 1,786,453	$ 114,923	$ 1,901,376	Montana	$ 1,250,000	$ -	$ 1,250,000
Alaska	$ 1,250,000	$ -	$ 1,250,000	Nebraska	$ 1,083,865	$ 166,135	$ 1,250,000
Arizona	$ 1,857,099	$ 965,470	$ 2,822,569	Nevada	$ 836,051	$ 413,949	$ 1,250,000
Arkansas	$ 1,250,000	$ -	$ 1,250,000	New Hampshire	$ 1,250,000	$ -	$ 1,250,000
California	$ 9,526,137	$ 5,796,069	$ 15,322,206	New Jersey	$ 2,393,995	$ 1,050,375	$ 3,444,370
Colorado	$ 1,673,950	$ 559,195	$ 2,233,145	New Mexico	$ 1,067,817	$ 182,183	$ 1,250,000
Connecticut	$ 913,181	$ 469,380	$ 1,382,561	New York	$ 5,219,021	$ 2,324,757	$ 7,543,778
Delaware	$ 927,233	$ 322,767	$ 1,250,000	North Carolina	$ 3,585,606	$ 481,504	$ 4,067,110
Florida	$ 5,856,159	$ 2,472,562	$ 8,328,721	North Dakota	$ 1,250,000	$ -	$ 1,250,000
Georgia	$ 3,503,081	$ 614,185	$ 4,117,266	Ohio	$ 3,757,703	$ 775,142	$ 4,532,845
Hawaii	$ 862,823	$ 387,177	$ 1,250,000	Oklahoma	$ 1,281,597	$ 252,852	$ 1,534,449
Idaho	$ 1,250,000	$ -	$ 1,250,000	Oregon	$ 1,388,745	$ 246,825	$ 1,635,570
Illinois	$ 3,519,156	$ 1,394,772	$ 4,913,928	Pennsylvania	$ 3,935,406	$ 1,029,000	$ 4,964,406
Indiana	$ 2,442,324	$ 168,322	$ 2,610,646	Rhode Island	$ 910,740	$ 339,260	$ 1,250,000
Iowa	$ 1,250,000	$ -	$ 1,250,000	South Carolina	$ 1,905,229	$ 91,359	$ 1,996,588
Kansas	$ 1,034,052	$ 215,948	$ 1,250,000	South Dakota	$ 1,250,000	$ -	$ 1,250,000
Kentucky	$ 1,598,690	$ 133,801	$ 1,732,491	Tennessee	$ 2,363,576	$ 284,668	$ 2,648,244
Louisiana	$ 1,802,727	$ -	$ 1,802,727	Texas	$ 8,038,804	$ 3,205,333	$ 11,244,137
Maine	$ 1,250,000	$ -	$ 1,250,000	Utah	$ 936,475	$ 313,525	$ 1,250,000
Maryland	$ 1,653,367	$ 691,050	$ 2,344,417	Vermont	$ 1,250,000	$ -	$ 1,250,000
Massachusetts	$ 1,655,720	$ 1,017,082	$ 2,672,802	Virginia	$ 3,109,689	$ 200,248	$ 3,309,937
Michigan	$ 3,080,874	$ 791,868	$ 3,872,742	Washington	$ 2,167,209	$ 785,724	$ 2,952,933
Minnesota	$ 1,870,033	$ 316,925	$ 2,186,958	West Virginia	$ 1,250,000	$ -	$ 1,250,000
Mississippi	$ 1,250,000	$ -	$ 1,250,000	Wisconsin	$ 1,997,414	$ 260,432	$ 2,257,846
Missouri	$ 2,083,827	$ 296,169	$ 2,379,996	Wyoming	$ 1,250,000	$ -	$ 1,250,000
GRAND TOTAL					$ 109,875,828	$ 29,130,936	$ 139,006,764

Source: Jared Walczak. State and Local Funding Totals Under the CARES Act. Tax Foundation, April 12, 2020 at https://taxfoundation.org/federal-coronavirus-aid-to-states-under-cares-act/.

The American Rescue Plan Act

The American Rescue Plan Act (ARPA) is a $1.9 trillion package of programs designed to provide relief from the economic and health impacts of the COVID-19 pandemic to individuals, families and governments. It was signed into law by President Biden on March 11, 2021 and is intended to build upon previous COVID-19 relief efforts (U.S. Congress, 2021). According to the U.S. Treasury Department, approximately $350 billion of the ARPA total were designated as State and Local Fiscal Recovery Funds and were designed to compensate state and local governments for revenues lost due to the effects of the pandemic. Each state received a minimum of $1.25 billion and the total amount to be allocated was originally estimated as (U.S. Department of the Treasury, 2021):

- $195 billion for state governments and the District of Columbia;
- $130 billion for local governments ($65 billion for cities and $65 billion for counties);
- $20 billion for tribal governments; and
- $4.5 billion for U.S. territories.

Approximately $26 billion of the funding earmarked for the states and the District of Columbia is being distributed equally while the remainder will be distributed according to unemployment rates. The local government share is being allocated equally between municipalities and counties with funding being provided in 2021 and 2022. The funds are to be spent between March 2021 and December 2024. There are a number of restrictions on the use of the ARPA funds: they may not be used for tax cuts, to fund reserves, to finance general infrastructure projects or to deposit into defined benefit pension funds and they must be used by the end of 2024. The allowable uses of the ARPA funds are replacement for revenues reduced as a result of the COVID 19 pandemic, pay for essential workers and investments in critical infrastructure for water, sewer and broadband projects (Government Finance Officers Association, 2021).

Figure 4. Estimated American Rescue Plan Act funding by amount

ESTIMATED AMERICAN RESCUE PLAN ACT FUNDING BY AMOUNT ($000s)							
	State Share	Local Share	Total		State Share	Local Share	Total
Alabama	$ 2,120,279	$ 1,739,419	$ 3,859,698	Montana	$ 906,418	$ 343,581	$ 1,249,999
Alaska	$ 1,011,788	$ 238,211	$ 1,249,999	Nebraska	$ 1,040,157	$ 662,955	$ 1,703,112
Arizona	$ 4,182,827	$ 2,643,688	$ 6,826,515	Nevada	$ 2,738,837	$ 1,040,963	$ 3,779,800
Arkansas	$ 1,573,121	$ 1,011,246	$ 2,584,367	New Hampshire	$ 994,555	$ 462,300	$ 1,456,855
California	$ 27,017,016	$ 15,897,566	$ 42,914,582	New Jersey	$ 6,244,537	$ 3,595,444	$ 9,839,981
Colorado	$ 3,828,761	$ 1,935,254	$ 5,764,015	New Mexico	$ 1,751,542	$ 704,729	$ 2,456,271
Connecticut	$ 2,812,288	$ 1,556,652	$ 4,368,940	New York	$ 12,744,981	$ 10,714,967	$ 23,459,948
Delaware	$ 924,597	$ 343,690	$ 1,268,287	North Carolina	$ 5,439,309	$ 3,410,739	$ 8,850,048
Florida	$ 8,816,581	$ 7,105,927	$ 15,922,508	North Dakota	$ 1,007,502	$ 242,497	$ 1,249,999
Georgia	$ 4,853,535	$ 3,510,277	$ 8,363,812	Ohio	$ 5,368,386	$ 5,289,397	$ 10,657,783
Hawaii	$ 1,641,602	$ 518,162	$ 2,159,764	Oklahoma	$ 1,870,417	$ 1,322,855	$ 3,193,272
Idaho	$ 1,094,018	$ 578,905	$ 1,672,923	Oregon	$ 2,648,024	$ 1,504,524	$ 4,152,548
Illinois	$ 8,127,679	$ 5,930,002	$ 14,057,681	Pennsylvania	$ 7,291,328	$ 6,158,947	$ 13,450,275
Indiana	$ 3,071,830	$ 2,587,845	$ 5,659,675	Rhode Island	$ 1,131,061	$ 536,834	$ 1,667,895
Iowa	$ 1,480,862	$ 1,173,577	$ 2,654,439	South Carolina	$ 2,499,067	$ 1,626,363	$ 4,125,430
Kansas	$ 1,583,680	$ 993,516	$ 2,577,196	South Dakota	$ 974,478	$ 275,521	$ 1,249,999
Kentucky	$ 2,183,237	$ 1,587,394	$ 3,770,631	Tennessee	$ 3,725,832	$ 2,281,391	$ 6,007,223
Louisiana	$ 3,011,136	$ 1,807,544	$ 4,818,680	Texas	$ 15,814,388	$ 10,439,643	$ 26,254,031
Maine	$ 997,495	$ 501,863	$ 1,499,358	Utah	$ 1,377,866	$ 1,099,163	$ 2,477,029
Maryland	$ 3,717,212	$ 2,322,461	$ 6,039,673	Vermont	$ 1,049,287	$ 200,712	$ 1,249,999
Massachusetts	$ 5,286,067	$ 3,388,355	$ 8,674,422	Virginia	$ 4,293,727	$ 2,909,954	$ 7,203,681
Michigan	$ 6,540,417	$ 4,406,991	$ 10,947,408	Washington	$ 4,427,709	$ 2,692,324	$ 7,120,033
Minnesota	$ 2,833,294	$ 2,132,390	$ 4,965,684	West Virginia	$ 1,355,489	$ 678,783	$ 2,034,272
Mississippi	$ 1,806,373	$ 947,199	$ 2,753,572	Wisconsin	$ 2,533,160	$ 2,322,817	$ 4,855,977
Missouri	$ 2,685,296	$ 2,472,816	$ 5,158,112	Wyoming	$ 1,068,484	$ 181,515	$ 1,249,999
GRAND TOTAL					**$ 193,497,532**	**$ 128,029,868**	**$ 321,527,400**

Source: Jared Walczak. State Aid in American Rescue Plan Act Is 116 Times States' Revenue Losses. Tax Foundation, March 3, 2021 at https://taxfoundation.org/state-and-local-aid-american-rescue-plan/.

Half of the $65 billion provided to cities will be divided between Community Development Block Grant (CDBG) jurisdictions and those that are not CDBG jurisdictions. The $65 billion provided to counties will be distributed on a per capita basis, although CDBG communities will receive a larger share of the funds (Government Finance Officers Association, 2021).

The chart below provides an estimate of the roughly $322 billion that is estimated to ultimately be distributed to state and local governments under the American Rescue Plan Act. Six states with small populations – Alaska, Montana. North Dakota, South Dakota, Vermont and Wyoming - will receive the minimum share of approximately $1.25 billion. California, Texas and New York will receive over $20 billion in funds.

Total COVID Related Stimulus Funding for State and Local Governments

Total federal stimulus funding from both the CARES Act and the American Rescue Plan Act provided to state and local governments to mitigate the economic and financial impact of the COVID-19 pandemic will total approximately $460.5 billion. Of that amount, 65.9%, or $303.4 billion, will provided to the states and the remaining $157.2 billion to local governments.

The State of Illinois

The State of Illinois has received a total of $11.6 billion in direct assistance from the federal government from the CARES Act and the American Rescue Plan Act. In addition to this funding, the State also borrowed $3.2 billion in two tranches from the Federal Reserve Bank's Municipal Liquidity Facility in 2020 to assist the state and larger local governments in dealing with cash flow issues resulting from the negative impacts of the pandemic. The first amount borrowed, $1.2 billion, was repaid in June 2021.

Figure 5. Total federal COVID-19-realted stimulus funding for state and local governments

TOTAL FEDERAL COVID RELATED STIMULUS FUNDING FOR STATE AND LOCAL GOVERNMENTS							
	State Share			Local Share			
State	CARES Act	ARPA	Subtotal	CARES Act	ARPA	Subtotal	Grand Total
Alabama	$ 1,786,453	$ 2,120,279	$ 3,906,732	$ 114,923	$ 1,739,419	$ 1,854,342	$ 5,761,074
Alaska	$ 1,250,000	$ 1,011,788	$ 2,261,788	$ -	$ 238,211	$ 238,211	$ 2,499,999
Arizona	$ 1,857,099	$ 4,182,827	$ 6,039,926	$ 965,470	$ 2,643,688	$ 3,609,158	$ 9,649,084
Arkansas	$ 1,250,000	$ 1,573,121	$ 2,823,121	$ -	$ 1,011,246	$ 1,011,246	$ 3,834,367
California	$ 9,526,137	$ 27,017,016	$ 36,543,153	$ 5,796,069	$ 15,897,566	$ 21,693,635	$ 58,236,788
Colorado	$ 1,673,950	$ 3,828,761	$ 5,502,711	$ 559,195	$ 1,935,254	$ 2,494,449	$ 7,997,160
Connecticut	$ 913,181	$ 2,812,288	$ 3,725,469	$ 469,380	$ 1,556,652	$ 2,026,032	$ 5,751,501
Delaware	$ 927,233	$ 924,597	$ 1,851,830	$ 322,767	$ 343,690	$ 666,457	$ 2,518,287
Florida	$ 5,856,159	$ 8,816,581	$ 14,672,740	$ 2,472,562	$ 7,105,927	$ 9,578,489	$ 24,251,229
Georgia	$ 3,503,081	$ 4,853,535	$ 8,356,616	$ 614,185	$ 3,510,277	$ 4,124,462	$ 12,481,078
Hawaii	$ 862,823	$ 1,641,602	$ 2,504,425	$ 387,177	$ 518,162	$ 905,339	$ 3,409,764
Idaho	$ 1,250,000	$ 1,094,018	$ 2,344,018	$ -	$ 578,905	$ 578,905	$ 2,922,923
Illinois	$ 3,519,156	$ 8,127,679	$ 11,646,835	$ 1,394,772	$ 5,930,002	$ 7,324,774	$ 18,971,609
Indiana	$ 2,442,324	$ 3,071,830	$ 5,514,154	$ 168,322	$ 2,587,845	$ 2,756,167	$ 8,270,321
Iowa	$ 1,250,000	$ 1,480,862	$ 2,730,862	$ -	$ 1,173,577	$ 1,173,577	$ 3,904,439
Kansas	$ 1,034,052	$ 1,583,680	$ 2,617,732	$ 215,948	$ 993,516	$ 1,209,464	$ 3,827,196
Kentucky	$ 1,598,690	$ 2,183,237	$ 3,781,927	$ 133,801	$ 1,587,394	$ 1,721,195	$ 5,503,122
Louisiana	$ 1,802,727	$ 3,011,136	$ 4,813,863	$ -	$ 1,807,544	$ 1,807,544	$ 6,621,407
Maine	$ 1,250,000	$ 997,495	$ 2,247,495	$ -	$ 501,863	$ 501,863	$ 2,749,358
Maryland	$ 1,653,367	$ 3,717,212	$ 5,370,579	$ 691,050	$ 2,322,461	$ 3,013,511	$ 8,384,090
Massachusetts	$ 1,655,720	$ 5,286,067	$ 6,941,787	$ 1,017,082	$ 3,388,355	$ 4,405,437	$ 11,347,224
Michigan	$ 3,080,874	$ 6,540,417	$ 9,621,291	$ 791,868	$ 4,406,991	$ 5,198,859	$ 14,820,150
Minnesota	$ 1,870,033	$ 2,833,294	$ 4,703,327	$ 316,925	$ 2,132,390	$ 2,449,315	$ 7,152,642
Mississippi	$ 1,250,000	$ 1,806,373	$ 3,056,373	$ -	$ 947,199	$ 947,199	$ 4,003,572
Missouri	$ 2,083,827	$ 2,685,296	$ 4,769,123	$ 296,169	$ 2,472,816	$ 2,768,985	$ 7,538,108
Montana	$ 1,250,000	$ 906,418	$ 2,156,418	$ -	$ 343,581	$ 343,581	$ 2,499,999
Nebraska	$ 1,083,865	$ 1,040,157	$ 2,124,022	$ 166,135	$ 662,955	$ 829,090	$ 2,953,112
Nevada	$ 836,051	$ 2,738,837	$ 3,574,888	$ 413,949	$ 1,040,963	$ 1,454,912	$ 5,029,800
New Hampshire	$ 1,250,000	$ 994,555	$ 2,244,555	$ -	$ 462,300	$ 462,300	$ 2,706,855
New Jersey	$ 2,393,995	$ 6,244,537	$ 8,638,532	$ 1,050,375	$ 3,595,444	$ 4,645,819	$ 13,284,351
New Mexico	$ 1,067,817	$ 1,751,542	$ 2,819,359	$ 182,183	$ 704,729	$ 886,912	$ 3,706,271
New York	$ 5,219,021	$ 12,744,981	$ 17,964,002	$ 2,324,757	$ 10,714,967	$ 13,039,724	$ 31,003,726
North Carolina	$ 3,585,606	$ 5,439,309	$ 9,024,915	$ 481,504	$ 3,410,739	$ 3,892,243	$ 12,917,158
North Dakota	$ 1,250,000	$ 1,007,502	$ 2,257,502	$ -	$ 242,497	$ 242,497	$ 2,499,999
Ohio	$ 3,757,703	$ 5,368,386	$ 9,126,089	$ 775,142	$ 5,289,397	$ 6,064,539	$ 15,190,628
Oklahoma	$ 1,281,597	$ 1,870,417	$ 3,152,014	$ 252,852	$ 1,322,855	$ 1,575,707	$ 4,727,721
Oregon	$ 1,388,745	$ 2,648,024	$ 4,036,769	$ 246,825	$ 1,504,524	$ 1,751,349	$ 5,788,118
Pennsylvania	$ 3,935,406	$ 7,291,328	$ 11,226,734	$ 1,029,000	$ 6,158,947	$ 7,187,947	$ 18,414,681
Rhode Island	$ 910,740	$ 1,131,061	$ 2,041,801	$ 339,260	$ 536,834	$ 876,094	$ 2,917,895
South Carolina	$ 1,905,229	$ 2,499,067	$ 4,404,296	$ 91,359	$ 1,626,363	$ 1,717,722	$ 6,122,018
South Dakota	$ 1,250,000	$ 974,478	$ 2,224,478	$ -	$ 275,521	$ 275,521	$ 2,499,999
Tennessee	$ 2,363,576	$ 3,725,832	$ 6,089,408	$ 284,668	$ 2,281,391	$ 2,566,059	$ 8,655,467
Texas	$ 8,038,804	$ 15,814,388	$ 23,853,192	$ 3,205,333	$ 10,439,643	$ 13,644,976	$ 37,498,168
Utah	$ 936,475	$ 1,377,866	$ 2,314,341	$ 313,525	$ 1,099,163	$ 1,412,688	$ 3,727,029
Vermont	$ 1,250,000	$ 1,049,287	$ 2,299,287	$ -	$ 200,712	$ 200,712	$ 2,499,999
Virginia	$ 3,109,689	$ 4,293,727	$ 7,403,416	$ 200,248	$ 2,909,954	$ 3,110,202	$ 10,513,618
Washington	$ 2,167,209	$ 4,427,709	$ 6,594,918	$ 785,724	$ 2,692,324	$ 3,478,048	$ 10,072,966
West Virginia	$ 1,250,000	$ 1,355,489	$ 2,605,489	$ -	$ 678,783	$ 678,783	$ 3,284,272
Wisconsin	$ 1,997,414	$ 2,533,160	$ 4,530,574	$ 260,432	$ 2,322,817	$ 2,583,249	$ 7,113,823
Wyoming	$ 1,250,000	$ 1,068,484	$ 2,318,484	$ -	$ 181,515	$ 181,515	$ 2,499,999
Grand Total	**$ 109,875,828**	**$ 193,497,532**	**$ 303,373,360**	**$ 29,130,936**	**$ 128,029,868**	**$ 157,160,804**	**$ 460,534,164**

Sources: Jared Walczak. State and Local Funding Totals Under the CARES Act. Tax Foundation, April 12, 2020 at https://taxfoundation.org/federal-coronavirus-aid-to-states-under-cares-act/ and Jared Walczak. State Aid in American Rescue Plan Act Is 116 Times States' Revenue Losses. Tax Foundation, March 3, 2021 at https://taxfoundation.org/state-and-local-aid-american-rescue-plan/

Another $690 million will be repaid in the middle of FY2022 and the remainder will be repaid over the next three fiscal years (Illinois General Assembly, 2021).

CARES Act

The State of Illinois received $3.51 billion from the federal government for COVID-19 pandemic relief under the CARES Act. The funds were received in two payments, $2.45 billion on April 21, 2020 and $1.06 billion on April 27, 2020. Illinois local governments received an additional $1.4 billion indirect federal assistance (Illinois Comptroller, 2022). These funds were to be used to cover pandemic related expenses incurred between March 1, 2020 and December 31, 2020. The table below shows the funds were distributed by purpose:

Figure 6. State of Illinois CARES Act funding distribution

State of Illinois CARES Act Funding Distribution ($000s)			
Agency	**Purpose**	**Amount**	**% of Total**
Emergency Management Agency	Operations for Emergency Management Agency & Department of Public Health	$ 1,500,000	40.7%
Healthcare & Family Services	Healthcare Providers	$ 830,000	22.5%
Revenue	Mortgage & Rental Assistance	$ 396,000	10.7%
Commerce & Economic Opportunity	Business Interruption Relief	$ 376,000	10.2%
Commerce & Economic Opportunity	Child Care Grants	$ 260,000	7.1%
Commerce & Economic Opportunity	Local Government	$ 250,000	6.8%
Human Services	Welcoming Centers	$ 32,000	0.9%
Human Services	Public Health Grants	$ 30,000	0.8%
Commerce & Economic Opportunity	Technical Assistance	$ 10,000	0.3%
Total		**$ 3,684,000**	**100.0%**

Note: For several appropriations amounts for federal awards were combined with other programmatic appropriations so that the total amount reported exceeds total CARES Act funding provided to Illinois.
Source: Governor's Office of Management and Budget. November 2021 Report to the Legislative Budget Oversight Commission, p. 6 at https://www2.illinois.gov/sites/budget/Documents/LBOC/LBOC-Report-November-2021-12.8.21.pdf.

- Roughly 40.7%, or $1.5 billion, was used to pay for operations at the Illinois Emergency Management Agency and the Illinois Department of Public Health.
- The next largest amount, $830 million, was earmarked for payments to long term care providers, mental health rehabilitation facilities, ambulance providers and other medical assistance providers.
- Approximately $396 million was set aside for affordable housing that the Department of Revenue provided to the Illinois Housing Development Authority for grants used for rental and mortgage assistance.
- Grants for businesses with operations interrupted by the pandemic were budgeted at $376 million from the Department of Commerce and Economic Opportunity (DCEO).
- DCEO also provided $260 million in grants to reimburse costs incurred by child care and daycare providers due to business interruptions or related issues and $250 million in grants and reimbursements to local governments, including their health departments, for COVID-19 related expenses.
- Smaller amounts totaling $72 million were earmarked for welcoming centers; public health grants for mental, health, substance abuse and counseling services; and technical support for community based nonprofit organizations.

American Rescue Plan Act (ARPA)

The State of Illinois received approximately $8.12 billion in funding from the American Rescue Plan Act. These funds must be used for expenses that are incurred through the end of calendar year 2024. Illinois will also receive $254 million from the Coronavirus Capital Projects fund (Illinois Governor's Office of Management and Budget, 2021).

The FY2022 Illinois State Budget appropriated $2.8 billion in ARPA funds. Of that amount, $1.8 billion will be used for operating expenses and $1.0 billion for capital expenses, focusing on water, sewer and broadband infrastructure. These one-time funds will be spent over several years. The remaining $5.3 billion will be allocated in the future (Illinois Comptroller, 2022).

Figure 7. State of Illinois American Rescue Plan funding distibution

State of Illinois American Rescue Plan Funding Distribution ($000s)			
Agencies	**Purpose**	**Amount**	**% of Total**
Various	Capital Infrastructure	$ 1,000,000	35.4%
Commerce & Economic Opportunity	Addressing Negative Economic Impacts	$ 573,700	20.3%
Healthcare & Family Services, Human Services, Public Health, Other Agencies	Healthcare Response	$ 406,000	14.4%
Emergency Management Agency	Eligible Operational Expenses for State Agencies	$ 380,000	13.5%
Human Services, Children & Family Services, Commerce & Economic Opportunity	Public Health	$ 163,800	5.8%
Illinois Criminal Justice Information Authority, Human Services, Children & Family Services, State Board of Education	Violence Prevention	$ 128,850	4.6%
Illinois Housing Development Authority, Human Services	Affordable Housing/Homelessness	$ 114,200	4.0%
Illinois State Board of Education, Illinois State Board of Higher Education, Illinois Community College Board, Illinois Student Assistance Commission	Elementary, Secondary and Higher Education	$ 55,800	2.0%
Total		**$ 2,822,350**	**100.0%**

Source: Governor's Office of Management and Budget. FY22 Federal ARPA Funding Budget Summary at https://www2.illinois.gov/sites/budget/Documents/Budget%20Book/FY2022-Budget-Book/FY22_Enacted_ARPA_Summary_6.21.21.pdf.

The next table shows the allocation of the $2.8 billion in ARPA funds appropriated in the FY2022 Illinois state budget. Roughly $1.0 billion, 35.4% of the total, will be used for capital infrastructure projects. The next largest amount, or $573.7 million, will be used for programs that address the negative economic impacts of the pandemic. Another $406.0 million is earmarked for a number of programs focused on healthcare responses to the pandemic. Additional amounts will be spent on programs addressing operational expenses, public health initiatives, violence prevention programs, affordable housing and homelessness mitigation programs and educational programs.

Cook County

Cook County will receive a total of $1.4 billion in funding from the CARES Act and the American Rescue Plan Act.

CARES Act Funding

In 2020, the County received approximately $429 million in coronavirus relief funding through the CARES Act. The finds were spent, as required, on COVID-19 related public health and safety expenses incurred between March 1 and December 31, 2020. These costs were allocated as follows: $288 million was used for operating expenses; $8 million was used for operational initiatives; $82 million was earmarked for economic development initiatives and the remaining $51 million was allocated directly to local governments (excluding the City of Chicago, which received its own CARES Act funds) (Civic Federation, 2021a).

The Cook County government allocated $51 million of the relief funds to 130 local units of government located within the County. The allocation was targeted to economically distressed communities in the southern and western suburbs of Chicago, including municipalities, townships and special districts (Civic Federation, 2021a). It was based on an equity-based formula developed by the County and the

Chicago Metropolitan Agency for Planning that weighed four factors: the percentage of the population in economically disadvantaged areas (40%); median income (30%); COVID related deaths per capita (20%) and tax base per capita (10%) (Yin, 2020).

American Rescue Act Plan Funds

Cook County is expected to receive approximately $1.0 billion in ARPA funding. Half of that amount was received in 2021 and the remainder will be received in 2022. The County will spend the funds over the next three years in equal increments. In FY2022,[1] $100 million will be used to replace revenues lost as a result of the pandemic and to fund administration and court personnel positions. The remaining $233 million will be used to pay for community program initiatives in accordance with the County's Policy Roadmap (Cook County, 2018) (Cook County, 2021). Because Cook County is in a relatively stable financial situation, most of the ARPA funds will not be used for current budgetary balancing purposes.

Cook County's Policy Roadmap report laid out a framework for the use of the County's ARPA funds. The monies will be used for the following policy priorities:

1. Health and Wellness;
2. Economic Development;
3. Criminal Justice;
4. Environmental and Sustainability;
5. Public Infrastructure; and
6. Good Government.

The County will classify projects using the four categories listed below. Initially, project monies will be directed toward near-term projects to be completed within a six-month period. The other categories will have a longer term horizon (Cook County, n.d.).

City of Chicago

The City of Chicago will receive a total of $2.37 billion in funding from the CARES Act and the American Rescue Plan Act.

CARES Act

The City of Chicago received $470.1 million in direct assistance from the CARES Act from the Coronavirus Relief Fund. Much of the funding is earmarked for costs associated with public health and safety personnel dealing with responses to the pandemic. In FY2022, this includes $173 million earmarked for increasing the City's ability to detect, prevent and respond to infectious diseases and $83 million for COVID 19 testing and vaccination efforts. Nearly $100 million from grants will be used for services to citizens and businesses impacted by the pandemic (City of Chicago, 2021b, p. 54). The Coronavirus Relief Funds are in addition to millions of dollars in funding provided to individuals, businesses, health care providers and airports through other programs (City of Chicago, 2021b, p. 53). Related Chicago governments such as the Chicago Transit Authority and Chicago Public Schools have also received $1.0 billion (Pratt & Byrne, 2020).

Figure 8. Cook county ARPA funding categories

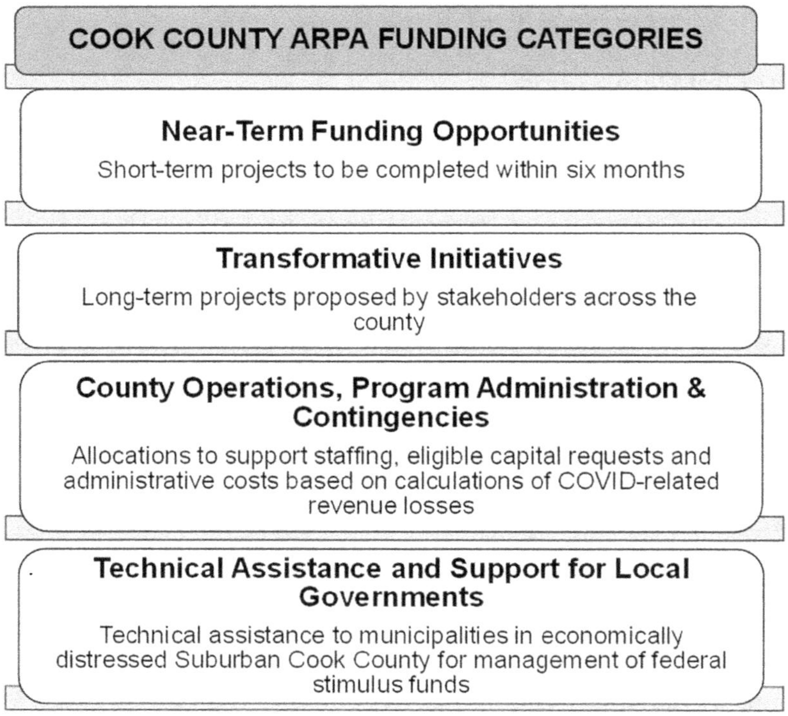

American Rescue Plan Act

The City of Chicago will receive nearly $1.9 billion in funding through the American Rescue Plan Act (National League of Cities, n.d.). It will supplement those funds with $660 million in bond funds. The City released a Chicago Recovery Plan in September 2021 to provide a framework for the use of this $2.5 billion in funds (City of Chicago, 2021a, p. 17).

Roughly 70%, or $1.3 billion, of the $1.9 billion in ARPA funding will be used to help cover budget deficits and pay for essential city services. Of that amount, $782 million will be used to cover the FY2021 budget gap, $385 million will be used to cover budget deficits in FY2022 and the remaining $152 million will be used in FY2023 (Civic Federation, 2021b, p. 5).

The remaining 30%, or $567 million, of the ARPA funds will be spent as shown in the chart below for top City policy priorities. Of that amount, $126 million will be used for programs assisting families in need, $103 million for health and wellness programs, $85 million for an increase in violence prevention program funding and $71 million for small business and workforce support. Smaller sums will be used for a variety of social service and economic development related programs. These funds are one-time revenue supports (City of Chicago, 2021b, p. 55). These programs were developed through a community engagement process. Many are short-term in nature; the City will decide in future years which programs to continue and how to fund them based in part from the results of a performance management system that will be developed to track outcomes and impact (Civic Federation, 2021b, p. 16). It is important to

Figure 9. City of Chicago use of ARPA funds to cover budget deficits

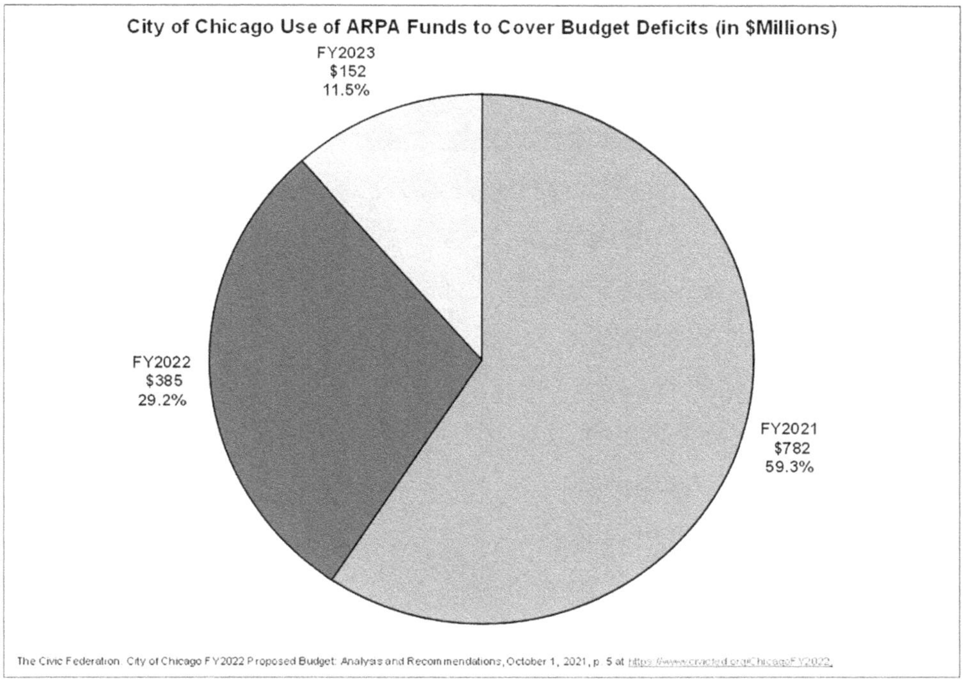

note that these funds will be supplemented by $660 million in bond funds, so that the full amount be spent on these initiatives will be $1.2 billion (City of Chicago, 2021a, p. 17).

CONCLUSION

States are very limited in their ability to use fiscal policies to address major economic disruptions such as the current coronavirus pandemic. Structural restrictions such as balanced budget requirements and debt limits as well as revenue capacity limitations make it nearly impossible for states to continue to provide key public services when faced with severe economic and revenue shocks. Only the federal government has the vast financial resources and the fiscal capacity to implement meaningful countercyclical fiscal policies that can mitigate these pressures and assist state and local governments. The billions of dollars in federal stimulus funds provided in 2020 and 2021 through the CARES Act and the American Rescue Plan Act have been critical to the continued provision of state and local government programs during the COVID-19 pandemic.

Figure 10. City of Chicago ARPA fund distribution for programs

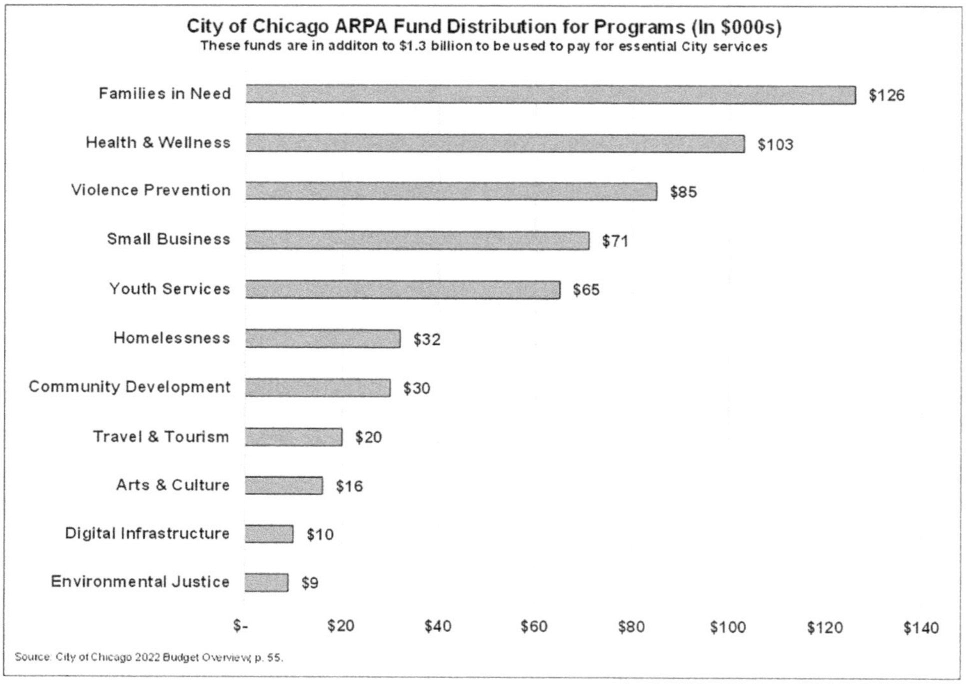

REFERENCES

Alesina, A., Campante, F. R., & Tabellini, G. (2008, September). Why is Fiscal Policy Procyclical? *Journal of the European Economic Association*, 1–2.

Baldacci, E., Gupta, S., & Mulas-Granados, C. (2012). *How Effective Is Fiscal Policy Response in Financial Crises?* Retrieved from International Monetary Fund: https://www.imf.org/external/np/seminars/eng2012/fincrises/pdf/ch14.pdf

Center on Budget and Policy Priorities. (2020, March 26). *How Much Each State will Receive from the Coronavirus Relief Fund in the CARES Act.* Retrieved from cbpp.org: https://www.cbpp.org/research/how-much-each-state-will-receive-from-the-coronavirus-relief-fund-in-the-cares-act

City of Chicago. (2021a, September 20). *Chicago Recovery Plan.* Retrieved from chicago.gov: https://www.chicago.gov/content/dam/city/depts/obm/supp_info/2022Budget/ChicagoRecoveryPlan.pdf

City of Chicago. (2021b). *2022 Budget Overview.* Retrieved from chicago.gov: https://www.chicago.gov/content/dam/city/depts/obm/supp_info/2022Budget/2022OverviewFINAL.pdf

Civic Federation. (2019, February 8). *Measuring the State of Illinois' Bill Backlog*. Retrieved from civicfed.org: https://www.civicfed.org/iifs/blog/measuring-state-illinois-bill-backlog

Civic Federation. (2020, April 15). *How Will CARES Act Funding Be Divided Among Illinois and Its Local Governments?* Retrieved from civicfed.org: https://www.civicfed.org/iifs/blog/how-will-cares-act-funding-be-divided-among-illinois-and-its-local-governments

Civic Federation. (2021a, March 5). *Final Cook County Coronavirus Relief Fund Allocations*. Retrieved from civicfed.org: https://www.civicfed.org/blog/final-cook-county-coronavirus-relief-fund-allocations

Civic Federation. (2021b, October 1). *City of Chicago Fy2022 Proposed Budget: Analysis and Recommendations*. Retrieved from civicfed.org: https://www.civicfed.org/ChicagoState

Cook County. (2018, November 14). *Policy Roadmap*. Retrieved from cookcountyil.gov: https://www.cookcountyil.gov/service/policy-roadmap

Cook County. (2021, October 7). *Executive Budget Recommendation, Fiscal Year 2022*. Author.

Cook County. (n.d.). *Roadmap to Recovery: Cook County's American Rescue Plan*. Retrieved from cookcountyil.gov: https://www.cookcountyil.gov/ARPA

Federal Reserve Bank of Chicago. (2020, October 20). *The Federal Reserve's Dual Mandate*. Retrieved from Chicagofed.org: https://www.chicagofed.org/research/dual-mandate/dual-mandate

Federal Reserve Bank of Chicago. (2021, January 26). *Statement on Longer-Run Goals and Monetary Policy Strategy*. Retrieved from Federalreserve.gov: https://www.chicagofed.org/monetarypolicy/files/FOMC_LongerRunGoals.pdf

Government Finance Officers Association. (2021, May 5). *American Rescue Plan Spending: Recommended Guiding Principles*. Retrieved from www.gfoa.org: https://www.gfoa.org/american-rescue-plan-spending-guiding-principles

Hou, Y., & Moynihan, D. P. (2008, January). The Case for Countercyclical Fiscal Capacity. *Journal of Public Administration Research and Theory, 18*(1), 141. doi:10.1093/jopart/mum006

Illinois Comptroller. (2022, February 9). *COVID-19 Response and Resources*. Retrieved from Illinois Comptroller: https://illinoiscomptroller.gov/covid19-information

Illinois Comptroller. (n.d.). *Backlog Voucher Report*. Retrieved from Illinois Comptroller: https://illinoiscomptroller.gov/financial-data/backlog-voucher-report-bvr

Illinois General Assembly. (2004, February 2). Illinois Public Act 93-660.

Illinois General Assembly. (2021, February 17). *FY2022 State Budget*. Retrieved from illinois.gov: https://www2.illinois.gov/sites/budget/Documents/Budget%20Book/FY2022-Budget-Book/Fiscal-Year-2022-Operating-Budget.pdf

Illinois Governor's Office of Management and Budget. (2021, June 21). *FY22 Federal ARPA Funding Budget Summary*. Retrieved from illinois.gov: https://www2.illinois.gov/sites/budget/Documents/Budget%20Book/FY2022-Budget-Book/FY22_Enacted_ARPA_Summary_6.21.21.pdf

Institute for Illinois' Fiscal Stability. (2019, February 13). *State of Illinois FY2020 Budget Roadmap: State of Illinois Budget Overview, Projections and Recommendations for the Governor and the Illinois General Assembly*. Retrieved from civicfed.org: https://www.civicfed.org/sites/default/files/illinoisroadmapfy2020.pdf

Investopedia. (2021a, August 29). *Monetary Policy*. Retrieved from Investopedia.com: https://www.investopedia.com/terms/m/monetarypolicy.asp

Investopedia. (2021b, October 10). *The Roots of Fiscal Policy*. Retrieved from Investopedia.com: https://www.investopedia.com/terms/f/fiscalpolicy.asp

Mikesell, J. L. (2018). *Fiscal Administration* (10th ed.). Cengage Learning.

National Association of State Budget Officers. (2019). *The Fiscal Survey of States*. NASBO.

National Conference of State Legislatures. (2010, October). *Fiscal Brief: State Balanced Budget Provisions*. Retrieved from ncsl.org: https://www.ncsl.org/research/fiscal-policy/state-balanced-budget-requirements-provisions-and.aspx

National League of Cities. (n.d.). *Local Allocations in the American Rescue Plan*. Retrieved from nlc.org: https://www.nlc.org/resource/local-allocations-in-the-american-rescue-plan/

Pew Foundation. (2021, December 22). *Fiscal 50: State Trends and Analysis*. Retrieved from pewtrusts.org: https://www.pewtrusts.org/en/research-and-analysis/data-visualizations/2014/fiscal-50#ind5

Pratt, G., & Byrne, J. (2020, April 9). *City expects federal coronavirus stimulus package to give $1.5 billion to Chicago government, CPS and CTA*. Retrieved from Chicago Tribune: https://www.chicagotribune.com/coronavirus/ct-coronavirus-chicago-stimulus-lightfoot-trump-20200409-e2rwavkp5rg2zpejape6
args4i-story.html

Reuben, K., & Randall, M. (2017). Debt Limits: How States Restrict Borrowing. Urban Institute.

Stone, C. (2017, July 28). *What's the Fed to Do? The central bank is navigating through uncharted waters*. Retrieved from US News and World Report: https://www.usnews.com/opinion/economic-intelligence/articles/2017-07-28/the-fed-struggles-with-the-unemployment-inflati
on-trade-off

Tapper, T. (2021, December 10). *Why Is Inflation rising Right Now?* Retrieved from Forbes.com: https://www.forbes.com/advisor/investing/why-is-inflation-rising-right-now

U.S. Congress. (2020, March 27). *H.R. 748 CARES Act*. Retrieved from congress.gov: https://www.congress.gov/bill/116th-congress/house-bill/748

U.S. Congress. (2021). *American Rescue Plan Act of 2021, sec. 9901, Public Law 117-2, codified at 42 U.S.C. 802*. https://www.congress.gov/bill/117th-congress/house-bill/1319

U.S. Department of the Treasury. (2021, March 18). *Fact Sheet: The American Rescue Plan Will Deliver Immediate Economic Relief to Families*. https://home.treasury.gov/news/featured-stories/fact-sheet-the-american-rescue-plan-will-deliver-immediate-economic-relief-to-families

Walczak, J. (2021, May 27). *State Aid in American Rescue Plan Act Is 116 Times States' revenue Losses*. Retrieved from Tax Foundation: https://taxfoundation.org/state-and-local-aid-american-rescue-plan

Yin, A. (2020, July 15). *Cook County crafts formula for CARES Act funding distribution with emphasis on struggling areas, aims to right inequities among suburbs during COVID-19 pandemic*. Retrieved from chicagotribune.com: https://www.chicagotribune.com/news/breaking/ct-cook-county-cares-act-equitable-funding-formula-20200715-5aaoc6zrcng5xc6uqj6ps7mfoy-htmlstory.html

ENDNOTE

1 The Cook County fiscal year is December 1 to November 30.

Chapter 2
Relationship Between Government Funding Supports and Innovation Performance of Latecomer Firms

Haoyu Wang
Illinois Institute of Technology, USA

ABSTRACT

As an important component of enterprise external environment, government funding supports play a significant role in the innovation of latecomer firms. Therefore, the support methods adopted by the government during the innovation and catching-up of latecomer firms should be extracted in this chapter to clarify the internal relationship between the intermediate mechanism and innovation performance affecting the performance of latecomer firms. It is useful for activating the new energy and motivation of latecomer firms, and it could be a scientific decision-making reference for the government to formulate relevant public policies.

INTRODUCTION

Innovation would not only boost enterprises to form powerful core competitiveness in foreign and domestic markets, but also be a critical motivation of national and regional competitive advantage. Therefore, how to support and encourage corporate innovation efficiently has been a highlight of governments at all levels.

However, it is a truth that most Chinese enterprises participating in the competition of international market are the latecomer ones, so their knowledge of cutting-edge core technology is insufficient with limited available innovation resources; however, they have to fight for the market in the industry-leading technology paradigm and core technology evolution track established by leading enterprises (Wu & Chen, 2018).

Compared with international leading enterprises, most latecomer firms in China are on small scale with limited resources. While the high investment of innovation activity forces them to face multiple

DOI: 10.4018/978-1-6684-2314-1.ch002

uncertain risks during their growth, which affects the increase of their innovation performance (Liu & Xu, 2018). As a supplying object of innovation mechanism, the Chinese government plays a critical role in the improvement of enterprises' innovation performance (Han & Gao, 2018), and the policy of government funding supports to corporation innovation has been a key point to affect the innovation performance of latecomer firms (Shou, Wei, & Liu, 2018).

It could be concluded that government funding supports have been a focus of the country and society during the improvement process of latecomer firms' innovation performance. It mainly includes: what is the influence effect of different funding supports on the innovation performance of latecomer firms? What are the variables that influence the innovation performance of latecomer firms in the process of government support? Figuring out these problems is good for enhancing the scientificity of government to stipulate public policies so as to optimize the innovation environment of latecomer firms systemically. It would provide theoretical and practical references for the improvement and enhancement of latecomer firms' innovation performance and the definiteness of government service paths for latecomer firms.

LITERATURE REVIEW

Government Supporting Methods (Providing Different Kinds of Funding Supports)

There are some studies about the government supporting methods. It is pointed out by Christian and Christopher that the methods of government supporting innovation are mainly the government-led research and development of scientific research institutions, tax preference for the subjects engaged in research and development activities and providing government subsidies for enterprises, and the most common methods are government subsidies and tax preference (Stadler & Nobes, 2018). Habib et al. study the impact of government financial subsidy, tax preference policy and other factors on the innovation activity of technology-intensive industry (Habib, Luo, & Zhong, 2018). They think that the impact of government support on the innovation of technology-intensive process enterprises is more significant. Chiara et al. divide the government support into guiding support and policy support; and the former includes a technological plan, financing service, public technology platform supported by the government while the latter is such policies as special funds and tax relief support provided by the government (Del Bo, Ferraris, & Florio, 2017). Shu and Wang et al. analyze the objective of government supporting enterprises to carry out innovation activities, and they point out that government should support enterprises to carry out technological innovation by implementing policies suitable for the enterprise development prospect and providing technical and funding supports for enterprises to carry out technological innovation (Shu, Wang, Gao, & et al, 2015). Zhao Yuanjun et al. classify the government supporting behaviors with bigger influence on enterprises into vertical ones and horizontal ones; the vertical supports should be the funds for enterprise R & D subsidy and research institute projects, and the horizontal supports should be innovation policy and tax relief (Zhao, Xu, Liu, & Xie, 2017). Zheng Ye and Wang Huan split the government support into such direct guiding policies as R&D subsidy, loan discount, planned projects and indirect guiding policies of tax credits and government procurement from the perspectives of government regulation theory, resource-based theory and so on; they consider that providing multi-level policies according to local conditions could effectively increase the innovation efficiency of enterprises (Zheng & Wang, 2017). Huang Yuting et al. hold the opinion that funding supports for technological activities of relevant government departments, the tax deduction for the R&D expenditure and tax relief for the high-tech enterprises would impose the biggest impact on industrial innovation (Huang & Li, 2015). Yan Tingbiao analyzes the motivation, positioning and method of government supporting scientific and technological innovation in the light of comparison of policies of government support for scientific and technological innovation in many countries, and Yan deems that government should support enterprises to carry out innovation through financial support, tax relief, organization and coordination and so on (Yan, 2014). Zeng Mingang et al. analyze the impact of local governments of our country participating in the innovation decision-making process of enterprises with the support of tax, land and other aspects on the activity of corporation innovation (Zeng, Ly, & Wu, 2014).

Definition of Innovation Performance and Measurement

"Innovation Performance" or "Innovation Success" would be used to describe the effect of corporation innovation in some literature, including the process achievements of the upgrading of corporation innovation ability, improvement of industrial structure and internal production process and the generation of new concepts for the interaction of the efficiency and effect of enterprises carrying out innovation activities as well as other factors during the innovation process. Just as the study of Ahuja shows that the innovation performance in a broad sense means the whole process from the generation of a new concept to the launch in the market, and it should focus on the technological innovation and the output and profit brought by commercialization (Ahuja & Lampert, 2016). Bongsun et al. suggest that the innovation performance of enterprise should be explained from the aspect of innovation result, and it mainly includes the number of product creativity and new concept design and the adaptability of enterprises to environmental changes and so on (Kim, Kim, Miller, & Mahoney, 2016). Kollmann and Stockmann divide the innovation performance into exploratory innovation performance and applied innovation performance; in their opinion, the exploratory innovation performance mainly means that the organization creates business value with the invention of new technology, new product and new service through the accumulation of new knowledge factors, and the applied innovation performance means that organizations could provide a better service for the present customers through the existing knowledge factors (Kollmann & Stockmann, 2014).

The studies of Chinese scholars on innovation performance is focused on the issue of performance of technological innovation, including the performance of technological innovation in all stages from the concept design, research and development and final launch of the product to show the whole process of technological innovation from the generation of vague concept to the product launch (Zhan, 2018; Han, Luo, & Zhong, 2016; Yun, Ma, & Chen, 2012).

Corporation innovation performance means the innovation achievement of enterprises after enterprises have interaction, linkage and cooperation with other organizations to undertake a series of innovation activities. The relevant literature measures the innovation performance through the single economic indicator, non-economic indicators and multiple comprehensive judgement indicators.

Here are the relevant studies. Panagiotis et al. measure the corporation innovation performance with the new product sales of high-tech enterprises, and they measure the impact of enterprise-scale, tax reduction and subsidy, internal R & D investment, and cooperation with external scientific research institutions and other factors on the corporation innovation performance with quantile regression (Piperopoulos, Jie, & Chengqi, 2018). Domingo et al. makes the number of invention patents owned by enterprises as the measurement indicator of initial innovation performance, and the sales rate of new products is deemed as the final measurement indicator of innovation performance; while the proportion of scientists and engineers and expenditure on technological transformation and new product development are the measurement factors for the impact degree of industrial input on innovation performance (Garcia-Perez-de-Lema, Madrid-Guijarro, & Philippe Martin, 2017). Gkypali and Trianni measure the corporation innovation performance with the knowledge creation ability and innovation diversity indicator in enterprises, and they also study the specific function degree of corporation innovation performance (Gkypali & Trianni, 2015). Ana et al. measures the performance with product sales, processes, organization and business conduct, and they make analysis on the role of integration of external and internal knowledge of enterprises on the innovation performance, so they conclude that different innovation policies would have different impacts on the performance (Serrano-Bedia, Piva, & Rossi-Lamastra, 2014). Jing and Aydm measure the corporation innovation performance with new product introduction and product innovation speed, and they also study the influencing effect of background factor and quality factor of the organization on the corporation innovation performance, so it is found that quality management would take effect on the corporation innovation performance by affecting the speed of new product and the product innovation quality (Jing & Aydm, 2014).

Wu Hang and Chen Jing choose the sales income of new product as an indicator to measure the corporation innovation performance. Based on the analysis of the relationship between high tech industrial agglomeration and enterprise innovation performance, they have a study on the moderating effect of corporate openness (Wu & Chen, 2018). Wang Lanfang and Hu Yue study the promotion effect of startup investment on innovation performance (Wang & Hu, 2017). Wang Kang and Zhou Xiao measures the corporation innovation performance with such indicators as R & D investment, R & D efficiency, R & D intensity, enterprise-scale, profit margin, ownership nature, and they hold the idea that R&D investment has a strong non-linear effect on corporation innovation performance (Wang & Zhou, 2017). Sun Zao and Song Wei make the per-capita patent output of the industry as the proxy variable of the industrial innovation performance, and they have a study on the functioning process of R&D investment on the industrial innovation performance. They reach a conclusion that the R&D investment of private-owned enterprises imposes a more significant positive impact on industrial innovation performance than that of state-owned ones (Sun & Song, 2012).

INTRODUCTION TO THEORIES, MODEL BUILDUP AND HYPOTHESIS

The Theory of Government Intervention and Its Applicability

The worldwide economic crisis from the 1920s to the 1930s announced the failure of "laissez-faire" enterprise development policy, while the "Keynesianism" advocating the intervention from the modern government had been a neo-orthodox school of western economics. Keynesianism thinks that the government should adopt a positive fiscal and monetary policy to stimulate consumption and increase investment to make up for the insufficiency of investment demand and consumption demand. Later, with the ceaseless struggle of economist inheriting the opinion of Keynesianism, the theory of Keynesianism has been revised and improved. The establishment of new Keynesianism represented by Samuelson and Phillips and their policy proposition have been widely spread, which provides theoretical support for designing and reshaping the new pattern of the relationship between government and market (Manuel, 2012).

Applicability begins from the aspect of the relationship between government and market, and the paper could find so much evidence of government intervening in the innovation of latecomer firms.

Government intervention is a general method that all countries around the world encourage corporation innovation. For example, America had started to provide tax support policies covering R & D expense deduction, tax deduction, net operating loss deduction, accelerated depreciation and so on for the technological innovation of enterprises in 1970. In France, a 42 billion Euro loan finance and support the development of small and medium enterprises and innovative enterprises was provided by a public investment bank in 2012. The intervention methods, intervention means and forces of governments in all countries for corporation innovation activities are varied, but the final result shows that all of them provide powerful support for the innovation activities of their domestic enterprises.

At the same time, the successful practice of over 40 years of reform and opening-up in China shows that the "supportive hand" of the Chinese government plays a key role, and the government is an irreplaceable helper in the corporation innovation activities.

Finally, the innovation activities of latecomer firms are featured with the indivisibility of the innovation process, the uncertainty of innovation result and sharing innovation profit. Along with the technology spillover, the short-term profit of latecomer firms' innovation would be greatly affected and their willingness to have innovation is restrained, which would cause a failure in the innovation behavior market. While the intervention of the government on the allocation of social resource would not only bring fund profit to enterprises directly through financial subsidies, R & D support and so on, it would also reach the objective to improve the corporation innovation performance.

In conclusion, with the guidance of government intervention theory, the paper could have a profound explanation of the influencing mechanism of various funding supports of government on the innovation performance of latecomer firms, so as to reach a systemic exploration on the possible path for government support to boost the improvement of latecomer firms' innovation performance.

Grounded Theory

The sociologists Glaser & Strauss proposed the grounded theory initially in 1967, and they consider that grounded theory is a specific study path and methodology. There are incomparable advantages in collecting data, defining core concepts, exploring the relationship between social phenomena, building new theories and related models and so on compared with other theories and study methods.

Since the study method of grounded theory could conclude, analyze and focus on the forming of conceptual framework or theory from data, so it could be applied to the field of public management to carry out the study of relevant problems (Jia, 2015).

Data Analysis

Open Coding

The essence of open coding is a convergence problem. The general process could be concluded to be "refining data—conceptualization—categorization" (Jia & Heng, 2016), and it mainly includes the decomposing and refining of the collected data, defining all kinds of phenomena to gain concept and confirming categories according to the logic relationship and similarity degree among concepts these three steps. To clearly show the whole process of open coding, the paper makes an open coding with the

Table 1. Open coding—with the sample of ZZCMM

Case data record of ZZCMM (Taking partial data fragment as an example)	Conceptualization
The former of ZZCMM is Zhengzhou Coal Mine Machinery. Since the establishment, the enterprise undertakes many scientific and technological key projects during the period from the 7th Five Year Plan to the 12th Five Year Plan. Many important scientific and technological innovations have been subsidized by the national R & D plan and special funds.	A_1 R&D subsidy A_2 Special funds
Since 2007, Hu Jintao and Li Keqiang, party and state leaders had visited ZZCMM, which confirmed the great contribution to the development of the coal mine industry in China. In 2007 and 2008, the fund for technological innovation projects, guidance fund, technological award and talent award fund granted by provincial and municipal governments would reach 13 million yuan.	A_3 Project fund A_4 Guidance fund A_5Technological award A_6 Talent award
Capturing the electro-hydraulic control system was the tough order released by General Secretary Hu Jintao for ZZCMM in 2007 in visiting the enterprise. With the support of the provincial government and State-owned Assets Supervision and Administration Commission of the State Council, ZZCMM undertook joint capturing with the cooperation of the Huazhong University of Technological, China University of Mining and Technology and other universities and R&D institutions and the supportive resources from governments through a combination of production, study and research, by the methods of building up a lab and technological innovation platform, carrying out technological result transfer and setting up special funds, etc.	A_7 Co-construction of lab A_8 Special fund for combination of production, study and research
ZZCMM started to plan the listing in 2007. However, China Security Regulatory Commission required that the original shareholder of the company to-be-listed should not exceed 200, so government-supported ZZCMM to transfer the equity of Bester company held by employees to investment institution and the executives of the enterprises through the transfer of shares for regulating the equity structure, and the enterprise was supported to have financing through multiple banks. In the same year, ZZCMM became the top in the world in the field of mining equipment of coal mine shaft work.	A_9 Transfer of shares A_{10} Financing service A_{11} Financing channel A_{12} Listing financing
Since 2007, along with the rapid development of Henan Province and Zhengzhou City, the local government has stipulated much more policies to support the innovation development of the manufacturing industry. ZZCMM had gained plenty of talent training subsidies, special subsidies and tax awards from financial support policies such as the special fund for the development of advanced manufacturing industry and the special fund for the introduction of scientific and technological talents (no specific statement here).	A_{13} Patent subsidy A_{14} Tax award A_{15} Training subsidy
The Henan State-owned Assets Supervision and Administration Commission supported ZZCMM to raise the matching funds through non-public issuance of A-shares in the securities market by founding Provincial Mechanical Equipment Investment Group Co., Ltd. And the auto part business of ASIMCO Technologies and the motor business of Bosch were purchased in 2017 so that ZZCMM could build up the top automotive motor and shock absorber business in the world to lay a foundation for the development of high-end manufacturing industry.	A_{16} Stock financing A_{17} Investment support

Data Source: The author sorts according to the open coding requirement of grounded theory.

sample of ZZCMM and Geely, which can be seen in Charts 1 and 2. For the limited paper, there would be no presentation of the open coding process of the other two enterprises.

Since the paper is adopted with the analysis method of multiple cases, the conceptualization result of ZZMCC and Geely should be a conceptual template. The sentence-by-sentence labelling is carried out for the rest of the case to revise and supplement relevant concepts to form the new template. After completing the open coding process of three cases in turn, there is a total of 28 concepts and 3 initial categories. See Chart 3 for specification.

Table 2. Open coding—with the sample of Geely

Case data record of Geely (Taking partial data fragment as an example)	Conceptualization
When Geely purchased Volvo in 2010, the central and local governments had provided a series of convenience for its filing policy of overseas M & A, much more support for overseas financing guarantee provided by domestic policy banks and approval procedure simplification. In addition, Shanghai, Chengdu, Daqing and other local governments provided vast financing for Geely in the forms of low-interest loan and intellectual property pledge.	A_{18} Financing Guarantee A_{19} Low interest loan A_{20} Intellectual property pledge
With years of struggle, Geely had gained vast of good performance of government procurement and another key account. Geely has been officially designated vehicles for G20 Hangzhou Summit. Geely Borui has been a foreign protocol car for years. Multiple types of Geely have been enlisted in public security police vehicle agreement supply catalogue and agreed on supply projects of official vehicles in various provinces and cities.	A_{21} Central procurement A_{22} Local procurement A_{23} Public business procurement
Under the background of national support for independent innovation of the automobile manufacturing industry, Geely has been gained with multiple political support. For example, the net profit of the enterprise reached 1.5 billion yuan in 2011, including the government subsidies and tax returns contribution of 877 million yuan. The net profit of the enterprise reached 1.02 billion yuan in 2012, but the government subsidies and tax returns contribution reached 634 million yuan. In addition, Geely also has much more income from government procurement. Geely is located in each city, and the local government gives large support in technological finance, information service, administrative procedures and research center construction.	A_{24} Government subsidy A_{25} Tax return A_{26} Tas relief A_{27} Government procurement A_{28} Technology finance

Data Source: The author sorts according to the open coding requirement of grounded theory.

Axial Coding

Axial Coding could achieve the relevance thinking between concept and category, aiming at finding and building the relationship among categories. The categories gained from the primary open coding are independent, there should be further analysis with axial coding technology.

The paper refers to the relationship among categories with the reference of the typical model "condition-result," so as to classify 3 primary categories into one main category. See the specification in Chart 4.

The role of the main categories is to form all text data information to be a completed evidence chain. Take one of the evidence chains of innovation performance for example. The causal condition is the

Table 3. Concept and category to form open coding

No.	Category	Concept and Its Explanation
AA_7	Tax Preference	Tax relief, tax return, tax award
AA_8	Financial Support	Listed financing, equity transfer, financing services, financing channels, financing guarantee, technological insurance, low interest loans, stock financing, investment support, technological finance
AA_9	Financial Support	Special funds, loan discount, R & D subsidies, project funds, guidance funds, technological awards, government subsidies, special funds, central procurement, local procurement, public business procurement, government procurement, talent training, Talent Awards, industry university research special funds

Data Source: The author sorts according to the open coding requirement of grounded theory.

Table 4. Result of axial coding

No.	Category	Primary Categories
1	Innovation Performance	Technological innovation, management innovation, process innovation, market innovation
2	Funding Supports	Tax preference, financial support, financing support

Data Source: The author sorts according to the axial coding requirement of grounded theory.

category of tax preference; the final result is that there is an improvement in the innovation performance of latecomer firms.

Selective Coding

Selective coding is called "core code," and it needs to choose one "core category" by systemic analysis on the found conceptual categories, so as to focus the study on the concepts and categories related to the core category.

Through the profound sorting of all concepts, primary categories and main categories and the comparison with the original materials, the typical relationship structure of selective coding is shown in Chart 5.

Table 5. Typical relationship structure and its connotation

Typical Relationship Structure	Connotation
Funding Supports —® Innovation Performance	The funding supports is an important factor to affect the innovation performance of latecomer firms, and it could directly affect the performance directly.

Data Source: The author sorts according to the selective coding requirement of grounded theory.

Hence, around the core problem of "the impact of government funding supports on the innovation performance of latecomer firms," the paper sorts out the storyline and concludes it to be: government funding supports imposing direct impact on the corporation innovation performance.

Buildup of Initial Theory Model

According to the conclusion gained from open coding, axial coding and selective coding, a storyline is formed around the core category to analyze the process of government funding supports affecting the innovation performance of latecomer firms. With reference to the outcomes of foreign and domestic researches, the primary theory model of the impact of government support on innovation performance of latecomer firms based on government intervention theory and innovation theory, shown in Figure 1.

Model Setup

In addition, the primary theory model shown in Figure 1 could be simplified to be the study model shown in Figure 2. The model is a basis to deepen the study on the impact of government funding supports on the innovation performance of latecomer firms and to propose the follow-up series of hypotheses.

Figure 1. Primary theory model of impact of government support on innovation performance of latecomer firms
Data Source: The author sorts according to the grounded theory.

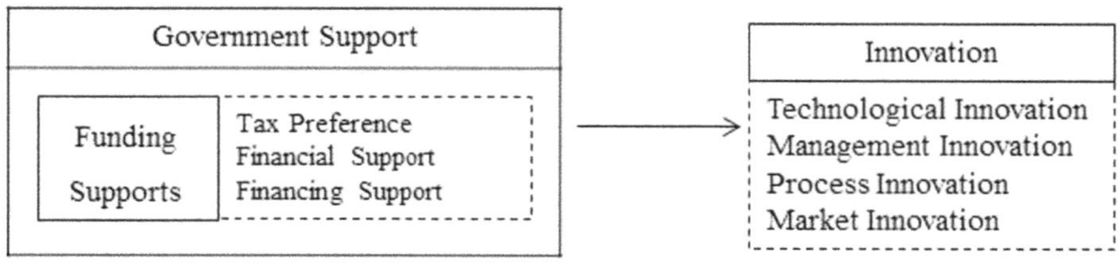

Figure 2. Study model of impact of government support on innovation performance of latecomer firms
Data Source: The author sorts according to the grounded theory.

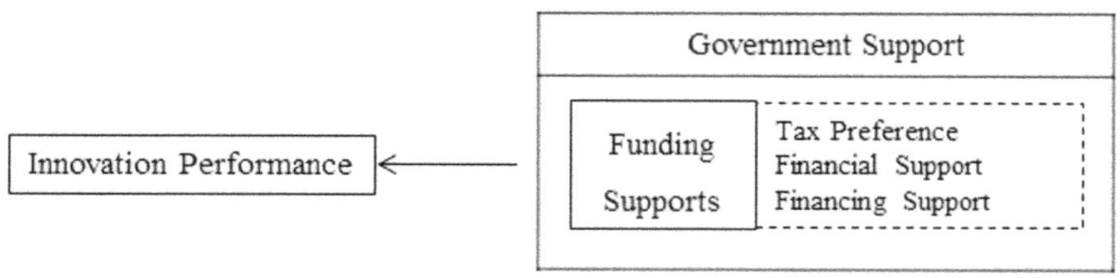

Hypotheses of the Impact of Government Funding Supports on Innovation Performance of Latecomer Firms

To encourage the enterprises to enlarge the innovation input, Chinese governments at all levels have stipulated a variety of funding supports policies, and the common methods are tax preference, financial support and financing support, etc. Hence, many scholars carry out studies on relevant content (Walter et al., 2018; Liu, 2016; Kang, 2013). The existing literature shows that government funding supports could effectively encourage enterprises to increase the innovation investment to enhance the innovation performance of enterprises.

For the latecomer firms, innovation should need vast investment, but the lag of output and the uncertainty of innovation results would enable enterprises to carry out innovation with higher risk. Obviously, the government adopting different funding supports policies for latecomer firms in the startup period, growing period and catching-up period imposes is a positive promoter for these enterprises to increase the innovation investment and improve the innovation performance.

The impact of government funding supports on the innovation performance of latecomer firms could be described from the impact of tax preference, financial support and financing support on the performance.

Impact of Tax Preference on the Innovation Performance of Latecomer Firms

Tax preference is a policy to support enterprises by reducing the tax burden or delay their taxation time. This is an effective approach for the government to reduce the innovation cost of enterprise and encourage them to carry out innovation activities to improve the innovation performance with direct or indirect taxation preference.

In view of so many dilemmas faced by latecomer firms in China, such as fewer resources, smaller scale and weaker risk tolerance, they are hard to catch up with the existing enterprises in a short time with their own strength. While the tax preference policy of the government could enhance the competitive power of enterprises in the aspect of talent introduction and cultivation, R&D investment, technological harvest transfer, new product promotion and other aspects, so as to boost the innovation development of latecomer firms and improve their innovation performance.

Impact of Financial Support on Innovation Performance of Latecomer Firms

Financial support means the policy to directly increase the income of the market subject through government expenditure. The government's financial support for enterprises takes up a tremendous inch in the development of society and economy as a national financial control policy.

For the dual risks of technology and the market faced by latecomer firms in China, corporate innovation is in a tough status. The government financial support could reduce the risk for enterprises by providing technical transformation funds and interest discount and other methods, so as to impel the latecomer firms to increase the innovation investment to carry out innovation activities and improve the innovation performance.

Impact of Financing Support on Innovation Performance of Latecomer Firms

Since most latecomer firms are featured with small scale, imperfect accounting information system and others, banks and fund market are difficult to estimate its financing risk precisely so that the enterprises are trapped into the financing dilemma and hard to carry out all kinds of innovation activities efficiently. The government could help latecomer firms to fix the financing dilemma by providing a financing guarantee and interest discount and other methods. Listing financing and issuance of additional bonds could facilitate enterprises to improve the financing ability and broaden the financing channels to improve innovation performance. At the same time, the government's support would have a significant "signal effect" for investors, and it is good to encourage the potential investors to increase the R&D investment for latecomer firms and participate in the innovation activities of the enterprises (Guo, He, & Xiao, 2011).

It could be known from what mentioned above that government funding policy could help the latecomer firms solve the funding shortage, lack of innovation talents, weak basic technology and worse anti-risk ability; on the other hand, it could help the latecomer firms to increase the innovation investment and have reasonable resource allocation as well as strengthening their independent innovation ability. It could be seen that government funding supports could effectively improve the innovation performance of latecomer firms. Based on it, the paper proposes the following study hypotheses:

H1 Government funding supports imposes positive impact on the improvement of latecomer firms' innovation performance;

H1a Tax preference imposes positive impact on the improvement of latecomer firms' innovation performance;

H1b Financial support imposes positive impact on the improvement of latecomer firms' innovation performance;

H1c Financing supports imposes positive impact on the improvement of latecomer firms' innovation performance.

EMPIRICAL ANALYSIS

Measurement Process of Explanatory Variables

The government funding supports (tax preference, financial support, financing support) in the paper are the explanatory variables. On the basis of the reference to the maturity scales of Andreas, Link and Linder, Zeng Peng et al., Guan Zhimin et al., the paper develops the demanded primary scale combined with the case study process of interview data (Welling, 2016; Guan, et al., 2014; Zeng, Liu, & Wu, 2016; Link & Linder, 2014). The specification is shown in Chart 6.

Measurement Process of Explained Variable

The innovation performance of latecomer firms in the paper is explained as variable. In the previous studies, the foreign and domestic scholars measure the innovation performance from the aspects of innovation profit and efficiency (Eojina, Liang, & Bosselman, 2018; Su & Liu, 2019). Therefore, the paper develops the demanded primary scale based on the study outcomes of Serrano-Bedia et al., Shang Hongtao and Huang Xiaoshuo, Li Xianjun et al. on the measurement of innovation performance (Serrano-Bedia, López-Fernández, & García-Piqueres, 2018; Shang & Huang, 2018; Li, Zhong, Wang, & Wang, 2018). The specification is shown in Chart 7.

Reliability and Validity Analysis

Reliability and Validity Analysis of Government Funding Supports

Reliability Analysis

As seen from Chart 8, the Cronbach's α coefficient of tax preference, financial support and financing support and another dimension of government funding supports are 0.896, 0.885 and 0.885, and all of them are higher than 0.7, so it means that there is high internal consistency. However, the CITC value of the question A4 and A8 is 0.471 and 0.455, which is lower than 0.5; what's more, the Cronbach's α coefficient increases after deleting the question A4 and A8, so the two questions should be eliminated.

KMO Measurement and Bartlett's Test

As seen from Chart 9, the KMO value of the scale of government funding supports is 0.911 while the P-value of Bartlett's test is 0.000; hence, the scale of government funding supports is suitable for factor analysis.

Table 6. Primary scale of government funding supports

Name of Variable	No.	Item
Tax Preference	A1	Enterprises get the support of tax relief policy from government.
	A2	Enterprises get the support of tax return policy from government.
	A3	Enterprises get the support of tax award from government.
	A4	Enterprises get the tax preference from the credit for the projects involved with technical innovation.
	A5	Enterprises get the tax preference from the risk investment in the field of technological R&D.
	A6	Government's preferential tax policy relief the financial pressure of enterprises.
Financial Support	A7	Enterprises get the technical R&D subsidy support from government.
	A8	Enterprises get the technological award support from government.
	A9	Enterprises get the fund support for technology from government.
	A10	Enterprises get the innovation guidance funding supports from government.
	A11	Enterprise' product or service is within the selection range of government procurement.
	A12	Enterprises' technical innovation project is funded by the government subsidy.
	A13	Governments provide loan interest discount for enterprises.
	A14	Enterprises get the support of technological achievements transformation fund set by government.
Financial Support	A15	The financial subsidy provided by government relieve the financial pressure of enterprises.
Financing Support	A16	Enterprises get the perfect financing channel support from government.
	A17	Enterprises get the risk investment support introduced by government.
	A18	Enterprises get the supports of technological achievements transformation policy in the aspect of credit from government.
	A19	Enterprises get the support for loan from government.
	A20	Enterprises get the support of startup financing and investment service from government.
	A21	Government support relieves the financing constraints of enterprises.

Data Source: It is sorted out by the author according to the existing study literatures and interviews.

Analysis on Exploratory Factors

The maximal rotation of variance is adopted to have the analysis on exploratory factors of the scale of government funding supports, and the result is shown in Chart 10.

The analysis result of the exploratory factors shows that factor 1 is composed of A1, A2, A3, A5 and A6; and factor 2 is made by A7, A9, A10, A11, A12, A13, A14 and A15. Factor 3 is composed of A16, A17, A18, A19, A20 and A21.

The cumulative variance contribution rate of the 3 factors is 81.719% and the factor loading is 0.5 above; besides, there is no overlapping among the measurement questions in the factors, which shows that there is a good discriminant validity in the scale of government funding support.

Table 7. Primary scale of innovation performance of latecomer firms

Name of Variable	No.	Item
Innovation Performance of Latecomer Firms	C1	The sales of new product of enterprises keep going up.
	C2	There is improvement in the product development and innovation technology.
	C3	Enterprises enhance the cooperation with stakeholders.
	C4	The speed of enterprises' new product is faster and faster.
	C5	There is a good market response in the improvement and innovation of products.
	C6	Enterprises could present new products faster than that of competitors.
	C7	There is significant improvement of enterprises' innovation technology through cooperation.
	C8	Enterprises form a competitive advantage of differentiation.
	C9	The market shares of enterprises are increasing continuously.

Data Source: It is sorted out by the author according to the existing study literatures and interviews.

Table 8. Reliability analysis of the primary scale of government funding supports

Name of Variable	No.	CITC	Cronbach's Alpha if Item Deleted	Cronbach's Alpha
Tax Preference	A1	0.814	0.841	0.896
	A2	0.856	0.803	
	A3	0.643	0.796	
	A4	0.471	0.994	
	A5	0.674	0.846	
	A6	0.683	0.819	
Financial Support	A7	0.842	0.791	0.854
	A8	0.455	0.899	
	A9	0.767	0.653	
	A10	0.671	0.669	
	A11	0.659	0.654	
	A12	0.792	0.745	
	A13	0.838	0.809	
	A14	0.829	0.792	
	A15	0.739	0.657	
Financing Support	A16	0.715	0.881	0.885
	A17	0.683	0.697	
	A18	0.792	0.751	
	A19	0.818	0.851	
	A20	0.833	0.757	
	A21	0.786	0.770	

Data Source: It is sorted by the author according to the data analysis result.

Table 9. Test result of KMO measurement and Bartlett's test

KMO Value	**0.911**	
Bartlett's Test	Approx. Chi-Square	2472.701
	df	142
	Sig.	0.000

Data Source: It is sorted by the author according to the data analysis result.

Combined with the analysis results above, the final scale of government funding supports is shown in Chart 11.

Reliability and Validity Analysis of Innovation Performance of Latecomer Enterprises

Reliability Analysis

Table 10. Analysis result of exploratory factors of primary scale of government funding supports

Question	Ingredient 1	Ingredient 2	Ingredient 3
A1	**0.768**	0.034	0.103
A2	**0.813**	0.042	0.021
A3	**0.743**	0.118	0.056
A5	**0.544**	0.145	0.005
A6	**0.739**	0.237	0.017
A7	0.036	**0.714**	0.162
A9	0.131	**0.689**	0.145
A10	0.161	**0.681**	0.125
A11	0.064	**0.664**	0.082
A12	0.018	**0.595**	0.304
A13	0.025	**0.727**	0.045
A14	0.261	**0.738**	0.182
A15	0.038	**0.662**	0.111
A16	0.112	0.088	**0.778**
A17	0.023	0.442	**0.685**
A18	0.041	0.036	**0.587**
A19	0.115	0.044	**0.675**
A20	0.008	0.075	**0.794**
A21	0.297	0.016	**0.833**
Variance Contribution Rate	32.635	28.473	20.611
Cumulative Variance Contribution Rate	32.635	61.108	81.719

Data Source: It is sorted by the author according to the data analysis result.

Table 11. Final scale of government funding support

Name of Variable	No.	Item
Tax Preference	A1	Enterprises get the support of tax relief policy from government.
	A2	Enterprises get the support of tax return policy from government.
	A3	Enterprises get the support of tax award from government.
	A4	Enterprises get the tax preference for the technical R&D risk investment.
	A5	Government's preferential tax policy relief the financial pressure of enterprises.
Financial Support	A6	Enterprises get the technical R&D subsidy support from government.
	A7	Enterprises get the fund support for technology from government.
	A8	Enterprises get the innovation guidance funding supports from government.
	A9	Enterprise' product or service is within the selection range of government procurement.
	A10	Enterprises' technical innovation project is funded by the government subsidy.
	A11	Governments provide loan interest discount for enterprises.
	A12	Enterprises get the support of technological achievements transformation fund set by government.
	A13	The financial subsidy provided by government relieve the financial pressure of enterprises.
Financing Support	A14	Enterprises get the support of multiple financing channels from government.
	A15	Enterprises get the risk investment support introduced by government.
	A16	Enterprises get the support of credit policy from government.
	A17	Enterprises get the support for loan from government.
	A18	Enterprise get the support of startup financing and investment service from government.
	A19	Government support relieves the financing constraints of enterprises.

Data Source: It is sorted by the author according to the data analysis result.

As seen from Chart 12, the Cronbach's α coefficient of innovation performance scale of latecomer firms is 0.865, which is higher than 0.7; so it means that there is high internal consistency. Besides, the CITC values of all questions are higher than 0.5 and all Cronbach's α coefficients are lower than 0.865 after deleting any question. Hence, all questions would be reserved.

KMO Measurement and Bartlett's Test

As seen from Chart 13, the KMO value of the innovation performance scale of latecomer firms is 0.962, and the P-value of Bartlett's test is 0.000. It could be concluded that the scale of innovation performance of latecomer firms is suitable for factor analysis.

Analysis on Exploratory Factors

The maximal rotation of variance is adopted to have the analysis on exploratory factors of the innovation performance scale of latecomer firms, and the result is shown in Chart 14.

Through the analysis on exploratory factors of the innovation performance scale of latecomer firms, it is extracted with 1 factor with eigenvalues greater than 1, and the question C1-C9 are in factor 1.

Table 12. Reliability analysis result of primary innovation performance scale of latecomer firms

Name of Variable	No.	CITC	Cronbach's Alpha if Item Deleted	Cronbach's Alpha
Innovation Performance of Latecomer Firms	C1	0.844	0.815	0.865
	C2	0.762	0.629	
	C3	0.808	0.713	
	C4	0.794	0.652	

Data Source: It is sorted by the author according to the data analysis result

Table 13. Test result of KMO measurement and Bartlett's test

KMO	0.926	
Bartlett's Test	Approx. Chi-Square	1859.473
	df	128
	Sig.	0.000

Data Source: It is sorted by the author according to the data analysis result.

The cumulative variance contribution rate is 70.184 and the factor loading is higher than 0.5; besides, there is no overlapping among the measurement questions in the factors. It means that there is a good discriminant validity in the innovation performance scale of latecomer firms.

Combined with the analysis results above, the final innovation performance scale of latecomer firms is shown in Chart 15.

Table 14. Analysis result of exploratory factors of primary innovation performance scale of latecomer firms

Item	Ingredient 1
C1	**0.675**
C2	**0.743**
C3	**0.826**
C4	**0.851**
C5	**0.762**
C6	**0.697**
C7	**0.845**
C8	**0.791**
C9	**0.688**
Variance Contribution Rate	70.184
Cumulative Variance Contribution Rate	70.184

Data Source: It is sorted by the author according to the data analysis result.

Table 15. Final innovation performance scale of latecomer firms

Name of Variable	No.	Item
Innovation Performance of Latecomer Firms	C1	The sales of new product of enterprises keep going up.
	C2	There is improvement in the product development and innovation technology of the company.
	C3	Enterprises enhance the cooperation with stakeholders.
	C4	The success rate of new product development of enterprises keeps increasing.
	C5	There is a good market response in the improvement and innovation of products.
	C6	Enterprises could present new products faster than that of competitors.
	C7	There is significant improvement of the cooperation innovation technology of enterprises.
	C8	There is significant improvement of the competitiveness of enterprises.
	C9	The market share of enterprises is increasing continuously.

Data Source: It is sorted by the author according to the data analysis result

Sample Description

To ensure the objectivity, universality and reliability of the study result, the selection of sample in the paper mainly follows the two principles: sampling enterprises should be latecomer firms and sampling enterprises should be covered with multiple industrial regions.

Firstly, sampling enterprises should be latecomer enterprises. The sample enterprises selected by the paper should go through the process from weak to strong, and all of them have oversea cutting-edged technology and innovation R&D project, so they could have a certain influence in their own industry and they could represent for the latecomer firms' group in China that is having innovation ability improvement.

Secondly, sampling enterprises must be covered with multiple industrial fields. The sampling enterprises selected by the paper is covered new energy technology, biology and new medical technology, electronic information technology, new material technology, aerospace technology, resources and environment technology, technology service industry and many other industrial fields.

The project team has released 628 copies of questionnaires to 189 latecomer firms, and it is recovered with 598 copies. 16 copies of incomplete questionnaires are deleted and there are 582 effective ones collected. The collection rate is 92.7%. Hence, it is confirmed that there are 189 effective sampling enterprises.

Reliability Analysis of Variables

The paper has a reliability test for the variables of large sample data with SPSS software. The reliability test result is shown in Chart 16. The reliability of tax preference, financial support, financing support, talent policy, intellectual property policy, the policy of combination of production, study and research, streamlining government and delegating authority and the innovation performance scale of latecomer firms are 0.899, 0.861, 0.886, 0.891, 0.873, 0.881, 0.879, 0.869, 0.884 and 0.887, which means that the data gained by formal research is reasonable and the analysis of research data could have a precise finding of the relationship between the government supports and the innovation performance of latecomer firms.

Table 16. Reliability test result of variables of large sample

Scale	Cronbach's Coefficient	Project Number
Tax Preference	0.899	5
Financial Support	0.861	8
Financing Support	0.886	6

Data Source: It is sorted by the author according to questionnaires.

Validity Analysis of Variables

Analysis on Exploratory Factors of Government Funding Supports

In Chart 17, the KMO value of the scale of government funding supports is 0.926 and Bartlett's Test of Sphericity is 0.000, which shows that government funding supports is suitable for factor analysis.

Table 17. Test result of KMO measurement and Bartlett's test

KMO	0.926	
Bartlett's Test	Approx. Chi-Square	2369.7852
	df	156
	Sig.	0.000

Data Source: It is sorted by the author according to questionnaires.

In addition, the maximal rotation of variance is adopted to have the analysis on exploratory factors of the scale of government funding supports, and the result is shown in Chart 18.

Three factors are extracted from the scale of government funding supports, and the cumulative variance contribution rate reaches 82.374%, which shows that there is good validity in the scale of government funding supports.

Analysis on Exploratory Factors of Innovation Performance of Latecomer Firms

In Chart 19, the KMO value of innovation performance of latecomer firms is 0.937 and Bartlett's Test of Sphericity is 0.000; hence, the innovation performance scale of latecomer firms is suitable for factor analysis.

In addition, the maximal rotation of variance is adopted to have the analysis on exploratory factors of the innovation performance scale of latecomer firms, and the result is shown in Chart 20.

One factor is extracted from the innovation performance scale of latecomer firms, and the cumulative variance contribution rate reaches 76.357%, which means that there is good validity in the innovation performance scale of latecomer firms.

Table 18. Analysis result of exploratory factors of scale of government funding supports

Item	Ingredient 1	Ingredient 2	Ingredient 3
A1	**0.695**	0.128	0.152
A2	**0.751**	0.015	0.064
A3	**0.799**	0.025	0.049
A4	**0.738**	0.106	0.158
A6	0.015	**0.771**	0.019
A7	0.026	**0.751**	0.194
A8	0.161	**0.684**	0.029
A9	0.131	**0.677**	0.201
A10	0.304	**0.597**	0.199
A11	0.128	**0.732**	0.079
A12	0.025	**0.781**	0.158
A13	0.087	**0.791**	0.167
A14	0.164	0.028	**0.678**
A15	0.221	0.217	**0.714**
A16	0.284	0.069	**0.726**
A17	0.064	0.259	**0.685**
A18	0.031	0.306	**0.591**
A19	0.285	0.059	**0.689**
Variance Contribution Rate	33.715	27.985	20.674
Cumulative Variance Contribution Rate	33.715	61.7	82.374

Data Source: It is sorted by the author according to questionnaires.

Confirmatory Factor Analysis

The confirmatory factor analysis could be used to test the applicability and authenticity of the buildup validity of the questionnaire. On the basis of study outcomes of Cheng Kaiming, Cheng Wenqi and Ge Hong, Xin Shibo et al., the paper chooses absolute goodness of fit and relative goodness of fit as the goodness of fit indexes of the model (Cheng K., 2006; Cheng & Ge, 2012; Xin, Chen, & Zhang, 2014); and the tool adopted by confirmatory factor analysis is AMOS. The specific goodness of fit indexes and the judgement standard is shown in Chart 21.

Table 19. Test result of KMO measurement and Bartlett's test

KMO	0.937	
Bartlett's Test	Approx. Chi-Square	2048.226
	df	139
	Sig.	0.000

Data Source: It is sorted by the author according to questionnaires.

Table 20. Analysis result of exploratory factors of innovation performance scale of latecomer firms

Item	Ingredient 1
C1	**0.784**
C2	**0.695**
C3	**0.805**
C4	**0.847**
C5	**0.852**
C6	**0.762**
C7	**0.816**
C8	**0.749**
C9	**0.814**
Variance Contribution Rate	76.357
Cumulative Variance Contribution Rate	76.357

Data Source: It is sorted by the author according to questionnaires.

Table 21. Goodness of fit indexes and evaluation standard of the model

Type	Indexes	Value Range	Evaluation Standard
Absolute Goodness of Fit Index	CMIN/DF(χ^2/df)	(0,+¥)	Less than 3
	Adjusted goodness of fit index (AGFI)	(0,1)	Greater than 0.8
	Goodness of fit index (GFI)	(0,1)	Greater than 0.85
	Root mean square error of approximation (RMSEA)	(0,+¥)	Less than 0.08
Relative Goodness of Fit Index	Normal fit index (NFI)	(0,1)	Greater than 0.9
	Incremental fit index (IFI)	(0,1)	Greater than 0.9
	Comparative fit index (CFI)	(0,1)	Greater than 0.9

Data Source: It is sorted by the author according to the existing study literatures.

First is the confirmatory factor analysis of government funding supports.

The test result of the measurement model of government funding supports is shown in Chart 22 and the fit result is shown in Chart 23.

The test result shows that the standardized first-order path coefficient and the second-order patch of variables pass the significance test. The fit result shows that is 2.119, less than 3; the value of AGFI is 0.978, more than 0.9; the value of GFI is 0.982, more than 0.9; the value of RMSEA is 0.002, less than 0.08; the value of NFI is 0.974, more than 0.9; the value of IFI is 0.996, more than 0.9; and the value of CFI is 0.997, more than 0.9.

It could be concluded that there is a good fit effect in the model and the measurement of government funding supports in the paper is effective.

Second is the confirmatory factor analysis of innovation performance of latecomer firms.

Table 22. Test result of measurement model of government funding supports

Dimension	Item	Coefficient of Second-Order	Coefficient of First-Order	Significance
Tax Preference	A1	0.879***	0.691	***
	A2		0.595	**
	A3		0.672	***
	A4		0.726	***
	A5		0.638	***
Financial Support	A6	0.916***	0.601	**
	A7		0.812	***
	A8		0.744	**
	A9		0.729	***
	A10		0.854	***
	A11		0.716	***
	A12		0.677	**
	A13		0.702	***
Financing Support	A14	0.832***	0.656	**
	A15		0.742	***
	A16		0.814	**
	A17		0.825	**
	A18		0.653	***
	A19		0.605	***

Note: *** means the significance level $p<0.001$; ** stands for the significance level $p<0.01$.
Data Source: It is sorted by the author according to questionnaires.

The test result of the measurement model of innovation performance of latecomer firms is shown in Chart 24 and the fit result is shown in Chart 25.

The test result shows that the standardized first-order path coefficient and the second-order patch of variables pass the significance test. The fit result shows that it is 1.631, less than 3; the value of AGFI is 0.958, more than 0.9; the value of GFI is 0.973, more than 0.9; the value of RMSEA is 0.012, less than 0.08; the value of NFI is 0.995, more than 0.9; the value of IFI is 0.996, more than 0.9; and the value of CFI is 0.993, more than 0.9.

It could be concluded that there is a good fit effect in the model and the measurement of innovation performance of latecomer firms in the paper is effective.

Table 23. Fit result of measurement model of government funding supports

Fit Index	χ^2/df	AGFI	GFI	RMSEA	NFI	IFI	CFI
Actual Value	2.119	0.978	0.982	0.002	0.974	0.996	0.997

Data Source: It is sorted by the author according to questionnaires.

Table 24. Test result of measurement model of innovation performance of latecomer firms

Dimension	item	Coefficient of Second-Order	Coefficient of First-Order	Significance
Innovation Performance of Latecomer Firms	C1	0.873***	0.761	***
	C2		0.694	***
	C3		0.715	***
	C4		0.813	***
	C5		0.689	**
	C6		0.895	**
	C7		0.739	***
	C8		0.762	**
	C9		0.839	***

Note: *** means the significance level $p<0.001$; ** stands for the significance level $p<0.01$.
Data Source: It is sorted by the author according to questionnaires.

Table 25. Fit result of measurement model of innovation performance of latecomer firms

Fit Index	χ^2/df	AGFI	GFI	RMSEA	NFI	IFI	CFI
Actual Value	1.631	0.958	0.973	0.012	0.995	0.996	0.993

Data Source: It is sorted by the author according to questionnaires.

TEST OF HYPOTHESES

Based on the analysis above, the correlation analysis method and regression analysis method of statistics could be used to test the research hypotheses deduced and concluded from the previous theories with SPSS, SMART and PLS2.0.

Correlation Analysis

The correlation among each variable should be analyzed before the regression analysis. The analysis result of the correlation among variables is shown in Chart 26. The result shows that there is a positive correlation between government funding supports (tax preference, financial support, financing support) and the innovation performance of latecomer firms, which is basically consistent with the study hypotheses, so it proves the feasibility of the study thinking of the paper.

What's more, the VIF value of all variables in the questionnaires is less than 10, which means there is no multicollinearity in the measurement of the study and the measurement result is reliable. Hence, the follow-up regression analysis could be undertaken in the paper.

Table 26. Correlation analysis result among variables

Variable	1	2	3	4	5	6	7	8	9	10	11	12	13	14	15	VIF
Nature of Enterprise	1															4.662
Age of Enterprise	0.331	1														3.336
Scale of Enterprise	0.168*	-0.118	1													1.342
Industry	0.256	0.013	0.185	1												3.561
Region	0.068	0.034	-0.213	0.166	1											1.377
Tax Preference	0.262**	0.398	0.070*	0.251	0.128	1										4.298
Financial Support	0.364	0.081	0.392	0.065	0.016	0.039	1									5.559
Financing Support	0.084	0.152	0.042	0.139	0.276	0.166	0.0209	1								2.367
Innovation Performance	0.405	0.034	0.228	0.019	0.306	0.112**	0.183**	0.384**	0.088**	0.023**	0.126**	0.308**	1			2.957

Note: *** means the significance level $p<0.001$; ** stands for the significance level $p<0.05$.
Data Source: It is sorted by the author according to questionnaires.

Impact Analysis of Government Funding Supports on Innovation Performance of Latecomer Firms

Test of Overall Impact of Government Funding Supports on Innovation Performance of Latecomer Firms

Hypothesis H1 suggests that the government funding supports impose positive impact on innovation performance of latecomer firms.

The innovation performance of latecomer firms is set to be a dependent variable, and the nature of the enterprise, age of enterprise, the scale of enterprise, industry and region are set to be controlled

Table 27. Analysis result of impact of government funding supports on innovation performance of latecomer firms

Variable	Innovation Performance of Latecomer Firms	
	Model I	Model II
Nature of Enterprise	0.147	0.128
Age of Enterprise	0.117	0.109
Scale of Enterprise	-0.0243	-0.0279
Industry	-0.073	-0.062
Region	0.293	0.277
Government Funding Support		0.558***
R Square	0.193	0.383
Adjusted R Square	0.156	0.339
F Value	5.683***	13.724***
VIF	2.013	1.729

Note: *** means the significance level $p<0.001$.
Data Source: It is sorted by the author according to questionnaires.

variables. Government funding supports is set to be an independent variable. The regression model is built with these variables to have a hierarchical regression, and the result is shown in Chart 27.

The innovation performance of latecomer firms is a dependent variable of the two models in Chart 27. The independent variables in model I only includes controlled variables while the government funding supports are added in model II on the basis of model I to test the impact of government funding support on the innovation performance of latecomer firms.

As seen from model II, the government funding supports impose a significant impact on the innovation performance of latecomer firms since the coefficient of 0.558 is far more than others. At that same time, the R squared value of model I is increased from 0.193 to be 0.383 after the variable of government funding supports is added in the model, which shows that government funding supports is an important exploratory role for the innovation performance of latecomer firms.

Hence, hypothesis H1 passes the test.

Impact Analysis of Tax Preference on Innovation Performance of Latecomer Firms

Hypothesis H1a suggests that the tax preference imposes a positive impact on the innovation performance of latecomer firms. The hypothesis H1a is tested with a regression model in the paper, and the result is shown in Chart 28.

The innovation performance of latecomer firms is a dependent variable of the two models in Chart 27. The independent variables in the model I only includes controlled variables while the tax preference is added in model II on the basis of the model I to test the impact of tax preference on the innovation performance of latecomer firms.

As seen from model II, the tax preference imposes a significant impact on the innovation performance of latecomer firms since the coefficient of 0.438 is far more than others. At that same time, the R squared value of the model I is increased from 0.217 to be 0.446 after the variable of tax preference is

Table 28. Analysis result of impact of tax preference on innovation performance of latecomer firms

Variable	Innovation Performance of Latecomer Firms	
	Model I	Model II
Nature of Enterprise	0.203	0.198
Age of Enterprise	0.0729	0.0394
Scale of Enterprise	-0.0459*	-0.0951*
Industry	-0.0288	-0.0173
Region	0.0469	0.0937
Tax Preference		0.438***
R Square	0.217	0.446
Adjusted R Square	0.202	0.293
F Value	3.794***	10.367***
VIF	2.113	1.946

Note: *** means the significance level $p<0.001$; ** stands for the significance level $p<0.05$.
Data Source: It is sorted by the author according to questionnaires.

added in the model, which shows that tax preference is an important exploratory role in the innovation performance of latecomer firms.

Hence, hypothesis H1a passes the test.

Impact Analysis of Financial Support on Innovation Performance of Latecomer Firms

Hypothesis H1b suggests that the financial support imposes a positive impact on the innovation performance of latecomer firms. The hypothesis H1b is tested with a regression model in the paper, and the result is shown in Chart 29.

The innovation performance of latecomer firms is a dependent variable of the two models in Chart 28. The independent variables in the model I only includes controlled variables while the financial support is added in the model II on the basis of the model I to test the impact of financial support on the innovation performance of latecomer firms.

As seen from model II, the financial support imposes a significant impact on the innovation performance of latecomer firms since the coefficient of 0.645 is far more than others. At that same time, the R squared value of the model I is increased from 0.221 to be 0.561 after the variable of financial support is added in the model, which shows that financial support is an important exploratory role in the innovation performance of latecomer firms.

Hence, hypothesis H1a passes the test.

Impact Analysis of Financing Support on Innovation Performance of Latecomer Firms

Hypothesis H1c suggests that financing support imposes a positive impact on the innovation performance of latecomer firms. The hypothesis H1c is tested with a regression model in the paper, and the result is shown in Chart 30.

Table 29. Analysis result of impact of financial support on innovation performance of latecomer firms

Variable	Innovation Performance of Latecomer Firms	
	Model I	Model II
Nature of Enterprise	0.132	0.165
Age of Enterprise	0.103	0.0672
Scale of Enterprise	-0.0139	-0.0148
Industry	0.0116	0.0239
Financial Support		0.645***
R Square	0.221	0.561
Adjusted R Square	0.193	0.285
F Value	3.297***	11.433***
VIF	2.928	1.669

Note: *** means the significance level $p<0.001$.
Data Source: It is sorted by the author according to questionnaires.

The innovation performance of latecomer firms is a dependent variable of the two models in Chart 6-29. The independent variables in model I only includes controlled variables while the financing support is added in the model II on the basis of model I to test the impact of financing support on the innovation performance of latecomer firms.

As seen from model II, financing support imposes significant impact on the innovation performance of latecomer firms since the coefficient of 0.514 is far more than others. At that same time, the R squared value of the model I is increased from 0.221 to be 0.561 after the variable of financing support is added in the model, which shows that financing support is an important exploratory role for innovation performance of latecomer firms.

Hence, hypothesis H1c passes the test.

Table 30. Analysis result of impact of financing support on innovation performance of latecomer firms

Variable	Innovation Performance of Latecomer Firms	
	Model I	Model II
Nature of Enterprise	0.0921*	0.1249*
Age of Enterprise	0.147	0.162
Scale of Enterprise	-0.0361	-0.0687
Industry	-0.0277	-0.0948
Area	0.0228	0.0173
Financing Support		0.514***
Adjusted R Square	0.106	0.279
F Value	3.294***	12.195***
VIF	2.068	1.694

Note: *** means the significance level $p<0.001$; ** stands for the significance level $p<0.05$.
Data Source: It is sorted by the author according to questionnaires.

Table 31. Test result of impact path of government funding supports on innovation performance of latecomer firms

Variable	Path	Standardization Coefficient	T Value
Government Funding Supports	Tax preference ® Innovation performance of latecomer firms	0.768	7.112***
	Financial support ® Innovation performance of latecomer firms	0.613	6.083***
	Financing support ® Innovation performance of latecomer firms	0.542	7.436***

Note: *** means the significance level $p<0.001$.
Data Source: It is sorted by the author according to questionnaires.

Test of Impact Path of Government Funding Supports

Based on the regression analysis, the partial least-square method is adopted in the paper to test the impact path of all dimensions of government funding supports on the innovation performance of latecomer firms. The analysis result is shown in Chart 31.

According to Chart 31, the standardization coefficients of three dimensions of financial funding supports, tax preference ® innovation performance of latecomer firms, financial support ® innovation performance of latecomer firms and financing support ® innovation performance of latecomer firms are 0.768, 0.613 and 0.542 respectively, which shows that the impact of tax preference on the innovation performance of latecomer firms is more significant than that of financial support and financing support.

Analysis of Test Result

(1) Test result analysis of impact of government funding supports on innovation performance of latecomer firms

The empirical test result shows that the governments funding supports are tax preference, financial support, financing support these three dimensions. And all of these three dimensions could significantly boost the improvement of the innovation performance of latecomer firms. The impact of tax preference on the innovation performance of latecomer firms is the most significant.

(2) Most significant promoting impact of tax preference on innovation performance of latecomer firms

The promoting impact of tax preference policy on innovation performance of latecomer firms is more significant than that of financial support and financing support. Here is the specific analysis:

Firstly, in view of the financial support policy of the government, there is a strong pertinence as a pre-incentives policy, but it is bad for latecomer firms to make the maximal play of the utility of optimal allocation of resources in the highly competitive market for the hard prediction of the implementation effect and insufficient flexibility. Obviously, as am after-event supportive policy, the tax preference policy of the government could effectively get rid of the shortage of the financial subsidy since the latecomer firms could enjoy relevant tax preference policies when the scale and display degree of the firms carrying out innovation reach the standard set by the government. Such conditions could have a better show of the government's intention to encourage the latecomer firms to carry out innovation. Hence, tax preference policy could be a more efficient incentive method to improve the innovation performance of latecomer firms.

Secondly, for the financing support policy of the government, it could solve the financing constraints of these latecomer firms to carry out innovation activities to some extent, and it could build a good financial market environment with a multi-layer financial market and abundant financing channels. However, compared with the universality of tax preference policy, the object selection of financing support of government is harsh since it would focus on the enterprises with better ability of repayment, better short-term profit and strong display degree of innovation outcomes; while those with higher risk, smaller scale and insignificant short-term profit are hard to get the support.

The test result of the hypotheses is shown in Chart 32.

Table 32. Test result of the hypotheses of the paper

Hypothesis No.	Hypothesis Description	Test Result
Hypothesis H1	There is positive impact of government funding supports on the innovation performance of latecomer firms.	Support
Hypothesis H1a	There is positive impact of tax preference on the innovation performance of latecomer firms.	Support
Hypothesis H1b	There is positive impact of financial support on the innovation performance of latecomer firms	Support
Hypothesis H1c	There is positive impact of financing support on the innovation performance of latecomer firms	Support

CONCLUSION

Government Funding Supports Impose Significant Promoting Impact on the Innovation Performance of Latecomer Firms

Government supporting enterprises to carry out innovation activities is an important method for latecomer firms to acquire heterogeneous resources for enhancing the competitive edge and transferring to be innovation performance. According to the result of the case study and the result of the empirical study, government funding supports has a significant promotion on the innovation performance of latecomer firms. Specifically, different funding supports provided by the government to help the enterprises increase the R&D investment and carry out innovation activities during the startup period, growing period and catching-up period through tax preference, financial support and financing support are the direct promoters, and they significantly improve the innovation performance of latecomer firms.

It is found in the study that, among the government funding supports, tax preference imposes more significant promoting impact on the innovation performance of latecomer firms, which means that the tax preference stipulated by governments for helping latecomer firms to have innovation development could provide much more universal financial support for these enterprises in undertaking innovation activities.

Suggestion on Policies

The previous study outcomes show that government provides innovation development fund for latecomer firms through tax preference, financial support and financing support, etc., which is a direct promoter for enterprises to increase the investment of innovation and to carry out innovation activities. It also significantly improves the innovation performance of latecomer firms. To keep motivating the innovation willingness of latecomer firms to keep improving the innovation performance of enterprises with the government funding supports, the government should improve the policy system of funding supports from the following aspects so as to keep enhancing the effect of innovative fund utilization of enterprises with the supports from the government.

Firstly, the government should build up a perfect tax preference policy system with industrial tax preference as the main ingredient and the regional tax preference as a supplement. According to the study result of the paper, as the most effective government supportive policy to boost the innovation performance of latecomer firms, tax reference reduces the subjective arbitrariness of government funding supports policy compared with that of financial support and financing support, and its universality eliminates the interest binding behavior between government and enterprise and power rent-seeking space. Therefore, the government should make the tax preference an important tool to encourage latecomer firms to positively undertake innovation activities. And it should keep raising the accuracy degree and incentive effect of tax preference policy. It should boost the continuous improvement of innovation performance of latecomer firms with the aim of ceaselessly raising the innovation willingness of latecomer firms. Based on it, the government should have an organic integration of tax preference policies distributed in multiple government departments to build up a tax preference policy system with the industrial tax preference as the main ingredient and the regional tax preference as a supplement to effectively encourage the latecomer enterprises' innovation development with the full coverage of the whole process of production and business.

Secondly, the government should build up a perfect supervision mechanism to ensure that the financial fund would be used for the innovation development of latecomer firms safely and efficiently. According to the study result of the paper, the effect of financial support of government is weaker than that of tax preference. On the one hand, it should further regulate the financial support policy to maintain some of them with significant effect while the ones with worse effect should be rectified or cancelled; on the other hand, the supervision force should be increased for some enterprises "cheating for" the financial support from the government. There should be precise control of the financial support fund's real use and flow direction when streamlining government and delegating authority, so as to ensure that the financial support fund could be fully used in the "key point" to push the innovation development of latecomer firms; and it could practically evoke the latecomer firms' innovation passion and improve their innovation performance.

At the same time, the government should practically solve such difficulties as "difficult financing" and "expensive financing" for latecomer firms through different financing methods according to their own scales and credits. It is known from the research that financing constraints are the "ordinary" problem faced by the innovation development of latecomer firms in China. Therefore, the government should provide purposeful financing methods for latecomer firms with different scales and credits, so as to feasibly solve the financing constraints of the latecomer firms.

Finally, the government should also improve the fund collaborative support mode with the main body of tax preference, financial support and financing support. To enhance the coupling and adaptation of government funding supports for the improvement of latecomer firms' innovation performance and to keep improving the implementation effect of government funding supports, the government should focus on coordinating various financial support portfolio policies to keep perfecting the fund collaborative support mode with the main body of tax preference, financial support and financing support, so as to encourage latecomer firms to keep increasing the innovation performance.

In conclusion, the government should build up a perfect tax preference policy system during the innovation process of latecomer firms; and it should set a perfect supervision mechanism to ensure that financial fund could be used for the innovation development of latecomer firms safely and efficiently. It should also practically solve the "difficult financing" and "expensive financing" for these enterprises with various financing methods. The collaborative support mode of government funds should be improved and perfected. Besides, it should improve the fund support mechanism and optimize the fund support structure continuously and ceaselessly. The application effect of coordinating various financial support portfolio policies should be viewed to achieve the "double-increase" of the effectiveness of fund policy. All of these would evoke latecomer firms' passion and motivation for continuous innovation and push the ceaseless promotion of the innovation performance of latecomer firms.

Limits and Expectation of Study

Being enlightened by the previous study outcomes, the paper builds up a model of the relationship between government supports and innovation performance of latecomer firms through the grounded root method with a comprehensive application of the government intervention theory and innovation theory. In addition, the effectiveness of relevant theoretical hypotheses is tested through a mathematical-statistical analysis method so as to conclude a series of conclusions that could be a reference to the stipulation of public policies in China.

However, there are some limits and imperfection in the study, and they are the main two aspects:

Firstly, the paper divides the government funding support into tax preference, financial support and financing support. The impact of each dimension on innovation performance of latecomer firms have been studied in the paper, and there is a comparison of different impact effects, but there is no profound study on the coordination mechanism of the dimensions involved in fund support on the improvement of latecomer firms' innovation performance.

Secondly, the paper makes the latecomer firms in China as study objects, so it is harder to have a series of deeper data collection. The measurement of variables such as innovation performance of the latecomer firms in the paper are based on the subjective questionnaire survey method, and there is a lack of objective indicators to reflect the innovation situation of these enterprises, neither the consideration of the difference of enterprise's subjective innovation initiative.

REFERENCES

Ahuja, G., & Lampert, C. (2016). Entrepreneurship in the large corporation: A longitudinal study of how established firms create breakthrough inventions. *Strategic Management Journal*, (22), 521–543.

Cheng, K. (2006). Characteristics and Application of Structural Equation Model. *Statistics & Decisions*, (10), 22–25.

Cheng, W., & Ge, H. (2012). Application of Structural Equation in Management Research. *Statistics & Decisions*, (22), 90–92.

Del Bo, C., Ferraris, M., & Florio, M. (2017). Governments in the market for corporate control: Evidence from M&A deals involving state-owned enterprises. *Journal of Comparative Economics*, *45*(1), 89–109. doi:10.1016/j.jce.2016.11.006

Eojina, K., Liang, T., & Bosselman, R. (2018). Measuring customer perceptions of restaurant innovativeness: Developing and validating a scale. *International Journal of Hospitality Management*, *74*, 85–98. doi:10.1016/j.ijhm.2018.02.018

Garcia-Perez-de-Lema, D., Madrid-Guijarro, A., & Philippe Martin, D. (2017). Influence of university-firm governance on SMEs innovation and performance levels. *Technological Forecasting and Social Change*, *123*, 250–261. doi:10.1016/j.techfore.2016.04.003

Gkypali, A., & Trianni, A. (2015). Evaluating the barriers to specific industrial energy efficience measures: An exploratory study in small and medium-sized enterprises. *Journal of Cleaner Production*, (82), 70–83.

Guan, Z., Wu, H., Tao, J., Cao, Z., Yang, J., & Wang, F. (2014). An Exploratory Study on the Role of Government Support and Success Factors in Industry University Research Cooperation: Based on the Survey Data of Enterprises and Universities/Scientific Research Institutions in Liaoning Province. *Science & Technology Progress and Policy*, (11), 43–48.

Guo, Z., He, W., & Xiao, X. (2011). Government Subsidies, Extra Behaviors and Changes of R & D Activities in Strategic Emerging Industries. *Macroeconomics*, (11), 63–69.

Habib, D., Luo, J., & Zhong, J. (2018). A literature survey of financial reporting in private firms. *Research in Accounting Regulation*, *15*(4), 1–7. doi:10.1016/j.racreg.2018.03.005

Han, Y., Luo, J., & Zhong, J. (2016). Research on the Influence of Dual Leadership on Team Innovation Performance: Based on the Perspective of Convention. *Chinese Journal of Management Science*, (1), 70–85.

Huang, Y., & Li, H. (2015). Research on Industry Characteristics, Government Support and Industry Innovation Performance. *Review of International Economics*, (9), 43–56.

Jia, X., & Heng, L. (2016). On the Construction Paradigm of Chinese Local Management Theory Based on "Grounded Spirit". *Chinese Journal of Management*, (3), 336–346.

Jia, Z. (2015). The Application of Grounded Theory in Public Management Research: Method and Practice. *Chinese Public Administration*, (3), 90–96.

Jing, Z., & Aydm, O. (2014). Structure of Small and Medium-Sized Enterprises in Turkey and Global Competitiveness Strategies. *Procedia: Social and Behavioral Sciences*, (150), 212–220.

Kim, B., Kim, E., Miller, D. J., & Mahoney, J. T. (2016). The impact of the timing of patents on innovation performance. *Research Policy*, *45*(4), 914–928. doi:10.1016/j.respol.2016.01.017

Kollmann, T., & Stockmann, C. (2014). Filling the entrepreneurial orientation-performance gap: The mediating effects of exploratory and exploitative innovations. *Entrepreneurship Theory and Practice*, *38*(5), 1001–1026. doi:10.1111/j.1540-6520.2012.00530.x

Li, X., Zhong, L., Wang, J., & Wang, W. (2018). The Influence of Open Innovation and Absorption capacity in Innovation Performance—Based on the Empirical Analysis of Auto Industry in China. *Science. Research Management*, (1), 45–52.

Link, S. S., & Linder, C. (2014). Business Model Prototyping—Using the Morphological Analysis to Develop New Business Models. *Procedia: Social and Behavioral Sciences*, *148*, 1–9.

Manuel, L. (2012). Network Governance of Innovation Policies: The Technological Plan in Portugal. *Science & Public Policy*, *39*(5), 655–668. doi:10.1093cipolcs043

Piperopoulos, P., Jie, W., & Chengqi, W. (2018). Outward FDI, location choices and innovation performance of emerging marke enterprises. *Research Policy*, *47*(1), 232–240. doi:10.1016/j.respol.2017.11.001

Serrano-Bedia, A. M., López-Fernández, C., & García-Piqueres, G. (2018). Complementarity between innovation knowledge sources: Does the innovation performance measure matter. *Business Research Quarterly*, *21*(1), 53–67. doi:10.1016/j.brq.2017.09.001

Serrano-Bedia, A. M., Piva, E., & Rossi-Lamastra, C. (2014). Open innovation and within-industry diversification in small and medium enterprises: The case of open source software firms. *Research Policy*, (43), 891–902.

Shang, H., & Huang, X. (2018). Dynamic Interaction Effects of Government Subsidies, R & D investment and Innovation Performance. *Studies in Science of Science*, (3), 446–455.

Shou, K., Wei, J., & Liu, Y. (2018). Portfolio Diversity Framework of Latecomer Alliances: A Qualitative Comparative Analysis. *Studies in Science of Science*, (7), 1254–1263.

Shu, C. L., Wang, Q., Gao, S. X., & Liu, C. (2015). Firm Patenting, Innovations and Government Institutional Support as a Double-Edged Sword. *Journal of Product Innovation Management*, *32*(2), 290–305. doi:10.1111/jpim.12230

Stadler, C., & Nobes, C. W. (2018). Accounting for government grants: Standard-setting and accounting choice. *Journal of Accounting and Public Policy*, *21*(5), 101–119. doi:10.1016/j.jaccpubpol.2018.02.004

Su, J., & Liu, C. (2019). An Analysis of the Paradoxical Relationship between political Embeddedness and Independent Innovation Performance. *Studies in Science of Science*, *2*, 375–384.

Sun, Z., & Song, W. (2012). The Influence of R & D Investment on the Performance of Industrial Innovation: Empirical Evidence from Chinese Manufacturing Industry. *Shuliang Jingji Jishu Jingji Yanjiu*, *4*, 49–63.

Wang, K., & Zhou, X. (2017). The Nonlinear Effect of R & D Investment on Technological Innovation Performance: An Empirical Analysis Based on Micro Data. *Statistics and Information Forum, 12*, 86-93.

Wang, L., & Hu, Y. (2017). Does Venture Fund Promote Innovation Performance? An Empirical Test based on Panel Data of Chinese Enterprises. *Journal of Financial Research*, *1*, 177–190.

Welling, A. (2016). The paradox effects of uncertainty and flexibility on investment in renewables under governmental support. *European Journal of Operational Research*, *251*(3), 1016–1028. doi:10.1016/j.ejor.2015.12.027

Wu, H., & Chen, J. (2018). The Innovation Effect of Enterprises' Dual Strategy of internationalization: With the Adjustment of Competition Intensity. *Studies in Science of Science*, (2), 334–341.

Xin, S., Chen, Y., & Zhang, C. (2014). Review on the Application of Structural Equation Modeling. *Journal of Industrial Technological Economics*, (5), 67–71.

Yan, T. (2014). The Motivation, Ways and Approaches of Government Supporting Scientific and Technological Innovation. *Economy Forum,* (10), 151-155.

Yun, J., Ma, W., & Chen, L. (2012). Research on the Interaction between Openness and Network Capability on Innovation Performance. *Science Research Management*, (7), 8–15.

Zeng, M., Ly, S., & Wu, Q. (2014). Research on the Relationship between Government Support, Trust and External Integration of Supply Chain. *Chinese Journal of Management Science*, (12), 48–55.

Zeng, P., Liu, Y., & Wu, X. (2016). The Impact of Government Support on Technological Innovation of Enterprises—From the Perspective of integration of Resource Based View and System Based View. *Economic Management*, (2), 12–26.

Zhan, Z. (2018). The Mechanism of Channel Network Embeddedness on Cooperative Innovation Performance. *Economic Survey: With the Mediating Variables of Relational Learning and Dual Ability*, 115-122.

Zhao, Y., Xu, G., Liu, Z., & Xie, M. (2017). Research on the Innovation Performance of Chinese Enterprises from the Perspective of Government Support. *Science Research Management*, (4), 412–418.

Zheng, Y., & Wang, H. (2017). Government Support for SMEs Innovation: Theoretical Basis, Policy Representation and Function Path. *Modern Economic Research*, (10), 126–133.

Chapter 3
A Policeman's Ethnography

Paul Mack
Illinois Institute of Technology, USA

ABSTRACT

This chapter is an ethnological examination of a police officer, the police culture, and the type of individual that makes up the "good cop." Through the lens of over 30 years' experience as a police officer in both small suburban and large city police departments, the author hopes to provide some insight into his experience. This chapter will most likely not affect anything institutional but may change the individual's view of police officers in the future.

INTRODUCTION

Beginning in 2014 with the media frenzy surrounding an Officer involved shooting in Ferguson Missouri, media fabrications, political condemnation, radical agendas, aggrandizement of both the frequency and severity of real and imagined Police misconduct, combined with intense scrutiny, and attacks on personal and professional character have led to an increasingly negative narrative and distasteful view of the American Police Officer. In this strange new era that can be described as increasingly hostile and unforgiving to those men and women in American Law Enforcement, I began asking myself about the very nature of police work and the shared systems of beliefs and personal attributes that make up the majority of our Law Enforcement Officers. What makes a good Police Officer? Why would any sane person join this profession?

This paper is an ethnological examination of a Police Officer, the Police culture, and the type of individual that makes up the "Good Cop." Through the lens of over 30 years' experience as a Police Officer in both small suburban and large city Police Departments I hope to provide some insight into my experience. This paper will most likely not affect anything institutional but may change the individual's view of Police Officers in the future.

DOI: 10.4018/978-1-6684-2314-1.ch003

METHODOLOGY

This is an ethnographic study of a Police Officer—me. Drawing upon over 30 years of experience in both suburban and big city policing, and as a Police supervisor for 21 years, I examine and re-examine the life and experiences that brought me to and allowed me to survive this profession. People are curious about Police Officers, and much of the available sources of information about law enforcement is gained through hearsay, limited interaction, often skewed media representation, and Hollywood. For this paper, I relied upon a recounting of my life, what and who prepared me for public service, and how it all related to my experiences as an Officer. In my attempt to answer the question, "What makes a Good Police Officer," I have reviewed many sources of literature that have helped me understand the complexities of motivation, new theories of leadership and ethics. Although enlightening, they fall short of providing a picture of the average and most commonly found Police Officer.

Limitations

As with any study, this paper has limitations. As an ethnographic study, this paper suffers from this more so, and I acknowledge those limitations. Perhaps the most significant limitation is the author who must rely on memories and experiences as primary source materials. Some memories come freely and naturally imperfectly. Other memories, purposely buried deep for my sanity or associated with negative incidents, were difficult and painful to recount. I understand that this study is colored by my personal experience, which is not every Officer's experience. I acknowledge that I am a Police Officer and I am incredibly fond of them! As such, I am biased regarding my opinion of Police Officers and Police Departments. I wished to interview a diverse group of Police Officers from a doctoral program to discover their experiences, views, and ideas of what a good Police Officer should look like but was unfamiliar with the Institutional Review Board (IRB) requirements. Unfortunately, there was insufficient time to submit, obtain approval, and take the required tests from the IRB that they require to conduct those interviews and surveys. It would have been nice to have more time to explore this topic and to have had interaction with the CPD Doctoral students; I believe they would have been illuminating. While studies on specific incidents or use of force determiners are numerous, there is a lack of current primary data about the Police Officer as a complete human being.

Literature Review

I have reviewed many sources of literature that have helped me understand the complexities of motivation, new theories in leadership, and ethics. Although enlightening, they fall short of providing a picture of the average and most commonly found Police Officer. Studies into the "Police Personality" have been limited, and modern studies are almost nonexistent. In Robert Balch's 1972 study, he wrote on the traits that make up the Police Officer and posited that like any stereotype, the Police may have fallen victim to crippling stereotyping that society accepts as truth. He references the fact that then, as in now, there is very little empirical evidence to quantify the question. Of the personality studies available, each used different techniques and scales, and there is little agreement between studies. (Balch, 1972) In 2005, Twersky-Glasner revisited the "Police Personality" question citing studies as far back as 1937 (Twersky-Glasner, 2005), but most having been completed in the 1970s. While I'm unable to say whether or not those studies apply today, the lack of modern research creates a gap; people, motivations, and accepted behavior change over time. The physical attributes required to work as a Police Officer have changed, could it be that what makes a good Police Officer has changed too? I found that literature, video, and film paint a broad and largely unflattering picture of America's Law Enforcement and most modern studies focus narrowly on a specific trait, act or incident. An ethnological examination may bridge the gap between identified traits, superficial aspects, and the complete Officer.

Analysis

First, let me state that I am a second-generation Police Officer and have been a one for over thirty years. My father was a suburban Police Officer for more than four decades, eventually becoming the Chief of Police in Addison, Illinois. I was fortunate to have worked in both suburban Cook County, and in the City of Chicago, where I've worked as a patrolman, detective, sergeant, Tactical Sergeant, Mounted Sergeant, Lieutenant, Tactical Lieutenant, Watch Commander, and currently as the Unit Commanding Officers of the Chicago Police Mounted Patrol, the Chicago Police Marine Unit, and the Chicago Police Helicopter Unit. I "grew up" on this job and have always been proud of my profession. I love Police Officers; I love the citizens that I serve, and the city that I protect.

Second, I never would have begun this endeavor if not for the encouragement and support of my dear Professor, Joanne Howard. Her suggestion that I should share my experiences and could somehow convey the face of the average Police Officer based upon what I find to be the shared morals, ethics, and conduct of my brothers and sisters in Law Enforcement was both exciting and a daunting challenge.

Childhood

When I look back, I can see that everything in my early life prepared me for a lifetime of public service. I guess that sounds a bit bleak unless of course, you feel as I do, that there is no higher calling than to serve; whether that be as an educator, healthcare worker, firefighter, soldier, state's attorney, public defender, municipal worker or police officer.

I was one of six children in a family that was blessed to have both parents in the home as active participants in the family structure. My parents planned to have a large family and agreed that my mother would quit her job as a nurse to raise the family while my father continued his work as a Police Officer in the village we lived. As you can imagine, feeding, clothing, and caring for two adults and six children in a single income home wasn't easy. With six kids all about 12 months apart, my dedicated and determined mother was run ragged twenty-four hours a day, seven days a week, managing and maintaining the household and performing miracles of budgeting, logistics, and childcare. My father's Police schedule rotated every twenty-eight days, from the day watch ("2nd Watch") 7:00 am to 3:30 pm, to the afternoon watch (3rd Watch) 3:00 pm to 11:30 pm, to midnights (1st Watch) 11:00 pm to 7:30 am, throughout my childhood. Almost every bit of his "free time" was spent picking up extra shifts at work, or at another of his part-time jobs; operating forklifts in the industrial park near us, unloading boxcars for Owens Corning, butchering deer for hunters during the hunting season, and working security at the local hospital Emergency Room and a hotel in Itasca, Illinois. Through immense personal sacrifice, determination, and sheer force of will, my parents ensured that we always had enough to eat, clean clothes on our backs, and a roof over our heads.

We weren't deprived, but we weren't handed anything either. Each of us learned and understood that we had to work to obtain things that we wanted because there was nothing left after providing for our essentials. We also learned that my mother would move heaven and earth to help us make our dreams come true. Our grandparents were a significant and positive presence in our lives. When they retired and moved to Florida, we desperately missed them and wanted to visit them. Knowing that we couldn't afford the trip, and my father couldn't take time off, we were all pretty sad—the "moping around" kind of sad. My mother, who probably missed them and their help as much as we missed their presence, found a part-time job that we could all do after school and on Saturdays to start saving for the trip. Yes, there were child labor laws, but this was my Uncle's business, and we could do this job in the safety and security of our home. The task we were given was to place large, thick gaskets into plastic caps that were used to seal barrels. We never actually saw a barrel, but I can still see those caps—thousands of them! In our dining room at our huge table, we formed a production line that would make Henry Ford proud. It was tedious work, but we made our fun by competing for the most finished caps and clowning around as little kids do. We didn't do this work every day and usually didn't work for more than a couple hours. My mother always supervised, and she did something that at the time, really irked me, but something that has paid me in dividends. You see, my mother knew how long our short attention spans were, and right at the time we began playing or griping more than working, she would bring us back on task for just a little bit longer before she would declare the job done. She did this until we could work and focus reasonably well for extended periods by always asking for a little bit more. As I grew older, I realized that this technique has allowed me to work and remain focused on tasks given to me—even the mundane ones—until the job is complete. Our reward for our work was my mother's smile and the proud feeling that we were helping to see our grandparents. She usually threw in a tasty snack to replenish our exhaustion. I remember the first check the family received, and although I don't know the amount, I remember the thrill and excitement of seeing our combined labor turned into "tons of money." Having minimal experience with money, I was somewhat dismayed that what I thought was a lot of money, was in fact, not. We continued with this job for only three months, but the next spring, my parents loaded up the station wagon, and we headed to Florida to see our grandparents. I didn't know what that good feeling was at the time, but I know now that it was a feeling of pride—we did it!

Rules & Manners

My parents were a united front when it came to raising the family. Before having us, they planned together what they wanted for their children, and how they could attain it. Together, they made conscious, deliberate decisions. I was raised on a steady diet of respect, accountability, manners, civics, right action, and chivalry. We had a very structured life of waking at 6:00 a.m., school by 7:15 a.m., dinner at 5:00 p.m., and bedtime at 8:00 p.m. We had assigned household chores given out by our age and ability, and my mother painstakingly taught each of her children how to be self-sufficient. My mother did not believe in gender-defined roles, and we all could cook, clean, and do laundry by the time we were 12. I could even iron military creases (on purpose), although my mother would never let me iron my father's uniform shirts! Ah, the many messes we made, the food we burned, and clothes we shrank or turned pink!

My mother's attitude to just about every issue or dilemma was, "We can do that," and "You can do that." I don't know if it was just the era (1960s–1970s), but she always told me that I could *be* anything and *do* anything I set my mind and talent to. We were taught to treat everyone with politeness and respect, and to "never judge a book by its cover." All adults were Mr., Mrs., or Miss; all requests were made using "please" and "thank you." Those times I was asked by an adult to do something, it was expected that it would be done immediately. (This was to cause me some anxiety as a new supervisor.) I understood accountability before I was able to spell it!

I've always marveled at children who got "allowance." What a wonderful thing! I've known of children getting an allowance for doing chores, going to school, getting good grades, or for just being themselves. Household chores, going to school, doing your best to get good grades, and behaving was *expected* of each of us as children. My parents always noticed when we did well, praised and rewarded us for going above and beyond, but held us accountable when we fell short—especially for reasons in our control.1 I didn't get an allowance and growing up that way instilled in me a sense of duty. It taught me, first and foremost, that we all had a duty to the "greater good" of the household when we helped and did chores. Each chore completed was a load taken from my mother, father, siblings, or made something more pleasant for everyone. A duty to ourselves when we put effort into school, though that sometimes takes a while to figure out. Each "stupid class" and "stupid assignment" that I put my effort into or that I tried my very best was a great learning experience, a positive reflection on myself, and my parents. It opened doors to me that has led to everything I desired.

School

Report-card day was always a bit stressful for us since my parents would get our grades and each of us would have a semi-private conference regarding them (there was no a lot of privacy in our large household). With grading scales A through F, we were expected to be in the A or B range. I honestly don't recall any of us having many C's, and certainly not a single D. I was, however, the only child in the Mack household to get an F. I was in the 7th grade, and my English teacher, who shall only be referred to as "Mr. X," gave me an "F" for the year. It was a complete shock since there was no warning, no "pre-fail" parent-teacher conference, and no note next to the grade with a reason. Needless to say, my meeting with my parents went abysmally; I had no idea how I could possibly have failed and could not account for what I thought was the worst of all things to happen in my short life. I was always a good student, probably not the brightest, but I tried pretty hard, and I took my grades very seriously. It was during this time, with Mr. X as my teacher between my 5th and 6th-grade years, that I developed a firm dislike of school that unfortunately, has continued to impact the way I feel about my continuing education.

Notice I stated, "...the way I *feel* about my continuing education," and not the way I *think*. Feelings are extraordinarily powerful, and the way a person feels about everything will most likely dictate their actions and reactions. The failing grade was not the reason; my treatment from Mr. X for two years was. This was one of the more painful times in my early life, and I'll recount some of it for you.

The summer before I entered the 3rd grade, I was diagnosed with Perthes disease of the left hip. Although not actually a disease, it's a softening and necrosis of the femoral head due to an inadequate blood supply. It's still unclear the cause(s) of the inadequate blood supply, but treatment and outlook are very different today. In the early 1970s, however, not much was known about the prognosis and treatment, and I faced the eventual avascular necrosis and collapse of my left hip. I was placed into a fifteen-pound leg brace that ensured no weight could be put on the leg or hip, and I had a right shoe that was built up a couple of inches to equalize the height differences. It was my "Frankenstein shoe," and I wore that brace and platform shoe for just over four years until right before entering the 8th grade. At one of the most active periods of childhood, I was unable to do everything that active children do. Even walking was an experience in pain as the surgical steel and leather bindings rubbed and tortured the flesh on my calf thigh and groin. During that period I was faced with the innocence, ignorance, and cruelty of children my age; the kindness and concern of some adults, and the cruelty, stupidity, and intolerance of others. Mr. X was a big, heavy man with a big personality and loud voice. He taught English and social studies in the public junior high school (grades 6th through 8th). In class, he carried a big stick that he would slam down on the desk of anyone he thought might not be paying attention to his lesson. He started class each day by coughing up a wad of sputum, walking to the window, and spitting it out onto a tree, where it sagged and dripped. He would say, "One man's garbage is another man's feast!" From the look of the tree, he had been doing this for years. It was without thought or hesitation that he belittled any wrong answers from the class. In the two years that I was his student, he never had cause to slam his stick on my desk.

What I recall was his outright dislike of me the first day in class when I could not sit properly in the one-piece desks due to the shape and limitation on my leg brace. I remember him pointing my issue out and embarrassing me. I don't recall his reactions to my wrong answers, because Mr. X wouldn't pick me when my hand was raised. Mr. X communicated to me through demeaning remarks about my infirmity, then later, about the fact that my father was a Police Officer. Throughout those two years, I was subjected to a daily unpleasant remarks about my physical limitations, like my inability to play sports like real men (though truth be told, Mr. X was so overweight that he was as far from an athletic man as I was!), or he would make derogatory statements about law enforcement. In my second year with him, in front of the entire class, he directed me to a "special desk," and a chair in the back of the room "made special for special people" like me. He ramped up his repertoire that second year with increasing numbers of snide remarks about law enforcement that culminated in direct assaults on my father. "Mack's dad can just pull a few people over to get money; the rest of us have to work for it." That last comment occurred a couple of months before the end of our school year, and it was one that I told my father about. At that time, my father arranged a meeting at the school with Mr. X and the principal, where *my* misunderstanding of the comment was clarified. Now, the "F" grade resulted in my parents arranging another meeting with the principal and Mr. X. I'll never forget that day, I was in there and my reputation—and my backside—were at stake. The meeting was in Mr. X's classroom where I was directed to sit in my chair in the back of the room while the adults spoke together at the front. Very quickly, my parents were told that I failed to turn in an important paper that was due the last week of class. My father asked why I did not turn in the paper, to which I fervently replied and eagerly maintained that I did turn it in and that I even illustrated it with my drawings. In front of my parents and the principal, Mr. X called me a liar, which went over very badly with the principal, my parents and me. I was being accused of not doing my work and of being a liar, and my calls of innocence seemed to fall on deaf ears. It was his word or mine. Oh, if this had only been modern times where computers and copy machines are in every home! I was completely demoralized, powerless to refute Mr. X's claim, and on the edge of real despair. In a generous gesture, Mr. X agreed that I could turn the paper in by the following Monday, and he would give me a passing grade of "D," which meant that I would not be doomed to repeat his class. I had never received a "D" grade, and somehow, the threat of repeating his class meant less at the moment than a "D" grade on my record and the injustice of the situation. While I sat in that in my special chair feeling powerless and dejected by the lack of justice, I turned around to face the back of the room. Heck, I was so sad, frustrated and angry, that I was beginning to cry. As I slowly looked up at the back wall, I gazed through liquid-filled eyes at a corkboard affixed there with very colorful drawings done by other classmates. I instinctively moved from my chair to the board and was greeted by the site of eight or ten student papers, slightly crowded, and pinned in place. Each one of these papers was illustrated by hand, by the author, and they were posted as examples of students that went the "extra mile." I looked at them wondering what was

Figure 1. Quote

"This is the oath of a Knight of King Arthur's Round Table and should be for all of us to take to heart. I will develop my life for the greater good. I will place character above riches, and concern for others above personal wealth, I will never boast, but cherish humility instead, I will speak the truth at all times, and forever keep my word, I will defend those who cannot defend themselves, I will honor and respect women, and refute sexism in all its guises, I will uphold justice by being fair to all, I will be faithful in love and loyal in friendship, I will abhor scandals, and gossip-neither partake nor delight in them, I will be generous to the poor and to those who need help, I will forgive when asked, that my own mistakes will be forgiven, I will live my life with courtesy and honor from this day forward."

— King Arthur, Le Morte d'Arthur: King Arthur and the Legends of the Round Table Quote By King Arthur: "This Is The Oath Of A Knight Of ... (n.d.). Retrieved from https://www.goodreads.com/quotes/530194-this-is-the-oath-of-a-knight-of-king-art

happening when Behold! The paper pinned at the bottom right, partially overlapped, was mine. Without excusing myself, I exclaimed, "Here it is! This is it! I told you I did it and handed it in!" Of course, Mr. X had to examine it closely to be sure, but justice was mine that day. In the end, and for whatever reason, I got an "A" that year, and I never seemed to come into contact with Mr. X again.

Lessons

I was always taught to respect others, and I learned that teachers were among the people that deserve to be respected most. We were taught that Police Officers, Fireman, the school nurse, and teachers were safe and could be trusted. Teachers are supposed to be some of the good guys. Well, they do deserve our respect, and they are part of the good guys. As an adult, I recognize that Mr. X, like all of us, was a flawed human being. I don't know the reasons behind his shortcomings, and I forgive him for being imperfect. Unfortunately, his position was one of power; power over students, and power to influence others—his students. Mr. X taught countless other young people how to treat me, and people like me. Some learned his lesson *very* well. He introduced, and at the very least reinforced a contempt for law enforcement and all authority other than his own. Instead of demonstrating the best in humanity and his profession, he showed the ignobility, coarseness and the petty nature of man; instead of fulfilling his duty to educate, he showed contempt and abused those he deemed lesser physically, intellectually and emotionally. For Pete's sake, he was teaching children; of course, he was physically, intellectually and emotionally more advanced! His corruption of the power for good given to him—not only as an educator of young people, purveyor of truth, good-guy, role model and authority figure but as someone in a position of great trust is, to me, unforgivable.

I was very much in touch with these thoughts and feelings at that time. My hip and brace gave me a lot of free time that couldn't be filled with running around acting like a normal kid. I filled that time with the stories of King Arthur and his Knights, The Legends of Charlemagne, Bulfinch's Mythology, chivalry, heraldry, good-guys and bad guys, and every topic that dealt with good triumphing over evil, and the strong standing for the weak. My dad did that; he was a modern-day knight. At that young age, I already knew that to be able to stand up for those who couldn't and to help those in need was about the coolest thing a guy could do. I was very proud of my father.

Strangely enough, I still seem to turn into that 11-year-old when I think of going to school. I've never lost the sense of foreboding, and the creeping, sick feeling of anxiety I associate with it. Mr. X wasn't

Figure 2. Scout oath

SCOUT OATH OR PROMISE

On my honor I will do my best

To do my duty to God and my country

and to obey the Scout Law;

To help other people at all times;

To keep myself physically strong,

mentally awake, and morally straight.

Boy Scout Scout Law, Oath, Motto, slogan And Outdoor Code. (n.d.). Retrieved from http://www.troop103.org/scoutlaw.htm

the first to treat me poorly or discriminate against me for my condition and limitations. He was simply the first adult, and one in a sacred position of authority and trust to do so. There would be others, few, but others. From this experience and my four years in the brace I learned patience and that some people are good, some are bad, and empathy for others.

Scouting

Scouting played a significant role in my parent's plan for us and was a crucial element in my development. My father recalled that my mother was the driving force behind this even before we were walking. I still marvel that my parents actually discussed what they wanted for their children and planned accordingly. Besides being happy and healthy, it was their goal to raise strong, kind children of good character, with fully developed moral compasses, ethically principled, civic-minded, and possessing the qualities of good leadership. They wanted their children to be better than them; to succeed where they failed; to strive for excellence, and to live good lives. My mother was involved in the Girl Scouts as a child, and she was adamant that all her children get into Scouting to help build those qualities. I was a Cub Scout and a Boy Scout, and I couldn't get enough of Scouting. The ideals espoused are a modern take on the knight's oath.

It was through Scouting that I learned the importance of honesty, ethics, cooperation, and team building. I gained invaluable team building and leadership skills that have served me well during my 30 years of public service. In fact, the training I received in citizenship, ethics, team building, and leadership while in the Boy Scouts far surpasses all training I have received in those areas since. To this day, I cannot think of a better way to train and prepare young people for their future. A future where they understand, value, and choose ethical behavior; where they practice fairness, right action, and good citizenship daily. These are the qualities ingrained in me.

I use the term, "Right Action" often, and my definition is simple:

- When faced with a choice to act, always make the right choice—not the easy one.
- Have courage in the face of adversity and adversaries.
- Choose to take action because it is ethically, morally and legally the correct thing to do. It is your duty.

Adolescence

My teen years were marked in much the same way as many young people at the time. I continued working hard through high school and was allowed to graduate in three years instead of the customary four. This I did, over the concerns of my parents who wanted me to stay at home and go to community college. I couldn't wait to start my life, and I would do it on my own. I needed to see the world. Well, Chicago is part of the world. I moved out of the house that summer, and through a friend, arranged to enter undergraduate school at the University of Illinois at Chicago the following spring. To fund this, I used Pell grants, loans, and worked after school at a hobby shop and on midnights sorting packages for UPS. A good friend's family living in the city provided me with room, board, encouragement, and a second home. I spent three unfruitful years at the university before dropping out. I could no longer sustain the work schedule and school. I worked right after school until 7:00 p.m., then home to eat and study until 10:00 p.m., then went to UPS from 11:00 pm to 3:00 a.m. My loans were frightful, my grades were abysmal, and I was miserable. Even if my pride would allow, my family could not provide monetary support, and I wouldn't allow myself to take up their offer to return home where I could have a roof over my head and three square meals a day. My friend and his family were wonderful and supportive, but I was sick and ashamed of my failure and could no longer impose on their love and hospitality. I moved out quickly, having signed a lease for a small "Garden Apartment" that I could barely afford near Clark and Irving in the Wrigleyville neighborhood. Two things of note: One; "Garden Apartment" means "dark basement," and I was lucky that it had a couple windows at sidewalk level. Two: In those days, the area around the baseball park was not nice, and because of that, rents weren't too high. My apartment was situated in a firmly entrenched Latin Eagles area of control (turf). A high-ranking member of the gang lived across the street from me, and he came out to meet me the day I moved in. It was a hot sunny day, and I just finished the move. As I waved goodbye to my friend, a thin, rangy Hispanic man with dark hair, medium complexion, no shirt, blue chinos, white tank-top stuffed in his back pocket and black high-top gym shoes hailed me from the steps of the apartment building across the street. I'll refer to him as "M." M was about my age, though it was hard to tell. He had a large number of the homemade skull and Spanish script tattoos on his chest, arms, and back, and one very professional Eagle tattoo on his left chest. He looked like a guy who had seen some rough days. He looked like a bad-guy. He most likely *was* a bad guy, but I really don't know, and I wasn't raised to judge a book by its cover. What I did know was that I would treat him the way I wished to be treated. He was my new neighbor! I believe we were both quite aware that this meeting would decide our relationship going forward. Somewhat like two dogs, we looked each other over and had to figure out the next course of action. "Hey," I said and extended my hand. In my memory, he slowly stood and walked off of the steps and extended his. Introductions were made, and he said he lived there. We made some small talk before a young woman and child came out from the apartment building and sat on the steps. As M looked over at the steps, I could see an uncontrolled smile cross his face, before looking back at me, all trace of the smile gone. I quickly asked if they were his (family). There was a slight look of alarm and possibly anger on his face before he answered, so I started talking about being away from my family. M relaxed slightly and told me, with pride, that those were his girlfriend and baby. I knew at that moment, when we exposed our shared humanity and common ground, that our relationship would not be adversarial. It never was. We seemed to talk for a good twenty minutes about the neighborhood, what I did (bouncer at a bar), what he did (mechanic at a muffler shop), and about the hordes of suburban yuppies that invaded the neighborhoods every weekend. I left that first meeting feeling good. Throughout my time there, M and

I remained in good standing, occasionally talking, but mostly just a quick wave and greeting. M had to know that I grew up in the suburbs because I asked questions that seemed to make him laugh and shake his head. A few weeks after I moved in, I was working on my motorcycle when M walked over. This time he had his shirt in his hand and a wry smile on his face, so I asked if he ever wore it or just carried it around to look cool. He laughed and called me something unflattering in Spanish. He was in a good mood, so I asked about his tattoos, and what they meant. He didn't want to talk about those except to say, "All men—all *real* men—have tattoos." A week or so later, I asked him again, and this time he told me that he was a Latin Eagle gang member and had been one since he was born. He wouldn't talk much more in-depth about them, except to point out his eagle very proudly and say, "This is who I am!" I didn't press him, and he gave me some help taking my carburetor off to clean it. Being a gang member, who I suspected as having some stature in the gang due to the deference others gave him, made him a bad-guy, right? But he was a proud father, funny, intelligent, and was trying to make ends meet like me! He even helped and advised me about keeping my bike in working order. I liked him; he was decent to me. I was on the verge of a major breakthrough in my thinking. Could it be that bad-guys can be good-guys to some people? On one memorable occasion, I was returning home from an errand, and there was quite a bit of traffic lined up on our street. M was in the middle of 8 or 10 grim looking people—both male and female—when he motioned for me to come across the street to him. When I crossed to him, he said to the group, "Hey, this is Mack," then he pointed to my motorcycle and said, "That's his bike. He's ok." Bewilderment must have shown on my face because he immediately said, "Man, there's some bad stuff going on, don't go around Southport and Irving. Don't go get gas there or eat over there. It ain't safe." Good enough for me! I asked if he was alright, and he just smiled. I thanked him and went home. I found out pretty quick that another gang was pushing boundaries into the Eagle's territory, and the conflict was escalating quickly and violently. M thought enough to look out for me and warn me. I'm thankful that at the time, gang hierarchies existed and were somewhat respected by the gangs. It wasn't exactly West Side Story where everyone agrees what weapons will be used; then they meet up in an empty lot to decide turf. No, brutality using every weapon imaginable was (and remains) their way of violence, but today's drive-by shootings weren't en-vogue then and didn't occur as frequently as they do now. Gang leaders generally weren't targeted when with their families, and gang-owned guns were for trusted security and enforcers. Indiscriminate shootings occurred, but they brought too much attention, so it was frowned upon. It's interesting how trends in gang violence changed and mutated over the years.

Several months later, I moved from the neighborhood. Surprisingly, it wasn't the gangs that made me want to move; it was the weekly invasion of multitudes of drunk, suburban Cub's fans fighting, urinating on lawns, kicking over my motorcycle and committing an assortment of property damage-related offenses that I could just no longer abide.

Police Exams

As time went on, I remained gainfully employed and well paid at a nightclub on the City's Northeast side. All of my friends at the time were waiting for the upcoming Chicago Police exam, and it was rumored that they would be doing massive hiring. My father was a suburban Police Officer, and I had the highest respect for their professionalism and service. I wasn't all that interested in working in the City since my experience with the Chicago Police had not been all that positive. Mind you; I was never physically abused or treated poorly. From what I saw, Chicago Police Officers had a pretty rough job, but they were rarely "squared away," and they always looked tired, wrinkled, and put out. Their appearance didn't inspire confidence or command respect. The Officers I saw just didn't *look* like professionals.

My initial experience with the CPD was while living in Wrigleyville. It seemed as though I was stopped several times per week, every week, and repeatedly whenever new Officers happened to be assigned to the area. My respect and admiration for Police Officers always meant that I was polite, helpful, and patient and I assumed that my manner of dress, old motorcycle, and the time of day (late at night and early morning) made me an interesting stop. But what I later learned was that the area I lived in was not only a gang area but a drug area that attracted young people from all over the City and suburbs. It was a significant narcotics distribution area in the City serving the gold coast and suburbs. I guess I knew this, but I never thought someone might look at me as a bad guy or someone who might be buying drugs! Apparently, I was a very attractive street stop for a narcotics investigation. How I learned the reason was quite by accident. After being stopped by a marked police vehicle, back-up officers arrived, and one happened to be a Tactical Officer who had stopped me in the past.

While the uniformed Officer was completing a name and license plate check in his vehicle, the Tactical Officer walked over to me and said, "What's up, Mr. Mack?" He was always friendly, and I said that I was going to be late to work, but "I get it." He asked me, "What do you get?" I said, "I know what I look like," and that "my father is a Police Officer in the suburbs." Of course, the last time my father saw me, he told me I looked like hell. Suddenly, the dynamic of the traffic stop and interview changed. The other Officers were now standing around me when the Tactical Officer asked if I had a business card for my father. I did and showed it to them.

They were not pleased and proceeded to read me the riot act about living in the area, looking like I looked, being in the area after dark, and, what was I thinking? These Officers explained that a lot of the young people coming into the area south of Addison after dark were purchasing heroin, acid or PCP. A portion of those were beaten, robbed, or worse. *Now*, I understood.

The thought that I might be able to walk in my father's footsteps meant that I would stop at nothing to become a Police Officer, so with some reservation, I signed up to take the Chicago Police Department (CPD) exam anyway. I also signed up for a Northwest Suburban Consortium exam which tested potential candidates for several suburban departments. Among them was Elk Grove Village, Arlington Heights, Evanston, and Glenview. In the spring of 1988, the physical portion of the consortium exam was given. It consisted of a 1.5-mile run; a timed run up "Mount Trashmore" (a 65-foot hill located in Robert E. James Park in Evanston, Illinois) weighted down with an old army belt containing lead shot and a five-pound vest. We did 30 push-ups, 30 sit-ups, a toe touch, vehicle push, and a simulation of a motorist in crisis. During the simulation part of the exam, we were required to enter a vehicle, release the seat safety belt, and pull out a simulated person (*very* heavy) who you must then drag 75 feet to safety. Easy. While I awaited those results, I took the Chicago Police exam. The physical exam was also a 1.5-mile run, toe touches, sit-ups, and threshold weight press (bench press a portion of your body weight). Chicago Police also had an obstacle course that was required after you're hired but before graduating the Police Academy as a recruit. Both written exams were similar. Questions ranged from basic, "How would you handle this situation," to "If you felt a law was unjust, what would you do?" Psychological exams were also given to examine a candidate's mental suitability. I would love to see how these have changed over the years, and how they account for the subtle differences we see in generational hiring.

While awaiting the results of the tests, City licensing changed and work as a "Bouncer" ceased to exist; we were now, "Doormen." It didn't matter what you called us, I still wore a leather jacket, stopped assorted silliness by patrons and staff alike, fought with drunks, soothed hurt feelings, and helped folks get cab rides when they needed them. We did the same job, which was becoming more and more unbearable. The thought of doing something "real" was all consuming and I was getting impatient. As the summer of 1988 wore on, good things began to happen. My excellent friend and fellow "doorman" introduced me to her one night after she laughed at me for asking for identification to prove her age. It wasn't the "Oh. You flatter me," type of laugh, it was the "Get real" type. A beautiful artist with rules of her own, I fell head over heels and remain so to this day. As September rolled around, I was extremely pleased to be dating my future wife and to learn that I had successfully passed the consortium tests. I was placed on the eligibility lists for all participating suburbs.

Hired

Within a week or two, I was offered a position as Police Officer for Elk Grove Village. I immediately took the job and started the Police Academy on October 9, 1988. Before the end of my academy training, I would receive three more offers for employment, but I had agreed to take the job in Elk Grove, so I remained in their employ. During that first week, we were sorted into home-rooms with Chicago Police Academy instructors assigned to each room. These instructors were veteran cops, many who had endured horrific ordeals on the streets and each had agreed to teach new Officers. Today's Academy Instructors, while undoubtedly experts in the fields they teach, seem to have been chosen for their communication and teaching abilities rather than their street experience and practical expertise. There also were no instructors with less than five years in the profession. I'll say subtle differences, but ones that I feel equal dramatic differences in the education of new Officers. In 1988, the CPD had the oldest Police Officers in the nation. Our instructors were adults in every way. They were often military war veterans and certainly CPD veterans who were stern and proficient. Their dress was impeccable, their bearing was confident and professional, and their knowledge of law and police procedure was tremendous. To a significant degree, we were in awe of them and wanted to emulate them. My homeroom instructor's (HRI) stated goals were to teach us the law, teach us procedure, show us how to survive, and to make us into the kind of Officers they'd like to work with. We ran 1.5 miles every morning, with push-ups, sit-ups, and plenty of leaning rest2 while awaiting our turn to perform another exercise. After morning calisthenics, we had classroom instruction until noon, then more physical training in arrests, control, and force options, before ending the day with more classroom and scenario-based instruction. Officer survival was emphasized at all levels. Calmness, communication, sound judgment, mental toughness, physical ability, technique, mastering the tools of your trade (your presence, voice, equipment, and weapons), and going home alive at the end of our tour of duty were constants in the curriculum. The training was unrelenting and became more demanding as one progressed. About halfway through my training at the Academy, I was approached by the CPD training staff and asked if I'd like to end my training for the suburbs and begin training for employment with the Chicago Police Department. I had taken and passed the CPD test, and a new class of CPD recruits would be going in the following week. I respectfully declined by explaining that I had accepted the position from the village and needed to honor that agreement. I was also only a few weeks from becoming a sworn Officer! Later that week, we were visited by a corpulent Commander from our employer, who unceremoniously informed us that we were misinformed about our wages and that we would be receiving $1,000.00 less per year than we had signed on for. Despite *that* news, I didn't give Chicago a second thought until a little over three years later. I was almost at the end of 18 weeks of training, and I couldn't wait to hit the streets, solve crime, and chase bad-guys!

Reality came crashing in on my first day at work as a suburban Police Officer. I had entered a world of extremes that I recall with some anxiety. Our welcome by the upper echelon was disconnected, disappointing and downright threatening. We were to conduct ourselves with the utmost professionalism and ethical conduct at all times or discipline, separation and prosecution would occur. We were probationary for the following 12 months and would be assigned to Field Training Officers (F.T.O.s) who would train us in policy, procedure and prepare us for the future service. The F.T.O.'s were responsible for our education and wellbeing, and their recommendations would determine whether an Officer would remain in the Village's employ. I did not doubt that I could successfully fulfill the requirements that were set forth, but I was taken back by the manner and tone of delivery. To make matters much worse, our original yearly wage agreement was $21,301.00, but as you recall, weeks before graduating and being certified as Peace Officers in the State of Illinois, we were told that our wages would be $20,301.00. Now, even those wages didn't add up after we received our pay. When this Commander asked if we had any questions, one of my fellow recruits brought it to his attention that there may be a problem since calculating our yearly wages only added up to $19,301.00. At this, the Commander leaned forward with a scowl on his face and informed us that there would be even less because we each had to pay for the training we received at the academy! I remember seeing the dismay on the faces of the other nine new Officers. We were already advised that we were prohibited from working secondary jobs during our 12-month probationary period. Some of these Officers had families, some left higher paying jobs, and about half of us were repaying student loans! The Commander could see pained expressions and some anger on our faces, so he added, "If you don't like it, there's the door" while pointing to the exit. The Commander looked quite satisfied with himself; his expression was gloating. We later learned that the repayment of training expenses would be refunded to each Officer if he/she remained with the Department for more than 12 months. He could have saved us all some aggravation with that information, but it was not in his nature. On that day, I remember him pointing to the door and looking directly at me. I smiled. My winning grin didn't endear me to that Commander, and he made sure that I could read that on his face. I pegged this man as a bully and tyrant, and I made sure not to cross his path unless necessary. I quickly learned that he was not respected by most of the Department's rank and file. Good always triumphs over evil—sometimes it just takes a while. Many years later, he retired in disgrace after briefly earning a local headline news story. It's been said many times in the past, "If you want the true measure of a man, look at how he treats those he deems lesser or inferior, not those he deems his equals." After that rousing welcome, we spent the rest of the day going over employment paperwork, drawing equipment, and requalifying with our weapons before being assigned to our F.T.O.s and a duty watch. I was assigned to an FTO on the 3rd Watch which began at 3:00 p.m. and ended at 11:30 p.m. The next evening, I arrived 15 minutes before roll call, spit-shined, polished, and somewhat apprehensive. I was right to be so; every Officer in the Department knew my father was a ranking Police Officer, and they expected me to be a typical "Police Brat." Unlike a "Military Brat" which doesn't have a negative association, a "Police Brat" does. It usually refers to someone whose parents were Police Officers, and when they themselves become an Officer, immediately assume a seemingly arrogant attitude, and display overconfidence in their abilities. (Interestingly, the Commander we'd met on the first day was one.) I was well aware that there would be veteran Officers working on my watch who knew, worked with, or worked for my father. They watched me closely those first few weeks. Thankfully, it's not in my nature or upbringing to be boastful or take much for granted, and I try to be a modest person. Although I felt great pressure to prove myself to these veterans, my youthful enthusiasm was significantly and thankfully suppressed by my Field Training Officer (FTO). A tough taskmaster, perfectionist, tyrant, and one of the most technically and tactically proficient Police Officers that I've ever known; I think he hated me in the beginning, and I found that I couldn't stand him much either! My time with Gary was some of the most stressful that I'd had up to that time. He never accepted less than excellence from me in my daily work and action, and resolutely refused to allow me an excuse for shortcomings. It seemed as though he could find fault with me in everything that I did. When I spoke with other rookies with "good" FTOs, they were having a great time. I was beginning to question why I had ever taken this job! I worked harder, had less success, and had been chewed-out more than I'd ever been in my life! Gary didn't believe in being idle, which was great, because I would rather be busy than bored. Through him, we handled every type of assignment available from parking and loud dog complaints, to domestic disturbances and fatal accidents. It was at one such accident that Gary was actually nice to me.

10-50PI

10-50PI is the code used by dispatchers in the suburbs to indicate that the assignment is an accident (10-50) with personal injuries (PI). We had taken the accident call late one night on Busse highway. A businessman leaving the office late fell asleep and rear-ended an 18-wheel tractor trailer as it pulled out of the industrial park. To give an idea of the speed of the auto as it struck the truck, the semi was pushed some 50 feet forward. The truck driver was bloody, dazed, and wandering in the street when we arrived. I immediately pulled our squad car across the two lanes of traffic with the emergency lights activated to block other motorists, and Gary called on the radio to ensure that an ambulance was en-route. Quickly exiting, Gary grabbed road flares to keep us visible and safe, while I approached the truck driver and led him to the safety of the parkway. He had a large cut to the side of his head from the force of the impact. Head wounds tend to bleed a lot, and the driver was becoming more focused and aware which was a good sign, so leaving him with my cotton handkerchief pressed to the wound, I approached the car—or what was left of it. The vehicles front end and engine compartment were crushed beyond recognition. Fluids and gasoline were everywhere. The windshield of the vehicle was smashed with a hole in the safety glass. Safety glass holds its shape when smashed so that passengers aren't injured by flying glass in a collision. There was dark fluid everywhere including half-way up the rear doors of the tractor-trailer. It was a bizarre mixture of the bright reddish transmission fluid over fluorescent yellow radiator fluid on glistening black spray. I hastened to the driver's door to check on the driver inside. What greeted me was something I had never seen before and have tried to forget. The driver was wearing his seatbelt, but upon impact, the vehicle crushed like an accordion. The driver was propelled forward through the windshield head first, then back through into his seat. His head tilted towards me, and one eye remaining in the head looked at me. The man had lost most of the skin on his head; ears, nose, eyelids and one eye was just—gone. There was a steering wheel where his abdomen and lower chest should have been, and a rasping sound coming from a partially opened throat. He was asking for help. I felt true distress; I was helpless. Just then, two Fire Department trucks and two ambulances arrived on the scene. "What we got?" faded away from the paramedic's mouth as he jogged up to me. That's when the yelling started, and two paramedics began triage and life support. As they attempted to get vital signs, the driver gurgled and moaned. The paramedic said, "Help me," as he forced an airway into the man's chest with a tube. As the paramedic began wrapping the driver's face in gauze, he told me to get him the ears, and other parts stuck on the glass. I handed him ears, then other pieces as I could get them; he just wrapped them around the driver's head with the gauze.

Everything was so slippery, and the smell of the vehicle, the driver, and the blood are all smells that I still involuntarily recall as I write. The driver died three times in my presence, and each time, the paramedics worked a miracle and brought him back. As the firefighters finished cutting him out of his vehicle, we placed the driver on the stretcher and got him into the waiting ambulance. Once the ambulance was underway to the hospital, I became aware of my FTO and Fire Chief approaching me. That is when I realized that I was soaking in blood and fluids. They helped me clean my face and skin, and the Fire Captain had his guys wash-down my pants and boots. I sat in the passenger seat on a blanket as Gary drove us back into the Police station for a more thorough wash and change of uniform. We didn't talk, but not because of emotional trauma. We were both just beginning to feel the total exhaustion that occurs after a huge adrenaline dump. We completed the tour of duty in the station writing reports with only occasional breaks in the silence. Leaving that morning was the first time Gary said, "Good job." From the moment we arrived on-scene, I moved unhesitant, with sure purpose and focus. I could do this; I was in pure work-mode, and I felt good. The horror of the scene and my actions came back to visit me many times later, but what hit me first and bothered me most, was the distress of that moment when my focus waned; the moment I felt helpless to save that man. Over the next few days, training progressed much as before, with no talk of the incident. Seemingly out of the blue, Gary ordered me to drive to the firehouse so he could use the facilities. Unknown to me at the time, his real reason was to arrange for us to speak with the fire and ambulance crews that were out there that night. When I think of this, I smile. I was 21 years old, and the fire crews were much older. What was said exactly—I don't recall, but after talking through the entire incident with experienced men who have handled and seen worse, I no longer feared to be helpless. I learned things that day; everyone feels helpless sometimes, so don't fear it.

Sometimes just being there with someone is enough. You can't save everyone, no matter how hard you try, and, the important thing is you do your best and never give up. Moreover, I began to feel a sense of brotherhood. We had all been through traumatic events. These men didn't know me, but they took the time to help me through the incident by showing me a way to feel differently about it. Gary knew that I—or we—needed this, and he made it happen. Throughout the incident, I didn't exactly know what Gary was doing; I just knew that he was doing everything I couldn't. It made me begin to appreciate partnership, ability, and competency. Everything was just a little bit different after that, and although I may not have increased in stature in his eyes, he certainly did in mine.

When my training ended, I was placed on a different watch, and I was happy to be on my own finally. I quickly realized that I knew procedure and I knew how to handle assignments and arrests that others in my class couldn't. Through Gary, I had done so much, dealt with every strange and challenging job, and was as prepared as I possibly could be. While another of my fellow rookies went the unfettered "Brat" route and garnered dislike and disdain by other Officers, I began to enjoy positive interaction with the veterans and supervisors. I saw that Gary knocked me down and kept me humble not allowing me to be a brat. He gave me every edge he could provide and did everything in his power to ensure I could be a competent success. Whenever I think about those days in training, it is with a mix of excitement, joy, dread, and embarrassment at my feelings and behavior with my FTO. I can never repay him for the job he did, or for giving me the tools I needed to succeed socially, culturally, and professionally. Gary taught me that true Police-work is more a product of personal intellect, professional attitude, and public service, rather than car chases and gun-fights. I *have* spoken to him since moving on to my present Department and assignments. Amusingly, having met him again after so many years, I reverted to that inexperienced 21-year-old rookie for a minute or two before regaining my composure. I was able to remain the veteran that I am long enough to sincerely thank him for being one of the lights in my career.

Police Families

I've found that we adult children of Police Officers are unusual. We grow up in and around a certain amount of Police culture. We're comfortable with Police Officers and relaxed with their tools and equipment. We even understand a certain amount of Police terminology and some regulations and laws. Our Police parents are our role models, and we often try to emulate them. Coming from a "Police Family" can help an officer to "fit in," or it really can be detrimental. There's always a microscope on cops from Police families; will they be like mom or dad, will they be "Police Brats," or will they be their own person? I have seen children of Police Officers who were not well liked to suffer, at least initially, for their parents' transgressions. My father was not universally loved, and some officers delighted in relaying that fact to me. He *was,* however, respected. The wrong parent, the wrong attitude, or a combination of those variables might determine how you're viewed and accepted (or not) by veteran Officers. It's not usually a permanent determination, but it can be tough to overcome coming at the beginning of a new career.

Street-Stop

The Police culture varies from department to department, but one constant remains; it takes more than wearing a uniform and badge to be a true brother or sister, it takes street experience, sacrifice, and trauma. Being a Police Officer almost certainly guarantees each. Shortly after my field training ended, I stopped a motorist on the far end of an industrial complex for speeding and swerving in his lane. I suspected alcohol. While approaching the vehicle, the driver exited and immediately stalked towards me. He was a 45-year-old male, approximately 5 foot ten inches tall, thin—weighing about 170 pounds, and appeared drunk and angry as hell. I was 22 years old, weighed 200 pounds, and was no stranger to fighting. Quickly and calmly, I spoke into the radio and requested a back-up unit. Just then, he attacked, and we met in a flurry of fists and elbows. The driver was taking the worst of the fistfight, but I could not get him to relent. He began grabbing at my arms and attempting to close with me. I was never good at wrestling, and this guy had a grip that was like iron. My strikes were making absolutely no difference to him; he would slow for a second, then renew his assault. I was retreating to open some distance between us, but he just advanced quicker. I could no longer withdraw as my back was against the squad car. As we began to wrestle, he began attempting to remove my revolver from my holster. Unlike modern holsters with weapon retention systems, our holsters of this time were simply leather secured with strap that snapped closed. Once unsnapped, the weapon was free to be removed or fall out. I was fighting for my life trying to overcome him while retaining my gun. As time slowed, it occurred to me that this guy wasn't struggling to escape or trying to get away; he was there to hurt or kill me. If he got my gun, he wouldn't walk away, and I would not be going home. I had never done anything to this guy, he was driving drunk, endangering everyone's lives, and I was doing my job protecting folks on the road. HE attacked ME! I became enraged and fought with everything I had. He was still trying to get my weapon, and my right hand was on his hand denying him access. A quick and lucky pivot of my right hip away from him broke his grip on my weapon's handle. This momentarily freed my right hand to strike him in the throat and deny him an open airway. Once he clutched his throat and staggered, I increased my efforts and was unrelenting until he went to the pavement. I saw red, and my head was buzzing. That's when I heard the sweetest sound; my back-up, along with four other squad cars were coming to help with their lights and sirens blazing. Officers were pouring in from all jurisdictions around. With the driver beneath me now and the help of what felt like an army of Officers, we finally were able to subdue and handcuff the offender. Every Officer from my watch arrived to help, and as I looked at Officers from the State Police, Sheriffs and an assortment of marked and unmarked squad cars from every town, I felt proud and part of something larger than myself and this small Police Department. How did they all know that I desperately needed help? My last transmission before the encounter was to request back-up. The dispatcher's response was repeatedly met by radio silence from me as I could not hear nor respond to the dispatcher during the fight. Our dispatcher immediately called for any available cars that could check on me, and they did! What seemed like hours of fighting was probably no more than 5 minutes. On the way into the police station, the arrestee renewed his assault and began kicking at the metal barrier between the front and rear seats as well as the back door. By the time we got him to the hospital, he had succeeded in kicking the back door out of its frame, bending the hinges out and making rendering it inoperable. It took eight officers to remove and then subdue the arrestee before he could be strapped down and eventually sedated by the Emergency Room staff. Much later after the arrestee's arraignment, I learned that the man had been a steelworker for 20 years and had just been fired. He was an alcoholic and a mean drunk. Friends and family testified that he was the kindest, most gentle person when he was sober. He apologized to me at his first court appearance.

I had just ten months on the job when I encountered the first person who, in a drunken rage, wanted to kill me. Luckily, I walked away from that one, and I learned a lot from my mistakes that day. Unfortunately, it wouldn't be the last time.

Brotherhood

Officers respect others in their profession for a variety of reasons. Those who are—or were "boots on the ground," or "from the trenches," or "do the job" gain respect quickly and are admired most. Why is that? Well, anyone who is in those categories has worked the streets — shared in the exhilaration, the boredom, anxiety, aggravation, frustration, sadness, and trauma., They've been cold, wet and hungry, missed holidays, birthdays, weekends, vacations, and the myriad of special events and family events that a significant portion of the population takes for granted. In short, you gain respect and become a brother or sister after you've made sacrifices. That fight in the industrial park changed the way I saw myself, my invulnerability, and my job, and it changed the way veteran Officer's interacted with me. It was like I passed a test that gives you weird a scar instead of an "A." One that subtly, but inevitably changes *everything*. I was now included in conversations with the veterans before roll call, and guys would stop by my assignments to help, make suggestions or talk.

Looking back on my entire career, I realize that my first traumatic event involving the willful, wanton act(s) of violence began an insidious phenomenon. Almost without knowing, I began to think about civilians and ask, "Do we have anything in common?" Not unlike soldiers who have been in battle, I began to believe that unless someone has seen, smelled, touched, done and endured the things I've had to, they couldn't possibly understand me. How could I ever explain any of this to someone who hasn't been in it?" Quite frankly, I've always felt that I—we—do and endure those things so that you, the public we serve, doesn't have to. Unfortunately, those thoughts and attitudes, though extremely common amongst us, only help to isolate Officers from society and begin an unhealthy cycle that only now is getting the attention it deserves and we need.

Thinking that nobody understands but other cops are one of the pitfalls that I was warned about from academy instructors. They told us to keep our friends, don't spend too much time with other Officers off-duty. Easier said than done. When I became an Officer, I had friends from just about every walk of life, every race, and many religions. To some, the day I swore that oath to serve and protect, I ceased being Paul, their buddy. I was now a cop. I was somehow less than trustworthy, my motives suspect, my beliefs twisted, and I was quickly and quietly set aside. I didn't understand at the time and was hurt by some of them. They *knew* me, but I became an enemy because of my job. I understood some reasons; I had friends that ran with rough crowds, and others *I* couldn't be around because of the paths they chose, but those were very few. As for the others, I believe they fell victim to near constant media representations of what Police Officers are, and assumed what I would become. In 1972, Robert Balch wrote about the "Police Personality." In his paper, he wrote, "If we can believe everything we read in magazines, journals, and sociology books, the typical policeman is cynical, suspicious, conservative, and thoroughly bigoted. This is not a flattering picture to be sure, but it recurs again and again in the popular and 'scientific' literature on the police." (Balch, 1972)

After ten months with the Village, I received a call from the Glenview Police Department, who advised me that they would like to hire me as a lateral transfer immediately. The representative went on to explain the benefits package, the professional development paths, and the general conditions of hire. I was working three rotating shifts (days, afternoons, and midnights) in an often-tyrannical Police Department and making about $18,000 *before* taxes. I wanted to marry but was too indebted, and I couldn't pay my bills *and* my rent together. Glenview paid a living wage and offered career paths, training, no residency requirement, and a future for me. I was very excited, but I had almost two months left until I had achieved the required one year with the Village, and $1500.00 was a lot of money to leave behind. Three months prior, the Arlington Heights Police Department made an offer for my transfer, but they could not wait. I knew that I wanted out and would take Glenview's offer no matter what, but I asked anyway. "Could you wait until I attained my one-year anniversary?" They couldn't have been more accommodating, and in the end, Glenview was every bit as good as advertised.

I began employment with the Glenview Police Department in the fall of 1989. My first day there was nothing like Elk Grove. I arrived and was met by the Chief of Police, his Commanders, and almost every Sergeant in the Police Department. The atmosphere was warm and friendly with the Chief formally welcoming me to the Department. From there, each bureau Commander and their Sergeants gave me a quick synopsis of the work they perform, and a tour of their respective areas. I was then escorted by a woman from the "Personnel Department" back to the Chief's office. Once inside, the Chief spoke about career development paths, which just astonished me!

Planning and developing "career paths" didn't exist in Elk Grove, and it doesn't exist in the Chicago Police Department today. The Chief's management philosophy was simple; treat everyone with respect. Pay people a living wage so that they can provide for their families and aren't tempted to do unethical things. Demand excellence at all times. Educate and train your people so that they may succeed. Ensure your people have the best equipment possible and provide them with additional skills and abilities so that Officers have more than simple patrol experience to fall back on. Trust in the Chief and his command staff was exceptional, and as close to unquestionable as I've yet seen. In a short time, I found him to be a very moral man, highly ethical, quick with a smile, and a great leader. I wish I could to speak with him or at least tell him the impact he had on my leadership. Unfortunately, Chief David Kelly passed before I ever thanked him properly.

I was immediately assigned to an extremely knowledgeable and highly competent FTO working the day watch. This was excellent as it allowed me to learn Glenview's winding streets and patrol areas in daylight. From my first day, I could see that the Police culture and work atmosphere were extraordinarily different from Elk Grove, where professionalism and performance were enforced through coercion and

Figure 3. Procedural justice steps

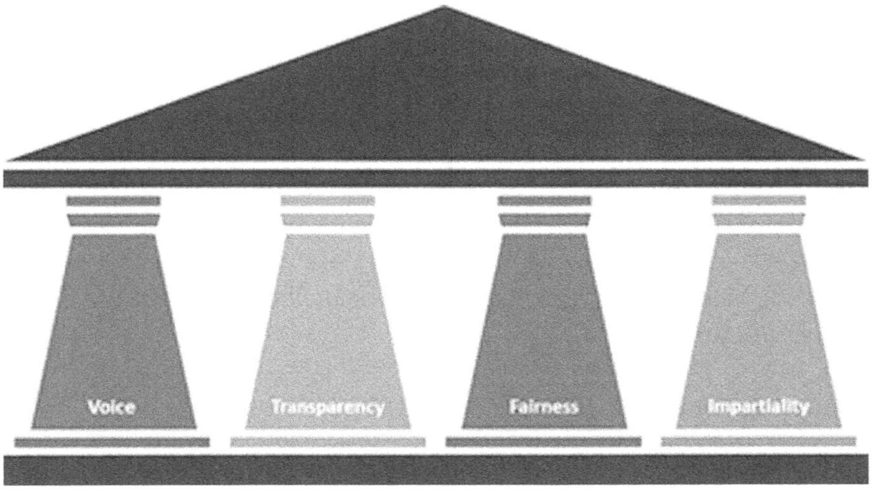

Adapted from Peterson, Emma, et al. (2017). "Procedural Justice in Policing: How the Process of Justice Impacts Public Attitudes and Law Enforcement Outcomes." *Illinois Criminal Justice Information Authority*, http://www.icjia.state.il.us/articles/procedural-justice-in-policinghow-the-process-of-justice-impacts-public-attitudes-and-law-enforcement-outcomes **pg3**.

discipline. The culture fostered by the Glenview Chief was that of willing compliance through shared values and beliefs. Officers did well, acted with professionalism and respect, and the gained the trust of the citizens because they were treated with what we refer today as, "Procedural Justice and Legitimacy." Dr. Tom Tyler's groundbreaking research in the late 1980s coincided with what the Chief already knew and practiced. Today, Procedural Justice is the axiom of proper management and better policing, and police departments like the Chicago Police Department are rapidly training Officers in its teaching. There are four principles, or "pillars" of Procedural Justice; voice, transparency, fairness, and impartiality.

Voice refers to providing an opportunity for people to be heard and instructs the Officer to listen. By giving a voice to those you interact with, you allow individuals to present their point of view, which makes them feel they have had some influence in the decision-making process and supports the notion of fairness in the interaction.

Transparency simply refers to informing those you interact with about the process they are part of and the basis for the decisions you're making.

Fairness is a concept that everyone desperately wishes for and can be a synonym for all the pillars. Impartiality, equality, objectivity, just treatment without bias, and evenhandedness are the concepts we always need to practice with each other. Fairness encompasses treating people with respect and dignity. Dr. Tyler's research showed that people are more likely to accept actions, decisions, and outcomes—regardless of whether those outcomes are good or bad—when they are perceived as fair.

Impartiality refers to the ability to remain neutral in disputes, decision-making, and actions. This pillar reminds and entreats Officers to interact with people without bias and make decisions based solely on objectivity and the law.

Based upon Dr. Tyler's research, it is believed that practicing these four pillars with the public will change the way citizens think and feel about the processes, decision-making and the outcomes of interactions with Police. It is also believed that practicing these concepts within Departments will change how Officers think and feel about their jobs, making them more likely to practice these beliefs with the public. In my experience, I believe that there is much truth in this theory, but I would argue that Procedural Justice is nothing new. Chief Kelly knew, and 30 years ago these tenets were drilled into our heads daily while we trained to become Police Officers. Every day we were expected to greet everyone as sir, mam, missus, miss, or young man. To this day, entering the Chicago Police Academy can be a bit amusing as every recruit in a multitude of recruits will stop and wish you, "Good morning, sir!" It didn't end with the greetings either. I was trained to greet, identify myself, state my purpose, listen, respond, and act objectively based on the totality of the events or situation.

Me: *"Good afternoon, Mam. I'm Officer Mack, and I've stopped you today for driving 60 miles per hour in a 40 mile per hour zone."*

Citizen: *Worried and agitated, "Oh my, was I really going that fast?"*

Me: *"Yes, mam, I have it on radar if you'd like to see. Do you have a driver's license?"*

Citizen: *Getting more agitated and worried, "Yes, here it is. I'm so sorry, I just got a call, and my kids are home alone. If I don't get back quick, they're going to kill each other!"*

Me: *I laughed, and citizen relaxed a bit. "How old are your children?"*

Citizen: *"Ten and twelve; a boy and girl."*

Me: *"Mam, I need to check your license and vehicle registration. If they both come back clear and valid, I'll get you out of here with a stern warning."*

Citizen: *Now much more relaxed, "Thank you, Officer."*

I made my decision based upon the totality of the circumstances. The traffic code was disobeyed; I had evidence to support the claim. The area where this occurred was an empty stretch of road with low traffic, no sidewalks, no pedestrians, and is bordered by forest preserve. The citizen offered a mitigating reason for the violation; her children were home alone. A check of the license and vehicle registration showed everything was valid with no history of moving citations issued to the driver. My goal of the traffic stop was to halt the unlawful behavior and attempt to impact the future conduct of this driver. Officers are allowed to use discretion in certain instances, and this is one of those, so I decided to use it. I successfully halted the behavior (speeding). Judging by the citizen's reactions, I felt a warning would be the most appropriate way to obtain compliance and make an impact on the citizen's future driving. Yes, a ticket for speeding could undoubtedly have been issued to force compliance, and often, that is the only way. However, issuing warnings can sometimes bring willing compliance without the added penalty of time and fines. In this case, I also had to take into account that the longer I delayed this driver, the longer her children would be left alone to get into trouble.

Good leadership can change the culture in a Police Department; however, it is difficult and takes time unless the majority (preferably all) of your management team subscribe to the new or emerging culture (known as "buy-in"). The longtime Chief of Police had buy-in from every one of his supervisors, and the Department was primarily veteran Officers. Supervisors understood the Chief's vision and management style, and they mimicked him in every critical area of operations and management. As I entered into this new Police culture, I felt that I found a home. Since I was already trained, I spent only four weeks with my FTO before being assigned to a watch as a one-person patrol car. Ken was a true gentleman who reinforced the notion that solving crime was an essential part of our job, but only a part of it: Public service, protection, and crime prevention were our primary duties. Knowing the community, keeping up on events and knowing the kids all help to accomplish those duties. He greeted and spoke to everyone when we patrolled and consequently knew an incredible number of families. He was trusted by the community, including the kids. He was an exceptional Officer; I never saw him lose his temper and he could talk most people down to avoid physical confrontations. He would say that anyone could make an arrest but solving a problem without having to make the arrest is the goal. He was right. Not too many arrests result in actual problems getting solved, and a good deal of them exacerbate existing issues. Still, arrests are necessary, and many are mandated.

Glenview was way ahead of the other Departments I've worked for in the areas of community policing, service-oriented policing, and crime prevention. The detective division, youth division, and traffic divisions all shared separate offices that were near the patrol roll call room. This allowed daily interaction and the free exchange and dissemination of intelligence.

This differed at the time from Elk Grove and currently differs from CPD. Having a relationship with the specialized units in your organization is an excellent way to tackle emerging crime and disorder trends. All Officers become knowledgeable of the issues facing each Unit and can make better patrol and enforcement decisions based on that knowledge.

Interestingly, I recently spoke with an Officer still working in Glenview who gave me an update. The Department changed a bit; new Chief, new Officers, an increase in the size of the Department, and they have a beautiful new state-of-the-art Police building. What he disliked was that the new layout of the building separates the officers and they no longer have contact with the detectives or traffic divisions. He said that instead of being a group working towards a common goal, they were becoming "us—doing what we do, and them—doing whatever they do."

I spent every day happy and proud to be a Glenview Police Officer. True to their word, after my six-month anniversary, the Village sent me to a week-long school for interviews and interrogation to begin my chosen career path in investigations. After my one-year anniversary, I had a string of good luck which put me in the right place at the right time to stop several in-progress crimes and arrest some pretty bad characters. Car thieves, car chases, burglars, guns, and gang-bangers made a deep impression on me, and I began to get restless. I loved the job, loved the village, and loved the citizens, but I wanted to take real bad-guys off of the street more often. Thanks in no small part to the Glenview Police working in concert with the community, Glenview didn't seem to have many bad-guys. It was during the next year that I learned that I was still on the list to be hired by Chicago PD.

New Job

An academy friend who was also approached by CPD while in the academy contacted me to see how I was doing. During the call, he told me that he was leaving the suburbs to become a Chicago Police Officer. He told me that even though he declined the initial invitation, CPD left his name active on their list. Later that week, on a Wednesday, I called my friend, and he provided me the name and number of the recruitment officer. I called right away, and after a few moments, the Officer had my personnel file. I was still active on their list! The recruitment Officer placed me on hold for about five minutes before returning to the phone and stating, "If you wanna be the Chicago Police, I gotta know by Friday. Monday starts the last class we're gonna make from your list, but I can get you in." My heart skipped a beat; I had so much to consider and so much to do. I spoke with my girlfriend and with some Chicago Police Officers that I knew, but I couldn't make up my mind. My father would tell me that I shouldn't go to the City, and I wouldn't tell my mother because she was already worried about me. I spoke to Ken (my FTO), and he suggested that I speak with the Chief. I made an appointment to talk to him the very next morning. It was a hard conversation for me to start; Glenview had been so good to me; it really was a dream job. He spoke with me for about 30 minutes while I waivered and angst over the decision. I asked if I could get a leave of absence to try Chicago out, and I'll never forget the fatherly smile on his face. The Chief told me that he had come from a bustling city before he came to Glenview, so he knew what I was longing for when it came to more "action." He told me that this decision was mine alone and he would be delighted if I stayed in Glenview, but only if I stayed and was happy with the decision I made. He said, "Paul, I'll give a leave of absence, but you *are* just like me, so I know that once you go and do that type of police work, you won't want to come back." I made up my mind right there and then and realized what I had done. I wanted to take this opportunity to become a Chicago Police Officer but wasn't brave enough to take the risk. I had placed the Chief in a bad position by asking him for a leave of absence to remove my risk. The Chief would have decided for me. I thanked him for approving a leave but told him that I could not take it. I informed him of my decision to go and apologized for placing him and the Department in this position. He shook my hand and wished me luck with "Be safe and let me know if you ever need something." After two wonderful years as a Glenview Police Officer, I cleared my locker out after duty on Friday. On Monday, I was back in the Chicago Police Academy.

The Chicago Experience

The first day back in the academy was somewhat of an eye-opener. Just like the previous time, we were assigned to a homeroom where our instructor asked the same question of the class that was asked three years earlier, "Why do you want to be a cop?" The first time this was asked while I was training for the suburbs, the answers could've brought a tear to your eye; "I want to give something back to the community that gave me so much." "I want to make society a better place." "I served my country, but I'm not done. I want to do more." "I want to be one of the good-guys," and the noble reasons went on and on. This time, the noble reasons were there, but there was also a smattering of, "Well, the benefits are good," "It's steady work," and "I don't know, I thought I'd give it a try." I was a little stunned at those reasons; I mean why would anyone want to do this job unless it was something they felt deeply about? There had been 711 Officers that died in the line of duty between 1988 when I began, and 1991. The Chicago Police Department accounted for 11 of the murdered3. Most of my Chicago recruit class were born and bred in Chicago, and the practicality of inner-city living and the weak economy was evident.

The training was most pleasant for me; I was in excellent physical shape, and the "Metro" training (suburban Officer training) seemed more difficult. I was a State of Illinois Certified Law Enforcement Officer with experience, and I was confident that I could successfully pass the academy requirements. I still took nothing for granted and kept my head down, my mouth shut, and my ears opened. I quickly discovered that some things had changed in the three short years since I was there last. Some of those changes were good, and others I felt were not for the best. I discovered one or two of the changes the hard way. The very first change that I noticed was the change-over of personnel. While there were still instructors whom I recognized and a couple who knew me, most of the training cadre was new, and the academy's ranking Officer had changed with the personnel. There was a distinct change in the culture which I did not care for. Instructors didn't have the length of service the 1988 academy had, and they were more likely to foster enmity with the recruits as they tried on the Hollywood drill sergeant role. Don't misunderstand; the 1988 training staff that I had contact with were tough, terrifying at times and unforgiving in most matters, but they refrained from belittling the recruits. They also didn't disparage the Metro classes for not being "The Real Police." This was something new, unnecessary, and unbecoming. Sure, I was a little sensitive about the "real police" comments because I worked with, and around some of the most talented and dedicated Police officers I've ever known, and they were suburban. I was bothered by it because, at a very impressionable stage in an Officer's training, those comments serve to teach recruits that all other law enforcement is lesser in everything. Many instructors refrained from that behavior, but in 1991, it seemed as though there was always more than a few of those guys around. I also think that it's a very slippery slope when you mark any other person or group of people as less worthy.

Next, I noticed that the physical training and tactics had changed considerably. Physical training wasn't as rigorous. We were still instructed to take control of every situation quickly, but "lawsuit" was the new "buzzword." Where daily morning cardio was never missed in 1988, we now ran only three days per week. Defensive tactics moved away from disabling the delivery system (disabling the arm or leg) to blocking offensive actions and redirecting momentum. Boxing was not taught or offered. Although these tactics were somewhat more suited to our role, it was a marked departure from only three years prior which shows a progression and response to changing demands.

As the training progressed, I was again honored to be named "Class Commander," and became immediately responsible for the daily care of sixty recruits. This made me responsible for ensuring all recruits were on-time, in proper uniform, and prepared for duty. It seemed as though I was getting chewed out three out of five days per week for the next three weeks until the class finally shaped up. It was relatively smooth sailing after that.

One benefit of being named Class Commander was that after academy training, I was allowed to pick my very first district of assignment. I wanted the busiest District I could find, so I chose the 21st District. Having the dubious honor of being the deadliest district in Chicago at the time, it was known as the Prairie Station. When asked for my choice, I quickly announced "21!" The room grew quiet and the Academy Commander politely dismissed me. The following week we graduated were assigned our stars and were sworn in as Chicago Police Officers. At that time, I was informed that I would not be going to the 21st District. I was told that my sergeant and the Commander felt my request was *crazy*—no one ever *chooses* to go to 21. Instead, I was assigned to the 23rd District for field training which was located at the corner of Addison and Halsted. As you may recall, I lived in the area earlier in my youth and spent some time with the Officers from the District who stopped me quite frequently. I was disappointed at first, but I quickly discovered that there was plenty of action and excitement there.

I was assigned to an unwilling veteran FTO who was ready to retire. Being within four months of his retirement date meant that he was not about to place himself unnecessarily in harm's way and certainly not with an unproven recruit. Needless to say, it was a very dull and unproductive training period. A very good thing that occurred because of my FTO was that more aggressive veteran Officers felt bad for me, so they tried to include me in their "capers" (arrests, investigations, or jobs). One of the Officers who used to stop me when I was younger was still working there and made it a point to introduce me to everyone and tell them how I used to have white hair and a motorcycle. I think he was making amends

Figure 4. Code of ethics

The Law Enforcement Code of Ethics is adopted as a general standard of conduct for all sworn members of the Department. It states:

a. "As a law enforcement officer, my fundamental duty is to serve mankind; to safeguard lives and property, to protect the innocent against deception, the weak against oppression or intimidation, and the peaceful against violence or disorder and to respect the Constitutional rights of all men to liberty, equality and justice."

b. "I will keep my private life unsullied as an example to all, maintain courageous calm in the face of danger, scorn, or ridicule; develop self-restraint, and be constantly mindful of the welfare of others. Honest in thought and deed in both my personal and official life. I will be exemplary in obeying the laws of the land and the regulations of my department. Whatever I see or hear of a confidential nature or that is confided to me in my official capacity will be kept ever secret unless revelation is necessary in the performance of my duty."

c. "I will never act officiously or permit personal feelings, prejudices, animosities, or friendships to influence my decisions. With no compromise for crime and with relentless prosecution of criminals, I will enforce the law courteously and appropriately without fear or favor, malice or ill will, never employing unnecessary force or violence and never accepting gratuities."

d. "I recognize the badge of my office as a symbol of public faith and accept it as a public trust to be held so long as I am true to the ethics of the police service. I will constantly strive to achieve these objectives and ideals, dedicating myself before God to my chosen profession . . . law enforcement."

and he took much better care of me than my FTO. For a month after my FTO training was complete, I was treated to working with some of the best Officers in the District. I was approached by the Vice team who asked if I would like to ride with them while one of their guys was out sick. I jumped at the chance; it was a plainclothes job, and the Vice Officer was a legendary cop. He taught me more in one week about hunting bad-guys than I knew in the prior 3 years. When you worked the "Vice Car," you worked in an unmarked police vehicle in plain-clothes. (jeans and t-shirt) This allows the Officers to get closer or even approach unobserved by those engaging in the vice activity. Vice activities were generally those associated with gambling prostitution, and drugs and they attracted some bad people. It was a late night at about10:45 pm when the call for help came out over the radio. A citizen called stating that he had discovered a wounded and severely bleeding man on Halsted Street in "Boys-Town." My Vice Officer was Ken, and we headed over with our emergency equipment and blue lights on. We arrived as the 2nd Police car on the scene but were unable to find the caller or victim. The location was an old car repair shop that was boarded up. Ken motioned to me to follow him around the back of the building where we observed the rear door ajar. It was dark inside, but there were very dim light sources emanating from somewhere within. Drawing our revolvers, we entered cautiously and soon discovered that the building had been turned into a brothel of sorts catering to many different clients. Announcing our office, "Police! Did someone call" turned the floor into mayhem with people pulling on clothes and running around looking for an exit. It was then that we found the victim in a small room. He lay on a blood-soaked mattress, and there were splashes of carnage on the walls. The man appeared to have been beaten until he was unrecognizable. He was approximately 5 foot 6 inches, with a large protruding stomach, his eyes were glazed and his breathing shallow. An ambulance was on the way, so Ken and I attempted to talk to him. Once he heard our voices, he became conscious, but could not speak with the mouthful of broken teeth that he began choking on. It seemed like an eternity as we rolled him on his side to clear his mouth and airway and waited for the ambulance. I could swear he was swelling up in the midsection. After the ambulance arrived, the victim lapsed into unconsciousness and began very labored breathing. The paramedics were having difficulty opening an airway on the scene, so we escorted the ambulance, lights, and siren, to Northwestern Emergency Room (ER). Helping the paramedics transfer the victim to the table was the last clean moment I had that night. ER Doctors immediately detected heavy internal bleeding and began blood infusions. The internal bleeding was preventing the victim from breathing, so in one movement, the Doctor made an incision into his torso, and a gushing fountain of blood erupted. In the end, they were able to save this man's life. However, he sustained considerable injury from a truly brutal beating. Ken and all the Vice Cops took this personal and discovered several other cases City-wide. The method of operation was to lure lonely, older men to secluded areas, rob them and in 2 cases, beat them to death. Every day after that night, the Officers of the 23rd District visited every bar, every tavern, and spoke to every contact they had or could make. It was a time in the Chicago Police Department where Officers became outraged that something like this could happen in our District, and we took it personally; this doesn't happen on our watch to our people! Three weeks and countless visits and interviews later, Officers of the 23rd took the Offender into custody after a bar patron thought a guy looked suspicious and called one of the Officers. Although I was transferred to another District by then, I learned that he was positively identified by our surviving victim and charged with his attempted murder. Murder charges were pending for the other two unfortunate victims, and I never learned the outcome.

Categories

Let me explain "hunting" bad-guys. In my experience, I've found there to be three main types of Officers working in any Police Department. Some subgroups range on each end of the spectrum and in each category, but I will not address them here:

Hunters: The most aggressive Officers who actively seek out evil and wrong-doers wherever they are. These Officers have made careful studies of human behavior and have honed their perception skills to notice details most of us don't. The way someone walks when he has a gun is different than someone unarmed. People walk subtly different when a weapon is in the waistband in the front, side, small of their back, or under the arm in a shoulder holster. These Officers tend to patrol only in the worst, crime-ridden areas.

There are "Hunters" in every district and municipality, and they are Good Cops.

Good Cops: These Officers make up the bulk of all the districts and departments I've worked in. They are the talented, capable, and well-rounded Officers that view public service as their duty and strive to discharge that duty to the best of their ability every day.

Good Cops see a bigger picture. A Vietnam War veteran and veteran Chicago Police Officer expressed it best; "A good cop uses his head, gets the job done, and keeps the peace without violence and arresting everyone. Any cop can arrest someone, but did that solve the problem? Any cop can use his hands or gun, but when you've gone there, it's over."

Mutts: Like any profession in every field, there are a small group of individuals who place themselves in this category. Thankfully, there aren't many of these Officers, but it seems they have a knack for getting noticed and remembered. The Mutt is that rare breed that seemingly stood in the wrong line at lunch and became a cop. He or She has no interest in policing or public service, and will try to tell you that they do the bare minimum because, "the job screwed them," or "it's all bullshit," or they actually rationalize that they're great cops because they're able to "handle the jobs without needing to make a pinch." (a pinch is slang for arrest). When they show up for an assignment, it's usually late, they're disinterested or unprepared or both, and they work hard at getting out of doing their jobs. The poor caller is left without service, a bad experience, and they either give up or are forced to call again hoping to have

Figure 5. District structure

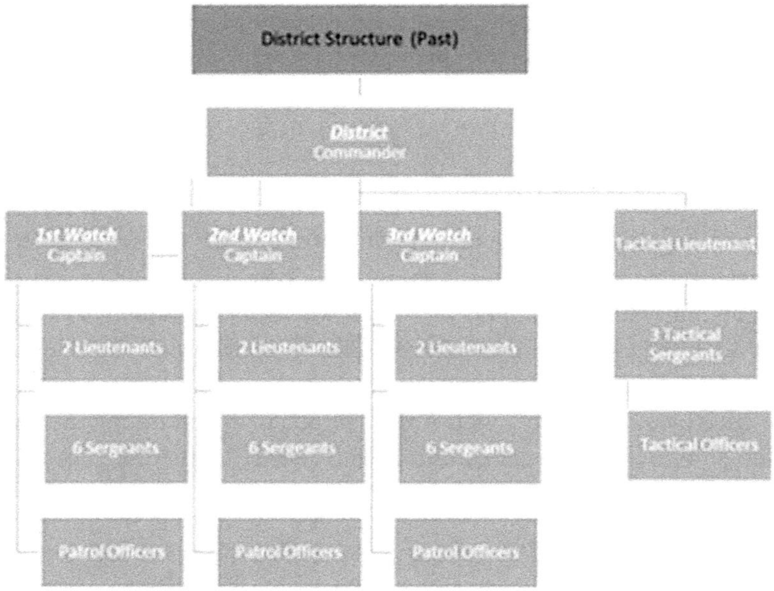

different Officers arrive. Every time one of these Officers renders service, he or she makes the rest of the profession look bad. Because their oath and duty mean nothing to these Officers, I have absolutely no use for this group — nor do they for me.

It is important to note that being a Hunter isn't better than being a Good Cop. NOTHING is better than being a Good Cop, and you must be one to be a Hunter. In my experience, it is common for newer Officers to "try on" the "Hunter" role and for Officers to bounce back and forth between categories #1 and #2. It's also common for veteran Hunters to naturally slow down as they age. What never happens is for a Hunter to turn into a Mutt, and a Mutt never turns into a Hunter. I don't know of any Mutt turning into Good Cop either.

A Chicago Police District can be viewed as a small community of like-minded people. Officers must rely on each other to keep the District crime and disorder to a minimum while trying to ensure a decent quality of life for the residents. Each District is led by a Commander, who sets priorities and goals based upon crime conditions and public needs. Three watches ensure 24-hour 365-day coverage, and at that time, rotated every 28 days. Today the watches are steady for one full year, and Officers bid for those watches based on seniority. (They do not currently rotate.) Each watch was led by a Captain (the Watch Commander), with 2 Lieutenants, six Sergeants, and the allotted body of Police Officers. Today, there is only one Captain in the District who works as the Executive Officer (XO) for the Commander. Two Lieutenants now run the watches with 9 Sergeants.

Shortly after my 1st anniversary when a recruit moves from probationary Police Officer to full-fledged Police Officer, I was given a permanent assignment in the 024th District—Rogers Park station. The 24th District was a fantastic place to work, with one of the most diverse communities in the City. Situated on Chicago's farthest Northeast side, it's an area of grand old buildings with huge apartments, beautiful lakefront beaches, Loyola University, and just about every racial, ethnic and religious group

Figure 6. District structure

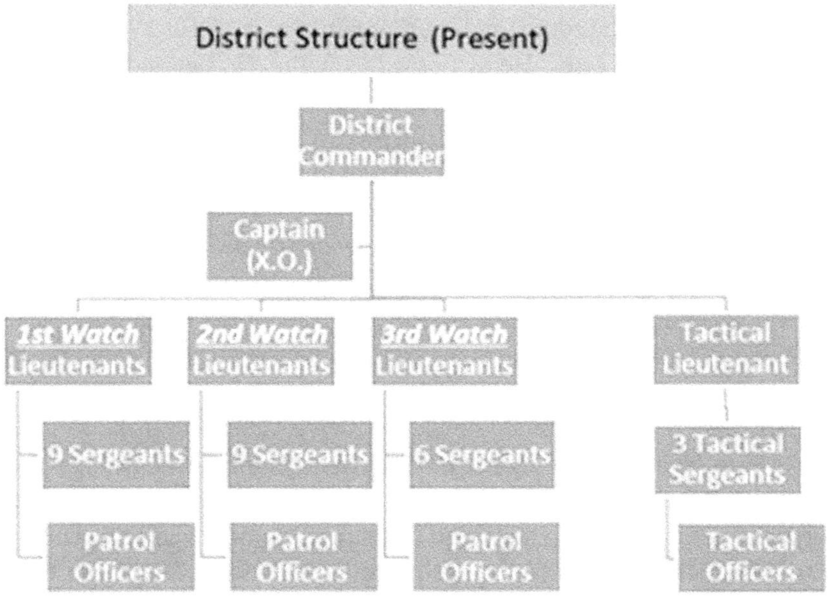

you can think of. I loved it. Beginning at Peterson Avenue on the south, it stretches North to Evanston, and west to Kedzie Avenue. There was plenty of action and just the right amount of beautiful areas to keep your head clear when you've had enough!

My first day in the District, I met with the Watch Commander who was quite old but capable looking, short on words, very direct and wearing two stars and 1 bar on his sleeve. Each sewn-on star means you've been with the Department for 20 years, and each bar equals five years. My new Captain had been a Police Officer for at least 45 years! This man had become a Police Officer in 1947 after WWII! He introduced himself, then told the sergeant to "Put him with somebody good." He was everything a Police Captain of old should be—awesome and terrible! That was it, he said nothing more to me and I was dismissed to go to roll call. The sergeant arranged for me to get my locker and had me fill out all the paperwork out for administrative things like weapon serial numbers, helmet number, and next of kin. I entered the roll call room and was left on my own. The room was about 75% old veterans, and 25% younger guys. Most of the old vets had seen the war in Korea or Vietnam. When the Captain came in for roll call, we stood until he inspected us. The Captain gave everyone their beat assignments for the night, relayed pertinent incidents from the prior watch, and gave each beat a priority issue to focus on in their beat. He then waved to the lock-up keeper (a Police Officer assigned to the holding cells) who brought in a handcuffed arrestee of about 20 years old who sneered at us. He was dirty, smelly, and had dried blood on his face. "This piece of work was selling after school on Juneway and fought the wagon. Take a good look." The Captain said a lot more in that sentence than appears; he wanted us to know that this individual sold heroin, and he sold it right after school, near the school, on the North side of the District. This dealer was exposing children to drug dependency and ruin. Now, if this guy fought with the wagon, that means that he fought with the two arresting Officers first, who had to call for the heavy transport vehicles known as Wagons, Meat Wagons, Meat Trucks, or Paddy-wagons. The bad-guy fought with at least 4 Officers before he could be arrested. Message clear, if we came across this guy at a later date, watch him, he's a dope dealer, and we should be prepared to fight if we have to arrest him. With that, the arrestee was removed from the room, and the Captain warned, "Everyone better have their hats on their head when out of the car or else." He dismissed us with, "Go out and do some good."

Let's talk about wagon-men. As my wife says, "Wagon-men were a whole other club!" They were usually the biggest, quietest, no-nonsense, and grim men you've ever met. We called it the Meat-Wagon or Meat-Truck because they were responsible for removing and transporting decedents, whether from natural, or unnatural causes. They all seemed to smoke cigars which help disguise the stench of decay, and they always had an extra fifty-cent Dutch-Masters when you needed one! Wagon-men spent most of their time around the dead, the violent, the infested, and diseased. All deceased, and all living persons requiring secure and separate transport went into the wagon, which meant that these guys had to have high thresholds for odors, horror, and violence. These were the men cops call when in need of heavy assistance. Like the cavalry coming to the rescue, seeing the wagon screaming in with lights and siren can make your heart soar! It was common knowledge on the street that if the wagon comes, somebody is going to jail. I need to point out that my use of the term "Wagon-Men" isn't purposely sexist, it's just that there were no women assigned to the wagons at this time. Most *men* didn't want to work the wagon!

One of the ordeals that a young cop had to go through at the time was to learn how to handle DOA's (all deaths, natural, homicide, and suicide). Technically, DOA stands for Dead On Arrival, but it is a short acronym used by Officers as a coverall term that leaves no doubt as to what is meant. Since we were not trained or prepared for such things, we'd be partnered with real wagon-men to get on-the-job training. During our first year, we'd be assigned to meet Wagon those situations arose so we could learn. Today, Officers do not handle or remove the deceased; they are removed by trained professionals with protective equipment and the correct tools.

My experiences assigned to the Wagon were memorable, no matter how hard I try to forget; I can still see each one like it just happened. My first experience was only a couple of blocks from where I was living. There, in an apartment on the 3rd floor, a young lady was found murdered after blood had seeped through the floor to the apartment below. She lay on her back, eyes partially open, with her arms and legs spread out. Arterial spray from the gash in her throat coated every wall, and the smell of blood and death was thick and sweet. There was so much blood that it was impossible not to step into it. I called for the Department Crime Lab, who were specially trained forensic investigators that gathered evidence to help the Detectives solve violent crimes. Today, the Chicago Police Crime Lab no longer exists. The City needed to cut costs, so we now use the Illinois State Police Crime Lab. I'm critical of this decision, not because the State isn't excellent at what they do, but because they handle such an incredible amount of evidence from every Police Department in the State that they're often very behind in their analysis. Also, when we staffed our own lab, the investigators came to the scene and were afforded an opportunity to observe, test, expand scenes and discover evidence that was sometimes overlooked by others. In the case of this homicide, the Crime Lab photographed everything and every area in the apartment. They bagged the Victim's hands in paper to preserve possible evidence under fingernails and to examine in detail, all defensive wounds. A quick probe of the throat confirmed that the neck had been cut so deep as to sever windpipe and both arteries. They made an important discovery when they lifted the toilet seat cover which revealed two condoms unflushed in the toilet bowl. This evidence was recovered and cataloged by the Crime Lab Officers even though the technology we have today for DNA analysis didn't exist. Today, the genetic contents would be of great value in positively identifying one of the last people to be in that apartment and quite possibly, the offender. While my veteran partner protected the scene, I spent about two hours inside with the Crime Lab Detectives. Throughout the entire time on this scene, the greying, fatherly, sixty-something-year-old Crime Lab Detective painstakingly brought me through their process, giving me insight into what I should be looking at, and what I needed to preserve.

During my time in that apartment, the horror of the event and scene didn't affect me like it later would. No, I had veteran Officers keeping me focused on technical aspects required for this assignment, so that emotions couldn't prevent or hamper me from doing this job that needed to be done well. The emotional element does come back. You *do* review the brutality and wonder, and hope, that the unfortunate Victim didn't suffer long. But for me, that's usually later and only when I close my eyes for the night. It's important to recognize that there were Sergeants and Lieutenants on the scene, but no ranking Officer needed to order a veteran to teach a new guy. It was a point of pride and a sense of duty that compelled the veterans to teach the new Officers. These veterans and many others over the last 30 years were "lights" in my career that helped me navigate through. Many of the lights have dimmed, and many more have gone out, but I smile when I think of them.

One of my sadder memories are of two elderly twin brothers who did everything together; they got married 40 years before to two girls, who were best friends, at the same ceremony. They vacationed together and lived in a two-flat building that they purchased together. The call came out, "2432, see the resident at… regarding a possible suicide." My partner Jeff and I pulled up, got out of the car and met one brother, who immediately and emotionlessly informed us that he had heard a muffled thump downstairs and discovered his brother had just killed himself in the 1st-floor bathroom. There were no tears but looking at his sadness was almost overwhelming to witness. We immediately called an Ambulance and made entry into the apartment. The Victim was located in the 1st-floor bathroom, slumped in the bathtub and missing a good portion of the top of his head. A .357 caliber revolver was on the floor and laying on the sink was a full, black knit winter hat oozing reddish fluid. A quick check of the man's vital signs assured us that he was deceased. In a note, the Victim wrote that he and his cancer had been a burden to his beloved wife until she passed, and he would not put his brother and sister-in-law through the same torment again. He wrote that there were ammunition and the receipt for the gun in his bedroom and that they should give them to the Police. "We will all meet again –" Signing it with love, the short note ended. When the ambulance arrived, they confirmed our findings. While the scene was being processed for evidence, my partner Jeff and I spoke with the surviving brother. He related that they were just planning a trip to Florida together at dinner last night and that he could not believe what happened. We learned that his brother had been diagnosed with cancer four years before which required quite a bit of care. Shortly after his remission, his wife of 40 + years had passed away. His cancer had just come back, and he did not expect to live.

After the scene had been processed for any evidence, Jeff and I rolled the brother into the black plastic body bag. He was very slight and thin in build, and it took us no effort. Moving to the knit hat, I found that it was initially on the Victim's head and had come off when the bullet exited his skull. Landing on the sink, it contained skull and brain matter. I carefully picked the hat up, careful not to spill or crush the contents, and placed it into the bag. While securing the ammunition and weapon receipt, I noticed a book lying on the bedside nightstand. It was a book that described in detail how to commit suicide, and it was marked at the chapter that addressed containing the mess that death leaves. Picking it up, I read the recommendation that a person uses the tub or shower so that clean-up would be a simple matter of washing it down the drain, and to wear a hat—knit or stocking, not baseball—to help contain any mess should the bullet exit the skull. Who would write something like this, and who would publish it? I don't like writing it here, now, and may edit this out later. I couldn't understand. I recovered it and inventoried it with the ammunition and gun receipt.

What happens after an incident like this? Simple, everyone leaves and someone—maybe the owner—cleans up. As Jeff and I got back in the car to finish our paperwork, I couldn't stand the idea of this brother cleaning his twin brother from the bathroom. I left the paperwork to Jeff and walked back into the apartment. I asked the brother if I could clean up. He said "no," that it was his brother and his responsibility, but I would not let him do this alone. He nodded, and as we scrubbed and wiped what remained, we worked in silence. I remember finding a skull fragment the size and shape of a pencil eraser at the top of the ceramic tile wall. We both stopped what we were doing, and not looking at each other; we cried together. When we were done, we shook hands, he grabbed my arm firmly and said, "Thank you." I never saw him again.

There were so many others; decomposing bodies in hot apartments, bodies being eaten by rats and insects, bodies leaking on your pants and shoes when you try to move them; the bloated corpses washing up on shore from Lake Michigan (called "Floaters"); the victims of gang fights, suicides, domestic-related homicides, child abuse and burning; removing boiled bodies and laughing until you cry at the absurdity of it all as a foot comes off in your hand. If you add searching every high-rise dumpster on the lakefront from Greenview to Loyola finding body parts and recovering a bag of hands from a lagoon, you may get a picture of what it was like to be a Chicago Police Officer thirty years ago. The smell of death stays with you, permeating everything and sticking to you and your clothing like glue. We had no formal training then, no personal protective equipment (PPE), no issued rubber or latex gloves, and no formal support group or counseling. What we did have, however, was each other, and "Choir Practice, where all saints get together to sing." This was our way to move forward.

It's been frowned upon, largely discontinued, and antiquated by newly available mental health programs but "Watch Parties" and "Choir Practice" were the acceptable, normal way to excise traumatic events, and to encourage partnership and brotherhood. This always involved the entire watch going to the local tavern to talk, blow off steam, then pour alcohol on top of it all to get over the day's events. It works for a while, but if anyone wonders why alcohol abuse was so widespread, one only has to examine the way traumatic events and stress were handled, and the lack of follow-up care that was available in the past. Thankfully, the Chicago Police Department, along with Department's across the nation, has changed. We still have quite a way to go, but we're moving in the right direction with our peer support and confidential professional counseling.

Promotional Exams

In my second year, the Department announced a new Detective and Sergeant test. I was really excited to take them both but almost didn't. You see, about two weeks before the test, I conducted a traffic stop on the west side of the district for a motorist driving through a red light. I was "10-99," which means I was alone, assigned to traffic enforcement that day. The violation was a close call; I believed the driver had time to stop on the yellow signal but decided to continue through the red. I spoke with the driver, checked the driver's license and registration, and issued a warning instead of the citation. It was a very typical street stop for me. The following day, I was called into the Captain's office where my Lieutenant, the Captain, and a Sergeant greeted me and informed me that they had just received a severe complaint. The driver of the vehicle that I had stopped on West Devon avenue the day before claimed that I drew my service revolver, and threatened, "If you don't stop driving that way, you'll be dead." The Captain explained that the Lieutenant was conducting a preliminary investigation and it would then be sent to Internal Affairs. Wow—my blood pressure zeroed, and I was speechless. I was allowed to outline the incident as it occurred, and to proclaim my innocence. I advised that I gave the dispatcher the location, license plate number, license number of the driver, and later the actions I had taken. I gave the driver a warning and did not remove my weapon from my holster or make threatening statements. All this was what my boss hoped and expected to hear, but the investigation would be conducted. I was worried sick. I knew I did nothing wrong, but it was my first complaint, and I knew it would come down to who's word was going to be believed. This was before body cameras and body microphones, and even before the intersections had cameras as they do now. Crestfallen, I couldn't believe someone could be that evil, especially when I let the driver off with a warning!

After a week of feeling depressed, one of the older Sergeants on the watch stopped me and asked what was wrong. I told him, and he smiled. "Paul, you're gonna meet people like that. Don't worry about them—there ain't that many of 'em. You keep doing what you're doing. You're doing good." As I shook my head, he asked if I was taking the promotion exams. I told him that I was going to but was re-thinking the whole thing after receiving this complaint. I also genuinely thought that I had no business being a Sergeant with only a couple of years' experience. The Sergeant shook his head and said, "Don't you do that. Look, if anyone believed you did that, you'd be down at IAD (Internal Affairs Division). It's BS. Now," he spun me around to show me another Sergeant who was among the least competent supervisors I've known, and said, "If *he* can be a Sergeant, you sure as shit can! Take those tests!" I think about Sergeant M often. Before that day, we had never really spoken, and the only interaction we had was at roll call and when he came to manage an assignment. I left him ready to take the tests. Another "light" that taught me how easy it is to show concern and care for Officers that would someday be under my command.

Guilty until Proven Innocent

Police Agencies have a tendency to make their Officers feel like they're guilty even if they are innocent. I'm confident that this not intentional, and it may be that there is no way around it. I recognize the need for timely action in response where deadly force is used and for complaints, but the quick action taken is often viewed by Officers as punishment. In the instance of deadly force, an Officer is required to surrender his firearm to be processed for evidence. This is a vital necessity. In practice, Officers are disarmed right away at the scene of these incidents in front of his peers and citizens alike by a Command staff member they usually don't know, then placed in the back of a Detective's vehicle. To a Police Officer, having your weapon taken in front of everyone looks terrible, and the back seat of any Police vehicle is for bad-guys, not good-guys. None of this is an indication of support to an Officer who has just gone through one of the most traumatic events a person can. Balancing the need to preserve and protect evidence with that of the Officer's physical and psychological needs could be easily accomplished by designating a supervisor to remain with the Officer with instruction that the Officer's weapon remains secured and unhandled in his or her holster until it can be inventoried at the Detective Area headquarters.

When it comes to complaints, due process isn't exactly one of a sworn Officer's rights. For instance; while working the West-side of Chicago, Narcotics dealers were making false claims about Officers to get them reassigned and out of their distribution areas. Unfortunately, it worked for a while because of the immediate need to remove an Officer, "just in case." There was no appeal to the decision. Up until recently, Officers were required to serve suspensions for transgressions before they could appeal the investigation or sentence. When the independent civilian review agencies began searching for Police misconduct (OPS, IPRA, COPA), their untrained civilian investigators found multitudes of Officers in violations that were proved false by trained investigators and hearing boards. Unfortunately, these agencies still fail to train their employees to any recognizable standards. I'm not sure that we can fully mitigate the necessary actions in these cases, but I am sure that we can do better.

Thanks to Sergeant M, I took those tests and within a year, the results were sent out. Of the thousands of Police Officers that took the tests, I was ranked number 9 on the Detectives list, and just under 200 on the Sergeants list. I knew that I'd be promoted to Detective right away, and Chicago's Mayor Daley pledged to promote 500 Sergeants to bolster the rapidly declining ranks. Naturally, and being a bit cynical, I put the idea of being promoted to Sergeant out of my head!

Detective Division

In January 1995, I was placed into "Detective School" where we were trained on policy and procedures affecting Detectives and given rudimentary instruction on typing and ethical investigations. I was promoted to the rank of Detective in February 1995 and assigned to the Area 5 Detective Division, located on the northwest side of Chicago at Grand and Central avenues. I was one of six new Detectives to be assigned to Area 5. As the name suggests, an "Area" is slang for the Detective division that investigates crime over an area of several Police Districts. An Officer might say, "I gotta stop at the Area and see the Dicks," which means he or she needs to stop in and see the Detectives assigned to the Police District. Nobody called us "Detectives" at that time unless we were in a formal or court settings. To the Officer on the street, we were the "Dicks." No, not an anatomical reference or a derogatory term, but one of brevity and endearment. I thought it a mispronunciation of "Dets," short for Detective, but it turns out that it is actually derived from the old comic strip hero "Dick Tracy." When an Officer has a big "caper" (an arrest or serious incident), he calls the "Dicks."

On my first day at my new job, we were hustled into the roll call room where we were to receive our Division assignments. The Detective Area was divided into specialty investigative divisions; Property Crimes Division and Violent Crimes Division (known as Property Crimes, or "Property," and Violent Crimes, or "Violent"). These Divisions were further specialized; Property Crimes was divided into "burglary," and "financial." Violent Crimes was divided into "general," "sex," "robbery," and "homicide." Of course, we all wanted to be assigned to homicide, but we everyone got assigned to the Property Crimes Division instead. Our sole purpose was to investigate the thousands of property-related crimes like burglaries, felony thefts, and felony damage to property.

Once again, we were assigned to veteran Detectives for field training, who were to provide on-the-job assistance and guidance. I'll be darned if I didn't get the retiree *AGAIN*! I had been through this before, so I knew I'd have to keep my eyes open and gather as much as I could from everyone else around me. He was gruff, and I thought pretty unhelpful since whenever I'd ask a question, he'd answer, "What do you think?" I came to appreciate this later when, long after he was gone and I was a Sergeant, I got it. He consistently made me come up with my own answer, then watched as it worked or failed. When my answer didn't work, he'd make a *little* suggestion—not a big one that would solve my problem. I don't think he would have ever stood by and watch me make a serious mistake, but it was maddening at the time. He always made me think, develop my own strategy, and act alone. By doing so, he helped me develop myself as an investigator and changed the way I thought about problem-solving. When faced with problems now, I always try to develop a solution, no matter how uncertain I am of its' success. As a supervisor, I never move a problem or issue up through my chain of command or to others without presenting my actions, "This is the issue, and this is what I've done so far / what I'd like to do / what I think could be done." This lets everyone know that you're attempting to solve your problem but require some assistance.

Detectives are a difficult group, and navigating their world was a delicate matter. This was unlike any group of Officers I had ever encountered up to that time. Egos ran rampant, and slights were often perceived where none existed. There was very little group or team cohesion, and there was always an undercurrent of suspicion and unpleasantness as everyone sought to be a star. Those in Property Crimes were somewhat looked down upon by the Detectives on the Violent side, and the veteran Property Dicks called the Violent Crimes Dicks "Prima-Donnas." Truth be told, the Detectives in Property Crimes used to be Violent Crimes Detectives and remained every bit as talented and motivated as any in the Area. The fact remains that Property Crimes was where the most senior, veteran Detectives went to work after grueling and heartbreaking years of investigating violence and monsters of all kind. Our Area Commander (and eventual Superintendent of Police) knew what he was doing when he started us in Property Crimes. I was afforded the opportunity to learn from some legendary Chicago Detectives and learned that investigations are about relationships and problem solving, and it is as much a skill as it is an art. It's important for me to include that I was never denied help by any of the veteran Detectives even when they were busy. Although they wouldn't say, I know most really appreciated being asked for their expertise and help.

As my Detective career moved forward, my partner and I were asked by the Commander to move to the Violent Crimes Division and work the "sex crimes" unit for three months. After that, the Commander said he'd move us to homicide if we wished. Of course, we'd move just because he asked, but the enticement was nice. Speaking together later, we both expressed apprehension over the new assignment. We had no training in handling traumatic events of this nature, and we were aware that the investigations tend to be very complicated, emotional, and often end unacceptably concerning prosecution. Using the investigatory skills we'd been taught, together with our experience and some guidance from former Sex Crimes investigators, we learned quickly.

Most people are ignorant of how serious misdemeanor and felony offenses move from an incident to the courtroom in Cook County. Typically, this is the progression: An offense is committed, and the Police are called. An investigation occurs to determine whether there is an actual violation of the law and evidence is gathered. If an offender can be placed into custody immediately, he or she is arrested. After the arrest, the offender is taken to the District or Area (depending on the severity of the offense), and the investigation continues which include interviews of all persons involved. Once again, if the elements of a crime present, the offender is charged with the violation committed. Now, in serious misdemeanors and all felonies, the Cook County State's Attorney is called *before* an individual is charged with those offenses. The Detective handling the case then speaks with or meets with an Assistant State's Attorney (ASA) to present all the available evidence in the case. The ASA then determines whether that offender is charged or not. The ASA determines the charges in *all* felonies, *not* the Police. I emphasize the words "*all*" and "*not*" because the newspapers just won't get it correct and citizens mistakenly believe the Police are the reason someone is charged and goes to court or not. I'd be remiss if I didn't inform the reader that the State's Attorney's office is a revolving door of attorneys, and a large portion of the ASA's are fresh from law school with little experience. There are some absolutely committed and talented attorneys there, but it seems that low wages, huge workloads, and political pressures push them away.

Without getting too deep into the facts of a particular case, it bears writing about a situation I encountered more than once concerning the arrest, charging, and prosecution of crime in general, and sex crimes specifically. My partner and I worked very hard investigating a sexual assault that occurred in our Area. We spend countless hours looking for witnesses, piecing together timelines, and interviewing everyone we felt might have information or evidence. A lot of time is spent with the Victim in cases like these who have to recount and relive the traumatic events repeatedly so that no detail might be missed. We identified the Offender and made the arrest. The Offender was high profile in his community, and this may or may not have been a factor in the decisions eventually made. An ASA came out to the Area to view the case evidence and interview the Victim, Witness, and Offender. While interviewing the Victim, it became evident that this ASA had no experience with interviews; he was brash and sounded skeptical and condescending from the start. After no more than 15 minutes with the Victim, he halted the interview and motioned us to leave the room to speak. Once away from the Victim, the ASA informed us that he didn't believe the Victim, and he would not approve charges—just like that. We could not persuade him to conduct further interviews or to reconsider. My blood boiled at this brand-new attorney, and it was all I could do not to grab him and make him explain his reasons to the Victim. He walked out the door while my partner and I were left to try to help the Victim understand something we couldn't understand ourselves. That same scenario happened one other time while in Sex Crimes, and our recourse is very limited. District Officers and Area Detectives experience these seemingly arbitrary refusals across the City daily, which has continued at an alarming rate today under our current State's Attorney.

True to his word, after three months, the Commander moved us into Homicide. The Detectives here were simply amazing. Yes, the egos were considerable, but the Homicide Unit did have something to brag about! These guys were consummate professionals; dedicated in every way and selfless in their work. At first, my partner and I were assigned to shadow and assist the veteran Homicide Detectives who were actually thrilled to have two new guys to train. The summer was heating up, and there was an emerging gang war in the 14th District. In one short week, I had worked on six shootings with eight homicide victims. As a patrolman in a District, mutual combatants who all engage in the criminal activity made it easier for me to view them as "Live by the Sword—Die by the Sword" homicides. That is until I was charged with their investigations. Death is always hard, and it's never gotten easier speaking with the loved ones of the deceased. I loved the work, though. It was always challenging and rewarding when I could identify and arrest a real bad-guy. Well almost.

Our very first solo homicide that my partner and I were assigned to was not a "Who Dunnit," but a senseless and brutal murder of a little girl by her biological father. We were called to the scene by the responding Officers. When they arrived, they were met by the father, who claimed that his daughter just lost consciousness during a nap and he could not wake her. The Officers did not see any visible signs of foul play, but the scene was moving very fast, and the paramedics began working the instant they arrived. The ambulance crew arrived at roughly the same time the Officers arrived and began working on getting some vital signs back. The girl was ultimately pronounced dead at when she arrived at the hospital. The father was very distraught and was en route to the hospital with an Officer and the paramedics. The girl's mother and family were not home when this occurred and were going to meet everyone at the hospital. Shortly, the mother would arrive at the hospital where grief counselors and hospital staff would inform her. Because this was an active investigation, as all child deaths are, the Officers had secured the scene of occurrence so the house could be entered to search and gather any evidence relating to the death. This is standard practice, and although you have to temper hope that a human wasn't responsible, you must approach the scene as a possibility. The residence was unremarkable inside. However, there was just something that didn't make visual sense. There were small moist areas in places on the floor, but not soaking spots. There were drips and drops, but no apparent source. When I looked in the bathroom, it was disheveled with toiletry items on the counters and had towels stuffed haphazardly into a full laundry hamper. The floor was clean. It looked like it had just been cleaned, there was no dirt, no hair, or other detritus. I searched through the hamper and discovered at the very bottom; wet child's clothing covered in what I believed was vomit and water.

Consulting with the veteran homicide Detectives that trained us, we immediately collected the articles for evidence. The entire scene was to be photographed and processed by the Crime Lab and would now be sealed pending the postmortem examination. Once at the hospital, it was apparent that other than brief statements, no comprehensive interviews could be conducted until the following day. The next morning the Medical Examiner's Office (ME's office) would conduct the post-mortem examination (called "the post") of the girl which we hoped would provide the cause of death. Following the example of our mentors, my partner and I always attended the "post" for all homicides we investigated because they yield a plethora of information in real time. The forensic pathologists at the ME's office are meticulous, and through their careful examinations, one can often discover traumas that were previously unknown or undetectable under normal circumstances. The investigator also has the opportunity to gain insight into the cause of death and injury quickly, discover the offending object or shape of the offending object, the amount of force used, and historical injuries that might indicate long-term abuse. The process for postmortems is well documented, and I won't go into them here. Just know that as sterile and professional as the Doctor and the environment is, it is still hard to see a child on that gurney. What we quickly discovered is that the child's head was severed at the spine which caused her death. The interior skin at the back of the child's head and neck showed that the child had been struck there with considerable force that effectively decapitated her. From an examination of her stomach contents, we discovered that she had received a powerful blow to her abdomen sometime proximate to her death which caused her digestive tract to stop working. The melted, undigested ice-cream showed that it was probable she was fed after the trauma, but prior to death. Unconsciousness and death would have been quick.

Through our interviews with the child's mother, we learned that the father had just been released from prison and wanted to meet his daughter and be part of their lives. Amidst protests from the family, the mother consented and allowed the father to move in. The day of her child's death was the first day he was left alone with her.

Interviews with the father were frustrating, and his account was inconsistent. My partner and I had an excellent idea of what happened there; an emotionally unprepared father did something that he will regret the rest of his life. The frustrating part was that both my partner and I felt that he *wanted* to tell us what actually happened, but he just could not. This young man was not a tough-guy, nor did he act with movie-bravado; he was in pain, and I swear he looked like he wanted us to help and make it okay. When one of our homicide mentors came by to check on us, we told him of our feelings that the suspect wants to tell us what really happened. To my surprise, the Detective got very serious and said, "Most of them do." He then asked if he could help us out and if he could speak with the suspect. Absolutely. We filled him in on everything we had learned and gave him a copy of the post exam. We all went into the interview room and introduced our mentor.

The veteran Detective began with his sincere condolences and then spoke about personal pain. Because he was older and had children, he became fatherly, reassuring and understanding. Within a few more minutes, the suspect began to cry and said he wasn't a monster. The veteran Detective reached over and placed his hand on the suspect's knee and stated, "I know you aren't." That was it, the offender—

suspect—father told us what and how it happened; that he snapped when she would not be quiet, so he punched her in the stomach. Then because her stomach was physically traumatized and hurt, she cried more. He tried to give her ice-cream, but when she ate it, she threw up. Now he had to wash her off and got water all over the floor. After changing her clothes, she still would not settle down, and in a fit of rage, he grabbed her by her legs and struck her head on the counter. "I'm not a monster."

Within months of that case, I was called into the Commander's office, and he asked, "Where do you want to go?" My blood pressure zeroed again, and I thought, "Oh G*d, what did I do *this* time?" The Commander saw my face and quickly congratulated me; I had just been promoted to Sergeant! After that, the Commander contacted a District Commander that he knew well in the 23rd District and arranged an interview for me. I heard him say, "You'll want this guy." Having his endorsement meant the world to me!

Sergeant

Sergeant school was, "interesting." First, we were absolved of our shortcomings as patrolmen and women, then told very firmly that we were now "them"—as in "Us and Them." From that moment forward we could no longer think like Patrol Officers because it was our new job to "get things done." They spent considerable time on disciplinary procedures, and while they retrained and refreshed us on Department policies and practices, there was no leadership training whatsoever. There was no class on management styles or evolving concepts in Police management. We learned how to prepare our activity logs, initiate complaint registers, and conduct complaint investigations. A definite display of the Department's priorities. In all fairness, the men and women teaching these classes were mainly Police Officers—grizzled veterans of the Department and were either in the military or had been brought up in that environment. It's entirely possible that they took it for granted that everybody had a clue about leadership principles. The week before school was over, we were sent on interviews. I met with 23rd District Commander who advised me that he was bringing me on as his new Sergeant and advised me not to interview anywhere else. I took his advice and was excited by the possibility of getting back to a great District.

I graduated from Sergeant training and was immediately sent to the 10th District—Marquette. When the Captain gave me my assignment, I involuntarily exclaimed, "Where the hell is that?" I was expecting to hear "23rd District" so it was a shock. Having never worked the south-side of Chicago, I had no idea, which tickled the Captain to bits. "Hey Northside, you spend time at 26th and Cal when you were a Dick?" "Yes, sir—a lot of time there," I replied. "Well that's where the hell 10 is—G*d help us. I hope you're better at Sergeant-ing than finding yer way around!" I got some good laughs out of that along with a wee bit of embarrassment, but it was all in good fun.

Leaving the Detective Division was difficult; I loved the kind of work I was doing. I loved the autonomy to manage my time and the ability to use my creativity to accomplish every task. I felt like I was treated like an adult, and I liked it. Now I know that it doesn't always happen the way we'd like, or in the manner or timeframe, but more than anything, I loved it because it was the one place where I knew for sure that good *does* triumph over evil. I worked for some great leaders, and I learned from their example.

Now it was my turn to lead. It was 1997, and I was going to the 3rd Watch in the 10th District. The District is bounded on the North by Ogden Avenue and on the South at 15th Street. The East boundary is Ashland Avenue, and the western border is the town of Cicero Illinois. The population of the District was mostly Hispanic and African American.

I worked for an excellent Captain who was always calm, and wise. He never raised his voice, and he had the air of always being in control. My Lieutenant was a likable guy; he made sure that his troops hit the street with a smile on their face every day. Having someone who strives to start your day out well was a blessing in a District like the 10th—it's a tough District. It was good to get back into patrol operations, and it was like going back in time when it came to good camaraderie and shared goals. The main difference here was that I wasn't one of them anymore, I was a Sergeant, and the difference was hard for me to process. I was "The Police!" I had been through shootings, fights, vehicle pursuits, foot pursuits, tavern brawls, and hostage situations. Now, when I "rode on a job," (answering a call for service) the assigned Officers wanted to know why I was checking up on them. I could no longer be back-up for assignments, and no matter what I *was*, I was no longer "us," I was "them." Well, that was okay, but I was still going to be "me" which meant that I would always ride on jobs, and I would check up on them because it was *my* job.

I learned quickly that the Officers who worried about me "checking up on them" needed me to. This attitude granted me acceptance with the veterans and Good Cops, but the Mutts hated me. My patrol Sergeant career ended after several Officers of the Mutt category decided that I could not continue to make them do their duty. They launched an attack via the union claiming that I threatened them, and they were now afraid to go to roll call when I was present. This went through the District like wildfire, and I quickly found myself in the Commander's office answering questions. This time, I was ready; I would not spend time angry, depressed or worried about the issue. I had, in fact, read the Officers the riot-act the previous evening for leaving for the night without being properly relieved, I warned them that should it ever happen again, I would write them up. This explanation, along with several veteran witnesses, effectively quashed the complaint.

Unfortunately, no matter how I tried to convince myself otherwise, I hated being a Sergeant and was seriously questioning why I left the Detective Division. I spent 95% of my time on less than 5% of Watch. This 5% were known as problem employees, but little did I know that they would not be my problems much longer. Two weeks after this incident, I was summoned to the Tactical Lieutenant's office. I knocked on the door and was told to enter. As I stood before the Lieutenant, he said, "What's this? I heard you threatened the whole 3rd Watch?" I was taken aback. "No sir, that's not what happened!" I protested.

The Lieutenant laughed and said, "I don't care. Why don't you come up and work for me?" I started my new job as the 1863B Tactical Sergeant on the following day. I had a nine-man, one-woman team of some of the most intelligent aggressive Hunters I've known. I earned three Department Commendations while there and had engaged in more police-work, search warrants, narcotics interdiction, and gang enforcement than I've had the pleasure of since. I really liked it, but I was at work all the time dealing with the absolute worst that humanity could provide, in the worst conditions, seeing just how horrible people could be to one another, and it was taking a toll on me. We were making arrests, seizing narcotics and weapons, but when we got to court, the bad-guys got a slap on the wrist and were out the next day. I felt that people were against us, the courts were against us, so what was the point? I began to feel frustrated, and I was becoming mean. What do you do when you lose faith and start feeling that everything you knew about good and evil was wrong? Evil seemed to win almost ALL the time. I was bringing it all home to my wife. She couldn't possibly understand, only my team could because they endured the daily crazy bad things with me. It was the lowest, darkest time in my life, let alone, my career. After accepting a painful ultimatum of "Do something, or I can't be with you," my wife suggested that I do something to clear my head—something I liked. The funny thing is, I couldn't think of anything I liked anymore. She had seen pictures of me and my father riding, and I always told her that I loved it, so she suggested horseback riding. I began my next day off, and I realized that I hadn't felt that feeling of joy in quite some time. Now, a portion of my overtime was spent on riding lessons, and I loved it. Later, a chance encounter with an Academy classmate who was assigned as a Training Officer in the Chicago Police Mounted Patrol Unit, provided me with an interview for an open Sergeant.

In 2001, I entered Mounted Patrol School and accepted the Sergeant position upon graduating. I knew it then, and I can say confidently now, that the horses and the Mounted Patrol Unit saved my family, my life, and my career. Working with horses is amazing, and to this day, just being near them eases my tension and helps make a better day. I wish every Officer in the City could work with horses for a week, just to "change their channel." I worked for a Commanding Officer who treated his supervisors like adults, expecting much for the autonomy in return and I would not disappoint him. Command of the Mounted Patrol Unit is by one Lieutenant who is the Commanding Officer, and four Sergeants who acted as watch Commanders and field supervisors. I was partnered with (then) Sergeant Paul Bauer, and together, we ran the 3rd Watch. Paul was a great partner and an excellent co-worker. I was suddenly in a world where on a daily basis, I had positive interaction with citizens all over the entire City. I forgot about the good people out there, and my assignment to the Unit renewed my faith that there are many more good people, than bad. The same year that I left the 10th District, I had to return with my Mounted Patrol Unit to a large festival held on May 5th. I saw the District in such a different light. Good people with their kids, along with some bad people that I recognized with their kids all having fun and acting as one big community. I no longer felt like an occupying army in hostile lands, and it did me a world of good.

Mounted Patrol Unit

My tenure in Mounted started in 2001 and ended in 2009. Those eight years were marked by George Bush junior's two-time presidency, the terrorist attacks on September 11th, the Space Shuttle Columbia disaster, the invasion of Iraq, Hurricane Katrina, North Korea's first nuclear bomb test, the capture, trial and execution of Saddam Hussein, the global economic crisis, Global Warming, arctic meltdowns, and record oil prices. Last, but certainly not least, was the election of the 44th U.S, President, Barack Obama. Each of these significant events led to national as well as world-wide civil unrest, violent protests, passionate demonstrations and clashes with the Police occurred every week. These events and the resultant disorder that occurred was to be the source of great learning and adventure. The Mounted Patrol Unit's primary focus is patrol. Highly visible, instantly recognizable, very approachable, and extremely maneuverable; horses can go almost everywhere that people can, but faster. I've found that unlike Officers on foot or in Police cars, citizens have little inhibitions about approaching a Mounted Officer on patrol to talk. While on Michigan Avenue, I watched as a citizen ran past an Officer in a squad car to report a robbery that was in progress one street over to Paul and me. Paul and I trotted to the corner and observed two Offenders wrestling a purse from a woman. The Offenders immediately saw the "Ten-Foot Cops" and split up running in different directions. Queuing our horses to the canter, we split up and caught the Offenders within 100 feet of where they started. So, why did the witness pass a Police car to report to the Mounted Officers? The answer is simple; we are highly visible and extremely approachable. This phenomenon repeatedly occurs to Mounted Officers, and it isn't limited to routine patrol. As masters of crowd management and control, the Mounted Patrol Unit is assigned to every large special event, protest and demonstration that occurs in the City. Having been assigned to the Bulls Celebration Riots between 1992 and 1997, I was no stranger to the chaos, fear, and uncertainty that surrounds large-scale disorder, but the anti-war / anti-Bush "protests" were something altogether worse. During the Bulls riots, the Police were not the real focus of the crowd's intent, although we became the focus whenever we acted. With the "Bush-era" demonstrations, there was a level of violence immediately directed at the Police, and that was concerning. Large groups of anarchists from all over the country streamed into Chicago to do masked combat with us. It was during two of these demonstrations that I was approached by demonstrators who provided me with information that was vital to prevent severe harm or death to Officers and horses. Both times, the information provided was confirmed as fact and the threats mitigated. The first encounter was a young woman and her friend wearing black, artfully ripped shirts, army fatigues, and combat boots.

The crowd was deafening that day at Federal Plaza, and I was part of a 30-horse skirmish line that was keeping the demonstration off of the street. We were stopped in a single column, nose to tail, and facing south with the event on our west (right side). The entire group including the two young women were yelling at us, "Get those animals off those horses," calling us fascists and other nonsense chants and insults for about 45 minutes. When it became apparent that we were not going to impede their free speech, the crowd grew somewhat quieter while they waited for their leaders to give them a new direction. At that time, one of the girls moved to my leg and asked—very quietly—if she could touch my horse. Usually, we would say "no," because they were working. I was a guarded because I wasn't sure of this person's motives, and I needed to protect my mount. However, on this occasion, I was tickled that a just few minutes before, with passion and hatred(?), she was calling me a fascist, and other foul names. I took a chance and said quietly, "Of course, his name is Knight, and he likes it best when you rub his shoulder." A covert smile spread on her face as she moved closer and secretly stroked Knight's right shoulder. Knight was my equine partner and a sweetheart, so he immediately turned his head and looked at the girl. She now lost all attitude and air of secrecy and breaking into a big smile, pulled her friend over and exclaimed pretty loudly, "You gotta see him, he's so sweet!" The friend scowled at me to let me know she still hated me, so I told her it was okay to touch him if she wanted. This turned into a small group of five protestors that were now petting my horse and the one behind me. After the short lull in the crowd's chanting, the leaders of the protest began again and all the insults and chanting renewed. This time, the two young women and the other five continued the anti-war chants, but they weren't shouting the insults anymore. As the demonstration wound up, we got word that it was going to move soon. As we prepared to move, the first young woman motioned that she wanted something from me. As I bent my head towards her, she said as quietly as she could, that we needed to be careful because "the guys with the bandanas have nails and batteries." I thanked her and waiting until she disappeared into the crowd, I radioed the information to the Incident Commander. A short time later, as we escorted the group through the streets, Officers were able to separate the identified individuals from the group and quickly discovered that they did, in fact, possess the batteries, as well as bent nails resembling children's jacks.

Batteries make small, very dense projectiles that can cause severe injury when struck. Throwing a battery at a person with even minimal force can cause injury. I was able to view the nails later after the protest ended. The devils had bent and welded the nails to hurt the horses. The proper name for the devices is "Caltrops," and they are a cruel and brutal medieval antipersonnel/anti-cavalry weapon. Strewn on the pavement, they always land with one point upwards. The caltrop pierces a person's boot or the horse's hoof and causing tremendous pain and panic. An out-of-control 1300 pound horse in a crowd situation could be deadly and would almost certainly require euthanizing the animal.

The second occasion was very similar to the first. Protestors that had just spoken to us and pet our horses notified us of hooks concealed on the ends of seemingly innocent poles holding protest banners. The hooks were to pull riders from their mounts. Closer examination of the banners revealed three sets of hooks (6 total with one set sharpened), deployed at different areas near our formation.

My times as a Mounted Sergeant were some of the best and undoubtedly most rewarding times on this job. As a Mounted supervisor, I was able to sharpen my people skills while further developing my

Figure 7. Caltrops

Caltrops. https://commons.wikimedia.org/w/index.php?curid=6696958

leadership skills and style. As a Tactical Sergeant, I learned about small unit leadership and team building. The Mounted Unit mirrors a Tactical team closely in form and motivation but differs dramatically in management. Mounted Officers are unique in that they care deeply for their mounts and do everything in their power to ensure their health and wellbeing. When a Mounted Officer goes on patrol, his or her concerns are for the safety of themselves, their mount, their human partner, and the partner's mount. All of that while still conducting enforcement and missions. They are devoted to the team concept and need little assistance in managing the necessity to work cohesively as a team. Their drive to get better at their craft is motivated by making the Unit better. As a supervisor in the Unit, one needs to concern themselves with all the Officers and mounts and concern themselves with logistical considerations such as managing food, water, distance, ground surfaces, and equine and rider ability. The supervisor must know each horse and rider's ability when tasking the team. A mismatch between skill and the difficulty of the task means the difference between success and failure of a mission.

I've found that horseback riding, is a lesson in leadership and building trust that translates to leading people surprisingly well. A trained team of horse and rider only work well when the rider gives clear, unhesitant direction and is trusted. When a trained horse seems unsure or hesitant it is usually due to fear or anxiety, and it can be indicative of a brand new experience for the horse, that clear direction is lacking, or trust is at issue. You build trust through clear direction and consistency in demands. Never demand behavior that hasn't been trained and learned. Perfect practice makes perfect; don't allow unacceptable behavior anywhere. Horses aren't leaders, but they will become one if the rider won't. When this happens, the team dynamic breaks, and it cannot perform its purpose or achieve the goal. Horses prefer a calm environment, and when that isn't possible, they require calm leadership from the rider. Leave preconceptions home; a horse may be said to be the worst, but often, a different rider can bring out the best.

I accept that those lessons might be considered "folksy wisdom," but, as silly as it might sound, I found that changing the words "Rider" for supervisor, Sergeant, or Lieutenant, and "Horse" for employee, Officer, or Team has worked for me in my management and leadership style.

Lieutenant

In 1996, The City offered a Lieutenant's exam. I had no interest in leaving, so I did not study. To my eternal, and utter shame, I bombed it accordingly, and I realized afterward, that I may have blown my one chance at further promotion. The City is notorious and has been openly criticized for only offering promotional exams once or twice in an Officer's entire career. Miraculously, one year later in 1997, the City offered a new exam. I still had reservations about taking the test because I loved working with horses, and I was only half-joking when I'd say, "I'd shovel horse-shit for the rest of my life if they would just let me work here!" I learned my lesson from the last exam; this might be the last opportunity, and I would put the effort doing well. I studied after work at the kitchen table every night until bed-time. One evening, Paul Bauer called. Paul did well on the last exam and was promoted and had to leave the unit. He asked what I was doing and if he could stop by. He was with the 12th District Commander, whom I liked and respected. I'll never forget that night; Paul and Ron (the Commander) came in, and after some talk, Ron asked, "Do you really want to be a Lieutenant?" I answered "Yes!" With a stern look and grave tone in his voice, he said, "If you want to be a Lieutenant, then you better get serious! Get out of here and go to a library where you have no distractions. Make studying your full-time job." Again, I felt the sting of the last failure. After they left, I spoke with my wife who had already suggested that I go to the library several times before Ron. She told said that I should put everything into studying. She would take care of everything at home and do everything in her power to make sure I could do it every day, uninterrupted. I didn't see much of her during that time. She made it, so I had nothing else to worry about except studying. It all paid off when I saw that of the hundreds of Sergeants taking the exam, I was ranked number 16 on the promotion list.

Turning Point

2009 marked another turning point in my life and career. The hotly contested presidential campaigns had ended with Barak Obama's historic win in Grant Park. I was there with the full complement of 31 Mounted Officers and horses, and we had worked all day. The area was densely packed with people of every description. The weather was perfect, the crowds were behaving beautifully, and the air was full of celebration and happiness. As the voting numbers came pouring in, a new Officer, riding a new horse that was scheduled for a break nervously asked if I would accompany him back to our horse trailers to water his mount. Knowing that it can sometimes be nerve-wracking when trying to walk through partygoers and "Horse-monsters" (anything that may startle a horse), I agreed—I needed a break too. I was riding my new mount "Rudy" who was the most capable, work-loving, and big (just under 17 hands tall, and very muscular) horses I'd ever had. Everything went well, and we got the horses fed and watered without incident. On the way back, however, a reveler ran up behind my new Officer and mount and slapped his mount on the rump. As he fought to regain control, his mount hit me and Rudy broadside, pushing us up onto a high granite curb. Granite is very hard and dense, and it is one of the surfaces that acts like ice when stepped on by our horseshoes. Rudy attempted to gain his balance and footing while I lost mine. Rudy stood straight up like he was rearing and came down hard on his rump. That slammed me to the ground, splitting my helmet and knocking it off before Rudy toppled over onto me. At the same time, I vividly remember looking straight up, and Rudy's wild left eye as his head turned, and he came down on his back. He landed on my right side, and I remember the sound of either my head or his hitting the sidewalk. It was very quiet, and my first thought was to get away because horses will scramble to get up very quickly when they go down, and I didn't want to get trampled too! At that moment, however, I realized that Rudy wasn't moving. I began pushing him and was able to free myself as he slowly moved up onto his side and tried to stand. Two young college-age women rushed to me and helped me to my feet. Rudy got up slowly and began to wander towards a line of SWAT personnel that was formed in a line in the street. Rudy just stood with them with his head down until I was able to walk over and get him. I don't remember the rest of the night or anything into the next day, but I know that I put my destroyed helmet back on and remounted. Rudy and I returned to duty and finished the night. The veterinarian diagnosed Rudy with a bad concussion, but otherwise, he was free of broken bones. It was about 12 months later that Rudy seemed to recover. I was diagnosed with a dual concussion and damage to my vestibular nerve. I didn't know it then, but my riding career was over; dizziness and lightheadedness are my constant companions.

018th District

Luckily for me, I was promoted to the rank of Lieutenant soon after. This time, Lieutenant school included an hour or so of some leadership fundaments taught by a well respected Deputy Chief who was a former Marine officer. It was excellent. As you progress through the ranks, every training period becomes shorter. Lieutenant training was over very quickly, and I was offered a position in the 018th District—"Near North" District. The 18th District is located in the heart of the city at Larrabee and Division and is home to the "Gold Coast," Michigan Avenue—The Magnificent Mile, Rush Street, North Avenue Beach, Oak Street Beach, Cabrini Green housing complex, Marshall Field Gardens, and more. It extends from the Chicago River at Wacker drive on the south, to Fullerton Avenue on the north, and from Lake Michigan on the east, to the North Branch of the Chicago River on the west. The 18th was always known as a desirable District and many Officers getting close to retirement would transfer there for the scenic areas, good food, and relatively low crime rate. I was familiar with the District because we patrolled most of its eastern expanses daily in the Mounted Unit.

My first day in the District, I met with the Commander who assigned me to the 2nd watch. The Captain on that watch was going into a medical status and would not return for an extended time. I was to shadow the Captain to ensure a seamless transition and faithful management practices according to the Captain's command style until his return to duty. In addition to watch personnel, I was responsible for working with a senior Lieutenant who maintained street duties. The goal was to maintain the Watch as the Captain would have. I would be acting as Captain until further notice. Oh, and I would be working with and directing the activities of a senior Lieutenant who will not be happy about my filling the position. This was going to require some delicate handling.

I started my tour that day meeting the Captain, who I found to be very agreeable with a great sense of humor. I would describe him as being somewhat "Old-School" in his management style. Unfortunately, that meant that once he made up his mind about you, that was it, there was no changing it. The Captain shared his views and opinions on every Officer in his command and made it thoroughly clear that he really disliked the other Lieutenant. This made me cautious, but as far as the Officers were concerned, they had clean slates with me. I spent a week with the Captain before he left, and I liked him. He had good people working for him, and it appeared to be a well-balanced and functioning watch.

That same week, I met the veteran Lieutenant, who was so short with the Captain and me that it was rude to me, and downright disrespectful to the Captain. These two came very close to hating each other, and every glance and word reaffirmed this. Neither could resist being snide to each other. It was appalling. My mind questioned how this occurred, and who allowed it to get to this point? I put those thoughts aside, knowing that I'd have to deal with it soon.

The veteran Lieutenant avoided contact with me until after the Captain left. My first day acting as the Watch Commander, I asked if he had some time to talk. Surprisingly, he was open and friendly, and it was as if a weight had been lifted in that office. He was aware that I had no responsibility in being chosen to run the watch and was gracious enough to help me with anything should I ask, but he said he was finished with the District and wouldn't be an active participant in the management of any Watch while assigned here. Wow. I said that I understood, but I didn't. There was too much information missing from the past for me to know how all of this happened, but I wouldn't concern myself with the past, we had a new beginning, and he was my new project. I wanted to get him back in the game and as an ally.

As a supervisor and manager in the Police Department, I expect those wearing rank to look at the bigger picture, and at least be polite and professional. I've always held that the moment you accept a rank promotion, you give up the right to act selfishly, hold grudges, and behave in ways that were acceptable in the position below. For instance, when one Officer doesn't like another Officer, those two Officers can avoid each other and not speak. That is considered acceptable behavior on a Watch among patrol Officers. Sergeants, Lieutenants and above also give up the luxury of "not dealing with" those whom he or she doesn't care for. They have a duty to supervise and manage everyone equally in order to accomplish our mission.

Officers everywhere are extremely curious, and they can be pretty suspicious. The moment that it's known a new Officer or supervisor is being assigned someplace, a tremendous internal engine coughs to life, and every attempt is made to get info on that person before he or she arrives. Phone calls are made, internal contacts thought to be "in the know" are interrogated, and spurious rumors become fact. Yes, there is a love for scuttlebutt among all Police Officers. Coppers always want to know who you are, where you come from, what your reputation is, and what you have "done" in your career. Unfortunately, where that person has been assigned and what their experience is, directly relates to how serious they'll be taken and how much initial respect will be given. For instance, having been a 10th District Ranger (slang for 10th District Tactical Officer) provides more initial respect than having worked as the Commander's administrative aide. Officers assigned to street duties sometimes devalue anyone not "in the trenches." Often, I've found that Officers don't know what someone else's responsibilities are, so they naturally assume the person does nothing. It's a strange and unfair phenomenon that happens in every District, Division, and Unit in the City. I know the phone lines were burning up attempting to get the "scoop" on me because it had been a week since I arrived, and I never had the opportunity to speak to them as a group. I was a week behind the rumor-mill and experience taught me that it's better to give them the facts before someone makes them up.

My first roll call alone with the Watch, I walked into a very quiet group. I was used to a good deal of talk and "horseplay" at Mounted, and it was apparent that the Watch was anxious about me. Looking around, I could read the faces of a couple of Officers wearing little, knowing smiles and who thought they knew about me. Most Officers were politely interested, and there were a few that appeared apprehensive. I introduced myself again and advised them that I would be filling in for the Captain during his extended absence. They knew this, of course. When I gave my background, I saw the face of one Officer change when he learned that I hadn't spent all my time as a "pony-cop." I was as proud of my time in Mounted as I was of anywhere else so I could care less about those who would deride it. I approached them open and honest, and the room turned visibly at ease.

I learned early in my career that everybody does better when they know the rules; I can't get angry or disappointed if I didn't tell them what I expect. I began with what they can expect from me; that I'll do everything in my power to help them get the job done and go home to their loved ones. I'll be there to support them, even if they make an honest mistake. If they need something that will help us accomplish our mission better, more efficiently or faster, tell me, and I'll do what I can to make it happen. If they have a question, ask me; if I can answer, I will. If I don't know the answer—I'll find out, and if I cannot answer for other reasons, I will tell them that I can't answer. I pledged that I would always tell them the truth, but caution them, as J.K. Rowling wrote (1997), "truth is a beautiful and terrible thing, and should, therefore, be treated with caution." Lastly, I made this clear, that everyone on the Watch has a clean slate with me and that the past will stay in the past. Moving forward, I believe everyone is accountable—even me.

I then gave the Officers my expectations, and they are simple:

- Be the heroes that they are.
- Always conduct themselves ethically, with respect, and proper decorum as representatives of the entire law enforcement community—not just the CPD.
- Without exception, I expect everyone to do their jobs, answer their calls, back each other up, and come clear promptly when finished with an assignment.
- I remind them that this is a team effort, and all laxity means more work for the person next to them.
- I expect them to do the right thing, not the easy thing, and that they'll do their best to do their duty.
- I remind them to be conscious of how we appear to the citizens when we're walking, talking and driving.
- I asked that they take ownership of their beats and remember that the good people are looking to us for help and we can't let them down.

There's nothing ground-breaking in these expectations, and I'm sure some supervisor or another has given some or all of these at one time in their career. Some may perceive them as corny, but as their supervisor, I set the tone. I always attempt to keep these expectations professional and positive, and I try not to let it be understood as, "Do this, or else." I gave the same speech to my Sergeants.

Everything went well during this time with few exceptions. The chronic problem employees chose to remain so, but I felt that the rest of the Watch flourished; medical usage declined considerably, enforcement rose, and camaraderie soared. I made the veteran Lieutenant part of every decision-making process and appealed to his incredible amount of experience and desire to be valued. He came to work on-time, anticipated the needs of the Watch, was bright and positive, and he really was a pleasure to work with.

Twelve months later, the Captain returned, and it was immediately apparent that he was not happy with me. He said very little after I briefed him on the Watch operations, along with our successes and failures from the past year. I was dismissed to go on patrol. After a couple of days of feeling his silent disapproval, I asked for a frank discussion. He did not hold back; I had usurped his authority while overstepping mine. I had fundamentally changed how his watch ran (though I'm not sure how), and worst of all, I treated with his enemies. I explained my "blank slate" philosophy and that I did what I needed to, and what I thought was the right, ethical choice to get the most from everyone and accomplish our goals. He shook his head and said, "You got a lot to learn." Over the next few weeks, things slid back in place for the Captain, and the feeling of constraint seemed to permeate the Watch. He re-arranged people's assignments, and I was assigned to Field Lieutenant duties with the "other" Lieutenant.

Being a Field Lieutenant was GREAT! I had a fraction of the responsibilities that I had the entire first year, and I was able to interact more frequently with my Officers. I used that contact to keep the Officers focused and on-task. I continued to feel the sting of the Captain every day that he worked. It was his condescending and petty attitude, and he bitterly pointed out differences in his opinion with my decisions on the street. It became apparent that I had answered one of the very first questions I asked myself after being assigned; the Captain encouraged and allowed the situations to deteriorate. Regardless of how it ended, I had a wonderful and incredibly valuable learning experience!

During my time as acting Captain / Watch Commander, I took leadership roles at a HAZMAT incident involving the accidental mixing and release of chlorine at a local drycleaning establishment, an underground C.T.A. train fire, several after-school violence incidents, gang narcotic activity in targeted locations, and unplanned protests and civil disturbances. I had increased productivity and morale and reduced medical abuse.

3rd Watch

Just after my Commander was promoted, the 1st Watch Captain was promoted to Commander to fill the vacancy. I was extremely pleased that he acknowledged my accomplishments, and I was asked that I take over the 3rd Watch when their Captain retires to do what I had done for the 2nd Watch.

I moved to the 3rd Watch and began the process all over. It was much more difficult than the day watch had been, and there was always so much happening that I would work all night without realizing that I hadn't taken a break or eaten lunch. After a few weeks, my administrative assistant noticed this, and every night after that, I was made to take a break for dinner and coffee. Each day, a different beat would stop by and make a coffee run for the inside people and me; team building was working. During this time, in addition to shootings, mob actions at the beach and on Michigan Avenue, officer-involved shootings, and the continuing unplanned protests and demonstrations, the Police Department was gearing up for the NATO Summit. History will show that we performed magnificently in all categories and especially so after the Chicago Police Department showed the world that Chicago could hold the NATO Summit without widespread violence and disruption.

Tactical

In 2013, the District Commander asked if I would leave the Watch Commander role and accept a position as the Tactical Lieutenant managing the District's Tactical, Robbery, and Burglary teams. I agreed, and for the next two years, I led sixty of Chicago's finest and most motivated Officers! The 018th District Tactical members were terrific; they conducted themselves with a level of ability, professionalism, and politeness that was inspiring. Working in such a diverse area made these Officers able to develop relationships and establish trust quicker than I had seen elsewhere. Over the next two years, I had very few complaints against my people because they built relationships and trust in the community. There were issues to address, and I gave my customary speech hoping that some of those issues might preemptively disappear. My reputation in the District was that I would make hard decisions, and I led by example.

Unfortunately, I would replace two Sergeants and three Officers for refusing or failing to rise to my standards. As uncomfortable as it was to do, it strengthened my resolve and provided the teams with proof that I had their interests at heart but would not negotiate my ethics or standards. I spent the next two years working in a culture where every Tactical Officer acted in my Unit worked seamlessly towards our goals and objectives. It was fantastic to be back in the Tactical environment where I could count on the job being completed correctly. The "easy way" just wasn't a path these men and women took.

Commanding Officer

In 2015, I was contacted by my old 018th District Commander—now the Deputy Chief of the Special Functions Division. He asked if I would like to return to the Mounted Patrol Unit as its Commanding Officer. I loved the Unit but had been away for over six years, and my riding status was in doubt. In the spirit of honest and full disclosure, I informed the Deputy, who related that he was aware of my accident and that his offer remained. He needed someone to get in there, get it straight, and be honest with him about capabilities. Before giving my answer, I spoke with my wife, who after securing a blood-oath that I would not ride again, consented. It's essential that I mention this because while the accident happened to me, she had to put my pieces back together, and is still helping me through. Having a Neurologist tell her that one more hit in the head and she would be spoon-feeding me justifiably sealed my fate.

I called the Deputy Chief back and accepted the position. I quickly found out that it was not the same Unit that I left. I had witnessed it several times while working in the 018th, and the Mounted Unit stood by, ineffective when they shouldn't have been. I quickly learned that a culture of permissiveness and neglect had turned my hard-working, horse-loving Unit into something unrecognizable. I approached the Unit in much the same way as the Watches but added I had been a riding Sergeant in the Unit for eight years. There were only five Mounted Officers that I knew from my old days left, and these had effectively taken over the Unit. Of the Sergeants, all were new to the Unit except one, and they lacked the courage, ability, and conviction to take control of their Watches. I heard things like from the Sergeants like, "I don't know, Lieutenant. The guys won't like this," and from the Officers, "This would be a great Unit if it weren't for the horses." I actually had a Sergeant tell me that they elected not to attend some scheduled details because they felt the horses weren't needed.

Prior to being promoted and leaving the Mounted Patrol, the Unit was required to complete basic horsemanship riding qualifications on a yearly basis to determine the training needs for the Unit for the winter season. The qualifications and "in-service training" had been largely ignored. The Head Training Officer is a trusted friend who was contemplating retirement because he could no longer tolerate the culture and watch as a Unit he was proud of for the previous 20 years fail. Together, but without revealing my reasoning, I immediately called for a mandatory day of in-service training. I planned to have the Head Trainer conduct some basic exercises without my presence, then run the Unit through some more practical and advanced horsemanship skills when I arrive. I intended to obtain an accurate picture of the 25 Officer's riding abilities and horsemanship, as well as the Unit's current operational capabilities. The Unit and personnel—except for three newer Officers—performed miserably. The Unit was also unable to operate as a team. I had my work cut out for me, and we began a regimen of basic horsemanship training daily for two weeks. I wanted to recreate an atmosphere similar to their initial Mounted training where they need to rely on each other. At the end of the two weeks, we would repeat the abilities inspection. If that went well, we'd continue with Unit capability training and follow the same two-week period. I knew that two weeks wasn't enough to see significant progress, but I needed to see *some* improvement in both categories quickly. It was during that time when three veterans Mounted Officers asked to speak with me separately. Each was concerned about the danger of riding a horse, two asked for preferential treatment because of their time spent in the Unit and the last advised me that he was planning on retiring in two years and didn't want to ride any longer. He asked that I find him a place in the Unit where he wouldn't have to ride. To all, I acknowledged that their concerns of danger were well-founded, but that this was our chosen assignment. They would be required to ride their horses, or they would have to leave the Unit. To the last, I informed him that there was no place for him "not to ride his horse," and that he should consider early retirement or a different unit immediately.

I needed to change the existing culture of the Unit to bring it back to a worthwhile and valued asset for the City. For the next year, I continued Mounted Unit training sessions and attempted to bring my Sergeants into line with my expectations. I deployed with the Unit to every detail and event, providing direction, instruction, and purpose to our movements. I wanted every Mounted Officer—regardless of rank—to know what I expected from them in every circumstance. I couldn't get angry or disappointed if they didn't know. It was a tough year as I was continually attempting to overcome the damage being done by my now extremely disgruntled veteran Officers. Their unofficial leadership and counter-efforts sought to undermine my authority and the Unit's excellence. They were not alone, however, and I soon identified two Sergeants who supported this group's efforts. Almost an entire year of hard work was negated and thwarted by these individuals. I realized that regime change is easy, but a change in culture is virtually impossible with embedded resistance and little support. After removing two Sergeants and warning a third, the veteran Mounted Officers began claiming injuries and moved into a medical—non-duty status. Although they were still on my assignment logs, they were no longer present at work to spread poison. I was soon able to bring a trusted friend and proven Sergeant into the Unit. I contacted him and told him what was going on. I said that needed a Sergeant I could trust and asked for his help. He immediately accepted, and he was assigned with 15 Officers to training. The Sergeant was one of three to pass the training class.

The following year, with the emphasis still on training and group performance, I continued my leadership at all details and events. I did not trust that my remaining two Sergeants would carry out my vision, and my new Sergeant had no experience. This allowed me to show the new Sergeant and two new Mounted Officers precisely what I wanted. This year was no easier than the last, with one irresolute Sergeant being directed by a strong-willed Sergeant who liked to refer to himself as the "Entertainment Sergeant." As a very charismatic leader, this Sergeant held considerable sway over the younger Officers and made it acceptable to perform the bare minimum and at the lowest skill level. When I was not on-duty, my new Sergeant had to battle the two Sergeants over operations to get them to perform according to my wishes. This was a tough year for him. His loyalty made him the "Bad Sergeant," which was reinforced daily in comments made from the other two Sergeants. It seemed that every day was a struggle for him. I made many mistakes during the last couple of years, and one was that I knew in my heart that the "Entertainment Sergeant" was telling me one thing and doing another, but I until now, I had no tangible proof on which to act. What I did have, was the spirit of a good Sergeant and loyal friend being continually tested and worn down. I shouldn't have waited on "proof," but that was not an option for me at the time. After two years of lies, deceit, and unethical behavior, I had what I needed for documentation, and had him removed from the Unit. As expected, he spread false rumors about the new Sergeant, individual Mounted Officers, and trainers, and sowed as much misery as he could before he left in a last-ditch effort to thwart the Unit's progress. I addressed the Unit, providing minimal backstory, and dispelled the rumors.

It was amazing to see how quickly things can change once obstacles are removed. The following year, I saw all the training and effort put in by everyone pay-off. I began turning over the details and events to my Sergeants to run and was rewarded with a new and increasing sense of pride in the Unit. I still had one Sergeant that seemed to always takes counsel of his fear, but I am working to him stop that bad habit. Now when I went out on major demonstrations, I was thrilled at their turnout, and my praise meant more to them than when I was always there. There was a new air of teamwork, and I saw my Mounted Unit becoming the capable, well-disciplined Unit I envisioned. Several anti-Police rallies later, we're being requested and complimented by the command staff.

Marine & Helicopter

Things became more difficult at the same time I began to breathe easy about the Mounted Unit. The Marine and Helicopter Units needed a Commanding Officer after the Captain in charge became sick with cancer. Captain Mark Marianovich was a good man, a tough man, and a bold leader. In short, he was everything that the Marine Unit needed, but it was not to be. I began filling in for him in early December, then the following January when he eventually lost his battle and passed. Again, I was contacted by the Deputy Chief and asked to remain as Commanding Officer for all three Units. It is true, my ego was stroked, but I would never have said "no" to my boss unless I physically couldn't accomplish his mission. Of course, I would still have tried.

In January 2017, and in addition to the Mounted Patrol Unit, I officially accepted the responsibility and became the Acting Commanding Officer of the Marine and Helicopter Units. The Helicopter Unit is situated very close to the Mounted stables in Chicago's Calumet Park on 95th Street. This Unit is as squared away as any I've known. Operating on Days and evenings only, the Unit's supervisors are excellent, and the pilots and Tactical Flight Officers (TFOs) are motivated and focused. Each man and woman assigned operates as a team. Since the 3rd Watch Sergeant was just brought in, I can write without reservation that the Unit's veteran 2nd Watch Sergeant has done a magnificent job managing all Unit assets including Officers, equipment, maintenance, and time.

The culture of the Marine Unit mirrors that of the Mounted Patrol Unit that I fought so hard to change. Assignment to this Unit is very much desired, and it remains prestigious among other specialized units. The Marine Unit operates 24 hours per day, 365 days per year. The Marine Unit personnel (called Marine Officers) are predominantly veteran Officers, having no less than ten years in the Unit. Taking stock over two months of the personnel, equipment, and facilities, I came to the following facts and conclusions: Commanding Officers were being assigned and reassigned or promoted away yearly and could provide no consistency, vision, stability or supervision. In the last five years alone, this Unit had gone through four Commanding Officers. Sergeants do not know their job as it relates to this specialized Unit. There was no training, and they were not performing their duty properly to keep the Officers focused, on task, and moving forward. Officers have become increasingly disaffected. Disgruntled Officers have become unofficial leaders, and their goals don't align with the Unit's mission or the Department's goals. The Unit is foundering.

I found the need for ethical, consistent, and fair leadership to be what has been lacking in the Unit. Old grievances were allowed to continue unabated and are as fresh today, as they were when they occurred in years past. The knowledgeable, respected veteran Sergeants in the Unit retired and were replaced by Sergeants with political divisions, no training, and much-perceived bias by the Officers. The replacement Sergeants failed to contend with the Officer's perceptions, and quite frankly, appropriated the attitude of the Officers while holding the mantle of Sergeant. Having to manage more than one unit has been challenging and has dramatically slowed progress. I am using every bit of my past 21 years' experience as a supervisor, and I'm finding the task very difficult. I am reluctant to admit that my efforts appear largely ineffective during this first year.

During the second year, I identified and retained the only knowledgeable and capable veteran Sergeant and succeeded in removing the ineffective ones. This veteran Sergeant has been key to moving forward, and he is untiring in his dedication. With the assistance and support of my Deputy Chief, I now have a full staff of replacement supervisors. Among them are a veteran Sergeant and ex-U.S. Marine, a (now reserve) Master at Arms 1st Class Petty Officer from the Navy, and a Lieutenant Commander from the Coast Guard. These new Sergeants bring a wealth of maritime experience, consistency, integrity, and honor with them. All my assigned Sergeants are performing as front-line Sergeants should. The Watch that requires the most help and leadership is the 3rd Watch. To those Officers, I placed my trusted ex-U.S. Marine who is quickly succeeding in focusing his Officers. Obtaining new Sergeants that "buy-in" to my vision for the Unit was my first step and wouldn't have occurred without my excellent chain of command. Providing these Sergeants with training, however, has taken over 12 months due to other personnel and seasonal constraints. "Rome wasn't built in a day," or so I've heard! The watches are in good hands, and as a first step, I'm optimistic.

As with most Departments and Units across the nation, the Chicago Police Department is struggling to do more with fewer Officers. The Marine Unit was eight Officers short when I began. The Deputy Chief provided me with 15 candidates for training last year, which yielded eight viable new Marine Officers. Before the Officers finished training, the Sergeants reported that their personnel were getting excited about the new arrivals. Not only were they excited, but they also began planning training for their new mates. The new Marine Officers have now been assigned to their Watches and have reinvigorated most of the veteran Marine Officers. Every day since the assignment of these new Marine Officers, the veterans on the Watches have scheduled training for a portion of their shift in some vital aspect of their duty. A noticeable change in attitude and teamwork is beginning to be evident. I expect that these new Marine Officers may do more towards changing the existing culture and attitudes that I could have ever imagined.

CONCLUSION

What makes a Good Cop? Upbringing? Empathy? A good sense of right and wrong? The answer? All of this made one Good Cop. I know I'm one, and I've worked hard to earn that title. I have met Police Officers from all over the country and world, and I find that we all share similar fundamental characteristics that drive us to this profession. Goodness, Community, Truth, Justice, Honor, Integrity, Duty; the list goes on. We are drawn to this profession; it is a calling. Police Departments and Agencies have done an excellent job of finding and hiring the nation's Police Officers. Yes, they make mistakes like every other job and profession, and yes, they can always do better—we all can.

For over 30 years, I have had the distinct pleasure of working with Good Cops and heroes. "Certainly, you've known bad cops," is the indelicate and rude statement I've heard more times than I can count, and from some surprising places. My answer is always taken with skepticism when I say "No." I've known Officers that were better or worse at one or more of the skills and abilities we value in Good Cops like communication, empathy, and calmness. Or Officers in crisis that, for reasons we all experience, have lost some compassion and understanding, but bad-guys are bad-guys; it doesn't matter if they're cops or not. Bad-guys don't hang around Good Cops because Good Cops don't tolerate bad-guys. I wouldn't tolerate one. Hollywood loves the tales of corruption and the one good cop that stands alone. They have it all backward. The Good Cops are legion, and it's the bad-guys who stand alone. The news media sells millions of papers based on portraying the actions of a few as the out-of-control actions of us all. The fact is that there are more good people in this world than there are bad. That means more good doctors, lawyers, nurses, paramedics, firefighters, teachers and in every job and profession; yes, that also means the Police.

This was and is my experience in law enforcement as a Chicago Police Officer. As an ethnography, it's an incomplete tale of a single experience that has spanned over 30 years. Reading it as a biography, I see that I was always destined to be a Police Officer and a Good Cop. There are so many people and many more incidents that I could have written about, and maybe, if this writing proves cathartic for me, I may include more. As Police Officers tend to shy from the spotlight, I've undoubtedly done the correct thing by leaving out the names of my coworkers, friends, and mentors. I, myself, am not entirely comfortable having my name on this, but to quote a favorite line, "I said those things I did those things. I can live with that."4 I *do* feel like I may have done them a great injustice too; Good Cops *should* be recognized. Everyone should know what they've done, and what they continue to do — day in and day out. Everyone should know that while they're warm, at home with their families, there's some Good Cop outside keeping watch over them.

My observations and categorizations are my own, and they don't reflect the ideas, ideals or truth of anyone or any entity but for me. I've tried to move through my career with honor, and integrity, preserving my sense of duty, and at all times to fulfill my oath to the citizens of Chicago. In this last statement, I feel that I speak for most Police Officers.

REFERENCES

Angelis, J. D., & Kupchik, A. (2009). Ethnicity, trust, and acceptance of authority among police officers. *Journal of Criminal Justice*, *37*(3), 273–279. doi:10.1016/j.jcrimjus.2009.04.007

Balch, R. W. (1972). The police personality: Fact or fiction? *The Journal of Criminal Law, Criminology, and Police Science*, *63*(1), 106. doi:10.2307/1142281

Bidarian, S., & Jafari, P. (2012). The relationship between organizational justice and organizational trust. *Procedia: Social and Behavioral Sciences*, *47*, 1622–1626. doi:10.1016/j.sbspro.2012.06.873

Chagnon, N. A. (1968). *Yąnomamö: The fierce people*. Holt, Rinehart and Winston.

Crank, J. P. (2003). Institutional theory of police: A review of the state of the art. *Policing*, *26*(2), 186–207. doi:10.1108/13639510310475723

Deane, C., Dine, K. C., Dolan, H. P., Gainer, T. W., Hudson, S., White, S., & Ramsey, C. (2013). *"Work of Policing" A 10th Peelian Principle? Creating Partnerships and Trust within Police Organizations*. Retrieved from http://www.bjaexecutivesessiononpoliceleadership.org/movie/04_A_10th_Peel_Principle.html

Dirks, K. T. (2000). Trust in leadership and team performance: Evidence from NCAA basketball. *The Journal of Applied Psychology*, *85*(6), 1004–1012. doi:10.1037/0021-9010.85.6.1004 PMID:11125648

Donald, H. M. (2017). *The war on cops: How the new attack on law and order makes everyone less safe*. Encounter Books.

Halbusi, H. A., Tehseen, S., Hamid, F., & Afthanorhan, A. (2018). A study of organizational justice on the trust in organization under the mediating role of ethical leadership. *Business Ethics and Leadership*, *2*(4), 89–98. doi:10.21272/bel.2(4).89-98.2018

Herr, R. M., Bosch, J. A., Loerbroks, A., Genser, B., Almer, C., Vianen, A. E., & Fischer, J. E. (2018). Organizational justice, justice climate, and somatic complaints: A multilevel investigation. *Journal of Psychosomatic Research*, *111*, 15–21. doi:10.1016/j.jpsychores.2018.05.003 PMID:29935749

Hillcourt, W. (1988). *Official Boy Scout handbook*. Boy Scouts of America.

Jackson, N. (2019). *Organizational justice in mergers and acquisitions: Antecedents and outcomes*. Palgrave Macmillan. doi:10.1007/978-3-319-92636-0

Kim, K. Y., Eisenberger, R., & Baik, K. (2016). Perceived organizational support and effective organizational commitment: Moderating influence of perceived organizational competence. *Journal of Organizational Behavior*, *37*(4), 558–583. doi:10.1002/job.2081

McDevitt, J., Posick, C., Zschoche, R., Rosenbaum, D. P., Buslic, M., & Fridell, L. L. (2011, February). National Police Research Platform. *Police integrity, responsibility, and discipline*. Retrieved from http://uicclj.squarespace.com/police-integrity-responsibili/

Mills, A. (2019, January 15). *Great Leadership Requires Humility*. Retrieved from https://www.policemag.com/501943/great-leadership-requires-humility

Morin, R., Parker, K., Stepler, R., Mercer, A., Morin, R., Parker, K., & Mercer, A. (2018, October 15). *What Police Think About Their Jobs*. Retrieved from https://www.pewsocialtrends.org/2017/01/11/behind-the-badge/

Murphy, K., & Tyler, T. (2008). Procedural justice and compliance behavior: The mediating role of emotions. *European Journal of Social Psychology*, *38*(4), 652–668. doi:10.1002/ejsp.502

Peterson, E., Reichert, J., & Konefal, K. (2017, November 7). *Procedural Justice in Policing: How the Process of Justice Impacts Public Attitudes and Law Enforcement Outcomes*. Retrieved from http://www.icjia.state.il.us/articles/procedural-justice-in-policing-how-the-process-of-justiceimpacts-public-attitudes-and-law-enforcement-outcomes

Reeves, S., Kuper, A., & Hodges, B. D. (2008, August 7). Qualitative research methodologies: Ethnography. *BMJ (Clinical Research Ed.)*, *337*(a3), a1020. Advance online publication. doi:10.1136/bmj.a1020 PMID:18687725

Rosenbaum, D. (2014, April 21). *Building Trust Inside and Out: Challenges Facing Police Leaders*. Retrieved from https://www.nij.gov/multimedia/presenter/presenterrosenbaum2/pages/presenter-rosenbaum2-transcript.aspx

Sargeant, E., Antrobus, E., & Platz, D. (2017). Promoting a culture of fairness: Police training, procedural justice, and compliance. *Journal of Experimental Criminology*, *13*(3), 347–365. doi:10.100711292-017-9296-0

Schulhofer, S. J., Tyler, T. R., & Huq, A. Z. (2012). American policing at a crossroads: Unsustainable policies and the procedural justice alternative. *Policing*, *35*(3). Advance online publication. doi:10.1108/pijpsm.2012.18135caa.003

Shjarback, J. A., Pyrooz, D. C., Wolfe, S. E., & Decker, S. H. (2017). De-policing and crime in the wake of Ferguson: Racialized changes in the quantity and quality of policing among Missouri police departments. *Journal of Criminal Justice*, *50*, 42–52. doi:10.1016/j.jcrimjus.2017.04.003

Twersky-Glasner, A. (2005, March). Police personality: What is it and why are they like that? *Journal of Police and Criminal Psychology*, *20*(1), 56–67. doi:10.1007/BF02806707

Tyler, T. (2017). Procedural Justice and Policing: A Rush to Judgment? *Annual Review of Law and Social Science*, *13*(1), 29–53. doi:10.1146/annurev-lawsocsci-110316-113318

Tyler, T. R. (2007/2008). Procedural Justice and the Courts. *Court Review: The Journal of the American Judges Association, 44*(1-2), 26-31. Retrieved from http://aja.ncsc.dni.us/publications/courtrv/cr44-1/CR44-1-2.pdf

U.S. Department of Justice, Bureau of Justice Assistance. (2014). *Legitimacy and procedural justice: A new element of police leadership. A report by the Police Executive Research Forum (PERF).* Author.

Wolfe, S. E., Rojek, J., Manjarrez, V. M. Jr, & Rojek, A. (2018). Why does organizational justice matter? Uncertainty management among law enforcement officers. *Journal of Criminal Justice*, *54*, 20–29. doi:10.1016/j.jcrimjus.2017.11.003

Worden, R. E., & McLean, S. J. (2017). *Mirage of police reform: Procedural justice and police legitimacy*. doi:10.1525/luminos.30

ENDNOTES

1. This is essential in good management skills.
2. Push-up position with arms straight out in front of you, supporting your body while maintaining a stiff plank appearance. Good for shoulder, chest, arm and core strengthening.
3. Source: Officer Down Memorial Page, https://www.odmp.org/
4. From "The Life Aquatic with Steve Zissou."

Chapter 4
Economic Development and Rail Infrastructure:
A Symbiotic Relationship

Kathryn Dominguez
Illinois Institute of Technology, USA

ABSTRACT

"Public transit" is a term usually associated with urban life. The term "commuter" is usually associated to suburban dwellers. One envisions rural dwellers as farmers, far from urban areas. Those who live in Northwest Indiana enjoy urban, suburban, and rural life, with easy access to the second largest city in the United States, Chicago. Access to a major metropolitan area allows inhabitants of Northwest Indiana to earn an income that is commiserate to an urban lifestyle, but with options of lower-cost housing, utilities, and amenities offered in suburban and rural communities.

INTRODUCTION

"Public transit" is a term usually associated with urban life. The term "Commuter" is usually associated to suburban dwellers. One envisions rural dwellers as farmers, far from urban areas. Those who live in Northwest Indiana enjoy urban, suburban, and rural life, with easy access to the second largest city in the United States, Chicago. Access to a major metropolitan area allows inhabitants of Northwest Indiana to earn an income that is commiserate to an urban lifestyle, but with options of lower-cost housing, utilities, and amenities.

Public transit is a means for any of these communities—urban, suburban and rural—to join other travelers in transiting distances together. Moving out of the comfort of one's own means of transportation; an automobile, to join in public transit is foreign to many rural dwellers. Suburban workers, who use public transit to access Chicago-based employment, use public transit for work, but continue to use their personal automobiles for all other transit needs (except air travel). Where suburban and rural dwellers shop and live is affected by access to public transit and personal automobiles.

DOI: 10.4018/978-1-6684-2314-1.ch004

Albeit there is opportunity in easy access to Chicago, Northwest Indiana inhabitants fear change of their controlled, comfortable communities by approving more public transit in Northwest Indiana. Public transit affords easy access to employment in urban areas for commuters in suburban areas, but also allows for access to suburban communities for those without personal automobiles in more urban areas. There is fear that development around public transit will be solely focused on the disenfranchised. Transit development should be planned for the community's benefit. All members of the community, those with and without means, should be able to take advantage of public transit opportunities; those that come from the transportation opportunity to Chicago as well as those opportunities that come from community development around the transit stations.

As a resident of Munster, Indiana, a commuter on Northwest Indiana Commuter Transit District (NICTD) and an employee of Metra; the commuter transit agency for the Chicago metropolitan area, I am very interested in the impact of NICTD's proposed extension to Southern Munster, Indiana. This extension of service will allow me to be close enough to the most southern station that I will be able to walk or ride my bike to access public transit. I welcome the positive developmental effect of being able to ride my bike to the station.

Access to public transit allows for businesses to spring up around the access points. Businesses that are planned to provide services and meet the needs of the public who ride the transit. I am excited about the opportunities that Munster will be afforded in this new transit line, but there are those who are vehemently against public transit in Munster.

I see the future of Munster as progressive; Munster is becoming a hub for commuters from further southern suburbs and rural areas. There are many businesses and services already along the proposed route of the new NICTD extension.

LITERATURE REVIEW

There are various success factors in transit-oriented development identified as part of achieving transit implementation success (Thomas & Bertolini, 2017). Transit-Oriented Developments can help off-set infrastructure costs by paying development costs up front, off-set capital construction costs and provide housing capital development near transit. Transit oriented development starts before the transit project can provide a tax base to help finance transit development (Fleissig, 2011). Several sections of our text provide information of development's impact on infrastructure and financing options based on public/private partnerships. Chapter 17, New Tools for Managing Infrastructure and the Environment provides particular insights that impact the Munster/Dyer station proposed for the NICTD extension (Grigg, 2010).

Transit Development is being funded by many levels of government. Large capital plans were discussed by various agencies per news articles that include several rail related projects, such as positive train control and the West Lake Corridor which ends in Munster/Dyer, Indiana. The funding provides for State of Good Repair money, as well as for other improvements, that are slated to improve transit in Northwest Indiana (Steele, 2018). Joint development projects, using both public and private investments, can be successful depending on the method of implementation, the region and use. Joint development in transit-oriented development can provide for efficient use of public funds and efficacy of land use (Zhao, Vardhan, & Larson, 2012).

The effect of physical design of transit-oriented development is crucial to coordinating intense land uses and multiple transit models (Jacobson, Justin, & Forsyth, 2008). Land use affects public transit.

The land use may be the draw for transit use, or particular transit stop use, thus making the transit stop the catalyst for development (Lee, Hickman, & Ton, 2013).

Approval for infrastructure upgrades in Northwest Indiana have been moving along, increasing appeal for the project. Indiana House approves funding for several transit-related projects, including the West Lake extension which ends in the Munster/Dyer region (Carden, 2018). Town planning and policy decisions affect transit-oriented development. Towns that plan and zone areas around railway lines for future public transit and transit-oriented development enhance their success. Use of public development agencies and heuristic public opinion methods enhance transit-oriented development (Curtis, 2012).

Approval for the infrastructure increase includes the economic development plan, which works symbolically with the rail infrastructure project. There is a demand for office rental space and economic development around transit in urban areas. Economic development increases close to transit and increases the economic efficiency of urban areas (Drennan & Brecher, 2012).

Public input always has its part to play in infrastructure development. A feisty community meeting was held that discussed possible transit-oriented development in the Munster/Dyer area. The meeting was meant to be informational, but was lively with comments and concerns. Most notably, townhome development was received in a favorable light, but not large rental unit buildings (Wilds, 2016). Household survey data indicates that transit-oriented development encourages walking while reduces driving activities. Proximity to the transit station positively correlates to increased walking activity (Noland & DiPetrillo, 2015).

DESCRIPTION OF INFRASTRUCTURE

The Northwest Indiana times provides much information on the NICTD extension project. The Munster/Dyer extension is an 8 miles extension from Hammond Indiana to the Dyer border at the end of Munster (Steele, 2018). This extension will provide a new main station for the South Shore line as well as the Munster Dyer Extension in Hammond. There will also be a station in Hammond with housing and retail development.

In Munster, there will be an economic development in downtown, with shops and a station. At the end of the line, will be a station just on the Dyer town border. Economic development, such as shops are expected to continue in that area, as a new Dunkin Donuts and an AnyTime fitness have opened close to where the station is slated to be.

News articles provide community commentary and project progress in funding and legislation. Development is positive, but there are those that may have to sell their homes and those that will have this proposed public transit within a short distance of their home. Measures are being proposed that will aid in mitigation of drastic changes to the community, but there will be changes if this project comes to fruition.

News articles discussed customer surveys on receptiveness to the development. As a community member myself and a NICTD rider, I agree there are pros and cons about this development. Articles mentioned riders expressing favorability with the project based on convenience, yet much worry about increased noise and traffic in Munster.

Project population growth and strategic planning possibilities with this new public transit extension and development are numerous. Transit-oriented development is a means to provide a community business, service and transit opportunities. It will be interesting to learn what peer reviewed journal articles, newspaper articles and the community at large thinks about NICTD's proposed extension to Munster Indiana.

MAJOR INFRASTRUCTURE CHALLENGES

The extension into the Munster area provides several challenges. The effect of physical design of transit-oriented development is crucial to coordinating intense land uses and multiple transit models (Jacobson, Justin, & Forsyth, 2008). Munster stems from an agricultural past, the has both hurt and saved the environment. Northwest Indiana is known for infrastructure projects that have had devastating ecological effects. Adhering to Federal regulations and ensuring compliance with codes and laws will be of utmost importance for project oversight.

Additionally, Munster strictly enforces building codes to a high standard and requires retailers to have ascetic standards that conform to development look and feel. Concerns that property values may drop could be realized.

An additional challenge is increased crime which may come with development. There are residents who do not want the rail line because they are concerned about transients. There may also be increased noise and pollution from increased traffic in the area. Increased economic development must be managed in order to maximize the economic benefits and reduce the problems.

CONCLUSION

The purpose of this paper was to show the symbiotic relationship between rail infrastructure development and economic development. I attempted to combine economic development and rail passenger transportation as mutually beneficial; multiplying the positive outcome. Transit-Oriented Development and NICTD's extension into Munster will both increase economic development for Munster, it will also sustain Munster's average household income level and desirability as a residential location.

Not only will my commute become easier, the commute of so many workers in Northwest Indiana will become easier with this development. Access to shopping and a walking community. Proximity to the transit station positively correlates to increased walking activity (Noland & DiPetrillo, 2015).

Along with family centered businesses and parks creates a residential area that Munster prides itself to be. Gone are the farms, but the warm development that comes from ecologically sustaining travel provided in public transit as well as economic development are growth factors for Munster.

REFERENCES

Carden, D. (2018, February 5). *Indiana house advances South Shore line financing plan to senate*. Retrieved from NWITimes.com: https://www.nwitimes.com/news/local/govt-and-politics/article_f9bd402b-ab51-5450-be9d-083578868e3a.html

Curtis, C. (2012, May). Delivering the 'D' in transit-oriented development: Examining the town planning challenge. *Journal of Transport and Land Use*, *5*(3), 83–99. doi:10.5198/jtlu.v5i3.292

Drennan, M. P., & Brecher, C. (2012, May). Does public transit use enhance the economic efficiency of urban areas? *Journal of Transport and Land Use*, *5*(3), 53–67. doi:10.5198/jtlu.v5i3.247

Fleissig, W. K. (2011, February 7). Reframing Transit & Development to TOD 3.0. In *TransACT, APTA CEO Seminar*. American Public Transportation Association.

Grigg, N. S. (2010). *Economics and finance for engineers and planners*. American Society of Civil Engineers.

Jacobson, J., & Forsyth, A. (2008). Seven American TODs: Good practices for urban design in transit oriented projects. *Journal of Transport and Land Use*, *1*(2), 51–88. doi:10.5198/jtlu.v1i2.67

Lee, S. G., Hickman, M., & Tong, D. (2013, June). Development of a temporal and spatial linkage between transit demand and land-use patterns. *Journal of Transport and Land Use*, *6*(2), 33–46. doi:10.5198/jtlu.v6i2.268

Noland, R. B., & DiPetrillo, S. (2015, February). Transit-oriented development and the frequency of modal use. *Journal of Transport and Land Use*, *8*(2), 21–44. doi:10.5198/jtlu.2015.517

Steele, A. (2018, February 4). *South Shore line capital plan total $1.2 billion over five years*. Retrieved from NWITimes.com: https://www.nwitimes.com/business/local/article_4186062c-7472-5e8c-af29-68caf4d3fb0c.html

Thomas, R., & Bertolini, L. (2017, October). Defining critical success factors in TOD implementation using rough set analysis. *Journal of Transport and Land Use*, *10*(1), 139–154.

Wilds, M. (2016, November 2). *South Shore extension meeting draws crowd in Dyer*. Retrieved from NWITimes.com: https://www.nwitimes.com/business/local/article_00f08ae9-8de8-5b8b-ba3e-352c67082490.html

Zhao, Z. J., Vardhan Das, K., & Larson, K. (2012, May). Joint development as a value capture strategy for public transit finance. *Journal of Transport and Land Use*, *5*(1), 5–17. doi:10.5198/jtlu.v5i1.142

Chapter 5
Selection of US Regional Electric Air Routes for Public Benefit Maximization

Henry White
https://orcid.org/0000-0002-6989-6832
Illinois Institute of Technology, USA

ABSTRACT

With electric commuter aviation a likely actualization within a few years, there exists an opportunity to utilize this technology to address externalities in the aviation sector. This study aims to answer the question of which US regional air routes would provide the most public benefit should they be operated by an electric fleet. Public benefit is considered along three dimensions: emissions reduction potential, noise reduction potential, and community alignment. The community alignment category contains tax base, workforce, economic development, and political priority considerations. The alternatives considered are the communities of the Essential Air Service, excluding Alaska. A comprehensive scorecard is developed for these candidate air routes, with a tier of nine top scoring air routes identified by this methodology. A potential short haul network appropriate for aircraft electrification is also identified. Recommendations are provided as to how a federal implementation authority may use these results to inform strategy around aircraft electrification policy.

INTRODUCTION

Aviation is an important segment of the transportation industry, connecting communities without the infrastructure cost necessary for rail or road. However, the climate crisis imposes a need to reevaluate aviation and its impacts, given the significant carbon footprint of this sector's activities. Policy options such as taxes and short-haul flight bans have been proposed in different parts of the world to reduce aviation activity (Gössling & Lyle, 2021, pp. 643–658); however, these tend not to be applicable for every community, especially where rail is not a feasible clean travel alternative. For many rural communities in the US, air travel is necessary for social inclusion and economic development. As such, a

DOI: 10.4018/978-1-6684-2314-1.ch005

more promising pathway towards reducing the carbon footprint of aviation is aircraft electrification, an exciting industry milestone likely only a few years away. While the technology is imminent, what still needs development is a realistic implementation plan for public benefit maximization.

Electric aircraft bring benefit to communities not only through emissions reduction but through noise pollution reduction and social and economic development. This study explores the extent to which these factors should be considered in evaluating air-routes for electric aircraft implementation and develops a scorecard for alternatives as a comparative analysis of the total benefits possible. The existing body of knowledge will inform the details of this scorecard methodology, and as a result recommendations about which areas are ideal for aircraft electrification will be provided. This will be contextualized with existing federal programs that could incentivize such an airspace transformation once electric aircraft are certified and available on the market.

BACKGROUND

Technology adoption is an area in which the role of the public sector may largely vary case by case. Often it is appropriate for market forces to drive the integration of new technology into community life as firms make choices that allow for better operating efficiency and consumers select new products with the most perceived value. However, new technologies may also pose solutions to problems with larger community impacts, giving rise to the case for public sector involvement in technology adoption. The modern aviation industry presents such an opportunity to address community issues. A correlation between air travel access and economic growth and social inclusion has been repeatedly established (Smyth, Christodoulou, Dennis, Marwan, & Campbell, 2012, pp. 53–59) but this benefit is paired with the existence of negative externalities, specifically noise and emissions. As these impacts are borne by members of the community not involved in the transaction of air travel, public sector intervention is appropriate in better distributing these costs.

While economic intervention can address these externalities, they may also be largely reduced by technological improvement and adoption. Specifically, new electric aircraft designs promise zero-emission regular operation and a significant reduction in aircraft noise. The technology needed to realize this vision is no longer a hypothetical; though they are currently awaiting FAA and ICAO certification they have a realistic path to commercial operation by 2025 (Schwab, Thomas, Bennett, Robertson, & Cary, 2021). These aircraft are ideally sized for regional travel, connecting rural communities to hub airports. The model most likely to enter the market first is Eviation's Alice, with test flights slated for 2022 (Anderson, 2019, pp. 10–11) but notably Bell, Pipistrel, Boeing, and Airbus also have proposed designs (Moua, Roa, Xie, & Maxwell, 2020, pp. 48–59). The Eviation design and competing prototypes of comparable performance would seat 8–19 passengers and an operating range approaching 1000 km (Secretariat, ICAO, 2019, pp. 124–130). Globally, flights under 1,000 km constitute more than 17 percent of all airline emissions (Esque, Riedel, & Riefer, 2021) so the substitution of existing craft with all-electric designs would have a significant impact. Studies in other countries have found net emissions reduction of over 60 percent when considering all operations of regional airports (Baumeister, Leung, & Ryley, 2020). Other designs under consideration include hybrid electric aircraft, which would also reduce the intensity of the negative externalities of emissions and noise to a significant degree (Prapotnik, Kamnik, Marksel, & Božičnik, 2019, p. 1864).

Negative externality abatement, while of high priority in the public sector perspective, constitutes only one portion of the factors driving the development of electric aircraft in the United States. A 2021 report from the National Renewable Energy Laboratory identified six factors motivating interest in aircraft electrification: Reduced operating costs, the regional travel market, emissions reductions, noise reduction, increased accessibility, and economic development implications (Schwab et al., 2021). Because airline operation in the United States is a private enterprise, the transition to aircraft electrification must be in-part encouraged by a profit-motive. Operating cost reduction is the most significant of these motivators. The two most likely successful developers of regional electric aircraft have reported anywhere from an overall 50 percent reduction in projected operating costs (Gent, 2022) to a 90 percent reduction in fuel costs with a 50 percent reduction in maintenance costs (Schwab et al., 2021). With the potential to generate more revenue per passenger, find new demand in the regional travel market, and generate more prosperity through community economic development, the profit motive certainly exists, allowing for consideration of the initial investment of a fleet overhaul required.

These aircraft electrification technologies, though seeming avant-garde, will soon be a reality. Reasonable expectations should be set in terms of these new aircraft's capabilities, a timeline for technology maturity, and the challenges faced in this development. As aircraft electrification encompasses not only substitutions for existing aircraft but also new innovations, the first all-electric aircraft to arrive to market will likely be smaller personal flyers for one to six passengers. The next phase would see electric vertical takeoff-and-landing (eVTOL) craft enter the market as aerial taxis. The projection from the National Renewable Energy Laboratory indicates these may enter the market by 2025, about the same time as regional commuter aircraft (Schwab et al., 2021). This is pending certification by the Federal Aviation Administration. More widespread development of large (greater than 70 seats) commercial electric aircraft may take an additional two decades and is dependent on the success of the earlier phases, emphasizing the importance for a successful implementation of the first generation of commercial electric aircraft (Domone, 2018).

The development of electric aircraft is also largely constrained by the rate of improvement to battery technologies. Often underappreciated is the importance of the fuel mass fraction to traditional aircraft performance, where the aircraft's range is largely determined by the reduction of its weight throughout the flight. Batteries are not only less energy-dense than current jet fuel, but the weight of spent batteries must still be carried for the entirety of the flight. Current projects exist in partnership between private industry, research institutions, and government agencies to develop high energy, low weight batteries (Tariq, Maswood, Gajanayake, & Gupta, 2017, pp. 93–103). New battery technologies in the private sector today have been largely driven by automobile applications, which don't necessarily demand the same weight reduction constraints. However, it is not just batteries themselves that will require upgrading to enable an all-electric commuter aircraft. The power grid itself must also be able to handle the load imposed by recharging.

While the climate crisis may be the primary motivator for investment in electric aircraft development, the noise pollution reduction potential of these designs also captures the interest of many communities. In general, aviation noise pollution has been linked to issues health issues such as sleep deprivation, cardiovascular disease, and stroke, but this is generally near airports with a consistent noise exposure level greater than 55 dB (Hansell et al., 2013, p. 347). However, even where there may not be adverse health impacts, there is community annoyance and social disruption. Over the last few decades, community annoyance with aviation noise pollution has risen, regardless of whether the noise events are increasing in frequency or intensity or remaining uniform (Janssen, Vos, van Kempen, Breugelmans, & Miedema,

2011, pp. 1953–1962). While airflow and turbulence around components such as the airframe, landing gear, and control surfaces still produces noise, engine exhaust and loading are often the biggest sources of aircraft noise pollution (Bertsch, Simons, & Snellen, 2015), making electric aircraft a promising innovation to address these concerns.

Regional airports are a source of great opportunity in most American communities. Most Americans live within 16 minutes of an airport, yet only 1.6 percent of all trips between 50 and 500 miles are taken by air (Antcliff et al., 2021). Given the identified social inclusion and economic development benefits of regional air travel to communities, federal programs exist to support their operation. Primary among these is the Essential Air Service (EAS). The EAS was born following the airline deregulation act of 1978, which shifted air passenger service to the private sector. With commercial airlines retaining the discretion to choose where they operated, many routes serving small communities were seen as non-viable as a reliable revenue source. As such, the EAS was created to provide subsidies to airlines to serve rural communities, keeping ticket costs low and guaranteeing a minimum level of service for its residents. Amendments to the initial EAS directive were passed by congress in 2000 and 2012, better defining which communities where eligible for EAS subsidies (Department of Transportation, 2017). The annual subsidies from this program as of March 2021 totaled $311,882,170 (Department of Transportation, 2021).

While this program has attracted criticism, being seen as inefficient by many, the data shows the effectiveness of this program. Given the demonstrated benefit of regional air travel to communities, this result is unsurprising. Studies have linked a 1 percent increase in air passenger traffic in EAS airports to a 0.12% increase in per capita income for the community (Özcan, 2014, pp. 24–29). This same study suggested that considerable net economic benefit may be obtained by communities if EAS utilization can be boosted without a significant increase in subsidy amounts. Other scholars consider measures of accessibility in developing EAS improvement suggestions. The current EAS is fairly inflexible to individual community considerations, especially around differing accessibility needs. However, to meet the ultimate goal of guaranteeing sufficient access opportunities of small communities to the National Airspace System, a non-uniform approach based on local community conditions may be appropriate (Park & O'Kelly, 2017, pp. 930–951).

In analyzing the current state of the EAS, the impact of the COVID-19 pandemic should not be overlooked. The air transport sector was one of the hardest hit industries during the pandemic, but EAS communities outperformed their non-subsidized peers. By the fourth quarter of 2020, these communities were nearer their pre-pandemic travel rates than others (Fuellhart, Dai, Grubesic, & Derudder, 2021). Though these impacts were not uniform for every EAS community, as an aggregate the group performed quite well.

The EAS illustrates that even in a highly privatized air travel market like that of the United States, there is still opportunity for government actions to ensure public benefit is generated. The subsidies of this program function as a market-based solution to the issue of National Airspace System access. Other market-based solutions utilized to promote NAS access in rural communities include the Small Community Air Service Development Program (SCASDP), providing grants to localities for a variety of airport improvement projects (Department of Transportation, 2021). Given these precedents, the most likely role the federal government could take in influencing the adoption of regional electric aircraft is through a subsidy or grant program. Such a program could target which airports and communities would receive funding to upgrade their power grid to handle the requirements of aircraft recharging. There even exists a case that the current EAS could be used to accomplish this objective, giving preference to bids from carriers intending to use electric aircraft. The current EAS selection process considers 5 factors when deciding on a carrier: (1) The demonstrated reliability of service provision, (2) the contractual arrangements on the applicant with larger carriers to ensure service beyond hub airports, (3) the interline agreements made with large carriers for ease of passenger transfer, (4) the preferences of the local community with their air service provider, and (5) the marketing plan of the applicant of its service to its intended community. As demonstrated by the emissions reduction, noise reduction, and community uplift potential of electric aviation, the fourth selection factor could be relevant in favoring electric aircraft implementation. However, in a broader context, scholars have indicated the EAS could benefit from more flexibility in the bid process in general, so these criteria could be due for reconsideration by congress.

The framework provided by the EAS and similar program indicates an existing relationship between the federal government rural communities around access to air travel. However, as new aircraft designs are introduced, the concept of technology adoption must be considered. For rural areas, it is observed that lack of financial resources often poses the greatest barrier to technology adoption (Fanelli, 2021, p. 430). However, firms are generally open to incorporating new technologies into their enterprises once these barriers are overcome. This emphasizes the importance of federal funding in a hypothetical aviation technology implementation exercise. When the focus shifts from the firms to the end users of this product, it should be recognized that trust in new aircraft must be developed through a transparent and comprehensive certification process. The designs of electric aircraft may look distinctly different than what the market is used to observing, with longer and skinnier wings for improved aerodynamic efficiency and engine placement differing from that of turbojets (Domone, 2018).

The implementation of future electric and hybrid electric aircraft shows a lot of promise for meeting the needs faced by the current climate crisis. However, in the interim period, transition policies are also recommended to reduce aviation's carbon footprint. Sustainable Aviation Fuel (SAF) is an area of application with great carbon footprint reduction potential through the recycling of substances such as cooking oils. Different taxes could affect both demand for air transport and motivate technology changes. Interim policy changes would target technology, transport demand, or social norm changes. Some of the most effective policy options for emissions reduction include carbon-related duty charges, options to purchase SAF flight, voluntary carbon offsets, and a value-added tax for all air travel (Gössling & Lyle, 2021, pp. 643–658). However, a long-term view of the problem in which the aforementioned economic development and social inclusion benefits of aviation are not lost must provide an electric aviation option. The impetus for this project exists, now what must be determined is the strategy to enable it.

RESEARCH QUESTION AND HYPOTHESIS

This study examines the potential public benefit brought by new electric aviation technologies but recognizes that diffusion of innovation considerations that accompany this technology's larger adoption. An effective primary implementation of electric aircraft in the first communities selected may be a determinant of the rate of more widespread adoption. As such, the central research question of this study is: Which air routes would provide the most public benefit should their current service be substituted for a new all-electric fleet?

Public benefit maximization requires a better definition of how this technology could bring about improvement to the wellbeing of their population served. Negative externality reduction is a key concern, as is the positive economic development potential. Community impacts should also be considered, such as trust in new technology and alignment of aviation improvements with existing locality priorities. The three dimensions along which public benefit will be considered in this study are:

1. *Emissions Reduction*—The total emissions that may be eliminated by substituting existing aircraft with electric craft along a specific route.
2. *Noise Reduction*—The human health improvements from lower noise levels in the community, as well as the impact on wildlife where applicable.
3. *Community Alignment*—How well the community's existing priorities and activities would support a technological shift in the aviation sector.

These different dimensions will comprise a scorecard for each air route under consideration in this study. Technical and political considerations will inform the relative weighting of these categories to one cumulative score per community.

The working hypothesis of this study is that electric aircraft adoption is most appropriate for rural communities with relatively larger populations with higher population densities. Public benefit would be maximized by bringing negative externality reduction to more individuals, a largely utilitarian view. This is dependent on the relative weighting of the different dimensions of the scorecard.

While this study will primarily discriminate air routes on an individual basis, there is a body of research that supports a short-haul network as the most appropriate application of electric aircraft (Salucci et al., 2021). Therefore, consideration will also be given to multiple high scoring routes within proximity, or all connected to the same hub airport. Should an appropriate short haul network present itself, a subsequent study of more narrowed scope may be recommended.

Methodology

This study uses a mixed methods approach, utilizing both quantitative and qualitative secondary data. To answer the research question, a comprehensive scorecard is developed using the identified dimensions of public benefit. Category scores are developed for each dimension of analysis with an appropriate methodology. For emissions and noise reduction, secondary quantitative data is used. For community alignment, a combination of qualitative and quantitative secondary data produces the score. The data for each category is normalized to a category score, then category weights are assigned.

The alternatives for consideration that are rated by this scorecard are the communities of Department of Transportation's Essential Air Service, excluding Alaska. Current aircraft serving these communities range between 8 and 50 seats (Department of Transportation, 2021) but it is conceivable that each could be serviced by the first generation of electric aircraft, with potentially more frequent trips per week than their current level of service. The rationale for the selection of these communities and air routes for consideration relies not only on the fact that aircraft are appropriately sized for these routes, but that generally only one air carrier operates the route at any time. Therefore, the implementation of electric aircraft on these routes would constitute a replacement of the existing fleet, guaranteeing net emissions and noise reduction. There are 110 communities included in the Essential Air Service that will be scored through this study.

In this study, emissions reduction potential is considered for the entirety of the air route traveled. This is reflective of a total carbon footprint reduction as opposed to measures of local air quality. This study imagines that electric aircraft will replace the fleet currently operating along these routes, and as such, the 2021 EAS report is used as a basis of information. The quantity of interest is a measure of cumulative miles traveled for each airline seat per week. This is obtained by multiplying the number of seats of the aircraft used by the number of round trips per week by the mileage of the trip route. A one-way trip is used for the route-milage, but the because the scores are normalized, the category score would remain the same if round trip mileage were used. For communities connected to two hub airports, the average route distance is utilized. The EAS report sources the information about current seats per aircraft and round trips made per week. The air route mileage is obtained Vincenty's formula and the map coordinates of the airports. This study does not provide an estimate for total emissions reduction directly but instead the comparative opportunity of the individual routes as alternatives under consideration. Each route earns a value for cumulative seat-mileage per week by the formula described above. These are converted to a category score by normalizing them by the maximum seat-mileage per week value possible.

Noise reduction potential in this study is considered with a utilitarian view of reducing noise pollution for the greatest number of individuals possible. Replacing the regional aircraft fleet with quieter vehicles is not likely to improve the noise related health impacts in the areas surrounding these large hub airports. The small communities served by the EAS generally do not experience these adverse health impacts because there are generally only 1 to 6 departures per day, not a sustained high level of noise. The true small community impact of regional aviation noise is more related to property values. From previous research, individual but expected noise events exceeding 55 decibels begin to have an adverse effect on property values (Sklarz & Miller, 2018). A commonly used government estimate for aircraft noise for light aircraft at 1000 ft, or 305 m, is 80 decibels (Spokane International Airport, 2014). By the inverse square law, sound measured at 80 decibels at 305 m will correlate to a pressure level of 55 decibels at 5.5 km. Assuming the loudest noise incident occurring at takeoff, this study considers individuals living within a 5.5 km radius of their regional airport runway as the parties standing to benefit from the noise reduction potential of electric aircraft. The online NASA SEDAC Population Estimation Tool was used to draw a circle of 5.5 km about the center of each regional airport airstrip and project the number of residents living within the drawn area. To convert this raw statistic to a score, the values were normalized by the largest population value of the candidate communities.

Community alignment was a dimension selected for this analysis with the rationale that an upgrade to the regional aviation industry in different areas should align with that region's political priorities and community needs. From a practical perspective, should the EAS be used as the program to incentivize electric aircraft adoption, community buy-in is a necessity. The factor used in the EAS bid process where sustainability and noise reduction considerations could be leveraged is the fourth criterion: the preferences of the local community with their air service provider. Therefore, it is important to consider whether electrified aviation aligns with each community's character. To score this category, four questions are posed of each community considered in this study, covering human resource, financial, sustainability, and economic development indicators.

1. *Is the community's airport currently served by similarly sized aircraft (8-17 seats)?* This addresses concerns about the national pilot shortage, as a community currently served by 50-seat aircraft asked to fly more frequently with smaller craft may have trouble attracted the necessary human capital for the operation.
2. *Is the community's population increasing?* Aircraft electrification may also entail local power grid improvements or other necessary infrastructure projects, which could be overly burdensome without an increasing tax-base.

3. *Does the community's budget document mention sustainability?* As the budget document is a representation of the community's political priorities, it is an appropriate place to look for an indication of whether sustainability practices are of importance to its leadership, and therefore its citizens.
4. *Does the community's budget document mention tourism or aviation specifically?* As tourism can provide an economic competitive advantage to communities and aviation supports this industry, a community recognizing this importance is likely to also desire a modernized air travel apparatus.

An affirmative response for each of these questions constitutes a quarter point in the category score, with an affirmative across all four questions constituting a full point in the community alignment category score. The EAS report is used to source answers to the first question, census data is used to source answers to the second question, and each community's budget document is used to answer the third and fourth questions. For communities with no performance budget available, or with minimal budget narratives, the city strategic plan, comprehensive plan, or economic development documents are referenced. If none of these are easily accessible, it is assumed that the community's priorities are not explicit, and no affirmative score is recorded for the question. Because of this approach, this is the dimension of the methodology that utilizes secondary qualitative data. While it is ideal that a community responds in the affirmative to all four questions, no one factor of these four can singularly form an impasse to not consider the community further.

With category scores developed along these three dimensions, relative category weights must be developed. It should be noted that these category weights are heavily dependent on the political preferences of the implementing agency, and therefore are subject to change with different administrations. The category weights used in this study reflect the current political priorities of the 2022 Department of Transportation, and the synthesized findings of the literature review. Emissions reduction potential was assigned a category weight of 0.5, given that this was a primary motivator for the development of electric aircraft. The US Department of Transportation has outlined innovation principles, key among them serving policy priorities. Addressing the climate crisis is explicitly listed in the summary of the current policy priorities (Department of Transportation, 2022). The next highest assigned category weight is for the community alignment score at a 0.3 weight. This is a largely practical matter for realistic implementation purposes. As outlined previously, should this program be adopted under the existing or similar framework as the EAS, the local community priorities will be the motivator for whether electric aircraft operators may be subsidized. Building a partnership with the local government and community is critical for a successful rollout but is also well-aligned with the previously mentioned Department of Transportation innovation principles. "The Department will embrace public private partnerships that share risk, foster purpose-driven innovation and protect the interests of the public, workers, and communities" (Department of Transportation, 2022). The final category score of noise reduction potential is assigned a category weight of 0.2. This is reflective of the nature of noise pollution from aviation in the communities proposed for this project, where it is more correlated with annoyance than health impacts given the sparsity of noise events. However, since there still may be a correlation between aviation noise and property values, even for these rural areas, the category is still deserving of fair consideration.

The stated category scores weights reflective the current moment in time and are subject to change with shifting political priorities and administrations. Given this understanding, individual category scores are given in the compiled scorecard following the conclusion section so that total scores may be recalculated under different weights.

Limitations

This preliminary study explores specific air routes and communities for aircraft electrification and provides justification for which are optimal for implementation on the basis of public benefit maximization. This specific area is not expressly addressed in the existing body of research and as such, this study faces limitations in the precision of the recommendations it can provide. Additionally, the time and information availability constraints on this project also bar a high level of precision in developing the scorecard.

Assumptions were made in the development of this study's methodology, including the timeline of electric aircraft implementation, a steady state of the Essential Air Service demand levels, and the existence of a political path to program implementation. When developing the category scores, simplifications were made that should be directly addressed. The emissions reduction category assumes a linear relationship between aircraft size (by seats) and total emission output. Noise reduction benefit assumes the population experiencing noise reduction reside within a constant radius from their regional airport. In reality, the region more closely resembles a highly eccentric ellipse whose major axis aligns with the primary runway. The noise estimate also assumes the same average noise level for all non-electric light aircraft models of 80 decibels. With these simplifications, the scores produced through this methodology should not be considered precise beyond one significant figure. Therefore, rather than a ranked list of ideal communities, this study will produce tiers of communities for which aircraft electrification will provide high to low public benefit.

Results

The scores for each community were computed following the prescribed methodology. In developing these scores, a few notable observations were made regarding specific communities that comment on both the implications of the chosen methodology and the hypothesis of this study. To reiterate the operating hypothesis of this study, it was believed that communities with larger populations and higher population densities would be the best candidates for public benefit maximization should aircraft electrification be adopted there. Following these individual observations, the comprehensive scorecard highlights are presented.

This analysis uses the current EAS program data to develop the average route mileage for each community. It is assumed that the best pathway to emissions reduction for each community would occur through the replacement of their existing fleet with electric aircraft. Therefore, a secondary implicit assumption is that the community is already operating in a manner to minimize emissions reduction, making this additional fleet improvement necessary. This is not always the case, as seen with Grand Island, Nebraska. This EAS community currently connects to the hub of Dallas/Fort Worth International Airport, 561 miles away. However, this is not the nearest hub airport, with Denver International Airport being 344 miles away and Chicago O'Hare International Airport located 544 miles away. The decision to fly from Grand Island to Dallas/Fort Worth as the subsidized air route is likely the result of other factors beyond individual route fuel efficiency, such as commuter demand or passenger end destinations. For this analysis, the current air route was used in the scoring for emissions reduction potential, but for future study, these alternative hubs should be considered as options for emissions reduction.

The operating hypothesis posits that communities with larger populations and higher population densities may be better candidates for aircraft electrification given the benefits brought by negative externality reduction. With the chosen methodology, this result would primarily manifest itself in the scorecard under

Table 1. Top scoring EAS communities for aircraft electrification

State	EAS Community	Hubs Served	Weighted Score
ND	Devils Lake	DEN	0.522
ND	Jamestown (ND)	DEN	0.486
SD	Watertown (SD)	DEN/ORD	0.456
NY	Ogdensburg	IAD/ORD	0.455
KS	Salina	DEN/ORD	0.452
NE	Grand Island	DFW	0.442
ME	Presque Isle/Houlton	EWR	0.425
MO	Joplin	DFW	0.418
NY	Plattsburgh	IAD	0.401

the noise reduction potential category. What the hypothesis does not recognize is the specific location of airports relative to the population centers they serve. The development of the scorecard illustrates several interesting examples of this. Garden City, Kansas, having a population exceeding 26,500 has an airport located well away from the city center along U.S. Highway 400. As such, the estimated population residing within the 5.5 km radius of the airport is only 183 individuals. An even more dramatic instance of this is observed for Canyonlands Regional Airport in Moab, UT. Though part of the EAS, this serves an already remote community and demand is largely driven by tourism. The airport is far removed from any population center, with the estimated residents within a 5.5 km radius being 0. These communities demonstrate that the initial hypothesis is insufficient in properly determining externality abatement, the location of the airport must be considered specifically.

Whereas the first two scoring categories rely on quantitative data, the determination of community alignment requires secondary qualitative data from each community's budget, strategic plan, or comprehensive plan. In converting these to a category score, some degree of subjective interpretation was required by the author, specifically in evaluating whether tourism was an active economic development strategy and whether new environmental and climate change technologies were part of the locality's political priorities. However, there were certain documents examined for which the language was so explicit that they deserve specific recognition. Watertown, South Dakota explicitly outlines "protecting environment" as one of the city's goals and objectives in their 2022 budget message. Laramie, Wyoming similarly outlines "environmental stewardship" as a goal in their adopted performance budget, even specifying the importance of renewable energy installations of efficiencies at city facilities. These examples illustrate the clearest instances of the city budget, a reflection of the priorities of the city government, confirming alignment of the community with the hypothetical aircraft electrification desired outcomes.

With the above specific examples framing the consequences of this methodology and the challenges to the initial hypothesis, the context for the full scorecard has been developed. As such, the results of the scorecard are reported below.

The communities in the top tier for aircraft electrification are the following:

As a basis of comparison for what distinguishes the most ideal communities for aircraft electrification, the lowest scored tier of communities is included as well.

Table 2. Lowest scoring EAS communities for aircraft electrification

State	EAS Community	Hubs Served	Weighted Score
PA	Altoona	BWI/PIT	0.045
AZ	Show Low	PHX	0.044
MT	Wolf Point	BIL	0.044
MT	Havre	BIL	0.043
MT	Glasgow	BIL	0.041
MO	Kirksville	STL	0.038
VT	Rutland	BOS	0.038
MT	Glendive	BIL	0.035
HI	Kamuela	OGG	0.030
NE	Chadron	DEN	0.028
NE	Alliance	DEN	0.026
HI	Hana	OGG	0.008

A more thorough exploration of the factors that resulted in these scores follows in the analysis section. Preceding the conclusion, a full scoresheet for all EAS communities considered may be found.

Analysis

The results shown in table 1 represent the full public benefit maximization along all scoring dimensions. There are some initial notable commonalities to discuss. It is observed that four hub airports are shared by at least two of the routes in the top tier of scores: Denver International Airport, Chicago O'Hare International Airport, Washington Dulles International Airport, and Dallas/Fort Worth International Airport. Similarly, there are many geographic similarities to these airport locations. In order to understand the characteristics possessed by the top tier communities that contributed to their scores, an analysis along each scoring category is performed.

The first and most heavily weighted category, emissions reduction potential, considered the total seat-miles per week flown along EAS routes currently. The data that contributed to this category score, and the category scores themselves, are shown for the top tier communities in table 3.

Given that the fifty percent of the total score weight was lent to this category, it is unsurprising that communities with high emissions reduction scores also have high total scores. However, it should be noted that there are other high scoring communities for this category that were not included in the top tier overall: Cody, Wyoming; Dickinson, North Dakota; Meridian, Mississippi; Kearney, Nebraska; Prescott, Arizona; and Sioux City, Iowa. All these communities had a better category score than Joplin, Missouri, which was had the lowest emissions reduction potential score while still being in the top tier. Similarities are observed in the operating schedules of the top tier flights. They average about 2 flights per day for twelve to thirteen flights per week, currently serviced by larger regional aircraft, generally the CRJ-200 or the ERJ 145 (Department of Transportation, 2021). Many are in neighboring states and utilize the same hub airport, which explains the common occurrence of longer route distance. This com-

Table 3. Emissions Reduction Potential category score data subset for the top tier communities

State	EAS Community	Seats	Weekly Round Trips	Hubs Served	Average Route milage	Seat miles per week	Emissions Reduction Score
ND	Devils Lake	50	12	DEN	639	383400	1.000
ND	Jamestown (ND)	50	12	DEN	573	343800	0.897
SD	Watertown (SD)	50	12	DEN/ORD	513	307800	0.803
NY	Ogdensburg	50	12	IAD/ORD	530	318000	0.829
KS	Salina	50	12	DEN/ORD	471	282600	0.737
NE	Grand Island	44	13	DFW	561	320892	0.837
ME	Presque Isle/Houlton	50	12	EWR	515	309000	0.806
MO	Joplin	50	12	DFW	434	260400	0.679
NY	Plattsburgh	50	12	IAD	444	266400	0.695

bination of large aircraft flown multiple times a day over long routes explains the high scores achieved for emissions reduction potential.

The noise reduction potential category scores were developed based on the estimated number of residents residing within 5.5 km of the airport, using the NASA SEDAC Population Estimation tool. This score was assigned a category weight of 0.2, given that the noise pollution impacts for regional airports were far less severe than aviation noise pollution discussed in general terms. Table 4 illustrates this category score and its development for the top tier communities identified.

Since this is the lowest weighted score category, it should be unsurprising that many of the communities of this top tier overall do not necessarily have the highest scores for this singular category. However, the distribution of these category scores should be considered as well. The community with the most residents within 5.5 km of the airport was Morgantown, West Virginia, which with the conglomerate of cities in the area had 73,646 residents for this statistic. This was the number used as the divisor in normalizing the data for this category. However, the average population within 5.5 km of the airport across all communities was 12,639. Therefore, there are multiple communities in this top tier with an above average number of residents who stand to benefit from the noise reduction potential of aircraft electrification: Jamestown, North Dakota; Watertown, South Dakota; Ogdensburg, New York; Salina, Kansas; Joplin, Missouri; and Plattsburgh, New York. In fact, two thirds of the top tier communities

Table 4. Noise Reduction Potential category score data subset for the top tier communities

State	EAS Community	Hubs Served	Residents within 5.5 km of Airport	Noise Reduction Score
ND	Devils Lake	DEN	8102	0.110
ND	Jamestown (ND)	DEN	13901	0.189
SD	Watertown (SD)	DEN/ORD	20112	0.273
NY	Ogdensburg	IAD/ORD	14727	0.200
KS	Salina	DEN/ORD	30560	0.415
NE	Grand Island	DFW	8750	0.119
ME	Presque Isle/Houlton	EWR	8184	0.111
MO	Joplin	DFW	28787	0.391
NY	Plattsburgh	IAD	19684	0.267

Table 5. Community Alignment category Score Data Subset for the Top Tier Communities

State	EAS Community	Seats	Increasing County Population?	Similarly Sized Aircraft?	Tourism as a Strategy?	Sustainability Priorities?	Community Alignment Score
ND	Devils Lake	50	No	No	No	No	0
ND	Jamestown (ND)	50	No	No	Yes	No	0.25
SD	Watertown (SD)	50	No	No	No	Yes	0.25
NY	Ogdensburg	50	No	No	Yes	Yes	0.5
KS	Salina	50	No	No	Yes	Yes	0.5
NE	Grand Island	44	No	No	Yes	Yes	0.5
ME	Presque Isle/Houlton	50	No	No	No	No	0
MO	Joplin	50	Yes	No	No	No	0.25
NY	Plattsburgh	50	No	No	No	Yes	0.25

would provide greater than average public benefit by noise production should they be selected for aircraft electrification routes.

The community alignment scores reflect the presence of four key indicators, as previously identified, correlating to tax base, work force, economic development, and political priority considerations. Tax base considerations looked to see if the population of the county was increasing. Workforce considerations were around pilot recruitment, with the indicator being the size of aircraft currently used for the community's air route (a positive result would be an aircraft with 17 seats or fewer). Economic development and policy priorities searched the community's performance budgets and strategic plans for key phrases or stated objectives. The results of this scoring dimension for the top tier communities are shown in table 5.

Notably in this table, each top-rated community is missing at least two indicators of community alignment for this hypothetical aircraft electrification project. If this category were weighted more heavily, it is possible that this would drive these communities out of the top tier of scores. In the entire analysis, only four communities possessed all four indicators of community alignment: Bar Harbor, Maine; Silver City/Hurley/Deming, New Mexico; Show Low, Arizona; and Kamuela, Hawaii. Also, for each the top tier communities, the aircraft currently flown are of the 50-seat variety, so to meet the same demand with a fleet of smaller electric aircraft, more daily trips must be made, and likely more pilots recruited. This is not an impossibility, as companies competing for EAS routes frequently promise the same level of service with a fleet of smaller aircraft. Replacing large aircraft with smaller narrow-body aircraft on short haul routes is already an existing fuel-saving measure (Givoni & Rietveld, 2010, pp. 159-167). Though unclear if it was motivated by fuel-savings, this exact phenomenon was observed in 2022 where Boutique Air bid on servicing routes previously operated by 50-seat CRJ 200 jets with a fleet of nine-passenger PC-12 turboprop craft (Waters, 2022). So long as pilot training for electric aircraft is not inherently more difficult than fore existing craft, this issue should be manageable.

Given that for most of these communities, the population is not increasing, a successful implementation plan should diligently and intentionally prevent the shifting of new cost burdens associated with the project to the community. Federal grants to fund the ancillary aspects needed for aircraft electrification, such as power grid improvements, should be considered for the most efficacious implementation. It is motivating to see that many of these top communities already have existing programs or priorities that well align with this initiative. A realistic implementation of aircraft electrification constitutes a partnership between federal and local governments and private airline manufacturers and operators. To have the priorities of these groups already aligned leads to more buy-in for the project from its key stakeholders.

As an additional point of consideration beyond the operating hypothesis, the development of a short-haul aviation network is also considered in the analysis of the weighted scores of EAS communities. Six of the top tier communities are part of neighboring states forming a contiguous region: North Dakota, South Dakota, Nebraska, Kansas, and Missouri. These communities are all connected to three hubs: Denver International Airport, Chicago O'Hare International Airport, and Dallas/Fort Worth International Airport. If the list of potential communities to include in this network is expanded beyond the top tier, Cody, Wyoming; Dickinson, North Dakota; Kearney, Nebraska; Sioux City, Iowa; and Pierre, South Dakota also emerge as candidates for this network to whom electric aircraft could bring significant public benefit. There are certainly additional airports that fall into this geographic region, but these are the locations that by this methodology merit the greatest consideration. This concept, hereby referred to as the Great Plains Short-Haul Electric Network, is pictured in Figure 1.

RECOMMENDATIONS AND FURTHER STUDY

The central research question of this study was "which air routes would provide the most public benefit should their existing fleet be substituted with electric aircraft?" Using the EAS communities as the candidates for comparison, this methodology yielded both a list of top tier communities and a network of short-haul routes that answered the research question. To translate this information into meaningful policy strategy, a series of recommendations are compiled here.

Within the next few years, it is a reasonable expectation for electric commuter aircraft to have been certified and purchased by existing regional airlines; what needs development is a means to connect these airline operators with the routes wherein they might provide the most public benefit. A case has been made for implementation in the existing framework using the EAS in its current state, specifically, the criterion of meeting community's needs. This criterion can be used to justify favoring electric fleets during the bid process. Should this strategy approach be selected, the recommended activities for the Department of Transportation or other federal implementing authorities are to begin cultivating relationships with the executives of the identified top tier communities' local governments to start a conversation around electric aircraft adoption. The path forward is one largely driven by partnership, and not just between these two levels of government. Airlines who intend to purchase electric fleets must also be brought into the conversation and persuaded to submit bids for the air routes identified in this study. Where the proposed Great Plains Short-Haul Electric Network is concerned, potential airlines ought to be persuaded to run the flight operations for all routes within this network. This will not only provide the greatest public benefit but makes good business sense as well for fleet strategy and management.

Another useful partner to consult is larger airline operators. Though these may not be the companies submitting bids for the specific routes, if they can build a business relationship with the smaller operators running electric fleets, these companies' bids become more compelling to the EAS. Criteria 2 and 3 of the EAS bid process examine whether small carriers can connect passengers beyond the initial hub airports through inter-airline agreements and contracts. If a smaller, newer air carrier emerges as the

Figure 1. Concept for the Commercial Flight Routes to be Included in a Great Plains Short-Haul Electric Network. Imagery Sourced through Google, TerraMetrics, and Great Circle Map

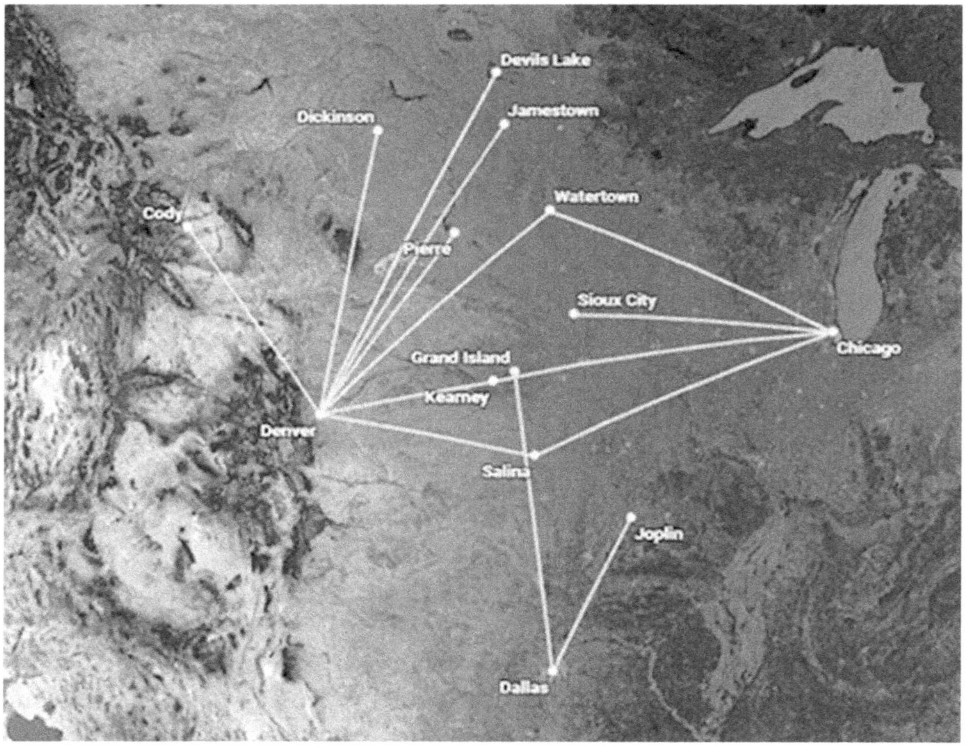

leader in electric fleet adoption, larger airline operators should feel compelled to initiate these agreements, so the former becomes a more competitive EAS bidder.

With these stipulations, and recalling a point made previously in the background section, it may be appropriate for the US congress to reevaluate and update the EAS. A new bid criterion should be giving favor to low or zero emissions fleets or minimal noise pollution aircrafts. Given the existing political landscape, this may be difficult to pass through congress, but this study would give reason for congress people from the states of the Great Plains Short-Haul Electric Network to view this amendment favorable. Even if the EAS is not amended, the previously described strategy is still workable in its current form. Ultimately the strategy recommended is one of communication and collaboration, where federal and local government and private enterprise can use these results to build consensus on where to target their efforts for the first fleets of electric aircraft.

Several limitations were detailed for this study, largely indicated that the scorecard may provide insights but at a low level of precision. Therefore, more rigorous further study is necessary. Specifically, the measures of this study largely demonstrated the comparative advantages of selecting these identified top tier communities over the other candidates. With further study, the expected benefits should be translated into more absolute measures to set specific policy goals, such as emissions reduction in terms of carbon mass per year, noise reduction in specific decibel levels, and community impact in terms of more rigorous cost analyses. Some of the simplifications of this model, such as treating all existing aircraft as equal in terms of emissions output per seat-mile or treating the noise-affected zone as a circle, can be improved upon, especially with time. As more accurate projections for the performance of the specific electric aircraft models become available, these estimates will become more reliable. Finally, demand forecasts should be developed for consumers to predict the diffusion of technology for this specific industry in the identified communities.

In the interim period where electric aircraft await certification and large-scale manufacturing, studies will continue to be released around related concerns such as power grid demand, recharging models, or workforce development. Thus far, these studies tend to select a hypothetical region to apply their models to and provide little justification for the selection. The proposed Great Plains Short-Haul Electric Network can know serve as a region of interest for future explorations on these topics, with this study serving as the justification for the selection.

CONCLUSION

This study yields not only recommendations for policy strategy to move towards an efficient and effective regional electric-aviation system, but also the methodology for a holistic analysis of route alternatives. While existing studies explored individual measures such as carbon emission reduction potential, this adds to the body of knowledge by suggesting a comprehensive scorecard approach that considers multiple dimensions of public benefit. The methodology presented incorporates, emissions reduction, noise pollution reduction, tax-base, workforce, economic development, and political priority considerations, along with appropriate category weights based on federal government priorities. The devised methodology on its own can and should be used in future studies comparing the effectiveness of electric air-route alternatives for public benefit maximization.

There exists a top tier of EAS communities most ideal for electric aircraft implementation, that being Devils Lake, North Dakota; Jamestown, North Dakota; Watertown, South Dakota; Ogdensburg, New York; Salina, Kansas; Grand Island, Nebraska; Presque Isle/Houlton, Maine; Joplin, Missouri; and Plattsburgh, New York. These communities all have a high weekly seat-mileage that translates to high emission reduction potential, significant noise pollution reduction potential, and in some cases, a good fit of local political priorities and economic development strategy. The Department of Transportation should look to these communities specifically as the ideal candidates for the roll out of the first Electric Aviation programs, through partnerships between federal and local government and private industry. To maximize the effectiveness of the realistic operation of electric airlines, the Great Plains Short-Haul Electric Network was proposed, incorporating other high scoring communities beyond the top tier. This is an excellent example to be used in further study on this topic or considered for business strategies by electric airline operators.

In summary, if electric aviation is to be a vehicle of public benefit as it has widely been marketed, the Department of Transportation needs to be proactive in considering where it should first operate to prove its effectiveness. This will address the climate crisis, bring local benefits to communities, and enable the future delivery of even greater carbon emission reducing technologies. While the timeline for these innovations is encouraging, the public policy strategy must keep pace to capture fully the promised benefits of electric aviation. The results of such a strategy will be long-lasting, positively impact all stakeholders, and reinspire the world to just how impactful technology can be in improving the lives of all, no matter where they reside.

Table 6. Compiled Scorecard for All EAS Communities Considered

State	EAS Community	Hubs Served	Emissions Reduction Score	Noise Reduction Score	Community Alignment Score	Weighted Score
AL	Muscle Shoals	ATL/PNS	0.123	0.158	0.5	0.243
AR	El Dorado/Camden	DFW/MEM	0.095	0.010	0.25	0.050
AR	Harrison	DFW	0.136	0.155	0.5	0.099
AR	Hot Springs	DFW	0.106	0.506	0.75	0.155
AR	Jonesboro	STL	0.085	0.548	0.75	0.152
AZ	Page	LAS/PHX	0.215	0.114	0.75	0.130
AZ	Prescott	DEN/LAX	0.707	0.055	0.5	0.365
AZ	Show Low	PHX	0.048	0.099	1	0.044
CA	Crescent City	OAK	0.235	0.188	0	0.155
CA	El Centro	LAX	0.101	0.694	0.5	0.190
CA	Merced	LAX/SMF	0.109	0.878	0.5	0.230
CO	Alamosa	DEN	0.280	0.121	0.25	0.164
CO	Cortez	DEN/PHX	0.151	0.037	0.5	0.083
CO	Pueblo	DEN	0.171	0.045	0.75	0.094
GA	Macon	BWI	0.558	0.200	0.25	0.319
HI	Hana	OGG	0.009	0.017	0.75	0.008
HI	Kamuela	OGG	0.022	0.094	1	0.030
IA	Burlington	ORD/STL	0.094	0.360	0.75	0.119
IA	Fort Dodge	ORD	0.509	0.227	0	0.300
IA	Mason City	ORD	0.451	0.081	0.25	0.241
IA	Sioux City	ORD	0.682	0.110	0.5	0.363
IA	Waterloo	ORD	0.397	0.213	0	0.241
IL	Decatur	ORD	0.244	0.216	0.25	0.165
IL	Marion/Herrin	BNA/STL	0.114	0.204	0.5	0.098
IL	Quincy/Hannibal, MO	ORD/STL	0.133	0.016	0.75	0.070
KS	Dodge City	DEN	0.457	0.219	0.25	0.272
KS	Garden City	DFW	0.649	0.002	0.25	0.325
KS	Hays	DEN	0.463	0.092	0.25	0.250
KS	Liberal/Guymon, OK	DEN	0.438	0.279	0.25	0.275
KS	Salina	DEN/ORD	0.737	0.415	0.5	0.452
KY	Owensboro	BNA/STL	0.075	0.627	0.25	0.163
KY	Paducah	ORD	0.624	0.077	0.5	0.328
ME	Augusta/Waterville	BOS	0.085	0.271	0.75	0.097
ME	Bar Harbor	BOS	0.177	0.037	1	0.096
ME	Presque Isle/Houlton	EWR	0.806	0.111	0	0.425
ME	Rockland	BOS	0.110	0.082	0.75	0.072
MI	Alpena	DTW	0.310	0.016	0.5	0.158
MI	Escanaba	DTW/MSP	0.475	0.177	0	0.273
MI	Hancock/Houghton	ORD	0.657	0.042	0.5	0.337
MI	Iron Mountain/Kingsford	DTW/MSP	0.507	0.189	0	0.291
MI	Ironwood/Ashland, WI	MSP/ORD	0.110	0.018	0.5	0.059
MI	Manistee/Ludington	ORD	0.090	0.050	0.75	0.055
MI	Muskegon	ORD	0.215	0.588	0.25	0.225
MI	Pellston	DTW	0.380	0.021	0	0.194
MI	Sault Ste. Marie	DTW/MSP	0.609	0.096	0	0.324
MN	Bemidji	MSP	0.363	0.208	0.75	0.223
MN	Brainerd	MSP	0.178	0.071	0.25	0.103
MN	Chisholm/Hibbing	MSP	0.272	0.026	0	0.141
MN	International Falls	MSP	0.399	0.180	0	0.236
MN	Thief River Falls	MSP	0.245	0.069	0	0.136
MO	Cape Girardeau/Sikeston	ORD	0.532	0.069	0.5	0.280
MO	Fort Leonard Wood	STL	0.112	0.258	0.25	0.108
MO	Joplin	DFW	0.679	0.391	0.25	0.418
MO	Kirksville	STL	0.073	0.008	0.75	0.038
MS	Greenville	BNA/DFW	0.124	0.016	0.25	0.065
MS	Laurel/Hattiesburg	IAH	0.582	0.026	0.25	0.296
MS	Meridian	IAH	0.692	0.171	0	0.380
MS	Tupelo	BNA	0.191	0.399	0	0.175
MT	Butte	SLC	0.607	0.280	0.75	0.359
MT	Glasgow	BIL	0.062	0.051	0.75	0.041
MT	Glendive	BIL	0.067	0.008	0.25	0.035
MT	Havre	BIL	0.065	0.055	0.25	0.043

continued on following page

Table 6. Continued

State	EAS Community	Hubs Served	Emissions Reduction Score	Noise Reduction Score	Community Alignment Score	Weighted Score
MT	Sidney	BIL	0.200	0.083	0.5	0.117
MT	West Yellowstone	SLC	0.427	0.023	0.5	0.218
MT	Wolf Point	BIL	0.069	0.046	0.25	0.044
ND	Devils Lake	DEN	1.000	0.110	0	0.522
ND	Dickinson	DEN	0.764	0.005	0.5	0.383
ND	Jamestown (ND)	DEN	0.897	0.189	0.25	0.486
NE	Alliance	DEN	0.051	0.003	0.25	0.026
NE	Chadron	DEN	0.056	0.001	0.5	0.028
NE	Grand Island	DFW	0.837	0.119	0.5	0.442
NE	Kearney	DEN/ORD	0.695	0.115	0.5	0.371
NE	McCook	DEN	0.054	0.109	0.25	0.049
NE	North Platte	DEN	0.355	0.038	0.25	0.185
NE	Scottsbluff	DEN	0.235	0.101	0.5	0.138
NH	Lebanon/White River Jct.	BOS/HPN	0.148	0.199	0.75	0.114
NM	Carlsbad	ABQ/DFW	0.123	0.048	0.5	0.071
NM	Clovis	DEN	0.362	0.031	0.25	0.187
NM	Silver City/Hurley/Deming	ABQ/PHX	0.118	0.000	1	0.059
NY	Massena	BOS	0.115	0.179	0.25	0.093
NY	Ogdensburg	IAD/ORD	0.829	0.200	0.5	0.455
NY	Plattsburgh	IAD	0.695	0.267	0.25	0.401
NY	Saranac Lake/Lake Placid	BOS	0.105	0.012	0.75	0.055
NY	Watertown (NY)	PHL	0.449	0.066	0.5	0.238
OR	Pendleton	PDX	0.079	0.212	0.25	0.082
PA	Altoona	BWI/PIT	0.059	0.076	0.75	0.045
PA	Bradford	IAD/PIT	0.093	0.025	0.75	0.051
PA	DuBois	BWI/PIT	0.119	0.016	0.5	0.063
PA	Johnstown	IAD/ORD	0.475	0.226	0	0.283
PA	Lancaster	BWI/PIT	0.098	0.739	0.75	0.197
PR	Mayaguez	SJU	0.050	0.572	0.25	0.139
SD	Aberdeen	MSP	0.469	0.231	0	0.281
SD	Pierre	DEN	0.603	0.145	0	0.330
SD	Watertown (SD)	DEN/ORD	0.803	0.273	0.25	0.456
TN	Jackson	ATL/STL	0.110	0.028	0.5	0.061
TX	Victoria	IAH	0.192	0.135	0.25	0.123
UT	Cedar City	SLC	0.346	0.544	0.75	0.282
UT	Moab	DEN	0.441	0.000	0.75	0.221
UT	Vernal	DEN	0.405	0.310	0	0.265
VA	Staunton	IAD/ORD	0.495	0.061	0.75	0.259
VT	Rutland	BOS	0.063	0.033	0.25	0.038
WI	Eau Claire	ORD	0.491	0.346	0.75	0.315
WI	Rhinelander	MSP	0.347	0.123	0.5	0.198
WV	Beckley	CLT	0.167	0.264	0	0.136
WV	Clarksburg/Fairmont	IAD/ORD	0.466	0.166	0.25	0.266
WV	Greenbrier/White Sulphur Springs/Lewisburg	IAD/ORD	0.524	0.054	0	0.273
WV	Morgantown	BWI/PIT	0.106	1.000	0.5	0.253
WV	Parkersburg/Marietta, OH	CLT	0.269	0.089	0	0.152
WY	Cody	DEN	0.714	0.151	0.5	0.387
WY	Laramie	DEN	0.177	0.072	0.75	0.103

REFERENCES

Anderson, M. (2019). US airline orders first passenger electric plane: The battery-powered nine-seater aircraft will enter service in 2022. *IEEE Spectrum*, *56*(09), 10–11. doi:10.1109/MSPEC.2019.8818579

Antcliff, K., Borer, N., Sartorius, S., Saleh, P., Rose, R., Gariel, M., . . . Oullette, R. (2021). *Regional Air Mobility: Leveraging Our National Investments to Energize the American Travel Experience*. Retrieved from NASA: https://sacd.larc.nasa.gov/sacd/wp-content/uploads/sites/102/2021/04/2021-04-20-RAM.pdf

Baumeister, S., Leung, A., & Ryley, T. (2020). The emission reduction potentials of first generation electric aircraft (FGEA) in Finland. *Journal of Transport Geography*, *85*(C), 102730. doi:10.1016/j.jtrangeo.2020.102730

Bertsch, L., Simons, D. G., & Snellen, M. (2015). Aircraft Noise: The major sources, modelling capabilities, and reduction possibilities (IB 224-2015 A 110 ed.) DLR.

Department of Transportation. (2017). *Essential Air Service*. Retrieved from transportation.gov: https://www.transportation.gov/policy/aviation-policy/small-community-rural-air-service/essential-air-service

Department of Transportation. (2021). *Subsidized Essential Air Service communities (48 Contiguous States, Hawaii, and Puerto Rico)*. Retrieved from transportation.gov: https://www.transportation.gov/office-policy/aviation-policy/subsidized-essential-air-service-communities-48-contiguous-states

Department of Transportation. (2022). *US DOT Innovation Principles*. Retrieved from transportation.gov: https://www.transportation.gov/priorities/innovation/us-dot-innovation-principles

Domone, J. (2018). *The challenges and benefits of the electrification of aircraft*. SNC Lavalin.

Esque, A., Riedel, R., & Riefer, D. (2021). *Reducing aviation emissions over the long and short haul*. McKinsey & Company. Retrieved from https://www.mckinsey.com/industries/aerospace-and-defense/our-insights/future-air-mobility-blog/reducing-aviation-emissions-over-the-long-and-short-haul

Fanelli, R. M. (2021). Barriers to adopting new technologies within rural small and medium enterprises (SMEs). *Social Sciences*, *10*(11), 430. doi:10.3390ocsci10110430

Fuellhart, K., Dai, L., Grubesic, T., & Derudder, B. (2021). The US Essential Air Service Program and SARS COV-2, 2019–2020. *Journal of Transport Geography*, 96.

Gent, E. (2022). *Eviation's Maiden Flight Could Usher in Electric Aviation Era*. Retrieved from IEEE.org: https://spectrum.ieee.org/eviations-maiden-flight-to-usher-in-era-of-electric-aviation

Givoni, M., & Rietveld, P. (2010). The environmental implications of airlines' choice of aircraft size. *Journal of Air Transport Management*, *16*(3), 159–167. doi:10.1016/j.jairtraman.2009.07.010

Gössling, S., & Lyle, C. (2021). Transition policies for climatically sustainable aviation. *Transport Reviews*, *41*(5), 643–658. doi:10.1080/01441647.2021.1938284

Hansell, A. L., Blangiardo, M., Fortunato, L., Floud, S., De Hoogh, K., Fecht, D., . . . Elliott, P. (2013). *Aircraft noise and cardiovascular disease near Heathrow airport in London: Small area study*. Retrieved from bmj.com: https://www.bmj.com/content/347/bmj.f5432

Janssen, S. A., Vos, H., van Kempen, E. E., Breugelmans, O. R., & Miedema, H. M. (2011). Trends in aircraft noise annoyance: The role of study and sample characteristics. *The Journal of the Acoustical Society of America, 129*(4), 1953–1962. doi:10.1121/1.3533739 PMID:21476651

Moua, L., Roa, J., Xie, Y., & Maxwell, D. (2020, August). Critical Review of Advancements and Challenges of All-Electric Aviation. In *International Conference on Transportation and Development 2020*. American Society of Civil Engineers. 10.1061/9780784483138.005

Özcan, İ. Ç. (2014). Economic contribution of essential air service flights on small and remote communities. *Journal of Air Transport Management, 34*, 24–29. doi:10.1016/j.jairtraman.2013.07.005

Park, Y., & O'Kelly, M. E. (2017). Exploring accessibility from spatial interaction data: An evaluation of the Essential Air Service (EAS) program in the contiguous US air transport system. *Environment & Planning A, 49*(4), 930–951. doi:10.1177/0308518X16680816

Prapotnik Brdnik, A., Kamnik, R., Marksel, M., & Božičnik, S. (2019). Market and technological perspectives for the new generation of regional passenger aircraft. *Energies, 12*(10), 1864. doi:10.3390/en12101864

Salucci, F., Trainelli, L., Bruglieri, M., Riboldi, C. E., Rolando, A. L., & García González, G. (2021). Capturing the Demand for an Electric-Powered Short-Haul Air Transportation Network. *AIAA SciTech 2021 Forum*. 10.2514/6.2021-0869

Schwab, A., Thomas, A., Bennett, J., Robertson, E., & Cary, S. (2021). *Electrification of Aircraft: Challenges, Barriers, and Potential Impacts (No. NREL/TP-6A20-80220). National Renewable Energy Lab.* NREL. doi:10.2172/1827628

Secretariat, I. C. A. O. (2019). Electric, hybrid, and hydrogen aircraft-state of play. *Climate Change Mitigation: Technology and Operations*, 124-130.

Sklarz, M., & Miller, N. (2018). *The Impact of Noise on Residential Property Value*. Collateral Analytics Research. Retrieved from https://www.collateralanalytics.com/wp-content/uploads/2018/10/CA-RESEARCH-The-Impact-of-Noise-on-Residential-Property-V
alues.pdf

Smyth, A., Christodoulou, G., Dennis, N., Marwan, A. A., & Campbell, J. (2012). Is air transport a necessity for social inclusion and economic development? *Journal of Air Transport Management, 22*, 53–59. doi:10.1016/j.jairtraman.2012.01.009

Spokane International Airport. (2014). *Aircraft Noise Analysis. Spokane International Airport Master Plan*. Retrieved from http://business.zlcms.com/core/files/business/uploads/files/Master%20Plan/Chapter%206.pdf

Tariq, M., Maswood, A. I., Gajanayake, C. J., & Gupta, A. K. (2017). Aircraft batteries: Current trend towards more electric aircraft. *IET Electrical Systems in Transportation, 7*(2), 93–103. doi:10.1049/iet-est.2016.0019

Waters, J. (2022). Denver Air Connection and Boutique Air seek Alamosa air route. *Alamosa News*. Retrieved from https://alamosanews.com/article/denver-air-connection-and-boutique-air-seek-alamosa-air-route

APPENDIX: List of Acronyms

EAS Essential Air Service
eVTOL Electric Vertical Take-Off and Landing
FAA Federal Aviation Administration
ICAO International Civil Aviation Organization
NASA National Aeronautics and Space Administration
SAF Sustainable Aviation Fuel
SCASDP Small Community Air Service Development Program
SEDAC Socioeconomic Data and Applications Center

Chapter 6
Participatory Governance for Institutional Transformation

José G. Vargas-Hernández
https://orcid.org/0000-0003-0938-4197
Posgraduate and Research Department, Tecnológico Mario Molina Unidad Zapopan, Mexico

Omar C. Vargas-González
https://orcid.org/0000-0002-6089-956X
Tecnológio Nacional de México, Ciudad Guzmán, Mexico

ABSTRACT

This chapter is aimed to analyze the institutional transformation of participatory governance from the socio-intercultural perspective and interethnic relationships. The analysis of the public culture assumes that socio-intercultural and interethnic relations is a broader social field considered in the context of the analysis of the institutions of governance to understand the social institutions and events. The method used is the reflective analytical based on the literature review and empirical study. It is concluded that these institutional transformations of participatory governance have been sourced and evolved into a governance structure to govern the behaviors of the communities, organizations, leaderships, and members.

INTRODUCTION

In this time of pandemic crisis, the health care systems around the world are being transforming their institutional governance at all levels by the market orthodoxy whereby the multilateral authority of the nation state is being supplanted by new socio-political actors, economic agents, and other multi-stakeholder governance arrangement systems (Dentico, 2020). The institutional transformation of participatory governance behaviors and structures must be based on the principle of maintaining the integrity of ecosystems.

The word governance was used in the 12th Century in France to designate the administration of a bailliage while in England designated the method of feudal power and organization (de Alcantara, 1998; Kooiman, 2003; and Plumptre and Graham, 1999). The term governance derives from the Latin gubernare with the meaning of rudder conveying the action of steering a ship. Governance is the set of "the

DOI: 10.4018/978-1-6684-2314-1.ch006

interactions among structures, processes and traditions that determine how power and responsibilities are exercised, how decisions are taken, and how citizens or other stakeholders have their say" (Graham, et al. 2003, ii).

Governance is a multi-dimensional concept that moves between several layers of discourses, institutions, governments, policy structures, bureaucracies, localities, activities, etc., which need to be real and tangible for people who are potentially concerned to facilitate change and opening a space for dialogue. The concept of governance is descriptive, normative, and analytical approaches of institutions, motivations, behaviors, cultural values, norms, and so on of a system, structure, policy, political environment, and processes perspectives.

The conceptualizations of governance translate into the organizational environment meaning that the conceptualizations of other communities may be totally different context of the organization (Morphy, 2007) or may form a cultural match (Cornell and Begay, 2004). The collective analyses of governance arise some theoretical propositions. Afterwards, this analysis concentrates on the relevant roles that play. Governance assumes conditions and features of uncertainty and open-endedness (Stoker, 1998) affecting the distribution of power, decision making and engagement in a distinction way that conventional government.

Institutional transformation is related to structures of power, institutional governance of culture, socio-interculturalism in governance, and cultures of governance, which are beyond the term good governance pushed of some governments. Organizational socio-interculturality is sometimes perceived as a museum of cultures problematic for good governance. Good governance is being perceived as a vague concept (Baron, 2003, Gaudin, 2002, Simoulin, 2003) linked to corporate governance with a managerial connotation. Its origins are French and adopted by Great Britain and United States (Le Roy, 2005).

Institutionalized practices of co-determination in functional conversion (Thelen, 2000) are becoming transformed to re-establish complementarity with the corporate governance system (Hoepner, 2001; and Hoepner and Jackson, 2001). The institutional structure changes to negotiate on issues that support efficiency, although the shareholders, agents and actors adapt their demands diversify quality production and new complementarity (Streeck 2001; and Beyer and Hassel 2002).

Governing socio-intercultural inter-organization relationships requires awareness of socio-intercultural activities and practices in the governance structure. The internal governance structures and standards should be focused on procedures to avoid debates on the contents. Social contacts foster socio-interculturalism (Morgan, 2005; Bagwell and Evans 2012). Creation of socio-intercultural spaces is an attractive place for people with diverse backgrounds to encounter each other, recognize and engage with cultural and human values without xenophobia. The membership in an association or organization in any constituency of a settler society is a bounded category and artefact of socio-intercultural space that make cause dynamic governance tensions between the influence of dominant groups.

The socio-intercultural pluralism dialogue open to alterity and complexity in a global perspective is the core of good governance. The governance approach selected implicates a process referred as plural selectivity (Bagshaw, 1977: 27). Socio-interculturalism is related to the knowledge systems of two cultures that are working together (Marika, Ngurruwutthun, & White, 1992, p. 28), and therefore the analysis of acquiring knowledge applies to others as much as to oneself (Abdallah-Pretceille, 2006, p. 477).

A multi-level governance system needs gateways and platforms for socio-intercultural dialogue to develop into socio-intercultural societies based on mutual respect, partnership, and cooperation among all the governance levels. The lower levels of governance have more opportunities to provide input into other higher levels of decision making. Multilevel partnerships governance arrangements are appropriate to coordinate the governmental responsibility in the solution of problems. Organizations may deliver collaborative good governance arrangements designed and implemented in multilevel institutions to achieve intended outcomes guided by value-based standards (Howlett and Rayner, 2006).

Devolved governance at multilevel systems occurs in tasks undertaken at decentralized level represented by all legitimized governing actors exercising their authority in conditions of integrity which provides the governance legitimacy which is consistent with communicative rationality (Habermas, 1981). Communicative rationality applies in contexts of governance where policy depends on trust developed between the participation of shareholders (Selman, 2001; Stratford and Davidson, 2002). An instrumental rational governance is based on a functional interconnectivity to build interdependencies across all the government, territory and policy scales and levels of (Dovers, 2005).

Institutional transformation of participatory governance is relevant in institutionalization theory that helps to understand the institutional environment through the historical, rational choice and sociological institutionalism. Institutional design is the normative perspective of institutional transformation that use the institutional-agent interactions as the media and tools in agency, governance, and coordination (Alexander, 1995). The institutional transformation of governance is part of the socio-cultural field (Gluckman, 1968). A socio-intercultural governance is based on the encouragement of innovation and risk associated in a socio-intercultural organizational system. The fields of socio-intercultural governance are constituted by deeply interwoven by similarities and differences of socio-cultural forms of thought, personhood, institutions, and actions leading to mutual exposure of engagements and transformations (Smith 2007; Gluckman, 1968).

The socio-intercultural space institutions, also known as the border zone, are sites of contestation for good governance, not always comfortable and untenable for effective and conducive governance arrangements. A hybrid socio-intercultural institutional and economy framework strengthens the institutional transformational adaptive capacities to manage governance for difference instead of governance for sameness. Hybrid and socio-intercultural form of governance operates in an increasingly creative and adaptive changing environment continuously addressing re-alignment challenges posed by the competing context influenced by the aboriginal and western forms of governance and social norms. These competing social norms must be managed and negotiated.

The analysis of the public culture based on socio-intercultural and interethnic relations as a broader social field must be considered in the context of the analysis of governance to understand the social institutions and events (Gluckman, 1968; Smith, 2007; Sullivan, 2005). These institutional transformations have been sourced and evolved into a participatory governance structure to govern the behaviors of the communities, organizations, leaderships, and members.

The analysis starts giving some background in this introductory note to continue analyzing the institutional dimensions of governance. Afterwards, the analysis concentrates on the relevant roles that play the socio-political actors and economic agents in the participative mechanisms. At this point, the analysis focuses on some of the conceptual, theoretical, and methodological issues related to contract governance and transaction costs to be able to highlight the implications of policy decision making and strategic governance. The theoretical treatment of institutional transformation of participatory governance has a significance beyond any specific single case. Finally, some concluding remarks are presented to wrap up this analysis

INSTITUTIONAL DIMENSIONS OF GOVERNANCE

Governance lies in institutions as the rules of the game as the glue for the way how things must be done to be considered as legitimating the practices (Cornell and Kalt, 2000; Kesteven and Smith 1984; Smith, 2007). Institutional building capacity is centered around the notion of institutions as the rules of the game, behavioral, socially, and culturally legitimate expectations. The rules of the game are the organizing processes and tools for governance. New institutional transformations of participatory governance acquire legitimacy through its outcomes produced by a consensuenced vision of its leadership (Newman, et al. 2004). The alliances based on socio-intercultural matches may support the governance legitimacy and effectiveness through some socio-cultural forms to match the local and indigenous control (Hunt and Smith, 2006: 18).

Socio-intercultural scale can be the basis to legitimate the dynamic structure and processes of the formal transformation institutions interwoven with the regional and local field of participatory governance. Formal and informal rules as governance institutions are generated by a transitional rule of innovation attempted to create workable solutions for challenging cultures of governance problems. Externally generated rules can easily undermine the institutional transformational culture of participatory governance and have less cognitive flexibility.

The long-lasting organizational and institutional dimensions activate the influential behaviors in determining the extent of local indigenous governance arrangements. These governance arrangements may be accommodated between formal and informal indigenous sociopolitical values. Cross (2008) investigates the contemporary indigenous governances in local authorities, institutions, relationships, and values that are opposed by the state governments and agencies. The institutional transformation strength must be developed from the individuals' choice of local indigenous people. Governments, indigenous local groups, and their agents may find and use appropriate governance institutions, values, processes and practices, related policies, and funding frameworks. The United Kingdom developed a standard for government and nongovernment agencies using public funding (TICGG, 2004).

The normative approach of global governance of organizations and intergovernmental organizations are supported by transnational rule-making organizations and related to institutional values such as accountability, transparency, inclusiveness, deliberativeness, etc., shaping and enacting their own identity. Accountability is a central notion to good governance. Governance accountability refers to the acceptance and allocations of responsibilities for decisions taken and actions in essential contexts for the credibility and authority, which may be distributed in vertical and horizontal accountability (Rosenau, 2000). Governance inclusiveness is referred to opportunities available for actors and stakeholders can engage in governance processes to participate in decision making processes.

A bidirectional accountability is a universal arrangement of good governance (Morphy, 2007). The accountability of the state to citizens is vertical while the horizontal accountability is by the state to the public institutions of accountability (O'Donnell,1999, Schedler, 1999, Schacter, 2000). Institutional horizontal accountability binds institutions of government buttressed by vertical accountability (Schacter, 2000) allowing the citizens to punish when they fail

Global governance organizations and institutions are changing their normative frameworks to include more socio-intercultural inclusive organizational fields and broader organizational structures to meet the social environments. Institutions and organizations need to develop good governance and anti-corruption policies supported by the normative and rulemaking dynamics of transnational governance schemes and organizations to include public, stakeholders and experts' consultations and deliberations despite the increase in the governance costs and the decrease of organizational autonomy. There are some organizational fields and issue areas that are more enthusiastic to accept the support of transnational governance while others issue areas are not able to accept transnational governance features such as the labor issues.

Power-based theories may serve to design and create governance models able to identify and regulate the power of agents and actors who are driving the international organizations to obtain concrete benefits form more participatory communication and decision-making processes, consultation, and deliberation among the different stakeholders. Power, norms, and interests are crucial factors for inner and transnational governance in the emergence and functioning of international institutions and organizations (Hasenclever, et al., 1997).

Power, economic, and political interests defined in terms of ideologies are factors relevant to transnational governance to norm the interactions and develop the governance rulemaking and modeling in institutional and organizational structures and processes. Colonists perceived local indigenous groups and unruly, lawless, and acephalous, but colonists were political, institutional, and social alien hieroglyph, enigmatic and incomprehensible symbols for local indigenous governance.

The western democratic concepts, governance institutions and structures have been imposed through the incorporation of social groups using hard and soft power mechanisms, authority, responsibilities and functions of the state, policy and legislative frameworks, diverse democratic systems of collective decision-making rights and individual citizenship and newly created legal categories of people. There is a cross cultural incongruity (Bagshaw, 1977: 69) between Western and Aboriginal forms and notions of governance. To maintain socio-intercultural checks and balances between Western mode of governance and customary aboriginal mode of governance and social norms must be mediated.

State power and bureaucratic institutions may assert through policy implementation processes to negotiate space for the regionalization of governance to reassert governance institutions and values. Certainty and security are built on the exercise of inclusive power and control. Local indigenous governance has been under state control and surveillance. Power dependence and institutional inequalities in the state identifies different types of governance as forms of construction of identity and institutional power, policy design, decision making, negotiation and contestation.

Thus, governance is seen like the states being supportive of authority and treated as *gubernare nullius* a kind of a *tabula rasa* with statecraft and control liberal institutions and norms. Good governance in liberal democracy does not give relevance to equality and fairness considering that people are not created equal, and leaders are not always elected under democratic principles. In some socio-intercultural contexts, women are taking power and authority positions in some activities, such as education.

The designing of transformational participatory governance institutions and organizations by members of a team making consensus decisions may develop a strong commitment to share visions, developing a sense of trust on self-governance and enabling them to be able to provide advice on government policy demands. Cultural collective shared views enhance workability enforcement and legitimacy of governance policies and rules and governing institutions. The state uses bureaucratic and statutory institutions, policy and regulations to govern their different systems of culturally based-institutions' culture of governance and governance culture to reassert the decision-making theory their legitimacy of governance arrangements.

Local cultural geographies strategically reinforce governance institutional transformational arrangements, structures, solutions and to resist externally imposed governmental institutions. The governance of culture is a symbiotic concept with cultures of governance both considered as tools to analyses the nature of engagements and interactions between different local and indigenous cultures farmed by institutional practices of government, communities, organizations, etc. The governance of cultures is an interrelated concept with cultures of governance to assert cultural geographies into a regionalization of governance trough the institutions inserting decision making processes to elucidate the nature of interactions and contestation between groups, communities, organizations, and the state.

Institutional transformation of government's culture of local participatory governance has implications on the government processes which may lead to government policy reversals an erratic form of governance of government. Culture of governance in local affairs is based on institutionalized policies, programs and funding's supported by financial compliance, transparency and accountability, technical, administrative, and financial reviews and audits as tools activated by government committees and agencies.

There are successful and outstanding local transformations of participatory governance capacities and institutions while others are dysfunctional having failed to deliver the basic rights to the represented population. Legitimacy of local governance and state nation governance may be inextricably linked through the institutions, norms, priorities, and so on. A policy of legitimate governance facilitates the institutional transformations and imperative designing of participatory governance innovation. Multiple agreements between public and private transformations of institutions can be used to deal complex issues of participatory governance and regimes aimed to give answers to the differing interests of stakeholder and states through comprehensive international agreements or bottom-up approach based on national initiatives (Hulme, 2010; Keohane and Victor, 2011).

The implementation of this strategy has advantages in governance culture, diversification and structural flexibility, accountability, diverse institutional capital, and leadership. Institutional capital is the result of the interacting cognitive, regulative, and normative components (Hunt and Smith, 2007; Oliver, 1997; Bresser and Millonig, 2003: 225–2; and Scott, 1995: 35–9).

ACTORS, AGENTS AND PARTICIPATIVE MECHANISMS

The organizational interactions are identified in global governance by the dynamics and shapes of the organizational fields as the structures and processes and their effects on all the involved stakeholders. Organizations are the subject of potential and significant economic component between the interests of involved agents that may derive in conflict to become the subject of an increasing element of contestation to the governance arrangements of local people.

Global governance stresses innovative forms of cooperation among the interactions between the different economic, social, and political agents, actors and stakeholders accepting core norms and gaining legitimacy (Dingwerth, and Pattberg, 2009). Of course, the interactions between these actors and agents are not exempt of functional and dysfunctional tensions, disputes, and conflicts of the pre-existing conditions in organizational operations at the different scales of the indigenous governance. The tensions between the orientations market-based governance and western and indigenous kin-based governance show that there is structural incongruence tracing towards adaptation of creative organizations.

Transnational rulemaking of organizational fields is understood as global governance organizations is an element of global governance that interact with other specific elements of intergovernmental governance organizations. The organizational fields micro-level dynamics should be incorporated into the analytical models to explain transnational regulation in the processes of global governance. Debilitated local governance need to develop a structure and process to rebuild their governance arrangements, to develop local capacities and articulate a strong governance model identified by external agents in its context. Organizational interactions lead to the adoption of social norms in accordance with the collective identity and expectations for the proper behavior of actors (Katzenstein, 1996: 5).

Different types of actors with disparities of power require the formation of a nation state and transnational rule-making organizational forces for private governance to regulate the interests among the actors. Their interrelationships may be contested despite the inherent complexities for the articulation of roles between regional and local organizations and the roles of the state government agencies. Local authorities and government are democratic when they have downward accountability to their communities, constituencies and people (Ribot, 2002).

Private governance emerges in areas of limited statehood, and in transnational contexts where there is vacuum of the states where the market retailers, consumers and other actors demand for governance non-state market driven (Börzel, and Risse, 2010; Cashore, Auld, Bernstein, and McDermott, 2007). Institutional transformation of corporate governance has been most pronounced in coordinated market economies with an impetus for and advocacy of change from the West economies, mainly from US (Lane, 2004; O'Sullivan 2000).

The structural relationship between the organizations related to governance should represent the socio-intercultural spaces along a continuum of exclusion – inclusion of the different political actors and economic agents. The socio-intercultural organizational structure of a different governance for the different populations tends to blend and accommodate indigenous social norms, codes of behavior and accountability with the western governance approach.

Indigenous and aboriginal populations actively involved in suitable organizational governance may invest in governance training for their bureaucrats due to their high turnover and because training has not been locally available before. The existence of other cultures as part of a socio-intercultural spaces of local organizations are incorporated in the vertical hierarchy of the state system including some features of governance arrangements taking more holistic approaches.

A hierarchical, command and control style governance (Davis and Rhodes 2000; Rhodes 2005) reverses self-determination for local indigenous people more aligned with collaborative partnership approaches. The unintended consequences of self-determination policy are the formation of western style advisers depending on partnerships with local aboriginal people. The informal and formal conditions of indigenous regional and local fields of governance are increasingly interweaving across the various scales and resulting in the ability of active and formal relationships of governance confirming the styles of indigenous sociopolitical governance. The enacted regional and local aboriginal forms of governance may be closely tied between the different involved stakeholders across the communities and the associated land ownership system.

International governance organizations and intermediaries working thorough their own channels, can cumulate more influence. Public regulators and regulated public and private agents engaged in direct relationship under the framework of old global relationship. The government´s regulatory scrutiny undermines the resilience of governance rather than enabling it while focusing on the fulfillment of external and financial compliance and responsibilities.

The context of governance must facilitate the collective participation with immediate practical use able to adapt to the changing governance needs. Good governance paradigm emerges through the participative, democratic, and interactive approaches between actors and stakeholders. The organizational dynamics embedded in broader social contexts, theoretically draws on appropriate global governance foundations on public-private partnerships and multi-stakeholder governance models. Mixed public–private system can be enhanced as a decentralized system to embed agreements, coherent architecture, decentralized initiatives, and leadership for private schemes filling the gaps of public governance. Good public governance requires compliance with legislation, standards, codes, etc., to have conformity with internal and external audits, as well as reporting requirements.

Larger regional aggregations may develop legitimacy, generate capacity, and respect indigenous local governance autonomy. A relative autonomy framework for socio-intercultural organizations such as the sites so called border zones as the places that create the hybrid and socio-intercultural interactive and meeting behaviors and forms (Clifford, 1997; Mattingly, 2006: 495) and cultural matches (Cornell and Begay, 2004).

The public–private governance is problematic when the authority is not well localized and is deeply entangle (Porter, 2009), although the distinction is crucial in social life (Pattberg and Stripple, 2008). The stakeholder participation norm in trans and international governance contributes to the diffusion of multi-sectoral partnerships. Governance issues can be treated, negotiated, and enforced according to the existing ecological norms and the cooperation of all the stakeholders and actors involved, such as in the case of land use. The institutional transformation of participatory governance should be sustained on the principle of maintaining the integrity of ecosystems.

Regulatory cooperation and orchestration schemes are mechanisms in which international governance organizations engage with other stakeholders such as private partners, business and industries groups and other intermediaries to influence their behavior toward the achievement of their targets (Abbot et al. 2010). Regulatory cooperation and orchestration as governance mechanisms strengthen centralized coordination of international governance organizations opposing to the current decentralized practices. The orchestration mechanism supporting existing or new schemes of the intermediaries and stakeholders can be used to advance and adopt public goals, policies, structures, and endorsement, facilitating formation and material assistance. However, despite that orchestration has some sovereignty costs it is a low-cost strategy with stronger actions and less resistance.

Orchestration efforts are used for biofuel governance by public regulators taking measures in the European Union actively supported by nation states and international organizations. However, there is little empirical evidence of the complications and benefits provided. Therefore, orchestration bonds third parties into governance arrangements (Abbott, *et al.* 2010, p. 1).

CONTRACT GOVERNANCE AND TRANSACTION COSTS

Contract governance is a new form of governance that has the potential to connect local socio-intercultural norms of a diverse partners. Contract and relational governance have an effective role on relationship commitment and performance between organizations which is used to govern interorganizational collaboration, although the impact is not well known. Relational governance supports information exchange and maintenance of the collaboration relationships to promote cooperation and potentially mitigating differences and conflicts. Contract governance effectiveness is related to the level of organization cultural intelligence capabilities which plays a relevant role in the implementation of collaboration. Effectiveness contract governance mechanism of organizations are being evaluated in terms of the detailed contract, coordination, information, and decision-making.

The interorganizational relationships, such as in the case of supply chains has relied on contract and relational governance leading to the fulfillments of joint and common objectives. The interorganizational relationship also needs collaboration and contract governance which are affected by the national culture and cultural intelligence as the moderating influence. Contract governance promotes cooperation and commitment to a partnership leading to fulfill joint objectives. The meta-cognitive and motivational cultural intelligence have positive effects on contract governance effectiveness for collaboration. Behavioral and motivational components of cultural intelligence moderate the relationships between collaboration and contract relational governance.

Cultural intelligence logics in contract governance is relevant in emerging economies where the political uncertainty is high, the transformation of the institutional environment and the rule of law are weak. Cultural intelligence is expressed in the behavioral flexibility and adaptability influencing the relationship between contract governance, collaboration, and social performance. Governance mechanism effectiveness of organizations is dependent on organization age and size (Zhu et al. 2012), the industry type and the experience of employers affect the social performance (Hair et al. 2010). Organizational governance performance information on all decisions should be transparent, accessible and available to all the stakeholders and anyone interested (Davidson and Stratford, 2000).

National culture and organizational culture have a contingent effect on the effectiveness of governance mechanisms and interorganizational cooperation (Handley, & Angst, 2015). The formal contract governance is associated with performance of collaboration. Activities and operations of organizations involved in contract governance benefit from collaborative knowledge and solutions. The legal bonds are laid out by the rights and obligations of parties involved in the relationship to safeguard the transactions. The contract governance should specify roles, obligations, expectations, and constraining opportunism of parties involved in interorganizational relational governance, incorporating legal bonds to foster commitment and improve performance.

The contract governance in interorganizational cooperation relationships is related to be more administrative effective in terms of transaction costs economics (Williamson, 2008, 1996, 1991) under conditions of cultural intelligence. The contract governance is based on transaction cost economics theory to promote the relational mechanisms governing exchanges though shared behavioral expectations of mutual control or understanding between the parties. Contract governance is interconnected to cultural intelligence capabilities to be able to promote socio-intercultural collaboration and cooperation between the partner's entities.

More administrative efficient organizations, from the transaction costs perspective (Williamson, 1996), is conducive to contract governance has positive effects leading to develop relationships of collaboration by decreasing behavioral opportunism. From the perspective of transactional costs economy, the high levels of meta-cognitive and motivational cultural intelligence enhance the socio-intercultural interactions and improves collaboration at the lower information exchange cost.

Cultural intelligence has effects on governance mechanism of the interorganizational relationships and cooperation. The dimensions of cognition, metacognition, behavioral, and motivational of cultural intelligence affect differently the socio-intercultural interactions and their impact on contract governance and collaboration relationships. Contract governance has a moderating effect with metacognition of cultural intelligence and more significant relationship for the collaboration, and the differences in metacognition of cultural intelligence are related with the level of collaboration and contract governance.

Cultural intelligence has effects on the relationship between contract-relational governance and collaboration (Ang and Inkpen, 2008) Cultural intelligence has a motivational component that leads to more cooperative behavior and socio-intercultural negotiations between members of different cultures while at same time moderates contract governance and collaboration. Metacognition of cultural intelligence has a moderating effect on contract governance and collaboration whose differences are associated with the levels of collaboration and contract governance.

Stakeholders should develop cultural intelligence capabilities as a source aimed to improve their relationship through contract governance to align their collaboration practices and activities. Some of these capabilities are the analytical and critical discussion, communicative and inspirational skills, as well as the capabilities to develop synergies through various methods for teamwork, learning and reflection.

POLICY DECISION MAKING AND STRATEGIC GOVERNANCE

Developing governance solutions may be an active process of innovation and adaptation of policy and decision making involving elected representatives and bureaucratic managers. The social organization nodes of highly decentralized governance systems enable decision making of nodal leadership and organizations that constitute the circuitry of authority and governing. Socio-intercultural leadership has emerged as a counterpoint of the colonial domination leadership providing a more culturally oriented and informed idea which proposes a cultural encounter considering all the fundamental characteristics of each specific and individual cultural (Coll, 2004, p. 27).

There is always a need to make decisions on the identity related to self-governance (Hunt and Smith 2006). Governance is about the politics of socio-interculturality and cultural identities more oriented towards local autonomy at the scales of cultural geography. Cultural geography focuses on indigenous and local governance, negotiation and contestation occurring in its boundaries, changing scales, and so on in the collective self in governance arrangements between and within governments and communities. These local aboriginal organizations extend the complexities of the governance styles including the aboriginal identity forms, localized population, types of land ownership, etc. Contemporary local indigenous governances have ontological frameworks components that are ignored or diminished in relevance by analysts (O'Malley, 1998, Christie, 2007, Howitt, 2001) or erased from its formal administrative structures and processes (Muller, 2008).

There is a wider regional level of connectedness related to indigenous governance structural and procedural arrangements which have implications on politicized and contested identity.

The disabling of these governance arrangements may have analytical and practical implications. This regional indigenous domain is located within the complexity of dimensions of a field governance environment. These dimensions or layers have been identified by Hunt and Smith (2006:76) as the individual, entity, inter-relationships, and environment.

The principles of governance have the tendency towards crossing boundaries and open-ended situations subject to negotiations (Williams, 1982) and values adhered. The governance principles are the platform to develop the governance, monitoring and evaluating instruments to apply in self-assessments and audits. These governance principles can be used to design and implement the institutional transformation of governance that must be legitimate, inclusive, transparent, accountable, fair, functional, structurally integrated, adaptable, capable, etc. A corporate governance principle has proposed for an evaluation of governance arrangements at Australian regional NRM organizations (Turnbull, 2005).

The common assumption that indigenous local cultures across the diverse settings of nation states are different that common design principles underpinning governance cannot infer needs to be rectify (Hunt and Smith 2007). The designing of these principles is a critical factor in strengthening indigenous local governance.

The existence of complex diversity and several different governance cultures operating in a broad field of governance such as the contested state governance. Organizations may embed the governance culture by promoting the norms and values such as fairness, respect, accountability, commitment, teamwork, autonomy, etc., which reinforce the legitimate collective governance. All these values and qualities are regarded as the collective support for the organizational cultural identity (Armstrong, 2007: 75, 2003) emphasized by members to maintain a style of governance. The governance culture is a process of building transformative institutional capital supported not only by deliberative leadership but also by the extended family organizations.

This governance socio-interculturality is required to attend the diversity of cultures. Socio-intercultural communication agency supported by local media can raise awareness of cultural diversity and socio-intercultural dialogue and the benefits practicing a cultural pluralism approach. Socio-intercultural dialogue challenges assumptions confronting different values, knowledge, worldviews, and beliefs, as well as exploring visions and aspirations of people to bring new and creative possibilities of living (UNESCO, 2008c) and providing an experiential opportunity to forge cultural links and knowledge exchanges. The socio-intercultural dialogue is valued for shaping social and cultural change processes (UNESCO, 2008a, 2008b).

Formal governance solutions must be included in an official document previously gained agreement. Forms of global governance have an impact on organizational strategies and therefore on the evolution of social norms and interactions at micro and private governance levels beyond the ideology, power, and efficiency of the nation-states. Socio-interculturality embraces the differences tolerated by the nation state by reducing the power asymmetries promoted by socio-intercultural projects determined by political and ideological frameworks. The state must make decisions on the value and benefits of resolving complex governance issues to facilitate the design and implementation of innovative strategies and policies. Governance was shunted aside when public bureaucrats at local governments took over it with extraordinary powers (Siewart 2007) after the implemented strategies of government reforms (Smith, 2004).

Local indigenous governance has been in continued policy complexity and contestation to the nation state that has not been able to deal with the indigenous identity and their political consequences on treating and control the affairs (Arabena, 2005: 28). The socio-intercultural process changes in complex multi-sited governance systems. Since the colonial times, indigenous local governance has been considered underdeveloped, unknowable, and invisible.

Transparent governance may facilitate early detection and correction of any policy mistakes and misallocations, an approach that may be demanding and time inefficient, it is expected that bureaucrats commit to this governance mechanism. A counterproductive policy implementation to the achievement of legitimate governance sometimes is maintained either by self-interest of negligence by policy makers or officials. When local government authorities are in organizational bankruptcy and perceived in parlous state constituting a stark crisis of governance (Behrendt, et al. 2007, Sanders, 2003, 2004 and Smith1995, 1996, 2007).

In a norm-based approach of organizational governance, the converging model may involve high costs of transnational regulations driven by ideological macro-social foundations of a transnational governance imposed on micro foundations of a sociological approach (Bernstein and Cashore, 2007). Organizational governance has formal and informal components, but informal governance is at the individual level working through the behavioral processes of conflicts, appeals, rewards, sanctions, etc., personal style, individual and collective identities, decision making, etc. Organizational governance also calls repeatedly for better evaluation of effectiveness despite the experiencing of internal tensions and the presence of complexity and uncertainty.

The improvement of the internal organizational governance arrangements can be the result of a negotiating empowering governance system in socio-intercultural spaces. The construction of values and responsibilities varies in function of the ideological political spectrum and the state model prevailing in government although some of the essential elements are given in a governance framework.

RESULTS

This study is based on the analysis focusing on the conceptual, theoretical, and methodological issues related to contract governance and transaction costs to be able to highlight the implications of policy decision making and strategic governance. 90 conceptual and theoretical research papers were analyzed based on the variables of the research, institutional transformation, and participatory governance. Out of these analyses, a reflective process leads to the following tendencies:

The spatial resources used by associations and organizations in participatory governance to advocate the reconstruction of spaces and development of a model of governance and public-civil partnership, that as users of spaces invest in the transformation into contemporary socio intercultural institutional governance. Institutional participatory governance is based on the interactions between public actors, organizations, and civil society, enabling the citizens to build their capacities to be used as democratic instruments for decision making to transform and improve the democratic quality of institutions.

Participation in institutional development governance faces structural, cultural, and transformative challenges. Cultural participation is a conceptual, operational, and interpretative foundations of cultural human rights based on institutional participatory governance policies such as the encouragement of social inclusive transformation. Social and cultural capital frameworks are fundamental resources for creation and development of settings based on institutional participatory governance, transforming territorial and locational communities.

The new institutions and innovations in public policies have transformative potential. Transformation of institutional participatory governance functions is remedied by operational functioning and established to the different actors and stakeholders involved in the non-institutional and institutional existing positions. Socio-intercultural participatory governance implies a critical awareness and respect for other cultural values that reflect diversity in the public transformations of public policies, institutions, public spaces, and civic culture that enable initiative and projects.

Policy scholarly agendas can help to understand the potential of institutions of participatory governance to transform the economic, social, and sustainable environment in which they are embedded. Policy making and activism are concerned about the specific contexts that better suite participatory governance to reframe process of transformation, although there is lack of knowledge about types of institutions given the limited resources available for institutional building.

CONCLUDING REMARKS

This analysis concludes that the institutional transformations of participatory governance have been sourced and evolved into a governance structure to govern the behaviors of the communities, organizations, leaderships, and members.

It is needed more robust institutional participatory governance arrangements to cope with this time of pandemic crisis around the world. The traditional governance arrangements need to be transformed at all levels in such a way that the multilateral authority of the nation state is being supplanted by new socio-political actors, economic agents, and other multi-stakeholder governance arrangement systems.

The institutional transformations of participatory governance have been sourced and evolved into a structures to govern the behaviors of the governments at all levels, communities, organizations, leaderships and members The practice of organizational governance should have to be more open to compromise and capacity building enable to create and develop more trust and autonomy to outweigh the benefits of outcomes performed by the synergetic support between the stakeholders, organizations and governments.

A broader organizational governance review may require including various local government agencies that may lead to make generalized recommendations that may not respond to clarify specific nature of the problems and the possible solutions to rectify them.

Imposition of governance solutions to internal bodies because the organization had received funding to carry out the review may bring more problems than solutions and the outcomes may have limited traction (Hunt and Smith 2007: xvi).

REFERENCES

Abbott, K. W., Genschel, P., Snidal, D., & Zangl, B. (2010) *IOs as Orchestrators*. Paper presented at the 7th Pan-European Conference on International Relations, Stockholm, Sweden.

Abdallah-Pretceille, M. (2006). Socio-interculturalism as a paradigm for thinking about diversity. *Socio-intercultural Education*, *17*(5), 475–483. doi:10.1080/14675980601065764

Alexander, E. R. (1995). *How Organizations Act Together: Interorganizational Coordination in Theory and Practice*. Gordon & Breach.

Ang, S., & Inkpen, A. C. (2008). Cultural intelligence and offshore outsourcing success: A framework of organization-level socio-intercultural capability. *Decision Sciences*, *2008*(39), 337–358. doi:10.1111/j.1540-5915.2008.00195.x

Arabena, K. (2005). *Not fit for modern Australian society. Aboriginal and Torres Strait Island people and the new arrangements for the administration of Indigenous Affairs*. Research Discussion Paper No. 16. AIATSIS.

Armstrong, L. (2003). *Financial management and business systems: the backbone of an effectively resourced capacity for governance*. Paper presented to the Building Effective Indigenous Governance Conference. http://www.nt.gov.au/cdsca/indigenous conference/web/html/papers.html

Armstrong, L. (2007). Finding Australia's soul: rebuilding our Indigenous communities. *The Circle*, *1*, 74–6. https://www.socialventures.com.au/files/pdf/TC%20mag%20Leah%20Armstrong.pdf

Bagshaw, G. (1977). *Analysis of Local Government in a Multi-Clan Community* [BA (Hons) Dissertation]. Department of Anthropology, The University of Adelaide.

Bagwell, S., & Evans, G. (2012). *Public Space Management, report to the socio-intercultural cities programme*. Council of Europe Publishing. www.coe.int/socio-interculturaLcitiezs

Baron, C. (2003). La gouvernance: Débats autour d'un concept polysémique. *Droit Social*, (54), 329–351. doi:10.3917/drs.054.0329

Behrendt, L., McCausland, R., Williams, G., Reilly, A., & McMillan, M. (2007). The promise of regional governance for Aboriginal and Torres Strait Islander communities. *Ngiya: Talk the Law. Governance in Indigenous Communities*, *1*, 126–166.

Bernstein, S., & Cashore, B. (2007). Can Non-State Global Governance be Legitimate? *Regulation & Governance*, *1*(4), 347–371. doi:10.1111/j.1748-5991.2007.00021.x

Beyer, J., & Hassel, A. (2002). The market for corporate control and financial internationalization of German firms. *Economy and Society*, 31.

Börzel, T., & Risse, T. (2010). Governance without a state: can it work? *Regulation and Governance, 4*(2), 113–34.

Bresser, R., & Millonig, K. (2003). Institutional capital: Competitive advantage considering the new institutionalism in organisational theory. *Schmalenbach Business Review*, *55*(3), 220–241. doi:10.1007/BF03396675

Cashore, B., Auld, G., Bernstein, S. and McDermott, C. (2007). Can non-state governance "ratchet up" global environmental standards? Lessons from the forest sector. *Review of European Community, and International Environmental Law, 16*(2), 158–72.

Christie, M. (2007). Knowledge management and natural resource management. In M. K. Luckert, B. Campbell, & J. T. Gorman (Eds.), *Investing in indigenous natural resource management* (pp. 86–90). Charles Darwin University Press.

Clifford, J. (1997). *Routes: Travel and Translation in the Twentieth Century*. Harvard University Press.

Coll, A. C. (2004). *The socio-intercultural challenge*. Pipal Tree.

Cornell, S., & Begay, M. (2004). *What is cultural match and why is it so important? Lessons from 14 years of the Harvard Project*. Paper presented at the Building Effective Governance Conference, Jabiru.

Cornell, S., & Kalt, J. P. (2000). Where's the glue? Institutional and cultural foundations of American Indian economic development. *Journal of Socio-Economics*, *29*(5), 443–470. doi:10.1016/S1053-5357(00)00080-9

Cross, S. (2008) *The Scale Politics of Reconciliation* [PhD. Dissertation]. Department of Human Geography, Macquarie University.

Davidson, J., & Stratford, E. (2000). *Building the knowledge base of the social and institutional dimensions of natural resource management*. Land and Water Resources Research and Development Corporation.

Davis, G., & Rhodes, R. A. W. (2000). From hierarchy to contracts and back again: reforming the Australian public service. In M. Keating, J. Wann, & P. Weller (Eds.), Institutions on the Edge? Capacity for Governance. Allen & Unwin.

de Alcantara, C. H. (1998). Uses and abuses of the concept of governance. *International Social Science Journal, 155*(155), 105–113. doi:10.1111/1468-2451.00113

Dentico, N. (2020). Editorial: The Vital Pedagogy of the New Coronavirus. *Development, 63*(2-4), 145–149. doi:10.105741301-020-00279-5 PMID:33311953

Dingwerth, K., & Pattberg, P. (2009). World Politics and Organizational Fields: The Case of Transnational Sustainability Governance. *European Journal of International Relations, 15*(4), 707–743. doi:10.1177/1354066109345056

Gaudin, J.-P. (2002). *Pourquoi la gouvernance?* Presses de Sciences Po. doi:10.3917cpo.gaudi.2002.01

Gluckman, M. (1968). The utility of the equilibrium model in the study of social change. *American Anthropologist, 70*(2), 219–237. doi:10.1525/aa.1968.70.2.02a00010

Graham, J., Amos, B., & Plumptre, T. (2003). *Governance principles for protected areas in the 21st century.* Institute on Governance, Parks Canada, and the Canadian International Development Agency.

Habermas, J. (1981). *The theory of communicative action: Reason and the rationalization of society.* Beacon Press.

Hair, J. F. J., Black, W. C., Babin, B. J., & Anderson, R. E. (2010). *Multivariate Data Analysis* (7th ed.). Prentice Hall.

Handley, S. M., & Angst, C. M. (2015). The impact of culture on the relationship between governance and opportunism in outsourcing relationships. *Strategic Management Journal, 2015*(36), 1412–1434. doi:10.1002mj.2300

Hasenclever, A., Mayer, P., & Rittberger, V. (1997). *Theories of International Regimes.* Cambridge University Press. doi:10.1017/CBO9780511521720

Hoepner, M. (2001). *Corporate governance in transition: ten empirical findings on shareholder value and industrial relations.* Discussion Paper 01/5. Max-Planck-Institut für Gesellschaftsforschung.

Hoepner, M., & Jackson, G. (2001). *An emergent market for corporate control? The Mannesmann takeover and German corporate governance.* MPIfG Discussion Paper 01/4. MPIf.G.

Howitt, R. (2001). *Rethinking resource management: Justice, sustainability, and indigenous peoples.* Routledge.

Howlett, M., & Rayner, J. (2006). Convergence and divergence in 'new governance' arrangements: Evidence from European integrated natural resource strategies. *Journal of Public Policy, 26*(2), 167–189. doi:10.1017/S0143814X06000511

Hulme, M. (2010). Moving beyond climate change. *Environment, 52*(3), 15–19.

Hunt, J., & Smith, D. (2006). *Building Indigenous community governance in Australia: preliminary research findings.* CAEPR Working Paper No. 31. CAEPR, ANU.

Hunt, J., & Smith, D. E. (2007). *Indigenous Community Governance Project: Year two research findings.* CAEPR Working Paper No. 36. CAEPR, CASS, ANU.

Katzenstein, P. J. (1996). Introduction: Alternative Perspectives on National Security. In P. J. Katzenstein (Ed.), *The Culture of National Security* (pp. 1–32). Columbia University Press.

Keohane, R.O., & Victor, D. (2011). The regime complex for climate change. *Perspectives on Politics, 9*(1), 7–23.

Kesteven, S., & Smith, D. E. (1984). Contemporary Land-Tenure in Western Arnhem Land: An Investigation of Traditional Ownership, Resource Development and Royalties. Report to the Australian Institute of Aboriginal Studies and the Northern Land Council.

Kooiman, J. (2003). *Governing as Governance.* Sage Publications. doi:10.4135/9781446215012

Lane, C. (2004). *Institutional transformation and system change: changes in corporate governance of Germancorporations* (Reihe Soziologie / Institut für Höhere Studien, Abt. Soziologie, 65). Wien: Institut für Höhere Studien (IHS). https://nbn-resolving.org/urn:nbn:de:0168-ssoar-220637

LeRoy, G. (2005). *The Great American Jobs Scam: Corporate Tax Dodgingand the Myth of Job Creation.* Berrett-Koehler Publishers.

Marika, R., Ngurruwutthun, D., & White, L. (1992). Always together, yaka gäna: Participatory research at Yirrkala as part of the development of a Yolngu education. *Convergence (Toronto), 25,* 23–39.

Mattingly, C. (2006). Pocahontas goes to the clinic: Popular culture as lingua franca in a cultural borderland. *American Anthropologist, 108*(3), 494–501. doi:10.1525/aa.2006.108.3.494 PMID:20706562

Morgan, G., Rocha, G., & Poynting, S. (2005). Grafting Cultures: Longing and Belonging in Immigrants' Ottaviano G.I.P., G. Peri (2005), Cities and cultures. *Journal of Urban Economics, 58,* 304–337.

Morphy, H. (2007). *Becoming Art: Exploring Cross-Cultural Categories.* Berg.

Muller, S. (2008). Accountability constructions, contestations, and implications: Insights from working in a yolngu cross-cultural institution, Australia. *Geography Compass, 2*(2), 1–19. doi:10.1111/j.1749-8198.2007.00087.x

Newman, J., Barnes, M., Sullivan, H., & Knops, A. (2004). Public participation and collaborative governance. *Journal of Social Policy, 33*(2), 203–223. doi:10.1017/S0047279403007499

O'Donnell, G. (1999). Horizontal accountability in new democracies. In A. Schedler, L. Diamond, & M. F. Plattner (Eds.), *The Self-Restraining State: Power and Accountability in the New Democracies.* Lynne Rienner Publishers. doi:10.1515/9781685854133-004

O'Malley, P. (1998). Indigenous governances. In M. Dean & B. Hindess (Eds.), *Governing Australia: Studies in contemporary rationalities of government* (pp. 156–172). Cambridge University Press.

O'Sullivan, M. A. (2000). *Contests for Corporate Control. Corporate governance and economic performance in the United States and Germany*. Oxford University Press.

Oliver, C. (1997). Sustainable competitive advantage: Combining institutional and resource-based views. *Strategic Management Journal, 18*(9), 697–713. doi:10.1002/(SICI)1097-0266(199710)18:9<697::AID-SMJ909>3.0.CO;2-C

Pattberg, P., & Stripple, J. (2008). Beyond the public and private divide: remapping transnational climate governance in the 21st century. *International Environmental Agreements: Politics, Law, and Economics, 84*(4), 367–88.

Plumptre, T., & Graham, J. (1999). *Governance and Good Governance: International and Aboriginal Perspectives*. Institute on Governance.

Porter, T. (2009). Global governance as configurations of state/non-state activity. In J. Whitman (Ed.), *Palgrave advances in global governance*. Palgrave Macmillan. doi:10.1057/9780230245310_5

Rhodes, R. (2005). The unholy trinity of governance. The Blake Dawson Waldron Lecture, National Museum of Australia, Canberra.

Ribot, J. C. (2002). *Democratic decentralization of natural resources: Institutionalizing popular participation*. World Resources Institute.

Rosenau, J. N. (2000). Change, complexity, and governance in globalizing space. In J. Pierre (Ed.), *Debating governance* (pp. 167–200). Oxford University Press.

Sanders, W. (2003). *Participation and representation in the 2002 ATSIC elections*. CAEPR Discussion Paper No. 252. CAEPR, ANU.

Sanders, W. (2004). *Thinking about Indigenous community governance*. CAEPR Discussion Paper No. 262. CAEPR, ANU.

Schacter, M. (2000). *When accountability fails: a framework for diagnosis and action. Policy Brief No. 9*. Institute on Governance.

Schedler, A. (1999). Restraining the state: conflicts and agents of accountability. In A. Schedler, L. Diamond, & M. F. Plattner (Eds.), *The Self-Restraining State: Power and Accountability in the New Democracies*. Lynne Rienner Publishers. doi:10.1515/9781685854133-021

Scott, J. C. (1998). *Seeing Like a State: How Certain Schemes to Improve the Human Condition Have Failed*. Yale University Press.

Selman, P. (2001). Social capital, sustainability, and environmental planning. *Planning Theory & Practice, 2*(1), 13–30. doi:10.1080/14649350122850

Siewart, R. (2007). *Ministerial powers to seize assets of service providers in prescribed areas within the Northern Territory*. Background Briefing, Parliament House, Canberra. http://www.rachelsiewert.org.au/files/campaigns/extras/Briefing_on_NT_seizure_powers.pdf

Simoulin, V. (2003). La gouvernance et l'action publique: Le succès d'une forme simmélienne. *Droit Social*, (54), 307–328. doi:10.3917/drs.054.0307

Smith, D. E. (1995). Representative politics and the new wave of native title organisations. In J. Finlayson & D. E. Smith (Eds.), Native Title: Emerging Issues for Research, Policy and Practice. CAEPR Research Monograph No. 10. CAEPR, ANU.

Smith, D. E. (1996). From cultural diversity to regionalism: The political culture of difference in ATSIC. In P. Sullivan (Ed.), Shooting the Banker: Essays on ATSIC and Self-determination. North Australia Research Unit, ANU.

Smith, D. E. (2004). *From Gove to governance: Reshaping Indigenous governance in the Northern Territory.* CAEPR Discussion Paper No. 265. CAEPR, ANU.

Smith, D. E. (2007). Networked governance: Issues of process, policy, and power in a West Arnhem Land regional initiative. *Ngiya: Talk the Law. Governance in Indigenous Communities*, *1*, 24–52.

Stoker, G. (1998). Governance as theory: Five propositions. *International Social Science Journal*, *155*(155), 17–28. doi:10.1111/1468-2451.00106

Stratford, E., & Davidson, J. (2002). Capital assets and intercultural borderlands: Socio-cultural challenges for natural resource management. *Journal of Environmental Management*, *66*(4), 429–440. doi:10.1006/jema.2002.0597 PMID:12503497

Streeck, W. (2001). *The transformation of corporate organization in Europe: an overview.* MPIfG Working Paper 01/8. MPIfG.

Sullivan, P. (2005). Searching for the socio-intercultural, searching for the culture, in The Independent Commission for Good Governance in Public Services (TICGG). *The good governance standard for public services*. http://www.opm.co.uk/icggps/download_upload/Standard.pdf

Thelen, K. (2000). Timing and temporality in the analysis of institutional evolution and change. *Studies in American Political Development*, *14*(1), 101–108. doi:10.1017/S0898588X00213035

Turnbull, W. (2005). *Evaluation of current governance arrangements to support regional investment under the NHT and NAP*. Departments of Environment and Heritage and Agriculture, Fisheries and Forestry.

United Nations Educational, Scientific and Cultural Organization (UNESCO). (2008a). Background Note. A Review of Education for Sustainable Development (ESD) Policies from a Cultural Diversity and socio-intercultural Dialogue Perspective. Unpublished document. UNESCO/CLT/CPD/CPO20/11/2008. Paris: UNESCO.

United Nations Educational, Scientific and Cultural Organization (UNESCO). (2008b). UNESCO Concept Note. Towards a New Cultural Policy Profile. UNESCO/CLT/CPD 01/08/2008. Paris: UNESCO.

United Nations Educational, Scientific and Cultural Organization (UNESCO). (2008c). ESD Lens, version 2, draft 1: Comments from a cultural diversity perspective. Unpublished document. Paris: UNESCO.

Williams, N. M. (1982). A boundary is to cross observations on Yolngu boundaries and permission. In N. M. Williams & E. S. Hunn (Eds.), *Resource Managers: North American and Australian Hunter-Gatherers*. Australian Institute of Aboriginal Studies Press.

Williamson, O. E. (1991). Comparative economic organization: The analysis of discrete structural alternatives. *Administrative Science Quarterly*, *1991*(2), 269–296. doi:10.2307/2393356

Williamson, O. E. (1996). *The Mechanisms of Governance*. Oxford University Press.

Williamson, O. E. (2008). Outsourcing: Transaction cost economics and supply chain management. *The Journal of Supply Chain Management*, *2008*(44), 5–16. doi:10.1111/j.1745-493X.2008.00051.x

Zhu, Q., Sarkis, J., & Lai, K.-H. (2012). Examining the effects of green supply chain management practices and their mediations on performance improvements. *International Journal of Production Research*, *2012*(50), 1377–1394. doi:10.1080/00207543.2011.571937

Chapter 7
Labor Management Relations in the Public Sector

Sam Hensel
Service Employees International Union, Local 73, USA

ABSTRACT

This chapter addresses public administration in the context of the government as an employer. In doing so, the relationship between a public employer and its employees is at issue. To understand public sector labor relations requires a basic understanding of legal principles that govern a public employer's rights and obligations to its employees. While this chapter does not, and cannot, address every aspect of labor management relations in the public sector, it provides an overview of the most important aspects of this relationship and how government can successfully function as an employer.

INTRODUCTION

The work of public administration cannot be done without a robust and dynamic workforce. Public sector workers, from police officers to firefighters, teachers, clerks, aides, and more form the backbone of government's day to day functions and provide for the vast majority of daily interactions between the people and their government. After a long period of oftentimes violent labor unrest, the passage of the federal National Labor Relations Act (NLRA) in 1935 granted most private sector employees the right to unionize and collectively bargain, and to otherwise band together for better working terms and conditions of employment with or without a union. National Labor Relations Act of 1935, 29 U.S.C. § 151, *et. seq* (1935). But the NLRA excluded public sector employees for a number of reasons. 29 U.S.C. § 152(2) (1935). Since the NLRA's passage, public sector workers have made great strides across the country in gaining the right to collectively bargain for the terms and conditions of their employment state by state. "Collective Bargaining in the Public Sector," *97 Harv. L. Rev.* 1676, 1680-81 (1984). Most states provide at least some public employees certain rights to collectively bargain, or to at least join a labor union. Id., n.30. For states that do not expressly grant the right to be a member of an employee association, they are nonetheless protected in doing so by the First Amendment's guarantee of freedom of association. Thomas v. Collins, 323 U.S. 516 (1945). Each state's laws are different, and therefore it is impossible to

DOI: 10.4018/978-1-6684-2314-1.ch007

summarize public sector labor-management relations uniformly. This chapter will seek to address public sector labor-management relations under regimens more generous towards public employees than those where employees have fewer rights. This chapter will also discuss many of the statutory rights employees have regardless of whether they are empowered to collectively bargain.

Collective bargaining is the process in which a labor organization or union and an employer negotiate over the hours, wages, and other terms and conditions of employment for employees. The NLRA guarantees employees the right to unionize and collectively bargain, and specifically exempts public sector employees from its protections. 29 U.S.C. § 152(2), 157 (1935). Accordingly, many states and some local jurisdictions have elected to pass their own laws to create public sector collective bargaining regimens for their own workers. Those laws are mostly modeled around the National Labor Relations Act and guarantee public sector workers many of the same rights, and impose many of the same obligations on unions and employers. Separate law governs public sector collective bargaining for certain federal employees. Federal Service Labor-Management Relations Statute, 5 U.S.C. § 7101, *et. seq.*(1970). This chapter will discuss the important aspects of labor management relations in the public sector and how public administrators can navigate and manage collective bargaining relationships.

The foundation of collective bargaining in the public (and private) sector is more fundamental than just the right to unionize and collectively bargain. It is the right to engage in concerted activities for the purpose of mutual aid or protection. An employee's engagement in concerted activity for the purpose of mutual aid and protection encompasses a broad category of activity. Employees have a right to discuss the terms and conditions of employment with their co-workers, including by sharing salary or pay information. Niles Co., Inc., 328 NLRB 411, 414 (1999). They may discuss health care and retirement benefits, disciplinary investigations (with some exceptions), scheduling, staffing levels, layoffs, workplace safety, and more. Flex Frac Logistics, LLC, 358 NLRB 1131 (2012). The discussion of any of these employment terms is fundamental to employees' right to communicate with each other before engaging in activity meant to better their lot and demand more from their employer. Employees have a right to bring their concerns directly to their employer if their doing so is meant to benefit employees as a whole. National Labor Relations Board v. Washington Aluminum Co., 370 U.S. 9 (1962). Employees may engage in concerted activity off or outside of work or while not on the clock, and with limitations during work and on work premises. Industrial Wire Products, Inc., 317 NLRB 190 (1995). Employees may generally wear pins, buttons, stickers, and other insignia that express their views regarding their terms and conditions of employment. Republic Aviation Corp. v. National Labor Relations Board, 324 U.S. 793 (1945). Employees also have a right to take their concerns about the terms and conditions of employment to outside third parties, such as the press, elected officials, customers or patrons of the employer, and others. Kinder-Care Learning Centers, 299 NLRB 1171 (1990). In addition to these rights being protected by labor law, in the case of public sector employees, these rights are more often than not likewise protected by the First Amendment right to free speech. Thomas v. Collins, 323 U.S. 516 (1945). Of course, employees also have the right to refrain from any or all of such activities, just as they have the right to vote against unionization. National Labor Relations Act, 29 U.S.C. § 157 (1935).

It is critical that public employers understand and respect these rights. This chapter will discuss the risks and consequences for employers who retaliate against employees later on. That being said, there are limitations on what employees may do. Some employee conduct crosses the line so that it is no longer protected by law, thus allowing employers to discipline or discharge them, subject to any other applicable limitations or restrictions. This activity can include disparaging a public or private employer's reputation or services, use language that is malicious, profane, demonstrably false, or stated with calculated intent to financially harm the employer. NLRB v. Local Union No. 1229, 346 U.S. 464 (1953). Needless to say, violence or unlawful threats as a form of concerted activity is not protected. NLRB v. Fansteel Metallurgical Corp., 306 U.S. 240 (1939). But outside of these exceptions, employees are free to band together to advocate for themselves and each other for purposes of getting better working conditions. Though there are exceptions among public employees, these legal protections only apply to non-supervisory employees. National Labor Relations Act, 29 U.S.C. § 152(3) (1935).

Supervisors, managers, and confidential employees generally do not have these legal protections, and by extension do not have a right to unionize, for the most part in public sector labor-relations, though there are exceptions. 29 U.S.C. § 152(3) (1935). In Illinois, for example, police sergeants have been permitted to unionize. Illinois Public Labor Relations Act, 5 ILCS 315/3(r)(1); Policemen's Benevolent and Protective Association, Unit #5, 36 PERI ¶ 113 (ILRB 2020). Many have called for school principals within the Chicago Public Schools system, who are obviously supervisors, to be given the right to unionize. Samantha Smylie, *Chicago principals are again trying to unionize. Will new momentum help?*, Chalkbeat Chicago (Mar. 2, 2022, 4:48 PM), https://chicago.chalkbeat.org/2022/3/2/22958917/chicago-principals-unionize-illinois-legislature. But in most circumstances, employers enjoy a right to rely upon their supervisors, managers, and confidential employees (such as executive assistants) in the execution of labor management relations. National Labor Relations Act, 29 U.S.C. 152(3). Allowing supervisors and managers the right to unionize would frustrate this managerial prerogative.

In many states, there is an official labor relations board, or government agency tasked with enforcement of public sector labor laws, be it for state, municipal, or otherwise local public sector employers and their employees. These labor relations boards largely mirror and are modeled after the National Labor Relations Board, which is tasked with enforcement of the NLRA and the adjudication of questions of law under the NLRA in lieu of courts. "Collective Bargaining in the Public Sector," *97 Harv. L. Rev.* 1676, 1680-81 (1984); 29 U.S.C. § 153 (1935). Illinois, for instance, has both a standard Illinois Labor Relations Board and an Illinois Educational Labor Relations Board strictly for public universities, school districts, community colleges, and other educational public employers, and their employees. Illinois Public Labor Relations Act, 5 ILCS 315/5; Illinois Educational Labor Relations Act, 115 ILCS 5/5. These labor relations boards are run by a board of members appointed and confirmed by state elected officials, and just like the National Labor Relations Board employ professional staff dedicated to enforcement of labor relations statutes. Id. They largely perform two functions: (1) processing petitions for labor unions to represent or no longer represent employees, and (2) investigating and prosecuting employers and unions for violations of labor relations statutes. Id. These violations are commonly known as an "unfair labor practices" or ULPs. Illinois Public Labor Relations Act, 5 ILCS 315/10; Illinois Educational Labor Relations Act, 115 ILCS 5/14.

Labor unions are not for profit organizations that exist to represent employees for purposes of collective bargaining with their employers for the terms and conditions of their employment, and for the enforcement of those terms when a collective bargaining agreement exists. Labor unions are frequently organized into different chapters. These chapters are most commonly referred to as locals. Some locals represent exclusively public sector employees, while some represent exclusively private sector employees. Many represent a mixture of both. While locals are each their own organization with their own constitution and bylaws, they are each ultimately subservient to their parent organization, with its own set of constitution and bylaws the locals must adhere to. The dynamics of internal union affairs and governance are beyond the scope of this chapter.

REPRESENTATION PETITIONS AND UNFAIR LABOR PRACTICES

When a labor union seeks to represent a unit of unrepresented employees, they must have support from a majority of the employees in the unit of employees they seek to represent. National Labor Relations Act, 29 U.S.C. § 159(a). Support for a labor union by employees often manifest in the form of cards signed by the employees stating that they wish to be represented by the labor union for purposes of collectively bargaining over the terms and conditions of their employment. Generally, if at least 30% of the employees have signed cards, the labor union may file a petition to represent the group of employees. National Labor Relations Act, 29 U.S.C. § 159(e)(1). After the union files the petition, the employer may voluntarily recognize the union, and the union will be certified to represent the employees provided that they have cards signed by a majority of employees within the proposed bargaining unit. National Labor Relations Act, 29 U.S.C. § 159(c)(1)(A). If the employer does not wish to voluntarily recognize the union, then the union must prevail in an election among the employees. National Labor Relations Act, 29 U.S.C. § 159(c)(1)(B). To win the election and be certified as the employees' exclusive bargaining representative, more than 50% of employees in the bargaining unit must vote in favor of unionizing for the labor union to prevail. Id.

Some states, including Illinois, allow for an election for a labor union to represent public employees to be bypassed through a "card check" procedure. This means that, if a labor union submits signed cards from a majority of employees in a bargaining unit, and so long as there is an appropriate unit for collective bargaining, the labor union is certified as the exclusive bargaining representative. Illinois Public Labor Relations Act, 5 ILCS 315/9(a-5); Illinois Educational Labor Relations Act,115 ILCS 5/7(b). The rationale for this rule is that if a majority of employees have signed cards that expressly state that they wish to be represented by the union, then there is little purpose in holding a vote to determine that very same question.

Labor relations boards also oversee other petitions that may be filed by unions, employers, and employees. These include petitions to decertify unions as the employees' representatives, petitions for unions to take over the right to exclusively represent a group of employees from another union (a process frequently and derogatorily known as a "raid"), and "self-determination" petitions to add new employee job titles to bargaining units already represented by a labor union. National Labor Relations Act, 29 U.S.C. § 159.

During organizing campaigns, employers have a right to talk to their employees about their perspectives on the advantages or disadvantages of organizing a union. National Labor Relations Act, 29 U.S.C. § 159(c). However, these conversations have their limit and cannot cross the line into becoming threatening or coercive. Id. Employers may not, for example, offer promises of higher wages or better benefits in exchange for not unionizing, or threaten to cause layoffs if the unionization effort succeeds. Dyncorp, 343 NLRB 1197, 1998 (2004), *affd.* Fed. Appx. 419 (6th Cir. 2007); Baker Machinery Co., 184 NLRB 358 (1970). Employers may generally not ask employees how they are going to vote. Struksnes Constr. Co., 165 NLRB 1062 (1967). In Illinois, it is illegal for a public employer to hire any third party, such as a "union avoidance" consultant, to speak to employees about unionizing. 5 ILCS 5/10(a)(6); 115 ILCS 114(a)(9).

Once an employer either voluntarily recognizes a labor union or once a labor union wins an election with majority support, the labor board will certify that union as the exclusive bargaining representative for the employees described in the certification. National Labor Relations Act, 29 U.S.C. § 159(e)(1).

THE PROCESS OF COLLECTIVE BARGAINING

Once a labor relations board certifies a union as the exclusive collective bargaining representative of a group of employees, the employer and union must bargain with one another over mandatory subjects of bargaining. National Labor Relations Act, 29 U.S.C. 159(d). That is, wages, hours, and other terms and conditions of employment such as employee benefits, staffing levels, discipline and discharge, and more. Id. Other subjects of bargaining, known as permissive subjects, may be bargained for in a collective bargaining agreement, but are not required to be. Central City Educ. Ass'n v. Illinois Educational Labor Relations Bd., 149 Ill.2d 496 (1992). If the terms of a permissive subject are not written into a collective bargaining agreement, then the public employer may unilaterally implement those terms of employment as it sees fit without bargaining with the union. Id. There are also prohibited subjects of bargaining, which the parties may not bargain over because doing so would be illegal. International Brotherhood of Teamsters Local 700 v. Illinois Labor Relations Board, 2017 IL App (1st) 152993.

With the duty to bargain over mandatory subjects comes a duty to bargain in good faith. National Labor Relations Act, 29 U.S.C. § 158(d). It is illegal for either an employer or a union to refuse to bargain in good faith. National Labor Relations Act, 29 U.S.C. § 158(a)(5), (b)(3). Bad faith bargaining can take on many forms. These include surface bargaining, in which a party goes through the motions of bargaining without any actual interest in reaching agreement. See Richfield Hospitality, Inc., 369 NLRB No. 111 (2020). Another example of bad faith bargaining is regressive bargaining, in which a party makes a proposal that is more favorable for themselves than a proposal they had already offered when the purpose is to frustrate efforts to reach agreement. Management & Training Corp., 366 NLRB No. 134 (2018). For example, if an employer proposes that employees make an hourly wage of $20 per hour and then the union rejects the proposal, it would be regressive for the employer to then propose their hourly wage be $18 per hour, since they already indicated a willingness to pay $20 per hour. A union or employer may also bargain in bad faith by conditioning the bargaining of a mandatory subject over the negotiation of a permissive subject. This too is illegal. NLRB v. Wooster Div. of Borg-Warner Corp., 356 U.S. 342 (1958). While the parties are not required to reach an agreement or any specific type of agreement, the legal duty to bargain in good faith drives the parties to work together to negotiate a final agreement. NLRB v. American National Insurance Co., 343 U.S. 395 (1952). When the parties reach agreement, there is an obligation on the employer to reduce that agreement to writing. The failure to do so is likewise a violation of the duty to bargain in good faith. Georgia Pacific Corporation, 275 NLRB No. 17 (1985).

Public employers are also frequently called upon to respond to information requests from the union. The purpose of information requests is to provide the union with the knowledge it needs to negotiate from an informed position and fulfill its obligation to represent its members. An employer's refusal to respond to an information request from a union it bargains with is generally illegal and stems from the refusal to bargain in good faith. NLRB v. Truitt Mfg. Co., 351 U.S. 149 (1956). For example, an employer that asserts it cannot afford to pay employees the wage that a union asks for at the bargaining table cannot then refuse to turn over their financial records that would support their claim of inability to pay. Employers are excused from providing information responsive to such requests generally only when the request is unduly burdensome, not relevant to the union's obligation to represent its employees, or if providing it would be illegal. Courtesy Bus Co., Inc., 354 NLRB No. 66 (2009). The duty to bargain in good faith also prohibits employers from engaging in "direct dealing" with employees in a bargaining unit. "Direct dealing" serves to bypass employees' exclusive bargaining representative when discussing terms and conditions of employment and frustrates the purpose of the labor-management relations under the law. Mercy Health Partners, 358 NLRB No. 69 (2012).

Sometimes, the parties will, after bargaining in good faith, reach a bona fide impasse and be unable to agree with one another on mandatory subjects of bargaining. What happens next depends on what is permitted by state or local law. Some jurisdictions prohibit strikes and will allow public employers to unilaterally impose their own terms and conditions of employment. FLA. STAT. § 447.403, 447.505 Others will also allow certain unions to strike. Illinois Public Labor Relations Act, 5 ILCS 315/17. And others, particularly where public safety employees like police officers and firefighters are involved, allow for interest arbitration. Illinois Public Labor Relations Act, 5 ILCS 315/14. Interest arbitration will be discussed more in depth later in this chapter.

Union Security and Dues Deduction Agreements

In the private sector and until recently in the public sector, labor unions would frequently negotiate for collective bargaining agreements to have "union security" clauses. William Gould, *How Five Young Men Channeled Nine Old Men: Janus and the High Court's Anti-Labor Policymaking*, 53 U.S.F. L. Rev. 209, 218-19 (2019). These clauses compel employers to only allow employees to work if bargaining unit members who are not dues-paying union members pay an "agency fee" to the union in exchange for the benefits of the collective bargaining agreement, along with the services the union provides in enforcing the agreement. Id. Some states, commonly referred to as "right to work" states, prohibit such agreements. National Labor Relations Act, 29 U.S.C. 164(b); Some contend that employees who do not wish to join a union should not have to pay a fee to the union in order to work for an employer. Supporters of unions contend that it is unfair to unions and to the employees who do pay dues that those who do not pay the union a fee get to nonetheless enjoy the benefits of a collective bargaining agreement and the services a union provides in terms of enforcement of that agreement. Critics of "right to work" laws frequently refer to them as permitting a system of "free riders." Heinsz, Timothy J., Nolan, Dennis R., & Bales, Richard A. (2009) *Labor Law Collective Bargaining in a Free Society*. Thomson/West, 892.

While the legality of union security agreements varies from state to state in the private sector, this is no longer the case in the public sector. In 2018, the U.S. Supreme Court held that union security clauses in collective bargaining agreements between labor unions and public sector employers violate the First Amendment rights of public employees who do not wish to pay agency fees. Janus v. Am. Fed. Of State, Cnty., and Mun. Employees, Council 31, 138 S. Ct. 2448 (2018). Accordingly, these agreements are unlawful, but public sector employees that are represented by a labor union may still join the union and pay dues if they wish. Id. In reality, public sector unions have, nationwide, retained almost all of their members following the U.S. Supreme Court's 2018 decision. The American Federation of State, County, and Municipal Employees (AFSCME) reported maintaining 94% of their members 9 months after the U.S. Supreme Court's decision. Gies, Heather, (2019). A Blow But Not Fatal: 9 Months After Janus, AFSCME Reports 94% Retention, *In These Times*. https://inthesetimes.com/article/janus-afscme-supreme-court-union-labor-agency-fees.

In addition to union security agreements are what are known as "dues deduction" agreements. A "dues deduction" agreement states that a public employer will agree to deduct the dues of union members from their employees' paychecks – just like they do for income taxes, Medicare, and Social Security – and remit the dues to the union directly. Dues deduction agreements are generally legal and are not scrutinized the same way as union security agreements. Hodges, Ann C., *Maintaining Union Resources in an Era of Public-Sector Bargaining Retrenchment,* 16 Employee Rts. & Emp. Pol'y J. 599 (2012).

Grievance Procedure and Arbitration

Once a collective bargaining agreement has been ratified, the public employer and the union work together to implement its terms. Of course, the drafting of contract language can lead to both latent and patent ambiguities in its language. For example, a contract can have patently ambiguous language such as providing that the public employer may only discipline or discharge an employee for "just cause." Brand, N. & Biren, Melissa H. (2008). Discipline and Discharge in Arbitration (2nd edition). *American Bar Association Section of Labor and Employment* Law, 30. Such a term is ambiguous on its face, and thus will inevitably lead to disputes over its meaning. A contract can contain a latent ambiguity that appears plain or having an obvious meaning on its face, but when applied to a particular situation that arises, can lead the public employer and the union to have reasonable disagreements over its meaning. When one of the parties to the collective bargaining agreement, usually the union, believes the other party violated a provision of the collective bargaining agreement, the party will file what is known as a grievance. Ware, Stephen J., *Labor Grievance Arbitration's Differences*, 51 Cumb. L. Rev. 275 (2020-2021). For purposes of this chapter's discussion, the union is always the party that files grievances. An individual that is the subject of the grievance, such as a person who was disciplined or deprived of another contractual right or benefit, is known as the grievant.

Grievances may sometimes be filed by any member of the bargaining unit, shop stewards on behalf of members, or only by agents of the union itself, depending on how the collective bargaining agreement is written. Id., n. 65.

Most collective bargaining agreements contain a grievance procedure that consists of several "steps." In each step, the grievant, and perhaps their steward and union officials will meet with officials representing the employer in an attempt to confer and come to a resolution of the issue. Zelek, Mark E., *Labor Grievance Arbitration in the United States*, 21 U. Miami Inter-Am. L. Rev. 197, 202 (1989). If the employer is unwilling to resolve the grievance in the manner that the grievant and union wish, then the union may advance the grievance to the next step. Id. There is no legal requirement for whom public employers must have representing them at each individual step, but public employers often start at the first step with the employees' immediate supervisor or the person above them, and then further up the hierarchy in subsequent steps. Collective bargaining agreements dictate which employer representative addresses the grievance at each step. Human Resources is often involved in grievance resolution, as it is tasked with the administration of collective bargaining agreements to begin with. The spirit behind designing the grievance procedure in this way is to ensure that a lower-level manager is not making decisions in a manner that their supervisors would deem arbitrary, and that every level of management would have an opportunity to review the issue before making a final decision. Virtually all collective bargaining agreements will then contain a step allowing the union to demand the matter be resolved at arbitration.

Since the 1960s, arbitration has become the undisputed, near-universal standard in both private and public sector collective bargaining for the resolution of disputes. AT&T Technologies v. Communications Workers, 475 U.S. 643 (1986). It is exceedingly rare for collective bargaining agreements to not contain procedures for the resolution of disputes arising under the contract language that include grievance steps and arbitration. In fact, Illinois law mandates that all public sector collective bargaining agreements contain grievance procedures, which must also include binding arbitration. Illinois Public Labor Relations Act, 5 ILCS 315/8; Illinois Educational Labor Relations Act, 115 ILCS 5/10(c). Arbitration is a relatively expeditious procedure that permits parties to resolve alleged contract violations outside of a courtroom, where litigation could take years and incur high financial and other costs on both parties. Ware, at 288. Grievances are also common and can be filed with a particularly high frequency if, for whatever reason, the public employer and union have a contentious relationship. Arbitration is a type of alternative dispute resolution (ADR) not limited to labor and employment relations, and has likewise been been utilized in consumer and commercial litigation, workers compensation claims, and more.

A public employer is generally required to arbitrate when a union demands arbitration. See, e.g., Illinois Uniform Arbitration Act, 710 ILCS 5/2 (Proceedings to compel or stay arbitration.) This is the case even if the employer believes the union's demand to arbitrate is premature, too late, or otherwise untimely. Amalgamated Transit Union, Local 900 v. Suburban Bus Div. of Regional Transp. Authority, 262 Ill.App.3d 334, 341 (1st Dist. 1994). In the context of labor arbitration, the employer and union will first work together to select an arbitrator. An arbitrator is a third party, neutral individual who decides disputes between parties that have been brought to arbitration. While there is no requirement that an arbitrator be a licensed attorney, many but not all arbitrators are experienced legal practitioners. *Survey of Arbitration in 1962*, in National Academy of Arbitrators, Labor Arbitration – Perspectives and Problems 304 (M. Kahn ed. 1964). Though not judges tasked with fairly and objectively interpreting the law, labor arbitrators are incentivized to be fair to the parties and not demonstrate bias in interpreting collective bargaining agreements, based on their previous affiliations or otherwise, if they want to be mutually agreed upon by the parties to be selected to hear a matter at arbitration. An arbitrator that is perceived by a party to be unfair or tilt too much to one side could be opposed for selection by the other side in the future, which would deprive them of work. This paradigm drives labor arbitrators towards the middle and compels them to be courteous, fair, and objective to the parties, and to perform higher quality work.

The method in which an arbitrator is selected is almost always described in the collective bargaining agreement. Some contracts will contain a short list of arbitrators by name for the parties to select from. Others will require the parties to simply agree on a person. Many contracts require the parties to enlist the assistance of the Federal Mediation & Conciliation Service (FMCS), a small federal agency tasked with facilitating the resolution of labor disputes (including grievances, contract negotiations, and strikes). Labor-Management Relations Act of 1947, 29 U.S.C. 173.

Once an arbitrator is selected, the parties will notify the arbitrator of their appointment and work with them to select a hearing date. An arbitration hearing is similar in many ways to a courtroom trial, but significantly less formal. Still, the parties present evidence in the form of witness testimony and exhibits. There is no requirement that each side's advocate be an attorney. However, each party will oftentimes assign attorneys to advocate for them at arbitration. Public employers either use in-house counsel, or retain the services of an outside law firm with a background in labor law. Loughran, Charles S. (2006) How to Prepare and Present a Labor Arbitration Case (2nd ed.), *BNA Books*, 4-5.

Once the parties have selected an arbitrator and agree to a hearing date, the parties will hold the hearing. If the grievance concerns a public employer's decision to discipline or discharge an employee, the public employer will present their case first and have the burden of proving to the arbitrator that there was cause to discipline or discharge the employee.If the grievance concerns a violation of another term of the contract unrelated to discipline or discharge, the union will present their case first and have the burden of proving to the arbitrator that the public employer violated the contract. Loughran, 19-20.

Once the parties have held the arbitration hearing and have made their arguments, the arbitrator will take time to review the record and write a decision, known as an award. Loughran, 509. The award is final and binding on the parties, and may not be appealed. There are extremely rare circumstances, however, in which an arbitration award can be voided in court. The first is if the terms of the award violate a public policy and its enforcement would be illegal. United Paperworkers Intern. Union v. Misco, Inc., 484 U.S. 29 (1987). The second is if the arbitrator acted in a manner that was outside the scope of their authority. Id. However, overturning arbitration awards is uncommon. Public employers and unions expect to be bound by the terms of the award, whether they agree with it or not.

In a discipline or discharge case, an arbitration award granted in favor of the union will oftentimes require the public employer to make the grievant or employee whole for losses. Brand and Biren, 462. This will require an employer to pay an employee who was suspended without pay, seniority, or benefits during their suspension period. Id. If the employee was discharged, the public employer could be ordered to provide backpay for the period of time in which the employee was terminated. Id. However, an employee is generally required to mitigate their damages by finding work elsewhere during this period of time, and the backpay a public employer would owe would be limited to the difference between what they would have been paid and what they were actually paid since their involuntary departure from their employment. Brand and Biren, 478. Arbitrators virtually never place public employers on the hook for damages other than the backpay that is owed to an employee. Brand and Biren, at 505.

Another form of arbitration alluded to earlier in this chapter is interest arbitration. Interest arbitration can oftentimes be required as a substitute to traditional economic weapons – like strikes – when the employees are firefighters and police officers and a work stoppage would jeopardize public safety. Illinois Public Labor Relations Act, 5 ILCS 315/14. This is the process by which the parties will submit last, best, and final offers on those mandatory subjects of bargaining in which agreement was not reached. An arbitrator is then selected to go proposal by proposal and select either the employer or union's offer, which will be binding on the parties for the new contract. Id.

The Duty of Fair Representation

Sometimes, labor unions can be compelled to advance grievances on behalf of members even when, for whatever reason, they would prefer not to. Every labor union owes a duty of fair representation to its bargaining unit members – whether they are card-carrying members of the union or not. Vaca v. Sipes, 386 U.S. 171 (1967). The contours of this obligation are generally two-fold: First, labor unions are afforded a great deal of discretion over what grievances to bring forward, and they are not obligated to bring forward grievances that they honestly or in good faith believe are lacking in merit, or would be prohibitively expense to prosecute. But second, a labor union may not engage in intentional misconduct by refusing to process a bargaining unit member's grievance for improper reasons. Such impropriety includes refusing to aide a grievant because of their race, gender, nationality, religion, or self-identifying characteristic, or because of the bargaining unit member's refusal to sign a membership card, or because they crossed a picket line, or because they opposed the union's officers in the most recent election. Id. at 191-193. Refusing to process grievances or otherwise represent employees for these reasons could subject a labor union to liability. National Labor Relations Act, 29 U.S.C. § 158(b)(1)(a); Illinois Public Labor Relations Act, 5 ILCS 315/10(b)(1); Illinois Educational Labor Relations Act, 115 ILCS 5/14(b)(1).

Weingarten and *Garrity* Rights

An important aspect of employee rights for public employers to understand are *Weingarten* rights. The U.S. Supreme Court held in 1975 that the right of employees to engage in concerted activity for mutual aid and protection includes the rights of employees to have union representation present when an employer conducts an interview of an employee that the employee reasonably believes could lead to discipline. National Labor Relations Board v. J. Weingarten, Inc., 420 U.S. 251 (1975). This principle has been applied in the public sector as well. *See, e.g.,* Bremen High School District 228, 37 PERI ¶ 94 (ISLRB 2021). The union or *Weingarten* representative can be a shop steward, a union representative, or another employee. Because *Weingarten* rights are considered to be concerted activity, employers may not retaliate against employees for invoking their *Weingarten* rights. National Labor Relations Act, 29 U.S.C. § 158(a)(1). An employee must actually invoke their right to representation before an interview that could lead to discipline. Weingarten, at 257. When an employee requests a representative, a public employer may delay the interview until the representative is available, to allow the employee to continue without a representative, or to terminate the interview altogether. During a meeting that could lead to discipline, *Weingarten* rights do not allow the union representative to tell the employee what to say. However, they may consult with their representative before answering. United States Postal Service v. National Labor Relations Board, 969 F.2d 1064, 1071 (D.C. Cir. 1992).

Unique to public sector employment relations are *Garrity* rights. When a public employer has to conduct an investigation into employee misconduct, they may have to ask employees questions that, if answered truthfully, would require employees to make incriminating statements. The prospect that an employee will be disciplined or discharged for refusing to cooperate with an investigation and make truthful, though incriminating, statements conflicts with the Fifth Amendment, which states that the government may not require a person to make self-incriminating statements. U.S. CONST. amend. V. A public employer, of course, is the government. Thus, *Garrity* rights provide a "work around" in which a public employee can cooperate with an employer's investigation, and make incriminating statements if necessary. Garrity v. State of N.J., 385 U.S. 493 (1967). In turn, those statements may not be used against the public employee as evidence in a separate criminal proceeding. Id. *Garrity* encourages public employees to be forthcoming during investigations by eliminating their motivation to lie, and is a useful tool for public employers to secure the cooperation of understandably reluctant employees. Generally, public employees are only protected by *Garrity* if they are compelled to come forward and make potentially incriminating statements. Id. A public employee that voluntarily makes incriminating statements to their employer of an investigator in response to a question they were not asked, of their own volition, might not be protected by *Garrity*. U.S. ex rel. Sanney v. Montanye, 500 F.2d 411, 416 (2d Cir. 1974).

Wage and Hour

Aside from the rules surrounding collective bargaining and organizing in the workplace, public employers are required to abide by many of the same laws as private employers when it comes to wage and hour issues, family and medical leave, and more. The federal Fair Labor Standards Act was passed to prescribe minimum workplace rules employers must abide by to help ensure a dignified workplace for their employees. Fair Labor Standards Act, 29 U.S.C. § 201, *et. seq.* (1938). Among those standards is a minimum wage, and a requirement that employees who work overtime, or more than forty hours per week, be paid one and a half times their normal rate of pay for those hours in excess of forty. Fair Labor

Standards Act, 29 U.S.C. § 206, 207. The U.S. Supreme Court has held that public sector employers are bound by the Fair Labor Standards Act in addition to private sector employers. Garcia v. San Antonio Metropolitan Transit Authority, 469 U.S. 528 (1985).

While paying overtime wages to employees can be costly for public employers, it is perhaps more costly for public employers to be liable for failing to pay overtime (or subminimum wages) to employees that are owed. Under the FLSA, employees can bring lawsuits against private and public employers alike for owed overtime or minimum wage pay up to the past two years, and for three years if the employer's decision not to pay overtime was willful. Fair Labor Standards Act, 29 U.S.C. § 255(a). Employees may also collect liquidated damages, attorneys' fees, and court costs associated with seeking recovery, thus giving employees more leverage in litigation and an incentive for employers to settle. Fair Labor Standards Act, 29 U.S.C. § 216(b). In addition, state laws provide additional relief to employees, in the form of a higher minimum wage than the federal standard, and additional damages and penalties to violators for minimum wage and overtime violations. *See, e.g.,* Illinois Minimum Wage Law, 820 ILCS 105/12(a) (permits damages in the amount of triple the nominal amount owed.) Public employers can be on the hook for serious damages associated with violations of federal and state minimum wage and overtime laws.

Importantly, public employers have certain protections and flexibility as well. For example, employers may pay employees in comp time rather than overtime. Fair Labor Standards Act, 29 U.S.C. § 207(o).

Family Medical Leave Act

The federal Family Medical Leave Act gives eligible public and private employees alike the right to take up to 12 weeks per year of unpaid leave to care for one's own illness or that of a family member, or to care for a new child. Family Medical Leave Act of 1993, 29 U.S.C. § 2601, *et. seq.* For a public employee to be eligible, two requirements must be met: The employee must have been employed for at least 12 months, and they must have worked at least 1,250 hours in those 12 months. Family Medical Leave Act, 29 U.S.C. § 2611(2)(A), (2)(B)(ii). Employers are entitled to advanced notice of an employee's FMLA leave, and it may be provided orally or in writing. Family Medical Leave Act, 29 U.S.C. § 2612(e). While an employee is not required to specifically mention FMLA, they are required to provide enough information so as to put the employer on notice as to the basis of their need for FMLA leave so that the employer can determine for itself whether the basis for the leave is covered by FMLA. Id.

When the need for FMLA leave is foreseeable (such as for taking care of a newborn child or to care for a family member following a scheduled surgery), an employer may require an employee to indicate how much leave is needed and when they can be expected to return. 30 days' advance notice is what is generally required. Id. The guiding principle of the nuances of FMLA is to balance the rights of employees who need to take leave for family and medical reasons with the needs of employers to experience minimal disruption to their operations. Family Medical Leave Act, 29 U.S.C. § 2601(b)(1). Employers are prohibited by law from interfering with or retaliating against an employee for exercising FMLA rights. Family Medical Leave Act, 29 U.S.C. § 2615.

Civil Rights

Of great importance to public and private employers alike is Title VII of the Civil Rights Act of 1964, which guarantees all employees in the private and public sectors alike a workplace free from discrimination on the basis of a variety of what is known as "protected classes," which include race, color, sex, national origin, disability, and religion. 42 U.S.C. § 2000e, *et. seq.* (1964). In a recent U.S. Supreme Court decision, sexual orientation and gender identity were added to the list of protected classes by virtue of an employee's "sex." Bostock v. Clayton County, Georgia, 140 S. Ct. 1731 (2020). The Age Discrimination in Employment Act also protects employees age 40 or over from discrimination as well. 29 U.S.C. § 621 (1967). Many states, such as Illinois, add additional protected classes through state civil rights laws such as the Illinois Human Rights Act. 775 ILCS 5/2, *et. seq.* (1980).

The prohibition on discrimination means that employers may not, on the basis of a protected class, discipline, discharge, refuse to hire, refuse to promote, demote, or commit any other sort of adverse employment action against an employee. 42 U.S.C. § 2000e-2; 820 ILCS 5/2-102(A). In addition, employees may not be subjected to a hostile work environment on the basis of being in a protected class. A hostile work environment is one in which working conditions are so abusive due to the actions of co-workers or supervisors. This can, and often does, include sexual harassment. Harris v. Forklift Systems, Inc., 510 U.S. 17 (1993); Sangamon Cnty. Sheriff's Dept. v. Illinois Human Rights Comm'n, 233 Ill.2d 125 (2009).

Public employers may be subject to liability by aggrieved employees for the discriminatory or abusive actions of not just its supervisors and managerial personnel, but of its rank-and-file employees as well when management is aware of the misconduct. Faragher v. City of Boca Raton, 524 U.S. 775 (1998). A public employer may avoid liability for the discriminatory actions of rank-and-file employees, including discrimination, the creation of a hostile work environment, or sexual harassment when it takes reasonable action to correct the issues so that employees are no longer subject to the misconducct that Title VII prohibits. Cerros v. Steel Technologies, Inc., 398 F.3d 944, 951-52 (7th Cir. 2005). This does not necessarily require the public employer to terminate managers or other employees, though that is a frequent solution. Employers may take other steps needed to rid the workplace of discrimination or sexual harassment. Id.

Employees who are victims of discrimination, sexual harassment, or an otherwise hostile working environment can bring charges against their employer through the Equal Employment and Opportunity Commission (the EEOC). 42 U.S.C. § 2000e-4. Employees also frequently bring similar charges before state equivalents of the EEOC, such as Illinois's Department of Human Rights. Illinois Human Rights Act, 775 ILCS 5/8-101. These agencies will send investigators will look into the charges brought against employers and issue findings concluding whether the charges are founded or unfounded. Regardless of the EEOC or state agency's findings, an employee is permitted to bring a civil rights lawsuit against the employer for monetary damages. 42 U.S.C. § 2000e-5(3). EEOC and civil rights claims are frequently brought by an employer's former employees, but they can sometimes be brought by current employees as well. Charges by current employers invites the risk that additional EEOC charges can be brought for retaliating against employees for filing the initial charges. Bernier v. Morningstar, Inc., 495 F.3d 369 (7th Cir. 2007). This can frequently put employers in a difficult place in dealing with such employees.

REFERENCES

Labor-Management Relations Act, 29 U.S.C. 173 (1947).

Age Discrimination in Employment Act, 29 U.S.C. § 621 (1967).

Amalgamated Transit Union, Local 900 v. Suburban Bus Div. of Regional Transp. Authority, 262 Ill. App.3d 334, 341 (1st Dist. 1994).

Anonymous. (1984). Collective Bargaining in the Public Sector. *Harv. Law Review*, *97*(1676), 1680–1681.

AT&T Technologies v. Communications Workers, 475 U.S. 643 (1986).

Baker Machinery Co., 184 NLRB 358 (1970).

Bernier v. Morningstar, Inc., 495 F.3d 369 (7th Cir. 2007).

Bostock v. Clayton County, Georgia, 140 S. Ct. 1731 (2020).

Brand, N., & Biren, M. H. (2008). *Discipline and Discharge in Arbitration* (2nd ed.). American Bar Association Section of Labor and Employment Law.

Bremen High School District 228, 37 PERI ¶ 94 (ISLRB 2021).

Central City Educ. Ass'n v. Illinois Educational Labor Relations Bd., 149 Ill.2d 496 (1992).

Cerros v. Steel Technologies, Inc., 398 F.3d 944, 951-52 (7th Cir. 2005).

Civil Rights Act, 42 U.S.C. § 2000e, *et. seq.* (1964).

Struksnes Constr. Co., 165 NLRB 1062 (1967).

Courtesy Bus Co., Inc., 354 NLRB No. 66 (2009).

Dyncorp, 343 NLRB 1197, 1998 (2004), *affd.* Fed. Appx. 419 (6th Cir. 2007).

Fair Labor Standards Act, 29 U.S.C. § 201, *et. seq.* (1938).

Family Medical Leave Act, 29 U.S.C. § 2601, *et. seq.* (1993).

Faragher v. City of Boca Raton, 524 U.S. 775 (1998).

Federal Service Labor-Management Relations Statute, 5 U.S.C. § 7101, *et. seq.* (1970).

FLA. STAT. § 447.403 (1974).

FLA. STAT. § 447.505 (1974).

Flex Frac Logistics, LLC, 358 NLRB 1131 (2012).

Garcia v. San Antonio Metropolitan Transit Authority, 469 U.S. 528 (1985).

Garrity v. State of N.J., 385 U.S. 493 (1967).

Georgia Pacific Corporation, 275 NLRB No. 17 (1985).

Gies, H. (2019). A Blow But Not Fatal: 9 Months After Janus, AFSCME Reports 94% Retention. *In These Times*. https://inthesetimes.com/article/janus-afscme-supreme-court-union-labor-agency-fees

Gould, W. (2019). How Five Young Men Channeled Nine Old Men: Janus and the High Court's Anti-Labor Policymaking. *U.S.F. L. Rev.*, *43*(209), 218–219.

Harris v. Forklift Systems, Inc., 510 U.S. 17 (1993).

Heinsz, T. J., Nolan, D. R., & Bales, R. A. (2009). *Labor Law Collective Bargaining in a Free Society*. Thomson/West.

Hodges, A. C. (2012). Maintaining Union Resources in an Era of Public-Sector Bargaining Retrenchment. *Employee Rts. & Emp. Pol'y J., 16*(599).

Richfield Hospitality, Inc., 369 NLRB No. 111 (2020).

Illinois Minimum Wage Law, 820 ILCS 105/12(a) (1971).

Illinois Educational Labor Relations Act, 115 ILCS 5/1, *et. seq.* (1984).

Illinois Human Rights Act. 775 ILCS 5/2, *et. seq.* (1980).

Illinois Public Labor Relations Act, 5 ILCS 315/1, *et. seq.* (1984).

Illinois Uniform Arbitration Act, 710 ILCS 5/2 (1991).

Industrial Wire Products, Inc., 317 NLRB 190 (1995).

International Brotherhood of Teamsters Local 700 v. Illinois Labor Relations Board, 2017 IL App (1st) 152993.

Janus v. Am. Fed. Of State, Cnty., and Mun. Employees, Council 31, 138 S. Ct. 2448 (2018).

Khan, M. (1964). Survey of Arbitration in 1962. In *Labor Arbitration – Perspectives and Problems 304*. National Academy of Arbitrators.

Kinder-Care Learning Centers, 299 NLRB 1171 (1990).

Loughran, C. S. (2006). *How to Prepare and Present a Labor Arbitration Case* (2nd ed.). BNA Books.

Management & Training Corp., 366 NLRB No. 134 (2018).

Mercy Health Partners, 358 NLRB No. 69 (2012).

National Labor Relations Act of 1935, 29 U.S.C. § 151, *et. seq* (1935).

National Labor Relations Board v. J. Weingarten, Inc., 420 U.S. 251 (1975).

National Labor Relations Board v. Washington Aluminum Co., 370 U.S. 9 (1962).

Niles Co., Inc., 328 NLRB 411, 414 (1999).

NLRB v. American National Insurance Co., 343 U.S. 395 (1952).

NLRB v. Fansteel Metallurgical Corp., 306 U.S. 240 (1939).

NLRB v. Local Union No. 1229, 346 U.S. 464 (1953).

NLRB v. Truitt Mfg. Co., 351 U.S. 149 (1956).

NLRB v. Wooster Div. of Borg-Warner Corp., 356 U.S. 342 (1958).

Policemen's Benevolent and Protective Association, Unit #5, 36 PERI ¶ 113 (ILRB 2020).

Republic Aviation Corp. v. National Labor Relations Board, 324 U.S. 793 (1945).

Sangamon Cnty. Sheriff's Dept. v. Illinois Human Rights Comm'n, 233 Ill.2d 125 (2009).

Smylie, S. (2022). *Chicago principals are again trying to unionize. Will new momentum help?* Chalkbeat Chicago. https://chicago.chalkbeat.org/2022/3/2/22958917/chicago-principals-unionize-illinois-legislature

Thomas v. Collins, 323 U.S. 516 (1945).

United Paperworkers Intern. Union v. Misco, Inc., 484 U.S. 29 (1987).

United States Postal Service v. National Labor Relations Board, 969 F.2d 1064, 1071 (D.C. Cir. 1992).

U.S. CONST. amend. V.

U.S. ex rel. Sanney v. Montanye, 500 F.2d 411, 416 (2d Cir. 1974).

Vaca v. Sipes, 386 U.S. 171 (1967).

Ware, S. J. (2021). Labor Grievance Arbitration's Differences. *Cumb. L. Rev., 51*(275).

Zelek, M. E. (1989). Labor Grievance Arbitration in the United States. *U. Miami Inter-Am. Law Review, 21*(197), 202.

Chapter 8
Anchor Organizations Embedded in Communities:
The Case of Centers for New Horizons

Joanne Howard
Illinois Institute of Technology, USA

ABSTRACT

Anchor organizations are typically, but not exclusively, not-for-profit organizations that are based in a city or town and are unlikely to move because their mission is intrinsically bound up in that area. The author has worked for non-profit-organizations embedded in residential communities. The communities may benefit from their relationship with the non-profit. Some non-profits and communities have a beneficial relationship. The author will review a nonprofit that has aligned its core functions to improve the socioeconomic conditions of the community where it is based. The analysis will be with Centers for New Horizons, a 52-year-old nonprofit located in the Bronzeville section of Chicago.

INTRODUCTION

Charitable, educational, and religious organizations are thousands of years old and some in the United States were founded in colonial times. The concept of "nonprofit organizations" as a unified and coherent "sector" dates back only to the 1970s. Over 90 percent of nonprofit organizations currently in existence were created since 1950 (Renz, 2010).

Anchor institutions are enduring organizations that are rooted in their localities. It is difficult for them to leave their surroundings even amid substantial capital flight. The challenge to a growing movement is to encourage these stable local assets to harness their resources to address critical issues such as education, economic opportunity, and health. It is difficult to imagine fragile local economies and widening social disparities changing without leveraging stable institutions, especially amidst a decline in government resources. These dynamics have given rise to the concept "anchors" as agents of community and economic development.

DOI: 10.4018/978-1-6684-2314-1.ch008

The City of Chicago is made up of neighborhoods and communities. In the 1920s, the Social Science Research Committee at the University of Chicago defined the community areas based on neighborhoods or groups of related neighborhoods within the city. The development of the system was led by sociologists Robert E. Park, and Ernest Burgess developed a system of naming the various communities that comprise Chicago. They developed 77 community areas that have become a part of the culture of Chicago.

The Economic Innovation Group (2016) analyzed community well-being across the United States. The report states:

Place matters. This simple concept has never been better understood than it is today. The American Dream is predicated on the idea that anyone from any place or background can climb to the highest rungs of the economic ladder. But there is a growing body of evidence that the more time an individual spends living in a distressed community—especially at childhood—the worse that individual's lifetime chances of achieving economic stability or success. And not all poor neighborhoods are alike, some offer vastly better chances of economic mobility than others. (Economic Innovation Group, 2016, p. 4)

The Economic Innovation Group identified geographic areas across the United States with significant dimension of distress and of basic community well-being. The analysis finds that for those living in distressed zip codes, the years of overall U.S. economic recovery have looked much more like an ongoing downturn. Large swathes of country are being left behind by economic growth and change. The phenomenon is taking place at many different scales: well-being diverges between cities and states but even more starkly within cities and at the neighborhood level.

The authors go on to report that while the features of distressed communities differ across regions, the following seven indicators of community well-being apply: (1) No High School Degree; (2) Housing Vacancy Rate; (3) Adults Not Working; (4) Poverty Rate; (5) Median Income Rate; (6) Change in Employment; and (7) Change in Establishments remaining open or closed.

The criteria of acknowledging geographic areas as distressed is a potent harbinger of community well-being or lack thereof. Chicago, Illinois, is listed as one of ten cities with the largest number of people living in distressed zip codes. A common feature unites this concentration of distress. The common feature is that the distress is caused by a struggle to transition from an economy based on legacy industries (often manufacturing) to a more advanced, knowledge-based one.

Harvard economist Raj Chetty says that, for white Americans, achieving the American dream is like climbing an income ladder. "If you've climbed up in one generation, that's basically where you're going to start the next generation, and then you can climb up further." But for Black Americans, and Black men in particular, "it's like being on a treadmill, where even after you've climbed up in one generation, there are tremendous structural forces that make it highly likely you're going to fall back down in the next generation and then you have to make the climb again" (Chetty, Friedman, Hendren, Jones, & Porter, 2018).

Over the past few years, the Harvard professor has received nationwide attention for his work on economic mobility in the United States. He and his colleagues created a map called the Opportunity Atlas, which uses census data and income tax returns to measure Americans' economic mobility over time in any given part of the country.

The Role of Nonprofits in the United States

The starting point for any discussion of nonprofits in the United States is Alexis de Tocqueville's *Democracy in America.* De Tocqueville's original conclusion was that local organized groups were one of the critical building blocks of the United States. These organizations were one of the most distinct aspects of America because they were separate and autonomous from the state and from higher-level political officials.

The nonprofit sector grew rapidly due to a set of social and economic conditions that sparked their growth. Kallman, Clark, Woo, and Lin (2016) identify five institutional logics that create tensions, synergies, and unevenness that can be seen in different proportions. They are Clientelism, Paternalism, Bureaucracy, Activism, and Professionalism.

Clientelism and patronage refer to the "trade of votes and other types of partisan support in exchange for divisible benefits" (Piattoni, 2001). Chicago is known for its political patronage and the utilitarian way some politicians approach the communities they represent at the local, state, or federal levels. The adage "what have you done for me latterly" resonates throughout the clientelism of Chicago.

Paternalism is widely identifiable in the nonprofit sector. Paternalism, unlike clientelism, is not a relationship that is meant to produce material or power benefits for a certain group, but an approach that emphasizes the condescending nature of interactions between the powerful and the powerless (Kallman, Clark, Woo, & Lin, 2016, p. 14).

Bureaucracy is a component of most well-functioning organizations. Max Weber, a German scientist, defined bureaucracy as a highly structured, formalized, and also an impersonal organization. He also instituted the belief that an organization must have a defined hierarchical structure and clear rules, regulations, and lines of authority which govern it. Nonprofits continue to learn and negotiate power sharing and responsibilities in conjunction with local or national arms of government.

Activism is a logic that is primarily seen among the grassroots organizations and volunteers who are impatient with the bureaucratic constraints of their institutional contexts and who are more open to using contentious practices to further their goals. The activist frame of many social movement and collective action discourses strongly values qualities of individual charisma, leadership, and flexibility, seeing themselves as a part of a social movement. Activism seriously enters the nonprofit sector after the 1968 uprisings in the United States (Kallman et al., 2016).

Lastly, professionalism is the process of transforming a job into a skilled profession, typically implying the establishment of accepted qualifications, professional norms, industry standards, professional bodies, and/or training programs. Professionalism became the rage in the 1930s and later in the 1960s as a signal of technical and systematic knowledge (Wilensky, 1964). It is an accepted practice in the nonprofit world that nonprofits draw on the five institutional logics mentioned above.

Bronzeville

Bronzeville, also known as the "Black Metropolis" and the "Black Belt," is the center of African American history on Chicago's South Side, just 10 minutes south of downtown. While the boundaries of Bronzeville are debatable, there is general agreement that the heart of Bronzeville is from 31st Street south to Pershing Road and east from today's Dan Ryan Expressway to Lake Michigan. Many consider Bronzeville to stretch from 18th Street all the way south to 67th Street (Illlinois Institute of Technology, 2022).

The Great Migration, when African Americans left the South for Chicago with the promise of better jobs and reduced oppression, began in 1916. The reality, however, fell far short of these promises, as conditions were still repressive and segregated. African Americans were restricted to live in the Black Belt in white-owned housing that was largely dilapidated and densely populated yet more expensive than housing in white areas.

Forced to live in this isolated area, Bronzeville's residents toiled hard and cooperatively to establish a full-fledged community with business, culture, and community institutions that did not have the racial restrictions enforced in most parts of the city. Bronzeville's institutions grew to have national influence rivaling, and even exceeding, those of New York's Harlem.

Founded by Jesse Binga, Binga Bank was Chicago's first Black-owned life insurance, realty, and financial institution. Daniel Hale Williams, an African American, pioneered open-heart surgery in Bronzeville's Provident Hospital. The *Chicago Defender* and *Chicago Bee* were African American daily newspapers of national influence and distribution. The Wabash Avenue YMCA established the first Black History Month. Venues like the Savoy Ballroom-Regal Theater complex and the Sunset Cafe rivaled Harlem's Apollo Theater in importance in music, film, and live performance.

Scores of this country's greatest entertainers, intellectuals, artists, and writers hailed from Bronzeville, including musicians Louis Armstrong, Nat "King" Cole, Sam Cook, Dinah Washington, Quincy Jones, and Herbie Hancock; gospel music pioneers Mahalia Jackson and Thomas A. Dorsey; choreographer Catherine Dunham; women's aviation pioneer Bessie Coleman; author Richard Wright; activist and writer Ida B. Wells; Olympic legends Jesse Owens and Ralph Metcalf; Negro League baseball founder Andrew Rube Foster; boxer Joe Louis; and Pulitzer Prize-winning poet Gwendolyn Brooks.

Today's Bronzeville is undergoing a revitalization driven by entrepreneurial African Americans who value its rich history and are dedicated to keeping that history and its lessons alive for generations to come. Renovated and restored historic homes complement new housing open to all income levels. Architectural landmarks, many of which have been restored, include the original Chicago Defender Building, Unity Hall, the Chicago Bee Building, Overton Hygienic Building, Michigan Boulevard Garden Apartments, The Forum, the Wabash Avenue YMCA, and the Supreme Life Building. Restaurants, shops, and other local businesses have begun to flourish, but Bronzeville's profound history remains the primary draw for both locals and tourists.

This community is known for its rich history and flourishing modern-day renaissance. Bronzeville's cultural contributions are vast—it brought the world Pulitzer Prize-winner Gwendolyn Brooks, civil rights activist Ida B. Wells, legendary musician Louis Armstrong, and more. Today, the area is embracing its legacy as a mecca for civil rights, jazz, blues, and gospel music. You'll find an array of coffee shops, galleries, libraries, monuments, and restaurants, alongside spectacular Victorian-era architecture and 19th-century mansions.

The Robert W. Roloson Houses, the only row homes that Frank Lloyd Wright ever built. Is In the midst of the Bronzeville history, look for striking modern public art installations, like a sculpture-adorned stretch of Martin Luther King Drive that features the Monument to the Great Northern Migration, The Bronzeville Walk of Fame, and The Victory Monument. Don't forget to dine on old-school Southern soul food at Pearl's Place and admire works by emerging multicultural artists at Gallery Guichard inside the Bronzeville Artist Lofts.

Centers for New Horizons: Anchoring Bronzeville

The City of Chicago is a city of neighborhoods and was identified as hyper-segregated in the 1980s by urban sociologist Douglas Massey, then a University of Chicago professor. Carl Nightingale (2012) in his book, *Segregation: A Global History of Divided Cities*, reports that "long-standing use of urban divisions" has led to the current situation where there are demarcations and dividing lines in Chicago. There are pioneers in various neighborhoods around the world who are influencers and whose imaginations are not stymied by racism and exclusion. Two such pioneers are Drs. Sokoni and Ayanna Karanja.

The Drs. Karnajas met as Adlai Stevenson Fellows and married shortly thereafter. They have enjoyed a loving marriage, filled with children and social activism. They are the founders of Centers for New Horizons. Centers for New Horizons is a nonprofit organization located in the Bronzeville community of Chicago. Prior to the formation of Center, the founders, Dr. walked the streets of the Robert Taylor Homes, State Way Gardens, and Ida B. Wells Chicago Public Housing Authority (CHA) projects to determine community needs. These three housing projects comprised over 30,000 residents and the leadership in each of the Local Area Councils (LACs) did not always see eye to eye with the Chicago Housing Authority (CHA).

When low-income housing came to Chicago in the 1930s, it was an improvement to the tenements where low-income people were forced to reside. The Great Migration of African Americans from the south to Chicago encouraged the building of housing complexes that grew and bore the names of prominent Chicagoans. Unfortunately, the housing projects were not well maintained. The projects came to be a source of embarrassment for the City of Chicago. The deteriorating buildings also became crime ridden and manifested all that was bad about public housing.

Enter Dr. Sokoni Karanja and his wife, Dr. Ayanna Karanja, urban pioneers, and educators. Dr. Sokoni, a doctoral prepared urbanologist from Brandeis, arrived in Chicago after a tour of Ghana and Tanzania. Dr. Ayanna Karanja, an anthropologist from The University of Chicago, had the desire to create a nonprofit to fill the gap of what residents in the Bronzeville community were experiencing (Sokoni & Sokoni, 2022).

The Early Years of Centers for New Horizon

Centers for New Horizons was founded in 1971 with a penchant for viewing community through the lens of the people who live in said place. Centers was founded after Chicago and more than 160 other cities had endured rebellions and urban inequality built on systematic, de facto and de jure discrimination that marginalized populations of color, and further solidified the "Two Americas" that Dr. Martin Luther King, Jr. proclaimed then as needing immediate attention (Cantor, Cooper, Brown, & Englot, 2019).

Centers for New Horizons expanded its services and offers childcare, youth services, adult care, violence prevention and workforce development services. The organization has 200 employees, has a \$18 million operating budget, and operates in five Chicago community areas. Center is headquartered in Bronzeville and has offices in the Englewood, Austin, Grand Boulevard, and Riverdale community areas of Chicago.

The organization has been in existence for 52 years. Like other high performing nonprofits, Centers is cognizant of its mission and its responsibility to continue the legacy of its founders. The mission statement hangs in the lobby of its small headquarters in the Bronzeville area, and every new employee is introduced to the legacy of the organization and the founders during orientation.

The Karanjas live in the Bronzeville section of Chicago. This is a key element in the success of Centers for New Horizons. The founders reside in the area and upon their retirements, they have maintained close contact and pay attention to the on-going success of the organization.

Dr. Karanja's successor was Christa Hamilton. Hamilton began her tenure with Centers in the workforce development area. She grew this component and was tapped to lead the organization for seven years. She maintained the focus of improving and enhancing the community and the financial well-being of the residents by continuing to deploy City of Chicago and Washington, DC financial largesse to Center's programs. The current executive director is Lakisha McFadden. Her focus is to continue the 52-year legacy of Centers by shoring up the internal controls and enhancing the financial well-being of the organization. She is working on diversifying the financial portfolio of Centers to include fundraising and grantsmanship.

The staying power of anchor organizations is the opportunity for growth and expansion. The realization that the Bronzeville community is changing demographically due to the enlargement of the downtown area of the City of Chicago. Centers for New Horizons will have to incorporate organizational change to accommodate the changing nature of the Bronzeville area.

HIGH PERFORMING NONPROFIT ORGANIZATIONS

Nonprofit organizations with staying power in Chicago have several commonalities: strong board engagement and oversight; strong staff and program management; and a strategy that involves a close eye on the bottom line. These organizations also know when there are gaps in their professional expertise and know when to reach out to consultants for assistance.

The Importance of the Board of Directors

The governing boards of nonprofits have increasingly become a part of the ongoing success of an organization. Boards are charged with leading nonprofits in an increasingly dynamic and complex environment, and the challenges of doing well have intensified interest in nonprofit boards and the work they do, how they are organized, and how they can and should contribute to the success and effectiveness of the organization they govern (Renz, 2004).

Ostrower and Stone (2006) in their survey of the nonprofit governance, observe that progress is being made yet "major gaps in our theoretical and empirical knowledge about boards continue to exist" (Ostrower & Stone, 2006, p. 12). Boards are complex entities and there are no sweeping generalizations that can be made about them due to their diversity. Part of the confusion that exists about boards is the governance and operations The board is the group of people entrusted with and are accountable for the leadership and governance of the nonprofit corporation. It is the board that has the ultimate authority and responsibility for the performance of the nonprofit, and they are ultimately accountable to the community, to the state, and to clients and beneficiaries.

Centers for New Horizons, like most small nonprofits, has a board of directors. The board is currently led by Jay Readey, a lawyer and entrepreneur. The development cycle the board undertakes annually is as follows:

- Define the work of the board

- Recruit and Select Members
- Build Member Capacity
- Build the Team
- Ensure Strategic Focus
- Implementation: Engage Members to Do the Work
- Conduct Effective Meetings
- Ensure Accountability

Each of these facets interdigitates with the other for an effective board cycle. The board of directors of Centers faces the challenge of integrating mission, money, and management strategies. Both the board and the chief executive play crucial and interdependent roles in meeting this continuing challenge.

The Importance of the Chief Executive Officer

The Chief Executive Officer of Centers for New Horizons is Lakisha McFadden. McFadden is steeped in the tradition of the organization as she ran the childcare program and the operations area before her appointment. The strength of Centers is the current and former leaders have taken responsibility for the organizational affairs and have provided facilitative leadership for the board; accepts and act on their psychological centrality; they accept and emphasize leadership beyond their organization's boundaries; and they think and act in political ways. The strong suit of any organization is the adoption of these four executive leadership strategies. Centers for New Horizons has exhibited these board leadership skills throughout its 52-year history.

Chicago is a city that repeats the adage "We Don't Want Nobody Nobody Sent" (Rakove, 1979), can be a saying for nonprofit organizations that grow their own talent. Nonprofit organizations that are service providers and operate on collaboration, cooperation, communication and seek new ways to partner for continuous improvement need spokes people who understand the nuances of their organizations The opportunity to retain the services of staff with a history allow for the mission of the organization to be advanced more effectively because of this narration. These board-centered external, and political leadership skills are what distinguish especially effective nonprofit chief executives.

The Role of External Consultants

There are 2 million nonprofit organizations in the United States. Larger nonprofits can recruit, retain, and reward their personnel for long-term security and growth. Smaller nonprofits that have a history of serving as anchors in their communities, there are problems with recruitment and retention and many times there are problems with fulling services both internally and externally. Smaller nonprofits have a difficult time competing for talent with larger nonprofits, government, and the private sector. In order to assist in filling the gaps smaller nonprofits have, in steps the need for services to from private sector firms to fill the skills the organization does not have.

First, consultants generally have a wide range of experience across a number of organizations and therefore may know what will work best for any unique organization. Compensation programs, especially with regard to benefits, are sophisticated and complex systems and even HR professionals with basic compensation knowledge may not have the breadth and depth of experience to develop and install programs that are a "good fit." (Renz, 2010, p. 713).

Centers for New Horizons had a difficult time retaining the services of internal financial support with the retirement of their chief financial officer. After multiple attempts to recruit a financial person, the organization recruited Quatrro Services, a leading accounting firm that provides accounting services to organizations. Quatrro organized, streamlined accounting services, and provided expert advice on investments and the sale of Centers' properties.

The opportunity to provide a strategic vision for the organization was developed by Conlon Public Strategies, a boutique consultancy to nonprofits in Chicago. Conlon provided a bridge to the future of Centers by loaning them a temporary executive that allowed them the space to interview and recruit their current Chief Executive Officer. These services allowed Centers to take a breath and decide the services and expertise they needed for future growth and development.

The changing context of the economy and moving to a post-pandemic world has changed the way organization's function. The fiscal challenges, the need to recruit employees who can work in hybrid environments, and the need to respond to the demands of employees has put a technological burden on organizations. Centers retained the services of Microtech for their information technology needs. Microtech has filled the void of the organization's inability to find the appropriate information technology staff to reside on the campus of Centers for New Horizons.

The major disadvantage of using consultants is, of course, cost. Sometimes several thousand dollars in consulting fees is money extremely well spent if it could provide the organization with results that maximize the value of the salary and benefit dollars that would be spent on an individual. Especially on an individual that may not be suitable for the nonprofit.

CONCLUSION

Nonprofit organizations pop up all the time and only those with strong boards, staff, volunteers, and a vision to remain competitive and true to their mission and constituency will remain viable. The challenges of finance, competition, effectiveness, and technology will be the determinant in the survival of nonprofit organizations.

There are emerging opportunities and major social and demographic shifts that are fueling changes in the nonprofit sector. New forms of philanthropy, greater visibility and policy changes, and the resumption of governmental spending on social welfare and other civil society programming will change the face of nonprofits.

Centers for New Horizons has played a significant and diverse role in the development of the Bronzeville community during the 1970s, 1980s, and 1990s. A new generation of leaders is taking the helm at these important organizations. This new generation understands the increasingly complex nature of the work they have signed on for with their respective organizations.

These are exciting times for Centers for New Horizons and the communities it serves. The capacity to deliver on the promises Centers has made to serve communities and citizens well hinges directly on the effectiveness of its leaders and managers. The author of this chapter believes they are up to the task.

REFERENCES

Cantor, N., Cooper, T., Brown, M., & Englot, P. (2019). *Tackling "The Two Americas" with City-wide Collaboration in Newark*. Rutgers University.

Chetty, R., Friedman, J. N., Hendren, N., Jones, M. R., & Porter, S. R. (2018). *The Opportunity Atlas: Mapping the Childhood Roots of Social Mobility*. National Bureau of Economic Research. doi:10.3386/w25147

Economic Innovation Group. (2016, February). *The 2016 Distressed Communities Index: An Analysis of Community Well-Being Across the United State*. Retrieved from EIG.org: https://eig.org/wp-content/uploads/2016/02/2016-Distressed-Communities-Index-Report.pdf

Illlinois Institute of Technology. (2022, May 1). *History of Bronzeville*. Retrieved from IIT.edu: https://www.iit.edu/community-affairs/about/history-bronzeville

Kallman, M. E., Clark, T. N., Woo, C., & Lin, J. (2016). *The Third Sector: Community Organizations, NGOs, and Non-Profits*. University of Illinois Press. doi:10.5406/illinois/9780252040436.001.0001

Nightingale, C. H. (2012). *Segregation: A Global History of Divided Cities*. The University of Chicago Press. doi:10.7208/chicago/9780226580777.001.0001

Ostrower, F., & Stone, M. M. (2006). Governance: Research trends, gaps, and future prospects. In R. Steinberg & W. W. Powell (Eds.), *The Nonprofit Sector: A Research Handbook* (pp. 612–628). Yale University Press.

Piattoni, S. (2001). *Clientelism, Interests, and Democratic Representation: The European Experience in Historical and Comparative Perspective*. Cambridge University Press. doi:10.1017/CBO9781139175340

Rakove, M. L. (1979). *We Don't Want Nobody Nobody Sent*. Indiana University Press.

Renz, D. O. (2004). Leadership, Governance, and the Work of the Board. In D. O. Rend (Ed.), *The Jossey-Bass Handbook of Nonprofit Leadership and Management*. John Wiley and Sons, Inc.

Renz, D. O. (2010). *The Jossey-Bass Handbook of Nonprofit Leadership and Management*. John Wiley and Sons, Inc.

Wilensky, H. L. (1964). The Professionalization of Everyone? *American Journal of Sociology*, *70*(2), 137–158. doi:10.1086/223790

Section 2
Healthcare

Chapter 9
An Assessment of Diversity From Senior Healthcare Executives

Diane M. Howard
Rush University Medical Center, USA

Kimberly Enard
St. Louis University, USA

ABSTRACT

The National Association of Health Services Executives and Deloitte Consulting administered a survey to assess the status of diversity, equity, and inclusion in March 2021 following social unrest in the United States. One-hundred and five NAHSE members responded to the topics on personal experience working in healthcare, organizational priorities and strategies in DEI, and opportunities in career advancement. A follow-up webinar in February 2022 with 211 participants explored compliance, accountability, and sustainability of diversity, equity, and inclusion initiatives. Sixty-seven percent stated there was no measurement in determining achievement of DEI goals. One-third of respondents stated there was no accountability if DEI goals were not achieved. The good news was that 53% of respondents thought the DEI initiatives developed at their organization would be sustained.

BACKGROUND

The National Association of Health Services Executives (NAHSE), working with Deloitte Consulting, surveyed the membership of NAHSE to determine what initiatives were being explored to address diversity, equity, and inclusion. Senior leaders from Deloitte worked with the NAHSE executive director and members of its Research Committee to gather survey data from NAHSE members and to gain insights into DEI activities in their respective organizations.

NAHSE is a personal membership group based in Washington, DC with 30 chapters throughout the country. Founded in 1968 for the purpose of promoting the advancement and development of Black

DOI: 10.4018/978-1-6684-2314-1.ch009

health care leaders and elevating the quality of health care services rendered to minority and underserved communities through mentoring, educational programming, and policy development.

Deloitte is a leading global provider of audit and assurance, consulting, financial advisory, risk advisory, tax, and related services. With more than 150 years of hard work and commitment to making a real difference, the organization has grown in scale and diversity—approximately 286,000 people in 150 countries and territories, providing these services—yet the shared culture remains the same. Deloitte serves four out of five Fortune Global 500® companies.

The Diversity, Equity, and Inclusion survey was administered in Year 2 of the pandemic (March 2021 to August 2021). There were social disruptions in the summer 2020 after the killing of George Floyd who was in Minneapolis police custody. The filming of his death by a 17-year-old with a cell phone brought attention to the unequal treatment of people of color. There was the rise of attacks on Asian, Jewish, Latinx, and Muslim persons around the country.

Survey Participants and Results

NAHSE and Deloitte designed and fielded an online survey to more than 2,000 NAHSE members in March 2021. A total of 105 respondents completed the survey (Deloitte Insights, 2021). The respondents were primarily Black women (91% identified as Black, and 68% identified as women). Respondents were C-level/executive management (22%), senior management (29%), mid-level management (30%), and entry-level/non-management (30%), and entry-level/non-management staff (8%). The remaining 12% were physicians, nursing leaders, or other clinicians. Most respondents worked at hospitals or health systems (57%), with 10% coming from universities or academic institutions, and the remaining respondents working at health care associations, medical device and digital health companies, and health plans. In addition, there were 10 executives leading DEI initiatives at health systems and health plans that Deloitte interviewed for further elaboration.

Two out of three respondents agreed that their management and leaders encourage them to continue with their professional growth and development. Four in five respondents reported their organization had active DEI committees or were launching initiatives. Sixty-one percent of these organizations had funding directed toward these initiatives/committees. Two in three respondents felt that all employees have not been fairly treated regardless of differences in background. Three in four respondents did not believe that everyone in their organization has the same general ability to get promoted regardless of gender, race, ethnicity, disability, sexual orientation, socioeconomic backgrounds, or other factors.

The respondents indicated that there were four strategies that bring DEI to life in an organization. The four strategies include: (1) make DEI enterprise wide where the entire C-suite is involved; (2) cultivate employee resource groups through executive sponsorship; (3) develop talent and leadership pipelines; and (4) measure DEI and lead assessments with data (Deloitte Insights, 2021).

In an accompanying chapter (see *Fifteen Years of Diversity, Equity, and Inclusion at Rush University Medical Center in Chicago*), the four strategies have been implemented.

Make DEI Enterprise-Wide and Involve the C-Suite

The Rush Health System CEO, Rush University Medical Center CEO, System Chief Diversity Officer, and University Provost are members of the Diversity Leadership Council that meets monthly to drive

DEI. They function as observers to the process and are able to take issues to the executive leaders in the organization.

Cultivate Employee Resource Groups

The Rush University Medical Center ERGs of prominence are described as case studies that are embedded in the Rush analysis. The Americans with Disabilities Task Force, Rush Community Service Initiatives Program (RCSIP), LGBTQ Initiatives, and Women's Leadership Council are ERGs that have been embedded into the culture of one organization.

Develop Pipelines

Rush developed a relationship with Community Colleges of Chicago to assist in developing a campus for health careers at Malcolm X College near the Illinois Medical District, of which Rush University Medical Center is a member. Rush serves as a destination university for students seeking the B.S. in health sciences who can matriculate to graduate degrees in nursing, medicine, or health sciences. Over 5 years, the Board of Trustees at Rush has earmarked $4.6M in scholarships to assist students of color in advancing through the academic pipeline.

Measure DEI with Data

Rush developed its 5-year strategic goals in DEI and invited an external consultancy to monitor its progress including recruitment and retention in the university for faculty and students and medical center clinical and support staff. While this is the more recent development of quantifying and assessing its diversity data, there was a transition of the information technology and data gathering systems to bring financial, operational, and human resources data platforms together.

A follow-up webinar to the Deloitte-NAHSE white paper on *Amplifying Black Voices* was held on February 22, 2022, to continue the dialog about diversity, equity, and inclusion (Atkins, Enard, Griffin-Hunter, & Howard, 2021). The speakers included executives from Deloitte Consulting, NAHSE's corporate office, a California hospital, and a Virginia health system. After the presentation, three questions were directed to the 211 participants via Zoom polling.

Does your organization have metrics to measure DEI goals?
Yes 8%
No 67%
Not sure 24%

Are members in your organization held accountable to achieve DEI goals?
Yes 33%
No 38%
Not sure 29%

Are your organizational DEI goals sustainable?
Yes 53%
No 19%
Not sure 28%

The good news is that organizations are pursuing diversity, equity, and inclusion goals because it is the right thing to do. What was interesting was that 38% of respondents thought there was no accountability for achieving DEI goals and 29% of the respondents were not sure if there was accountability in achieving DEI goals. The encouraging sign from the respondents was that 53% of the respondents felt their organizations commitment to DEI could be sustained over time.

CONCLUSION

The death of George Floyd while in Minneapolis police custody that was caught on cell phone and transmitted around the world brought attention to police brutality and the harm done to people of color. The violence against Asian, Jewish, Latinx, and Muslim citizens always existed, but a light was directed to violence perpetrated against them for little to no reason. Corporations started to react and direct resources to diversity, equity, and inclusion to enhance the work environment and to start dialog about ethnic, racial, religious, and gender differences. The National Association of Health Services Executives in conjunction with Deloitte Consulting canvassed its membership to determine that there were four strategies that bring DEI to life in an organization. The author identified Rush University Medical Center in Chicago as an example of an organization that had deployed the four initiatives.

REFERENCES

Atkins, P., Enard, K. R., Griffin-Hunter, K., & Howard, D. (2021, July 22). *Amplifying Black Voices: What health care organizations can do to advance diversity, equity, and inclusion in the workforce*. Retrieved from Deloite.com: https://www2.deloitte.com/us/en/insights/industry/health-care/diversity-in-healthcare-workforce.html

Deloitte Insights. (2021). *CHS Health Care D&I Workforce NAHSE*. Retrieved from NAHSE.org: https://www.nahse.org/wp-content/uploads/2021/08/Deloitte-and-NAHSE-Amplifying-Black-Voices-7-22-21.pdf

Chapter 10
NAHSE and the 2020 Presidential Elections

Diane M. Howard
Rush University, USA

Kimberly Enard
St. Louis University, USA

Rhonda BeLue
University of Texas, San Antonio, USA

Ebbin Dotson
School of Public Health, University of Michigan, USA

Keith Elder
Mississippi College, USA

Angel Evans
Governors State University, USA

Rupert Evans
Governors State University, USA

Allyson Hall
University of Alabama, Birmingham, USA

Dale Sanders
Alma College, USA

Laurie Shanderson
Methodist College, USA

Jacqueline C. Wiltshire
Indiana University, USA

ABSTRACT

In Summer 2020, prior to the U.S. November 2020 elections, the "NAHSE Political Leadership in the United States" survey was administered to 2,000 members with a 12.6% response rate to assess member views on the Presidential candidates. The purpose of the survey was to assess healthcare concerns of the membership, which would help frame the organization's public policy agenda. Of the respondents, 98% stated they would definitely vote with 80% very confident or confident that their votes would be counted. Approximately 65% of respondents plan to vote in person on the day of the election or through early voting opportunities, and 35% intend to vote via mail or absentee ballot, with 1% stating they do not plan to vote. The top five issues the membership recommended to be addressed by the new President of the United States are (1) COVID-19, (2) criminal justice/police brutality, (3) race relations/police brutality, (4) jobs/economic insecurity, and (5) economy.

DOI: 10.4018/978-1-6684-2314-1.ch010

BACKGROUND

The U.S. Presidential election of 2020 had two candidates—the current occupant of the White House President Donald Trump and former Vice-President Joseph Biden—running for the new term. The vitriol between the candidates, the Democratic and Republican party competition, the public's anger over the handling of COVID-19, the resulting shut-down of the economy, and the introduction of public health principles mandating face-masking that some constituencies refused to support added to the election controversy.

The murders of Ahmaud Arbery (February 23, 2020), Breonna Taylor (March 13, 2020), and George Floyd (May 25, 2020) resulted in a summer of "Black Lives Matter" marches to demand justice for the murders of unarmed Blacks. The recording of George Floyd's death on a cell phone captured international attention and brought young people to the streets to march for social justice during the pandemic.

The general election was held on November 3, 2020, with voters directly selecting their state's members to the U.S. Electoral College. On November 7, most national media organizations projected that Biden had clinched enough electoral votes to be named the U.S. president-elect (*The New York Times*, 2022). Unlike in previous elections where the incumbent candidate lost and congratulated the newly elected president, there was no acknowledgement in the Trump circle that the Trump Administration would not advance to a second term of office.

Survey Administration

The purpose of the "NAHSE Member Survey of Political Leadership in the United States" was to identify healthcare priorities, needs and concerns of the member's organizations and communities regarding the political and policy landscape during the health pandemic and time of national transition. Approximately 2,000 members of the National Association of Health Service Executives (NAHSE) received invitations to participate in the survey, and 252 members responded (12.6% response rate). Sixty-three percent of respondents were residents of nine states: Florida (8%); Georgia (9%) Illinois (10%); Michigan (4%); Missouri (5%); New York (4%); Pennsylvania (6%); Tennessee (5%) Texas (12%). The remainder were distributed in smaller numbers across several remaining states.

The respondents were 62% female and 38% male; 86% were between the ages of 25 and 64, and 11% were over 65. Relative to academic preparation and highest degree earned, 67% of respondents hold a master's degrees; 20% hold doctoral degrees; 12% hold bachelor's degrees and less than 1% have associate degrees. Eighty-one percent of the respondents were employed full-time; student respondents accounted for 5%, retired persons 4%, and unemployed 5%. Also included were "other" at 5%, and the combination of consultants, entrepreneurs, or working in another industry outside of healthcare was 5%.

How COVID-19 Affected Members' Professional and Personal Lives

Based on 261 responses, 210 (80%) indicated that they had "no," limited, or temporary reductions in their compensation and/or benefits. Of the 261 respondents, 210 individual responses (66%) indicated that their employment benefits were not impacted by the COVID-19 pandemic. However, 7% had their pay reduced but it had been restored; in addition, 8% were furloughed/laid off/hours and/or benefits reduced temporarily but were restored to baseline.

Table 1. NAHSE Member Health Care Priorities: 2005, 2018, and 2021

2005 **n=150**	**2018** **n=214**	**2021** **n=252**
1. Healthcare disparities	1. Healthcare disparities	1. COVID-19
2. Health professional shortage	2. Quality of care	2. Criminal justice/police brutality
3. Medicaid reductions	3. Funding and financial reimbursement	3. Race relations/racism
4. Federal and state deficits	4. Recruitment and retention	4. Jobs/economic insecurity
5. Access to healthcare	5. Medicaid reduction	5. Economy

Of all respondents, 51 respondents (20%) were furloughed, laid off, benefits/pay/hours reduced, and/or unemployed/looking for work. Sixty-six percent of the respondents were not impacted professionally by the COVID-19 pandemic.

Perceptions and Activities Related to the 2020 Elections

The overwhelming majority of respondents (>99%) indicated they would definitely (97.6%) or probably (1.6%) vote in the 2020 election. Many states in the United States had started to implement voter suppression policies, which made voting more difficult, particularly for members of marginalized populations (e.g., non-white and female voters) (The Brennan Center, 2022). In the last two presidential elections, voter registration issues were exacerbated by partisan rule, long lines, and challenges to voters' eligibility (Wang, 2012). Due to the pandemic which forced social distancing measures in states, voter suppression issues included redistricting, mail-in and early voting restrictions, and social distancing fear mongering due to COVID-19.

Members expressed concern that voter suppression would impact the elections was shared by 92.28% of respondents. This was reflected in 227/246 of respondents choosing very concerned or somewhat concerned, 160 and 67, respectively. The concern for voter fraud impacting the 2020 election was shared by 58.34% of respondents. One out of every eight respondents were not at all concerned that voter fraud would impact the 2020 election results.

An overwhelming majority of respondents, 91.47%, favored states allowing voters to vote by absentee/mailed ballots in the 2020 election. This is reflected in 225/246 of respondents choosing strongly favor or favor, 178 and 47 respectively. Only 6.10% of respondents were undecided. Approximately 65% of respondents plan to vote in person on the day of the election or through early voting opportunities. Approximately 35 planned to vote via mail or absentee ballot. Only 2 respondents do not plan to vote in the 2020 election (<1%). The survey asked respondents to identify voter engagement activities in their community and if they participated. The majority of respondents (43.2%) did not contribute to voter engagement activities, however, 22.2% reported making financial contributions to voting rights advocacy groups, 10.3% helped with voter education, 9% helped with voter registration, and 9.8% made other contributions.

The Direction of the Country and Health Care Priorities

The majority of the respondents, over 92% (n=220) feel that the country is on the wrong track. Only five respondents felt that the country was generally going in the right direction (<3%) and thirteen respondents were unsure (5.5%). Forty two percent of respondents ranked the COVID-19 pandemic as the #1 problem to be addressed by the next administration; overall, 65% ranked COVID-19 among the top 5 problems. Nearly half of respondents ranked criminal justice/police brutality (49.0%); health care access and costs (48.6%); or race relations/racism (48.2%) among the top 5 problems. Also ranked among the top 5 problems by a large number of respondents were health inequities (36.5%); jobs/economic insecurity (36.1%); the economy (33.7%); and education (32.1%).

Surveys conducted in 2005 and 2018 identified the top 5 priorities of the NAHSE members. The top 5 initiatives appear in Table 1.

In 2005 and 2018, the member priorities focused on health disparities related to access, insurance reimbursement, and workforce recruitment and retention (Howard, 2018). After the COVID-19 pandemic, public health issues related to criminal justice, racism, economic insecurity, and the economy were center stage. The focus went from medical delivery issues around hospitals/facilities to macro-level issues that involved communities and broader existential threats to populations (NAHSE Research Committee, 2021). Since the majority (60%) of the NAHSE membership has been employed in hospital/health systems, the health care priorities have been influenced by the needs of the institution where they were employed (Howard, 2018). With COVID-19, the social unrest related to the deaths of unarmed Blacks, and the upcoming Presidential elections, the members focus transcended a facility focus to that affecting a broader scope of issues that would indirectly affect a hospital/health system.

CONCLUSION

In attempting to address the 2021 health care priorities, the NAHSE members suggested the organization pursue two broad categories of initiatives: 1) education and advocacy and leadership and collaboration. Specific ideas included developing white papers; leveraging website communication and newsletters; speaking engagements and educational forums; collecting and sharing data with Congress; Capitol Hill visits; coordinated advocacy efforts to reduce health care costs and inequities; promoting diversity in administrative, clinical, and executive levels; and partnering with other organizations to lead on important issues.

The political landscape did change. Joseph R. Biden and Kamala Harris were elected President and Vice-President, respectively, of the United States. Prior to their inauguration on January 6, 2021, former President Trump instigated an insurrection to overturn the election results. Nonetheless, the inauguration went forward on January 20, 2021 and the Biden/Harris Administration identified its priorities as COVID-19, Climate, Racial Equity, Economy, Healthcare, Immigration, and Restoring America's Global Standing (The White House, 2021). The NAHSE members 2021 top 5 priorities mirror the White House's priorities. The medical delivery and public health sectors have long been viewed as two separate systems in the U.S. and perhaps under a new administration, the focus can be on the better integration of these sectors.

ACKNOWLEDGMENT

The National Association of Health Services Executives (NAHSE) is a nonprofit association of Black health care executives founded in 1968 for the purpose of promoting the advancement and development of Black health care leaders and elevating the quality of health care services rendered to minority and underserved communities.

NAHSE's purpose is to ensure greater participation of minority groups in the health field. Its basic objective is to develop and maintain a strong viable national body to more effectively have input in the national health care delivery system. It has provided a vehicle for Blacks to effectively participate in the design, direction and delivery of quality health care to all people.

REFERENCES

Brennan Center. (2022). *Fact Sheet: The Impact of Voter Suppression on Communities of Color.* Retrieved from Brennan Center: https://www.brennancenter.org/our-work/research-reports/impact-voter-suppression-communities-color

Howard, D. (2018). Demographic Profile of NAHSE Members. In D. Howard (Ed.), *Celebrating Our Future by Remembering Our Past: NAHSE at 50* (pp. 353–359). NAHSE.

NAHSE Research Committee. (2021). *Election 20200: NAHSE Member Survey of Political Leadership in the United States.* Retrieved April 21, 2022, from http://www.nahsechicago.com/uploads/1/2/0/2/120299982/nahse_survey-members_020_presidential_election_2-5-21.pdf

The New York Times. (2020, November 3). Presidential Election Results: Biden Wins. *The New York Times*. Retrieved April 8, 2022, from https://www.nytimes.com/interactive/2020/11/03/us/elections/results-president.html

The White House. (2021). *The Biden-Harris Administration Immediate Priorities (2021).* Retrieved April 21, 2022, from https://www.whitehouse.gov/priorities/

Wang, T. (2012). *2012 Election Lessons Learned: How Voters Stood Up Against Suppression, ID, and Intimidation.* Demos. Retrieved from https://www.demos.org/policy-briefs/2012-election-lessons-learned

Chapter 11
COVID-19 and a Professional Organization's Member Responses

Diane M. Howard
Rush University, USA

Kimberly Enard
St. Louis University, USA

Rhonda BeLue
University of Texas, San Antonio, USA

Ebbin Dotson
School of Public Health, University of Michigan, USA

Keith Elder
Mississippi College, USA

Angel Evans
Governors State University, USA

Rupert Evans
Governors State University, USA

Allyson Hall
University of Alabama, Birmingham, USA

Dale Sanders
Alma College, USA

Laurie Shanderson
Methodist College, USA

Jacqueline C. Wiltshire
Indiana University, USA

ABSTRACT

The National Association of Health Services Executives issued a national survey to determine how its membership was responding to COVID-19 at its initial outbreak. Of the 201 respondents, 84% stated they were employed full-time; 4% were students; 4% were retired; and 4% were consultants, entrepreneurs, or working outside of the healthcare industry. More than half (53.5%) were employed by a hospital or hospital system, 12% worked at a university or academic institution, 9% were employed by consulting firms, with the remaining 14% employed in a variety of settings. Fifty-nine percent of respondents indicated they were always or usually working remotely, 13% worked remotely sometimes, and approximately 28% indicated that they rarely worked remotely. The survey results revealed COVID-19 had changed the way individuals interfaced at their work environment based on the nature of the work conducted and the age of the respondents and if they had school-aged children at home.

DOI: 10.4018/978-1-6684-2314-1.ch011

BACKGROUND

In December 2019, a suspicious flu-like condition was reported in Wuhan, China and started to circumnavigate the globe. By March 2020, the United States began a shut-down of services with school and employer closings. While the Federal Government was reluctant to issue formal statements that would impact the economy, deaths from COVID went from 16 cases in March 2020 to 231,024 by December 31, 2020. As of March 2022, there have been 79 million cases in the United States resulting in 952,000 deaths (Stevenson, A., & Chien, A. C., 2022). The population most severely affected were older adults and people with severe underlying medical conditions with heart or lung disease or diabetes (Stevenson, A., & Chien, A. C., 2022). Of the ethnic and racial groups and employees severely affected were African American, Latinx, and front-line workers.

The National Association of Health Services Executives

The National Association of Health Services Executives (NAHSE) is a personal membership group based in Washington, DC with over 30 chapters throughout the country. NAHSE was founded in 1968 for the purpose of promoting the advancement and development of Black health care leaders and elevating the quality of health care services rendered to minority and underserved communities through mentoring, educational programming, and policy development. NAHSE has over 2,000 members in senior leadership and middle management health care health systems, hospitals, consulting, insurance, association, and supplier firms. The membership included faculty and students from undergraduate and graduate health management programs. Sixty-percent of the members were female and 40% were male. Forty-eight percent of the members were under 40 years of age, 49% percent were between 41 and 59 years of age, and three-percent were over 60 years of age. Sixty-six percent of the membership had a master's degree, 5% have a Ph.D., 4% have a J.D., and 3% have a M.D. (Howard, 2018).

The COVID-19 Survey

One of the NAHSE organization's committees is the Research Committee which was developed in 2004 to supplement the Policy Committee initiatives. In May 2020, the NAHSE Research Committee issued the COVID-19 survey to determine how the NAHSE membership was responding to the COVID-19 pandemic. In addition, the membership was canvassed on their plans to attend the 2020 Annual Meeting in Atlanta. With 64% stating the meeting should not be face-to-face and 85% of the respondents stating they would attend a virtual meeting due to the pandemic and limitations being put on company travel, the NAHSE educational program was moved to a digital platform.

In addition, the survey solicited information on how NAHSE members were faring in the pandemic. Members were asked to respond to questions about the impact of COVID-19 on their professional lives and their impressions about some of the longer-term effects of COVID on their organizations and communities. Members were also asked about their perceptions of the national response to COVID. Approximately 2,000 NAHSE members received invitations to participate in the survey, and 201 members responded (10% response rate) between June 1 to June 15, 2020.

The Survey Results

Sixty-three percent of respondents were female; 37% were male. Fifty-six percent of the respondents were under 45 years of age; 35% were between 46 and 64 years of age; and 8% were 65 years or older. Respondents were geographically diverse. More than 31 NAHSE chapters in 28 states were represented among the respondents. Sixty percent of respondents were residents of nine states: Maryland (9%); Texas (8%); Florida (7%); Georgia, Illinois, New York, and Pennsylvania (6% each); and Michigan and North Carolina (5% each).

Eighty-four percent of respondents were employed and working full-time; students (4%) and retired persons (4%) are also included among the respondents; other respondents (4%) were consultants, entrepreneurs, or working in another industry outside of healthcare. More than half (53.5%) were employed by a hospital or hospital system; 12% worked at a university or academic institution; 9% were employed by consulting firms; the remaining 15% were employed in a variety of organizations, including law firms, medical device companies, community-based pharmacies, or as third-party insurance administrators. The majority of respondents (59%) were affiliated with American College of Healthcare Executives (ACHE): 44% are members and 8% are fellows of ACHE.

How is COVID-19 Affecting Professional Lives

The survey asked the members if they were working remotely. Fifty-nine percent of respondents indicated they always or usually worked remotely; 13% worked remotely sometimes; approximately 28% indicated they worked remotely rarely or never. The majority of respondents indicated they were extremely or very confident (81.6%) that their institution could adequately support them through the pandemic. However, nearly 20% of participants still had concerns about receiving adequate support from their institution. Over 90% strongly agreed or agreed that their institution communicated a clear plan in response to COVID-19. Slightly less than 10% of respondents were ambivalent or indicated that their institution did not have a clear communication plan.

Most respondents reported being extremely confident (36.7%), very confident (30.9%) or somewhat confident (20.9%) of their safety from COVID-19 infection in their work or school environments. Slightly more than 10% of respondents indicated that they were not so confident (7.3%) or not at all confident (4.2%) of their safety at work or school. Nearly 80% of respondents reported being at least a little worried that they may experience job loss, pay cuts or reduced benefits due to COVID-19 related financial losses experienced by your organizations. Approximately 22% of respondents indicated they were not at all worried about experiencing job loss, pay cuts or reduced benefits.

A majority of respondents (76.3%) indicated that they were coping well living and working virtually; (11.6%) indicated that they were barely coping or not coping; 12% of respondents responded "other" to this question and specified that they were not working remotely and they were going into the office (5%) or refused to respond (3%). The remaining 4% stated:

- It comes and it goes. Most days I'm fine but there are moments when I miss what life used to be.
- Coping was maybe too harsh of a word, but it was a big adjustment.
- Every day was different. It depended on the day but I'm mostly coping well.

What are the longer-term effects of COVID-19 on Members' Organizations and Communities?

There was no clear consensus among respondents about whether social distancing will stay in force indefinitely. Thirty-one percent of respondents answered yes when asked if social distancing was here to stay; 35% answered no, and a 33% were unsure. The majority of respondents (87%) indicated support for laser thermometer testing to check for fevers before employees returned to work (63% were very likely and 24% were likely to support laser thermometer testing). Less than 10% of respondents indicated they were unlikely or very unlikely to support laser thermometer testing.

Most respondents indicated that their organizations served more than one type of community. Approximately 85.9% of respondents reported that their organization served city or urban communities; 59.9% served suburban communities, and 41.2% serve rural communities.

The resources most frequently named by respondents as being most important to helping their communities respond to the COVID-19 pandemic were: employment (18.8%), hospital and emergency services (13.7%), telehealth (14.7%), groceries (9.6%) and banking/financial (8.1%). In addition, 18.8% reported that "other" resources were important to helping their communities respond to COVID-19. Where "other" was indicated, the respondents thought all the listed resources were critical to the community and they did not want to identify one service over another (14%). The remaining respondents reported that their survey would not allow them to indicate a specific resource and the "other" category was the only category they could check. The majority of respondents (82.5%) had either a very negative or negative impression of the federal leadership's response to COVID-19 pandemic. The remaining respondents had a neutral (14%) or positive (3.5%) impression of the federal response.

Three main themes emerged from qualitative responses to this question. First, respondents indicated that the federal government needs to send clear, fact-based messaging about the pandemic. Communication should be based on guidance and facts from medical and scientific experts, without bias or a political agenda. Second, the federal government should address racial and ethnic disparities associated with COVID-19. Finally, coordination between federal, state, and local governments should be improved.

WHERE ARE WE NOW?

It has been two-years since the COVID-19 2020 survey was administered. The 2020 presidential election ushered in Joseph R. Biden and Kamala Harris as president and vice-president, respectively. Immediate attention was directed at promoting vaccinations with a vaccination rate of 65% as of February 2022 (New York Times, 2022). The Centers for Disease Control became the central agency to record and publish COVID rates and issue directives on masking. Scientists rather than politicians became the voice of COVID protocols from the White House podium. The Federal Drug Administration issued emergency authorization for Johnson & Johnson's single-shot COVID-19 vaccine and subsequently put its administration on pause due to reports of blood clots in people who received the shot. The pause was subsequently lifted determining that the benefits of the shot outweighed potential risks.

President Biden mandated vaccines for federal workers and contractors. Some states had already adopted mandates that applied to state employees and health care workers (AARP, 2022). The delta variant became the dominant strain in the U.S. and worldwide in September 2021 which was replaced by the omicron variant as the dominant strain in December 2021. A level of frustration crept into the population that had grown tired of masking, social distancing, and working remotely. The fear of COVID was replaced by frustration and anger. At the start of March 2022, two-years after the COVID pandemic was made official, there were over 78 million confirmed cases in the United States and approximately 950,000 deaths (Stevenson, A., & Chien, A. C., 2022).

The NAHSE membership held its 2021 meeting remotely, the second time the annual meeting was moved to a digital platform. Its Leadership Retreat in December 2021 was held as a hybrid meeting. Approximately 30 members attended in-person in New Orleans while 30 members attended digitally. Clearly COVID has changed how people meet. The airplane travel has been replaced with digital meetings that are less expensive and easier to schedule and manage. Anecdotally, the membership is anxious to see each other and socialize, but there remains an anxiety around meetings where there are restrictions based on vaccination status and masking.

In general, the nature of work has changed. The pandemic has taught people lessons of work-life balance. The daily grind of being at the desk, responding to e-mails, running from meeting to meeting with little opportunity to reflect, the luncheon and evening meetings have been replaced with thoughtful and more deliberate management of time. There is variability in how each generation of NAHSE member responds. For those members over 55 years of age and approaching retirement, there is the realization that their health is important and getting the two-dose vaccination and booster is key to remaining healthy. For those members with children, the pandemic has created havoc in their lives. Their children's vaccination status has influenced how they interface with the world. School closures with digital class work moved the membership into the home and working remotely in a home office became de rigueur. Emerging leaders found that moving away from the politics in the office was satisfying. In January 2022, the Centers for Disease Control published it recommendations that most children and all teens could get COVID-19 vaccinations (CDC, 2022).

In February 2022, California was the first U.S. state to wind down its restrictive COVID-19 measures and move the state from its pandemic to an endemic orientation to the disease (Serrin, 2022). New York, New Jersey, and Connecticut followed suit and lifted their restrictions on mask-wearing, business closures, and vaccination requirements. As COVID-19 cases fell along with hospitalizations, cities and states are opening, and at times outpacing the CDC and its guidelines (Tucker, E., Alonso, M., & Johnston, C., 2022). Many U.S. states, led by Republican governors and legislatures refused or had relaxed standards in following COVID-19 masking and vaccination standards.

Hybrid models of remote work are likely to persist in the wake of the pandemic, mostly for highly educated, well-paid minority of the workforce (Lund, S., Madgavkar, A., Manyika, J. & Smit, S., 2020). Cultural and technological barriers have been removed that prevented remote work in the past. The issue is maintaining contact with colleagues, reaching consensus, and moving decision-making to benefit the organization rather than hiding behind computers. In healthcare delivery, many of the jobs require collaborating with others or using specialized machinery; other jobs, such as conducting CT scans, must be done on location; and some, such as managing supply chain deliveries, must be performed onsite (Lund, S., Madgavkar, A., Manyika, J. & Smit, S., 2020). This will create disparities in healthcare delivery as advantages are given to those with education who have the ability to work from home. The converse is also true that political advantages are given to those who have the luxury of coming to work and interfacing with senior executives face-to-face.

On the academic side, admissions committee interviews have moved from face-to-face onsite interviews to digital platforms. Classes that were once face-to-face and moved to remote learning can now be face-to-face, remote, and hybrid. The personal relations and development of interpersonal skills that were once so important have been interrupted by technological interface. It is yet unclear what the future holds and how the world of work will be affected.

What we do know is that in the two-years since COVID, the U.S economy has rebounded after losing 22 million jobs in spring 2020. The share of Black Americans who are either working or looking for work, known as the labor force participation rate, was equal to the share for White workers in both January and February 2022 (Marte, J., 2022). The Labor Department reported that over the last year, payrolls have remained robust averaging more than 550,000 a month with unemployment under 4% (Marte, J., 2022)

CONCLUSION

While we have no data to address post-COVID response from the NAHSE membership, there are plans to return to its face-to-face programming in May 2022. The reluctance to gather in meeting space has slowly ebbed as it has across the country. Members want to connect and develop the camaraderie they experienced before COVID. The psychological after-effects of COVID have not been captured through surveys. There is only anecdotal information that members want to put the trauma of COVID behind them and move on to whatever is the "new normal."

REFERENCES

AARP. (2022). *List of Coronavirus-Related Restrictions in Every State*. Retrieved March 22, 2022, from https://www.aarp.org/politics-society/government-elections/info-2020/coronavirus-state-restrictions.html

CDC. (2022). *Covid-19 Vaccines for Children and Teens*. Retrieved March 5, 2022, from CDC: https://www.cdc.gov/coronavirus/2019-ncov/vaccines/recommendations/children-teens.html

Howard, D. (2018). Demographic Profile of NAHSE Members. In D. Howard (Ed.), *Celebrating our Future by Remembering our Past: NAHSE at 50* (pp. 353–359). NAHSE.

Lund, S., Madgavkar, A., Manyika, J., & Smit, S. (2020). *What's Next for Remote Work: An Analysis of 2,000 Tasks, 800 Jobs, and nine Countries*. Retrieved November 23, 2020, from https://www.mckinsey.com/featured-insights/future-of-work/whats-next-for-remote-work-an-analysis-of-2000-tasks-800-jobs-and-nine-countries

Marte, J. (2022). *The Evolving Post-COVID U.S. Job Market in five Charts*. Retrieved March 16, 2022, from Reuters: https://www.reuters.com/world/us/evolving-post-covid-us-job-market-five-charts-2022-03-04/

New York Times. (2022). Retrieved March 22, 2022. https://www.nytimes.com/interactive/2021/us/covid-cases.html

Serin, G. (2022). *Gov. Newsom Lifts All, but 5% of COVID-19 Executive Actions. Here's What Remains*. Retrieved March 22, 2022, from KCRA: https://www.kcra.com/article/gov-newsom-lifts-all-but-5-covid-executive-actions-heres-what-remains/39233442#

Stevenson, A., & Chien, A. C. (2022). *Covid Live Updates: As Asia grapples with omicron, cases rise again in Europe*. Retrieved March 16, 2022, from The New York Times: https://www.nytimes.com/live/2022/03/16/world/covid-19-mandates-cases-vaccine

Tucker, E., Alonso, M., & Johnston, C. (2022). *Growing Number of States, Major Cities Lift COVID-19 Restrictions*. Retrieved March 6, 2022, from CNN: https://www.cnn.com/2022/02/19/us/covid-mandates-vaccine-indoor-dining/index.html

Chapter 12
Fifteen Years of Diversity Leadership at an Academic Medical Center in Chicago

Cynthia E. Boyd
Rush University Medical Center, USA

John Andrews
Rush University Medical Center, USA

Paula J. Brown
Rush University Medical Center, USA

Angela L. Davis
Rush University Medical Center, USA

Sheila A. Dugan
Rush University Medical Center, USA

Sharon Gates
Rush University Medical Center, USA

Diane M. Howard
Rush University Medical Center, USA

Wrenetha A. Julion
https://orcid.org/0000-0002-5197-9955
Rush University Medical Center, USA

Christopher Nolan
Rush University System for Health, USA

ABSTRACT

The diversity and inclusion initiatives at a Chicago academic medical center are reviewed in the context of its activities over 15 years. The team of leaders discuss how the diversity initiatives were introduced and the strengths, weaknesses, opportunities, and threats of pursuing diversity, equity, and inclusion, as staff move in and out of the organization. Five employee resource groups and initiatives that serve as the backbone of the DEI initiatives are discussed including Rush community service initiatives program, Americans with Disabilities, business diversity, Women's Leadership, and LGBTQ programming.

BACKGROUND

The diversity leadership initiative at Rush University Medical Center was initiated in 2007 after a formal diversity plan was developed. Accountability for diversity at Rush was accepted by the Executive

DOI: 10.4018/978-1-6684-2314-1.ch012

Leadership Council. Rush diversity goals were established in 2008 and annual reporting on diversity recommendations began with an energized organization. In 2012, *Diversity and Inclusion: A Report of Progress* was published to inventory the strides made in making the Medical Center a diverse and inclusive environment (2012). The D&I initiatives were to sustainable with activities to benefit the community, including patients, students, faculty, staff and people that Rush serves (2012).

A five-year plan was initiated led by senior leadership under the Executive Leadership Council with participation by the President/CEO. The Rush vision was adopted: To be a diverse and inclusive patient care, educational, research and community service institution of the highest caliber with measurable goals. Accountability for diversity at Rush

The Medical Center located in an ethnically diverse community with minorities representing over 65 percent of those living in the area (2012). In quantifying its internal constituency, it described itself as being 70 percent female; over 45 percent minority, approximately 40 percent physician residents and fellows are minority, almost 75 percent of students are women, almost 30 percent of students are minority.

In supporting the D&I initiatives, the Medical Center formed two bodies to achieve diversity goals over a 5-year period and to meet a 2016 deadline to accomplish the goals established. Those entities, Executive Leadership Council and Diversity Leadership Council (DLC) were to collaborate on the specified goals developed. The core stakeholder groups were management, faculty and students. The Management Subcommittee focused on the university and medical center sectors. The Student and Faculty Subcommittees focused on the university sector.

Goal Setting and the Work of the Subcommittees

The Management Subcommittee's key goals were 1) gender diversity, 2) ethnic diversity, and 3) inclusion of people with disabilities. A key decision of the group was that Rush look like its customers.

The goals of the subcommittee were:

Goal 1: Achieve and maintain gender diversity of 50 percent female/male for Executive Leadership Council, Associate Vice President, Assistant Vice President and Director positions.

Goal 2: Achieve and maintain ethnic diversity by 20 percent among management to reflect Rush's patient population and availability of talent.

Goal 3: Establish an organization that continues to distinguish itself as being the place for those with disabilities to work and to receive care.

The Faculty Subcommittee's two goals were:

Goal 1: Faculty and academic leadership will be reflective of the patients, students and other communities served with a target of 5 percent above ethnic availability.

Goal 2: Build cultural awareness and competency among faculty and graduates by building comprehensive learning experiences and prepare graduates to be providers in a diverse and global society.

The Student Subcommittee recognized that students consider matriculation based on the diversity of the faculty and so faculty recruitment was considered vital.

Goal 1: Ensure matriculation of students who are underrepresented in medicine is at or above 16 percent of the available number from programs throughout the U.S. The focus was on students from biological science programs.

Goal 2: Create a welcoming, multicultural environment for all students.

Our fearless leader – J. Robert Clapp

J. Robert Clapp ("Bob") joined Rush University Medical Center in 2005 as Senior Vice-President of Hospital Affairs. He was responsible for the day-to-day operations of the hospital and was critical to the 10-year comprehensive renovation of the Rush campus. Bob was a faculty member in the graduate program in Health Systems Management at Rush University where he taught the Capstone course. He was highly rated for his teaching and served as a mentor for students and managers. A graduate of George Washington University's MHA program, he held senior leadership roles at Tenet Healthcare Corporation and Duke University Medical Center prior to coming to Rush.

Bob established and chaired the Rush Diversity Leadership Group, the advisory body on Medical Center diversity. In 2009, Rush established an annual award in his name which is given to an individual or group for promoting or creating diversity and inclusion at Rush. Bob was diagnosed and succumbed to pancreatic cancer in 2012. A much-admired healthcare executive, his loss as the chair of the Diversity Leadership Group was significant because he worked at the System, Medical Center, and University levels. Also, as a White Southerner who worked internationally, he brought a geographic perspective, both regional and international that was difficult to replicate.

When Bob conceived of developing the diversity initiative at Rush, he convened a planning group composed of leadership from human resources, Equal Employment Opportunity Commission (EEOC) and support services. The group developed an executive briefing which Bob shared with senior executives at Rush and colleagues from Innovations International and a former colleague with whom he developed the diversity initiative at Duke University Medical Center. In 2006, the diversity plan and corporate diversity goals were developed. In May 2006, a conversation on diversity was held at Rush with 50 attendees. From these attendees, the Diversity Leadership Council was developed. The 27 original members of the DLC formed a close bond because each member discussed their personal journeys through diversity. The sharing of stories created a bond between these early DLC members which has endured over the 15-years of the DLC.

Scholarships

In 2012, the Diversity Leadership Council was intentional in setting up scholarship support to increase diversity in the student population. During the span of time between 2012 and 2021, the number of African American & Latinx students in the University increased from 12-19%, and the absolute numbers of URM students increased from 266 to 508 (17-30%). While there had been a dramatic increase in the total dollar total dollar amount of scholarship dollars allocated for the University from all sources between 2012 and 2021, the time-period between 2019 and 2021 saw the largest increases ranging from 3.6 million to 6.4 million. The grand total in scholarship dollars over the past 10 years is $23 million. The break down in scholarship support to the University based upon the source of the funding for FY 21 follows below.

The Rush System for Health provided $4.6 million or 72% of total scholarship dollars to the University. Individual college level DEI scholarships to students over the past 3 years varied according to identified need. The College of Medicine saw diversity scholarship numbers increase from 42 to 68 students. The College of Nursing scholarships ranged from a low of 48 in 2019 and 2020 to 106 in 2021. The College of Health Sciences received DEI scholarship support for 30 to 82 students. The average number of students supported by DEI scholarships in the Graduate College was 22 (high of 30 in

2021). Additional institutional DEI scholarship support is available to the four colleges for fiscal years 22 through 25 at the current level of funding in the amount of approximately 5 million dollars. Even so, there are disparities in funding based upon the colleges with the CHS and COM receiving 2-3 times as much as the Graduate College and the CON. The next steps are to craft a 4-year funding plan that will extend from 2026 – 2030. The four colleges will reassess the levels of DEI funding necessary to remain competitive. The institutional commitment to future scholarships would remain intact because the funding would continue to come from non-operating income. Future implications for DEI scholarships include developing uniform metrics that exemplify return on investment, advancing equity and compliance with DEI legal guidelines, and considering a potential shift to philanthropic support.

EMBEDDED CASE STUDIES:

Case Study 1: Rush Community Service Initiatives Program (RCSIP) - Sharon Gates

The student led outreach effort named Rush Community Service Initiatives Program (RCSIP) began organically in 1991. Peter DiGolia, a Rush medical student, began volunteering his time to teach parishioners in the basement of St. Basil's Church the meaning behind the numbers of their blood pressure results. When his classmates heard what he was doing, they wanted to join Peter. The group decided to bring the idea to the attention of the medical college to make it a learning experience for all students and involve faculty, thereby, gaining a deeper reach into the community. The students met with Dr. Ed Eckenfels, department Chair for Religion and Health, along with Dr. Larry Goodman who, at the time, was the Senior Associate Dean of the Medical College. They both approved of the creation of RCSIP stating it would be a benefit to the community and to the student experience. The founders of RCSIP agreed the program must not be required nor should the experience be reflected in the students' official transcripts. They decided the mission should be centered around humanism and bring to life the vision of improving the health of the individuals and families on the westside of Chicago. The first RCSIP experiences were St. Basil's Church and Franciscan Outreach.

RCSIP evolved around the needs of the community with programming positioned where the participants live, attend school, church and community centers. This made it convenient for participants to become involved. For example, there was a rise in asthma attacks in children at the Henry Horner Housing Development located next door to Rush across the Eisenhower Expressway. Students and staff visited the site regularly holding workshops for youth on how to prevent asthma attacks and helping educate parents about the dangers of smoking around the children.

The volunteers of RCSIP have always been responsive to the community. When AIDS became a reality for us all, a student created a fictional character called Cyrus the Virus. His desire was to educate teachers, students, anyone in the community interested in learning the truth about AIDS and how to avoid acquiring the virus. These types of student led efforts are supported by faculty who guide students in applying evidence-based research to their curriculum.

The many programs under the umbrella of RCSIP take different shapes. Such as when the levees broke in New Orleans after Hurricane Katrina hit land. Due to the massive flooding, families were relocated to northern cities to provide safe shelter until the waters receded and the community rebuilt. Chicago received over 10,000 people who were rescued from the Super Dome. Partnering with the Salvation

Army, RCSIP volunteers met the new arrivals at Fosco Park providing them with emotional support and assisting city personnel connecting the survivors with resources. In 2012, a call to Rush came in from the new founding principal of Richard T. Crane Medical Preparatory High School to partner. With a $10,000 donation to fund the partnership with a directive to establish a program involving ten students. Instead, RCSIP adopted the entire school and folded multiple programs into the school such as career exploration, health education, exposure days at Rush, college prep, paid summer internships for more than 500 students and targeted programming that included a Health IT initiative.

The new initiative was funded by the JPMorgan Chase Foundation. For three years over 65 youth were taught courses to become certified in Epic which is software for an electronic medical record. Epic is a billion-dollar company that provided training at their headquarters in Verona, Wisconsin. The goal for the youth enrolled in this program was graduation from high school, admission to college with scholarship dollars and certification in Epic. People with a high school diploma, Epic certification and two years of experience have the potential to earn a six-figure job within in the health care industry. Today, 100 percent of the students in the Health IT Initiative have graduated from high school and admitted to college with scholarship. A handful of students received over $1 million in individual scholarship offers. Many in the first graduating class of the new Crane graduated from college in the spring and winter of 2021. Several are preparing for their next step in applying to a graduate program in healthcare. A Crane alum who graduated early from college was admitted to the Rush College of Nursing and she has completed term three of their classes. Now that the funding from Chase is over, other opportunities have been created to keep the students engaged in a career in Health IT through Revenue Cycle. Interesting, this experience was funded in June of 2021 by The Crane Company. Richard T. Crane High School bears the name of the company's founder. Also, programming to encourage students to pursue a career in health are ongoing at the school through RCSIP volunteers. The overarching goal is to break the cycle of generational poverty.

Another extremely important time that brought change to RCSIP was the pandemic of 2020 – COVID-19. When Rush leadership decided to keep students and staff safe while the world waited for a vaccine, the students demanded to be included in the continued care of the people they saw weekly in the shelters. After signing a waiver, they began volunteering again by screening the men and women at the shelters twice daily in the beginning. The process played like a symphony – individuals were screened, if they were symptomatic, they were taken to a testing site. Should the person have COVID, they were admitted to a Rush College of Nursing respite site. During this time, Rush applied for the Spencer Foreman National Award for Community Service which was presented by the Association of American Medical Colleges (AAMC). Rush became the 2020 recipient of the award due to the seamless execution of our community outreach efforts for the past 30 years.

The benefits of RCSIP aren't limited to the community residents and stakeholders. Student volunteers gain great benefits from the experiences as they connect to the community, learning the history of the people and challenges they face; especially those who are of a different race than the student provider. This is essential given Rush is located on the west side of Chicago and the institution's patient census is predominately from marginalized neighborhoods located in Rush's backyard. As the student progresses with their professional career, they won't be limiting their care to people whom they resemble or practice their religious belief. They will have to learn how to connect with their future patients to earn their trust. Students are learning the needs of the people they serve along with the daily challenges that are embedded in structural racism. When working with families at a shelter, a student recently said he now realizes there is no difference between the wants and desires of his parents and the parents he met at the shelter, "they all want a healthy meal in their child's belly, a roof over their head and a good education". RCSIP is giving students these experiences as they work to bridge the gaps in the community.

RCSIP's commitment to the community is sustainability. Given the programs are led by a team of student volunteers who have academic requirements, a strong structure is required to assure that Rush sees to the programs continuing. The organization chart includes general volunteers, steerers, RCSIP Core leaders which is the governing body for RCSIP consisting of one leader per program and the RCSIP Core co-presidents. This hierarchy works to elevate the voices of all programs and address their needs. Clinical programs have licensed supervision and non-clinical programs have faculty advisors. As the steerers progress in their academic journey, they select their successors. The peaceful transition of power happens at the start of the new school year, followed by orientations and training. The entire process is overseen by a staff person who is true to the mission, raises the money to keep the programs running, advocates for the students and partners with community stakeholders.

Case Study 2: ADA – Paula Brown

History of RUMC Americans with Disabilities Act (ADA) Task Force

The Rush Americans with Disabilities Act Task Force was created in 1991, just a year after the passage of the Americans with Disabilities Act in 1990, as defined by Section 504 of the Rehabilitation Act. At that time, Rush University Medical Center was one of the first, if not the only medical center in the nation that created a Task Force solely to create a culture of inclusion for persons with disabilities.

The processes and programming around inclusion for persons with disabilities were broad and powerful. The catalysts for the work began with upholding RUMC's ICARE values of Inclusion, Collaboration, Accountability, Respect, and Excellence. The goal of the organization was to become a best practice and national leader for empowering people with disabilities. The goal was accomplished through the promotion of exceptional education to and clinical treatment of people with disabilities. The tools used to become THE national best practice included the following:

- Education
    - Disability Speaks series
    - Online Educational Modules
    - Creation of a Disability web page
    - Trauma training
- Engagement
    - Thonar Award Program

Named after Eugene J-MA Thonar, Ph.D., a world renowned biochemist. Being on the task force from its inception, Dr. Thonar, born in Belgium and raised in South Africa. He dreamed of being a professional soccer player as a child, but was diagnosed, at age 14 with ankylosing spondylitis, a chronic inflammation of the spine, a condition that for many years his doctors misdiagnosed as tuberculosis. As a teenager, he spent years confined to a bed in a convalescent home, where he received only an hour of schooling a day from visiting teachers. Dr. Thonar used his disability and his passion for helping others with disabilities into "turning a disability into a possibility." Annual celebrations of people with disabilities were supported and encouraged across the enterprise, and it helped overtime, to change the perceptions and abilities of people with disabilities. People who won the award did not have to have a disability, but they had to have helped this population in some significant way. People who won the award crossed all segments of the medical center and university, from doctors, nurses, administrators, faculty, students, and volunteers. Dr. Thonar was noted as saying "I think Rush has gone further than almost any medical center in the country and probably in the world in making this place accessible. For many years now, Rush has taken a proactive approach to improving the Medical Center for people with disabilities."

The significance of his influence in this area is evident in the fact that the ADA task force chose to name its annual award for him. He often said there was nothing he was prouder of than the award being given in my name, and the work I've done with the task force." He was profoundly gratified that he was able to change the culture of such a prestigious institution.

Other engagement activities came from:

- RU Student Disability Assessment Team [RUSDAT]
- PACE Program
  - § Rush encouraged a relationship and internships with this program that stemmed from National Louis University; that specialized in Paths to Academics, Community, and Employment,
    - Outreach
- Chicago Area Health Education Center
- Healthcare and Family Services of Illinois
- Safehaven
- Symposiums on updates in the field of pediatric care for children with special needs
- ADA Employment Forums
  - Scholarships
- Journal entries
- Conference presentations
- Student capstones
  - Collaborations
- Road Home Program/The Center for Veterans their Families at Rush
- Access Living
- Mayor's Office for People with Disabilities
- Michael and Julie Tracy Foundation
- Office of the State Guardian
- Illinois Department of Public Health
  - Actions taken included:
- Nursing Care Plans
- Creating Mocktracers for patients with Intellectual Developmental Disabilities (IDD)
- Service Animal Policy
  - § Rush was the first medical center in the nation to create a Service Animal Policy. The lead committee members charged with its creation was a blind pharmacist who worked for the Poison Control Center. The highlight of this policy was once emphasized by a patient who told administrators that they came to Rush solely because of Rush's Service Animal Policy. They noted that no other medical center they contacted would accept them as a patient because they had a service animal. The patient had no family or friends to care for him or his animal, so Rush became their lifesaver.

The results of these continuous efforts over time were ultimately to gain patient satisfaction, as well as to create a culture of inclusion for its employees. To that end, the following were highlights of Rush's creations and accomplishments:

§ 24 programs for improved access and services.
§ 45 instances of accommodations and accessibility
§ Local and National recognition and awards for our efforts.

The improvements continue because, what we learned over time was that, every life has value....

Case Study 3: Business Diversity – John Andrews

The Rush University Medical Center Business Diversity Program, launched in 2007, began as an initiative embedded in the Leadership and Accountability Sub-Group of the Diversity Leadership Group (DLG), now the Diversity Leadership Council (DLC). The program position statement was clear in terms of focus and intent:

Consistent with the Rush commitment to Equal Opportunity, Diversity and Affirmative Action, Rush is establishing a Business Diversity Program to ensure that qualified diverse and local suppliers will have equal access to opportunities to do business with Rush.

Rush's leadership dedicated time and effort outlining the business case for developing and supporting the program including:

- Shifting demographics in business ownership
  - MBE and WBE business ownership has doubled in last 10 years
- Opportunity to supports the small business community
  - Creates jobs & helps to build businesses of scale
  - Estimated that 120MM people employed by small business
  - Local hiring, small businesses typically hire within 2-3 mile radius of business location
- Helps to create local and diverse vendors of scale
- Creates competition between current and potential vendors
- Helps to create value in the supply chain and drives cost savings
- Promotes innovation through the introduction of new products, services, and solutions
- Demonstrates Rush's commitment to doing business in diverse and local markets
- Showcases Rush's commitment to the economic vitality of all communities

The program has focused on several key diverse vendor groups including certified minority and women-owned businesses, small businesses, and business owned and operated by person with disabilities.

Local procurement, defined as within in the Chicago city limits, has also been a focus area since the program's inception. More recently, Rush launched its Anchor Mission Strategy, which has a "Buy Local" pillar aimed at supporting the vendor community in Chicago's West Side neighborhood. This initiative calls for moving millions of dollars of annual operational and capital supply spend to vendors within a targeted catchment area. The goals of the initiative include increasing annual spend with West Side vendors, working to build West Side businesses of scale, and increase local hiring by the supported businesses.

Additional, as part of our Anchor Mission Strategy, Rush was an early signatory of the Healthcare Anchor Network's (HAN) Impact Purchasing Commitment, which focused on growing local procurement spend, community wealth-building, and expanding sustainability efforts within the healthcare industry.

To ensure a successful and sustainable program, Rush has instituted several policy and procedures aimed at encouraging increased of local and diverse business including:

- Created a business diversity manager role in Purchasing and Contracting
- Developed business diversity metrics and dashboard
- Tracking prime vendor and Tier II spend annually
- Created annual diverse and local vendor spend goals
- Added supplier diversity reporting language to request for proposals (RFPs) and contracts
- Engaged and supported business diversity assist agencies and affinity groups
- Launched a comprehensive business diversity outreach strategy
- Hosted an annual diverse vendor fair

Over the past decade, the Rush Business Diversity Program has been able to have real economic impact by using its considerable spending power to support the local and diverse vendor community. More importantly, the Rush supply chain and organization has benefitted significantly from its support of the many qualified and successful small, minority and women-owned businesses within the Chicago market.

Case Study 4: Women's Leadership – Sheila Dugan

In 2017, the gender equity group, the Women's Leadership Council (WLC) presented to the combined Senior Leadership Team (SLT) and Executive Leadership Council (ELC) about the state of gender equity at the institution. The invite came from the CEO and was related to recent conversations with the Chair of the WLC. It was brought to his attention that, per usual, the Semi-Annual Medical Staff Meeting included one, mostly white, male after another reporting out from each sector of the corporation, although the work reported out was done by diverse teams of individuals, including many women. In fact, almost 75% of the paychecks at the institution go to women. The recent publication of a picture of the Section Chiefs in Internal Medicine was another reminder that although half of the medical school students are women, the Chiefs were all male, and only one was non-white. The WLC led off the meeting with a slide comparing the 2017 Internal Medicine Chief picture with the 1971 photo of the all-white, all-male department. What about feminism in academic medicine? The #MeToo movement exposed widespread sexual harassment across many industries; medicine was no exception. Our gender equity work was relevant and crucial.

For some background, the WLC was the final iteration of a group of women leaders that had been meeting related to gender equity and the climate for women at the institution since the early 2000's. Initially the group hailed from the Medical College (the Women's Advisory Group to the Dean) and later encompassed University women leaders (the Provost's Committee on Gender). One thing was clear to women leaders across their networks: corporate women faced similar challenges. We knew we were stronger together. The next iteration, the Women's Leadership Council, aimed to include all women leaders. The intentional name change aligned the WLC with the Diversity Leadership Council (DLC) nomenclature. Beyond the name, it also aligned the WLC work with the DLC's scope and goals. The intersection of gender and race result in even greater pipeline issues for BIPOC women. In reporting out to the group of like-minded individuals in the DEI space, the WLC could benefit from best practices, insights about organizational sponsors and pitfalls, and maintaining positivity and long term perspectives.

Next we set to aligning our work with institutional priorities, an important step in garnering resources for diversity work. Ahead of the SLT and ELC meeting presentation, we queried women leaders, including University Professors and Associate Vice President level and above, about their lived career experience. Themes about gender inequity surfaced including perceived salary inequity: limited family friendly benefits and policies; lack of talent management, succession planning, and transparency related to jobs in leadership roles; and a male dominated climate. After the presentation, the CEO and President requested a five year plan and budget toward gender equity.

One key ingredient in successful advocacy is recognition. Prior to 2017 we were a group of dedicated women who were working in a vacuum. Therefore, we budgeted for a WLC space, including private office and conference furniture to gather and train; a lending library; and a lactation space. Thus, allowing us to strategize, share successes and challenges, informally mentor one another, and expand our social and professional networks. Our budget also included visiting speakers, book clubs, travel to present at gender equity meetings, and salary support for a half time administrator and .2 FTE Chair position. Leadership training was budgeted to support women attending internal HR and university based and national women's leadership training including ELAM and the Carol Emmott Foundation. We have worked with HR in support of their Total Benefits package with a broader range of family friendly benefits like support for child care. We continue to meet about conveniently located lactation rooms. In addition, we have an annual report out from the Office of Institutional Equity regarding the number, type and disposition of hotline complaints, learning that the vast majority are in the sexual harassment followed by racial bias category.

We continue to support a stronger Talent Management effort but find that the pandemic has shifted the focus to recruitment due to myriad openings. Internally, we launched and completed two mentorship programs. The first linked WLC mentees with SLT/ELC mentors. More recently, the WLC mentorship program connected women leaders across the entire system of hospitals and the University in mentor/mentee pairs to broaden opportunity recognition. We are particularly focused on increasing the number of women in leadership positions, in particular BIPOC women. Since women participate to a greater extent than men in unpaid, and possibly unrecognized DEI work, we focus on women's wellness. At our institution, women are more likely to use the Wellness Center programming; we work collaboratively with the Wellness Center to provide women's focused programs. We published findings of several targeted multivariate salary analyses that concluded there was no statistically significant differences by gender in salaries but work to change covariates like the number of men versus women promoted to Professor or in high paid specialties.

The gender equity work continues to inspire and at times frustrate the WLC. Institutional support gives us a stronger platform, yet we have work to do related to the sexism most of us have grown up with, understanding that healthcare is no exception.

Case Study 5: LGBTQ Leadership – Christopher Nolan

Rush University Medical Center has routinely been at the forefront of lesbian, gay, bisexual, transgender, and queer health equity initiatives. From an inclusive affirmative action policy dating back to the 1970s, being an early adopter of same-sex domestic partner benefits since 2000 and creating an LGBT student organization in the early 2000s, Rush has been committed to enhancing and improving health and well-being. Upon the creation of the Diversity Leadership Council (DLC) in 2008, Rush doubled down on its commitment to the LGBTQ community. In 2009, Rush participated in the Human Rights Campaign (HRC) Foundation's Healthcare Equality Index (HEI). Not only did Rush participate, but it became the first academic hospital in the State of Illinois to receive a perfect score and be named a Leader in LGBT Health Equality. This effort then led to Rush receiving the HRC Corporate Equality Award in 2009.

In 2014, upon annual completion of the annual HEI survey, it was clear that while Rush was still earning Leader status, there was still work to be done to ensure healthcare equity for the LGBTQ+ community. As a result, in consulting the best practices published by the HRC HEI, completing an organizational scan, as well as a strengths, weaknesses, opportunities, threats (SWOT) analysis, it was clear that more could, and should, be done. As a result of this, the LGBT Health Committee was formed by employees dedicated to bringing about best practices for the community. In order to ensure that this effort was well supported, the co-chairs made sure to build the committee into existing Rush structures. As such, the then Rush University Medical Center President as well as DLC Chair were consulted, with a recommendation that the Committee be formed under the DLC. The LGBT Health Committee was officially adopted by the Diversity Leadership Council in Spring of 2014. The committee was then tasked with bringing best LGBT practices to Rush, including the aim to have Rush's community hospital in Oak Park, Illinois, Rush Oak Park Hospital, participate in the HEI. In forming the committee, the aim was to have all of Rush's respective arms represented in the effort: both hospitals, the university, and the medical group. There were also champions enlisted from legal, human resources, and marketing/communications, and the Rush General Counsel was appointed the Executive Sponsor.

The LGBTQ+ Leadership Council began implementing many initiatives to achieve health equity for the LGBTQ+ community and has made incredible strides since its founding. The following is a brief timeline of major LGBTQ+ highlights at Rush that have either been led or influenced by the LGBTQ+ Leadership Council.

2014

- Completed LGBT SWOT/organizational scan and identified best practice opportunities
- LGBT Health Committee officially forms under Diversity Leadership Council
- Rush Oak Park Hospital completes its first Healthcare Equality Index survey, earning a perfect score and Leader status

2016

- Rush became the first health system in Illinois to offer comprehensive affirming insurance coverage for transgender employees and students
- Rush led the way with EPIC (Electronic Health Record) integration of Sexual Orientation and Gender Identity (SOGI) data to ensure Rush could accurately and respectfully document patient identity
- LGBTQ+ liaison role created in order to help Rush employees and community members navigate the Rush system

2018

- Rush Copley Medical Center participated in its first Healthcare Equality Index, resulting in all three Rush Hospitals being awarded LGBTQ+ Leadership status by Human Rights Campaign Foundation
- Adopted inclusive signage and formalized a policy allowing all people to use the bathroom that most closely aligns with their gender identity
- Recruited Medical Director for LGBTQ+ efforts

2019

- All 3 Rush hospitals joined the WERQ! Chicago job fair with an aim for more LGBTQ+ hiring
- Growing LGBTQ+ services led to 3 full-time employees being hired: a Manager of Social Work and Navigation Services, a full-time Patient Care Navigator, and a Program Coordinator
- Rush begins its first gender affirmation surgeries
- Rush begins new volunteer program at Vital Bridges Food Pantry in Garfield Park with monthly volunteer opportunity to serve those living with HIV/AIDS
- Rush struck down it's infertility definition in the employee benefit plan, positively impacting single women and lesbian couples engaging in fertility treatment
- Implemented an adoption benefit for Rush employees, positively impacting LGBTQ+ employees

2020

- Launch of Affirm: The Rush Center for Gender, Sexuality, and Reproductive Health - the first interdisciplinary LGBTQ+ center in the Chicago region, which received coverage by The Chicago Tribune, Becker's Hospital Review, ABC 7, and Windy City Times
- Gender-Inclusive Care Training integrated into MA Onboarding and Nursing Transition to Practice
- Rush named a "Business Championing Diversity and Inclusion" by Crain's Chicago Business in the award's inaugural year, citing its LGBTQ+ efforts
- Staff, students, and employees able to be identified by their chosen name and gender for all documentation purposes
- In its first year, Affirm served over 350 patients and trained over 1800 RUSH employees

2021

- Affirm expanded LGBTQ clinical services to include pediatrics as well as increased mental health services for those that are uninsured as well as adolescents
- Advised Human Resources on development of Trans-inclusive employee policies
- Representation on Patient Education Materials Review Board to ensure that all patient education materials are inclusive and respectful towards LGBTQ+ patients
- Affirm provided various different trainings including affirming youth approaches for school-based LCSWs, behavioral health trainings for Cicero Family Services, LGBTQ affirming sex education for Chicago Public Schools, and the needs of the LGBTQ community during the COVID-19 pandemic

- Collaborated with the TaskForce to facilitate support groups for trans women of color in the Austin neighborhood
- Raised over $12,000 through t-shirt sales and donations during Pride Month for West Side LGBTQ+ community partners

In conclusion, Rush continues to make strides in LGBTQ+ health equity and will continue to raise the bar. The Affirm program has navigated over 660 patients and educated 3,000 Rush employees to date and will be expanding in 2022 as it aligns with efforts to fully develop a gender affirmation surgical program. The Rush leadership is committed to healthcare equity and diversity, equity, and inclusion and the health system has become a National leader in these efforts and will not stop until equity is achieved for all.

The Way Forward, 2022

As the DEI initiatives at Rush University Medical Center move into a new calendar year, there has been a change in the Diversity Leadership Council chairmanship, retirements and recruitment of new members, the designation of diversity officers for the hospital system and university, and a reevaluation of strategic pillars to pursue in terms of diversity. A new five-year plan is currently being unveiled and a sub-committee of DLC leaders to drive change are meeting regularly. The goal is to reinvigorate the DLC, raise its visibility in the organization, designate successors to its current members, and recommit to the initiatives that honor J. Robert Clapp, Jr. and advance diversity, equity, and inclusion in the organization.

REFERENCES

Buse, K., Bernstein, R. S., & Bilimoria, D. (2016). The Influence of Board Diversity, Board Diversity Policies and Practices, and Board Inclusion Behaviors on Nonprofit Governance Practices. *Journal of Business Ethics, 133*(1), 179–191. doi:10.100710551-014-2352-z

Clapp, J. R. & Ad Hoc Advisory Group on Diversity Leadership. (2007). *Becoming a Better Organization: Promoting Diversity as a Part of the Culture at Rush University Medical Center.* Chicago: Rush University Medical Center.

Coleman, A., Palmer, S. R., Rippner, J., & Riley, R. W. (2009). *A 21st Century Imperative: Promoting Access and Diversity in higher education: A Policy Paper on Major Developments and Trends.* www.collegeboard.com/access

Diversity Leadership Council. (2014). Diversity Leadership Informational Handbook. Rush University Medical Center.

Diversity Leadership Council. (2020). Diversity Leadership Informational Strategy PPT. Rush University Medical Center.

Gauss, J. W., & Jessamy, H. T. (2007). *The Board's Role in Developing a Diverse Leadership Team. American Hospital Association Trustee Magazine.*

Hernandez, M., Barilla, D., & Bass, K. H. (2022). *Boards Must Address Equity Competencies: Health leaders' attention, connection and empathy will help guide difficult conversations*. American Hospital Association Trustee. https://trustees.aha.org/boards-must-address-equity-competencies

Appendix 1

Table 1. SWOT ANALYSIS

Strengths 1. Foundational work has been done 2. Cadre of professionals invested in DEI **3.** Organizational structure that supports DEI	Weaknesses 1. Longevity of the original DLC membership who may be stuck in the past **2.** The absence of a 'call to action' for leaders and staff across the organization 3. competing for resources for DEI versus community engagement-I hope we can word smith this to reflect it as a global issue as well as local pitfall.
Opportunities 1. Board financial investment 2. BLM and its elevation of interest in DEI 3. Recognition that things need to change	**Threats** 1. Changing leadership where historical philosophy behind the DLC is getting lost 2. Retirements of the original DLC committee members 3. Frustration that creeps in from progress not being made

APPENDIX 2

Diversity Leadership Topics

Ten-Year Celebration

Year 1: October 28, 2009

"Quantifying the Value of Diversity in Healthcare and Education"

Moderator: Lois Halstead, Ph.D., R.N., Vice-Provost and Vice-President, University Affairs, Rush University Medical Center

Speaker Panelists:

- Martin R. Castro, J.D., Vice President of External Affairs, Aetna Foundation
- J. Robert Clapp, Jr., FACHE, Senior Vice-President for Hospital Affairs,

Rush University Medical Center and Executive Director,
Rush University Hospitals

- Sue L. Gin, Chairman/CEO, Flying Foods and Board Member,

Rush University Medical Center

- Dwight McBride, Ph.D., M.A., Dean of the College of Arts and Sciences,

University of Illinois at Chicago

- Peter Weil, Ph.D., Vice-President, American College of Healthcare

Executives, Chicago

Year 2: January 27, 2011

"The Challenge of Embracing The Other"

Moderator: *Clayton Thomason, J.D., M.Div.*

Bishop Anderson Professor of Religion and Ethics in Medicine and Chairperson, Department of Religion, Health and Human Values, Rush University Medical Center

Speaker: Fr. Vaughn Fayle, OFM, Ph.D. (native South African), Professor of the Philosophy of Religion and Director of Philosophical Studies, Catholic Theological Union, Chicago

Year 3: February 9, 2012

"Should the Pursuit of Quality be a Diversity Initiative: Alignment, Action, and Accountability?"

Moderator: Beverly Huckman, Associate Vice-President, Equal Employment

Speaker: Quint Studer, Founder and President, The Studer Group

Year 4: February 5, 2013

"The Military-Civilian Collaboration – Before you treat me, You must know me"

Moderator: Dino Rumoro, D.O., Chairman, Department of Emergency Medicine and Associate Professor, Internal Medicine/Rush Medical College

Speaker: Col. Nathaniel Todd, Director of Health Financial Policy, Office of the Army Surgeon General, Washington DC

Year 5: February 26, 2014

"A Conversation with the Cook County Board President"

Moderator: David Ansell, M.D., Chief Medical Officer and Senior Vice-President, RUMC

Speaker: Toni Preckwinkle, Cook County Board President

Year 6: February 18, 2015

"Who is Responsible for Population Health?"

Moderator: Thomas Deutsch, M.D., Provost, Rush University and Dean, Rush College of Medicine

Speaker: Donald Burke, M.D., UPMC-Jonas Salk Chair in Global Health and Dean, School of Public Health, University of Pittsburgh

Year 7: February 17, 2016

"Building a Health Care Workforce to Improve Population Health"

Moderator: Charlotte Royeen, Ph.D.

Dean, College of Health Sciences, Rush University

Speaker: Christy Harris Lemak, Ph.D., FACHE

Professor and Chair, Department of Health Services Administration, University of Alabama at Birmingham

Year 8: February 15, 2017

"Equity by Design: Making Progress in Providing Equitable Health Care"

Moderator: Marquis D. Foreman, PhD, RN, FAAN, John L. and Helen Kellogg Dean of Nursing Professor, Department of Adult Health and Gerontological Nursing, Rush University College of Nursing

Speaker: Thomas A. LaVeist, Ph.D., Professor and Chairman, Department of Policy and Management, Milken Institute School of Public Health, The George Washington University

Year 9: March 15, 2018

"Health Equity Progress and Missed Opportunities"

Moderator: Steven K. Rothschild, M.D., *Associate Professor, Departments of Preventive Medicine and Family Medicine, Rush Medical College and Vice Chairperson, Department of Preventive Medicine and Associate Chairperson for Clinical Programs, Department of Family Medicine*

Speaker: Wayne Giles, MD, MS

Dean, School of Public Health, University of Illinois at Chicago

Year 10: March 6, 2019

"Educating the Next Generation of Health Science Leaders: Challenges and Opportunities"

Moderator: Larry Goodman, M.D., CEO, Rush University Medical Center and Rush System for Health

Speaker: Sherine Gabriel, M.D., MSc., President, Rush University

Year 11: February 26, 2020

"LGBTQ Advocacy in Medicine: Your Secret Super-Power "

Moderator: Colin Sperry, Graduate Student, Health Systems Management and President, LGBTQ Student Forum

Speaker: Magda Houlberg, M.D., Chief Medical Officer, Howard Brown Memorial Clinic

Years 12 and 13: February 2021 and 2022

Programming suspended due to COVID-19 pandemic

1-21-22

Chapter 13
Burnout Syndrome in Health Professionals in Portuguese Public Hospitals During the Pandemic Context

Vânia Borges Valério
Instituto Superior de Contabilidade e Administração do Porto, Portugal

Óscar Fontes Bernardes
Instituto Superior de Contabilidade e Administração do Porto, Portugal

ABSTRACT

The pandemic caused by COVID-19 triggered several adverse mental health situations in everyone's lives, particularly in health care professionals, especially those on the frontline. It is in this context that the starting question arises: Is COVID-19 enhancing the burnout syndrome in Portuguese public health professionals? This is the main objective of this research, and to this end a quantitative study based on a systematic review of the literature will be conducted to assess changes in burnout levels and to identify predictors of burnout in health care professionals. It was concluded that in the study by Almeida et al. conducted in Portugal, the majority of health care professionals do not have burnout symptoms, only 32.1%; while the factors that imply burnout prevalence were identified as having a medium or low level of resilience (OR=6.8), the perception of lack of social/family support (OR=5.4), and having more concerns about the future post-pandemic (OR=4.5).

INTRODUCTION

The pandemic caused by COVID-19, was first identified in the city of Wuhan in China in late 2019, and quickly spread to the five continents of the world (Lana et al., 2020).

In the past, there have been several types of infectious diseases, very similar to COVID-19, such as Ebola, Influenza, and MERS, through which it was possible to observe several impacts of mental nature,

DOI: 10.4018/978-1-6684-2314-1.ch013

on healthcare workers, such as, anxiety, depression, post-traumatic stress, and Burnout. The latter was predominant in the periods during and after the pandemic, having as predictors: being younger, having fewer years of experience, the lack of social support, stigma and isolation (Barreto, 2020; Cabello et al., 2020; Zhang et al., 2020).

Due to the pandemic, health organizations, especially the entities of the National Health Service (NHS), have been forced to modify their work environment to meet a basic need, which is to ensure public health. Thus, the NHS was overburdened due to the large increase in users who use these services.

In this context, one of the consequences is the disturbance of the mental health of health professionals, which implies the development of the Burnout Syndrome, since it is likely that the workload has increased, working hours may have changed, and lack of resources, either organizational or human, may have emerged.

Burnout is defined as a state of physical, emotional and mental exhaustion, which usually arises as a result of working with people over a long period of time, and the work situations are emotionally demanding (Pines & Aronson, 1983; Shaufeli & Greenglas, 2001).

Taking into account the current panorama, the mental health of health professionals can undergo drastic changes due to several factors, such as the stress caused by work overload, i.e. changes in working hours that translate into long working hours, which leads to increased time in direct contact with patients (Marôco et al, 2016; Cruz et al., 2018; Reith, 2018; Tachtsoglou et al., 2018), on the other hand, decisions are made under pressure, the confrontation with death, poor working conditions and the lack of specialized resources, whether human or organizational (Ferreira & Luca, 2015; Marôco et al., 2016; Mosteiro et al., 2018; Chemali et al., 2019).

LITERATURE REVIEW

Definition of Burnout Syndrome

The first approaches to Burnout Syndrome emerged in the 1970s in the United States of America (Freudenberger, 1974). The problem of Burnout was initially pointed out as something characteristic in the "helping professions", in individuals who "work with people", as is the case of care occupations and human services, namely, health care, mental health, social services, criminal justice system, religious professions, counseling and decision-making (Maslach, 2003).

The word Burnout comes from the English expression " to burn out ", which means (burn) outside (out), that is, to burn to exhaustion, which indicates that the individual who suffers from this disease has physical and emotional damage. Due to their state of exhaustion (Maslach & Schaufeli, 1993).

The concept of Burnout was used to characterize a state of physical and mental fatigue, which is felt by many groups of professionals in the area of health and human services, being a direct consequence due to the chronic emotional tension and the excessive effort that the contact presupposes. continuous with other people, especially when they have problems (Maslach & Jackson, 1981).

The evolution of Burnout syndrome stems from an exhausting and overloaded professional life that disables workers to perform their tasks with quality due to prolonged or chronic professional stress (Trigo et al., 2007).

The definition of Burnout Syndrome, currently most accepted, is based on the socio-psychological perspective proposed by psychologist Christina Maslach and colleagues, who classify Burnout as a syndrome that encompasses three dimensions: emotional exhaustion, depersonalization and decreased personal fulfillment., which occurs among individuals who work with other people (Carlotto, 2002).

The first fundamental aspect of Burnout Syndrome is the increase in feelings of emotional exhaustion; in this sense, the emotional resources of professionals are exhausted, and they feel that they are not able to deliver more of themselves at a psychological level. The second aspect focuses on the development of negative and cynical attitudes and feelings toward the recipients of their services, these negative reactions with customers may be related to emotional exhaustion. The third aspect is the tendency that the professional has to evaluate negatively aspects related to his work, he also develops a habit of feeling unhappy with himself and dissatisfied with his work (Maslach & Jackson, 1981).

The World Health Organization (WHO) started to include Burnout in the list of diseases on May 27, 2019, it is then a Syndrome caused by the state of physical and mental exhaustion due to the exercise of professional activity, characterized by a feeling of exhaustion, as well as negative feelings related to work and reduced professional effectiveness (SNS, 2019).

Maslach, Schaufeli & Leiter (2001) state that, taking into account the various definitions of Burnout, although some are divergent, it is possible to find five common elements: the emphasis on behavioral and mental symptoms and not on physical symptoms; the relationship between symptoms and work; the predominance of symptoms related to mental and emotional exhaustion, fatigue and depression; the decrease in effectiveness and performance at work, which occurs because of negative attitudes and behaviors; the symptoms manifest in "ordinary" people who did not suffer from psychopathological disorders before the Syndrome appeared.

Burnout Dimensions

According to Maslach (2006), Burnout Syndrome encompasses three dimensions, such as emotional exhaustion, depersonalization and decreased professional fulfillment (figure 1).

- Emotional exhaustion translates into a feeling of emotional overload combined with the absence of emotional and physical resources to deal with adverse situations. The main reasons for this exhaustion are work overload and interpersonal conflicts at work, in this way people feel emotionally and physically exhausted, without energy replacement. It is not something that is simply felt, it also provokes reactions of emotional detachment, in interpersonal relationships, from oneself and from work, presumably it is a strategy to deal with work overload (Maslach et al., 2001; Guedes, 2009; Ruviaro & Bargadi, 2011; Borges et al., 2021).
- Then, depersonalization consists of an attempt by the individual to distance himself from himself and the recipients of his services, thus ignoring the qualities and characteristics that make people unique and engaging. The professional resorts to cognitive distancing, developing an attitude of indifference or cynicism when he is exhausted and/or discouraged. Detachment is an immediate reaction to exhaustion, revealing a strong relationship between exhaustion and depersonalization (Maslach et al., 2001). Depersonalization is often the result of loss of motivation, increased irritability and anxiety, which leads to the appearance of negative feelings and actions, indifference and insensitivity towards the people around him, representing the interpersonal component of Burnout (Maslach et al., 2001; Vieira, 2010; Borges et al., 2021).
- Finally, the decrease in professional fulfillment represents the dimension of Burnout self-assessment, it refers to feelings of incompetence, lack of fulfillment and productivity at work (Maslach

Figure 1. Dimensions of Burnout
Source: Own elaboration

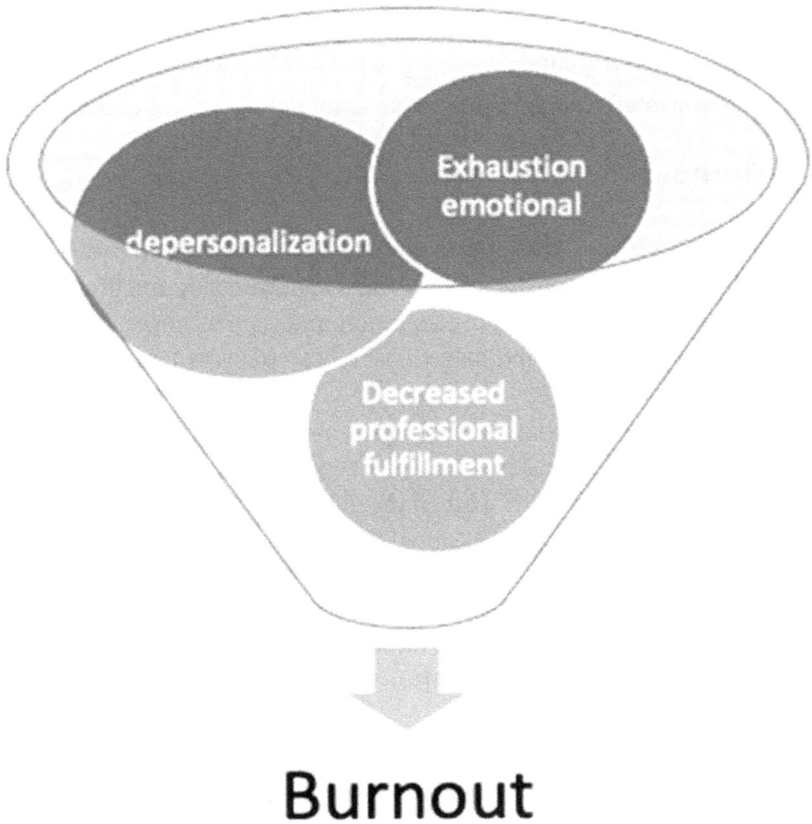

et al., 2008). The decrease in personal fulfillment results from the negative self-assessment that the professional makes of himself, feeling ineffective at a professional level and dissatisfied with his personal fulfillment at work. The feeling of ineffectiveness is associated with depression and the inability to cope with the demands of work, and can be exacerbated by the lack of emotional support and opportunities to develop professionally (Vieira, 2010; Borges et al., 2021).

The relationship of the last dimension with the other two dimensions is complex, as the decrease in personal fulfillment can arise due to one of the different two dimensions or a combination of the two. The reduction in personal satisfaction causes a feeling of professional ineffectiveness, as the individual cannot have positive feelings, such as personal fulfillment when he feels exhausted. At the same time, emotional exhaustion and depersonalization appear from work overload and interpersonal conflicts.

Bibeau (1989) presents a diagnosis of the syndrome based on criteria for determining its degree, in which the main symptom of Burnout is fatigue, which is related to the first dimension (emotional exhaustion) developed by Maslach et al., (2006). Emotional exhaustion is often accompanied by feelings of professional incompetence and job dissatisfaction, as the author Maslach refers to these symptoms in the third dimension (decreased professional fulfillment) (Maslach, 2006). There are other factors to be considered, such as anguish, concentration problems, irritability and negative feelings, which are described in the second dimension (depersonalization), as a rule, individuals become insensitive, impersonal and emotionally rigid. In their interpersonal relationships, in a professional context (Maslach, 2006).

Symptoms of Burnout

According to Cordes & Dougherty (1993), the symptoms of Burnout syndrome can be physical, emotional, interpersonal and behavioral. The consequences of this syndrome are manifested through various types of problems, which are physical, such as fatigue; emotional such as anger and sadness; interpersonal as the difficulty in dealing with people; and behavioral factors such as lack of commitment to work, high irritability and absenteeism.

Gallego and Rios (1991) report that the symptoms associated with Burnout can be psychosomatic, that is, chronic fatigue, body aches, excess or lack of sleep, gastrointestinal problems, weight gain or loss, hypertension, allergies and in the case of women the alteration of the menstrual cycle, in a general way, can be observed by the behavior of the professional through absenteeism, together with the consumption of psychoactive substances such as alcohol and drugs, the behavior is violent or the individual can put himself in a risky position in some way. Burnout symptoms can also be emotional, and are observed through distancing, irritability, difficulty concentrating, poor memory, low self-esteem and, ultimately, suicidal tendency; and finally, the symptoms of Burnout can be translated into defensive behavior, which is based on the denial of emotions to be strong, irony and cooling of relationships.

Benevides-Pereira (2002) argues that Burnout Syndrome has been considered a problem of an extremely important social nature. It is associated with high costs for the organization, such as turnover, absenteeism, low productivity, and quality. According to the author, there is an extensive list of manifestations of Burnout symptoms, being subdivided into physical, psychological, behavioral, and defensive. Physical symptoms are characterized by constant and progressive fatigue, sleep disturbances that translate into insomnia, nightmares or oversleeping, persistent muscle pain, headaches, migraines, nausea, and gastrointestinal disorders. Psychic symptoms include lack of attention and concentration, poor memory, impatience, low self-esteem, and emotional lability. Behavioral symptoms are irritability, aggressive behavior, inability to relax, increased consumption of substances (alcohol, tobacco, drugs, tranquilizers), increased risk behaviors, and suicidal tendencies. Only physical, emotional, psychological and behavioral can also be defensive, in this sense, the professional isolates himself, thus adopting this defense strategy, feelings of frustration and incapacity are constant, loss of interest in work, which can lead to abandonment At work, irony and cynicism are frequent to suppress the emotional state of the individual (Benevides-Pereira, 2002).

In short, both Gallego and Rios and Cordes and Dougherty argue that the symptoms of Burnout are predominantly physical, as can be seen in Figure 2, while Benevides-Pereira adds that the symptoms are defensive, based on strategies that could lead to absenteeism or even abandonment of the job.

Figure 2. Summary of Burnout Symptoms
Source: Own elaboration

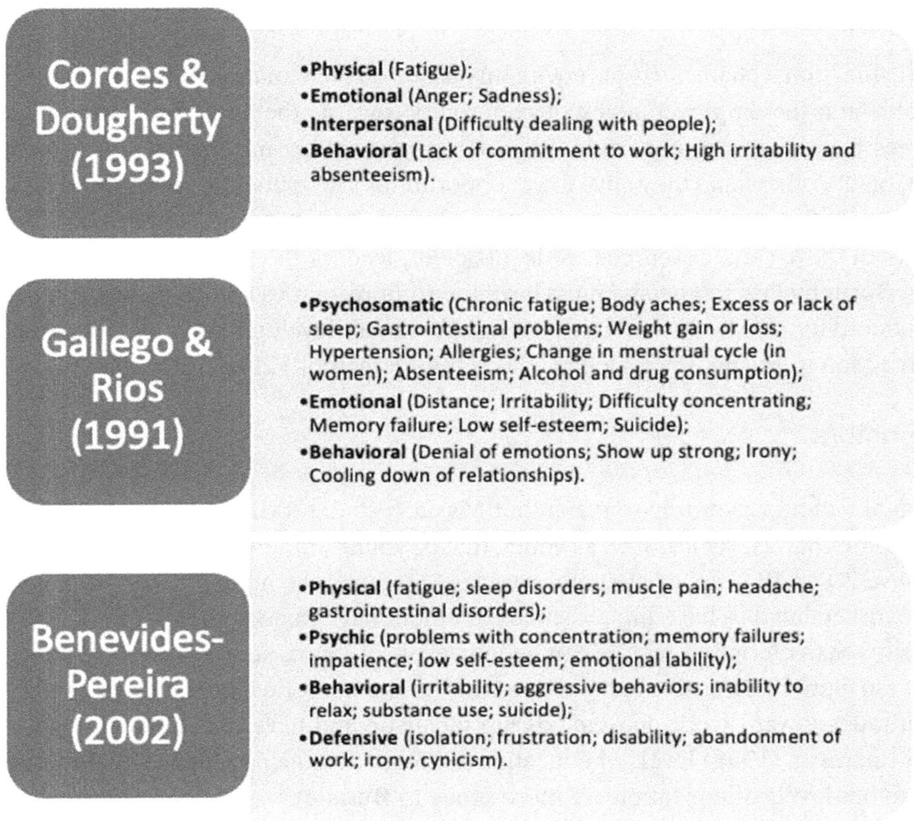

Risk Factors that Enhance Burnout

Burnout syndrome results from a combination of several risk factors according to several authors. Maslach et al. (2001) divides these factors into two groups, being situational and individual (figure 3). The situational factors are directly related to the work environment, such as work overload, unstable and conflicting environments. Individual factors are associated with the individual, such as self-efficacy, the excessive pressure and attribution of responsibilities, and neurotic tendencies.

Situational factors

As for the situational factors characterized by Maslach et al. (2001), starting with work characteristics, the worker feels that he/she has too much work for the time available, that is, the worker feels overloaded; role conflict, where the individual has to perform conflicting actions; role ambiguity, that is, there is a lack of adequate information and the individual does not know what is expected of him/her; lack of social support; lack of support from superiors, as well as lack of feedback.

On the other hand, in the occupational characteristics, it is possible to highlight problems in the interaction with the client, if applicable, and in a more specific context, for example, health professionals have frequent contact with chronic or terminally ill patients and the confrontation with death (Maslach et al., 2001).

Finally, organizational characteristics are mainly based on the violation of the psychological contract, which translates into the employer's lack of reciprocity towards the employee's effort, i.e. on the one hand employees have to spend more time, have to put more effort into their work and still have to be more flexible, on the other hand they have fewer opportunities for career promotion and less job security. For Bakker et al. (2005), work resources, even though they are less related to burnout, show a negative relationship when these same resources are insufficient, leading the worker to burnout. Therefore, for a worker to perform his/her job he/she must have the right resources and available in a timely manner, otherwise productivity will be lower, as well as professional development, cost reduction will also be lower and protection to Burnout prevalence (Bakker & Demerouti, 2007).

Individual Factors

As for individual factors, according to the author Maslach et al.,(2001), there are three factors, the first being demographic characteristics, such as youth, that is, young employees have higher levels of Burnout than those above 30 or 40 years of age; male workers tend to have higher values of depersonalization, while female workers tend to have higher values of emotional exhaustion.

In personality characteristics, factors can be low levels of vigor, people who have a form of extreme responsibility attribution, defensive and passive coping, and neurotic tendencies (Maslach et al., 2001).

Finally, attitudes toward work, individuals are idealistic and have high expectations. According to Schaufeli and Enzmann (1998) levels of education are related to the prevalence of Burnout, and professionals with higher levels of education are more prone to Burnout.

Burnout in Healthcare Professionals

Health professionals face particularly adverse and demanding working conditions (Dallacosta, 2019) that can trigger problems in their psychological well-being, such as occupational stress and Burnout, having a negative impact on all aspects of their lives (Gonçalves et al., 2019). Through some studies, it is possible to affirm that Burnout Syndrome develops predominantly in nurses and operational assistants rather than in doctors, administrative and technicians (Chou et al., 2014), other studies indicate that nurses, administrative and technicians are those who present a high level of emotional exhaustion, when compared to doctors and operational assistants (Marques et al., 2018).

In fact, nurses have a high level of emotional exhaustion due to factors such as long work shifts, the insufficient number of professionals in the National Health Service in Portugal, the non-existent career progression in terms of salary, the daily contact with suffering of their patients, as well as pain and death. In this way, nurses must focus on greater control over their emotional and mental state, in order to face the adverse situations they are faced with on a daily basis in their work (Maslach et al., 1996).

The Mental Health Action Plan 2013-2020, being extended until 2030, proposed by the WHO, states that nurses are in the group of those most prone to mental health problems, due to the close contact they establish with their patients, at monitoring they make of their suffering, their physical and psychological pain and also for the expectation of improvement or decline in their health status. And most of the

Figure 3. Predictors of Burnout
Source: Own elaboration

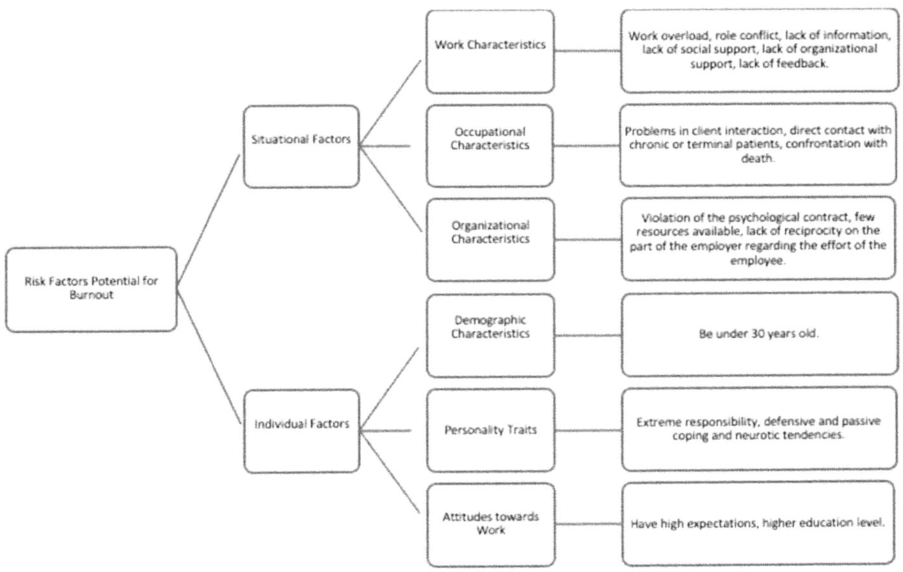

time, these are the professionals who report information about the health status of their patients to their families, where they are not always able to accept the disease, the treatment and the possible loss of their loved one (WHO, 2021).

A factor that can put the health professional at an increased risk of developing Burnout is the lack of working conditions (Ferreira & Lucca, 2015).

In a previous study carried out at national level, in 2013, about 21.6% of the sampled health professionals had a high level of Burnout and 47.8% had moderate levels (Marôco, et al., 2016). About 44% of physicians had high Burnout, while in nurses the percentage of high Burnout was around 50%, that is, comparing the professional groups it is possible to say that in the case of nurses, they are considered a risky profession because the percentage of Burnout is greater, this is due to the precariousness of working conditions (Marôco, et al., 2016), this study corroborates the assertions of Ferreira and Lucca (2015). The poor working conditions can be justified by the increase in stress imposed on professional practice in situations that do not allow achieving a good quality for the provision of medical or nursing care (Bragard et al., 2015).

Burnout in Health Professionals in the Context of a Pandemic

During the pandemic, several changes took place in the daily lives of individuals, such as the obligation to periods of quarantine and social isolation, the closure of services and schools, separation from family and friends, and the obligation to telework (Freide 2020; Duarte et al., 2020), which may in a certain way have an impact on the psychological well-being of health professionals, often leading to the development of Burnout Syndrome (Melo, et al., 2021). Additionally, individuals experience several fears: fear for their health, safety, family, finances and employment, which are transversal to all (Taylor, 2019).

Several aspects contribute to Burnout, such as work factors that include excessive workloads and working hours, on the other hand, personal factors such as the imbalance between the professional's private life, inadequate support and sleep deprivation, and finally the organizational factors, namely insufficient rewards, interpersonal communication and leadership (Shah et al., 2020). But, the lack of control over the procedures implemented as well as the measures for the spread of the virus, the mistaken notion of safety precaution, the poor communication and disinformation (Wilson et al., 2020), the lack of preparation and emotional support, inadequate personal protective equipment (The Lancet, 2020) and the high perceived mortality rate are a set of factors associated with Burnout (Shah et al., 2020; Lai et al., 2020).

Indirect exposure to the media can be a stressor, that is, the confrontation with repeated news and the number of confirmed cases or deaths causes anxiety in health professionals (Lima et al., 2020). Social networks can have a protective effect, as they help professionals or even people who have to be in isolation and away from their families to have the possibility to stay in contact with their families and friends (Lai et al., 2020).

One of the leading causes of the development of Burnout is based on the fear of the professional being socially censored (Lai et al., 2020), for working directly with the virus and the concern about transmitting the disease to their family and friends (Lai et al., 2020). Waring et al., 2021).

It is also necessary to mention that frontline health professionals are more predisposed to the development of Burnout, compared to other professions, due to the direct exposure to the adverse effects on mental health, derived from Covid-19 (Melo et al., 2021). In this sense, personal protective equipment, which is used for several hours by health professionals, becomes uncomfortable (Melo et al., 2021). Despite this, with the safety measures adopted in health institutions, it was observed that many health professionals developed skin problems due to excessive hand hygiene, where they used chemical products (Sanghera et al., 2020). The consequences of these measures adopted, in the health professionals who work in the front line, are diverse, being them, lack of motivation, feelings of frustration, increased feelings of technical inability to care for their patients, susbtance abuse, and suicidal ideation (Zhang et al., 2020).

Social isolation and the obligation to quarantine imposed to stop the spread of the virus worsened emotional exhaustion, and consequently led to the development of psychosocial problems (Galanis et al., 2021).

All these risk factors can lead to the triggering of psychological problems, such as Burnout, in health professionals, with a negative impact on the response capacity of health systems (Zhou et al., 2020).

Some consequences of Burnout were evidenced through contact with patients and in the reduction of working hours, that is, the professional works more and with less time available, this is a fact that contributes to the work overload. In studies carried out during other epidemics, it was found that absenteeism and the increase in behaviors that somehow affect their functions (Maunder, et al., 2006), associated with psychosocial variables and variables related to working conditions, where a greater number of contacts, for example with patients with SARS, is related to greater emotional exhaustion (Marjanovic et al., 2007).

These previous investigations reinforced the impact of these pandemics on the mental health of individuals, as did some studies carried out during the Covid-19 pandemic, where some symptoms such as fear, anxiety, emotional stress and post-traumatic stress were observed in the general population., and in particular health professionals (Shah et al., 2020).

During the initial phase of Covid-19 in China, about 70% of health professionals reported problems associated with mental health, such as insomnia, anxiety in depression and psychological distress (Lai et al., 2020), with the use of personal protective equipment throughout the workday (Bansal, et al., 2020), was considered one of the biggest promoters of anxiety (Montemurro, 2020), as was the lack of personal protective equipment or inadequate equipment (The Lancet, 2020).

Some initial studies carried out in Wuhan, China, with a sample composed of health professionals, it is concluded that the fact of being a woman, being a nurse, being on the front line, being involved in diagnosis and treatment and providing care to patients with Covid-19, professionals showed symptoms of depression, anxiety, insomnia and anguish (Lai, et al., 2020). Another study conducted in Wuhan, China, points out that being female, having more than 10 years of experience, having chronic illnesses, family history of mental disorders, and family members with confirmed or suspected cases of Covid-19, healthcare workers are more susceptible to having symptoms of stress, depression, and anxiety (Zhu et al., 2020).

Some recent studies show that burnout prevalence rates are higher in health professionals during the pandemic when compared to previous studies, relating this fact to the high workload, more significant time pressure, and lack of organizational support (Morgantini et al., 2020).

BURNOUT COMPARISON BEFORE AND DURING THE PANDEMIC

Before the pandemic, studies on Burnout were scarce due to the relatively recent definition of Burnout Syndrome. Despite this, it is deduced that there will be a progressive increase in Burnout levels.

Comparing the periods before and during the pandemic, emotional exhaustion has a predominant presence during the pandemic, in this sense, Burnout is considered a public health problem because it affects health professionals and other professional groups that work on the front line in the fight to COVID-19 (Ortiz et al., 2020).

Most countries affected by the COVID-19 pandemic have imposed various measures to combat COVID-19, such as quarantine, isolation, and restriction of movement (Ribeiro et al., 2020). In previous pandemics, it was observed that some mental problems can be triggered due to social isolation, such as increased anxiety and depression. Some factors such as insecurity, fear, and lack of knowledge about the duration of the pandemic, together with work overload, contribute to the increase of mental problems in health professionals (Faro et al., 2020).

A study conducted by Pereira et al. (2020) points out that several symptoms of Burnout were identified in health professionals, more specifically, in nurses, due to the fact that they are carrying out their activity on the front line in the fight against COVID-19, because of this they are in a work environment with a high risk of contamination, and also due to the large number of patients in their care, through which they develop a feeling of insecurity and professional impotence, they also tend to face adverse situations at work and the need to take quick decisions (Pereira et al., 2020).

It is possible to conclude that health professionals, such as nurses, are likely to have higher levels of Burnout, compared to other professional groups. Due to feelings of frustration, insecurity, emotional exhaustion, direct contact with death, due to the fact that they deal with patients with infectious diseases that put nurses under pressure due to the risk of contagion, making it a profession in which in the exercise of their functions proves to be challenging and of increased risk (Gomes et al., 2009).

In Portugal, a study carried out by Marôco et al., (2016), it is concluded that, in the periods between 2011 and 2013, about 21.6% of health professionals presented a moderate level of Burnout and 47.8% with high Burnout. At the beginning of the pandemic, in a study carried out in Wuhan, it was found that half of health professionals (51.7%) had burnout, and of which about 15% had high Burnout (Zhang et al., 2020). In a study carried out by the National School of Public Health, 72.2% of Portuguese health professionals had medium or high levels of emotional exhaustion and similar values in Burnout, this study was carried out in three moments during the pandemic (National School of Public Health, 2020). Another study carried out in Portugal, during the pandemic, estimated that about 53.1% of health professionals had a high level of work-related Burnout (Duarte et al., 2020). In Portugal studies on Burnout are still scarce.

CONSEQUENCES OF BURNOUT ON HEALTH PROFESSIONALS

Burnout Syndrome causes several devastating consequences, leading to the degradation of physical and mental health, professional performance, and the individual's relationships, whether in the workplace or in private life (Carlotto, 2012).

The main consequences of Burnout Syndrome in health professionals are serious, being divided into four groups: individual disorders, behavioral changes, difficulties at work and consequences for hospitals (Perniciotti et al., 2020).

In individual disorders, for example, post-traumatic stress disorder, substance and alcohol use, persistent psychosomatic complaints, depression and suicidal thoughts (Lazerescu et al., 2018). Behavioral changes are associated with job dissatisfaction, lack of motivation and involvement, and work abandonment (Waterman et al., 2007; Maslach et al., 2008).

Difficulties at work include absenteeism, professional errors and poor results in patient safety measures (Moss et al., 2016). The accumulation of the consequences of Burnout results in a decrease in the quality of life of health professionals and their effectiveness at work, which will directly resonate negatively in the quality of care provided to the patient (Carlotto et al., 2008). Subsequently, these factors will trigger errors in the professional act, which translates into losses for the professional himself, such as loss of confidence in his work, difficulties in sleeping, reduced satisfaction at work, increased occupational stress and damage. On its reputation (Waterman et al., 2007).

About the consequences for hospitals, starting with the abandonment of work that increases the turnover of professionals, which consequently entails high costs for the organization to replace employees (Moss et al., 2016), with previous studies stating that hospital organizations have to bear high costs with early retirements and reduced hours worked (Dewa et al., 2014).

METHODOLOGY

The methodology phase is divided into four stages, the first of which is the definition of the study objective, the second stage concerns the study design, then the identification of the instrument and, finally, the selection of the population and sample.

GOAL

With the present study, the starting point was the following question, is COVID-19 potentiating Burnout syndrome in Portuguese public sector health professionals? Through which, it is intended to explore Burnout, in health professionals, during the COVID-19 pandemic:

1) To measure the effect of the pandemic on mental health in health professionals, in particular those who were on the front line in the treatment of patients with COVID-19
2) Analyze the determinants of vulnerability and protection;
3) Evaluate the various moments in the course of the pandemic, covering the final period of confinement and the subsequent period of deconfinement.

The purpose of this study is essential to characterize the impact of the pandemic on the evolution of Burnout Syndrome, in particular in health professionals.

STUDY DESIGN

The data for the preparation of the present study were collected from the report entitled "Mental Health in Pandemic Times (SM-COVID19)", from the National Institute of Health Doutor Ricardo Jorge do INSA, carried out by Almeida and collaborators (2020).

The data collection process was carried out between May 22, 2020, which corresponds to moment T0, and August 14, 2020, which corresponds to moment T1, based on the application of an online, self-completed questionnaire survey, that is, a population-based survey.

The questionnaire used in the first moment (T0) consisted of the total set of questions, while in the second moment of data collection (T1), a simplified version of the original questionnaire was used. More precisely, eight questions were eliminated because they were considered to be information with a low probability of having been changed between the first and second moments of observation.

The language and content used in some questions were adapted to the second moment of data collection, as it took place at a different stage of the pandemic, for example, questions about general concerns about the lack of definition were included. With this, it is possible to conclude that the moment T0 refers to the period of confinement and the moment T1 corresponds to the phase of deconfinement.

INSTRUMENT

In the study conducted by Almeida and collaborators (2020) the data collection instrument was developed and released in the LimeSurvey® software, where the questionnaires are filled out online, it consists of four sections:

1) mental health and well-being indicators;
2) indicators of access to health services and means of protection;
3) indicators of changes in life and expectations for the future;
4) sociodemographic, professional and situation indicators regarding the pandemic.

Section 1 consists of a set of questions that aim to assess different dimensions of mental health and well-being, with a special focus on the Burnout dimension. Sections 2 and 3 include a set of indicators that assess work-family balance, work status and financial income, leisure activities and lifestyles, expectations for the future and perceived social support. Finally, in section 4, participants are asked about sociodemographic and general professional data, regarding the household and their housing conditions, and also about their individual and family situation in the face of the pandemic.

The evaluation of the Burnout Syndrome of the participants, who were performing their duties at the time of data collection, was performed using the Shirom-Melamed Burnout Measure (MBSM) instrument. This scale consists of 14 items, organized into 3 subscales, which correspond to the dimensions of physical fatigue (6 items), cognitive fatigue (5 items), and emotional exhaustion (3 items). More specifically, participants are asked about their feelings or difficulties regarding their work, such as tiredness, fatigue, difficulty concentrating, and interpersonal relationships, the answer is given based on a Likert-type frequency scale that varies from 1 (never) to 7 (always or almost always) points. Subsequently, the score of the items of each subscale and also of the global scale was calculated, where the score on the global scale was obtained, in which it was classified from 1 to 3 points (without burnout) and from 4 to 7 points (with burnout). Additionally, the same participants were asked about their work performance in the last four weeks, and a visual analogue scale was used, where they positioned their perception in this domain, in which 0 corresponded to the "Worst performance at work that someone could have" in their role" and 10 "Performance of the best worker in this same role". Responses were considered in non-integer numbers, up to the order of tenths (Kessler et al., 2003).

POPULATION AND SAMPLE

In the study that follows, two populations were considered, the first being the adult population residing in Mainland Portugal and the Azores and Madeira Archipelagos and the second concerning Portuguese health professionals. Taking these populations into account, it is possible to obtain two different samples, namely people resident in Portugal, aged 18 or over and health professionals, from various careers and professional categories, such as doctors, nurses, senior health and/or diagnostic and therapeutic technicians and medical assistants. Regarding the communication and subsequent dissemination of the study, different means of communication were used, such as the Website itself and a Flyer, both of which served to disseminate the SM-COVID 19 project and its questionnaire survey in digital format.

The SM-COVID 19 study obtained 6859 completed questionnaires, only about 6079 were considered valid. Of the total set of 3982 respondents, correspond to the general population, and about 2097 respondents constitute the sample related to health professionals. In the second evaluation moment, 2291 questionnaires were obtained, of which only 2073 were considered valid. Among these, 1385 are the sample of the general population and 688 refer to health professionals. In a longitudinal perspective, data from 1592 individuals were considered, of which 1040 are part of the sample relating to the general population and 522 to health professionals.

To meet the objective of this study, the selected sample concerns health professionals, from the different groups of professionals in the health area, through which a total of 815 respondents were considered, with a sample mostly female with about 546 respondents and 269 were male, which corresponds to 67% and 33%, respectively.

DATA ANALYSIS AND DISCUSSION

In the tables in annexes I and II, it is possible to observe that about 32.1% of the healthcare professionals present Burnout symptoms, but no sociodemographic variable is significant to evaluate Burnout symptoms. On the other hand, the group of health professionals, presenting Burnout symptoms, when we analyze work/family reconciliation, are those who most frequently reveal that they have not been able to reconcile work and home life tasks (58.0%), work has interfered with family and personal life (41.6%).

Annex III shows the table of the logistic regression model with Burnout as the independent variable, with or without Burnout, in the sample of health professionals. On the other hand, based on the simple regression models (appendix III), it is possible to verify an association with the following variables gender; age group; education; net monthly income; career/professional category; work in a hospital; regular and face-to-face contact with patients; treatment of COVID-19 patients; need to be away from the family; changes in working hours; level of resilience; work-family balance; work and financial income; social and family support; lifestyle and leisure activity; access to health services and care; period of deconfinement; future after the pandemic, are a set of factors that influence burnout in the sample of health professionals.

According to the simple regression model (Appendix III), it was concluded that some variables are considered predictors of Burnout in health professionals, which was measured using the MBSM scale, and then the variables are presented in descending order of risk (OR) added to the implication of Burnout (Almeida et al., 2020):

- Have a medium or low level of resilience (OR=6.8)
- The perception of lack of social/family support (OR=5.4)
- Having more concerns about the post-pandemic future (OR=4.5)
- Having difficulties in reconciling work-family (OR=4.3)
- Having difficulties in maintaining a habitual lifestyle or in the practice of leisure activities (OR=4.2)
- Having difficulties in terms of work/income (OR=.1)
- The professional categories of medical assistants (OR=2.5), nurse (OR=1.9) and physician (OR=2.1)
- Having the need to move away from the family (OR=2.2)
- Perception of difficulties in accessing health services/care (OR=2.0)
- Treating patients with COVID-19 (OR=2.0)
- Being over 59 years old appears as a protector against burnout (OR=0.22)

When considering the variables mentioned above, in the multivariate model, or in the final model, it is verified that a lower resilience, a lower capacity to conciliate work-family and in the maintenance of lifestyle/activities, difficulties in terms of work/income, less social or family support and still having concerns about the future after the pandemic are the factors that most explain the prevalence of Burnout.

In health professionals, the results point to higher percentages of psychological distress, such as moderate to severe anxiety. Those most affected are those who are treating patients with COVID-19, as they have a higher risk of psychological distress than those who are not treating these patients. It is also in this group of health professionals that Burnout levels (physical and emotional exhaustion) are highest (32%).

Difficulty in reconciling work and family, concern with maintaining work or preserving income, the perception of less social or family support and concern about the future are determining factors of mental health problems in health professionals.

It should be noted that 32% of health professionals report symptoms of Burnout, the factors that contribute to the change in Burnout levels during the pandemic are the fact that they are in regular contact with patients (31%), are treating patients with COVID-19 (38%) and the increase in the number of working hours (36%), in this sense, the results obtained in this study corroborate the results of a study carried out by Lai et al., (2020), at the beginning of the pandemic, in Wuhan, China.

Strategies to Fight Burnout

Hospitals should implement programs that aim to improve the mental health of professionals: continuous training with modules addressing coping strategies, exemplifying adverse situations in the profession, should also carry out a self-diagnosis of the professional and his professional practices. These sessions should focus on communication, skills, conflict management, time management, priority management, managing expectations and emotions, proximity and distance as well as the dynamics of the doctor/patient relationship, and encouraging healthy lifestyles. (Frasquilho, 2003)

The structuring of medical care services, aligned with the specific needs of health professionals, will have to be ensured by an entity and supported by medical associations (Order and Unions). On the other hand, access to these treatments may be facilitated, for example, through a non-face-to-face consultation by telephone (Frasquilho, 2003).

On the other hand, creating a website that includes information on psychiatric and psychological support contacts with links to publicize these contacts, namely telephone lines, telemedicine and psychotherapy teleconsultations, as well as information related to the context of the pandemic with purpose of reducing the effects of Burnout (Almeida et al., 2020).

During the pandemic, some strategies were reported to reduce the impacts of *Burnout*, such as holding workshops where techniques are shared, which makes professionals learn new techniques (Oliveira et al., 2021).

Death Cafés are a practice that consists of holding meetings where the main theme is death, in this case, health professionals share their experience of confronting the death of their patients, how they feel, how they were, and their feelings. in view of these losses, during the pandemic, in the impossibility of performing in person, the best format would be online (Oliveira et al., 2021).

CONCLUSION

There is international evidence on how the pandemic is having a significant impact on mental health and well-being (Huang et al., 2020; Lai et al., 2020; Mazza et al., 2020; Wang et al., 2020; Wang et al., 2020; al., 2020).

The main objective of the present study was to characterize Burnout in the context of a pandemic, in health professionals, from different categories or professional careers, such as doctors, nurses, superior health and/or diagnostic and therapeutic technicians auxiliaries of action doctor.

The health professionals who participated in this project (OR= 1.95) indicated being on the front line in caring for COVID-19 patients. In comparison with other studies found, it is possible to observe that these health professionals are more likely to have a high level of psychological distress compared to those who do not treat patients with COVID-19, according to the simple regression model used (Lai et al., 2020; Pappa et al., 2020; Vindegaard et al., 2020). Still in the group of health professionals, it is possible to observe that burnout levels, such as physical and emotional exhaustion, correspond to about 32.1% of respondents with Burnout.

The perception of lack of access to social and family support by health professionals has a negative impact on mental health, the higher the perception and quality of this support, the lower the implication for the prevalence of Burnout. In this study, this factor was identified as a strong predictor of Burnout (OR= 5.4), which is in line with previous evidence (Liu et al., 2020).

On the other hand, the difficulty in reconciling private life with professional life is a risk factor for psychological suffering, requiring a more in-depth analysis of its relationship with the fear of infecting the family or close people and the work context (increase in the number of working hours, rest periods, rotation of teams and tasks, among others) that explains this effect.

On the other hand, it is possible to conclude that pandemics have several consequences at a global level, starting with the restriction of free movement between countries and within the country itself, it is also important to mention that its impacts are observed in the drop in productivity, which contributes for problems of an economic and social nature, this situation can translate into an increased risk for the mental health of all those involved, as the dubious financial situation, the increase in unemployment and uncertainty about the future, contribute to the increase in problems of mental health (Drydakis, 2015).

REFERENCES

Almeida, T., Heitor, M., Santos, O., Costa, A., Virgolino, A., Rasga, C., & Vicente, A. (2020). *Relatório final: SM-COVID19 – Saúde mental em tempos de pandemia*. Instituto Nacional de Saúde Doutor Ricardo Jorge.

Bakker, A., & Demerouti, E. (2007). The Job Demands-Resources model: State of the art. *Journal of Managerial Psychology*, *22*(3), 309–328. doi:10.1108/02683940710733115

Bakker, A., Demerouti, E., & Euwema, M. (2005). ob Resources Buffer the Impact of Job Demands on Burnout. *Journal of Occupational Health Psychology*, *10*(2), 170–180. doi:10.1037/1076-8998.10.2.170 PMID:15826226

Bansal, M. (2020). Cardiovascular disease and COVID-19. *Diabetes & Metabolic Syndrome*, *14*(3), 247–250. doi:10.1016/j.dsx.2020.03.013 PMID:32247212

Barreto, C. (2020). Prevalência de burnout é maior em médicos que atuam na linha de frente da Covid-19. *PedMed*, *8*(6), 1781–1790.

Benevides-Pereira, A. (2002). *Burnout: quando o trabalho ameaça o bem estar do trabalhador*. Casa do Psicólogo.

Bennet, H. (2003). Humour in medicine. *Scientific Medical Journal*, *96*(12), 1257–1261.

Bibeau, G., Dussault, G., Larouche, M., Lippel, K., Saucier, F., Véniza, M., & Vidal, M. (1989). *Certaine aspects culturels, diagnostiques et juridiques de burnout*. Condefération de Syndicats Nationaux.

Borges, F., Aragão, D., Borges, F., Borges, F., Sousa, A., & Machado, A. (2021). atores de risco para a Síndrome de Burnout em profissionais da saúde durante a pandemia de COVID-19. *Revista Enfermagem Atual In Derme*, *95*(33), 1–15. doi:10.31011/reaid-2020-v.94-n.32-art.835

Bragard, I., Dupuis, G., & Fleet, G. (2015). Quality of work life, burnout, and stress in emergency department physicians: a qualitative review. *European journal of emergency medicine: official journal of the European Society for Emergency Medicine, 22(4)*, 227-234.

Cabello, I., Echavez, J., Ripoll, M., Navarro, D., Roque, M., Moreno, G., & Bradley, D. (2020). Impact of viral epidemic outbreaks on mental health of healthcare workers: a rapid systematic review. MedRxiv, 1-92

Carlotto, M. (2002). A Síndrome de Burnout e o Trabalho Docente. *Psicologia em Estudo*, *7*(1), 21–29. doi:10.1590/S1413-73722002000100005

Carlotto, M. (2012). *Síndrome de Burnout em Professores Avaliação, fatores associados e intervenção*. LivPsic.

Carlotto, M., & Câmara, S. (2008). Análise da produção científica sobre a Síndrome de Burnout no Brasi. *PSICO*, *39*(2), 142–158.

Chemali, Z., Ezzeddine, F., Dosset, M., Salameh, J., Bizri, M., Dubale, B., & Fricchione, G. (2019). Burnout among healthcare providers in the complex environment of the Middle East: A systematic review. *BMC Public Health*, *19*(1), 19. doi:10.118612889-019-7713-1 PMID:31640650

Chou, L.-P., Li, C.-Y., & Hu, S. (2014). Job stress and burnout in hospital employees: Comparisons of different medical professions in a regional hospital in Taiwan. *BMJ Open*, *4*(2), 1–7. doi:10.1136/bmjopen-2013-004185 PMID:24568961

Cordes, C., & Dougherty, T. (1993). A review and an integration of research on job burnout. *Academy of Management Review*, *18*(4), 621–656. doi:10.2307/258593

Cruz, R., Andrade, J., Moscon, D., Micheletto, R., Esteves, G., Delben, P., & Carlotto, P. (2020). COVID-19: Emergência e impactos na saúde e no trabalho. *Revista Psicologia Organizações e Trabalho*, *20*(2), 1–3.

Dallacosta, F. (2019). Estresse e Síndrome de Burnout: quando a saúde do trabalhador pede socorro. Saúde (Santa Maria), 45(2).

Dewa, C., Loong, D., Bonato, S., Thanh, N., & Jacobs, P. (2014). How does burnout affect physician productivity? A systematic literature review. *BMC Health Services Research*, *14*(325), 1–10. doi:10.1186/1472-6963-14-325 PMID:25066375

Drydakis, N. (2015). The effect of unemployment on self-reported health and mental health in Greece from 2008 to 2013: A longitudinal study before and during the financial crisis. *Social Science & Medicine*, *128*, 43–51. doi:10.1016/j.socscimed.2014.12.025 PMID:25589031

Duarte, I., Teixeira, A., Castro, L., Marina, S., Ribeiro, C., Cristina, J., & Nunes, R. (2020). Burnout among Portuguese healthcare workers during the COVID-19 pandemic. *Research Square*, *1*, 1–16. doi:10.21203/rs.3.rs-87357/v1

Duarte, I., Teixeira, A., Castro, L., Marina, S., Ribeiro, C., Jácome, C., & Nunes, R. (2020). Burnout among Portuguese healthcare workers during the COVID-19 pandemic. *BMC Public Health*, *20*(1), 1–10. doi:10.118612889-020-09980-z PMID:33287794

Escola Nacional de Saúde Pública. (2020). *Escola Nacional de Saúde Pública*. Obtido de Resultados do Questionário 3: Profissionais de saúde exaustos, para além de um número pouco aceitável de infetados?: https://barometro-covid-19.ensp.unl.pt/resultados-do-questionario-3-profissionais-de-saude-exaustos-para-alem-de-um-numero-pouco-aceitavel-de-infetados/

Faro, A., Bahiano, M., Nakano, T., Reis, C., Silva, B., & Vitti, L. (2020). COVID-19 e saúde mental: A emergência do cuidado. *Estudo Psicologia*, *37*, 1–29. doi:10.1590/1982-0275202037e200074

Ferreira, N., & Lucca, S. (2015). Síndrome de burnout em técnicos de enfermagem de um hospital público do Estado de São Paulo. *Revista Brasileira de Epidemiologia*, *18*(1), 68–79. doi:10.1590/1980-5497201500010006 PMID:25651012

Frasquilho, M. (2003). Eu sou actor do meu stress. *Segurança*, *154*, 28–30.

Freide, R. (2020). Uma reflexão sobre as medidas iniciais adotadas no combate à Covid-19 no Brasil. *Revista Augustus*, *25*(51), 15–30. doi:10.15202/1981896.2020v25n51p15

Freudenberger, H. (1974). Staff Burn-Out. *The Journal of Social Issues*, *30*(1), 159–165. doi:10.1111/j.1540-4560.1974.tb00706.x

Galanis, P., Vraka, I., Fragkou, D., Bilali, A., & Kaitelidou, D. (2021). Nurses' burnout and associated risk factors during the COVID-19 pandemic: A systematic review and meta-analysis. *Journal of Advanced Nursing*, *77*(8), 3286–3302. doi:10.1111/jan.14839 PMID:33764561

Gallego, A., & Rios, F. (1991). El síndrome de "burnout" o el desgaste profesional. *Revista de la Asociación Española de Neuropsiquiatría*, *11*(39), 257–265.

Gomes, R., & Cruz, F. (2009). Occupational stress in health professionals a study with Portuguese nurses. *Psicologia: Teoria e Pesquisa (Brasília)*, *25*(3), 307–318. doi:10.1590/S0102-37722009000300004

Gonçalves, M., Fontes, L., Simães, C., & Gomes, R. (2019). Stress and burnout in health professionals. In P. Arezes (Ed.), *Occupational and environmental safety and health,* (pp. 563–571). doi:10.1007/978-3-030-14730-3_60

Guedes, D. (2009). Estresse ocupacional e produtividade: um estudo exploratório em torno da síndrome de burnout com docentes do ensino superior. *XXIX Encontro Nacional de Engenharia de Produção*, 1-12.

Huang, Y., & Zhao, N. (2020). Generalized anxiety disorder, depressive symptoms and sleep quality during COVID-19 outbreak in China: A web-based cross-sectional survey. *Psychiatry Research*, *288*, 288. doi:10.1016/j.psychres.2020.112954 PMID:32325383

Lai, J., Ma, S., Wang, Y., Cai, Z., Hu, J., Wei, N., Wu, J., Du, H., Chen, T., Li, R., Tan, H., Kang, L., Yao, L., Huang, M., Wang, H., Wang, G., Liu, Z., & Hu, S. (2020). Factors Associated With Mental Health Outcomes Among Health Care Workers Exposed to Coronavirus Disease 2019. *JAMA Network Open*, *3*(3), e203976. doi:10.1001/jamanetworkopen.2020.3976 PMID:32202646

Lana, R., Coelho, F., Gomes, M., Cruz, O., Bastos, L., Villela, D., & Codeço, C. (2020). Emergência do novo coronavírus (SARS-CoV-2) e o papel de uma vigilância nacional em saúde oportuna e efetiva. *Cadernos de Saude Publica*, *36*(3), 1–5. doi:10.1590/0102-311x00019620 PMID:32187288

Lancet, T. (2020). COVID-19: protecting health-care workers. *PubMed Central* .

Lazarescu, I., Dubray, B., Joulakian, M. B., Blanchard, P., Chauvet, B., Mahé, M. A., & Thureau, S. (2018). Prevalence of burnout, depression and job satisfaction among French senior and resident radiation oncologists. *Cancer radiotherapie: journal de la Societe francaise de radiotherapie oncologique, 22*(8), 784-789.

Lehrer, P., & Woolfolk, R. (2021). *Principles and Practice of Stress Management,* (4th ed.). The Guildford Press.

Lima, C., Carvalho, P., Lima, I., Nunes, J., Saraiva, J., Souza, R., & Neto, M. (2020). The emotional impact of Coronavirus 2019-nCoV (new Coronavirus disease). *Psychiatry Research*, *287*, 287. doi:10.1016/j.psychres.2020.112915 PMID:32199182

Liu, X., Shao, L., Zhang, R., Wei, Y., Li, J., Wang, C., & Zhou, F. (2020). Perceived Social Support and Its Impact on Psychological Status and Quality of Life of Medical Staffs After Outbreak of SARS-CoV-2 Pneumonia: A Cross-Sectional Study. *Lancet*, 1–21.

Marjanovic, Z., Greenglass, E., & Coffey, S. (2007). The relevance of psychosocial variables and working conditions in predicting nurses' coping strategies during the SARS crisis: An online questionnaire survey. *International Journal of Nursing Studies, 44*(6), 991–998. doi:10.1016/j.ijnurstu.2006.02.012 PMID:16618485

Marôco, J., & Marôco, A., Leite, Ema, Bastos, C., Vazão, M., & Campos, J. (2016). Burnout in Portuguese Healthcare Professionals: An Analysis at the National Level. *Acta Medica Portuguesa, 26*(1), 24–30. PMID:26926895

Marôco, J., Marôco, A., Leite, E., Bastos, C., Vazão, M., & Campos, J. (2016). Burnout in Portuguese Healthcare Professionals: An Analysis at the National Level. *Acta Medica Portuguesa, 29*(1), 24–30. PMID:26926895

Marques, M., Alves, E., Queirós, C., Norton, C., & Henriques, A. (2018). The effect of profession on burnout in hospital staff. *Occupational Medicine (Oxford, England), 68*(3), 207–2010. doi:10.1093/occmed/kqy039 PMID:29546385

Maslach, C. (2003). Job Burnout: New Directions in Research and Intervention. *Current Directions in Psychological Science, 12*(5), 189–192. doi:10.1111/1467-8721.01258

Maslach, C. (2006). Stress and Quality of Working Life: Current Perspectives in Occupational Health. Information Age Publishing.

Maslach, C., & Jackson, S. (1981). The measurement of experienced burnout. *Journal of Organizational Behavior, 2*(2), 99–113. doi:10.1002/job.4030020205

Maslach, C., Jackson, S., & Leiter, M. (1996). *Maslach Burnout Inventory Manual,* (3rd ed.). CPP, Inc.

Maslach, C., & Leiter, M. (2008). Early predictors of job burnout and engagement. *The Journal of Applied Psychology, 93*(3), 498–512. doi:10.1037/0021-9010.93.3.498 PMID:18457483

Maslach, C., Schaufeli, W., & Leiter, M. (2001). Job Burnout. *Annual Review of Psychology, 52*(1), 397–422. doi:10.1146/annurev.psych.52.1.397 PMID:11148311

Maslach, C., & Wilmar, S. (1993). Historical and conceptual development of burnout. *Professional burnout: Recent developments in theory and research*, 1-16.

Maunder, R., Lancee, W., Balderson, K., Bennett, J., Borgundvaag, B., Evans, S., & Veldhorst, G. (2006). Long-term psychological and occupational effects of providing hospital healthcare during SARS outbreak. *Emerging Infectious Diseases, 12*(12), 1924–1932. doi:10.3201/eid1212.060584 PMID:17326946

Mazza, C., Ricci, E., Biondi, S., Colasanti, M., Ferracuti, S., Napoli, C., & Roma, P. (2020). A Nationwide Survey of Psychological Distress among Italian People during the COVID-19 Pandemic: Immediate Psychological Responses and Associated Factors. *International Journal of Environmental Research and Public Health, 17*(9), 3165. doi:10.3390/ijerph17093165 PMID:32370116

Melo, S., Strobel, A., Soares, B., Bastos, B., Silva, I., Silveira, L., & Reis, B. (2021). Síndrome de Burnout nos profissionais de saúde durante a pandemia da COVID-19: Uma revisão narrativa. *Revista Eletrônica Acervo Saúde, 13*(11), 1–7. doi:10.25248/reas.e9225.2021

Montemurro, N. (2020). The emotional impact of COVID-19: From medical staff to common people. *Brain, Behavior, and Immunity*, *87*, 23–14. doi:10.1016/j.bbi.2020.03.032 PMID:32240766

Morgantini, L., Naha, U., Wang, H., Francavilla, S., Acar, O., Flores, J., Crivellaro, S., Moreira, D., Abern, M., Eklund, M., Vigneswaran, H. T., & Weine, S. (2020). Factors contributing to healthcare professional burnout during the COVID-19 pandemic: A rapid turnaround global survey. *PLoS One*, *15*(9), e0238217. doi:10.1371/journal.pone.0238217 PMID:32881887

Moss, M., Good, S., Gozal, D., Kleinpell, R., & Sessler, N. (2016). An official critical care societies collaborative statement: burnout syndrome in critical care healthcare professionals: a call for action. *American Journal of Critical Care*, *44*(7), 1414–1421. PMID:27309157

Mosteiro, M., Almeida, M., Baptista, P., Zaballos, M., Diaz, F., & Diaz, M. (2019). Síndrome de burnout em trabalhadores de enfermagem brasileiros e espanhóis. *Revista Latino-Americana de Enfermagem*, 1–9.

Oliveira, T., Silva, K., Floriano, L., Xavier, P., & Righi, L. (2021). Possíveis estratégias de enfrentamento do Burnout entre profissionais de saúde durante a pandemia do coronavírus. *Revista de Medicina (São Paulo)*, *100*(6), 586–592. doi:10.11606/issn.1679-9836.v100i6p586-592

Ortiz, J., Quintero, D., Córdoba, C., Ceballos, F., & Córdoba, F. (2020). Consecuencias de la pandemia de la COVID-19 en la salud mental asociadas al aislamiento social. *Colombian Journal of Anesthesiology*, *48*(4), 1–8.

Pappa, S., Ntella, V., Giannakas, T., Giannakoulis, V., Papoutsi, E., & Katsaounou, P. (2020). Prevalence of depression, anxiety, and insomnia among healthcare workers during the COVID-19 pandemic: A systematic review and meta-analysis. *Brain, Behavior, and Immunity*, *80*, 901–907. doi:10.1016/j.bbi.2020.05.026 PMID:32437915

Pereira, M., Torres, E., Pereira, M., Antunes, P., & Costa, C. (2020). Sofrimento emocional dos Enfermeiros no contexto hospitalar frente à pandemia de COVID-19. *Research. Social Development*, *9*(8), 1–21.

Perniciotti, P., Júnior, C., Guarita, R., Morales, R., & Romano, B. (2020). Síndrome de Burnout nos profissionais de saúde: Atualização sobre definições, fatores de risco e estratégias de prevenção. *Revista da SBPH (Belo Horizonte)*, *23*(1), 35–52.

Pines, A., & Aronson, E. (1983). Combattinhg burnout. *Children and Youth Services Review*, *5*(3), 263–275. doi:10.1016/0190-7409(83)90031-2

Reith, T. (2018). Burnout in United States Healthcare Professionals: A Narrative Review. *PubMed Central, 10*(12).

Ribeiro, L., Vieira, T., & Sousa, K. (2020). Síndrome de burnout em profissionais de saúde antes e durante a pandemia da COVID-19. *Revista Eletrônica Acervo Saúde*, *12*(11), 1–10. doi:10.25248/reas.e5021.2020

Ruviaro, M., & Bardagi, M. (2011). Síndrome de Burnout e satisfação no trabalho em profissionais da área de enfermagem do interior do RS. *BarBaroi*, 194–216.

Sanghera, J., Pattani, N., Hashmi, Y., Varley, K., Cheruvu, M., Bradley, A., & Burke, J. (2020). The impact of SARS-CoV-2 on the mental health of healthcare workers in a hospital setting—A Systematic Review. *Journal of Occupational Health*, *62*(1). doi:10.1002/1348-9585.12175 PMID:33131192

Schaufeli, W., & Enzmann, D. (1998). *The burnout companion to study and practice: A critical analysis*. Taylor & Francis.

Schaufeli, W., & Greenglass, E. (2001). Introduction to special issue on burnout and health. *Psychology & Health*, *16*(5), 501–510. doi:10.1080/08870440108405523 PMID:22804495

Shah, K., Chaudhari, G., Kamrai, D., Lail, A., & Patel, R. (2020). How Essential Is to Focus on Physician's Health and Burnout in Coronavirus (COVID-19) Pandemic? *Cureus*, *12*(4). doi:10.7759/cureus.7538 PMID:32377486

SNS. (2019). *Serviço Nacional de Saúde*. https://www.inem.pt/2019/05/29/oms-inclui-burnout-na-lista-de-doencas/

Tachtsoglou, K., Lera, M., Iliadis, C., Frantzana, A., & Kourkouta, L. (2018). Occupational Burnout of Health Care Professionals in Hospitals. *Journal of Healthcare Communications*, *3*(38), 1–7.

Taylor, S. (2019). The psychology of pandemics: Preparing for the next global outbreak of infectious disease. In Cambridge Scholars Publishing (Ed.). Cambridge, Scholars Publishing.

Trigo, T., Teng, C., & Hallak, C. (2007). Síndrome de burnout ou estafa profissional e os transtornos psiquiátricos. *Rev Psiq Clín*, *34*(5), 223–233. doi:10.1590/S0101-60832007000500004

Vieira, I. (2010). Conceito(s) de burnout: Questões atuais da pesquisa e a contribuição da clínica. *Revista Brasileira de Saúde Ocupacional*, *35*(122), 269–276. doi:10.1590/S0303-76572010000200009

Vindegaard, N., & Benros, M. (2020). COVID-19 pandemic and mental health consequences: Systematic review of the current evidence. *Brain, Behavior, and Immunity*, *89*, 531–542. doi:10.1016/j.bbi.2020.05.048 PMID:32485289

Wang, C., & Zhao, H. (2020). The Impact of COVID-19 on Anxiety in Chinese University Students. *Frontiers in Psychology*, *11*, 1–8. doi:10.3389/fpsyg.2020.01168 PMID:32574244

Waring, S., & Giles, S. (2020). Rapid Evidence Assessment of Mental Health Outcomes of Pandemics for Health Care Workers: Implications for the Covid-19 Pandemic. *Frontiers Public Health* .

Waterman, A., Garbutt, J., Hazel, E., Dunagan, C., Levinson, F., & Gallagher, T. (2007). The emotional impact of medical errors on practicing physicians in the United States and Canada. *Joint Commission Journal on Quality and Patient Safety*, *33*(8), 467–476. doi:10.1016/S1553-7250(07)33050-X PMID:17724943

Weiss, L. (2004). *Therapist' s guide to self-care*. Routledge. doi:10.4324/9780203340110

WHO. (2021). *Obtido de Comprehensive mental health action plan 2013-2030*. World Health Organization. https://www.who.int/teams/mental-health-andsubstance- use

Wilson, N., Ravaldi, C., Scoullar, L., Vogel, P., Szabo, A., Fisher, W., & Homer, E. (2020). Caring for the carers: Ensuring the provision of quality 48 maternity care during a global pandemic. *Women and Birth; Journal of the Australian College of Midwives*, *33*(3), 205–308. PMID:32241720

Zhang, Y., Wang, C., Pan, W., Zheng, J., Gao, J., Huang, X., Cai, S., Zhai, Y., Latour, J. M., & Zhu, C. (2020). Stress, Burnout, and Coping Strategies of Frontline Nurses During the COVID-19 Epidemic in Wuhan and Shanghai, China. *Frontiers in Psychiatry*, *11*, 1–9. doi:10.3389/fpsyt.2020.565520 PMID:33192686

Zhou, X., Snoswell, C., Harding, L., Bambling, M., Edirippulige, S., Bai, X., & Smith, A. (2020). he Role of Telehealth in Reducing the Mental Health Burden form COVID-19. *Telemedicine Journal and E-Health: The Official Journal of the American Telemedicine Association, 26*(4), 377-379.

Zhu, Z., Xu, S., Wang, H., Liu, Z., Wu, J., Li, G., & Wang, W. (2020). *COVID-19 in Wuhan: Immediate Psychological Impact on 5062 Health Workers*. MedRxiv., doi:10.1101/2020.02.20.20025338

APPENDIX A

Figure 4.

Profissionais de saúde			
	Sem *Burnout* n (%)	Com *Burnout* n (%)	Total, n (%)
TOTAL	**553 (67.9%)**	**262 (32.1%)**	**815 (100%)**
Situação face à doença			
Não estou nem nunca estive infetado/a com o novo coronavírus	530 (67.6%)	254 (32.4%)	784 (100%)
Estou quarentena, em isolamento ou já recuperado da COVID-19	23 (74.9%)	8 (25.1%)	31 (100%)
Sexo			
Masculino	176 (65.6%)	93 (34.4%)	269 (100%)
Feminino	377 (69%)	169 (31%)	546 (100%)
Grupo etário			
18-29 anos	68 (63.7%)	39 (36.3%)	106 (100%)
30-39 anos	169 (67.6%)	81 (32.4%)	249 (100%)
40-49 anos	121 (68.5%)	56 (31.5%)	177 (100%)
50-59 anos	148 (64.9%)	80 (35.1%)	228 (100%)
60+ anos	46 (88.8%)	6 (11.2%)	52 (100%)
Escolaridade			
Até ao 9º ano	71 (61.8%)	44 (38.2%)	115 (100%)
12º ano	168 (67.3%)	82 (32.7%)	250 (100%)
Ensino Superior	314 (69.7%)	136 (30.3%)	450 (100%)
NUTS II			
Norte	243 (65.3%)	129 (34.7%)	373 (100%)
Centro	107 (64.9%)	58 (35.1%)	164 (100%)
Área Metropolitana de Lisboa	140 (71.1%)	57 (28.9%)	197 (100%)
Alentejo	27 (82.7%)	6 (17.3%)	33 (100%)
Algarve	10 (77.9%)	3 (22.1%)	12 (100%)
Região Autónoma dos Açores	5 (62.6%)	3 (37.4%)	8 (100%)
Região Autónoma da Madeira	5 (100%)	0 (0%)	5 (100%)
Rendimento líquido mensal			
Mais de 2000 euros	59 (71.9%)	23 (28.1%)	82 (100%)
1001 a 2000 euros	225 (70.6%)	94 (29.4%)	319 (100%)
Até 1000 euros	255 (64.1%)	143 (35.9%)	398 (100%)
Situação profissional			
Empregado/a	553 (67.9%)	262 (32.1%)	815 (100%)
Desempregado/a	0	0	0
Reformado/a	0	0	0
Outra	0	0	0
Forma de trabalho			
Em casa, em teletrabalho	35 (83.2%)	7 (16.8%)	42 (100%)
Em teletrabalho parcial	12 (66.3%)	6 (33.7%)	19 (100%)
No local de trabalho	496 (67%)	244 (33%)	740 (100%)
Outra	10 (70.3%)	4 (29.7%)	14 (100%)

APPENDIX B

Figure 5.

Profissionais de Saúde			
	Sem *Burnout* n (%)	*Com Burnout* n (%)	Total, n (%)
TOTAL	**553 (67,9%)**	**262 (32,1%)**	**815 (100%)**
Conciliação trabalho família			
Tenho conseguido conciliar o meu trabalho com as tarefas da vida doméstica			
Não concordo	55 (42%)	76 (58%)	131 (100%)
Não sei ao certo	21 (38,1%)	35 (61,9%)	56 (100%)
Concordo	462 (75,9%)	147 (24,1%)	609 (100%)
O meu trabalho tem interferido com a minha vida familiar e pessoal (mais do que antes da pandemia)			
Não concordo	198 (91%)	20 (9%)	217 (100%)
Não sei ao certo	35 (58,1%)	25 (41,9%)	61 (100%)
Concordo	296 (58,4%)	211 (41,6%)	508 (100%)
Acesso aos serviços e cuidados de saúde			
Continuo a ter o mesmo acesso aos cuidados de saúde de que preciso, no Serviço Nacional de Saúde (centros de saúde, hospitais ...)			
Não concordo	170 (60,5%)	111 (39,5%)	281 (100%)
Não sei ao certo	85 (66%)	44 (34%)	129 (100%)
Concordo	245 (73,7%)	88 (26,3%)	332 (100%)
Continuo a ter o mesmo acesso aos serviços de urgência			
Não concordo	89 (58,9%)	62 (41,1%)	152 (100%)
Não sei ao certo	62 (60,7%)	40 (39,3%)	101 (100%)
Concordo	324 (72,4%)	124 (27,6%)	448 (100%)
Tenho acesso fácil a linhas de apoio psicológico e emocional			
Não concordo	55 (56,2%)	43 (43,8%)	97 (100%)
Não sei ao certo	138 (61,1%)	88 (38,9%)	226 (100%)
Concordo	145 (69,6%)	63 (30,4%)	208 (100%)
Tenho acesso fácil a apoio psicológico e emocional presencial			
Não concordo	108 (58,4%)	77 (41,6%)	184 (100%)
Não sei ao certo	146 (62,85%)	86 (37,2%)	232 (100%)
Concordo	92 (75,2%)	30 (24,8%)	123 (100%)

APPENDIX C

Figure 6.

	Modelos simples		Modelo final	
	OR	IC 95%	OR	IC 95%
Sexo				
Masculino	—	—	—	—
Feminino	0.86	(0.50-1.48)	0.88	(0.51-1.52)
Grupo etário				
18-29 anos	—	—	—	—
30-39 anos	0.84	(0.49-1.45)	0.57	(0.31-1.03)
40-49 anos	0.81	(0.44-1.48)	0.61	(0.31-1.22)
50-59 anos	0.95	(0.47-1.92)	0.51	(0.23-1.12)
60+ anos	**0.22**	(0.11-0.46)	0.31	(0.15-0.67)
Escolaridade				
Ensino superior	—	—		
Ensino básico/secundário	1.21	(0.73-2.00)		
Rendimento líquido mensal				
Mais de 2000 euros	—	—		
1001 a 2000 euros	1.06	(0.73-1.55)		
Até 1000 euros	1.43	(0.84-2.44)		
Carreira/categoria profissional				
Outra	—	—	—	—
Auxiliar de ação médica	**2.47**	**(1.37-4.46)**	1.90	(0.98-3.69)
Enfermeiro	**1.91**	**(1.29-2.82)**	1.54	(0.92-2.57)
Médico	**2.12**	**(1.40-3.21)**	1.56	(0.91-2.66)
Trabalho em hospital				
Não	—	—		
Sim	1.27	(0.81-1.99)		

OR, Odds Ratio; IC, Intervalo de Confiança; OR ajustados através de modelos de regressão logística aplicados a amostras complexas; Modelos simples: OR brutos; Modelo final: ajustado para todas as variáveis expressas (Pseudo R2 = 0.42); Valores a negrito: $p < .05$

Figure 7.

	Modelos simples		Modelo final	
	OR	IC 95%	OR	IC 95%
Estilos de vida e atividades de lazer				
Manutenção de estilo de vida / atividades de lazer	—	—	—	—
Dificuldades na manutenção de estilo de vida / atividades de lazer	**4.22**	**(2.46-7.22)**	**2.76**	**(1.62-4.73)**
Acesso a serviços e cuidados de saúde				
Acesso fácil a serviços/cuidados de saúde	—	—		
Dificuldades no acesso a serviços/cuidados de saúde	**1.97**	**(1.25-3.09)**		
Período de desconfinamento				
Sem preocupações relativas ao desconfinamento	—	—		
Com preocupações relativas ao desconfinamento	2.55	(0.74-8.81)		
Futuro depois da pandemia				
Sem preocupações relativas ao futuro	—	—	—	—
Com preocupações relativas ao futuro	**4.47**	**(2.05-9.73)**	**3.26**	**(1.25-8.50)**

OR, *Odds* Ratio; IC, Intervalo de Confiança; OR ajustados através de modelos de regressão logística aplicados a amostras complexas; Modelos simples: OR brutos; Modelo final: ajustado para todas as variáveis expressas (Pseudo R2 = 0.42); Valores a negrito: $p < .05$

Figure 8.

	Modelos simples		Modelo final	
	OR	IC 95%	OR	IC 95%
Contacto regular e presencial com doentes				
Não	—	—	—	—
Sim	1.31	(0.62-2.77)	1.19	(0.59-2.38)
Tratamento de doentes COVID-19				
Não	—	—	—	—
Sim	**1.95**	**(1.18-3.22)**	1.48	(0.88-2.49)
Necessidade de se afastar da família				
Não	—	—		
Sim	**2.22**	**(1.38-3.57)**		
Alterações ao horário de trabalho				
Reduziu o horário de trabalho	—	—		
Manteve o número de horas de trabalho	0.83	(0.38-1.80)		
Aumentou o horário de trabalho	1.61	(0.74-3.51)		
Resiliência				
Nível alto de resiliência	—	—	—	—
Nível médio/baixo de resiliência	**6.75**	**(4.03-11.3)**	**5.22**	**(2.94-9.24)**
Conciliação trabalho família				
Capacidade de conciliação trabalho família	—	—	—	—
Dificuldades de conciliação trabalho família	**4.27**	**(2.43-7.48)**	**2.26**	**(1.24-4.13)**
Trabalho e rendimento				
Trabalho/rendimento preservado	—	—	—	—
Dificuldades ao nível do trabalho/rendimento	**3.09**	**(1.90-5.05)**	**1.94**	**(1.14-3.31)**
Apoio social e familiar				
Acesso a apoio social/familiar	—	—	—	—
Falta de apoio social/familiar	**5.38**	**(3.02-9.58)**	**3.27**	**(1.76-6.09)**

OR, Odds Ratio; IC, Intervalo de Confiança; OR ajustados através de modelos de regressão logística aplicados a amostras complexas; Modelos simples: OR brutos; Modelo final: ajustado para todas as variáveis expressas (Pseudo R2 = 0.42); Valores a negrito: $p < .05$

Chapter 14
Underappreciated and Undervalued:
Nurse Dissatisfaction and the COVID-19 Pandemic

Ursula Hersh
Ilinois Institute of Technology, USA

ABSTRACT

This chapter seeks to analyze the impact the COVID-19 pandemic has had on nurses and how it has affected the prevalence of compassion fatigue, moral injury, and overall job satisfaction. It examines current intervention strategies and frameworks and offers recommendations for how these systems may be improved to better support nurses. Numerous instruments have been developed in an attempt to study compassion fatigue. One of the most widely used of these instruments is the professional quality of life (ProQOL) scale. Using the ProQOL scale as a foundation, the author conducted an anonymous survey of nurses (n = 91) employed at a major university-affiliated hospital in Chicago. The author also conducted two longer individual interviews with nurses who are employed at this hospital. The pandemic has profoundly harmed nurses and triggered a cascading stream of consequences. The pandemic has increased the prevalence of both compassion fatigue and moral injury. Nurses are chronically overworked and lack critical resources and support from hospital management.

INTRODUCTION

"By choosing to enter the profession of nursing, we are choosing to be in service to others. But we did not sign up to be martyrs."

The COVID-19 pandemic has changed the healthcare landscape in complex and unpredictable ways. Healthcare providers have been forced to rapidly adjust to increasingly intense working conditions during a time of tremendous uncertainty. Nurses, who are at the forefront of patient advocacy and caregiving,

DOI: 10.4018/978-1-6684-2314-1.ch014

have borne the brunt of many of the intense and traumatic consequences of the pandemic. This prolonged exposure impacts the well-being and mental health of nurses. Compassion fatigue (CF) is defined as stress and declining emotional capacity that results from repeated interactions with traumatized individuals. In nurses specifically, CF may emerge from prolonged exposure to the suffering of others. Cocker and Joss describe CF as the intersection of secondary traumatic stress (STS) and cumulative burnout (BO), a state of physical and mental exhaustion brought on by an inability to function in one's everyday environment (2016). The COVID-19 pandemic "forces frontline health-care workers to make difficult medical decisions that may result in moral injury. Understanding the extent to which physicians, nurses, and other health-care workers experience moral injury while working in a pandemic is of critical importance to establish preventative measures and trauma-informed treatment" (Litam & Balkin, 2021). The COVID-pandemic has also aggravated the nursing shortage in the United States. The American Hospital Association (AHA) reports that the United States is experiencing a critical nursing shortage that is expected to persist until at least 2030 (AHA, 2021). Without intervention, this shortage is expected to worsen.

Healthcare providers regularly face intense, high-stress situations that affect their own mental well-being. Those working in Intensive Care Units (ICUs), in particular, regularly care for critically ill patients with higher mortality rates than those in other units. "A growing body of evidence suggests that burnout among ICU nurses and ICU physicians is a remarkable result of the demanding and continuously high-stress work environment. It has been suggested that ICU professionals could be emotionally affected by end-of-life issues, ethical decision making, observing the continuous suffering of patients, disproportionate care or medical futility, miscommunication, and demanding relatives of the patients" (Van Mol et al., 2015). Understanding these potential unit-specific variables is important in developing effective and targeted intervention strategies.

REVIEW OF LITERATURE

Defining Compassion Fatigue

While compassion fatigue (CF) is a widely used term, especially within healthcare, the construct of CF and how it is measured remains debated. Researcher Kathleen Ledoux concluded that "there are multiple and diverse understandings and definitions of what compassion fatigue is. So much so, there are equally multiple, diverse and conflicting strategies to mitigate it"(2015). To better understand what compassion fatigue really is, Ledoux began by exploring and defining what compassion itself means. Interestingly, Ledoux found that the tools most often used to measure nurse compassion fatigue do not appear to measure the construct of compassion. None of the multiple definitions of nurse compassion fatigue that were explored actually aligned with an understanding of compassion. This has important implications for how CF should be measured and the effectiveness of current interventions.

Emily Peters, BSN, RN, defines compassion fatigue as "declining empathetic ability from repeated exposure to others' suffering" (2018). By clarifying the concept of compassion fatigue, Peters argues, methodologies of treatment and intervention for CF in nursing may be improved. Peters conducted a concept analysis of compassion fatigue by reviewing the following databases: OVID, CINAHL Complete, Science Direct, Academic One File, Criminal Justice Abstracts, Education Full Text (H.W. Wilson), PsycARTICLES, PsycINFO, Social Work Abstracts, and Teacher Reference Center. Through this research, Peters concluded that CF occurred across disciplines. However, nurses in particular were especially vulnerable to compassion fatigue due to the nature of their work. The consequences of CF "negatively impacted the nurse, patient, organization, and healthcare system" (Peters, 2018). Extensive research has been conducted in an attempt to measure the research trends and scientific analysis of burnout and compassion fatigue among healthcare providers. There is a general consensus among researchers that this is a chronic and pervasive issue; despite this, few measures have been taken to improve working conditions for nurses to reduce the prevalence of CF.

Unit-Specific Variables

Research has suggested that nurses working in certain units may be more vulnerable to emotional distress. Intensive care units (ICUs) are widely considered to be particularly high stress and emotionally draining environments that may have an especially consequential impact on employees. Van Mol et al. conducted a systematic review of literature regarding the prevalence of compassion fatigue and burnout among healthcare providers in intensive care units. Interestingly, they found significant variation in the reported prevalence of compassion fatigue, secondary traumatic stress, and burnout: notably, "the reported prevalence of burnout in the ICU varied from 0% to 70.1%" (Van Mol et al., 2015). This suggests that further research may be needed, as well of a standardization of how these conditions are defined and measured. Furthermore, a "wide range of intervention strategies emerged from the recent literature search, such as different intensivist work schedules, educational programs on coping with emotional distress, improving communication skills, and relaxation methods" (Van Mol et al., 2015). This paper concludes that the true prevalence of burnout, compassion fatigue, secondary traumatic stress and vicarious trauma in ICU healthcare professionals remains uncertain. The authors recommend that emotional distress in relation to skills and performance be studied further in order to develop successful preventive strategies.

Berger et al. (2015) conducted a similar study, but focused specifically on pediatric nurses. They found that CF negatively affects both the quality of patient care and the well-being of nurses themselves. Berger et al. conducted their study using the Professional Quality of Life survey to assess the prevalence of compassion fatigue, which informed the approach used in this survey. The authors of this study found that nearly 30% of their nurse participants had high burnout and secondary traumatic stress. This study was from 2015, suggesting that current numbers may be even higher. Berger et al. concluded that "nurses under 40 years of age, with 6–10 years of experience and/or working in a medical-surgical unit had significantly lower compassion satisfaction and higher levels of burnout" and that "secondary traumatic stress from caring for children with severe illness or injury or end of life was a key contributor to compassion fatigue" (2015). These factors indicate that the unit in which nurses work is an intervening variable in determining their risk of burnout and compassion fatigue.

Ortega-Campos et al. conducted research to explore the prevalence of compassion fatigue, compassion satisfaction, and burnout among oncology nurses. The authors theorized that due to the characteristics of this unit, CF, burnout, and low compassion satisfaction are more likely to arise. Ortega-Campos et al. analyzed 15 studies: they found that "there are levels of risk of suffering burnout and compassion fatigue among nursing professionals, affecting more women and nurses with more years of experience, with nurses from oncology units having one of the highest levels of burnout and compassion fatigue," (2020). These authors argued that identifying the factors that make certain populations more vulnerable to burnout and CF will be critical in developing successful and targeted intervention strategies. This paper also reviewed the specific factors in the healthcare field that make employees more susceptible to burnout.

Cavanagh et al. (2020) conducted a survey among 296 direct care providers at St. Louis Children's Hospital using the Professional Quality of Life Scale, Version 5. They sought to assess levels of compassion fatigue, burnout, and secondary traumatic stress, and to determine how those variables impacted job satisfaction, patient satisfaction, productivity, and several other factors. Their research indicated that healthcare providers who work in pediatrics and care for seriously ill children and their families are at increased risk for compassion fatigue; "constant exposure to children who are suffering, in combination with workplace stressors and personal issues, may contribute to the development of compassion fatigue" (Cavanagh et al., 2020). This study found that while compassion fatigue, burnout, and secondary traumatic stress scores did not differ statistically by age, work category, level of education, or work experience, there were significant differences in scores as a function of nursing unit. Nurses who worked in the pediatric intensive care unit, in particular, reported lower compassion satisfaction scores and higher burnout and secondary traumatic stress scores. These results strongly support the need to develop a compassion fatigue intervention program for direct care providers.

Compassion satisfaction is sometimes referred to as the antidote to compassion fatigue. Kelly et al. (2015) examined compassion fatigue and compassion satisfaction in acute care nurses across multiple specialties in a hospital-based setting. The authors surveyed 491 nurses to measure their professional quality of life, looking at burnout, secondary traumatic stress, and compassion satisfaction. Kelly et al. found that significant predictors of burnout included lack of meaningful recognition, having more years of experience, and belonging to the "Millennial" generation (21–33 years of age when this research was conducted). Receiving meaningful recognition, reporting higher job satisfaction, belonging to the "Baby Boomer" generation (then 50–65 years of age), and having fewer years of experience significantly predicted compassion satisfaction. Interestingly, this study noted no significant differences across nurse specialties, units, or departments (Kelly et al., 2015). This study offered strong evidence that recognition and appreciation for employees may help to mitigate compassion fatigue. The authors concluded that "meaningful recognition may increase compassion satisfaction, positively impact retention, and elevate job satisfaction" (Kelly et al., 2015).

Pandemic Context

One of the key considerations in current studies of compassion fatigue is understanding how the COVID-19 pandemic has affected healthcare providers. Some argue that it has exacerbated already-pervasive issues, contributing to the severe nursing shortage across the country. Litam and Balkin sought to study moral injury specifically in the context of the COVID-19 pandemic. They conducted a national survey of 109 healthcare workers and assessed whether secondary traumatic stress was significantly associated with moral injury. The authors then examined potential interventions to improve the mental health of healthcare providers. Their research indicated that "mental health professionals may reduce treatment barriers by offering flexible sessions, nontraditional hours, and short-term interventions through telemental health platforms to support health-care workers experiencing trauma symptoms" (Litam & Balkin, 2021). This study was one of the first to link high levels of secondary traumatic stress to moral injury and burnout among frontline healthcare workers during the COVID-19 pandemic. The COVID-19 pandemic has presented unprecedented challenges for frontline healthcare workers that "may result in secondary traumatic stress and consequently, moral injury and burnout" (Litam & Balkin, 2021).

Current Intervention Strategies

Intervention strategies aimed at a reduction of compassion fatigue exist, but are not widely used in hospital settings. Cocker and Joss (2016) conducted a systematic review of the effectiveness of interventions to reduce compassion fatigue in healthcare, emergency, and community service workers. Compassion fatigue (CF) here is defined as stress resulting from exposure to a traumatized individual: "CF has been described as the convergence of secondary traumatic stress (STS) and cumulative burnout (BO), a state of physical and mental exhaustion caused by a depleted ability to cope with one's everyday environment" (Cocker & Joss, 2016). This paper identified and reviewed thirteen relevant studies, ten of which focused on nurses. Seven of these studies reported a significant difference post-intervention in BO or STS. The effectiveness of CF interventions is a new and largely unexplored topic. Cocker and Joss recommend "more research to determine how best to protect vulnerable workers at work to prevent not only CF, but also the health and economic consequences related to the ensuing, and more disabling, physical and mental health outcomes" (2016). The mental health of nurses is often a secondary consideration for hospital administrators. Mental health resources, when offered at all, are frequently inadequate and/or ineffectual.

METHODOLOGY

"When the pandemic began we were heroes. Now it's just an expectation."

For the purpose of this paper, the primary focus was on gathering data from the perspective of nurses who have worked during the COVID-19 pandemic. The sampling case for this research was nurses from a major university-affiliated hospital in Chicago. Respondents completed a survey comprising a combination of qualitative and quantitative questions. No personal information was collected so that all participants may remain anonymous. 91 nurses completed the survey. Nurses from across 18 units and specialties responded to the survey.

Questions were sorted into five categories: staffing, burnout, mental health, workload, and COVID-19 precautions. Participants were also given the option to respond to several open-ended questions at the end of the survey. To account for potential selection bias, this survey was presented as "an opportunity to share your experiences as a nurse," rather than initially using keywords that might allude to burnout or dissatisfaction. The majority of the online survey comprised multiple choice questions. There were six optional open-ended questions at the end of the survey (responses to these open-ended questions are in the appendix):

1. What could your employer do to make you feel more supported in the workplace?
2. What could your employer do to improve your work environment?
3. What other changes could be implemented in order to improve your work environment?
4. What would you like people to know about what it's like to work as a nurse?
5. How has the pandemic changed your experience working as a nurse?
6. Is there anything else you would like to add?

Table 1. Survey

Unit	Count
Neonatal ICU	29
In-patient Medical/Surgical Unit	13
Adult ICU	8
Adult Post Anesthesia Care Unit	6
Pediatric ICU	5
Pediatric ER	4
In-patient Pediatrics	4
Adult ER	3
Adult and Pediatric ER	3
Outpatient IV Therapy	3
Labor and Delivery	3
Adult OR	2
Adult In-patient Float Pool	2
Cardiovascular Thoracic Surgery	2
Postpartum	1
Interventional Radiology	1
In-patient Adult Oncology	1
Neurology/Neurosurgery	1

Two nurses also agreed to participate in longer individual interviews. Both are employed at the same hospital from which respondents were digitally surveyed. They were interviewed individually and asked to answer a series of eight questions, which built upon the foundation of the online survey:

1. Tell me a little bit about your background in nursing.
2. What made you gravitate towards a specific unit?
3. How do you think the COVID-19 pandemic has affected the hospital?
4. How has the pandemic affected you personally? How has it affected your work environment?
5. Do you believe that the pandemic has decreased the quality of patient care?
6. Have you felt supported by your employer/supervisor? Have they made resources available to support nurses? Has there been any intervention from management?
7. Do you think that the pandemic has exacerbated compassion fatigue/burnout?
8. Researcher Emily Peters, a nurse herself, argued that CF prevention may be achieved through professional boundaries, self-care measures, self-awareness, and education on the concept at the individual and organizational level. Do you think that this is a complete solution?

Figure 1. "Do you believe that your hospital is understaffed?"

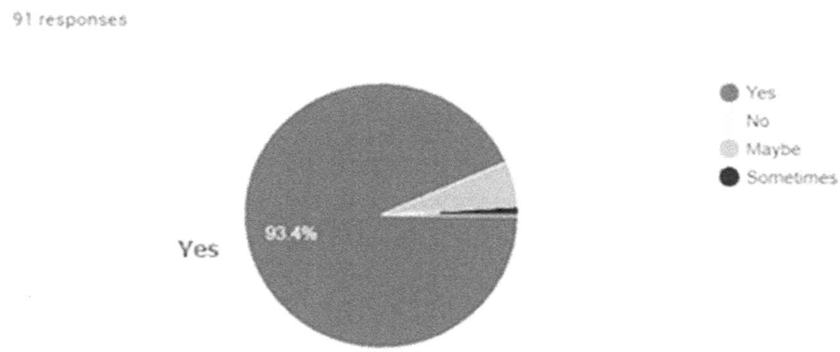

RESULTS

"Nurses want respect, not pizza parties."

Staffing

In the first section of the survey, general demographic information was collected: participants were asked what unit they worked in, whether they were currently full- or part-time employees, whether they typically work day or night shifts, what the lengths of their shifts are, and how long they had been nurses. 46.2% of respondents had been working as nurses for over fifteen years. The second section of the survey contained questions about staffing. Respondents were asked how often they work overtime, with choices being outlined as regularly, sometimes, occasionally, rarely, and never (with corresponding explanations for interpretations). For this question, there was a fairly even split with the responses, with 36.3% of respondents never working overtime, 28.6% occasionally working overtime, 15.2% regularly working overtime, 13.2% sometimes working overtime, and the remaining percentage submitting an alternative response. Next, respondents were asked if, in the past six months, overtime had been needed to ensure their unit was sufficiently staffed, to which 96.7% responded yes; 53.8% of respondents said they had felt pressured to work overtime. In cases where they did end up working overtime, 79.1% reported that their unit was still short staffed. Figure 1 shows that 93.4% of respondents believed their hospital is understaffed. Figure 2 indicates that 95.6% of respondents believed this is negatively impacting the quality of the care that is provided. And finally, 91.1% believed that the pandemic has impacted the quality of care that is provided to patients (Figure 3).

Burnout

The third section of the survey focused on burnout. Respondents were first presented with a definition of compassion fatigue and burnout. 65.9% of respondents said they had felt significantly more stressed at work in the past two years, since the onset of the pandemic; and 28.6% felt slightly more stressed. When asked to respond to the statement "I regularly feel burned out at my job," 60.4% of respondents

Figure 2. "If so, do you believe that this is negatively impacting the quality of care that is provided?"

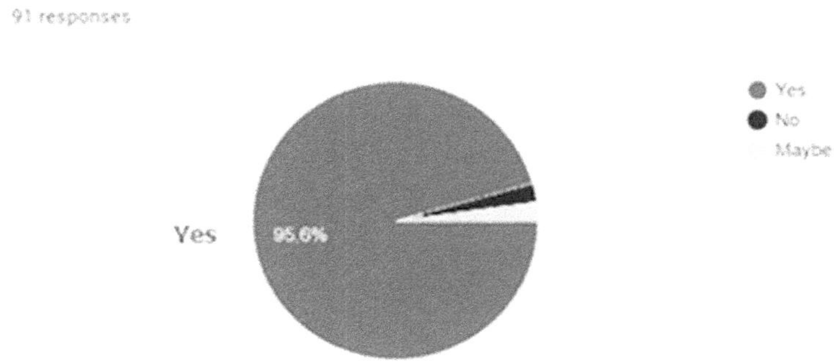

Figure 3. "Do you believe that the pandemic has impacted the quality of care that is provided to patients?"

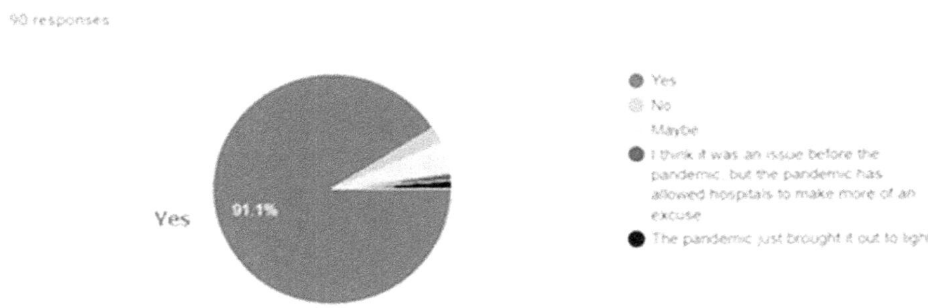

strongly agreed, while 31.9% slightly agreed. In responding to the statement "Burnout has affected my performance at work," 33.4% of respondents strongly agreed, and 42.2% slightly agreed. Participants were asked if they had considered leaving their job in the past two years, to which 86.8% responded yes. Of those who responded yes, feeling unsupported in the workplace was a top reason, followed by feeling overworked.

Figure 4. "In the past two years, have you felt more or less stressed while at work (on average)?"

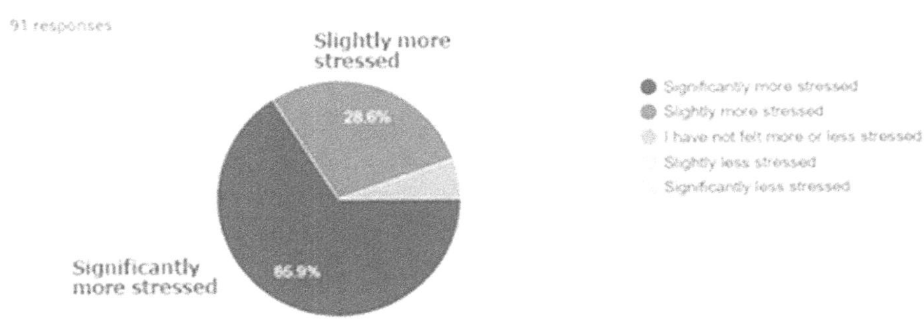

Figure 5. "Please respond to the following statement: I regularly feel burned out at my job."

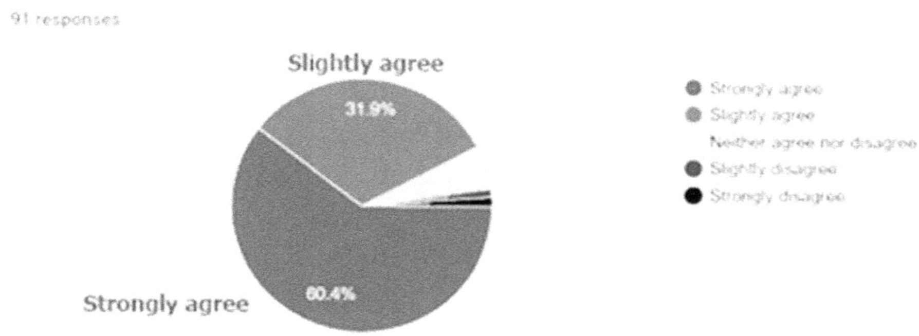

Mental Health

The next section of the survey covered mental health. 80.2% of respondents said that workload had negatively impacted their mental health. Of those respondents, only 32.9% reported seeking treatment; 76.9% of respondents did not feel that their workplace takes the mental health of employees seriously. When asked if they believed that their workplace provides sufficient support and access to mental health resources, only 8.8% of respondents said "yes."

Workload

The following section dug deeper into workload. Respondents were asked if they were able to take their guaranteed break(s) at work always, sometimes, rarely, or never. Only 12.1% of participants responded always. When asked to rate their level of agreement with the statement "My employer supports a healthy work/life balance," 34.1% of respondents strongly disagreed, and 27.5% somewhat disagreed.

Figure 6. "Please respond to the following statement: Burnout has affected my performance at work."

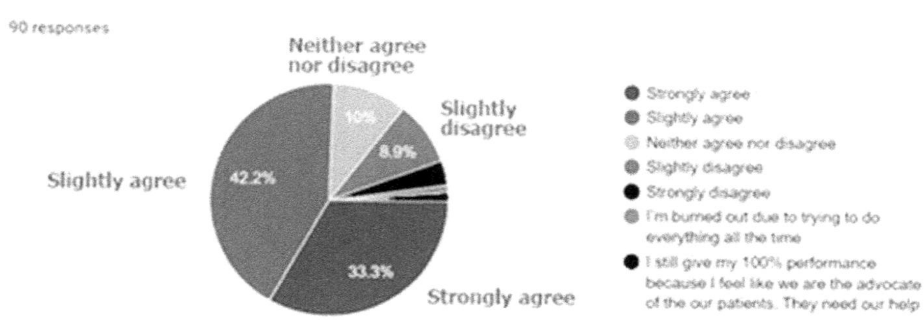

Figure 7. "Has your workload ever negatively impacted your mental health?"

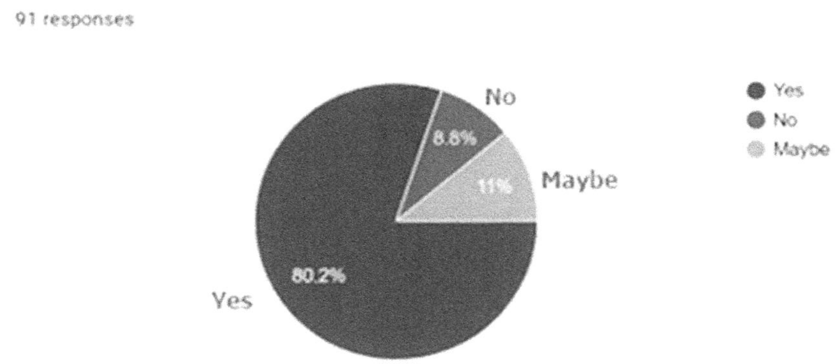

Figure 8. "If so, have you sought treatment?"

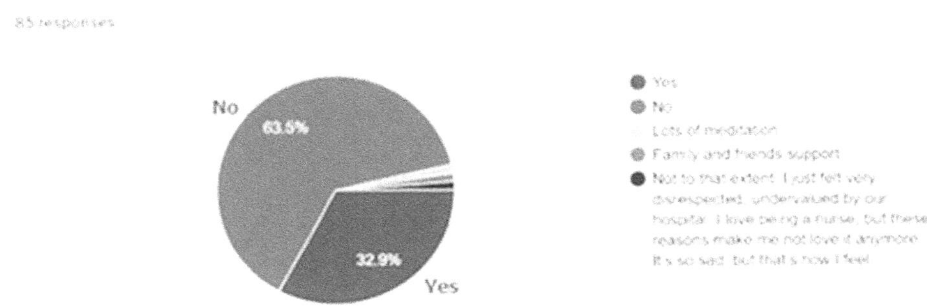

COVID-19 Precautions

The final section pertained to COVID-19 precautions within the workplace. Of participants who responded, 61.1% answered "yes" when asked if they felt their workplace had taken appropriate COVID-19 precautions. Yet only 34.4% reported that they always had access to the supplies and resources neces-

Figure 9. Do you feel that your workplace takes the mental health of employees seriously?"

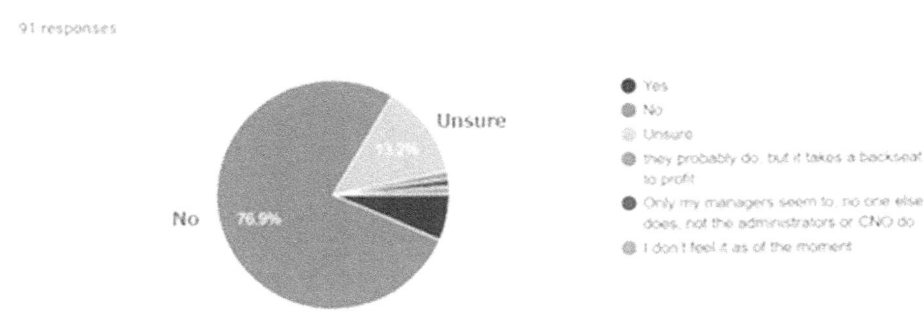

Figure 10. "Do you believe that your workplace provides sufficient support and access to mental health services?"

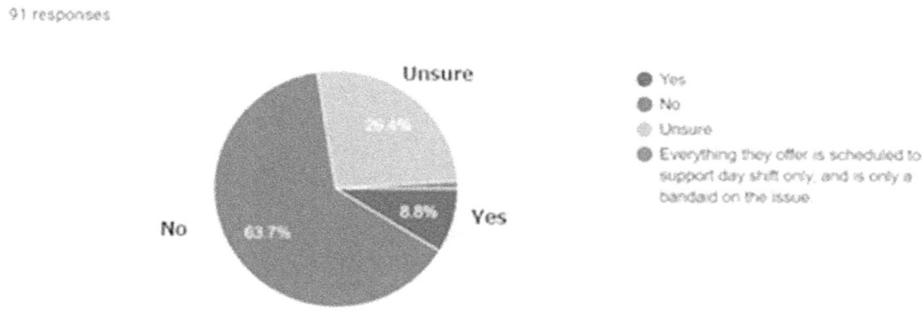

Figure 11. "Are you able to take your guaranteed break(s) while at work?"

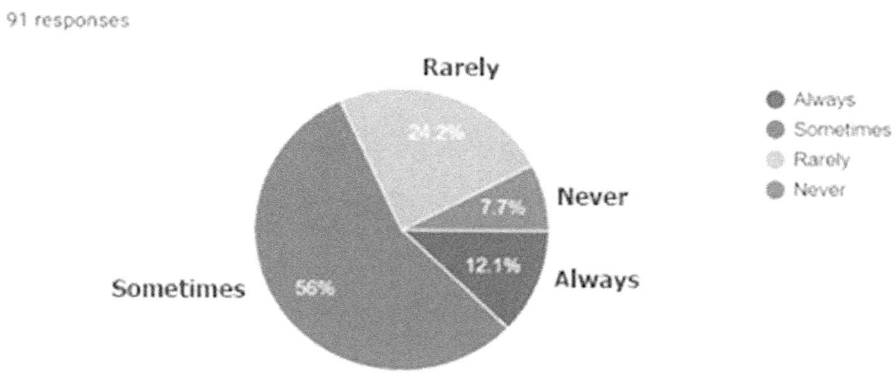

Figure 12. "Please rate your level of agreement with the following statement: My employer supports a healthy work/life balance."

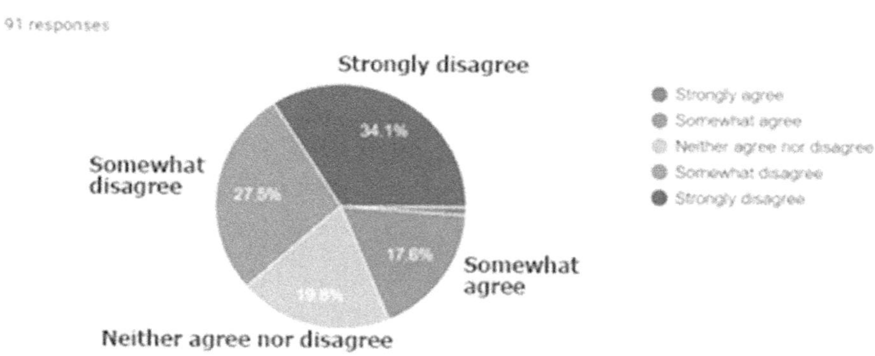

Figure 13. "Do you feel that your workplace has taken appropriate COVID-19 precautions?"

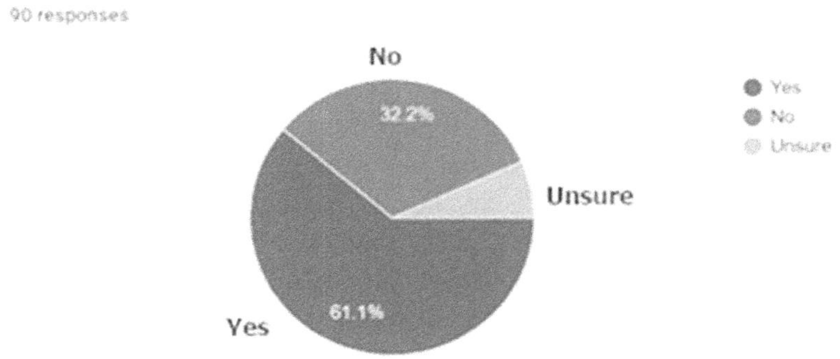

Figure 14. "Do you have access to the supplies and resources necessary to protect yourself and do your job?"

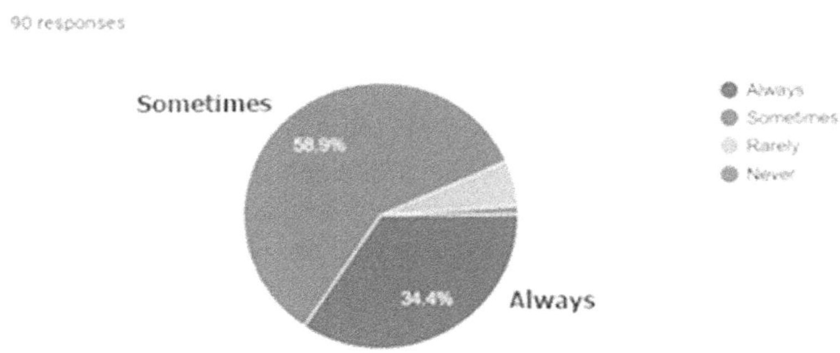

Figure 15. "Has your employer communicated expectations (regarding practices during the pandemic) in a clear and timely fashion?"

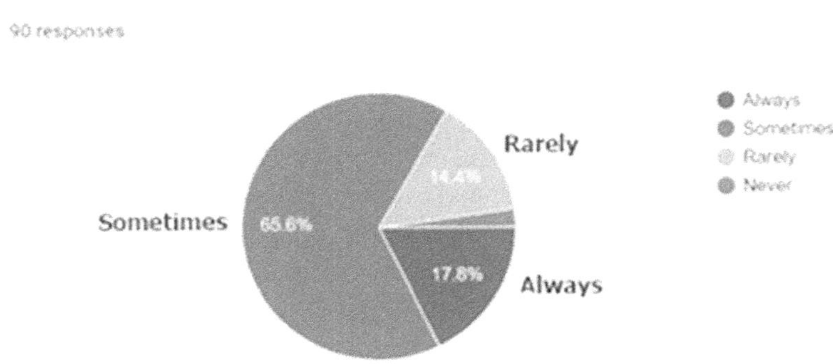

sary to protect themselves and do their jobs. Only 17.8% of respondents believed that their employer had always communicated expectations regarding standards of practice during the pandemic in a clear and timely fashion.

Two nurses who had responded to the online survey also participated in longer individual interviews (all names have been changed to protect their identity). Susan has worked as a nurse in the Neonatal Intensive Care Unit for the past eleven years. Before that, she worked in pediatrics at a different hospital. Kathryn has been a nurse for a total of twelve years. For the past three years, she has worked in the surgical trauma ICU. Before that, she worked in the NICU, then the PICU, at this same hospital. Both women agreed that the pandemic has harmed nurses in particular, and both reported feeling unsupported by the institution in which they work. They were both highly critical of how their institution has handled its response to the pandemic. "At the beginning of the pandemic," Susan said, "a lot of the nurses I work with were paying close attention to what was happening around the world and feeling fairly certain that it was just a matter of time before everything changed for us at work. Several nurses in my unit started wearing masks at work as a precaution right away, and they were actually called into the office and reprimanded for doing so. They were told that it would make patients' families feel uncomfortable and that there was no reason to wear masks. One week later, masks were required for all of us."

As the pandemic progressed, Susan said, "there didn't seem to be any comprehensive plan for how to provide adequate protection for employees, patients, or families. The rules changed arbitrarily and there weren't standards across the institution, meaning that rules were different between units. It seemed that the hospital missed the opportunity to provide appropriate PPE [personal protective equipment] because they were so invested in utilizing the just-in-time supply chain (based on the idea of keeping a real-time inventory and order supplies as needed, rather than keeping a stockpile), which quickly became impossible as there were shortages of supplies. To a lot of us, it seemed like the hospital should have been able to anticipate needs. It seemed like they were just focused on trying to save money instead. The hospital accepted many donations of cloth masks, which were all different sizes and shapes and designs. Most of them didn't fit us correctly. And that was all we had to protect ourselves in the very beginning." Susan noted how shockingly lacking the protective equipment made available to nurses at her hospital was in comparison to the supplies provided in other countries: "You looked at images of healthcare workers in other countries wearing this extensive protective gear, just top of the line. They had Tyvek suits and N95 masks from the start. And eye protection and face shields. And we had these flimsy cloth masks. We had no sort of standardized masks or protective equipment[…]Why wasn't our hospital providing actual equipment that we know provides protection?[...]There were so many things that we could have anticipated. Things that should have been common sense. It just created an atmosphere of distrust." The debate over the effectiveness of masking was especially discouraging within this particular institutional setting. Before the COVID-19 pandemic, nurses were already wearing masks when entering the rooms of patients with contagious illnesses such as influenza and tuberculosis. Susan felt as though the upper management at her hospital refused to acknowledge the information that was already known regarding the value of PPE such as masks in preventing the spread of illness.

Kathryn echoed many of the same sentiments. She and Susan both described the persistent tendency to put the needs of nurses last. "I think the thing is," said Kathryn, "while managers want to be supportive, they listen more to the people above them. That always trumps what is better for the nurses. I know that they're getting heat on the back of their neck to do certain things. And I unfortunately feel like the hospital runs like a business. Dollars and cents. What's better for the bottom line? Instead of what's better for the staff and patients. Staff comes last. It's money, patients, then staff. There's a running joke among nurses that management tries to fix everything with pizza parties. We ask if we can have fair pay, better staffing, and they hand us free food. We don't want more pizza parties." Variations of this attitude appeared numerous times in responses to the initial online survey. Multiple respondents cited the only interventions by management as being related to providing free food or other superficial distractions.

Susan further outlined the hierarchy that she feels exists within her hospital: "The institution has made decisions to protect administrators and physicians from exposure risk which left nurses and respiratory therapists providing even more of the physical care of patients than usual as well as completing phlebotomy and janitorial tasks normally completed by other departments. The resources provided seemed cursory and inadequate–cookies or a $5 gift card or online mediation. I never felt like anyone with decision-making authority ever took the time to ask nurses what we needed. Management was absent but not actually missed because they are so out of touch with what is needed to take good care of patients and employees." Susan described multiple cases where she felt the health and safety of doctors was prioritized over the well-being of nurses. In an instance where she was caring for a COVID-positive patient, she stated that the attending physician was unwilling to enter the patient's room, and "said that he needed to protect himself and his fellows from COVID exposure." The expectation, she said, was that she would shoulder the burden of risk by doing any physical assessments and direct care.

Kathryn and Susan both described staffing as a critical issue. They both felt that their units were consistently understaffed. When asked about specific staffing concerns, Kathryn reported that "It seems like there are tons of nurses daily who are leaving. They go to agencies to make more money. Go back to school to make more money. Or they leave the career entirely. Lots of nurses, if they have the option, are retiring early. Constantly, I feel like we're having a staffing issue at the hospital. There's always a unit that is understaffed. When we do have the staff we need, they pull people and move them to other units. It's like they want everyone to be "equally short staffed." This sentiment aligned with the consensus that was illustrated in the initial online survey, where nearly all respondents felt that their units were consistently short staffed.

"I feel like there's this mentality that a nurse is a nurse," Kathryn continued, "but that's so wrong. We all have our specialties and comfort zones. Pulling nurses into unfamiliar units with very different expectations does not create a good environment for them. And it certainly makes things worse for patients." Susan felt the same way. "During the pandemic," she said, "hospitals were forced to create so many overflow units. Nurses that had a specialty, who were used to taking care of a certain kind of patient, suddenly found themselves taking care of patients they did not have the expertise to take care of. You saw trauma patients being cared for in the oncology unit. My own mom, after her hip replacement, was put on a neuro floor where nurses were trained to take care of stroke patients. They simply did not know how to take care of her."

When asked if they believed that the pandemic has exacerbated compassion fatigue and burnout, both Kathryn and Susan fiercely agreed. However, Susan added that she has "difficulty in accepting the terminology because what is really happening seems to be that nurses are being asked to do completely different jobs than they were hired to do. If we don't like those new jobs we are labeled maladaptive in some way and encouraged to take care of ourselves and meditate. I'm not burned out at all by taking care of patients, but I am frustrated with some of the unrealistic expectations that have been imposed on my work day. The documentation burden is very heavy, and non-nursing departments add tasks for nurses to complete without soliciting feedback from nurses. It feels like we are told what to do and never asked how we think we should do things." This assessment has serious implications for understanding the criteria impacting high job dissatisfaction among nurses. While so-called compassion fatigue clearly presents among nurses, it seems that there are deeper reasons for burnout and discontent within the profession.

DISCUSSION & CONCLUSIONS

"I never felt like anyone with decision-making authority took the time to ask nurses what we needed."

The results of this survey present a deeply concerning trend: nurses feel unsupported, frustrated, and even vilified. Current intervention strategies are deeply lacking, and often perceived as infantilizing. Perfunctory and superficial protocol is simply not enough to address such a complex and deeply pervasive issue. Emily Peters, a nurse herself, argued that CF prevention may be achieved through professional boundaries, self-care measures, self-awareness, and education on the concept at the individual and organizational level (2018). However, this is far from a complete solution. It illustrates the dubious tendency of forcing nurses to serve as their own advocates. Furthermore, it shifts the burden to nurses, rather than institutions, to create solutions. Numerous respondents expressed their frustration with the self-care measures that were being thrown at them. They described them as largely meaningless, and even demeaning. It is impossible for nurses to set professional boundaries when they are constantly being pushed by managers to work overtime, or when they face extreme pressure to perform. Their needs are not being met by institutions, which are being run with profit as the top priority. Despite critical shortages, nurses are still viewed as expendable. They are pushed to their breaking points by hospitals that do not prioritize their safety or well-being. Then, their frustration is pathologized as compassion fatigue or moral injury.

While the concept of compassion fatigue is certainly valid and unfortunately prevalent within the nursing profession, it is symptomatic of a much larger problem. The current institutional framework of healthcare allows for critical policies to be imposed upon nurses without their feedback or insight. Nurses are being asked to perform tasks that extend far beyond the scope of their training and expertise. There is a deeply problematic tendency to view nurses as a homogenous group, rather than recognizing the unique challenges that stem from different specializations and units. The underlying issue behind so many of these challenges is a fundamental lack of understanding and meaningful respect for nurses and the profession. The recent trend of designating nurses - and healthcare providers in general - as heroes does little to meaningfully support or empower them; rather, it poses a much more sinister consequence. It glorifies martyrdom and justifies the risks that nurses endure on a daily basis. Rather than emphasizing the importance of protecting our frontline workers, the United States has taken a stance that allows institutions to operate without taking proper precautions to keep them healthy and safe. Susan stressed her personal concerns with the term hero: "By choosing to enter the profession of nursing, we are choosing to be in service to others. But we did not sign up to be martyrs."

The criminal prosecution of Tennessee nurse RaDonda Vaught, who unintentionally administered the wrong drug to a patient in 2017, resulting in the patient's death, was brought up by both Kathryn and Susan. According to a report from the National Public Radio (NPR), "a lead investigator in the criminal case testified[…]that state investigators found Vanderbilt University Medical Center had a "heavy burden of responsibility" for a grievous drug error that killed a patient in 2017, but pursued penalties and criminal charges only against the nurse and not the hospital itself" (2022). Many nurses fear that Vaught's trial sets a dangerous precedent for future prosecutions: "[In the RaDonda case], all of that fell on the nurse. That's how nurses feel that things work in general," Kathryn said. "You have all of these system issues, and yet everything falls on the nurse in the end."

The scope of the responsibilities that nurses are expected to bear has increased exponentially since the start of the COVID-19 pandemic. The pandemic has resulted in increasingly complex patient cases, often presenting with comorbidities. Nurses face ever-increasing workloads and very limited support from their managers and institutions. The hierarchical structure of healthcare, which is deeply ingrained in social norms, places doctors above nurses. Frequently, doctors are afforded more safeguarding than nurses against COVID-19. Doctors are not as present at the bedside, yet are granted accommodations and protections against the pandemic that nurses are not. This is not to say that doctors should not be supported, but rather that nurses should receive the same benefits. In many ways, doctors are also failed by institutions and administrative practices that prioritize monetary incentives over patient care. So many of the practices of healthcare institutions in the United States are intrinsically flawed. They practice a top-down approach to devising and implementing policies, when instead they should defer to a bottom-up perspective. Radical intervention is required to shift the course of healthcare and nursing. The first step toward change is taking the time to listen to nurses.

REFERENCES

AHA. (2021, May 26). *Fact Sheet: Strengthening the Health Care Workforce.* American Hospital Association. https://www.aha.org/fact-sheets/2021-05-26-fact-sheet-strengthening-health-care-workforce

ANA. (n.d.). *Nurses, ethics, and the response to the covid 19 pandemic.* American Nurses Association. https://www.nursingworld.org/~495c6c/globalassets/practiceandpolicy/work-environment/health--safety/coronavirus/nurses-ethics-and-the-response-to-the-covid-19-pandemic.pdf

Berger, J., Polivka, B., Smoot, E. A., & Owens, H. (2015). Compassion fatigue in pediatric nurses. *Journal of Pediatric Nursing*, *30*(6), e11–e17. doi:10.1016/j.pedn.2015.02.005 PMID:25800590

Cavanagh, N., Cockett, G., Heinrich, C., Doig, L., Fiest, K., Guichon, J. R., Page, S., Mitchell, I., & Doig, C. J. (2020). Compassion fatigue in healthcare providers: A systematic review and meta-analysis. *Nursing Ethics*, *27*(3), 639–665. doi:10.1177/0969733019889400 PMID:31829113

Cocker, F., & Joss, N. (2016). Compassion fatigue among healthcare, emergency and community service workers: A systematic review. *International Journal of Environmental Research and Public Health*, *13*(6), 618. doi:10.3390/ijerph13060618 PMID:27338436

COW. (2022). *New Mayo Clinic Report Sheds Light on Healthcare Professional Well-Being.* Champions of Wellness. https://www.championsofwellness.com/new-mayo-clinic-report-sheds-light-on-healthcare-professional-well-being/

House, S., & Havens, D. (2017). Nurses' and physicians' perceptions of nurse-physician collaboration: A systematic review. *JONA: The Journal of Nursing Administration*, *47*(3), 165–171. doi:10.1097/NNA.0000000000000460 PMID:28157818

Kean, K., & Gettinger, A. (2020, April 20). Now recovering from COVID-19, ICU nurse describes work at UCMC through a pandemic. *Hyde Park Herald*. https://www.hpherald.com/news/local/now-recovering-from-covid-19-icu-nurse-at-describes-work-at-ucmc-through-a-pandemic/article_50ff7e90-834a-11ea-a6e7-83e59cf618be.html

Kelly, L., Runge, J., & Spencer, C. (2015). Predictors of compassion fatigue and compassion satisfaction in acute care nurses. *Journal of Nursing Scholarship*, *47*(6), 522–528. doi:10.1111/jnu.12162 PMID:26287741

Kelman, B. (2022, March 24). *At nurse RaDonda Vaught's trial, testimony points to Vanderbilt's responsibility: Shots—Health News*. NPR. https://www.npr.org/sections/health-shots/2022/03/24/1088397359/in-nurses-trial-witness-says-hospital-bears-heavy-responsibility-for-patient-dea

Ledoux, K. (2015). Understanding compassion fatigue: Understanding compassion. *Journal of Advanced Nursing*, *71*(9), 2041–2050. doi:10.1111/jan.12686 PMID:25981240

Litam, S. D. A., & Balkin, R. S. (2021). Moral injury in health-care workers during COVID-19 pandemic. *Traumatology*, *27*(1), 14–19. doi:10.1037/trm0000290

Matziou, V., Vlahioti, E., Perdikaris, P., Matziou, T., Megapanou, E., & Petsios, K. (2014). Physician and nursing perceptions concerning interprofessional communication and collaboration. *Journal of Interprofessional Care*, *28*(6), 526–533. doi:10.3109/13561820.2014.934338 PMID:25003547

Ortega-Campos, E., Vargas-Román, K., Velando-Soriano, A., Suleiman-Martos, N., Cañadas-de la Fuente, G. A., Albendín-García, L., & Gómez-Urquiza, J. L. (2020). Compassion fatigue, compassion satisfaction, and burnout in oncology nurses: A systematic review and meta-analysis. *Sustainability*, *12*(1), 72. doi:10.3390u12010072

Peters, E. (2018, October). Compassion fatigue in nursing: A concept analysis. *Nursing Forum*, *53*(4), 466–480. doi:10.1111/nuf.12274 PMID:29962010

Sweileh, W. M. (2020). Research trends and scientific analysis of publications on burnout and compassion fatigue among healthcare providers. *Journal of Occupational Medicine and Toxicology (London, England)*, *15*(1), 1–10. doi:10.118612995-020-00274-z PMID:32684943

Van Mol, M. M., Kompanje, E. J., Benoit, D. D., Bakker, J., & Nijkamp, M. D. (2015). The prevalence of compassion fatigue and burnout among healthcare professionals in intensive care units: A systematic review. *PLoS One*, *10*(8), e0136955. doi:10.1371/journal.pone.0136955 PMID:26322644

APPENDIX: OPEN-ENDED RESPONSES

What could your employer do to make you feel more supported in the workplace? Safe staffing, & allowing employees to take the vacations, breaks they so need to recharge & perform better at their job. Also, compensate us for the extra work they are adding to our already long list of stuff to do. Put on some scrubs and come work the unit when we are short! Stop allowing families to threaten/ disrespect staff with no consequences Be physically present to help. When we are short staffed, jump in and help.

Make sure we have adequate supplies for patient care.

Make sure we have appropriate PPE for the shift prior to the start

Give month vacations

Managers could staff the department but don't have the same nursing skill set as we do and are of limited use. There is a constant feeling that management is always short lived and not committed to the position of the staff or the organization.

Focus also on employee satisfaction with the same importance as patient satisfaction.

Listen to staff regarding concerns in patient care. Agency/supplemental nurses are not adequately trained. We should receive a retention bonus.

Help out on the unit when it's chaos.

Incentives, support staff

Upper leadership to stop trying to squeeze more from less. Hire staff not increase ratios

Listen and be realistic

Offer retention bonuses, more sick time pay (greater number of hours of sick time pay given to nurses so we don't work while sick)

Treat me like a human. It became painfully obvious during the pandemic (although alluded to previously) that nurses were expendable bottom dollars, both in my organization and nationally. We had no information from our employer, subpar PPE, and constraints about taking sick time for mental health.

Give us our PTO (paid time off)

Timely communication of risk and exposure information regarding COVID

Actually listen to staffs concerns and facilitate change to support nursing

Improve communication. Listen. Management put themselves on the frontline, not stay safely at home or in their offices, walk the walk. Provide us with the staff, equipment, and supplies to do the job. Give us our accrued time off. Give the nurses back the money they stole by freezing our pensions during the pandemic citing loss of revenue during the early stages all the while collecting large sums of money from the federal government.

Communicate faster in emails. Assist us better with scheduling our work days.

Listen to our concerns. Shadow a day in the life of a nurse and see what it has been like doing many other job duties other than RN. Food service, EVS, transport, etc. Dealing with many unsatisfied patients because we don't have enough staff or enough support staff trained in N95 to do their own job, specifically in Covid rooms

Staff us per safe ratios and pay raise

Money incentives

I strongly believe that leadership (managers) could be helpful on the unit by assisting us, answering our questions, ensure that we take adequate breaks, and have our backs

Have back up

Show more appreciation other than food. Offer more incentive to pick up shifts

Give us appropriate time off

Increase staffing, when pts come in for admission or surgery get all covid testing done stat not routine. Nurses support systems are not working, i.e., phlebotomy, transportation, dietary

Retention bonus. Improve hourly rates.

Approve time off

Pay more hire more and staffing

Hire more staff

Adequate staffing

Organize time for every nurse to get a break

Listen

Help us in days we are short staff

Be visible. Involve us in discussions about changes

Act like they care

Provide adequate staffing hospital wide

Let us take vacation, adequate staffing and following the contract

Adequate staff, quality management

Be more supportive

Recognize burn out and fully staff the units instead of relying on overtime

Honor day off requests.

Adequate staffing and addressing mental health.

Leaders model the behavior. More visibility from leaders. Supplies

Come onto the unit to see what's going on

Hire qualified people

Stay out of their offices and be in the unit more.

They always just send emails about new rules and policies instead of coming to the units and actually talking to the nurses about what they can do to actually support us.

Provide a phlebotomist.

Breaks! Recognition! Pay!

Better staffing, better resources, adequate supplies, guaranteed and covered complete lunch breaks, better communication.

They could show empathy to the workers. They just keep giving orders and they do not know what it is like to be on the frontline.

Actively listen to nurses' concerns.

Have more staff have safe patient ratios, support staff to help nurses with daily activities of patients, a resource nurse to ensure staff has adequate breaks.

Help and round on the unit to see what our needs are.

Give us retention bonuses, pandemic pay, supplies, support and stop treating us like children (pizza parties, calling us heroes but not helping us)

Retention pay for nurse who haven't left

Better staffing. Better pay. Listen to us

More Staffing

Have supplies we need; give us the time off we have; be aware what's going on in the unit

Round and ask us how are you doing.

Be replaced

Support a work/life balance by actually approving your earned paid time off. I am THE senior nurse in a situation where seniority is the basis for approval of PTO, but I am routinely denied my time off. I am actually at the limit of vacation time. This means I can no longer accrue vacation time, but they continue to deny my requests to use it.

More staff

Offer to come help when we are short. Listen to our feedback on the new hires.

Hire enough staff

Be genuine about understanding what we are going through and how this negatively impacts patient care

Higher pay. Incentive pay

To assign enough staff to work on our shift not to float some RNs because we will end up overwhelmed because of lots of admissions in the middle of the night.

Be considerate of work/ life balance and outside obligations

Therapy

Hire more nurses in a timely manner!

Support the nurses more by making sure concerns are being heard instead of brushing them off

Better staffing

Bonus; Hazard/COVID pay

Grant our holiday time off, grant days off for our CEUs, staff our unit adequately, ensure we have working equipment, ensure we have enough supplies, allow us to have potlucks and other celebrations again since Covid numbers are down

Be more flexible with time off when needed.

What could your employer do to improve your work environment?

Hire more staff

More staff

Take us seriously when we say we're burned out. Hear us out because without nurses, who are the backbone of the hospital, they cannot operate. Nurses can help other departments with their job, but who helps the nurses? No one!

Provide supplies needed, equipment that works

Be physically present

Recognize the overtime workers and not guilt them into doing additional OT shifts.

Hire better people that fit your particular Department

Get equipment that works and isn't 27 years old (our EKG machine for example)

Be sure supplies are available

Our unit is not as clean as it should be. Better cleanliness and sanitizing need to be implemented

Offer more classes & pay OT to train newer nurses to learn ECMO & charge so it doesn't always fall on the same people.

Proper PPE

Hire RNs and support staff

Hire competent leadership

Hire people to ensure I get my breaks. 12+ hours is a long time not to have a break.

Units are consistently staffed per a hospital's budget on paper. We are always understaffed because that fails to take into account real life scenarios, where multiple people are sick or on leave on any given day, and further doesn't take into account patient acuity, which is still variable on a unit where minimally we are staffed 1:1 with patients. We cannot make it the norm to force employees to work 12 hours with no breaks, come in on their "off" days to help out the unit, or float to other units when adequately staffed. So, staffing. It would also benefit everyone to have open communication regarding supply chain issues, new packaging, etc.

The culture of communication is very reactionary, if there was a bit of proactive communication, we could actually be prepared to do our jobs.

Supplies, we are often out of basic necessities like linen.

Hire more staff.

Better staffing, more involvement/visibility in the unit. Supporting nurses concerns

Provide us with the staff, equipment, and supplies to do the job. Improve communication!

Building up team morale

Safe nurse to patient ratios

Staff the unit

Ensure sufficient breaks are taken, hire more staff, and stop being in so many meetings and be more present on the unit.

Improve problems with other departments

My manager is amazing but there's some bullies on our unit that just get a pass because that's how they've always been

Get IV pumps that work, scd machines that work. More supplies, too much time is being wasted looking for things.

Staff according to acuity

Be present and jump in to help

Higher pay

Adequate supplies

More nurses for a better nurse patient ratio and implementing breaks

Staff properly

Be present and help the nurses

It's a known punitive environment. It does not foster honesty or education

Be more supportive to staff and truly listen

Limit family visitation

Follow the contract

Adequate supplies and staff

Be more inviting

Staff appropriately

Acknowledge verbal and physical violence nurses experience during patient care.

More supplies or adequate supplies. Visibility from leaders including upper management to CNO

Increase staffing and supplies

Make the supplies and equipment that we need more readily available to us

Give us the supplies and staff we need in order to do our jobs instead of just adding more and more things to our plates

We are told our phones will soon scan meds. Right now we only have a few computers on the floor that scan meds

Breaks and support

Have better security to assure my safety, better surveillance of visitors, check their belongings prior to entering our premises to assure they're not bringing paraphernalia inside and to search patients belongings too. They say they have zero tolerance for abusive and combative patients— I have not seen ANY support in ANY of the units I work in. We are still being forced to care for these abusive patients.

Find a way to retain nursing staff.

Have more staff, have safe patient ratios, support staff to help nurses with daily activities of patients, a resource nurse to ensure staff has adequate breaks. Have safety protocols and adequately train the staff to protect the staff and other patients.

Get the supplies we need

Get sustainable equipment instead of cheap solutions

Better staffing. Better communication.

More transparency regarding union rules

Make rounds with us, let us know we are appreciated.

Better pay, actually show appreciation and mean it

Support r/t abusive families, adequate staffing, adequate supplies.

Anything to increase staff morale, provide positive feedback

Stop putting more demands and responsibilities on an already short and stressed staff.

Provide adequate staffing

Enough staff and supplies

More staff and approve requested time off

More staff. Saying no to the docs who want to admit without the nurses

Force the resignation of our medical director

Stop taking away benefits and stop making payroll mistakes

Better communication

Hire and RETAIN staff

Be properly staffed with well trained nurses.

What other changes could be implemented in order to improve your work environment?

Safe staffing ratio, giving us breaks, allowing us to take vacations as needed & proper compensation.

Increased ways of showing us some sort of appreciation, stop singling out nurses and calling them to work OT. Creates stress and guilt and does not support a work/ life balance

Stop sweating the little things so much.

They could get our paychecks correct. They could pay out the bonuses for retention. They could figure out why nurses don't feel supported and actually FIX it instead of putting a bandaid on it. Stop charging us through the nose for healthcare that we get at our own organization.

Supportive management team/they always look for what is wrong. Also, manager's discretion in personal situations lacks empathy.

The hospital needs to realize that nurses are not interchangeable between specialties and units.

More incentive for nurses to improve and expand their skills.

Definite lunch breaks, manager support

Allow scheduled time off

Mental health days, on unit support

Provide benefits that allow you to access mental health providers not associated with the facility. There is still so much stigma surrounding seeking care that many are reluctant to utilize services provided for fear of retaliation by management.

Our work area is filthy

More flexible work shifts (shorter hours, varied start times)

Supply nursing with the tools to do our job be it staffing, supplies, support staff(secretaries, evs, nsa) pharmacy. When dealing with shortcomings in other areas it actually takes away from our job at the bedside.

Address the negative feelings and atmosphere in the unit (not sure how this could be done). Improve safety on the unit. Hold parents accountable for their actions and words, healthcare provider abuse is real.

Decrease Floating, utilizing peds staff in adult areas regularly

Hire more staff. Base staffing on acuity of patients in addition to nurse to patient ratio.

Women coming to UC for deliveries are getting sicker and sicker and comorbidities.

100% breaks so that nurses can take their lunch and not just "fit" this time anywhere within a 12 hour shift

More staff, no tolerance with patients and family members

Approve our well earned vacation time. Give us mental health days

Do some team building exercising

Nurses stop doing secretary and aid work because those people aren't available for the unit.

Change the times pharmacy restocks.

Better staffing ratios

Change the ratios so make the workload better

Staffing ratios

Time off

Have a manager that is caring and accommodating, not cold hearted and stuff like mine.

Better follow up and resources for new hires following orientation

More paid time off

More concern about people and less about money

Change the culture of older nursing

Paying us for what we're worth

Change starts with leadership. They can implement and promote better morale, resources and staff.

Not sure. But mental health days or granting days off

A good cleaning. Better education and mentoring

Better staffing

Having supporting roles be more present in the hospital instead of being in their offices or at home and communicating via email. Nurses don't always have time to read their email. We're busy actually saving lives

A pharmacy that will make sure the meds are available

Have clear communication with all departments, support us don't demand more when there is no more to give, recognize we are working our butts off

Better staffing!

Allow for time off

Supplies

Safe staffing ratios, and security staff that protect staff.

More staff

Better staffing

Having a resource nurse always available

Supplies

Staffing, EVS, TRANSPORT, TECHS, Lab! You know a health care system where everyone is held accountable for not doing their job and not just nurses

Actually having the supplies we need

Make sure all equipment and needed supplies are accessible and are well maintained in good working condition.

Accountability for all ancillary staff in completing their job responsibilities

Better security, more breaks and food available

Teamwork and good communication

Allow for registry staff to help with staffing issue on unit

Staff. Break nurses. Being able to step off the unit

Have our backs when it comes to unruly and rude visitors/family members and have them escorted out of the facility!

Staff safety

Better Staffing and supplies schedule

Management demonstrating their appreciation for staff.

Installing an ice and water machine inside our unit for the parents

Have adequately staffed and trained personnel in the ancillary departments with which you work.

What would you like people to know about what it's like to work as a nurse?

Honestly, I used to feel that it was rewarding even if it entails a lot of hard work. But now, it's not rewarding anymore, and the work is even harder. Patients abuse us, our hospitals don't support us. It's very disheartening. I've been a nurse for 24 years, & I don't want to do it anymore.

We aren't there to hurt you, we are on the same team and want the best for you and your families. We advocate for you and we take our patients home with us. We don't leave our jobs at the door when we leave.

Overtired

Under appreciated

Frustrated

The flow of Covid 19 protocols has been confusing for exposed parents

Mentally exhausting telling people to pull their masks up…even after 2 years or how to wear the mask

If you are doing it for the money…..god help you because it's a bad investment.

It can be very rewarding. It is who I am as a person in so many ways...but I am so many more things. Not all employers will recognize this. It really feels like the bottom dollar is all they care about.

It requires all of you when you are working.

If you work in a hospital, expect to work weekends and holidays.

Hard work that bears a great deal of responsibility with little appreciation by management.

It's mentally & physically exhausting & often times thankless.

Exhausting

We are humans not machines

It's hard tiring and you need a lot of compassion

Your performance is never good enough for patients or hospital administrators. No matter how fast you work, if you follow all the policies and procedures, it's never enough.

It is not about taking care of people and making them feel better. Nurses are mostly the last stop before all kinds of errors would reach you. We are fail safes and safe guards and it is taxing to constantly be questioning everything and not trusting your team.

We don't have a choice to work from home. We work weekends, holidays and odd hours instead of being with our families, we are guilted into coming when the weather is terrible. It's physically and emotionally taxing. People complain about wearing a paper or cloth mask for a half hour at the grocery store, try wearing an n95 for a twelve hour shift!

You are expected to sacrifice yourself in order to deliver care that is 100% with supplies and support that will only get you 75% of the way there.

After all is said and done it is one of the most rewarding professions. I have never regretted my decision, but I am truly saddened by the current state of hospital nursing.

It is an incredibly difficult job that requires extensive knowledge, and takes a physical and mental toll on its people. Nurses are the last line between you and mistakes. Nurses will take the fall for mistakes that went through multiple people. We are responsible for the lion's share of your care.

It is what you make of it. If you're unhappy, find another unit or facility. Don't be afraid to branch out.

You work with some great coworkers! Keep pushing every day because there are many days that make it worth the struggles in the past 2 year.

There are no words to describe the many roles of a nurse. One of the hardest jobs out there.

It is hard! We bare the responsibility of the shortcomings of other departments and when it comes to quality measures we are constantly scolded about our numbers or percentages when in reality we are doing our absolute best

It was great until this past year when patients and family members started verbally attacking the nurse in everything.

Nursing is hard. We are overworked and underpaid and often punching bags.

Everything for that patient is put on your shoulders. For 12 hours we are stressed, so be gentle with judgements

Nursing is an Art backed by scientific principles. It is the hardest work I have ever performed, Nursing has given me purpose and satisfacción beyond all understanding . It has been a privilege and my highest honor to serve my pt's, my community.

It's become increasingly more challenging - covid aside - patients are more sick, more demanding and it all falls on the bedside nurse. Throughput is a focus and we are always full yet we don't have the staff to support the amount of patients and the tasks required. There is very little respect and it's a thankless job. 3 days a week of "work" but you need more time to recover.

It used to be an admired profession, and now I feel as though it's a frowned upon job. We are just a number; a replaceable employee.

Don't do it

How hard and emotionally draining it can be

Very very hard

This pandemic has been mentally taxing for many nurses across a variety of units with heavier workloads and less staffing.

A thankless job

It's a tough job. A nurse wears many hats. A nurse has to be an aide, housekeeper, a therapist, PT, a secretary, a phlebotomist, but no one can be a nurse and do all the job of a nurse but a nurse!!!

It's a calling and a cause and not just a job. If it's not viewed that way the care delivered will suffer along with the outcomes

It's stressful and rewarding

Physical and verbal abuse is an everyday part of nursing life

The majority of us genuinely care. We put our hearts and souls into our patients, and it's about time that we're fairly compensated for literally standing between life and death

The responsibilities of nurses are vast. When nurses are overwhelmed, patients' outcomes are negatively affected.

It is exhausting. Few days I feel accomplished and as though I've made a difference.

I love nursing but I feel it is changing. It isn't a passion but just a job for many and it reflects in care.

Good nursing is intellectual, physical and emotional. Serving as a patient advocate is an incredibly important part of the job especially as Covid restrictions have limited the ability of families to be at the bedside. I want to have true interdisciplinary collaboration. Hospitals would run better if more control was given to the people who work at the bedside. I have the feeling that hospital administrators are the least important and most overpaid people in the institution. Nurses want respect, not pizza parties.

That's it's very difficult right now

It's hard work

It has fallen on the nurses' shoulders to do the jobs of so many other people especially since a lot of the supporting roles have moved to work from home

It's physically and mentally challenging and should be paid at a much higher rate than at present

It is demanding mentally, physically, and emotionally. We are expected to know everyone's job and how to do it. The finger is always pointed back at the nurse. It can be rewarding but in the last few years it has changed. Nursing is a calling and I will always have passion for what I do.

But being a nurse means being able to handle being beat up, literally, with the question what could you have done differently.

A lot of things are not in our control (though we wish it were), we are on your side, we're here to help and heal. We are trying our best, so don't project your anger at the world towards us.

We are literally the ones managing EVERYTHING in your care. Be kind to us.

It really is a great profession but if you have no support it is really difficult.

I find joy in taking care of my patients

We truly love what we do, it's not a job everyone can do. This pandemic has shown us the value of a nurse to the public as well as to management, and the hospital. We give our all to every patient, even on our worst days.

We're drowning and I don't see a way out if employers can't get their act together and realize how important we are.

It's not fun anymore. It used to be fun.

It is tiring and unrewarding. Working a job that people think is customer service when my job is to do what is best for someone despite their opinion on the matter.

The job would be much more fulfilling if I had more time to spend with my patients and my assignments were appropriately spread out among the 9-10 nurses that we never have..but I guess that's wishful thinking.

It is the BEST job due to its versatility. There are so many careers one can have as a nurse. It's also very physically, emotionally and mentally challenging to be a nurse working 12 hour shifts in a hospital.

On our feet to make sure you are able to stand on theirs.

It's not worth it

It was my lifelong joy & pride. No longer. It's sad how difficult it has become. There is no support or change from management to create a positive atmosphere.

Overworked and underappreciated

That it is an amazing career choice but it isn't for everyone. And that it's not always like this

It can also be very rewarding.

We are responsible for everything.

Do not go into the profession if you want to be treated as a human

It is bitter and sweet. Sometimes you will get burn out but most of the time I enjoy taking care of people, learn from them, witness them get well

It's REALLY exhausting. Emotionally and physically.

It's the most mentally exhausting yet rewarding job. No one wants to hear about our bad days, but it's always your fellow RN's that help pick up all the pieces and support one another

Nursing is saving lives not hotel service

Stressful

We can't, but currently have to do, all jobs

It is so much harder than you think it is. We see horrible, sad, tragic things every single day but we never talk about them (except with our coworkers) because we don't want to make our loved ones sad or for them to feel sorry for us.

It is a tough job and not for the faint of heart, but the job can also be very rewarding.

How has the pandemic changed your experience working as a nurse?

Yes

It just heightened the lack of support, respect & value towards nurses. Saying that we are heroes does not mean anything. I don't feel any sincerity when our hospital said that. I felt like it's more for press release. They never really valued us. To them, we are disposable, easily replaced. I could go on forever, but it's just going to stress me more.

Chronic short staffing has made me learn how to work in conditions that are stressful and caused me to be be more resourceful and rely on me peers even more when I need help

Initially we were seen as heroes…now we are holding patients hostage from their loved ones.

Wearing a mask for 12-20 hours can be tiring as you re-breathe your CO2 for such long periods of time.

It hasn't however it brings to light how political healthcare is

I let a lot of things go that normally I would have cared about. Like Housework and food and everyday messes. Life is too short to get worked up about that

I am anxious for retirement.

Yes. I am more comfortable setting limits with patients.

It's made me realize that hospitals will cut corners in any way they can. Nurses are expendable because they will do everything necessary to protect the patient even if it means the nurse is not protected.

No longer as rewarding as it used to be

Has increased stress; highlighted the undervalued culture we have been conditioned to think was okay

I realized that my employer really does not value its nurses at all

I go to work dreading it.

It has been horrifying to see our already stressed healthcare infrastructures move toward the point of collapse with the pandemic. We cannot treat patients adequately without supplies or staff, and the mental burden of that has been incredibly hard. It is especially difficult to not see an end in sight due to new variants, and the general disregard for science and public health policies by our world.

I loved my job, now I'm thinking of early retirement.

Fearing physical safety at work due to virus exposure as well as stressed/ angry patients and families.

Definitely

People are more on edge and more self-centered, further changing how they interact with nurses. It is more dangerous than ever. In addition, hospitals have used the pandemic to further remove financial support, time off, and staffing from nursing. Nurses have been vilified as greedy, not just seeking the compensation compensate with their education, skill, and responsibilities.

I feel more burnt out and overworked

More anxiety

It made me realize that even though nurses were considered "heroes" we are actually unappreciated and disposable

Drove me back to school to leave bedside

It has opened my open eyes to the downsides of healthcare and how we as employees are seen to higher ups.

Yes. I think it's nerve wracking getting new patients with respiratory symptoms.

It has started me to thinking that it is time to leave a profession that has given me so much purpose and satisfacción. Nursing is my identificación. I am getting emotional taking your survey.

I want new opportunities and I can work at other places in less stressful jobs for slightly less pay. Dollar general for $25/hour stocking and scanning?

In some cases the agency nurses don't have the same skill sets and care is missed. In addition the new nurses coming out of school are needing extra support since they didn't have a lot of hands-on learning opportunities and then they get a year of training and leave for better paying jobs or don't like the profession at all. Bedside nursing is leading to burnout but there are lots of other nursing jobs.

Negative

It has felt very stressful at the peak of it where it made me consider leaving the hospital setting.

Feel less valued

As a nurse I always never of the risk/potential of being exposed to harmful contagious disease so in the beginning I was afraid but once I had the necessary equipment to do my job I did it. It has made me tired but tougher!

It has definitely made it physically and mentally more challenging. Just wearing a mask affects stamina, deep breathing and effects communication

Yes

Unchanged

Yes. I don't enjoy it as much anymore

Loss of quality coworkers

It has increased the workload due to coworkers being out sick. It has affected our interaction with patients. It's difficult wearing a mask for long hours a day. Supplies are more difficult to obtain.

Yes. The burnout is significantly higher.

Lack of contact. Isolation

Because I don't work on a Covid unit I experienced some feelings of guilt and fraudulence as nurses were framed as "heros" a term I greatly dislike because it creates the expectation of martyrdom. Nurses have been thrust into dangerous and unsustainable positions while other employees give orders from the safety of their homes. I feel disrespected, misunderstood and unappreciated.

Yes

It's very tiresome

I no longer feel like we have support from the community

I have experienced really sick kids from covid.

Gave me wrinkles, made me emotionally burnt out with the feeling of absolute hopelessness. I used to love to help save lives and make a difference, even just one patient. Now it has given me compassion fatigue. I don't know how to cry anymore.

I'm not the same tolerant, patient, empathetic person I was before. A lot of unkind and selfish patients took that from me.

Well, when the pandemic began we were heroes. Now it is just an expectation.

I have anxiety and insomnia sometimes prior to my scheduled work day.

Yes it made me realize hospitals no longer care about taking care of people, they care about money and making profit.

I never thought I'd feel so unsupported by my job and the public.

I didn't think I'd ever get tired of it. Now I dread it.

It has made me bitter and jaded. It has shown me how unappreciated nurses are to hospital systems

Honestly there was a week or two where covid was spreading among staff which made our assignments more difficult to balance but this is a day by day situation.

Stress but knowing God is truly God.

I have lost my love of the profession. It's not just the pandemic, it's the public attitude of entitlement & abuse we are subjected to on an everyday basis.

Feel insignificant

It has made it much harder to with the supplies not being stocked, harder to support families, harder to care for myself and my family.

It has made me appreciate my fellow nurses even more.

Yes, it shows how much less respect the Healthcare system has for nursing staff

Hospitals do not care about their nursing staff

Challenging experience in all aspects

Yes- it makes me want to leave the hospital not out of fear for the pandemic, because of the way the hospital treats it employees related to the vaccine

I've become numb.

We've lost so many amazing nurses to lucrative travel contracts. Glad they can take advantage of the pay we should all be receiving, but I still miss them

Made it more stressful because attitudes towards nurses are more hostile when things don't go the patients' way

Emotional and stress

It hasn't changed anything personally.

It has made me lose complete empathy for people who did not take Covid seriously, did not believe in wearing masks, or did not get vaccinated.

During the beginning and height of the pandemic, work procedures were constantly changing. It made me become more flexible in how my nursing care was provided.

Is there anything else you would like to add?

Just because our profession is about caring does not mean we cannot complain, & make demands.

Yes, we chose this profession, but it does not mean that we are to endure all the hardships that get thrown at us. We don't deserve to be abused, & expected to just stay quiet & carry on with our jobs. Enough is enough.

My respect for my coworkers has grown immensely. The support and encouragement I have received during all of this has come from them. Nurses are an amazing group of people!

Take naps. Take your time off that you are entitled to. Take care of yourself. Don't sweat the small stuff. Go on a trip. By yourself even. Talk to people and get help if you need it. I did. And because I did I am still here.

I have been burned out, not appreciating my work as much as I used to, for almost eight years.

I just transferred to a new unit that is (hopefully) less intense. I could no longer deal with the disorganization and unprofessionalism on my old unit.

I wouldn't recommend anyone to be a nurse.

We went from hero to zero in no time flat.. these last 2 years have really soured my view of nursing. I used to love my job I can't say that anymore

This is important research and thank you for bringing these topics to light!

Full disclosure, I was burned out before the pandemic. It has only been exacerbated by the pandemic.

I was a CNA for a long time before being a nurse and I think they're going through the same things with less than half the pay.

Nurse burnout was already an ongoing problem before COVID started. COVID just exposed this problem and made it worse.

I truly feel patient care is suffering and nurses need support. Mental, physical and emotional.

Despite awful conditions in the hospital I still love my job taking care of patients.

When I became a nurse I did it to help people. I love people of all kinds! I thought I could make a difference. I didn't know that I would be abused by patients and management. The expectations of a nurse are so much. I didn't know I would be so emotionally, mentally, physically drained. I would choose another career.

We need better laws to protect our nurses and to ensure their safety!

Not really…hardest and best job ever

Great project much success.

I pray that changes bring the profession of nursing back to what it was.

Busting your butt through a pandemic and worrying you'll bring this virus home to your family is hard enough and now we have the government trying to cap pay that travel RN's can make.

Who is going to help then?

I have never felt "glad" that someone gets ill or has health problems, but since this debacle with Covid I have actually found myself wishing a bad case of Covid on certain people because for some reason I feel like they "deserve" it. I have never had those kinds of thoughts before and honestly I am very ashamed of these feelings. This is not the kind of person I am and it is very distressing to have these feelings.

Section 3
Community and Education

Chapter 15
Perspectives on Building Racial Equity in Science, Technology, Engineering, Math, and Health Science Education and Workforce Systems

Rukiya Curvey Johnson
Rush University Medical Center, USA

Natalia Gallegos
Rush University Medical Center, USA

Angela Freeman
https://orcid.org/0000-0002-6485-6348
Rush University Medical Center, USA

ABSTRACT

Persistent and deeply entrenched systemic racism too often contributes to the lack of Black and Latinx people from low-income communities ascending and succeeding at the highest levels of STEM and healthcare careers. The authors examine the relationships between equity-centered innovations in K-12 STEM education, persistence, and attainment. The authors identify community-specific constructs with potential to engage partners and increase collective capacity for more Black and Latinx youth. They focus on how to structure social-emotional health into STEM and health science learning models, occupational identity development, and specific work-based learning strategies for students. Data and infrastructure are considered, and approaches to program design are discussed from a methodological point of view. This analysis considers these elements through its case study of the rush education and career hub (REACH), a pipeline and workforce intermediary. REACH is distinct for its position within Rush University Medical Center, an anchor institution on Chicago's west side.

DOI: 10.4018/978-1-6684-2314-1.ch015

INTRODUCTION

People of color are dramatically underrepresented in STEM fields—according to a recent Pew Research Center report, just 2.2% of Latinos, 2.7% of African Americans, and 3.3% of Native Americans and Alaska Natives have earned a university degree in STEM fields (Funk & Parker, 2018). The same Pew report surveyed current STEM professionals, finding that 52% of those surveyed believed this lack of representation was due to a lack of educational opportunities for people of color and 45% believed the cause was people of color not being encouraged at an early age to pursue STEM-related subjects (Funk & Parker, 2018). Finally, around one-third of those surveyed also attribute this underrepresentation to a lack of belief in their ability to succeed in these fields, the lack of diverse role models in these fields, and racial/ethnic discrimination in recruitment, hiring and promotions (Funk & Parker, 2018).

There is a great and growing demand for workers in the STEM and healthcare fields. It is projected that between 2016 and 2026, health sector employment will grow at a significantly higher rate than employment in all other sectors (Lacey, Toossi, Dubina, & Gensler, 2017). Health sector employment is projected to grow from nearly 16.5 million jobs in 2016 to more than 19.5 million jobs in 2026, an increase of 18%, compared to only 6% growth for jobs in all other employment sectors. The U.S. Bureau of Labor Statistics employment projections show that by 2029, jobs within STEM fields are expected to grow at more than double the rate for all occupations (Zilberman & Ice, 2021).

There is an imperative to improve the representation and the trajectory for Black and Latinx workers in healthcare and STEM and to improve health outcomes through a diverse, culturally competent workforce. The diversity gap within the STEM and healthcare fields directly impacts the economic opportunities for Black and Latinx workers and also has disastrous health impacts for patients of color. Less than 10% of nurses and physicians are Black and Latinx (Association of American Medical Colleges, 2019). Black and Latinx patients consistently experience negative health outcomes, in comparison to White patients, even when controlling for other variables-including income and health insurance status. The infant mortality rate in the black population is twice that of whites. Black men are seven times more likely than white men to receive a diagnosis of H.I.V. and more than twice as likely to die of prostate cancer. Black women are 40 percent more likely to die from breast cancer (Tweedy, 2015). Research demonstrates that when Black, Indigenous, People of Color (BIPOC) patients receive care from BIPOC doctors, the outcomes improve exponentially. A recent study by Stanford University found that increasing the number of black physicians could lead to a 19 percent reduction in the black-white male cardiovascular mortality gap and an 8 percent decline in the black-white male life expectancy gap (Alsan, Garrick, & Graziani, 2019).

Persistent and deeply entrenched systemic racism throughout systems impacting students and families, including K-12 education too often contribute to the lack of Black and Latinx people from low-income communities who are succeeding at the highest levels of STEM and healthcare careers. Students of color, especially Black and Latinx students, routinely demonstrate dramatically lower test scores than their White peers. A report from the National Assessment of Educational Progress (NAEP)—which measures whether students can apply tech and engineering skills to real-life situations—revealed a 38-point gap between Black and White students (Strauss, 2019). Nationally, more than half of White students across grade levels score at or above average on STEM standardized tests, compared with 28 percent of Latinx and 18 percent of Black students (Smith & Reeves, 2020). These gaps are exacerbated by the lack of access to high-quality and culturally relevant STEM education for students of color within the k-12 educational system. The 2018 National Survey of Science and Mathematics Education found only about a quarter of middle school and about a third of high school science teachers have participated in

36 hours or more of science professional development in the last three years, with very few elementary teachers receiving any professional development (Banilower, et al., 2018).

Anchor Institutions: Economic and Social Potential of Place-Based Partnerships

The labor market in the United States is vast and complex. Frequently quoted measures, such as the unemployment rate or payroll employment, reflect distinct aspects of labor market activity, but it's not uncommon for these indicators to give contradictory signals about labor market circumstances or overall strength of the US economy (Chung, Fallick, Nekarda, & Ratner, 2014). COVID-19 caused severe disruption in certain communities introducing an array of social and economic precarities with respect to employment, housing, and financial security. Researchers Perry et al. from Indiana University capture this idea of pandemic precarity and its consequences,

As unemployment reached near-Great Depression era levels during the early stages of the pandemic, questions remain about the potential of the COVID-19 pandemic to exacerbate historically high levels of socioeconomic inequality in the United States, raising the possibility that social inequities, preexisting and current, have weakened economic resiliency and reinforced disadvantage. (Perry, Aronson, & Pescosolido, 2021)

The pandemic has refocused attention on perennial issues of equity and access, with a particular focus on rethinking and reimagining jobs and the workforce in a post-COVID reality. All sectors of the economy will need to assess the lasting impact of the pandemic on labor demand, workforce readiness, shortages, and resiliency, however the healthcare sector must consider the long-term impacts of COVID-19 from the perspective of both patient and provider. How has the COVID-19 pandemic affected the health care workforce? And how will the pandemic reshape the health care workforce going forward?

A growing body of evidence indicates asymmetrical patterns COVID-19 morbidity and mortality across racial and ethnic groups (Bambra, Riordan, Ford, & Matthews, 2020; Romano, et al., 2021). An initial assumption was that cities were epicenters of COVID disease spread due to housing density, however, researchers have determined that the driving forces behind disparities on COVID health outcomes are much more complex. There are several mechanisms through which the social and structural environment can shape risk of exposure to, and infection by infectious diseases. The underlying factors that contribute to these dramatically disparate outcomes are often varied, multidimensional, and geographically influenced. Differences across socioeconomic factors like educational attainment, affordable housing, income, and labor force participation contribute to the acute vulnerabilities of communities of color. These inequities stem from a pattern of historical social and racial injustice not created but exacerbated by COVID.

Disparities, or notable differences across groups, like the ones observed in COVID-19 stem from systems and structures that make it harder for those living in poverty, or who are members of historically excluded groups. These inequities harm community health, economic vitality and overall well-being. The pandemic raises renewed concerns about inequality, and the role of institutions in improving economic mobility, health, and quality of life for the communities they serve (Perry, Aronson, & Pescosolido, 2021). The observable influence of anchor institutions on the economic, cultural, and social fabric of a community forces consideration on their role in driving the economies of the future. Anchor institutions are large, usually nonprofit organizations tethered to their communities, like universities, medical centers, or local government entities (Zuckerman, Ansell, & Davis, 2019; Ubhayakar, Capeless, Owens, Snorrason, & Zuckerman, 2017; National Academies of Sciences, Engineering, and Medicine, 2017). They have significant economic and social impact on their communities, and they also have an economic self-interest in making sure these communities are healthy and safe (National Academies of Sciences, Engineering, and Medicine, 2017).

A number of strategies that leverage institutional assets can be undertaken as part of anchor mission building. Common anchor strategies include (Dragicevic, 2015):

- Directing a greater percentage of purchasing power toward local vendors.
- Hiring a greater percentage of the workforce locally.
- Providing workforce training for people needing assistance in the community.
- Incubating the development of new businesses, including social enterprises as well as nonprofits.
- Leveraging real estate development to promote local retail, employer-assisted housing, and community land trusts.
- Using pension and endowment funds to invest in local job creation strategies and to provide community venture capital for nonprofits, entrepreneurs, and employee-owned firms (Dragicevic, 2015).

Encouraged by these alternative approaches to economic development, many institutions across the country are engaging with their surrounding communities to discover the best ways to build sustainable ecosystems that support equitable outcomes and directly benefit local residents. However, harvesting the economic and social potential of these place-based partnerships requires deliberative community engagement to co-produce programming for systemic change and lasting effect. As outlined by Kliewer and Priest,

The purpose of any anchor mission-oriented strategy should be to engage in collaborative learning and action with community members, advance connections to the organizations, enhance the public presence of the groups, and build a sense of empowerment around important issues facing the communities these institutions serve. (Kliewer & Priest, 2019)

ENGAGING COMMUNITIES THROUGH TIMES OF CRISIS AND CHANGE

Community engagement is a hallmark of public health practice and research and remains the key component for pragmatic partner engagement. During the COVID-19 pandemic, such engagement had to be curtailed and alternatives needed to be formulated rapidly. This crisis event provided opportunities for those working in community engagement to re-think and re-engage with the fundamental principles of meaningful and authentic engagement, and how to re-image community engaged practices to rise to the challenges and exigencies of COVID and beyond (Marsh et al., 2021). There is emerging consensus that engaging communities in a meaningful way means shifting current paradigms to accelerate engagement outcomes and create measurable progress towards equity and systems transformation (Organizing Committee for Assessing Meaningful Community Engagement in Health & Health Care Programs & Policies, 2022).

As the country reaches a turning point in the COVID-19 pandemic and we collectively begin to chart a cautiously optimistic path forward towards endemicity and coexistence with the virus, it is imperative to consider long-term strategies towards racially equitable recovery and the role of community engagement in fostering change. The complex social problems and injustices exacerbated by COVID-19 did not develop over night, but are the accumulation of disinvestment, discrimination, and systematic exclusion over generations. Historical racial segregation and neighborhood disinvestment have blocked upward mobility for Black and LatinX communities and sustained social and economic inequities still observed today (Greene, Turner, & Gourevitch, 2017). Addressing long-term needs and core problems of these communities will need immediate and ongoing investment. From a workforce systems perspective, several domains of engagement may contribute to the overall transformations towards more equitable societies.

Community engagement, in its most basic form, aims to better involve the community in the production of long-term and sustainable results, processes, connections, discourse, decision-making, or execution of its identified priorities (Jones et al., 2009; Ahmed & Palermo, 2010; Wallerstein et al., 2015). Its strategies should be attentive to the local environment, to adequately address issues affecting health, well-being and overall quality of life. To achieve success, community engaged strategies should incorporate a variety of techniques, emphasizing the need of establishing and enhancing trust as a key component of long-term active civic participation. Leveraging the principles of community engagement can strengthen organizations and the people that lead them who are working to change systems in communities that have historically received little support.

A significant body of research confirms that even in the presence of increased production of college graduates observed over time, the United States is still falling short in identifying and navigating potential barriers at key transition points throughout the 'cradle to career' continuum and subsequently inadequately preparing students for the world of work. These gaps in the system generate huge ramifications including the enduring inequitable educational, economic, and civic opportunities that are disproportionately borne by Black, LatinX and Indigenous communities (Pew Research Center, 2020). Developing broad community power for future education and workforce systems is necessary to uncover policy solutions for how to best prepare students for college, career, and civic participation in a rapidly changing workforce and society. COVID-19 and growing inequality exacerbated pre-existing deficits of historically marginalized communities, however, organizations can better weather the instabilities of the moment, deepen their understanding of the structural gaps in education and workforce training systems, and adequately prepare for the future of work through community-engaged partnerships.

The National Academy of Medicine further discuss the opportunities within meaningful engagement of communities and how it is necessary in power sharing and equitable transformation of historically marginalized communities.

Meaningful community engagement is "a powerful vehicle for bringing about environmental and behavioral changes that will improve the health of the community and its members. It often involves partnerships and coalitions that help mobilize resources and influence systems" (CDC, 2011). An approach focused on leveraging community engagement to improve health outcomes, relies on broad-based efforts to fundamentally work towards the creation of thriving communities that are structured to be less transactional an instead work to continuously earn the trust of people in their communities. (Organizing Committee for Assessing Meaningful Community Engagement in Health & Health Care Programs & Policies, 2022)

Five indicators that suggest engagement has led to thriving communities (Organizing Committee for Assessing Meaningful Community Engagement in Health & Health Care Programs & Policies, 2022):

- Physical and mental health
- Community capacity and connectivity
- Community power
- Community resiliency
- Life quality and well-being

The term "community engagement" at times has been vague, but consistent in its practice is the collaborative effort of people to effect change and give voice to what matters to them. If racial equity is the goal, then organizations and decision-makers must be called to lead by those shared values and ideals, bonding them in purpose with the communities that they serve. There is a responsibility to work collaboratively in addressing the fundamental conditions (policies, regulations, etc.) that cause these systems to behave the way they do in the production of inequitable outcomes.

CASE STUDY: THE RUSH EDUCATION AND CAREER HUB

On a Mission to build a best-in-class pipeline to STEM and healthcare careers for underrepresented groups

My favorite motto is: If not you, then who? REACH has taught me to not doubt myself and to have the confidence to help out my community. I've grown with REACH, not outgrown REACH.

—REACH alum and Youth Advisory Council Member, University of Illinois-Chicago class of 2025 and aspiring oncologist

Overview

First launched in 1990 as the Science and Math Excellence (SAME) Network, the Rush Education and Career Hub (REACH) is a strategic education and workforce initiative of Rush University Medical Center (Rush), Chicago's longest standing healthcare institution and the largest non-governmental employer on the Near West Side of Chicago. Set in the Illinois Medical District near Chicago's Loop, the nation's largest urban medical district, Rush University Medical Center is part of a hub of leading-edge patient care, research and education. It has won a wide range of distinctions-in 2020 Rush ranked among the top 50 hospitals in nine specialties, with two in the top five nationally and three are the highest-ranked programs in Illinois (Rush University System for Health, 2022).

The mission of the Rush University System for Health is "to improve the health of the individuals and diverse communities we serve through the integration of outstanding patient care, education, research, and community partnerships." REACH advances Rush's health equity strategy, which is designed to address the fact that average life expectancies in some West Side Chicago communities are 16 years shorter than nearby wealthier neighborhoods (Chicago Department of Public Health, 2016).

REACH supports education from cradle to career by providing innovative, hands-on STEM learning to underrepresented youth so they can reach their academic and professional potential, increasing postsecondary education success and interest in healthcare and STEM careers. The health care sector offers meaningful, well-paying jobs that can put young people on track to a brighter future—but unfortunately, educational inequality and inequitable access to these jobs persist. We know that too few Black and Latinx students are deeply engaged in science, technology, engineering, and math (STEM) learning. As a result, too few of them are well prepared for high-demand healthcare jobs or equipped to advance into STEM careers that require higher skill levels.

Work-based learning (WBL) experiences involve students engaging with professionals in workplace environments. WBL is an educational approach that combines classroom instruction with practical work experience that is directly related to a program of study, with the mission to enhance student knowledge by combining classroom learning with hands-on work experience. WBL can take numerous forms, ranging from job shadowing to apprenticeships, but these real-world experiences shape students in profound ways. These experiences can often be the opportunity to give students a clear direction for their postsecondary learning and career goals. The past decade has seen increased coordination of workforce development systems across geographies and industries. Workforce Intermediaries are labor market institutions that mediate the relationship between specific employers and job seekers with the goal of increasing access to family-sustaining careers (Fitzgerald, 2004; Giloth, 2004; Holland, 2016). While strategies differ by sector, workforce intermediary partnerships:

- Bring together education providers and employer partners to assess the training needs by sector or region
- Help to customize the training, apprenticeship, and educational curriculum
- Cultivate the partners needed to produce the training
- Recruit oftentimes from low-income or historically underrepresented communities
- Ensure that those individuals who invest in their employment security will be rewarded with meaningful advancement along a career ladder.

What follows is a case study of the Rush Education and Career Hub approach to WBL as a workforce intermediary for STEM and health science. To explore how industry specific workforce development programs might build on institutional resources and community partnerships, this profile examines the strategies and promising practices of REACH to support STEM and health science accessibility for Black and Latinx youth and young people experiencing poverty through: (1) increased awareness of and interest in STEM and healthcare career options; (2) improvement of college readiness, student development, and achievement; (3) access to hands-on practical experiences that help prepare them to pursue careers in health sciences, medicine, IT, and other STEM-related fields; and (4) increased postsecondary success in college and career for healthcare and STEM-related fields.

Barriers to Health and Wellness

The nine neighborhoods that comprise Chicago's west side have life expectancies that are considerably less than other neighborhoods in Chicago and the United States overall. For example, residents of the West Garfield Park neighborhood have a life expectancy of 69 years, in the Loop, just six miles away, the average life expectancy is 85 (Chicago Department of Public Health, 2016). This tremendous gap is simply unacceptable in a resource-rich city like Chicago. In response to this tremendous health inequity, Rush has committed to improving health and economic vitality by not only addressing healthcare inequities but by also simultaneously addressing social determinants of health that impact these communities. Educational attainment is one of the most important drivers to increase health, improve life expectancy and reduce hardship (Olshansky et al., 2012). People with more education have better jobs, earn more, and have better access to resources such as healthy food, transportation and health care (Heiman & Artiga, 2015).

Career Pathways & Informal STEM Education in Black & Latinx Communities

Due to persistent equity gaps in STEM careers, researchers and practitioners have turned to innovations that are growing in popularity: career pathways and informal (out-of-school) STEM education interventions (McCombs, Whitake, & Yoo, 2017), to improve STEM outcomes for underserved students and diversify the STEM workforce. Incorporating (high quality) summer interventions may also help prevent the "summer slide," where students, particularly those from disadvantaged communities, experience learning loss (Quinn & Polikoff, 2017). Effective career pathways, which integrate basic education, career training, and post-secondary education, can help reduce potential equity gaps in the workforce as well as in achievement (Eyster & Gebrekristos, 2018). However, for career pathways to be successful, elements of STEM career pathways courses and experiences must align with principles of effective STEM learning. Considering the current strains on the health care workforce, health systems have a unique opportunity to engage their communities around careers in STEM and the health sciences while supporting employment opportunities and job training for Black and Latinx youth and young people experiencing poverty.

Recognizing the Challenge

- Large gaps in educational attainment and aspirations
- Lack of diversity among active physicians; high-skilled STEM professionals
- Disparities in education, employment and earning potential, affecting health and economic outcomes

Chicago youth need workforce development programs that incorporate holistic approaches to develop learners personally and professionally to address society's most pressing health challenges. Black and Latinx youth and young people experiencing poverty have unique perspectives on the places that they live and have a critical role to play in addressing health disparities and building more equitable communities. The Rush Education and Career Hub will reshape its proven model of connecting with students, parents, educators, and staff to spark and catalyze STEM/Health Sciences learning in and outside the classroom and develop career connected paid work-based learning opportunities where youth are provided classroom education, technical certifications and innovate models for case management and whole person support.

Solidifying the Approach: The Rush Education and Career Hub

Complex health needs persist in communities across the United States, influenced largely by social and structural determinants. So, what is the role of academic medical centers in creating the next generation of community problem-solvers, the healthcare workforce of the future? Viable solutions require creativity and contemporary approaches to the perennial problem of equitable access to education and employment opportunities. Education and training programs in the health sector in the United States have a role in developing a workforce that is equipped to rise to the challenges a post-pandemic healthcare landscape will present. Recognizing the importance of this moment, REACH sought to identify opportunities to simultaneously support student learning, community partnership development, and competency-based career pathways programs for STEM and the health sciences and restructured Rush's overall strategy for youth workforce development in 2017. The most promising transformational strategies implemented by REACH in the past two years utilizes the local community and environment as a starting point to teach concepts in health sciences across the education continuum and provide work-based learning experiences. Place-based education promotes learning locally in the natural, built, historic, and cultural environment. Strong, long-term partnerships with both Chicago Public Schools and City Colleges of Chicago create additional opportunities for under-represented learners to earn early college credit and receive substantive advising, increasing career relevant learning and reducing barriers to postsecondary degree attainment.

Projects and programs encourage partnerships between students, teachers, and community members; between K-12, higher ed, and community organizations that strengthen student achievement, community vitality, and a sustainable path forward.

Through partnership with NORC at the University of Chicago, a sequential three-phased approach was used to (1) develop a visual theory of change, (2) define curricular components, (3) indicate pedagogical methods, and (4) determine data and evaluation approaches with specific indicators for measuring the quality of program implementation and participant outcomes. In this, two key themes emerged as drivers of the work: alignment of skills and abilities to labor market demand and the strategic role of Rush as an anchor institution and community-engaged workforce intermediary. Leveraging Rush's institutional influence on the local economy was specifically important in critically assessing and rethinking engagement with the community around youth career exploration, and how REACH could be positioned to produce targeted community benefits for Black and Latinx youth and young people experiencing poverty through collaboration and capacity building. REACH's approach with exposure, engagement and participation supports occupational identity development in STEM and healthcare through:

- Access to high quality STEM learning experiences from Pre-K to College
- Paid work-based learning experiences paired with professional & personal development
- Articulated career pathways aligned to labor market demand and ability to earn industry recognized credentials
- Mentoring and network-building experiences to strengthen connections and sense of belonging
- Wraparound supports and mentoring to facilitate student and family participation and engagement.

Developing Occupational Identity

The adolescent period is crucial to developing imagined occupational identities. REACH begins providing experiences for young people to explore careers at the onset of adolescence and offers multiple entry points for work-based learning over the high school and college years.

> [Adolescence] is a critical window for decision making for occupational pathways, and for introducing youth to career-relevant experiences and opportunities. The majority of students who pursue STEM degrees make that choice before they enter college (Maltese and Tai 2010). Researchers have identified the period of middle school as a particularly important time for choosing to pursue STEM versus non-STEM careers (Barton et al.2013; Kang et al. 2019). These findings suggest that adolescence is a sweet spot where children are still open to identity experimentation, but in ways that are tied to realistic planning and skill development. (Callahan, Ito, Campbell, & Wortman, 2019)

Figure 1. The Rush Education and Career Hub Theory of Change

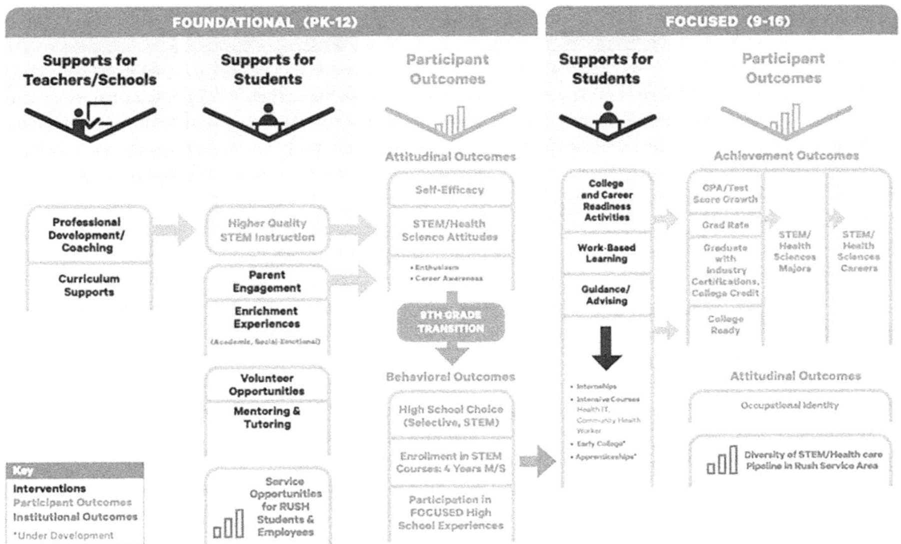

The Rush Education and Career Hub Theory of Change

The logic model guided the design of the evaluation and provides a framework for ongoing program revision through describing a structured set of learning experiences that include providing professional development to teachers; engaging families/stakeholders; creating, modeling, and supporting curriculum additions, and supporting enrichment and career learning experiences both in and outside of school. The logic model and pathway trajectory illustrate the continuum of support and intentional focus from developing awareness and interest in STEM/healthcare topics to supporting the development of academic and professional skills alongside opportunities to explore healthcare careers. The model also reflects differing levels of investment and focus on the part of both Rush and students.

REACH Cradle to Career Pipeline of STEM/Healthcare Programs

REACH programs provide multiple points of entry and opportunities for Black and Latinx students from 9th grade through college to: (1) increase awareness of and interest in STEM / healthcare career options; (2) improve college readiness, student development, and achievement; (3) gain hands-on practical experiences that help prepare them to pursue careers in health sciences, medicine, IT, and other STEM-related fields; and (4) increase postsecondary success in college and career for healthcare and STEM-related fields. REACH's pipeline approach provides opportunities for students to earn stackable credentials over the course of their high school and college career, which lead to door-opening, entry-level jobs that provide a family-sustaining wage and serve as a springboard to higher skilled occupations with continued education.

Table 1. Programs

Grade Band	Primary Focus	Programs	Key Outcomes
Pre-K - Grade 5	Early Exploration in STEM and Career Awareness	STEMagineers: Builds a foundational interest in STEM (science, technology, engineering and mathematics) and health care with students in preschool through 5th grade.	Interest in STEM Foundational academic skills Awareness of own interests Early career aspirations Enrichment experience
Grade 6 - 8	Career Awareness, Skill and Attitude Building	VITALS for STEM Success: Vitals for STEM Success is an after-school program for highly motivated middle school students who are interested in STEM or health care careers. Vitals for STEM Success exposes students to different career paths in the field of healthcare, helping them understand the different tracks available and what it takes to get started. Future Ready Learning Lab: An enrichment elective incorporated into the school day at select West Side elementary schools focused on building interest and awareness of STEM/health care careers, increasing self-efficacy, developing 21st century learning skills and supporting the transition to high school.	Ability to collaborate Planning, goal setting Career awareness, aspirations Connections between school and work College-going attitude
Grade 9 - 12	Career Exploration, Exposure, Strengthening Skills	MedSTEM Explorers: MedSTEM Explorers is a paid enrichment program for rising high school sophomores and juniors. There is one, 6week summer session (120 hours) in which students attend classes at Rush University Medical Center exploring various STEM and healthcare careers, developing workforce skills, and researching real-world issues that affect their Chicago communities. MedSTEM Pathways: MedSTEM Pathways is a paid internship program for rising high school juniors through recent high school graduates. Students spend up to 150 hours 6 weeks, gaining work-based learning skills while interning in departments throughout Rush University Medical Center and several other partner organizations. During the summer session, students also spend three day per week strengthening college readiness and life skills through academic and professional development classes.	Employability and life skills College preparatory Industry-recognized credentials Social capital and network Belonging Self-efficacy Occupational identity
College & Beyond	Career Pathway Training and Development	College Career Pathways: Supports under-represented youth between the ages of 18 and 24 through paid internships, college and career advising, professional and technical skill training, and employment assistance with STEM and Healthcare employers in their desired field.	Technical training Workplace experiences Social capital College persistence and graduation Employment in healthcare or STEM
	Center for Community Health Equity (CCHE) Summer Internship	Provides paid 8-week summer internships to undergraduates from under-represented communities who have a strong interest in research, health disparities and community relations and are considering graduate studies in health and social sciences.	Technical training Workplace experiences Social capital College persistence and graduation Employment in healthcare or STEM
	Mentoring and RU Ready Prep	The RU Ready Prep Center is a virtual space where Chicago high school students can develop writing skills, study habits, and workforce readiness. It also includes SAT preparation courses, math enrichment, and professional development workshops.	

Considering Equity in Data and Infrastructure

From *A toolkit for centering racial equity throughout data integration,* Actionable Intelligence for Social Policy, 2020:

Black, Indigenous, and people of color (BIPoC) and/or people living in poverty are often over-represented within government agency data systems, and disparate representation in data can cause disparate impact. Laws, policies, business rules, and narratives are permeated by structural racism, which is the root cause of the racial disparities evident in system outcomes. Such disparities are often sterilized by well-intentioned names (e.g., "disproportionate contact" in criminal justice or the "achievement gap" in education) that hide the social consequence of structural racism: that, as a group, Black, Indigenous, and people of color in America have worse outcomes in many human service system outcome measures regardless of socioeconomic status. And yet, many agency solutions and data initiatives are largely disconnected from this root cause, and the "hunt for more data is [often] a barrier for acting on what we already know." (Nelson, et al., 2020)

The underrepresentation of Black and LatinX professionals in STEM and the health sciences reflect several factors arising from structural and socioeconomic conditions that shape the places we live, however making these connections within our existing body of evidence remains a challenge. REACH documents the evidence and explores how Black and LatinX youth engage with STEM and health science career exploration and experience work-based learning experience in health care environments. We are acting on what we already know but seek to go further in generating actionable data and strategies to advance racial equity in STEM and the health sciences.

Data sharing and systems integration enable the transformation of individual-level information collected both internally by REACH and externally by our community partners into actionable intelligence that can be used to (1) understand urgent and long-term labor market needs and trends in STEM/health science; (2) improve the quality of direct services that REACH provides for students, families and the community; (3) develop innovative curriculum streams and programs; and, (4) ultimately, improve the health and economic vitality of the communities we serve. Yet, efforts to setup the infrastructure to share data between REACH and educational/community partners remains an area of future opportunity and in thinking of the "big picture" even once established, the focus would then need to shift towards considerations around the way that that data has been collected, cleaned, analyzed, its intended use and weight in decision making/strategic planning. If not done with an eye towards equity and the social environment from which this data is produced, these factors have the potential to introduce significant bias into our data and "at-best" not move the needle towards better outcomes for Black and Latinx youth and at worst reproduce inequities or harm with these populations.

There seems to be a need for those working in data science to reshape thinking around data access, use and strategy. The Rush Education and Career Hub curriculum employs multiple modalities to integrate public health, health care and service learning into STEM/Health science academic enrichment. These sessions provide students with training and career exploration in the health sciences and focus on application of these concepts to clinical settings, the community, as well as students' future roles as STEM/Health leaders in our 21st century health systems.

A pilot year evaluation provided an opportunity for REACH to consider these elements in evaluation of its programs and demonstrated that REACH serves a diverse population of students, providing valuable learning experiences and building their commitment to health careers.

Key Evaluation Findings

- *REACH participants:* REACH programs serve a diverse population of middle and high school students from the schools and neighborhoods surrounding our hospital campus.
- *Top impacts on interns:* The top impacts reported by REACH interns mix broad professional skills with skills specific to preparing for a health career.
- *Learning for students, contributions for Rush departments:* Rush employees who hosted REACH interns in their department confirmed growth in their skills and report that interns made significant contributions to the work of the department.
- *Persistence in the pipeline:* Once students participate in a REACH program, particularly the internship, they tend to stay in the pipeline.
- *Strengthened commitment to health careers:* Most students started their internship already strongly interested in a health career. By giving students exposure to the range of health careers and clarifying their specific interests, the REACH internship made most students even more committed to working in health.

On Social-Emotional Learning

REACH utilizes the CASEL 5 definition (Collaborative fro Academic, Social, and Emotional Learning, 2015), a widely recognized and often studied theory of SEL. The CASEL 5 includes self-awareness, self-management, social-awareness, relationship skills, and responsible decision-making. These elements are often considered also as indicators of well-being (Linton, Dieppe, & Medina-Lara, 2016) and social capital (Scales, Boat, & Pekel, 2020). Social-emotional health cannot solve education inequality alone, however, it can "promote understanding, examine biases, reflect on and address the impact of racism, build cross-cultural relationships, and cultivate adult and student practices that close opportunity gaps." For example, people who see themselves (and individuals who look like and are similar to them) in STEM are more likely to imagine themselves working in that field (Harvard Gazette, 2020). In addition, positive, ongoing student relationships with adults can dramatically enhance students' level of motivation and therefore promote learning (Education Trust & MDRC, 2020).

A Pandemic and Supporting Students through Crisis

A global pandemic during the spring semester of the 2019-20 academic year required significant changes to REACH programs, which affected student participation and program evaluation. COVID-19 and statewide stay-at-home orders of Spring 2020 presented unforeseen challenges, compelling REACH to find innovative ways to deliver instruction, experiences, and support virtually. With rigorous evidence of program effectiveness and a "think and do" approach, REACH navigated these unprecedented logistical challenges while remaining committed to the provision of career-connected learning and the communities we serve. During the shutdown, REACH worked hard to stay connected to both students and families, providing wraparound supports that included technology assistance; help with emergency resources such as healthy food, utility payments, transportation, and housing; and virtual discussion groups that gave students and parents a place to talk about the challenges of life and learning during a pandemic and civil unrest.

Support to students, families and teachers during the pandemic also included:

- Movement of all programming virtually, provision of wellness kits, and digital instruction/lesson plans to teachers.
- A community resource email newsletter to share free resources for remote learning; mental health and wellness; emergency assistance for food, housing and employment; and COVID safety.
- Hosting bilingual webinars and discussion groups on topics ranging from how parents can care for themselves and support their children to ways teens can manage mental health and prepare for college even during the uncertainty of the pandemic.
- Launching wraparound supports and emergency assistance funds for students and families in need.
- Providing laptops, internet hotspots, headsets and other technology to students who lacked reliable devices for learning.

Lessons Learned

With increased evidence available about the impact of work-based learning and hands-on, experiential learning in STEM and health care, our programs are pivotal to expanding and diversifying the educational and career pipeline for youth in STEM and health care professions.

Chicago youth need workforce development programs that incorporate holistic approaches to develop learners personally and professionally to address society's most pressing health challenges and lead from a place of awareness in uncertain times. Critical to our success has been the integrated academic and career technical content, problem-based instructional strategies, work-based learning opportunities, professional development and support services preparing students to navigate and transition to the next phase of learning and employment.

The Rush Education and Career Hub curriculum employs multiple modalities to integrate public health, health care and service learning into STEM/Health science academic enrichment. Community health coursework is woven through-out the work-based learning experiences. These sessions provide students with training in core public health and focus on application of these concepts to clinical settings, the community, as well as students' future roles as STEM/Health leaders in our 21st century health systems. Our approach spans three dimensions: (a) that youth development is predicated on a strengths-based approach, (b) that a socio-ecological approach to youth leadership development is a prerequisite for substantial and enduring change, and (c) that the larger intent of developing youth is encompassed in advancing equity, of which a student-centered learning environment is a critical component.

FINAL THOUGHTS AND FUTURE DIRECTIONS

Equity and opportunity are at the center of everything REACH does. REACH's comprehensive model includes training, engagement, advising and support that address critical barriers and challenges for underrepresented youth from pre-kindergarten all the way through college. Since 2017, REACH has served more than 10,000 students and community members through academic enrichment, college and career preparation, mentorship, and internships.

Meeting the challenges of racial and economic inequities in society will continue to be the organizations' overall goal, but in the era of coronavirus, these challenges have been heightened. More than any other time in REACH's history, 2020 and beyond continues to test the perseverance and grit of Chicago's communities. While none have been immune to the immense change and challenges of the global pandemic, those who were in already under-resourced communities have felt this brutal period more keenly. While the events of the year stretched capabilities, REACH found ample opportunity to continue to advance health equity, provide timely career connection experiences for young people, change outcomes, support our neighbors, and build better communities. REACH plays a unique role as an intermediary between youth and their future employment, providing enrichment programming that helps students build the skills they need to succeed in school and prepare for the 21st-century workforce: communication, collaboration, critical thinking, creativity, and leadership.

REFERENCES

Ahmed, S. M., & Palermo, A. (2010). Community engagement in research: Frameworks for education and peer review. *American Journal of Public Health, 100*(8), 1380–1387. doi:10.2105/AJPH.2009.178137 PMID:20558798

Alsan, M., Garrick, O., & Graziani, G. (2019). Does diversity matter for health? Experimental evidence from Oakland. *The American Economic Review, 109*(12), 4071–4111. doi:10.1257/aer.20181446

Association of American Medical Colleges. (2019). *Diversity in medicine: Facts and figures 2019*. Association of American Medical Colleges.

Bambra, C., Riordan, R., Ford, J., & Matthews, F. (2020). The COVID-19 pandemic and health inequalitites. *Journal of Epidemiology and Community Health, 74*(11), 964–968. PMID:32535550

Banilower, E. R., Smith, P. S., Malzahn, K. A., Plumley, C. L., Gordon, E. M., & Hayes, M. L. (2018). *Report of the 2018 NSSME*. Horizon Research, Inc.

Callahan, J., Ito, M., Campbell, R. S., & Wortman, A. (2019). *Influences on Occupational Identity in Adolescence: A Review of Research Programs*. Connected Learning Alliance.

Chicago Department of Public Health. (2016). *City of Chicago*. Retrieved from CityofChicago.org: https://data.cityofchicago.org

Chung, H. T., Fallick, B., Nekarda, C. J., & Ratner, D. D. (2014). Assessing the Change in Labor Market Conditions. *Finance and Economics Discussion Series*. Washington, DC: Divisions of Research & Statistics and Monetary Affairs, Federal Reserve Board.

Collaborative fro Academic, Social, and Emotional Learning. (2015). *Fundamentals of SEL*. https://casel.org/fundamentals-of-sel

Dragicevic, N. (2015). *Anchor Institutions*. Mowat Publications.

Eyster, L., & Gebrekristos, S. (2018). *Fulfilling the Promise of Career Pathways*. Urban Institute.

Fitzgerald, J. (2004). Moving the workforce intermediary agenda forward. *Economic Development Quarterly, 18*(1), 3–9. doi:10.1177/0891242403259992

Funk, C., & Parker, K. (2018). *Women and men in STEM often at odds over workplace equity*. Pew Research.

Giloth, R. P. (2004). Introduction: A case for workforce intermediaries. In Workforce Intermediaries for the Twenty-first Century, (pp. 3-30). Temple University Press.

Greene, S., Turner, M. A., & Gourevitch, R. (2017). *Racial residential segregation and neighborhood disparities*. US Partnership on Mobility from Poverty.

Harvard Gazette. (2020). *This is What a scientist looks like*. Harvard. https://news.harvard.edu/gazette/story/2020/07/i-am-a-scientist/

Heiman, H. J., & Artiga, S. (2015). *Beyond health care: The role of social determinants in promoting health and health equity*. Kaiser Family Foundation.

Holland, B. (2016). Both sides now: Toward the dual customer approach under the Workforce Innovation and Opportunity Act in the Untied States. *Local Economy, 31*(3), 424–441. doi:10.1177/0269094216640476

Jones, L., Norris, K., Meade, B., & Koegel, P. (2009). The vision, valley, and victory of community engagement. *Ethnicity & Disease, 19*(4), S6. PMID:20088076

Kliewer, B. W., & Priest, K. L. (2019). Building collective leadership capacity: Lessons learned from a university-community partnership. *Collaboration: A Journal of Community-Based Research and Practice, 2*(1), 16. doi:10.33596/coll.42

Lacey, T. A., Dieppe, P., & Medina-Lara, A. (2016). Review of 99 self-report measures for assessing well-being in adults: Exploring dimensions of well-being and developments over time. *BMJ Open, 6*(7), e010641. doi:10.1136/bmjopen-2015-010641 PMID:27388349

Lacey, T. A., Toossi, M., Dubina, K. S., & Gensler, A. B. (2017). Projections overview and highlights, 2016-26. Monthly Labor Review. doi:10.21916/mlr.2017.29

Linton, M. J., Dieppe, P., & Medina-Lara, A. (2016). Review of 99 self-report measures for assessing well-being in adults: Exploring dimensions of well-being and evelopments over time. *BMJ Open, 6*(7), e010641. doi:10.1136/bmjopen-2015-010641 PMID:27388349

Marsh, E. E., Kappelman, M. D., Kost, R. G., Mudd-Martin, G., Shannon, J., Stark, L. A., & Carrasquillo, O. (2021). Community engagement during COVID: A field report from seven CTSAs. *Journal of Clinical and Translational Science, 5*(1), e104. doi:10.1017/cts.2021.785 PMID:34192058

McCombs, J. S., Whitake, A., & Yoo, P. (2017). *The Value of Out-of-School Time Programs*. Rand Corporation. doi:10.7249/PE267

Natinoal Academics of Sciences, Engineering, and Medicine. (2017). *Communities in Action: Pathways to Health Equity*. National Academies of Sciences, Engineering, and Medicine.

Nelson, A. H., Jenkins, D., Zanti, S., Katz, M. F., Berkowitz, E., Burnett, T. C., & Culhane, D. P. (2020). *A toolkit for centering racial equity throughout data integration*. Actionable Intelligence for Social Policy, University of Pennsylvania.

Olshansky, S. J., Antonucci, T., Berkman, L., Binstock, R. H., Boersch-Supan, A., Cacioppo, J. T., & Jackson, J. (2012). Differences in life expectancy due to race and educational differences are widening, and many may not catch up. *Health Affairs*, *31*(8), 1803–1813. doi:10.1377/hlthaff.2011.0746 PMID:22869659

Organizing Committee for Assessing Meaningful Community Engagement in Health & Health Care Programs & Policies. (2022). Assessing Meaningful Community Engagement: A Conceptual Model to Advance Health Equity through Transformed Systems for Health. NAM Perspectives, National Academy of Medicine. doi:10.31478/202202c

Perry, B. L., Aronson, B., & Pescosolido, B. A. (2021, February 5). Pandemic precarity: COVID-19 is exposing and exacerbating inequalities in the American heartland. *Proceedings of the National Academy of Sciences of the United States of America*, *118*(8), e2020685118. doi:10.1073/pnas.2020685118 PMID:33547252

Pew Research Center. (2020). *Most Americans Say There Is Too Much Economic Inequality in the U.S., but Fewer Than Half Call It a Top Priority*. Pew Research Center.

Quinn, D., & Polikoff, M. (2017). *Summer learning loss: What is it, and what can we do about it*. Brookings Institution.

Romano, S. D., Blackstock, A. J., Taylor, E. V., Felix, S., Adjei, S., Singleton, C. M., & Boehmer, T. K. (2021). Trends in racial and ethnic disparities in COVID-19 hospitalizations, by region—United States, March-December 2020. *Morbidity and Mortality Weekly Report*, *70*(15), 560–565. doi:10.15585/mmwr.mm7015e2 PMID:33857068

Rush University System for Health. (2022). *Recognitions and Accreditations*. Rush University System for Health.

Scales, P. C., Boat, A., & Pekel, K. (2020). *Defining and measuring social capital for young people: A practical review of the literature on resource-full relationships*. Search Institute.

Smith, E., & Reeves, R. V. (2020). *SAT math scores mirror and maintain racial inequity*. Brookings Institute.

Strauss, V. (2019, November 1). The common mistake Betsy DeVos made aboutn new NAEP scores—and other problems with her "sky is falling" narrative. *The Washington Post*, pp. 1-19.

Tweedy, D. (2015). *Black man in a white coat: A doctor's reflections on race and medicine*. Picador/Macmillan.

Ubhayakar, S., Capeless, M., Owens, R., Snorrason, K., & Zuckerman, D. (2017). *Anchor Mission Playbook*. Rush University Medical Center and The Democracy Collaborative.

Wallerstein, N., Minkler, M., Carter-Edwards, L., Avila, M., & Sanchez, V. (2015). Improving health through community engagement, community organizations, and community building. *Health Behaviro: Theory, Research and Practice, 5*.

Zilberman, A., & Ice, L. (2021). Why computer occupations are behind strong STEM employment growth in the 2019–29 decade. *Computer, 4*(5), 11-15.

Zuckerman, D., Ansell, D., & Davis, M. (2019). Rethinking the Mission of Health Systems: Improving Community Health as Anchor Institutions. In J. L. Michener, B. C. Castrucci, D. W. Bradley, E. L. Hunter, & C. W. Thomas (Eds.), *The Practical Playbook II: Building Multisector Partnerships that Work*. Oxford University Press.

Chapter 16
Motherhood:
Parent-Child Separation

Sandy Orozco
Illinois Institute of Technology, USA

ABSTRACT

The incarceration of women and the impact on children, families, caregivers, and the prisoner in terms of motherhood and parenting has become an increasingly prominent area of interest within the criminal justice system. The number of women in state and federal prisons has dramatically increased; however, gender-responsive policies and practices that address incarcerated women's needs and circumstances have been limited. These findings give rise to concern regarding the number of women in jail or prison who are mothers of minor children. This paper investigates the differences between inmate mothers' and fathers' reported incarceration rates and examines the associations between early mother-child separation behaviors and children's outcomes. The impact of COVID-19 will also be included to address the ongoing harms to the lives of female prisoners. Based on these findings and other studies, prisons and jails need to develop a comprehensive strategy to fully address the needs of incarcerated mothers and reduce the harmful impact of incarceration on their children.

INTRODUCTION

The United States has the highest incarceration rate of women in the world, "between 1980 and 2019, the number of incarcerated women increased by more than 700%, rising from a total of 26,378 in 1980 to 222,455 in 2019" (Incarcerated Women and Girls, 2020, p. 1). While many more men are in prison than women, women are incarcerated now more than at any other point in U.S. history. This rapid, unprecedented growth is predicted to continue. This results from "more expansive law enforcement efforts, stiffer drug sentencing laws, and post-conviction barriers to reentry that uniquely affect women" (Incarcerated Women and Girls, 2020, p. 1). While there has been data collected about individuals who have been or are under some form of criminal justice system control, "very little is known about the approximately 10 million children in the U.S. who are under 18 and have had one or both incarcerated parents. Who are invisible to the larger society," (Reed & Reed, 1997, p. 152). More than 60% of women

DOI: 10.4018/978-1-6684-2314-1.ch016

Figure 1. Number of People in Federal Prisons for Drug Offenses, 1980–2013
Source: Sourcebook of Criminal Justice Statistics Online; Carson, E.A. (2014). Prisoners in 2013. Washington, D.C.: Bureau of Justice Statistics.

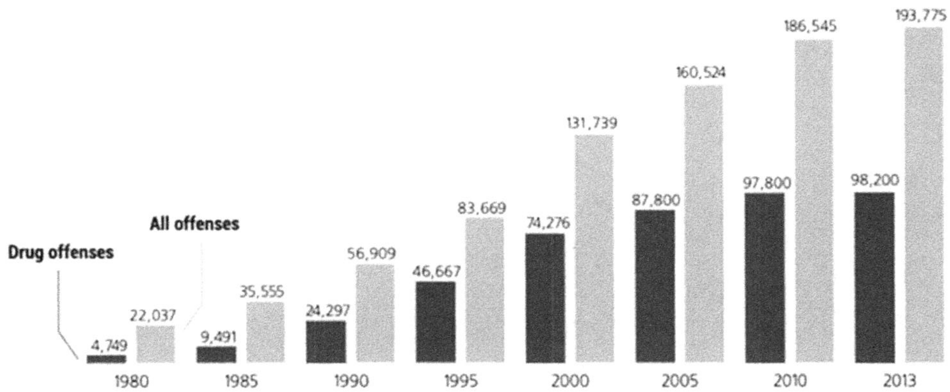

in state prisons have a child under 18 (Incarcerated Women and Girls, 2020, p. 1). The national trend in women being incarcerated guarantees that children will continue to be adversely affected by policies enacted without considering the harm done to family systems. This report aims to examine what is presently known about motherhood and includes the child's experience as their lives are disrupted. We begin by placing women's increase in incarceration in its larger historical and political context and conclude with recommendations to address and alleviate the problems resulting from mother-child separation.

Imprisoned Mothers and Their Children: "War on Drugs"

Studies have shown that the increase in numbers of incarcerated women is largely due to the "War on Drugs." According to Sharp and Eriksen (2003, p. 119), "[t]he United States is waging war on poor women and their children." Over the past two decades, there have been increasing numbers of women imprisoned due to the sentencing for drug possession. This drug policy moved to the forefront of criminal justice policy during the 1980s and early 1990s (Wonders, 1996). The proportion of imprisoned women convicted of a drug offense increased from 12% in 1986 to 26% in 2018 (Incarcerated Women and Girls, 2020, p. 1). As a result of the draconian drug laws, there has been an increase in U.S. women's prison population.

The War on Drugs was an effort of the United States to combat illegal drug use and increased penalties, enforcement, and incarceration for drug offenders (see Figure 1). According to Bush-Baskette, the "War on Drugs" was first declared in 1972 by President Nixon and then re-declared 10 years later by President Reagan" (2000, p. 1). These statutes forced drug offenders to serve longer prison terms and now applied minimums to any member of a drug trafficking conspiracy. This holds an individual liable for any activity within the drug-related crime. Mandatory sentences uniformly punished any member and offered a low chance of judicial discretion.

The "War on Drugs" disproportionately targeted women. Even though men are sought out by drug law enforcement more frequently, many of the war on drugs targets have been women (see Figure 2) (Women, Prison, and the Drug War, 2018, p. 1). The Anti-Drug Abuse Acts of 1986 and 1988 imposed lengthy

Figure 2. Female Drug Arrests, 1980–2012
Source: Bureau of Justice Statistics.

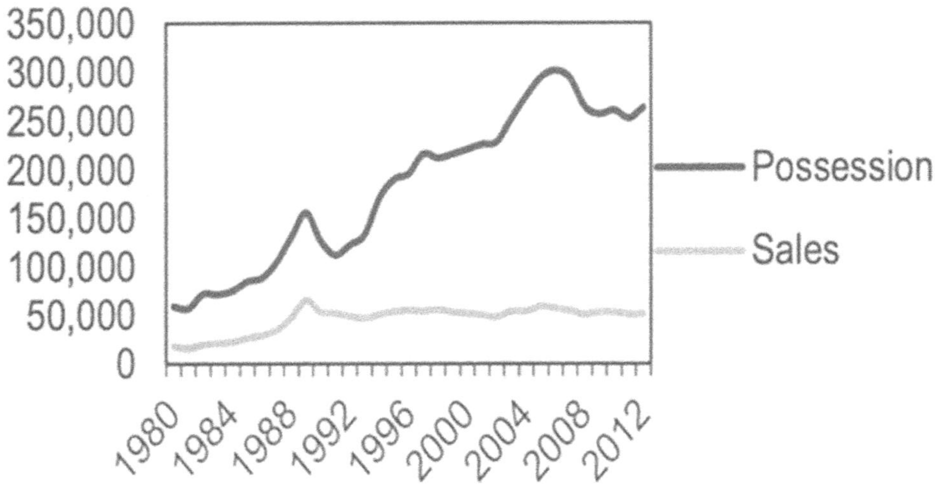

mandatory minimum sentences with the intent to prosecute high-level drug offenses. However, these laws resulted in an influx of women into the criminal justice system who may not have been directly tied to the use or selling of drugs but simply by the affiliation of someone involved in a drug-related crime.

The passage of the Anti-Drug Abuse Act of 1986 and 1988 has been harmful to families and communities. According to Bush-Baskette, the increased "incarceration of young women may have even greater long-term effects and dire consequences" (B 2000, p. 1). While these women may not have had a criminal record earlier but were directly or indirectly linked to the involvement in the dealing or possession of the drug were eligible for the harsh mandatory minimum by the Anti-Drug Abuse Acts of 1986 and 1988. These harsh mandatory minimum sentences may keep women incarcerated for a prolonged period. Women are now a fast-growing segment of the U.S. prison population (see Figure 3).

In the United States, women in state prisons are more likely to be convicted for a drug or property offense. "Twenty-six percent of women in prison have been convicted of a drug offense, compared to 13% of men in prison; 24% of incarcerated women have been convicted of a property crime, compared to 16% among incarcerated men" (Incarcerated Women and Girls, 2020, p. 1). It is evident that the policies implemented under the so-called tough on crime, "War on Drugs" approaches to policing have led to an explosion in the U.S. women's prison population (see Figure 4).

Women are convicted at a higher rate for these offenses than men and suffer lifelong consequences, such as an increased risk of parent-child separation, among others.

Incarcerated, women must navigate the systems, practices, and policies that are designed for men. With limited resources, jails and prisons are ill-equipped to address women's challenges once they enter the criminal justice system. Before communities, policymakers, and justice-system officials can broaden efforts to reform their use of jails for women; they must expand their data collection. To gather more information about women involved in the criminal justice system and use it as a basis for future evidence-based analysis and policymaking.

Figure 3. Rise in Women's Incarceration, 1980–2019
** Prison figures are from year-end 2019 while jail figures are from year-end 2018, the latest available data from the sources used. Sources: Bureau of Justice Statistics. Historical Corrections Statistics in the United States 1850-1984 (1986); Prison and Jail Inmates at Midyear Series (1997-2018), Prisoners Series (1986-2019). Washington, DC.*

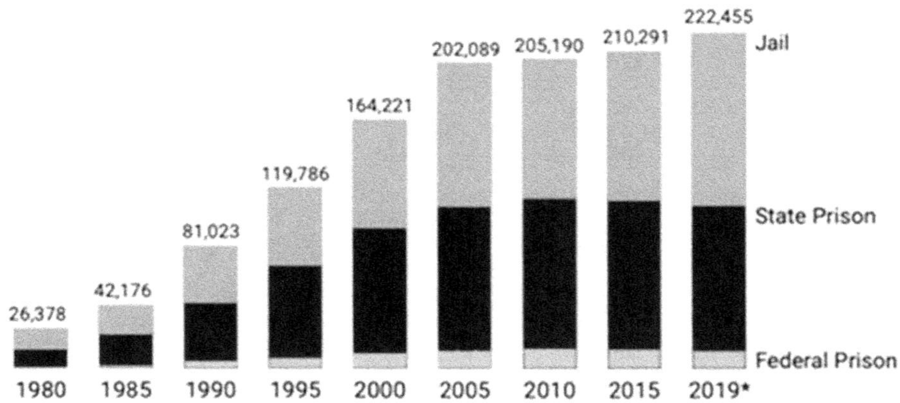

Race and the "War on Drugs"

The public has concerns over the effectiveness of the War on Drugs and increased awareness of the racial disparity of the punishments meted out by it. Because women are more likely than men to be in prison or jail for nonviolent, low-level drug-related crimes, women, especially poor women of color," bear this burden of this 'war,'" (Clark et al., 2013, p. 779). While drug use occurs at similar rates across racial and ethnic groups, women of color are far more likely to be criminalized for drug law violations and other offenses. Racial disparities in drug law enforcement and sentencing affect children who are routinely and increasingly separated from their imprisoned mothers under the drug war logic that has infiltrated our child welfare system. The war on drugs has disproportionately affected women of color who are likely to be incarcerated for a drug offense. Based on race and ethnicity data collected from prisons:

Figure 4. Offense Type by Gender in State Prisons, 2018
Source: Carson, E.A. (2020). Prisoners in 2019. Washington, DC: Bureau of Justice Statistics

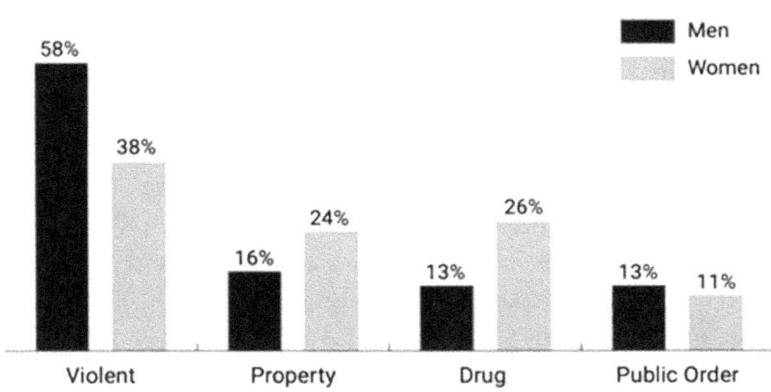

Figure 5. Imprisonment by Gender, Race, and Ethnicity per 100,000: 2000 vs. 2019
Source: Prisoners Series. Washington, DC: Bureau of Justice Statistics.

		2000	2019	% Change
White	Women	34	48	**41% increase**
	Men	449	385	14% decrease
African American	Women	205	83	60% decrease
	Men	3,457	2,203	36% decrease
Latinx	Women	60	63	**5% increase**
	Men	1,220	979	20% decrease

- "In 2019, the imprisonment rate for African American women (83 per 100,000) was over 1.7 times the rate of imprisonment for white women (48 per 100,000)
- Latinx women were imprisoned at 1.3 times the rate of white women (63 vs. 48 per 100,000" (Incarcerated Women and Girls, 2020, p. 1).

Gender & Offenses

Women in prison are a vulnerable group who experience a lack of acknowledgment for their gender and parenting-related needs once involved in the criminal justice system. Many women are already vulnerable and marginalized in multiple ways; many are pregnant or will give birth. According to Clarke et al., "The majority of women in prison and jail are in their reproductive years with a median age of 34. Between 5 and 10 percent of women enter prison and jail pregnant, and approximately 2,000 babies are born to incarcerated women annually" (2013, p. 779). Once women are incarcerated, they face direct and collateral consequences and difficulties in motherhood.

According to Swavola et al., "the majority of women in jail are charged with non-violent crimes. The vast majority (82 percent) of women are in jail for non-violent offenses. 32 percent of women in jail are there for property offenses, 29 percent for drug offenses, and nearly 21 percent for public order offenses" (2016, p. 9). Most of these women are on "low-level charges" and are booked into jail on misdemeanor charges (Swavola, 2016, p. 9). One consequence of this dramatic increase is that more mothers with dependent children are incarcerated. Women, especially women of color, are often ignored in this conversation and are significantly overrepresented in state and federal prison populations (see Figure 5).

Roughly 60 percent of women in state and federal prisons are mothers of minor children. Two-thirds of these parents are incarcerated for non-violent offenses, a substantial proportion of which are drug law violations" (Alliance, 2018, p. 2). The criminal justice system drug war crisis makes a noticeable contribution to the extraordinary growth in incarceration rates for women and the number of children affected. Specifically, the segments of the population that share the burden of parental incarceration are children of color. "African-American children and Hispanic children were 7.5 times more likely and 2.3 times more likely, respectively, than white children to have an incarcerated parent" (Martin, 2017, p. 2).

It has been reported that some long-lasting penalties and exclusions follow a women's drug conviction. This has created a second-class status for millions of Americans but can significantly affect women, and women of color, who are the primary caregivers of children.

The "War on Drugs" sentences significantly influenced an incarcerated mother's ability to help her dependent children. "Most women behind bars are mothers, many of them sole caregivers" (Women, Prison, and the Drug War, 2018, p. 1). Incarcerated women "have lower incomes than their male counterparts, making it more difficult for them be able to "afford cash bail, phone calls from prison, and ancillary services (such as babysitters) which they might require to meet all of their probation requirements" (Women, Prison, and the Drug War, 2018, p. 1).

The imprisonment of mothers due to the "War on Drugs" policies disproportionately targets women of low socioeconomic status, who are "often banned from voting, from getting a job, securing a student loan and accessing housing or other forms of public assistance, such as Temporary Assistance for Needy Families (TANF) and Supplemental Nutrition Assistance Program (SNAP)" (Women, Prison, and the Drug War, 2018, p. 2). A report in 2013 found that more than "180,000 women have been affected in the twelve states that maintain a fulltime ban for people with drug convictions" (Women, Prison, and the Drug War, 2018, p. 2).

The massive rise of incarceration "has not been without repercussions for society, as research details incarceration can generate a wide range of consequences for individuals, families, and communities who lives have been directly or vicariously impacted by the carceral system" (Jackson et al., 2022, p.1). Women face social stigma and those who are mothers face difficulty in experiencing motherhood in a criminal justice system designed for men. Immediately destabilizing the relationship and has negative consequences on a child's outcome (see Figure 6).

Children of an incarcerated mother suffer serious harm. Black women are no more likely than white women to use illicit drugs during pregnancy, and they are far more likely to be reported to child welfare services for drug use (Women, Prison, and the Drug War, 2018, p. 2). A "seminal study published in the *New England Journal of Medicine* found that black women were 10 times more likely than white women to be reported to child welfare" (Women, Prison, and the Drug War, 2018, p. 2). These consequences are attributes of disadvantaged children, independent of parental incarceration. The discriminatory incarceration of people of color and women of color is an important cause of children's array of cognitive and noncognitive outcomes from the trauma of an incarcerated parent.

Studies describe the racial disparities that are seen in the incarceration population replicate themselves among the children left behind: "by 2008, one in nine (11.4 percent of) black children, one in 28 (3.5 percent of) Latino children and one in 57 (1.8 percent of) white children had an incarcerated parent" (Women, Prison, and the Drug War, 2018, p. 2). This data supports the notion that children of color disproportionately see the effects of women's incarceration.

COPING WITH ACTUAL SEPARATION DUE TO IMPRISONMENT

Impact of Incarceration on Women

Most of the incarcerated population in the United States is male. While female inmates represent a small percentage of the overall prison population, their numbers steadily increase (see Figure 7). Most criminal justice research focuses on the male population and neglects female inmates' diverse and unique needs. The steady growth in the female inmate population indicates the need for further research to understand the impact of incarceration on women. It appears entirely valid that an incarcerated mother would experience considerable difficulty and distress concerning her child's welfare and changes to their relationship.

Figure 6. Children with an Incarcerated Parent
Source: Western and Pettit, Pew Charitable Trusts, 2010.

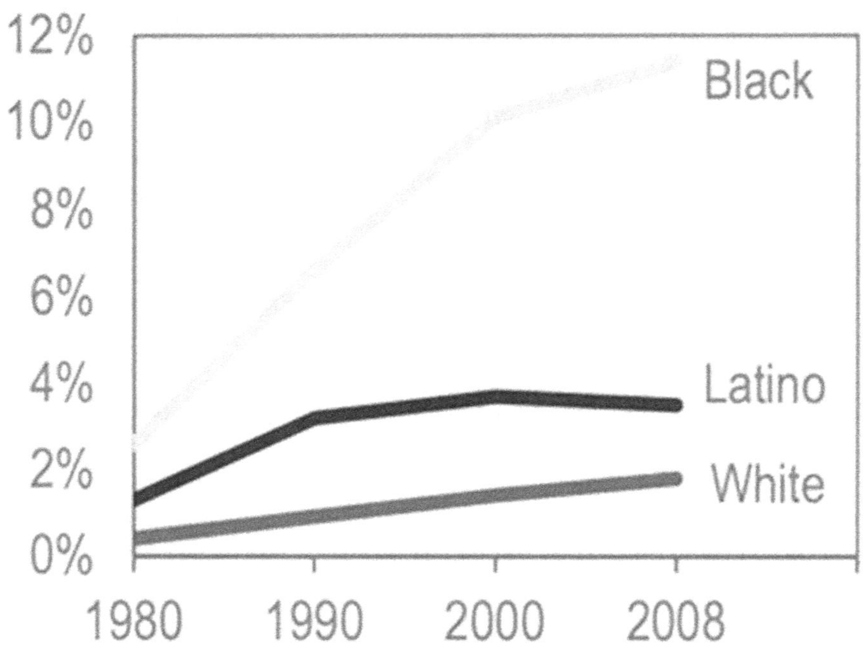

Figure 7. Women under Control of the U.S. Corrections System, 2018–2019
Source: Incarcerated Women and Girls, 2020, p. 1.

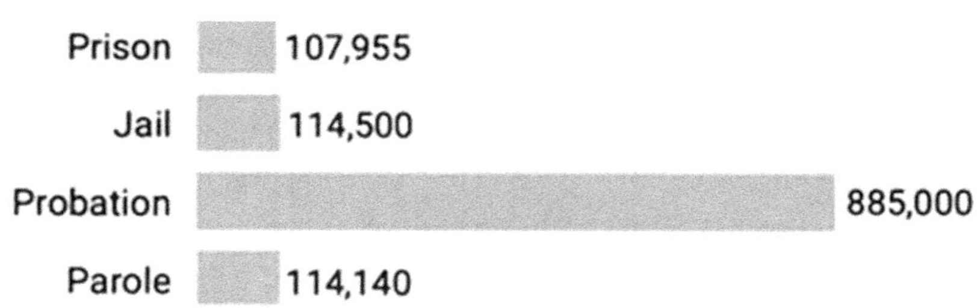

"There are 1.2 million women under the supervision of the criminal justice system" (Incarcerated Women and Girls, 2020, p. 1). The rate at which women are incarcerated has a significant effect on the ability of the mother to fulfill many of the maternal responsibilities of a mother. Women of reproductive age may experience pregnancy and mothering in a correctional environment designed for men. As the number of incarcerated women has increased, pregnancy during incarceration has become a significant concern. "Correctional facilities are not mandated to track or report pregnancy-related data, and most facilities do not have any routine process for collecting such information" (Friedman et al., 2020, p. 1).

When they are incarcerated, pregnant women must navigate or contend with a healthcare system that frequently fails to meet even the basic standards of care for expectant mothers.

Further studies have revealed that incarcerated women face distinct challenges with mother-child separation. Approximately half of the men incarcerated in the US are fathers and are typically not the primary caregiver for their children prior to their imprisonment (Kinner et al., 2007). Most incarcerated women are single women who are the sole source of support for their children (Hyppolite, 2017A). When a child is separated from their mother, they have a financial loss as the mother contributed to family expenses.

There are additional barriers to visitation for incarcerated women, including that because there are fewer women's prisons, there are greater distances between mothers and children. The separation of a mother and child causes psychological suffering to the mother due to the limited or prohibited contact between mother and child. Mothers often have increased concerns for their children's emotional well-being and physical safety. Not to mention incurred feelings of guilt about having "failed their child," increased levels of anxiety, and remorse for committing the acts that caused them to be separated from their children.

Parental Incarceration and Child Risk Factors

"There are an estimated two million children with a parent currently incarcerated, and that number does not include children whose parents have been previously incarcerated and released or those whose parents are under some community supervision such as probation or parole" (see Figure 8) (La Vigne et al., 2008; Graham and Harris, 2013). When a child's parents are incarcerated, there are challenges associated with incarceration that substantially impact a child's well-being. A "parent's incarceration poses several threats to a child's emotional, physical, educational, and financial well-being" (Martin, 2017, p. 2). Research on the children of incarcerated parents has shown psychological problems and antisocial behavior. One study, for example, "found that African American children and children who have both a mother and a father incarcerated exhibited significant increases in depression" (Martin, 2017, p. 3). A child of an incarcerated parent has an increased risk for depression and change in childhood behavior. An incarcerated parent cannot provide the nurturing and guidance a child needs, leading to an increase in negative emotions. Lengthy parent-child separations often occur because of maternal imprisonment.

Society often forgets that when incarcerated women enter prison or jail, they leave children and their families behind. Children and families are then forced to carry the burdens of the parents' crime with grief and confusion. While the incarcerated mother has a unique set of risks, such as stigma, shame, and depleted resources, it is important to consider the child's economic well-being. The removal of a parent creates unique and individual challenges and stressors for children that often go unnoticed or are underestimated by others. It is difficult to predict a child's outcome when separated from a parent; however, having a parent in prison can impact a child.

Several studies have stressed the negative implications of disruptions between children and their incarcerated mothers. Children react emotionally to separation from their mothers at the time of imprisonment. The most common consequence of parental incarceration appears to fall under the umbrella of antisocial behavior, "which describes any number of behaviors that go against social norms, including criminal acts and persistent dishonesty" (Martin, 2017, p .3). A meta-analysis was conducted of 40 studies on children of incarcerated parents and found that "antisocial behaviors were present more than any other factors, including mental health issues and drug use" (Martin, 2017, p. 3). This study found that parental incarceration was strongly associated with "externalizing behavioral problems" (Martin, 2017, p. 3).

Figure 8. Number and Percentage of Children with a Parent Incarcerated, USA 1980–2015
Source: Author's calculations from the Surveys of Inmates, Bureau of Justice Statistics Annual Inmate Counts, and the Current Population Survey.

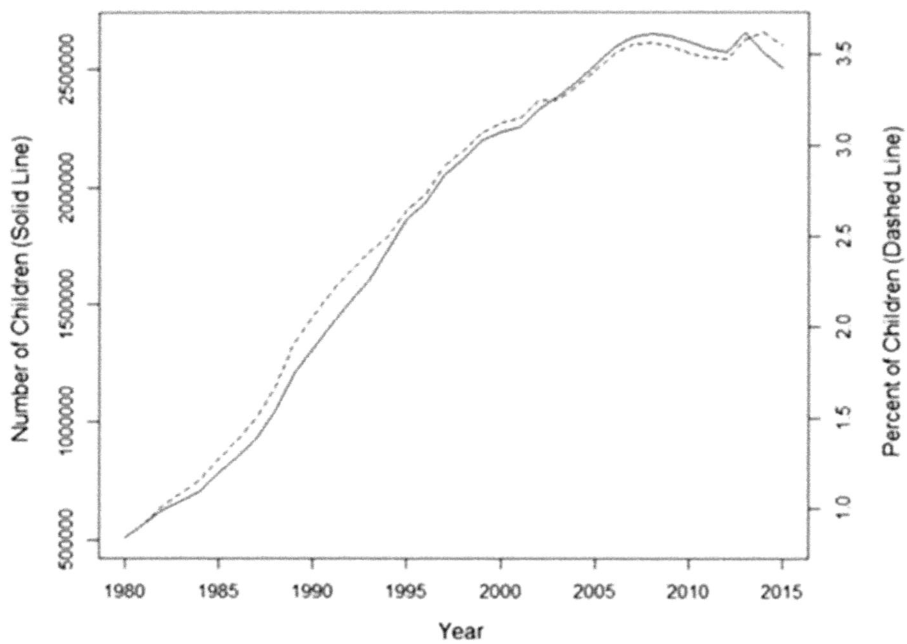

As stated by Hyppolite, "the risks in children's lives often co-occur and overlap in time" (2017B, p. 1). Another study found that the children of incarcerated parents faced multiple adverse childhood experiences throughout development, and other issues also persisted into adulthood. According to Martin, research has frequently found an association between children's "low educational attainment and parental incarceration" (2017, p. 3). A separate study found that children of incarcerated parents are "significantly more likely to be suspended and expelled from school" (Martin, 2017, p. 3). In addition to children facing and coping with their mother's diminished capacity to provide active mothering, they face the emotional burdens of the mother-child separation, increased behavioral problems, and physical and mental health conditions than their peers.

Hyppolite (2017B) created what they call a "multiple risk model" (see Figure 9) to explain the risks that parental incarceration, as well as other factors, have on a child's life.

As Hyppolite explained,

That allows for control of other prominent risk factors in a child's life. The impact of four primary parental risk factors (parental mental illness, parental substance abuse, and poverty) on seven childhood outcomes (school failure, criminal behaviors, being arrested, behavioral difficulties, emotional difficulties, alcohol use, and drug use) was examined. (Hyppolite, 2017B, p. 1)

Hyppolite utilized a program logic model that is a schematic representation that describes the impact of parental incarceration on a child's life. According to Hyppolite, "multiple risk factors in a child's life was found to significantly increase the likelihood that several negative outcomes would occur" (2017B, p. 1).

Figure 9. (Modified from source: A Multiple Risk Model—Poverty, Parental Substance Use, Parental Mental Illness, and Parental Incarceration (Hyppolite, 2017B)

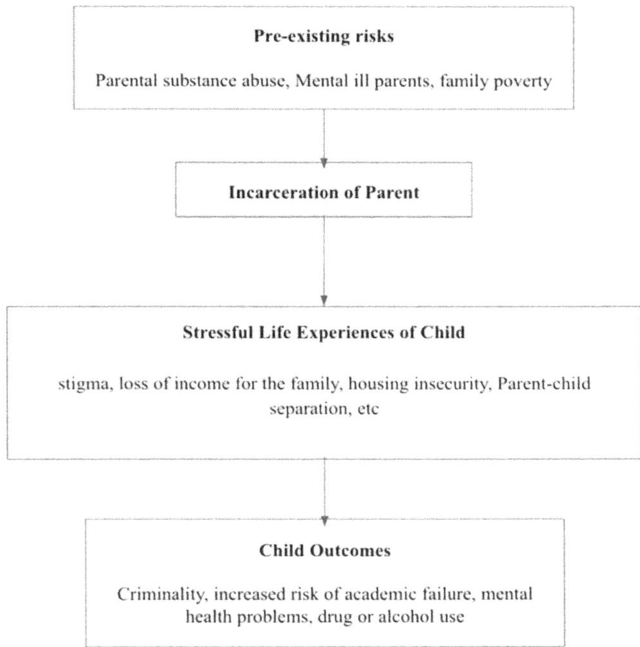

The author notes that while the model appears linear, this may not occur in a child's life. A child may experience these factors all at once, or "they are present and addressed, then return later in a child's life" (Hyppolite, 2017B, p. 5). This study uses a multiple risk model to include parental incarceration as a risk factor, as it "relates to other risks in a child's life and the subsequent child outcomes—parental incarceration" (Hyppolite, 2017B, p. 5). It would be difficult to argue that the incarceration of a mother would not have a significant impact on a child's life. Research has supported that a parent's incarceration causes traumatic and stressful moments that characterize the lives of these children. According to Hyppolite,

When a parent is separated due to incarceration, it is ambiguous and often difficult for children to understand. Their parents are alive, yet absent from their lives. Children of incarcerated parents are likely to feel ashamed and fear rejection from others in their environment if it is discovered. (Hyppolite, 2017B, p. 3)

Parental involvement in a child's life has been linked to positive outcomes throughout life. Yet, children of an incarcerated parent tend to face multiple risks contributing to negative outcomes.

Figure 10. COVID Oubreaks in Correctional Facilities
Source: World Health Organization, 2022.

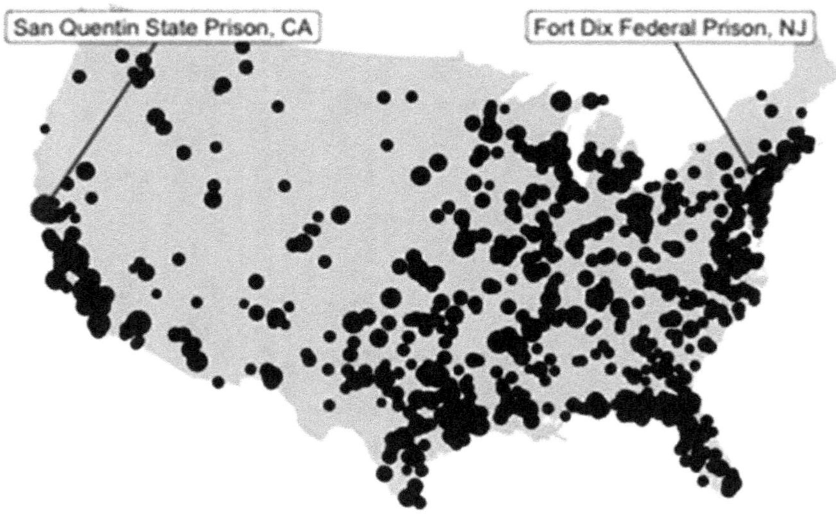

THE COVID-19 PANDEMIC

The COVID-19 pandemic has increased public scrutiny on overcrowded prisons.

"By mid-November 2020, novel coronavirus disease 2019 (COVID-19) outbreaks had occurred at more than 850 jails and prisons across the United States, and new cases continued to rise rapidly" (WHO, 2022, p. 4). This is alarming, as COVID-19 cases and deaths continued to rise within correctional facilities. "These trends are especially concerning given that the U.S. has the largest incarcerated population in the world, with approximately 2 million people behind bars" (WHO, 2022, p. 4). COVID-19 especially impacted state and federal prisons and women in several ways (see Figure 10). Data has supported that racialized women are disproportionately incarcerated. The women population has faced the separation of their children and families and were also vulnerable to the mishandling of social distancing measures from the COVID-19 pandemic and subsequent outbreaks.

Prisons have consistently lacked resources to improve their health, and the pandemic has caused ongoing concern due to over-crowding. While limited data exist on women specifically it is still important to conceptualize how ill-equipped social distancing is in prison systems and how the incidence of COVID-19 impacted inmates.

WHO (2022) created what they call a "COVID-19 OUTBREAKS IN CORRECTIONAL FACILITIES" to illustrate how prisons in the United States have spread COVID-19 among incarcerated individuals, who are the most vulnerable. "Nationwide estimates for COVID-19 infection rates among prisoners are five times higher than in general population" (Altibi et al., 2021, p. 1). Due to limited physical distancing strategies, it was difficult to mitigate the COVID-19 spread, as inmates were confined together. According to Altibi et al., "despite this mortifying public health crisis, current federal and state-level healthcare policies failed to respond adequately in a manner that would lead to "flattening the curve" in U.S. prisons" (2021, p. 1). The prison population, and in this context, women faced the impact of being placed in cramped and under-resourced prison systems. The outbreak caused the conditions of prisoners to worsen.

In this report, the focus is on women and for several reasons, there are limited reported cases among women prisoners: regarding infection rates, confirmed cases, and death toll numbers. The reported numbers of prisoners tend to be grouped; however, undoubtedly prison health systems have often neglected gender-specific approaches, and women inside prisons may have not been tested and symptomatic cases are also factors in unseen risks with those incarcerated.

In March 2020, "days after formally declaring the disease a pandemic, the World Health Organization warned that global efforts to tackle the spread of COVID-19 would fail without proper attention to infection control inside prisons" (WHO, 2020). This supports the notion, that being incarcerated also impacted the rapid transmission of the disease and overwhelmed the prison system. The officials responded and implemented measures to manage the prison population numbers. The official's "responses ranged across three main areas: managing prison population (though inflow constraints and expanded release measures) to reduce overcrowding and facilitate social distancing; suspending or restricting visits from family members and others and halting temporary leave for home visits, work or other previously permitted purposes" (Altibi et al., 2021, p. 8). This increased the isolation of prison inmates and women who faced a lack of health and community safety.

Women who were detained faced the risk of contracting COVID-19 and those who were pregnant, and mothers had increased vulnerability. Public health concerns often focused on the communities outside of the prison system and neglected the poor health services prisoners often face. In this aspect, women in prison environments faced the burden of COVID-19 and increased risks due to the lack of empathy for them as inmates and as mothers. COVID-19 exacerbated a greater threat to the health and welfare of women and demographically women of color who lack poor health conditions (physical layout limited social distancing).

Women and mothers faced disproportionate risks and consequences, as gender inequality and the COVID-19 pandemic deepened pre-existing disparities. Intersectionality exists as race, gender, patriarchy, ethnicity, and economic background are all sources of subornation (Berkhourt et al., 2020). These intersections of "race, gender, economic position, and mitigation overlap to heighten risks for particular women especially" (Berkhourt et al., 2020, p. 6). As stated by Berkhourt, the prison setting has experienced higher infection rates and overwhelmingly has impacted women, especially minorities.

Women in correctional facilities had new challenges as the effects of COVID-19 also increased undeniable effects on individuals' social, physical, and mental health. As the world went on "lockdown" to slow the spread of COVID-19, female prisoner's faced increased psychological concerns about staying safe and healthy. Those who were mothers had even more stress in understanding how they could care for their children and family outside of the correctional institution. Prisoners had limitations in contact with the outside world and regimes were in place to reduce the risk of infection from prisoners to outside communities.

The perspectives of incarcerated women and specifically incarcerated mothers are often excluded in research and in health policy. The needs of women and children needs to be at the forefront of criminal justice reform. Limited research exists on how incarcerated mothers feel during their custody in terms of their physical, mental, and behavioral health from the separation of their children. Furthermore, the lack of family services during incarceration complicates the ability of mothers to foster a relationship with their children. If no parenting program is designed or implemented to foster the connection between mothers and their children, then the relationship will only worsen.

Regarding the COVID-19 pandemic, to improve the well-being of mothers their needs must be conceptualized in the intervention context, as their voices have been excluded in guiding policy. There must be efforts to ensure mothers' and children's experiences are considered when a health crisis occurs as these groups are vulnerable to isolation.

LIMITATIONS & DIRECTIONS FOR FUTURE RESEARCH

This report aimed to address emotional, social, economic, and racial disparities for women who are incarcerated mothers and the outcomes for their children in the U.S. criminal justice system. This research aims to understand the complexity and need to address how the arrest of a parent can be traumatic for a child and how further research needs to be done to find strategies to mitigate the consequences of parent removal in a child's life. It is important to acknowledge that this paper is limited—it is not comprehensive in reviewing all the research or data on children of incarcerated parents.

This report aims to inform others about the need to implement gender-responsive policies and practices that will address the needs of incarcerated mothers. To promote better outcomes for mothers and children. This report highlighted the barriers incarcerated mothers face in correctional facilities. The various literature reviews used in this report examined mothers' and children's psychological and socio-emotional well-being after separation.

This report focused on motherhood and a child's risk factors in attachment disruption. The separation of a child and mother were explored, and evidence supports the notion that a mother-and-child separation increases the risk factors for children. Research findings indicate hidden consequences for the impact of incarceration on dependent children. Children of incarcerated parents face profound and complex threats to their emotional, physical, and financial well-being. Therefore, this report examined a mother and child's attachment.

For further research on this topic, this report can be used as an analysis framework to expand how unfair, and ineffective policies in the criminal justice system have led to disparities in social, economic, and environmental conditions for women, specifically women of color and their offspring.

Further research efforts can reinforce the interest in criminal justice reform with an emphasis on the parenting role and relationship of incarcerated mothers with their children before incarceration and during custody. Directions for future research are to focus on the prison environment and how it fosters the mother-child relationship or the lack thereof.

The identities and roles of women must be used in the decision-making process, and studies should be done in linking a mother's trauma to their criminal activity/behavior. The primary role of mothers is to provide for their child or children, and their criminal behavior may be a component of an intergenerational cycle of violence. A mother's background must be evaluated and assessed on how this could have impacted her life experiences and decisions prior to incarceration. A mother's engagement in crime without the context of generational trauma or the need to protect their child is often not used to reduce in the courtroom in reducing their sentence. Women of color often face additional barriers in mitigating factors available to reduce their prison term. Policy needs to incorporate child welfare and family services when reforming the criminal system. A mother's parental rights need to evaluate to ensure that the outcomes for mothers and children are improved.

Recommendations include the need for strong leadership at the state level with a conscious effort to improve and address the adverse outcomes of parental incarceration. Based on the handful of studies in this area of maternal incarceration, there needs to be more research to assess the risk of disorganized attachment:

1. To better understand the extent of children at risk following a mother's incarceration, there must be better estimates of the number of children affected by their mother's imprisonment.
2. More research can be done to understand how children with a history of displacement from their mother, siblings, and school are affected in correlation to a child's academic performance or attendance.
3. Child and social welfare systems need to conduct a comparison report of the child of an incarcerated parent and one who is not to identify risk factors unique to these children.

Children of inmates are often the "hidden victims" of crime because they have been understudied. When a child is separated from their mothers, data has supported that a child will face additional risk factors. Understanding the extent of a significant life event such as the removal of a parent is crucial to making informed policy decisions that can improve a child's outcome.

CONCLUSION

Breaking the cycle of a child entering prison due to their mother's criminal history is important for reduced criminal sentencing in the United States. There is an urgent need to have a family-focused approach to the criminal sentencing of mothers. A child of an incarcerated mother faces a hidden cost of punitive criminal sentencing policies that neglect the specific needs of children and act as a barrier to maintaining a mother-and-child bond. This report aimed to increase awareness of the negative consequences of a mother-and-child separation and recognizes the need for additional research to understand and estimate the adverse outcomes of having an incarcerated mother.

REFERENCES

Alliance, D. P. (2018). *Women, prison, and the drug war*. Academic Press.

Altibi, A. M., Pallavi, B., Liaqat, H., Slota, A. A., Sheth, R., Al Jebbawi, L., George, M. E., LeDuc, A., Abdallah, E., Russell, L. R., Jain, S., Shirvanian, N., Masri, A., & Kak, V. (2021). Characteristics and comparative clinical outcomes of prisoner versus non-prisoner populations hospitalized with COVID-19. *Scientific Reports*, *11*(1), 1–9. doi:10.103841598-021-85916-w PMID:33753786

Berkhout, S. G., & Richardson, L. (2020). Identity, politics, and the pandemic: Why is COVID-19 a disaster for feminism(s)? *History and Philosophy of the Life Sciences*, *42*(4), 1–6. doi:10.100740656-020-00346-7 PMID:33048278

Clarke, J. G., & Simon, R. E. (2013). Shackling and separation: Motherhood in prison. *AMA Journal of Ethics*, *15*(9), 779–785. doi:10.1001/virtualmentor.2013.15.9.pfor2-1309 PMID:24021108

Eddy, J. M., & Poehlmann-Tynan, J. (Eds.). (2019). *Handbook on children with incarcerated parents: Research, policy, and practice*. Springer Nature. doi:10.1007/978-3-030-16707-3

Friedman, S. H., Kaempf, A., & Kauffman, S. (2020). The realities of pregnancy and mothering while incarcerated. *The Journal of the American Academy of Psychiatry and the Law*, *48*(3), 365–375. PMID:32404363

Graham, J. A., & Harris, Y. R. (2013). Children of color and parental incarceration: Implications for research, theory, and practice. *Journal of Multicultural Counseling and Development*, *41*(2), 66–81. doi:10.1002/j.2161-1912.2013.00028.x

Hyppolite, M. (2017A). Examining Four Major Vulnerabilities Faced by Families. *Community Mental Health: Challenges for the 21st Century*, 159.

Hyppolite, M. L. (2017B). Understanding child outcomes within a multiple risk model: Examining parental incarceration. *Social Sciences*, *6*(3), 82. doi:10.3390ocsci6030082

Jackson, D. B., Testa, A., & Turney, K. (2022). Unpacking the connection between parental incarceration and parenting stress: The mediating role of child health and health care strains. *Journal of Criminal Justice*, 81.

Kinner, S. A., Alati, R., Najman, J. M., & Williams, G. M. (2007). Do paternal arrest and imprisonment lead to child behaviour problems and substance use? A longitudinal analysis. *Journal of Child Psychology and Psychiatry, and Allied Disciplines*, *48*(11), 1148–1156. doi:10.1111/j.1469-7610.2007.01785.x PMID:17995491

La Vigne, N. G., Davies, E., & Brazzell, D. (2016). *Broken bonds: Understanding and addressing the needs of children with incarcerated parents*. Academic Press.

Poehlmann, J. (2005). Representations of attachment relationships in children of incarcerated mothers. *Child Development*, *76*(3), 679–696. doi:10.1111/j.1467-8624.2005.00871.x PMID:15892786

Reagan, B. (1990). The war on drugs: A war against women. *Berkeley Women's Law Journal*, *6*, 203.

Sharp, S. F., & Eriksen, M. E. (2003). Imprisoned mothers and their children. *Women in prison: Gender and social control*, 119-136.

Sheet, F. (2015). *Trends in US corrections*. The Sentencing Project.

Sufrin, C., Beal, L., Clarke, J., Jones, R., & Mosher, W. D. (2019). Pregnancy outcomes in US prisons, 2016–2017. *American Journal of Public Health*, *109*(5), 799–805. doi:10.2105/AJPH.2019.305006 PMID:30897003

Swavola, E., Riley, K., & Subramanian, R. (2016). *Overlooked: Women and jails in an era of reform*. Vera Institute of Justice.

Women, I. (2020). *Girls*. The Sentencing Project.

World Health Organization. (2020). *Preparedness, prevention and control of COVID-19 in prisons and other places of detention: interim guidance 15 March 2020* (No. WHO/EURO: 2020-1405-41155-55954). World Health Organization. Regional Office for Europe.

World Health Organization. (2022). *Health in prisons-COVID-19. Minimum dataset: summary of data reported from May 2020 to October 2021* (No. WHO/EURO: 2022-4752-44515-63010). World Health Organization. Regional Office for Europe.

Chapter 17
The History and Future of School Finance Reform:
The Abbott v. Burke Case

Joanne Howard
Illinois Institute of Technology, USA

ABSTRACT

The Education Trust singled out New Jersey as a state that has made real progress in terms of funding. In 1997, the state had a funding gap of $787 per student in cost-adjusted dollars. By 2002, the gap had been erased, and the state had a $566 positive difference for low-income students. Starting in 1998, spurred partly by the state's long running Abbott v. Burke school funding lawsuit, the state implemented a series of new funding programs designed to help low-income students. This chapter details the progress.

INTRODUCTION

The Education Law Center, a nonprofit organization that tracks school financing issues, reports that lawsuits challenging state methods of financing public schools have been filed in 45 states (Education Law Center, 2022). Founded in 1973, The Education Law Center is the nation's legal defense fund for public education rights. ELC is widely recognized for successfully advancing education equity, opportunity and justice in New Jersey, New York, and states across the country. ELC pursues its advocacy mission through litigation, public engagement, policy development, research, and communications.

ELC seeks to elevate the urgent need for school funding fairness as a state and national imperative for improving student outcomes and school performance through in-depth, state-specific analyses and reports, targeted communications, and support for the Partnership for Equity & Education Rights (PEER).

After narrowing in better economic times, the financial gap between poor and wealthy school districts has widened (Education Trust, 2004). State and local money account for more than 90 percent of all education spending, but higher poverty districts typically receive less per student from those sources in 2002 than did their counterparts with relatively few poor children.

DOI: 10.4018/978-1-6684-2314-1.ch017

The Education Trust report singled out New Jersey as a state that has made real progress in terms of funding. In 1997, the state had a funding gap of $787 per student in cost-adjusted dollars. By 2002, the gap had been erased, and the state had a $566 *positive* difference for low-income students. Starting in 1998, spurred partly by the state's long running *Abbott v. Burke* school funding lawsuit, the state implemented a series of new funding programs designed to help low-income students.

Abbott v. Burke is a like a mystery novel with a great deal of twists and starts. The case is of particular interest to the author because she was born in Trenton, New Jersey, and received an excellent kindergarten through high school education in Bordentown, New Jersey. Bordentown (Exit 7 on the New Jersey Turnpike) is a twenty-minute drive from Camden, New Jersey (Exit 4 on the New Jersey Turnpike), the home of Raymond Arthur Abbott, the lead plaintiff. This case has remained in the author's heart and mind for more than thirty years because the process of reconciling two school districts that are twenty minutes from one another produce substantially different results for its graduates.

There have been twenty-seven iterations of *Abbott v. Burke.* In general, research on school finance appears to be disconnected from education reform. Advocates for school finance reform tend to focus attention on how equal the funding is and how it is distributed, and economists and educational sociologists appear to be more interested in determining what the outcomes are.

BACKGROUND

History of Public School Litigation and Underlying Theories

The idea of "America as a land of opportunity" captures an essential part of the national spirit and heritage, and public education is often viewed as the institution that can transform the ideal into reality. An equitable system of education is one that offsets those accidents of birth that would otherwise keep some children from having an opportunity to function fully in the economic and political life of the community (Berne & Stiefel, 1999, 1984).

Public education is the largest area of state and local government spending in the United States, accounting for almost one-fifth of direct state and local government expenditures in 1996 (Statistical Abstract of the United States 1999, table 504). Given the enormous resources involved and the critical private and societal benefits that education produces, the distribution of educational opportunities across communities has generated considerable interest among policy makers, the public, and the courts (Moser & Rubenstein, 2002).

In most states in the United States, elementary and secondary schools are financed primarily through a combination of local property taxes and state aid. Although the relative proportion of state to local funding varies substantially across states, local property taxes provide a significant share of school funds in many states. Real property wealth is not distributed equally across taxing districts, however, and differences among districts in property-tax wealth per pupil can be dramatic. This unequal distribution of property wealth, coupled with continued reliance on local property taxes, introduces inequities into school funding (Blanchard & Duncombe, 1998; Berne & Stiefel, 1999; Lukemeyer, 2003).

Districts with higher property-tax wealth per student can tax themselves at lower rates, but still provide more school revenue per pupil than property-poor districts (Odden, 1992; Levinem 1991). School districts with high property wealth per pupil tend to have higher educational spending per pupil (Reschovsky, 1994).

The legal battles that characterized education reform in the 1950s and 1960s were solely about ridding schools of the vestiges of segregation and expanding civil rights. During the 1970s, the battle over court-ordered busing proliferated. Educational reformers, aggrieved parents and students, social movement activists, and public interest litigators almost reflexively relied on judicial intervention in public education to transform institutions of learning (Reed, 2001, 1998, 1996). Access to education has been achieved for all children in the United States; however, the battle by education reformers for nearly forty years has been to make the resources of poorly funded schools and school districts more closely mirror what was expended on schools in higher property valuated districts.

School finance reformers have been attracted to the judicial arena by the stunning victories won there in the name of civil rights and civil liberties. With *Brown v. Board of Education* (1954) as an implicit model, activist lawyers pursuing egalitarian goals often shun popularly elected legislators and executives and attempt to achieve their objectives through the decisions of judges who are insulated from public opinion. Successful lawsuits reinforce the view that, rather than reserving litigation as a last resort, it should be used earlier in the process.

Since the 1960s in America, individuals and groups seeking an increased level or share of valued public benefits have often turned to courts for assistance, hoping to achieve their goals outside the traditional political process. Courts have been especially receptive to these pleas when they are made by the politically powerless and deal with matters of fundamental importance (Minorini & Sugarman, 1999a, 1999b).

Campaigns to reshape public policies have no choice but to rely on litigation because groups in power may refuse to negotiate with the powerless without the threat of judicial action. Lehne reports that reform through legislation is a cumbersome process, which can require financial resources and public support that are beyond the reach of reformers. He goes on to report that, under such circumstances, failure to invoke judicial procedure becomes, in effect, a ratification of the status quo. By any standard, reformist litigants have been successful in winning favorable judgments from both state and federal courts in their efforts to alter the content of public policy (Lehne, 1978).

As this judicial activism started taking hold, lawyers and scholarly advocates turned their attention to the financing of public schools; school finance concerns the distribution and use of money for the purpose of providing educational services and producing student achievement. They focused on the way in which most states have historically relied on local property taxes as a substantial source of funding public education (Enrich, 1995). Those early advocates viewed equity (focuses on an examination of how states distribute resources across districts that serve various student populations) as an essential component of the principle of basic fairness because they argued traditional school finance arrangements created grave inequities for children in the availability of educational resources and opportunities (Lukemeyer, 2003).

During the late 1960s, several scholars and lawyer activists began examining America's system of school finance. These newcomers to the world of school finance learned what experts in the field had long known—that, by giving local governments the primary power and responsibility to raise funds and set spending levels in public schools, states had created systems that substantially favored some children over others. Notwithstanding the publication of the Coleman Report (1966), which raised doubts about how much money really mattered in improving student outcomes, these scholars and activists found a great deal unfair about the funding of the nation's public schools (Minorini & Sugarman, 1999b).

Arthur Wise, then a doctoral student in the School of Education at The University of Chicago, argued that education was a fundamental right, and that the equal protection clause required that education must be provided equally across all school districts (Wise, 1968, 1983). He further argued that variations in educational expenditures across districts in most states did not reflect uniformity of educational offerings, because expenditure variations were not related to educational need (Odden & Picus, 2004, p. 31). His dissertation, which he subsequently turned into a book, *Rich Schools, Poor Schools,* advanced the equity argument for litigation in the 1970s.

Around the same time, John Coons, a law professor at Northwestern University, and two of his law students, William Clune and Stephen Sugarman, began to frame another argument: that education funding created a suspect classification defined by district property wealth per pupil (Coons, Clune, & Sugarman, 1970). They argued that local school districts were creations of state governments and that by making school financing heavily dependent on local financing, states gave school districts unequal opportunities to raise educational revenues, because the property value per child varied widely across school districts. Their contention was that education could not be dependent on local wealth, but only on the wealth of the state as a whole (Odden & Picus, 2004). The work of Wise, Coons, Clune, and Sugarman was the foundation for litigation strategy in state courts.

During the late 1960s, reformers began bringing constitutional challenges to these disparities in education funding, first in federal courts, and then in state courts. Over forty states have now faced court challenges to their school funding systems (Minorini & Sugarman, 1999a, 1999b; Evans, Murray, & Schwab, 1997). Legal scholars (Levine, 1991; Thro, 1990) divide this litigation into three "waves." Each wave is characterized by a distinct legal theory underlying reformers' claims and by different rates of plaintiff's victories.

Wave I

Wave I of school finance reform litigation produced two leading cases. The first was the California Supreme Court's 1971 decision overturning the California school finance system in *Serrano v. Priest.* The second case marking the end of Wave I was the United States Supreme Court's decision favoring the state in *San Antonio Independent School District v. Rodriguez* (1973). In both cases, plaintiffs argued that the school finance system, with its heavy reliance on local property taxes, created wide disparities in funds available to school districts and in both spending and educational opportunities across school districts.

In *Serrano I,* the California court held that the finance system differentiated among students on the basis of a suspect classification: wealth. The court concluded that education represented a fundamental interest because it is crucial to a democratic government, individual well-being, and individual economic mobility. For these reasons, the court found that the California finance system did not pass constitutional muster (Lukemeyer, 2003).

In *Rodriguez,* the United States Supreme Court addressed the issue of whether the disparities in funds available to Texas school districts amounted to a violation of the equal protection clause. The funding system and distribution of school revenues and resources were very similar to those confronting the *Serrano* court. Unlike the court that decided the *Serrano* decision, the U.S. Supreme Court concluded that this "large, diverse, and amorphous" class did not exhibit a history of discrimination or disability that would command "the extraordinary protection from the majoritarian political process" accorded a suspect class *(Rodriguez, 411 U.S. at 28).* The court next addressed whether education was a constitutionally protected fundamental right. The Court concluded that fundamental rights were limited to those implicitly guaranteed by the Constitution. The court characterized the Texas finance system as an attempt to provide a basic education to all students while allowing substantial local control and participation (Lukemeyer, 2003; Firestone, Goertz, & Natriello, 1997).

Serrano v. Priest was the first case filed using the Coons, Clune, and Sugarman strategy in California. The case was filed in 1968 and the California Supreme Court determined in 1971 that (1) the case was justiciable, using the fiscal neutrality standard; (2) education was a fundamental right and property wealth per pupil was a suspect class; and (3) the California school finance system was unconstitutional. This was a precedent-setting opinion, gaining nationwide media, policy, and legal attention, and immediately spawning a series of similar court cases in other states. The court determined that this funding scheme was invidiously discriminatory against the poor since it made the quality of a child's education a function of the wealth of his parents and neighbors. In determining that education was a fundamental interest not conditioned on wealth, the court could find no compelling reason to uphold the system of financing. This decision placed the burden of financing education firmly on the state. It did not, however, state that the use of the property tax in financing schools was unconstitutional (Lukmeyer, 2003; Firestone, Goertz, & Natriello, 1997; Odden & Picus, 2004).

Rodriguez v. San Antonio was decided in 1973 by the United States Supreme Court and ended Wave I. The ruling that Texas's school finance formula did not violate the Equal Protection Clause and that education is not a fundamental right under the U.S. Constitution, and therefore, poor school districts are not a protected class was a blow to litigants. The Court refused to apply strict scrutiny analysis because wealth was not a suspect classification, and education was not a fundamental right. Employing the rational basis test, the Court ruled that the state's reliance on property taxes was rationally related to the legitimate governmental interest of promoting local control. This decision by the U.S. Supreme Court effectively precluded plaintiffs from using the equal protection clause of the U.S. Constitution by declaring it applies to individuals, not governmental entities.

Wave II

The second wave of school finance reform concentrated on state constitutional claims, and they took two forms. First, most state constitutions include clauses that have been interpreted as conferring protections similar to those of the federal equal protection clause (Enrich, 1995). The plaintiffs continued to press claims that school finance systems violated state equal protection clauses. All state constitutions contain provisions imposing some duty on the state to create a public school system, so during this wave, plaintiffs pressed claims that the state's school funding system violated constitutional obligations imposed by these constitutional provisions. Wave II lasted from 1973 to 1989 but yielded relatively few victories for reformers (Thro, 1993; Levine, 1991).

In Wave II, plaintiffs argued that school finance formulas violated the equal protection clauses of state constitutions. This litigation strategy required plaintiffs to distinguish state equal protection provisions from the Equal Protection Clause of the U.S. Constitution. Although plaintiffs have been occasionally successful, most state courts in second wave cases have upheld the constitutionality of state funding systems. Scholars have cited several reasons for the failure of second wave claims, including the difficulty of defining the concept of equity, the doctrine of separation of powers, and the concerns of rich school districts (Reed, 2001, 1998; Reschovsky & Imazeki, 1998; Reschovsky, 1994; Lukemeyer, 2002; Fischel, 1998).

Wave III

In the third wave, which started in 1989 and has run to the present, plaintiffs argued that states have failed to provide poor districts with an adequate level of education. This strategy uses state education clauses, which define the state's constitutional duty to provide an education. Adequacy approaches have several problems that have limited their overall effectiveness. Some courts have deferred to the state legislatures' definition of an adequate education, thus guaranteeing that the plaintiffs will be unable to succeed in their adequacy claim. Adequacy formulations (providing sufficient funds for the average district/school to teach the average child to state standards, plus sufficient additional revenues for students with special needs) might actually impose greater restrictions on local control than equity approaches, because a court could determine how school districts spend their money (Ladd, 1975).

Plaintiffs have had more success under the third wave than the second wave. Courts in thirteen states have invalidated their school finance systems in whole or in part, while courts in twelve states have upheld their school finance systems. Supporters argue that adequacy arguments are more likely than equality arguments to rebuff objections based on local control. Adequacy does not conflict with local taxation because school districts are not required to provide equal resources. Moreover, adequacy approaches do not conflict with local governance of schools because districts can still dedicate additional resources or develop distinctive education programs.

According to Peter Enrich,

...adequacy arguments must confront not only the problems faced by equality arguments in determining whether the relevant dimension for measurement is school funding, or educational inputs, or student outcomes, but also the additional questions of what quantity of funding, what level of services, or what degree of student achievement suffices to meet the constitutional demand. (Enrich, 1995)

Third wave cases attempted to deemphasize equal protection analysis and, instead, focus on education clauses in state constitutions. These cases placed a heavier emphasis on adequacy rather than equity. Plaintiffs in the first two waves of school funding cases tended to emphasize the reduction of spending disparities. They focused on input measures like per-pupil spending. Plaintiffs in third wave cases concentrated on the sufficiency of school funding and postulated the existence of a constitutional floor of minimally adequate education to which public school students are entitled. When courts have found the education afforded students to be below this minimum, they have ruled in favor of plaintiffs.

According to Michael Rebell, Executive Director of the Campaign for Fiscal Equity in New York, "Although plaintiffs prevailed in the early litigation, by the early 80's, defendants were winning most of these cases, primarily because the courts had great difficulty in devising solutions for the problems of funding inequities." Rebell sees the third wave cases as offering a benefit to the courts in terms of providing more tangible solutions. "Instead of dealing with equal funding concepts and complex property tax reforms, the adequacy approach allows courts to focus on the concrete issues of what resources are needed to provide the opportunity for an adequate education to all students and the extent to which those resources are actually being provided" (Rebell, 2002).

Wave IV

Since 2011, California has led the way to a fourth wave that would combine equity and adequacy to focus on student achievement in relation to state curriculum standards. These four waves are discussed in relation to the recent history of declining resources and student achievement in California.

THE MULTIPLE DEFINITIONS OF FAIRNESS IN SCHOOL FINANCE LITIGATION

Numerous scholars, economists, and legal commentators have noted that a variety of school finance outcomes might be the goal of reform efforts (Minorini & Sugarman, 1999a, 1999b; Berne & Stiefel, 1999, 1984; Enrich, 1995; Reschovsky, 1994; Clune, 1992; Levine, 1991; Monk & Brent, 1997). Proponents of reform are not always clear about which goal they are seeking. This lack of clarity or consistency sometimes characterizes judicial decisions as well (Friedman & Wiseman, 1978).

Berne and Stiefel (1984), Monk and Brent (1997), and Duncombe and Yinger (1996) provide a useful method for analyzing the goals of school finance reform efforts. They characterize reform goals in terms of two dimensions: equity objects and equity standards. Equity standards describe what is considered a fair distribution of spending or resources or some other object. Equity objects describe what is being equalized or otherwise distributed.

Three categories of potential equity objects appear relevant to this litigation: (1) spending per pupil; (2) school resources and services such as teachers, curricular offerings, library materials, counseling programs; and (3) student outcomes or achievement. As Duncombe and Yinger (1996) point out, while school finance litigation focuses on disparities in per-pupil spending, expenditures are actually a relatively poor proxy for the goals that reformers seek. Lukemeyer (2003) reports that, when there are differences in the cost of resources (for example, differences in salaries needed to attract good teachers), equalizing spending across districts is unlikely to result in equalizing either resources or school services. The Coleman Report (1966) reported that family characteristics may play an even larger role in the level of student achievement.

Lukemeyer (2003) indicates there is a second dimension involved in standards used to assess equity or fairness in the distribution of the chosen object. Four standards are useful for analysis of school finance reform litigation: minimum adequacy, equality, access equality, and fiscal neutrality. Each of these may be paired with spending-per-pupil or with any of the equity objects.

A minimum adequacy standard requires all schools to provide some minimum level of spending per pupil. Local districts are free to provide any amount of educational services beyond the amount defined as "adequate," but every district must provide its students some defined level of spending, educational resources, or skills. The level defined as adequate may be high or low. Reed (1998) reports that the state constitutional claims that plaintiffs have made in school financing suits generally fall into two categories: equity claims and adequacy claims. Often which claim is invoked depends on the language of the state education clauses and the state equality provisions. He also reports that legal activists make strategic considerations when deciding which approach to take. Equity claims seek to equalize expenditures among districts, while adequacy claims often seek to boost the resources of the worst-off districts, without requiring parity among districts.

Under the equality standard, expenditures per pupil must be equal across school districts. Alone, an equality standard implies no absolute minimum, and is satisfied as long as all districts spend equally, regardless of level.

Access equality attempts to counter differences in tax bases across school districts and to equalize each district's revenue-raising capability. This standard is met when each school district can produce equal amounts of the chosen equity object with a given tax effort. Reform efforts (such as district power equalizing grants) that address this goal typically attempt to ensure all districts tax themselves at the same rate and are able to raise the same revenue per pupil (Ladd & Yinger, 1994). This goal allows school districts to continue to determine rates of property tax and levels of school spending per pupil. Therefore, this system maintains local control over educational spending and enhances local control among poorer districts by allowing them easier access to higher levels of spending (Minorini & Sugarman, 1999b; Levine 1991). It does not, however, require all districts either to tax themselves or to spend at the same rate.

Under a fiscal neutrality standard, the selected equity object may not vary with a district's tax base or fiscal capacity. A funding system in which poorer districts consistently provide fewer resources per pupil violates this principle. Nevertheless, the fiscal neutrality standard allows different districts to provide widely different levels of resources so long as the level of object is not systematically related to district tax base or fiscal capacity.

Historical Framework for Education in New Jersey

Elwood Cubberly (1947), Dean Emeritus of the School of Education at Stanford University, wrote the seminal work on the history of education in the United States. He recounts the creation of school districts and their funding. The first schools in America were clearly the fruits of the Protestant Revolts in Europe. The reformers in Europe had insisted upon the necessity of a knowledge of the Gospels as a mean to personal salvation. The inability to realize their ideals of life and worship in their European homelands resulted in large numbers of religious congregations leaving Europe to come to America.

The Scottish and Scotch-Irish Presbyterians settled in New Jersey, as did Germans. The provision of education, aside from certain rudimentary and religious instruction thought necessary for religious purposes, and aside from the apprenticing of orphans and the children of the very poor, was left largely for those who could afford to pay for an education. Of the different denominations, the Quakers, in particular, rendered notable service in the founding of schools in New Jersey, particularly for educating paupers (Cubberly, 1947).

In the early history of New Jersey, the state was classified as a pauper-parochial-school state of the five Middle Colonies. Education was the province of the church and charitable organizations. A state school fund was not established until 1816. In 1820 permission to levy a local tax for schools was granted. In 1828 a report showed that one-third of the children of the State were growing up without a chance for any education. Largely as a result of this, the first general school law was enacted in 1829. This law provided local taxation and made a state appropriation of $20,000 a year to help establish the system. The next year, however, it was repealed as a result of bitter opposition from private and church-school interests.

In 1830 and 1831, laws limited state educational effort to aiding schools for the education of the children of the poor. In 1838 the beginnings of a state public school system were made, and in 1844 state aid was limited to public schools. The first state constitutional mention of education was in 1844.

A number of societies began to crop up around the country to support public education. In New Jersey the "Society of Teachers and Friends of Education" held conventions, drew up memorials and petitions, and its members visited all parts of the State advocating general education at public expense, and especially the elimination of the pauper-school education system, which was based on class and was out of place in a Republic founded on the doctrine that "all men are created equal, and endowed by their Creator with certain inalienable rights."

Between 1828 and 1838 several conventions of friends of free public schools were held in the State, and considerable work was done to promote education for children. In 1828, the state conducted a study to learn about the condition of education. According to the study:

- Many children were still unable to attend school;
- One in every five voters was unable to read or write; and
- State residents wanted a free public school system (New Jersey Department of Education, 2001).

At a convention in 1838, "the most notable convention of the friends of the common schools ever held in the State," a committee was appointed to prepare an "Address to the People of New Jersey" on the educational needs of the State. This Address, coupled with the speakers that were sent around the State to talk to the people on the subject, so aroused the people that positive action soon followed. That "every free State must provide for the education of all its children," and that the education of the people is indispensable to the preservation of free institutions, were held to be axiomatic. The pauper-school idea was vigorously condemned. Concerning this, the "Address" said:

We utterly repudiate as unworthy, not of freemen only, but of men, the narrow notion that there is to be an education for the poor as such. Has God provided for the poor a coarser earth, a thinner air, a paler sky? Does not the glorious sun pour down his golden flood as cheerily on the poor man's hovel as upon the rich man's palace? Have not the cotter's children as keen a sense of all the freshness, verdure, fragrance, melody, and beauty of luxuriant nature as the pale sons of kings? Or is it on the mind that God has stamped the imprint of a baser birth, so hat the poor man's child knows with an inborn certainty that his lot is to crawl, not climb? It is not so. God has not done it. Man cannot do it. Mind is immortal. Mind is imperial. It bears no mark of high or low, of rich or poor. It asks but freedom. It requires light (Cubberley, 1947, p. 197).

This study and the work of reformers proved to be the impetus for various legislative measures over the next 50 years. During this period, laws were enacted to provide for state and local funds for the operation of schools; prohibit spending school funds for purposes other than education; permit local districts to appoint school superintendents; establish a state board of education and a state superintendent of public instruction with authority to enforce school law; and require schools to be free to all children age five to eighteen.

Jean Anyon (1997) writes that in 1871, when the New Jersey legislature compelled all of the state's municipalities to offer a 9-month school term and prohibited tuition charges, the state became the last in the nation to guarantee free public education. Even though New Jersey was late in providing free public education, the spirit of the action seems to have been generous. As a result of this 1871 act, for almost ten years education in New Jersey became primarily a state responsibility. The state government assumed 75 percent of school costs of all districts exclusive of construction and repairs (*Robinson v. Cahill* 1973, p. 266; Burr 1942).

In 1875, the New Jersey Constitution was amended to address the subject of education opportunity. The Legislature reviewed recommendations of an 1873 constitutional commission, including the commission's proposals that addressed state financing and maintenance of a public education system with emphasis on "rudimentary" education. The Legislature further enhanced the commission's recommendation in the 1875 constitutional amendment that stated:

The Legislature shall provide for the maintenance and support of a thorough and efficient system of free public schools for the instruction of all the children in the state between the ages of five and eighteen years (New Jersey Constitution, Article 8, Section 4, Paragraph 1, Amended to the 1844 Constitution in 1875).

During the 20th century, education in New Jersey continued to change and expand. Public schools became free for everyone between the ages of five and twenty, and education was made compulsory for all students between the ages of six and sixteen. Kindergartens, nursery schools, and child daycare centers became more common, and special classes and services were developed for gifted students as well as for those who were physically, mentally, and emotionally handicapped.

Anyon (1997) reports that while business leaders in the cities and the rural elites believed that education was a cure for the problems resulting from industrialization and immigration, they were unwilling to pay for the enactment of the "thorough and efficient" amendment for very long. After nine years, an 1881 law returned 90 percent of state school taxes to the county of origin. The state's extensive railroad property was exempt from taxation, and the legislature's historic reliance (since 1670) on the property tax for school funds confined most money to the wealthier districts (Salmore & Salmore, 1998). Thus, the 1881 law reinstated a trend that would contribute to extreme fiscal disparities in school districts—a reliance, as in almost all states, on local support of education (Anyon, 1997; Carnoy, 1982).

The demand for secondary education grew, resulting in the creation of junior high schools and local county vocational schools. Many school districts without high schools arranged to send pupils to neighboring districts, and legislation enabled small districts to merge financially in order to construct high schools and form regional districts.

Between the end of World War II in 1945 and the early 1970s, the state's population exploded. The need for more schools and teachers made dramatic demands on taxpayers. By the early 1970s, state aid to public schools had declined to 28 percent. This set the scene for a reorganization of education financing.

In Henry J. Aaron's book, *Who Pays the Property Tax* (1975), he reported that New Jersey was one of four states (along with Connecticut, Massachusetts, and New Hampshire) that contributed more than 35 percent of its local funds for public schools. Laura Mansnerus (2002) reported in The New York *Times* that "much more than most states, New Jersey relies on the property tax. New Jersey already has the highest per-capita property taxes in the nation."

To provide services, municipalities must levy taxes and prepare a budget. New Jersey's local governments depend almost entirely on the local property tax, which provides 98 percent of locally raised revenues, as compared to about 74 percent nationally (U.S. Advisory Commission on Intergovernmental Relations, 1989). Property taxes are collected by municipalities, but their governing bodies receive and spend a rather small portion. Municipal governments are the collection agents for counties, whose budgets also depend heavily on property taxes. A large share of local taxes goes to finance local public schools, and this money is allocated by separate boards of education. New Jersey has even more school districts (610) than it does municipalities (567) and more mostly elected school-board members (4,780) than elected local officials (3,376). Most municipalities have fiercely resisted proposals for regionalized schools (Salmore & Salmore, 1998). Fred Burke (personal communication, December 1, 2003), former Commissioner of Education for New Jersey, lamented his failure to convince policymakers, school boards, and stake-holders in New Jersey to consolidate school districts. "I tried to get the State Legislature and others to cut back from 600 plus school districts to 100. You can't imagine the uproar. Everyone was concerned that their individual roles would be diminished."

Expenditures for public education consume nearly a third of the state budget, and New Jersey has ranked first or second in spending for elementary and secondary education among the states for some years. The state's proportional fiscal contribution is below the 50-state average, and local property taxes in New Jersey remain among the highest in the nation.

Nowhere else is the state's home rule tradition more apparent than in the realm of public education. Almost all New Jersey municipalities have their own elementary schools, and high schools of barely 500 students are the rule rather than the exception. Arguments for curricular enrichment or economies of scale pall when they mean eliminating the institution most central to the identity of New Jersey's towns—where high school football is practically a ritual, reinforced by the historic absence of major professional or even collegiate competition in the state.

New Jerseyans are barely inclined to redistribute their school tax dollars outside their own communities, much less to redistribute their children. Battles over public education—who should control it and how to fund it—have devoured more debate time in New Jersey in the last two decades than even the tax system to which they are intimately connected (Salmore & Salmore, 1998; Burtless, 1996; Barro, 1992).

Tiebout's (1956) classic theory of local expenditures describes the phenomenon of "voting with your feet" when individuals choose to live in the area that offers a mix of public services most closely matching their preferences. The nearly 15,000 school districts in the United States provide an example of Tiebout's theory. For example, realtors report that homebuyers frequently ask about the quality of local schools. Clearly, many people make decisions about where to live, at least in part, on the basis of their perception of the quality of local educational services (Odden & Picus, 2004). There are more than 600 school districts in New Jersey and 581 are adequately funded (Education Week, 2001). It is the thirty-one special needs districts that clearly warrant the attention of policymakers.

New Jersey has had two school finance cases that have spanned three decades. *Robinson v. Cahill* was filed in 1970 and a decision was handed down in 1973. This case occurred in the second wave of state court cases, several months after the U.S. Supreme Court decided *Rodriguez,* the case that effectively ended Wave I. *Abbott v. Burke* is considered the "son of *Robinson v. Cahill*" (Salmore & Salmore, 1998, p. 197) and the first decision was handed down in 1985. *Abbott* has had ten iterations, each deciding a different point for the plaintiffs. These cases are at the heart of New Jersey's school finance litigation.

In 1973, New Jersey's system of financing public education was ruled unconstitutional by the State Supreme Court in *Robinson v. Cahill*, a lawsuit brought by a child and his parents against Governor William T. Cahill. The court also ruled that the system was preventing many of the state's children from receiving the educational opportunity guaranteed them under the state's constitution. Three years later, the Public School Education Act of 1975 was enacted (Chapter 212 created a new state funding formula for public schools, but lawmakers did not raise taxes to pay for it). This measure specified how the state should prepare all students to function successfully in society. The New Jersey Gross Income Tax of 1976 funded this law. State education in the 1980s and 1990s in New Jersey was dominated by school finance issues. The issue of finance equalization continues to resonate to this day in New Jersey and other states around the country.

Abbott v. Burke was filed in 1981 and ten decisions were made on behalf of low-income children between 1985 and 2004. In each instance, the New Jersey Supreme Court and various lower courts in New Jersey ruled on behalf of low-income school-aged children in the state.

TAXES IN NEW JERSEY SCHOOL FINANCE CASES

The property tax is perhaps the most hated and flawed tax the public is required to pay. Netzer indicates

...the American property tax abounds in anomalies. During the past century, no major fiscal institution, here or abroad, has been criticized at such length and with such vigor; yet no major fiscal institution has changed so little in modern times...The demise of the property tax as a major factor in the American fiscal scene has long been heralded; yet it continues to finance more than one-fifth of the civilian general expenditures of federal, state, and local governments. (Netzer, 1966, p. 1)

According to Aaron (1975), Berne and Stiefel (1984), and Monk and Brent (1997) the property tax is a tax on wealth that takes the form of property. Property can take numerous forms, and states vary in how they treat different types of property for tax purposes. In general, property can be classified in any one of three broad groups: real property, tangible personal property, and intangible personal property. Real property refers to land and any permanently attached improvements, such as commercial buildings and residential houses. Tangible personal property is comprised of assets other than real property that have physical substance. Tangible personal property includes such property as business equipment, inventory, automobiles, and computers. In contrast, intangible personal property includes assets that do not have physical substance that are held by taxpayers because of the use of the rights or exchange value they confer to the owner. Examples of intangible personal property are cash, stocks, bonds, copyrights, patents, and trademarks. One reason real property is always used in determining the tax base for property tax purposes is that it is an immobile asset that is difficult to conceal. This is less true for personal property (Monk & Brent, 1997, pp. 39-40).

Fairness is an important principle in tax policy. It is generally believed that all individuals in society should contribute to the public good and be treated in uniform ways. But it is also recognized that not all taxpayers are in the same financial condition when taxes are due. The ability-to-pay theory states that taxpayers should contribute in accordance with their economic capacity to support public services. Rather than demanding absolute equality in tax payments, the principle calls for an examination of individuals' abilities to contribute (Swanson & King, 1997, p. 94). This standard was advanced by Adam Smith as early as 1776:

The subjects of every state ought to contribute towards the support of the government, as nearly as possible, in proportion to their respective abilities: that is, in proportion to the revenue which they respectively enjoy under the protection of the state...In the observation or neglect of this maxim consists what is called the equality or inequality of taxation (Smith, 1993 (original 1776), p. 451).

This ability-to-pay standard applies to schools, and in New Jersey the value of one's property is what buys a good education. New Jersey has always put an unusual reliance on local property taxes to fund its public schools. Taxes on property began in 1670. Three centuries later, the local property tax was still the linchpin of government finance. As late as 1962, it generated 65 percent of all state and local tax revenues in New Jersey, compared to a 38 percent average for all the states.

Even in 1989, long after New Jersey imposed broad-based sales and income taxes, property taxes still accounted for 43 percent of state and local tax dollars, compared with a national average of 30 percent (Froojian, 1991). Only three states—Montana, New Hampshire, and Oregon—collected a larger proportion of income form this source. New Jersey still relies more heavily on the property tax than any other state with both sales and income taxes (Augenblick, 2001).

By the mid-1950s, thirty-one states had a state income tax, thirty-three states had a general state sales tax, and only three—including New Jersey—had neither. About two-thirds of New Jersey's state revenues came from excise taxes and fees (e.g., on public utilities, motor fuels, vehicle registration, cigarettes and alcohol, and racing); most of the rest was from corporate taxes. In 1956, New Jersey state taxes, as a percentage of all own-source revenues, were at half the national average.

High local property taxes accounted for the divergence. On average, state and local taxes contributed about equally to a state's own-source revenue in the 1950s. In New Jersey, local revenues—virtually all from the property tax—still contributed four times as much. Its county and local leaders saw broad-based taxes as the "greatest threat to the endurance of the home rule tradition" (Felzenberg, 1978. p. 67).

Extraordinary dependence on the local property tax produced vast inequalities among counties and municipalities. Residents with low or fixed incomes especially suffered from a tax that had a limited relationship to ability to pay and no protection against housing inflation. The tax system discriminated against urban areas with shrinking tax bases and increasing demands for public services. In 1951, assessment ratios (the assessed valuation of a property as a proportion of its market value) were at least 50 percent above the state average in eight of the thirteen largest municipalities (Beck, 1958).

As cities imposed high tax rates to pay for constantly growing needs, businesses and middle-class residents fled, intensifying a vicious cycle (Goldman, 1988). New Jersey developers seeking cheap land and home buyers and businesses seeking low taxes produced "a premature spreading out of urban development, the creation of an automobile-dependent society, and the deterioration of established cities" (Lehne, 1975, p. 249).

Beginning mid-century, the tax system relied on local property taxes that were insensitive to economic fluctuations, had little relation to ability to pay, and covered only a small proportion of income-producing assets. It accelerated cities' decline by depressing urban property values and was based on unstandardized and inequitable assessments (Beck, 1978, p. 578).

By the mid-1960s, the climate finally seemed right for cautious tax reform (Lehne & Rosenthal, 1979). However, in New Jersey the adage that it is easier to raise an existing tax than to impose a new one continued to hold sway. Governor Richard Hughes (1962–1970), a Democrat with a Democratic legislature, put through a 3 percent sales tax. It was less regressive than many state excise taxes in that it exempted both food and clothing.

When William Cahill, a Republican, became governor, he raised the sales tax to 5 percent and helped to establish a state-run lottery, a painless source of revenue (Salmore & Salmore, 1998; Goertz, 1992). Cahill established a Tax Policy Committee to study the entire tax system. The Committee recommended generating state and local revenue in approximately equal proportions from income, sales, and property taxes. The proposal shifted much of the tax burden from localities to the state, from property to income, and for an overall increase in revenues. The plan cut local property taxes by about half the amount of an increased state tax burden of $1.5 billion, and the committee also recommended a ceiling on property tax rates (Salmore & Salmore, 1998). A lack of Republican backing ultimately led to a defeat of the plan, and resulted in Cahill's defeat when he sought re-election in 1973. Even when contemplating taxes, the old adage, "the devil you know is better than the devil you don't know" has relevance.

The Democratic governor Brendan Byrne took office in January 1974 after campaigning on a platform of no new taxes in "the foreseeable future," but was forced to push for an income tax to pay for court-mandated revenue for public education. Byrne oversaw the passage of a public referendum legalizing casino gambling in Atlantic City in 1977. The principal motive behind the casino policy was to revive Atlantic City and to generate additional revenue for the state.

The economy improved under Republican governor Thomas Kean, but with surpluses the politicians looked for a way to return some of the bounty to the taxpayers. In September 1985, the Democratic majority in the legislature passed a credit against income tax bills for homeowners and tenants. Like Cahill, Kean created the State and Local Expenditure and Revenue Policy (SLERP) commission in December 1984 to study the effects of mandated spending and the impact of the tax system on the economic vitality of the state. A delay in appointing members to the Commission to keep the issue of taxes on the back burner slowed down their work. In the end, they concluded that new taxes were not required, and that tax reform should be revenue neutral.

By 1987, the effects of the Reagan-era federal cuts were obvious. The state share of revenue continued to rise as a result of increased sales and income tax rates. SLERP recommended that Trenton assume the cost of the state court system, the local share of welfare costs, and county expenditures for psychiatric centers and centers for the developmentally disabled. Additionally, the state was to contribute a greater proportion of the costs of the public schools and county colleges.

Problems continued to dog the state because of the disparity in assessment ratios and tax rates between cities and suburbs. In 1986, the effective tax rate in Princeton was $1.94 per $1,000 of assessed valuation, while Trenton, in the same county, had an effective rate of $4.85—as against a state average of $2.38. A former state treasurer calculated that if all municipalities were taxed at the statewide average rate, Newark's rate would drop by half and the rates in Camden and East Orange by two-thirds (Goldman, 1988).

Other factors also helped suburban property owners and hurt their urban counterparts. For one, businesses paid 30 percent of all local property taxes and they sought to locate in places like the Princeton area with its low rates, open space, and prestigious address. Tax exemptions and special rates also favored rural area and discriminated against urban areas. Cities contained the most tax-exempt property devoted to public use, such as government buildings, public universities, parks, airports, and seaports (Bordentown Register News, 2005; Winter, 2004; Wong, 1999; Salmore & Salmore, 1998).

Taxing and spending continue to be centralized in the state capital, Trenton. Just beneath the surface is an extreme distrust of politicians that bear bad tidings about taxes. There also continues to be suburban indifference to the plight of urban areas in the state. As a review of the *Robinson* and *Abbott* cases in the next chapter will indicate, no good deed goes unpunished when it comes to trying to apply fairness in the distribution of education dollars in New Jersey.

Successful School Financing Legislation in California

The strategy to allow the court to provide legal cover for education officials appears to occur in other states. Sharon Weitzman Soltman was the lead attorney in the *Corey H.* (1998) case in Illinois that led to the mainstreaming of disabled children into regular classrooms so they could receive a normal education and master the standard education curriculum, consistent with the most current federal law (Individuals with Disabilities Education Act or IDEA). Ms. Soltman has indicated that education officials may believe children with disabilities should be mainstreamed into regular classrooms or that poor children deserve an excellent well-funded education, but it is much easier to carry out when a court mandates that it happen (Soltman, 2003).

At the same time the *Robinson* case was filed, Paul Tractenberg, a professor at Rutgers University School of Law in Newark, was assisting the Newark Chapter of the National Association for the Advancement of Colored People (NAACP) to file an *amicus curiae* brief to support the need to equalize funding in New Jersey. Mr. Tractenberg had concluded that New Jersey's school financing scheme was unfair and signed onto the case. In 1973 with a grant from The Ford Foundation, he would also found the Education Law Center. The organization came into existence at the beginning of Wave II of school finance reform cases in the country. Mr. Tractenberg is known as the "dean" of school finance reform in New Jersey, he is a nationally recognized scholar on the subject.

After two years at the helm of the Education Law Center, Mr. Tractenberg resumed his position at Rutgers University School of Law in Newark. He indicated the Robinson case would take many years to settle prior to signing on to the case. When he returned to the classroom, he left the organization in 1979 in the hands of Ms. Marilyn Morheuser, a former nun and law student of his at Rutgers. Mr. Tractenberg assumed a seat on the Education Law Center's board of directors. He continues to serve on the board of directors today.

By all accounts, Ms. Morheuser was tenacious in her struggle to make New Jersey's school-financing system more equitable for the state's poorest districts. She was the organization's lead counsel for the plaintiffs in *Abbott v. Burke* when the case was filed in 1981 to challenge the state's Quality Education Act of 1980 (a result of *Robinson v. Cahill, 1973).* Christopher Kilbourne (1994) wrote in the Bergen County Record that "it was a classic mismatch: a former nun, leading a shoestring crusade to win equal education funding for underprivileged children, going up against the arsenal and inertia of New Jersey state government. The state never had a chance." The article goes onto report that Ms. Morheuser's role in the case went far beyond that of lead attorney. Paul Tractenberg said, "she is the case; the case is her. It has been a labor of love and a major part of her life… If a major law firm were handling this, they'd have ten people doing it."

The inseparability of Morheuser and the crusade for school funding equity had colleagues wondering who would carry the banner for the state's urban schoolchildren once she died from cancer in 1995. They need not have worried. David Sciarra became the third executive director of the Education Law Center in 1996. Mr. Sciarra was recruited to the Education Law Center after serving as a civil rights attorney in New Jersey, including ten years at the Office of the Public Advocate. Under Mr. Sciarra's leadership, the Education Law Center has greatly expanded its capacity to provide services to individual parents and groups seeking legal assistance in the resolution of problems affecting the education of poor children and children with disabilities.

Professor David Mayrowitz, with the School of Education at the University of Illinois at Chicago and a former consultant with the Education Law Center, described Mr. Sciarra as resilient and extremely hardworking. "His commitment to social justice and his advocacy for the right of all children in New Jersey to have a quality educational experience cannot be overstated. He is a master of the long work day and the consum-mate public service attorney." This writer can attest to Mr. Sciarra's work schedule as he granted her a three-hour interview on Thanksgiving eve in 2003, immediately following an all-day meeting with the thirty school superintendents of *Abbott* districts.

Dr. Fred G. Burke was Commissioner of Education in New Jersey from 1974 to 1982. He was appointed by Governor Brendan Byrne. Prior to joining the Byrne administration, he was Commissioner of Education for the state of Rhode Island. The *New York Times* (2005) described his tenure as "stepping into the center of a storm." Over the eight years, Dr. Burke, a Democrat, became a target of teachers' unions, school boards, disgruntled taxpayers, and political foes as he pushed for accountability by students, teachers, and administrators, while New Jersey imposed its first income tax to reverse the slide of a school system that discriminated against children in poorer districts.

Brendan T. Byrne was the Democratic governor of the state from 1974 to 1982. Prior to being elected governor, he served as a lawyer, prosecutor, and Supreme Court judge. His legacy includes signing the state's first income tax into law, preserving the Pinelands (a pine tree-lined area identified by Rutgers University as an area in need of protection against overdevelopment), and bringing casino gambling to Atlantic City. In an interview for station NJN (New Jersey News), he said he wanted his legacy to be that he "fought for a better educational system and better treatment of the underprivileged" ((Byrne, 2004).

Thomas Kean was born in New York City in 1935 to a long line of New Jersey politicians. He attended the elite St. Albans School and Princeton and Columbia Universities. Originally a teacher of history and government, he was elected in 1967 to the New Jersey Assembly. He served as the New Jersey House Speaker in 1972, and was minority leader in 1974. He served as the Republican Governor of New Jersey from 1982 to 1990.

James Florio was born in New York City in 1937. He graduated from Rutgers University Law School in 1967. He was a Democratic member of the New Jersey Assembly from 1970-1974, a member of the U. S. House of Representatives from 1975–1989, and Governor of New Jersey from 1990 to 1994.

Christine Todd Whitman was born in 1946 in New York City and raised in New Jersey. She attended the Chapin School in New York City and was a 1968 graduate of Wheaton College. She was the Republican Governor of New Jersey from 1994-2001, when she left the governorship to serve in the Bush Administration as Secretary of the Environmental Protection Agency.

James McGreevey was born in Jersey City and attended St. Joseph High School in Metuchen. He attended The Catholic University of America before graduating from Columbia University in 1978. He later earned a law degree from Georgetown University in 1981 and a master's degree in education from Harvard University in 1982. He was the Democratic governor of New Jersey from 2002 to 2004 when he resigned from office.

Raymond Arthur Abbott, the lead plaintiff in *Abbott v. Burke*, was a twelve-year-old Camden Public School student when the Education Law Center filed the case. The names of the twenty children were arranged in alphabetical order and he came to represent all the children from urban school districts in New Jersey. Contrary to public opinion, his mother was a teacher in the Camden Public School system and his natural father (who died when Abbott was nine) was a Presbyterian minister, and his stepfather was an assistant principal (Kladko, 1997).

Sheldon Elliott (1959), in his book titled *Improving Our Courts,* wrote that "New Jersey's [judicial] system embodies a combination of the features proposed as models… [They] have placed New Jersey in the vanguard of the states." The judicial system and the judges who comprise the system played a major role in both the *Robinson* and *Abbott* cases. The story of the judicial system in New Jersey will be discussed in the next chapter.

NEW JERSEY COURTS

D. W. Brogan wrote,

If you want to see the old common law in all its picturesque formality, with its fictions and its fads, its delays and uncertainties, the place to look for them is not London, not in the Modern Gothic of the Law Courts in the Strand, but in New Jersey. Dickens, or any other law reformer of a century ago, would feel more at home in Trenton than in London. (Brogan, 1943)

The 1947 constitution brought change to all of New Jersey's political institutions, but especially to the courts. The popular phrase "Jersey Justice" was a pithy description of the pre-1947 judicial system. It was a contemptuous allusion to "the most complicated scheme of courts existing in any English-speaking nation" (Hendrickson, 1957). Based on a model Britain abandoned in the nineteenth century, an archaic structure of separate law and equity courts and a welter of inferior courts reflected the state's innate parochialism and hostility to change.

Yet "Jersey Justice" also had a positive meaning. Politics infused the judiciary as it did everything else, but a certain propriety occurred when choosing high court judges. When making nominations, governors followed a tradition of bipartisan balance. Even reformer Arthur Vanderbilt—first chief justice under the new constitution and long-time opponent of the Hudson County machine—admitted that county party organizations lifted up talented jurists. Vanderbilt thought it wrong to foresee "a governor and a senate appointing bad judges to the court of last resort" because "with a very few exceptions over the last hundred years" this had not happened. Organizational deficiencies, not the caliber of the justice dispensed, were the major impetus for the 1947 judicial reforms.

The new constitution's judicial clause called upon the new chief justice to implement massive reforms. The job fell to Arthur T. Vanderbilt, dean of the New York University Law School, and long-time Essex County political leader, and nationally known court-reform scholar. Vanderbilt's ten years as chief justice left an indelible mark on the organization and administration of the courts (Salmore & Salmore, 1998, pp. 182-183).

Before 1947, New Jersey had separate law and equity courts; several county and state courts with overlapping roles; a misleadingly named "supreme court"; and a court of errors and appeals, to which cases from the supreme court and some other courts could be appealed. The court of errors and appears had sixteen members, including ten lay judges. A 1947 constitutional convention delegate described it as a "little larger than a jury, little less than a mob" (Rich, 1957, p. 173).

The new constitution abolished the separate law and equity courts that required resort to the law courts and their adversarial process for assessing damages and to the equity courts for fact-finding, injunctions, and other court orders. Instead, it created a single three-tier court system, with equity and law divisions. The system was also reorganized functionally and geographically.

The superior court has jurisdiction over all matters originating in the state courts. Its law division handles all civil and criminal actions, including small claims cases assigned to the special civil part. The equity division deals with requests for injunctions, orders compelling performance of contracts, probate of contest estates, and family concerns (e.g., juvenile delinquency, domestic violence, adoptions, and divorces).

Superior court judges sit in fifteen vicinages, headquartered in county courthouses. Eleven counties have separate vicinages. There are two multi-county vicinages in the south (Atlantic and Cape May; Gloucester, Cumberland, and Salem) and two in the west (Morris and Sussex; Somerset, Hunterdon, and Warren). In each vicinage, an assignment judge devises the calendar for all its judges. Judges generally hear cases of a single type (civil, criminal, or equity). Superior court cases are heard by a single judge, and only murder cases must have jury trials.

The appellate division of superior court sits in Hackensack, Newark, and Trenton. Two- or three-judge panels hear appeals of lower-court and administrative-law decisions and publish written opinions. The appellate division may not overturn such decisions, but may reduce sentences or damages. Appellate judges review procedures, jury instructions, and statutory interpretations.

Atop the system is the seven-member supreme court, sitting in Trenton. It is the only New Jersey court in which all of the member judges hear all of the cases. The high court only accepts cases with substantial constitutional questions, a dissent in an appellate court decision, or the imposition of a death sentence. At least three justices must agree to hear a case. Because of the court's strict interpretation of its jurisdiction, it hears fewer cases than most state supreme courts. In a comparison of New Jersey with five other states (California, Kentucky, Michigan, Nebraska, and Arizona) the New Jersey Supreme Court issued the fewest opinions (Fino, 1987; Salmore & Salmore, 1998).

When Arthur Vanderbilt became the new system's first chief justice, he paid as much attention to his administrative role as he did to deciding cases. He pushed his judges to decide cases within four weeks and admonished them if they took longer, and he would insist that they submit weekly status reports. His successors have required the same efficiency. The legacy he left the court is best indicated by Bernard Swartz, a leading judicial scholar, when he ranked New Jersey first among the states in judicial power over rulemaking and third in centralized management of the courts (Glick, 1979).

New Jersey's judges have long been noted for their high caliber and professionalism. Judges on the Supreme Court are also known for their activism. In a 1988 article by Tarr and Porter, they describe the distinctive ethos of New Jersey judges as emanating from the states' political culture (Tarr & Porter, 1988). Under New Jersey's first constitution of 1776, the governor was chief magistrate, and the legislature gave this role to the state's most distinguished citizens. Even during the heyday of the party machines under the second constitution of 1844–1947, there was respect for the role of judges. The court has continued to insulate itself from the prevailing political culture in the state and created a distinctive state legal culture.

Since 1947, each of New Jersey's chief justices has previously served as an elected or appointed official, and none has disdained "the political thicket." As party organizations weakened and the legislature's power centers fragmented, the courts were increasingly called on to resolve difficult political issues. As the legislature gained independence from the governor, both branches looked to the courts to resolve disputes between them (Salmore & Salmore, 1998, p.188).

All New Jersey judges must be members of the bar for at least ten years when named to the bench. All are nominated by the governor and confirmed by the senate. After a seven-year probationary period, judges reconfirmed by the senate receive tenure and may serve until mandatory retirement at age seventy. The system is unusual in several respects. Only seven other states have no judges elected by the public or the legislature. In most states, judges undergo periodic review. Only Rhode Island grants life tenure initially; only Massachusetts and New Hampshire, in addition to New Jersey, grant tenure after a probationary period until age seventy (Council of State Governments, 1987).

Despite their diminished role, county party organizations are still active in naming judges. Vacancies in the lower courts are first identified as "belonging" to the Democrats or Republicans, in accord with bipartisan tradition. Informal negotiations among county party organizations, bar organizations, and local state senators produce names to submit to the governor, who may also have other candidates in mind. In this competition for judgeships, "rarely does the individual without 'connections' and without a record of partisan political activity do well" (Salmore & Salmore, 1998, p. 189). In publicly reprimanding two superior court judges for accompanying politically active spouses to Governor James

Florio's 1990 inaugural ball, Chief Justice Wilentz acknowledged many jurists' past political activity, but asserted, "that stops completely and without exception on becoming a judge…The prohibition is absolute" (Carter, 1990).

In an interview conducted with Fred Burke, former commissioner of education under Brendan Byrne, Dr. Burke indicated when he

…was Commissioner of Education in Rhode Island, Brendan Byrne cast a wide net for his cabinet members. He had people in his Cabinet that were from as far away as Israel. He sent an attorney to interview me. The attorney later became the Chief Justice of the New Jersey Supreme Court, Robert Wilentz. While I was in agreement with all of the Abbott decisions, I couldn't say it at the time. As a political scientist, I was intrigued by the case and all the machinations that went on behind the scenes. Judge Wilentz gave me autographed copies of Abbott II. He died in 1996 and I attended his funeral along with Brendan Byrne (personal interview conducted December 1, 2003).

Dr. Burke cherished the signed copies of the decisions by Judge Wilentz. Dr. Burke also related during this interview that Brendan Byrne hosted an annual dinner of members of his cabinet. The interconnectedness of a personal relationship with a political relationship, particularly between an activist judge (Wilentz), a former activist judge and governor (Byrne), and an activist commissioner (Burke) cannot be overstated.

Outside observers and the justices themselves repeatedly describe the New Jersey Supreme Court as a leader among "activist" state courts. "Activism" has many guises. One is a reliance on state grounds to find new or expanded constitutional rights. Another is limited attention to precedent. Most fundamentally, an "activist" court involves itself heavily in public policy.

New Jersey's high court meets all these criteria. Its justices are much less likely than those of other states to say that precedent is important and are more likely to say that policy-making is a proper judicial function. The New Jersey court also more often has before it issues depending on state statutes (Salmore & Salmore, 1998, p. 191). Tarr and Porter (1988, p. 247) write that New Jersey's high court is often "unwilling to defer to the expertise or stature of the United States Supreme Court."

Tarr and Porter provide a useful list of the major categories of state supreme court policymaking. Courts may be innovative by overturning or filling in gaps in state policy and imposing a specific policy. Secondly, they can set a policy agenda by upsetting traditional policies without specifying a new alternative. Third, their decisions may be complementary by aiding legislative policy goals or "taking the heat" for the legislature. Fourth, they may be elaborative by extending federal precedent. Alternatively, they can be restrictive by limiting or evading U.S. Supreme Court decisions. Finally, they can seek to advance the judicial institution by preserving the autonomy and integrity of the courts and seeking sufficient financial support for the court system (Tarr & Porter, 1988, pp. xvi-xviii).

The New Jersey Supreme Court has involved itself in two controversial policy-setting arenas: school funding and land-use regulation. These interventions, which affect every municipality and many individuals, and which challenge New Jersey's home-rule tradition, have brought the court to public attention. The New Jersey high court has not hesitated to involve itself in state policy-making. Its role, however, is even greater than this inventory suggests. When called upon, as it frequently is, to referee disputes between the branches of government, it also affects policy significantly. The court has not hesitated to impose remedies when it perceives legislative irresolution or irresponsibility (Baker & Green, 2002).

DEFINING MOMENTS FOR EDUCATION IN NEW JERSEY

Robinson v. Cahill: The Antecedent of Abbott v. Burke

Rosenburg (1991), in his book *The Hollow Hope,* argued that courts can achieve significant social transformations only under very carefully specified conditions. Because courts lack the institutional tools to undertake major social restructuring, the success of their agendas depends on other branches of government and popular support (Reed, 2001, p. 15).

When *Robinson v. Cahill* was filed in 1970, several New Jersey Supreme Court justices were nearing retirement. The case was decided in 1973, and only three members of the Weintraub court, which served through the 1960s, were still sitting. By the fall of 1974, they would all be gone. Salmore and Salmore (1998) reported that Weintraub preferred a three-pronged strategy when dealing with public officials. First, he thought it important to leave lawmakers wondering—and worrying—what the court would do next if they did not act. Second, he believed interim remedies should be distasteful enough to all parties to provide a strong incentive to act. Third, to encourage quick action, any remedy should also withhold government benefits from everyone affected.

Shank (1969) reported in *New Jersey Reapportionment Politics* that Weintraub successfully employed this strategy to achieve a constitutionally acceptable legislative reapportionment plan in the late 1960s and early 1970s. The court never specified detailed reapportionment plans, but rather used Weintraub's devices to compel politicians to come up with them.

Lehne (1978) reports that when Justice Weintraub retired, former governor Richard Hughes became Chief Justice. Justice Hughes chose to allow the state legislature to formulate proposals to resolve the issue but also granted the legislature a year's delay. There were people in New Jersey who saw this delay as a sign of retreat and indecision. Considerable political wrangling enveloped the state legislature and the New Jersey Supreme Court.

The *Robinson* case immersed the court in the details of the state's school finance formula, and the justices, not being trained in education finance, needed help in understanding the formula's complexities. The court addressed specific questions to the New Jersey State Department of Education, which provided details on expenditures district-by-district. Since the department was the only source for the information and the department was in fact one of the defendants, this made for a very unusual situation.

Reed (2001); Firestone, Goertz, and Natriello (1997); and Lehne (1978) reviewed how actively engaged the courts and the Byrne Administration were in seeing that the problem was resolved. Governor Byrne had personally addressed the court and advised the judges that they had their own reputation to protect in making the *Robinson* decision.

The New Jersey Superior Court based its 1973 ruling in *Robinson v. Cahill* on the constitution's "thorough and efficient" (T&E) education clause. The court defined the constitutional requirement as "that educational opportunity which is needed in the contemporary setting to equip a child for his role as a citizen and as a competitor in the labor market" (*Robinson v. Cahill*, 1972), and ruled that the school funding system was unconstitutional. It recounted the history of the thorough and efficient clause in the context of a 19th century concern for ensuring that a free public education be extended to all students in the state in order to secure "the common rights of all" (New Jersey Constitution of 1844 by amendments adopted in 1875, p. 287). The court's ruling was based on the gross inequities that the property-tax-based system of funding created. The bulk of the decision was dedicated to listing the various deficiencies in poor school districts throughout the state, due to the fact that they had insufficient revenues.

The ruling spoke of closets serving as libraries, people teaching for over twenty years with only "emergency" teaching certificates, and science textbooks dating back thirty years, when walking on the moon was still considered fiction. It assailed the concept of local control as a defense of the current system of funding through property taxes, declaring that "local control and responsibility cannot be used to justify a system that breed substantial disparities in the quality of education…local control is illusory. It is control for the wealthy, not for the poor" (*Robinson v. Cahill*, 1972).

The New Jersey Supreme Court slightly modified, but substantively affirmed, the ruling (*Robinson v. Cahill,* 1972). Upon hearing further arguments from the state, however, the Court, out of deference to separation of powers, allowed the current funding system, which was to remain untouched until there was sufficient time for legislative action to be taken. The Court set a deadline of December 31, 1974, for the legislature to enact a new, more equalized funding system, which was to take effect no later than July 1, 1975 (*Robinson v. Cahill,* 1972).

In May of 1975, the Court issued a ruling that extended the legislature's deadline; although it allowed the current system to apply for one more year, the Court warned that it would impose its own provisional system for the 1977-78 school year unless the legislature complied with its prior rulings (*Robinson v. Cahill,* 69 N.J. 449, 1975). Following this ruling, however, the legislature passed the Public Education Act of 1975. The law stated that

The goal of a thorough and efficient system of free public schools shall be to provide to all children in New Jersey, regardless of socioeconomic status or geographic location, the educational opportunity which will prepare them to function politically, economically, and socially in a democratic society. (New Jersey State Assembly, 18A:7A-4)

The Court, in its ruling on the constitutionality of the law, reaffirmed a position it had taken since its first *Robinson* decision—"if the local government cannot carry the burden of adequately funding education, the State must itself meet its continuing obligation" (*Robinson v. Cahill,* 1976). The Court found that the law did not fully address this obligation, but it did not specify from where state funds would come to fulfill this duty. "The 1975 Act is silent as to how this contingency of local fiscal inability is to be met. It does not say, in so many words where the money is to come from in the event of a showing that a local school district is performing inadequately due to a fiscal insufficiency." Nevertheless, the Court upheld the constitutionality of the law, "assuming it is fully funded" (*Robinson v. Cahill*, 1976).

The legislature did not authorize funding for the bill the next year, so the case was again presented before the Supreme Court. As a result, the Court ruled that "the existing unconstitutional system of financing the schools into yet another school year cannot be tolerated" (*Robinson v. Cahill*, 1976). The Court declared that "On and after July 1, 1976, every public officer, state, country or municipal, is hereby enjoined from expending any funds for the support of any free public school" (*Robinson v. Cahill,* 1976). The case had now come before the court for the seventh and last time. The court finally applied a Weintraub-like stratagem, making the outcome unfavorable and untenable for everyone involved, and shut down the schools.

The New Jersey Supreme Court shut down the unconstitutionally funded public school system. It was summer, and 100,000 children in summer school and in year-round programs for the handicapped were affected. On July 9, 1976, the legislature passed an income-tax package and funding plan acceptable to the Court, and *Robinson v. Cahill* came to an end. But it was only an apparent end, because the plan still contained constitutional defects justices had previously criticized. There was education "peace" for five years, and then the longest running school finance reform case, *Abbott v. Burke*, was filed (National Conference of State Legislatures, 2005; Salmore & Salmore, 1998).

Richard Lehne, professor of political science at Rutgers University and author of *The Quest for Justice: The Politics of School Finance Reform*, chronicled the *Robinson v. Cahill* saga. Professor Lehne writes that

…this study of the Robinson v. Cahill litigation did not see a supreme court resolve a long simmering conflict; to the contrary, in this case a court ignited such a dispute. In New Jersey, the courts were used to bringing an important matter before the legislature, which the busy and reluctant members would have preferred to ignore. Much to their displeasure, the New Jersey Supreme Court placed the issues of education, school finance, and taxation squarely before the two chambers, and the legislators had no choice but to deal with them. The court raised the issues and then granted the legislature surprising latitude to develop its response. The posture of the New Jersey court was so permissive in this case that it eventually approved a new education program that reinstated many of the constitutional defects that it had previously criticized. In this instance, the New Jersey Supreme Court was not making decisions about the content of public policies, but was raising issues for consideration by other governmental institutions. The court performed here an agenda-setting function rather than a decision-making one. (Lehne, 1978)

Lehne describes the characteristics of the *Robinson* decision and used the following words: *ambiguity, persistence, visibility, immediacy, legitimacy,* and *intrusive.* The court was ambiguous because it refused to define precise policy standards in its opinion because it consciously sought to fill the agenda-setting role, because it wanted to circumscribe the legal implications of its ruling, and because it did not know itself what policy standards it favored. The persistence of the court's mandate complicated the state's policy formation task even more. Since the decision would not go away, it became the vehicle for many groups in the state to attempt to promote business efficiency of school operations, others sought to enrich specialized educational activities, and still others saw in it the need to enact a personal income tax.

While the debate over the case lasted more than three years from April 1973 to July 1976, the court did set deadlines for the legislature to respond.

The New Jersey Supreme Court focused attention on education issues at a time that would not have been selected by the department, the legislature, or the education community in general. During the mid-1970s, negative views of education were ascendant in Trenton, and the department was less prepared to cope with basic issues than it had been in the past or would be in the future. Robinson articulated the cares and aspirations of the 1960s, but it suffered from the excesses of those years and from the restraints of the 1970s. By the mid-1970s, organizational concerns about the problems of urban and disadvantaged communities were not as prominent in New Jersey education circles as they once had been, and the funds from federal and state sources did not flow as freely. (Lehne, 1978, p. 205)

Judicial involvement in *Robinson* also gave the issue a legitimacy and a visibility it otherwise would not have had, since local newspapers wrote about the decisions on the front pages and indicated it was a problem that had to be dealt with. The final quality Lehne (1978) describes is the intrusiveness of the case. The case would not go away, and hence it forced all of the policy organizations to deal with education and its financing.

ABBOTT V. BURKE: SON OF ROBINSON V. CAHILL

Toward Equal Educational Opportunity

The notion of educational opportunity and equality must compete with individualism and social mobility in the United States (Coons, Clune, & Sugarman, 1970). As seen in *Robinson v. Cahill*, the best intentions of the New Jersey Supreme Court, the Byrne Administration, and the state legislature could not deter education activists in the state from following up with another round of litigation.

Abbott v. Burke I

In February 1981, the Education Law Center filed *Abbott v. Burke*. The new case was brought against Fred G. Burke, Commissioner of Education, on behalf of twenty students from Camden, East Orange, Irvington, and Jersey City, and similarly situated students in other urban school districts in the state. It charged that the new income-tax package and funding plan passed under *Robinson* was insufficient to provide for education of poor children in the state. The case alleged that the state's school-financing formula, which relies in large part on local property tax revenues, denies poor children the same educational opportunity afforded students attending public schools in wealthier communities. Urban school boards and advocates for the poor argued that "the continued funding disparities between wealthy and poor school districts have a direct correlation to the quality of education provided to students" (Sheil, 2000).

Savage Inequalities (Kozol, 1991) details, in a chapter entitled "Children of the City Invincible," the disparities between schools in Camden and Cherry Hill, a seven-minute ride from one another. It juxtaposes the fact that students in Camden learn how to type on old Olympia typewriters while children from Cherry Hill or Princeton learn on computers. Additionally, the chapter describes how children in science classes in Camden are forced to study chemistry and physics by merely reading the textbooks because they do not have the requisite laboratories to conduct the experiments.

When Fred Burke was named commissioner of education in 1974, he was required to represent the Byrne administration's vision of "thorough and efficient" education. He told this researcher quite candidly, "I was met with the question, what am I going to do about T&E, when I arrived in New Jersey? I had no idea what the heck these people were talking about" (Burke, 2003). Soon he would learn that the people in the legislative branch of government wanted to impose accountability standards that would involve testing. It would be his responsibility to develop the Byrne administration's position. Dr. Burke was adamantly opposed to the accountability component that would call for mandatory testing. Dr. Burke believed that "education is a continuous cycle of obtaining and synthesizing new information and it cannot be tested at grades 3, 8, and 10" (Burke, 2003).

The Education Law Center learned from the *Robinson* case to form alliances with members of the education community and other activist groups to make a strong case for *Abbott.* They were joined by the Greater Newark Urban Coalition, a group of civic and social leaders in the state that had considerable stature in their respective communities. They agreed that testing was a way to promote accountability, and test scores were a tangible way to verify that additional money did make a difference in outcomes for urban school children.

The Education Law Center drafted the language for the bill mandating that tests and state standards become a part of the educational process. Within weeks, the bill passed the state assembly with support from both sides of the aisle. The bill was altered when it reached the state senate based on considerable lobbying by the New Jersey Education Association (NJEA). The NJEA was concerned that, if children could not pass a requisite test, then the classroom preparation that led to the failure would not only be the fault of the student and parents, but would also lead to teachers being held accountable. The largest teachers' association (National Education Association) has consistently resisted accountability measures that would impose teacher standards on their respective memberships (Ravitch and Finn, 1987; Ravitch, 1987).

There was considerable horse-trading around the notion of accountability and how it would be operationalized in the state. Finally, with the amendment that the senate agreed to, and with the support of the watered-down accountability measures the NJEA could support, the "state guidelines and local standards" were adopted by the State Board of Education in February 1978. These guidelines essentially defined "thorough and efficient" in process terms. The state was to monitor all schools annually on over 300 items, including financial management, curriculum planning, goal setting, and facilities planning, as well as basic skills achievement. Passing scores for the basic skills tests were set low enough that urban pass rates would not be fatally embarrassing, but high enough to require tangible support for schools. A study of participants in local goal-setting meetings found many attendees to be NJEA members or their relatives (Felzenberg, 1978; Salmore & Salmore, 1998). The tax issue ostensibly cost William Cahill the governorship. Brendan Byrne, Cahill's successor, was not going to be another casualty of taxpayer ire.

Judicial review of legislative acts enjoys a long and vibrant history in New Jersey (Williams, 1997; Sheil, 2000). The two authors report that the judicial branch's actions define the reputation of the court. The New Jersey Constitution, however, has an "express separation of powers doctrine." Specifically, it states "The powers of the government shall be divided among three distinct branches, the legislative, executive, and judicial. No person or persons belonging to or constituting one branch shall exercise any of the powers properly belonging to either of the others, except as expressly provided in this Constitution" (Williams, 1997).

Abbott v. Burke I claimed the *Robinson* remedy did not ensure urban students a "thorough and efficient" education. It reiterated that Chapter 212 violated the state constitution's equal protection and antidiscrimination clauses. When the New Jersey Supreme Court ruled in *Abbott I* in 1985, the Court recognized the presence of constitutional claims but determined that the case should be remanded to an administrative judge for factual matters to be established such as:

1. whether the plaintiffs suffered substantial educational deficiencies;
2. if the Act's funding scheme resulted in gross disparities among school districts and endangered inequalities in educational resources;
3. if the State's obligation to provide a constitutionally-mandated education to special-needs children could be met only by increasing financial aid to their schools.

Abbott I was a procedural mandate that put the case in the hands of an Administrative Law Judge. After nine months of hearings, Administrative Law Judge Steven Lefelt rendered a 607-page decision in August 1988. Judge Lefelt ruled for the plaintiffs:

I find the pervasive nature of the political intrusion into Jersey City's school system shocking and harmful to the school children and qualitatively and quantitatively different from the pressures present in most other property-poor districts. The expenditure differences are in some cases greater now than before Chapter 212 was enacted. I have concluded that the funding law contains systemic defects which contribute to the continued inequity. (Abbott v. Burke, 1985)

By the time the ruling was issued, Fred Burke was no longer Commissioner of Education. When Thomas Kean was elected governor and took office in 1982, he named Saul Cooperman to be Commissioner of Education. Dr. Saul Cooperman rejected Judge Lefelt's reasoning and issued his own 234-page response on February 3, 1989:

No one has ever determined there is a minimum amount of funding necessary to provide a thorough and efficient education. Rather, the opposite is true. If a district is found to meet the criteria established by the State for T&E, then its spending is, by legal definition, adequate. (Goertz, 1979)

The factual findings documented extreme disadvantages and unmet needs faced by the students in the special needs district. The case was then appealed to the Supreme Court due to the Commissioner's refusal to mandate equal programs and expenditures for the urban districts.

Abbott v. Burke II

On June 5, 1990, the New Jersey Supreme Court concurred with Judge Lefelt and ruled that Chapter 212 was unconstitutional as it applied to poorer urban districts bcause the education delivered to the students was neither thorough nor efficient (*Abbott II*). The justices found that:

...under the present system...the poorer the district and the greater its need, the less the money available, and the worse the education... Education has failed there, for both the student and the State (Abbott II at 295).

Firestone, Goertz, and Natriello report that

...in these two Abbott decisions, the court expanded the constitutional standard for a thorough and efficient education to one that assures disadvantaged students the opportunity to compete in, and to contribute to, the society entered by their relatively advantaged peers. (Firestone, Goertz, & Natriello, 1997, p. 23)

"Thorough and efficient means more than teaching the skills needed to compete in the labor market" *(Abbott II at 363),* the definition the court had established in *Robinson I.* It means the ability to fulfill one's role as a citizen; participate fully in society, in the life of one's community; to appreciate music, art, and literature, and to share that with friends. The justices wrote:

We have decided this case on the premise that the children of poorer urban districts are as capable as all others; that their deficiencies stem from their socioeconomic status; and that through effective education and changes in that socioeconomic status, they can perform as well as others. Our constitutional mandate does not allow us to consign poorer children permanently to an inferior education on the theory that they cannot afford a better one or that they would not benefit from it. (Abbott II at 340)

The court then determined that the constitutional mandate of a thorough and efficient education had not been satisfied in poorer urban districts. It based its conclusions on both the absolute level of education in those districts and on the comparison of educational programs in science, foreign language, computers, music and art, industrial arts, and physical education with those in affluent suburban districts (Firestone, Goertz, Natriello, 1997; Sheil 2000; Kozol, 1991). Chief Justice Robert Wilentz wrote the unanimous opinion.

The court did not directly address the question of whether low property values caused lower spending, though it obviously believed that they did. The notion that poor children should accept an education that was inferior to suburban children appeared to offend the Supreme Court justices (Schrag, 2003). Justice Wilentz denounced the thinking of state education authorities by indicating

...the social and economic pressures on municipalities, school districts and citizens of these disaster areas...are so severe that tax increases in any substantial amount are almost unthinkable. To pejoratively label...resistance to increased taxes as "political" fails to recognize the situation that some school boards face. (Abbott v. Burke, 1990)

The Court agreed that twenty-eight (1990) poorer urban districts be classified as special need districts.

After 1976, the legislature fully funded the aid formula only in fiscal year 1981 and fiscal year 1985, both gubernatorial election years. Governor Thomas Kean (1982-1990) would not expend his enormous political capital on the case, so it was left to the education advocates and the judiciary to continue to push for additional funding. The court went on to define which students were, in terms of dollar "inputs," being denied a "thorough and efficient" education. They relied on data from the Department of Education dividing school districts into eight economic District Factor Groups, labeled A, with lowest per-pupil spending, through J, with highest per-pupil spending (New Jersey Department of Education, 2005; Mackey, 2002; Sheil, 2000).

The legislature was given a year to "devise any remedy...as long as it achieves a thorough and efficient education as defined herein for poorer urban districts." The program could be phased in over five years. New Jersey's Supreme Court thus became the first to define educational equity for students in poor districts as the level of effort on behalf of students in the wealthiest districts.

In concluding their landmark opinion, the justices noted that with New Jersey's minority student population approaching a third of all students—highly concentrated in urban districts—"it is not just that their future depends on the state, the state's future depends on them...After all the analyses are completed, we are still left with these students and their lives. They are not being educated. Our constitution says they must be."

As a result of the *Abbott II* decision, twenty-eight districts were identified as special needs districts: Asbury Park, Bridgeton City, Burlington City, Camden City, East Orange City, Elizabeth City, Garfield City, Gloucester City, Harrison Town, Hoboken City, Irvington Township, Jersey City, Keansburg Borough, Long Branch City, Millville City, New Brunswick, Newark, City of Orange Township, Passaic City, Paterson, Pemberton Township, Perth Amboy, Phillipsburg Town, Pleasantville City, Trenton, Union City, Vineland, and West New York Town. As a result of petitioning to be considered an *Abbott* district, Neptune Township and Plainfield were added in 1999. Salem City was added in 2004, bringing the current list of *Abbott* districts to thirty-one.

In May 1990, Governor James Florio introduced the Quality Education Act (QEA) in anticipation of a Supreme Court decision in favor of the *Abbott* children. He introduced a $2.8 billion state tax increase to pay for the new law and the budget deficit he inherited from the Kean years. In June 1990, the New Jersey Supreme Court ruled in *Abbott II* that inadequate and unequal funding denies students in urban districts a thorough and efficient education and requires the State to equalize funding between suburban and urban districts for regular education and to provide extra or "supplemental" programs to "wipe out disadvantages as much as a school district can."

Unfortunately, Governor Florio did not sell a plan for a "One New Jersey" educational policy, nor did he wait for an audit to find new revenues. He proposed $1.4 billion in increased income taxes dedicated to education aid and property tax relief as part of the $2.8 billion tax package. The complex Quality Education Act (QEA) was pushed through the legislature in 22 days and passed in June 1990 with no Republican support. Implemented over four years, almost half the new aid would go to 30 urban districts with low "educational inputs"—decaying school buildings, inexperienced teachers, outdated curricula, and inadequate equipment. The other half would go to "middle class districts," mostly in the southern half of the state where property values were lower. About a quarter of all districts, with a fifth of the students, would gradually lose all state equalization aid over four years. The number of districts affected and the plan cost went far beyond the mandate of *Abbott v. Burke.* Dissatisfaction with the QEA came from school boards teachers and citizens (Salmore & Salmore, 1997, p. 274; Firestone, Goertz, & Natriello, 1997; Masell & Fuhrman, 1994; Goertz, 1995).

The Court in *Abbott II* and in subsequent rulings ordered the State to assure that urban school children received an adequate and constitutional education through a comprehensive set of programs and reforms, including standards-based education supported by parity funding, supplemental programs, preschool education, and school facilities improvements. The Court explicitly limited the programs and reforms to a class of school districts identified as "poorer urban districts" or "special needs districts." Under *Abbott II*, twenty-eight districts were identified as *Abbott* districts based on the following criteria:

- Must be classified by the Department of Education as urban;
- Must be those with the lowest socio-economic status, thus assigned to the lowest categories on the Department of Education's District Factor Group (DFG) scale;
- "Evidence of substantive failure of thorough and education." including "failure to achieve what the Department of Education considers passing levels of performance on the High School Proficiency Test (HSPT)";
- A large percentage of disadvantaged students who need "an education beyond the norm";
- Existence of an "excessive tax [for] municipal services" in the locality where the district is located; and
- A large percentage of students of color.

Governor Florio, although born in New York, spent a considerable amount of his professional career in Camden, New Jersey, and wanted urban education to be his highest priority. "We want to have one New Jersey as opposed to multiple New Jerseys…We don't have one New Jersey in terms of its education system." Governor Florio advocated equalized funding and acknowledged the political task of his administration would be to persuade people that education was not an "us and them—it is us" (Braun, 1990, p. 1).

On July 3, 1990, one month after the *Abbott v. Burke* decision, Governor Florio signed into law a new school-funding formula. At the time of its passage, it was hailed as a major step toward achieving education equity in New Jersey. However, over the course of nine months of its introduction, it was buffeted with criticism from citizens and major education interest groups throughout the state. In March 1991, four months before the QEA was to take effect, it was watered down to provide for greater property tax relief and less aid to the financially strapped urban school districts (Firestone, Goertz, & Natriello, 1997).

Due to the uproar around the state, Governor Florio in March 1991 signed an amendment to the Quality Education Act that diverted $360 million to property tax relief (www.edlawcenter.org). *Abbott* required the state to have transition aid, categorical aid, and established expenditure caps for district and state aid. In July 1992, the Education Law Center reactivated the *Abbott* case charging that the QEA failed to comply with the 1990 *Abbott II* ruling.

Abbott v. Burke III

In July 1994, the New Jersey Supreme Court issued a ruling in *Abbott v. Burke*. In this round of litigation, called *Abbott III*, the court declared the Quality Education Act unconstitutional because it did not equalize funding or guarantee needed supplemental programs in the special needs districts. The court ordered the state to adopt a new funding formula by September 1996 that would assure substantial parity, "approximating 100 percent," and provide for special education needs for the 1997-98 school year. It also charged the state to address the existing disparity in the upcoming school years of 1995-96 and 1996-97. The court retained jurisdiction over the case and agreed to entertain applications for relief if the state did not meet the court's timetable (Education Law Center, 2002-2022; Firestone, Goertz, & Natriello, 1997).

The New Jersey Department of Education released a blueprint designed to achieve equalization between suburban and urban districts by reducing spending in the suburban districts in February 1995; the negotiations continued between legislators, the teachers' union, and education activists. During November 1995, Governor Christine Whitman unveiled a plan to change the school funding formula by capping spending in suburban districts at a minimum level by directing implementation of the New Jersey Core Curriculum Content Standards. In December 1996, Governor Whitman signed into law the Comprehensive Education Improvement and Financing Act (CEIFA) that incorporated her plan, without the spending caps in suburban districts. CEIFA authorized spending in suburban districts at existing levels, and limited spending in urban districts at $1,200 per pupil below the suburban average.

Abbott v. Burke IV

In January 1997, the Education Law Center returned to the Supreme Court to challenge the failure of CEIFA to comply with the 1990 and 1994 *Abbott* rulings. Because CEIFA's regular education funding provisions failed to guarantee parity of educational expenditures between poorer and wealthier school districts, the court declared CEIFA unconstitutional as it applied to the Special Needs Districts. There were eleven *amicus curiae* briefs filed in support of the plaintiffs, among them the City of Newark, the League of Women Voters of New Jersey, the Black Ministers Council, the New Jersey School Boards Association, and the New Jersey Education Association. In May 1997, the New Jersey Supreme Court in *Abbott IV* declared CEIFA unconstitutional and ordered state officials to immediately increase funding for urban schools to parity with suburban schools.

The court also ordered a special hearing before Superior Court Judge Michael Patrick King to determine the supplemental programs needed by disadvantaged children and to determine facility needs in urban districts. After two months of hearings, Judge King recommended to the Supreme Court an implementation package of supplemental programs, including preschool, at an additional cost of $312 million a year, and a program to renovate or replace urban school facilities.

Abbott V

In 1997, the Supreme Court remanded aspects of the school financing case to Superior Court Judge Michael Patrick King to conduct hearings and make findings and recommendations on the need for supplemental programs and facilities improvements in Abbott school districts. Judge King, with the approval of the Supreme Court, designated Dr. Allan Odden, Professor of Educational Administration at the University of Wisconsin-Madison, as Special Master. Dr. Odden, a national expert on public school finance, submitted to Judge King his recommendations on the supplemental services and facilities improvements that he felt were needed to provide the special needs districts with a thorough and efficient education.

Dr. Odden recommended that a whole school reform program called *Success for All* be one of the remedies in effectuating change in the special needs district. The Education Law Center had its own experts: Dr. Margaret Goertz, Professor in the Graduate School of Education at the University Pennsylvania; Dr. Gary Natriello, Professor of Sociology and Education in the Department of Human Development at Teachers College, Columbia University; and Dr. William Firestone, Director of the Center for Educational Policy Analysis and Educational Policy at Rutgers University. They each recommended all day pre-school training for children and extended-day programs for all elementary, middle, and high school students in Abbott districts.

In May 1998, the New Jersey Supreme Court issued *Abbott V* and ordered an unprecedented series of entitlements for urban school children, including whole school reform, full-day kindergarten and preschool for all three- and four-year-olds, and a comprehensive state-managed and -funded facilities program to correct code violations, to eliminate overcrowding, and to provide adequate space for all educational programs in the *Abbott* schools. The supplemental programs also advanced were health and social services, increased security in the schools, technology alternative education, school-to-work programs, and after-school and summer-school programs. New Jersey became the first state in the nation to implement a court-mandated public pre-school for three- and four-year-olds.

Abbott VI

In July 1999, the Education Law Center once again returned to the New Jersey Supreme Court to challenge the State's failure to implement a well-planned, high-quality preschool education for all children in the *Abbott* districts. In March 2000, the New Jersey Supreme Court ruled on *Abbott VI* that the State had failed to implement preschool education as directed, and ordered the New Jersey Department of Education to overhaul its programming for the 2000-2001 school year.

Abbott VII

In May 2000, the New Jersey Supreme Court reaffirmed its prior ruling that the State must fully fund the *Abbott* school construction program, and in July 2000, the legislature enacted the Educational Construction and Financing Act authorizing a school construction program for *Abbott* districts and school districts statewide.

Abbott VIII

On September 25, 2001, the New Jersey Supreme Court listened to arguments on the State's continuing failure to implement preschool. In October 2001, the Appellate Division of Superior Court heard arguments on the failure of the State to establish clear, effective, and comprehensive guidelines for local school and district implementation of Abbott programs and reforms. The Supreme Court issued the first ruling of Abbott *VIII*, and directed the timely state decisions of preschool plans and budget and expected the administrative appeal process to resolve disputes between districts and the Department of Education over the plans and budgets. The Supreme Court issued its second decision on February 21, 2002, and lent additional texture and clarifying points on the requirements for State implementation of the *Abbott V* preschool mandate, as augmented by *Abbott VI.*

James McGreevey assumed office in January 2002 and wanted to have a less combative relationship around funding for education in the state. Governor McGreevey's wife is a former teacher, and he wanted to promote the state as being one that is progressive and hospitable to education issues. The Education Law Center, the attorneys for the Abbott plaintiffs, and the McGreevey Administration established the Abbott Implementation and Compliance Coordinating Council, pursuant to Executive Order #6, bringing together the parties to Abbott, including the Education Law Center, the Governor's office, the Attorney General, Commissioners of Education, Human Services, Higher Education, and the Economic Development Authority to identify implementation problems and solve them.

The Education Law Center in March 2002 agreed to support the McGreevey Administration's application before the Supreme Court for a one-year freeze on further implementation of Abbott remedies at 2002-2003 levels. In exchange, the McGreevey administration agreed to boost preschool spending by $150 million and maintain parity with an additional $83 million in a year when budget deficits required flat State funding to all other school districts.

Abbott IX

On June 4, 2002, the New Jersey Supreme Court issued an order in *Abbott IX* directing the one-year freeze on further implementation of Abbott remedies due to a state budget crisis. Justice James H. Coleman, the first African-American appointed to the State Supreme Court under Governor Christine Todd Whitman, dissented from the decision. Justice Peter Verniero, the former attorney general in the Whitman Administration who was responsible for representing the Department of Education before the court, did not participate in the decision.

Justice Coleman dissented because he did not think there should be a delay or a moratorium put on any of the Abbott implementation plans. He stated that *Abbott IV* and *V* were not based on the state's projected income, and that this change in income should not be a basis for reformation of implementation; he did not agree that there should be a reduction in funding. This marked the first time in the decisions where there appeared to be disagreement and not a unanimous opinion.

Abbott X

Prior to this ruling, the McGreevey Administration issued Executive Order #24 and established the School Construction Corporation. Governor McGreevey wanted to build high-performing schools in not only construction, but instruction. The state continued to be buffeted by financial woes brought on by the Whitman Administration's tax cuts. The Abbott Implementation and Compliance Coordinating Council, established in February 2002, agreed to discontinue meeting because of strong rumors that the McGreevey Administration would seek a second year freeze on funding Abbott and would seek to further roll back the court-ordered mandates.

In March 2003, the McGreevey Administration applied to the Court to remove the mandates for whole school reform and supplemental programs. In April 2003, the Supreme Court directed the parties to mediate the disputed matters before Judge Philip Carchman. Throughout this time, the Education Law Center and the Department of Education engaged in ten days of mediation. In June 2003, the Supreme Court accepted the mediation agreement. The Supreme Court accepted the following points:

- Every Abbott elementary school shall continue to implement whole school reform as required by Abbott V;
- Every Abbott elementary school shall continue to implement selected whole school reform models and establish a set of standards that will help in the remediation of low-performing schools;
- The Department of Education will have jurisdiction in this area and be able to determine if the remediation is sufficient;
- Schools that have not been identified as either low or high performing will continue to commit to whole school reform.

The Supreme Court directed the Department of Education in July 2003 to fund the districts at amounts sufficient to maintain expenditures authorized in the 2002-2003 budgets. In August 2003, a Cooperative Rulemaking group ordered in Abbott X concluded its work on new Abbott regulations. Their work resulted in the New Jersey Department of Education accepting some recommendations and ignoring others.

In addition to the complaints heard from the existent thirty-one Abbott districts, the Appellate Division heard appeals by 21 districts challenging the State's failure to provide $150 million in disputed state aid in January 2004. Meanwhile, the secondary workgroup that was ordered in Abbott X began meeting to develop research-based reform initiatives for Abbott middle and high schools. In February 2004, the evaluation workgroup ordered in Abbott X began meeting to develop protocols for an independent evaluation of Abbott implementation, ordered in Abbott V but not delivered by the Department of Education (Education Law Center, 2002-2022).

MONEY AND GOOD INTENTIONS

New Jersey has gone through more than thirty years of school finance litigation. Beginning in 1973 with the first *Robinson v. Cahill* decision and through ten iterations of *Abbott v. Burke,* school funding has dominated the education landscape in the state. The thirty-one special needs districts with approximately 300,000 public school students have certainly received additional funding; however, there has been no systematic restructuring of New Jersey's finance system (Reed, 2001). The thirty-one school districts gained new programs (full-day kindergarten, early reading literacy, dropout prevention programs, and elementary parent involvement), new resources, new buildings, and some hope that the educational system would improve their children's life chances. An evaluation of the outcome for students in these districts is currently underway by external reviewers.

The New Jersey Supreme Court attempted to settle the matter with their rulings; however, the legislature, in fear of losing their clout and perhaps even their offices, would not advance the cause of the urban districts at the expense of their own. Fennimore (2005) and Anyon (2005) explore the concept of civic responsibility in regard to urban public school equity conflicts and the dilemmas that crop up when people with good intentions for their own children allow themselves to be co-opted by the labels placed on schools. The terms magnet, small school, school choice, charter schools, inter-district open enrollment plans, and voucher programs have created elitist inequitable structures within the public school system. Their contention is the social contract between citizens of the United States makes it important to demand that every child in this country receive a quality education, complete with certified teachers, parental involvement, strong accountability system, clean and safe environment with extracurricular activities, and great libraries.

All children should be equally valued and receive equal consideration, parental choices should not obscure public school accountability for equitable distribution of resources, best practice should remain a universal commitment to all children, full intellectual development should be an unwavering goal for all children, and all choices and options should exist within a full, systemic commitment to equity and excellence. (Fennimore, 1996)

Kozol reports that in New Jersey "far more than incremental gains have been achieved" as a result of *Abbott v. Burke:*

Up until 1997, the funding gap between high-poverty districts and successful, affluent districts was more than $1,000 for each pupil. By 2004, per-pupil spending in high poverty districts had increased to $11,000, the same amount that was being spent, on average, in the schools that served the children of the privileged; and the state has also made available an additional $2,000 for each pupil in the poorest districts to support "at risk" and supplemental programs. Meanwhile, the state has instituted full-day kindergarten and a full-day, full-year pre-K program for all three- and four-year-olds in the low-income districts and is spending an initial allocation of $6 billion to replace or to update school buildings in these districts. (Kozol, 2005, p. 261)

In an interview (2002) with David Sciarra, Executive Director of the Education Law Center, and in subsequent personal correspondence (2004), he indicated that

New Jersey is the first state where funding for children in high-poverty districts like Newark and Camden was equalized at the level spent on children in Cherry Hill and Princeton. Additional funding to the thirty-one special needs districts has also generated additional services like pre-school services and school repairs and building that funding for children in special needs districts are receiving more than their counterparts in wealthier districts.

The research and writings of Kozol (2005); Rebell (2004); Rebell and Wardenski (2004) and Sciarra (2002 and 2003) from research performed by Firestone, Goertz, and Natriello (1997) and the report from *Education Week* (1997) describe that additional resources did make its way to the urban school districts. The Education Law Center worked in partnership with the major education groups, groups representing urban districts, foundation aid districts, and wealthier suburban districts, who each toiled separately and in concert with one another over the course of many years, to reach compromises so the children of New Jersey could all receive a quality education.

A CLOSER LOOK AT THE ABBOTT DISTRICTS

What Does Increased Funding Buy?

In response to *Robinson v. Cahill* (1973) and *Abbott v. Burke* (1985), the New Jersey Supreme Court struck down incarnations of the state's school finance formula four times from 1973 to 1997. In *Abbott*, the high court took the unique step of ordering the state to ensure that public schools in the poorest urban districts are able to spend at the same level as those in the wealthiest suburbs. The court's 1998 blueprint also remains unusual for being highly detailed and prescriptive (whole-school reform models, court mandated full-day kindergarten and preschool, broad social-service programs, enhanced school security and technology, high school dropout programs, and smaller class sizes, as well as a major facilities program to overhaul sub par buildings). Additional programs, such as summer school, could receive funding with demonstrated need, the court said. "We must reach the point where it is possible to say with confidence that the most disadvantaged school children in the state will not be left out or left behind," said a unanimous court in 1998.

Funding

When the class action was filed on behalf of New Jersey's urban school children, the state's poorest districts were spending 40 percent less than its wealthiest ones. Now, with huge infusions of court-required state aid, the *Abbott* districts spend approximately $13,000 per pupil, very nearly what the richest districts spend. That parity of spending, advocates and critics alike contend, can only yield better results in closing the performance gap between privileged and underprivileged children (Gewertz, 2005).

Education Week (2005) reported that policymakers and observers on all sides of the school funding debate nationwide have watched and continue to watch the *Abbott* case closely as a test of whether raising spending levels in poor districts to parity with the wealthiest can significantly improve achievement for students from low-income families. Activists also use it as a case study of how a court's deep involvement in schools' inner workings has benefits—or limits.

Literacy and the Achievement Gap

Gordon MacInnes, Assistant Commissioner of Education in charge of the Abbott District Implementation, agrees that the *Abbott* decisions have greatly enhanced the quality of education in the thirty-one special needs districts. "The achievement gap is closing" but he insisted "there is still more to do. Literacy is the key to the success in all the Abbott districts. If students can learn to read, they will have the ability to perform well in math" (2005).

Seven years into New Jersey's bid to put poor districts on a financial footing with the wealthy districts has provided a mixture of promise and struggle. A review of the outcome information for the school districts in the state appears to bear this out. More than three-hundred elementary schools in the *Abbott* districts have phased in court-ordered, whole-school reform models (school-wide strategies to overhaul instruction and management), and there is an attempt to move the *Abbott* high schools into the whole-school reform model.

New Jersey's language arts test for general education students in the fourth grade shows those in *Abbott* districts improving at a faster rate than students statewide, and those in the worst-performing *Abbott* districts and where state administrators have been conducting intensive intervention in literacy skills are improving as well. *Abbott* districts improved their average passing rate on that test from 63 percent to 75 percent, nearly 13 percent, between 2001 and 2004, compared with the state's 5 percentage point gain. For example, Long Branch, an *Abbott* district, saw 74 percent of its fourth graders pass the language arts test in 2001. In 2004, 85 percent passed, though that proportion still trailed the state average of 90 percent (MacInnes, 2005; Gewertz, 2005; Ritter & Lauver, 2003).

Many of the improvements that *Abbott* elementary schools have experienced continue to be elusive when the topic turns to middle schools and high schools. Gordon MacInnes along with members of the *Abbott* Implementation Division (Office of Early Childhood Education; Office of Student Achievement and Fiscal Support (OSAFS); three Regional OSAFS offices located in northern (East Orange), central (Trenton), and southern (Sewell) Jersey; Office of Middle Grades Literacy and Secondary Education Programs; and the Office of Urban Literacy) are working to provide a coordinated effort to boost education for all education levels of the thirty-one special needs districts.

Fred Carrigg, former Executive Director for Academic Programs with the Union City Public Schools, is "on loan" to the New Jersey Department of Education as the Special Assistant to Gordon MacInnes. Mr. Carrigg is in charge of the Office of Urban Literacy, where he is responsible for assisting *Abbott* districts implement intensive literacy programs and where he works with low-performing schools in accordance with *Abbott* regulations. In a recent interview with *Education Week* (2005), he described the progress the special needs districts are making as "promising and significant."

The plan for Abbott districts is a "road map to a destination," says MacInnes. The achievement disparities in the Fourth Grade Assessment Language Arts exam from 1999 to 2005 have decreased considerably. The achievement gap appears to also be significant in mathematics. The achievement gap and meeting standards on the state's fourth-grade tests have increased markedly. Results at the eighth grade and high school levels have been flat so far (Davis, 2003).

State officials and school advocates theorize that the fourth grade tests are the first evidence that the court's mandates on whole-school reform are beginning to pay off. But some experts say that because some schools and districts have had more success with whole-school improvement than others, and no state evaluation has been performed, ascertaining exactly what is working and why is tricky. Bari A. Erlichson, an education consultant and former Rutgers University professor of public policy who has studied the *Abbott* mandates, has also indicated it is difficult to determine what elements have led to the improvement (*Education Week*, 2005).

PreSchool

The most astounding change has been to the number of children enrolled in *Abbott* preschool programs. Education experts have said this one mandate has changed the education landscape in many New Jersey districts. Preschool enrollment in the *Abbott* districts more than doubled from 19,000 in the 1999-2000 school year, the year the program began, to a projected 43,000 in 2004-2005, more than 80 percent of the three- and four-year-olds in those districts. Some districts, such as Long Branch, have conceived their own programs, while others, such as Trenton, rely largely on community providers. Sharon Shields,

Program Manager for At-Risk Children in the Camden School District, concurs. "The preschool program has been incredible and it has really made a difference to the preparation of children proceeding to kindergarten and first grade." Ms. Shields also reports that "things have been dicey with the middle and secondary schools" (Shields, 2005). Lee and Burkam (2002) recount the acquisition of language by young children because they have attended pre-school.

Since January 2002, the Abbott Implementation Division under the direction of Gordon MacInnes has been driven by two goals set by the New Jersey Supreme Court, and endorsed by the Legislature, taxpayers, parents, and educators. First, Abbott students should master the New Jersey Core Curriculum Content Standards as determined by state assessments; and second, this mastery must be achieved in the most efficient manner possible. He is also concerned that all students in the thirty-one Abbott districts graduate from high school prepared to handle the academics in a four-year university. Mr. MacInnes has indicated he wants the same standards for those graduates who want to pursue college, enter the labor force, or join the military.

The Abbott Implementation Division did not exist four years ago, and Mr. MacInnes has been the Assistant Commissioner for two years. As a former state senator, he is aware that his division operates at the discretion of the Governor.

Particularly on matters of finance and operations, the division abides by policies and schedules set by the administration and legislature, which do not always coincide with the court-ordered schedules for Abbott districts. The fact that Abbott district budgets are rarely settled until after the legislative budget is enacted, introduces a continuous budgeting process not experienced by other districts. (MacInnes, 2005)

In the division plan presented by Mr. MacInnes, there have been "observable" changes to the way the opportunities for education enrichment and school administration have been handled. He reports the division has placed an emphasis on schools providing a more coordinated effort to selecting standards-based instruction remedies that boost student achievement for the more than 454 schools in the 31 districts. There is more of a focus on budgeting efficiency, and there is a "radical decentralization of authority, decision-making, and budgeting down to the school level." The division has also assisted in promoting the preschool program that has more than 40,000 participants.

Education Content Standards

New Jersey, like many districts nationwide, has an accountability component that requires children to master the content of their state examinations. Previously underperforming districts like Orange, Jersey City, Perth Amboy, and Pleasantville have made impressive gains that have persisted. Still, there are particular instructional issues for English language learners and students with disabilities that need to be addressed since almost 40 percent of all Abbott students are from non-English-speaking family backgrounds or are disabled.

The division has performed a Herculean duty for the state with its fifteen professional staff and three support personnel. It has made strategic use of faculty members from area universities and school districts with considerable expertise in early childhood education, English as a second language, reading, mathematics, fiscal accountability, and program evaluation. Mr. MacInnes (2005) reports that the Abbott Division has treated each Abbott district as a unique entity and they have been cognizant of its demographics, leadership, faculty experience and competence, instructional philosophy, practice, and curriculum.

One of the significant consequences of placing so much time and energy in preschool education is that it makes it easier to recruit teachers because they know they will not have to spend a great deal of time on remediation when children enter grade school. This appears to be one of the critical elements in retaining a productive faculty. The division has also engaged teachers and administrative staff from the Abbott districts to get their input. Professional development for faculty and administrative staff has been a necessary ingredient in order to build capacity within the special needs districts.

Facilities

The most controversial piece of the court mandates was a call to improve the physical facilities of many of New Jersey's older school districts. Controversial because of the expense of replacing and upgrading hundreds of aging school buildings. The court's mandate has produced more than $660 million in repairs, such as replacement of leaky roofs and removal of asbestos. More than 500 renovations, additions, or new buildings are planned, with more than 200 in some stage of approval, design, or construction. While a dozen projects have been completed so far, all 500-plus of the planned projects will be completely state-financed. The original law passed in 2000 to pay for the court mandate authorized $6 billion in spending in the *Abbott* districts, but experts in school facilities believe the price tag could double by the time the projects are completed (Gewertz, 2005). This particular *Abbott* remedy requires that every school building in the *Abbott* districts be made safe, healthy, and educationally adequate to promote high student performance. The Abbott School Construction Program was formed to fund and manage all of the needed facilities improvements in these districts. Research confirms that students learn best in an environment that is healthy, comfortable, naturally lit, clean, and in good repair (Schneider, 2002; Ponessa, 2004).

A report published by the 21st Century School Fund, entitled "For Generations to Come: A Leadership Guide to Renewing Public School Buildings," states that a growing body of research suggests that

> *...poor building condition and design are a liability to students and teachers, and that neither students nor teachers perform their best in unhealthy, crumbling, or overcrowded schools. New state standards and federal mandates hold teachers and principals to higher levels of accountability, yet many continue to work in sub-standard buildings that are desperately in need of repair or modernization. Improving school facilities is an important part of ensuring that high standards for teacher effectiveness and student achievement can be met. (21st Century School Fund, 2002, p. 13)*

A recent front-page New York *Times* article (Gettleman, 2005) confirms that even judicial mandates cannot always make this occur. The article reports "that hundreds of people have been pushed out of their homes for school projects that, it turns out, were only dreams. They were displaced as part of a once-celebrated $8.6 billion program that, instead of creating new schools, has in several instances created new slums." The New Jersey Schools Construction Corporation established by former Governor James E. McGreevey in 2002 was intended to save money on economies of scale on school construction in the *Abbott* districts. While the agency was built for speed to bring new schools to Abbott districts, recent investigations have exposed millions of dollars wasted on excessive bonuses, exorbitant fees, and design errors. Gerald Murphy, the agency's chief operating officer reports in the *Times* article (2005) that "in an effort to build schools quickly, state officials streamlined the process so that property acquisition, design, surveying and other tasks were all moving ahead at the same time—and at the same time, school funds were disappearing."

More than two hundred projects in Abbott districts are now stalled at the New Jersey Schools Construction Corporation without funding, including more than ninety projects under design by architects. In addition, the Education Law Center's web site reports numerous projects in other districts are at risk because the corporation has run out of funds to support them. The Education Law Center, legal counsel for the *Abbott* districts, will host a conference in November 2005 to update the public on the status of facilities improvements and building in the special needs' districts.

Construction in *Abbott* districts has become a subject in the November 2005 New Jersey gubernatorial election between U.S. Senator Jon S. Corzine and his opponent businessman Douglas R. Forrester; they both have issued statements on how they will pay for the construction and renovation of schools in poor and urban districts. This issue remains open for discussion and review.

CONCLUSION

Summing Up

School finance reform is an extremely complicated set of issues that involves local, state, and federal revenues. Not only must people be civic minded, but they must be willing to go against their own self-interest to achieve a goal that was first promulgated when the United States Supreme Court decided *Brown v. Board of Education* (1954).

When speaking of urban schools, one primarily talks about the schools that black, Latino, and lower-income children attend. In Fred G. Burke's 1990 book, *Public Education: Who's in Charge?* he very pointedly wrote:

By the turn of the century, more than one third of the children in our public, tax-supported elementary and secondary schools will be black or Hispanic. Despite recent evidence that the nation's minority citizens are beginning to flex their political muscle, it is not likely that they will soon exercise influence proportionate to their numbers. Nor is it likely that they will soon aggregate sufficient voting power to counter that of the dominant majority, most of whom do not have children in public schools and who are less and less inclined to support taxation to pay for the education of other people's children. This eventually is all the more likely if the myriad of expensive, locally episodic, often haphazardly installed reform efforts do not show evidence of stemming the educational decline. If costly expanding enrollment, especially of minority children, is accompanied by media-publicized failure of the expensive reform programs, public and political support can be expected to decline even further.

Between 1986 and 1990 the public school population will have increased by more than 2 million children. Even if everything else remains unchanged, this fact alone will require an extraordinary increase in annual expenditures for education. The costs of an array of expensive programs designed to improve teacher quality with a view to significantly improving the performance of students will have to be funded, of necessity, over and above what is dictated by an expanding school population. The long-range implications of such fiscal realities to the future of the educational reform movement are placed in stark *perspective when it is noted that the implementation of only those reform proposals recommended by the National Commission on Excellence would entail a twenty percent per pupil increase in educational expenditure. The recommendation of the Carnegie Forum on Education and the Economy would require additional revenues of approximately $48 billion over a ten-year period.*

Once the political mileage in education runs out, it is unlikely that governors and would-be governors will campaign on platforms advocating massive increases in educational expenditure. In most states the local property tax remains the mainstay supporting the nation's schools. Property taxpayers are disproportionately representative of the population without children in the public schools. Therefore, it is unrealistic to anticipate from a predominantly white middle-class, middle-aged population with few, if any, of their own children in the public schools' substantial political support in favor of increased levels of taxation to support additional educational expenditures. (Burke, 1990, p. 107)

Dr. Burke's words are as prescient as they are disturbing. In an advanced society like the United States, there is an implied social and civic contract citizens have with government. An outgrowth of that contract is the belief that citizens will each be afforded services and opportunities that will enhance the ability to become self-sustaining and contributing members of society.

New Jersey has the second highest per capita income in the nation, and yet has four of the country's poorest cities, along with a few others that would qualify as the poorest cities in most states. New Jersey's predominantly white suburbs have some of the most valuable property in the nation, booming economies, and excellent schools. The cities, on the other hand, have little property wealth, stagnant or declining economies, and poor education conditions. The cities also have less than one-quarter of the seats in the state legislature. Blacks and Latinos constitute close to 25 percent of the public-school population, yet New Jersey has one of the most segregated school systems in the country (Carr & Fuhrman, 2003).

In contrast with the national trend toward school district consolidation, New Jersey has actually created more school districts and now has over 600. Fred Burke (2003) indicated he tried to consolidate and reduce New Jersey's multiple school districts down to 100 in the 1980s. Gordon MacInnes (2005) also indicated New Jersey needs to go to a county-wide system like they have in Maryland. However, each school district has a vested interest in maintaining local control of its own resources and education policies. Although the lack of district consolidation is inefficient, regionalization of school districts is a political taboo because of racial, class, and ideological implications.

In response to the *Abbott* decisions, there appears to be greater collaboration between stakeholders; however, there continues to be a need to have an advocacy group like the Education Law Center with the threat of going back to court to keep everyone honest. The gains generated by the urban school districts because of the decisions have been substantial; however, there is an "opportunity cost" for each decision.

Unintended Consequences of Creating the Abbott Districts

Education policy experts (Ritter & Lauver, 2003) and economic experts (Hanushek, 1998, 1996; Card & Krueger, 1992) offer a set of provocative skepticisms regarding the parity spending in New Jersey. Ritter and Lauver have studied the financial consequences of the *Abbott* decisions and found that middle-income districts and low-income non-Abbott districts have higher tax rates than Abbott or wealthy districts, yet they still end up with less money. The roots of the inequities lie not in the court mandates, but in the state's aid system. "There continue to be 'winners' and 'losers' in the school finance scheme and only the faces have changed" (Education Week, 2005). Hanushek continues to focus on student outcomes, and he writes that seven years of near-parity spending between rich and poor districts has not closed the achievement gap significantly enough.

David G. Sciarra, the lead attorney for the school children in the *Abbott* districts, agrees that the near future must hold a reckoning when the state stares down the inequities of its finance system and finds a way to provide for all children the same high-quality programs from which *Abbott* children are benefiting. He also adds "...we cannot be satisfied until every child has what they need to be thoroughly and efficiently educated" (2003).

There is a very difficult political equation being written in New Jersey. Perhaps the election of a new governor with a commitment to education will continue to drive school finance reform. Two ex-governors, Brendan Byrne and James Florio, have provided cover for the New Jersey State Legislature by promoting a constitutional convention to revamp the state tax policy. Property taxes are the "third rail" issue in the state, and only a change to the constitution could reduce the State's over reliance on property taxes for local and state functions (Peterson, 2004).

Only pressure from advocacy groups working in tandem with politicians and policymakers with a deep commitment to education will continue to drive education opportunity to the school children in high poverty areas in New Jersey. At this moment in history, politicians in New Jersey do not appear to have the will to alter how schools are paid for in the state. All parties will have to play a game of watchful waiting to see how the push for increased adequacy, coupled with accountability, will play out in the state.

AFTERWORD

Politics of the State

Jon S. Corzine was elected Governor of New Jersey on November 8, 2005, and took office in January 2006. His first major speech since winning the governor's race was at the annual conference of the New Jersey State League of Municipalities. He warned that solving New Jersey's budget and property tax problems would require plenty of "tough choices and pain." He told the audience that he would keep his campaign promise to convene a special session of the Legislature next year to develop a plan to reduce property taxes. It is his intention to offer voters a solution on property taxes in a ballot proposal next November. "I don't look at this as a hopeless exercise" (Chen, 2005).

Governor Corzine will inherit a budget deficit of $5 billion, school construction and transportation funding that has virtually dried up, and a $1 billion pension payment due in 2006. What does this portend for the Abbott districts? The Democratic Party in New Jersey has control of both houses in the state legislature; however, this is not a guarantee that the new governor will have an easy time finding support for his agenda, which includes education. "If we're going to have real reform with property taxes, it won't be something you accomplish because you just work with Democrats" (Kocienewski & Holl, 2005).

As a senator, Jon Corzine supported the No Child Left Behind Act (NCLB), an education reform program that requires states to set high standards for students and that strengthens federal incentives to boost low-performing schools and significantly improve educational achievement. In his campaign literature for governor of New Jersey, a web site spells out his commitment to education reform. Education reform efforts cannot be effective without sufficient resources, and he is working to provide adequate funds to help states and school districts implement the new reforms.[1]

As a senator, Mr. Corzine co-sponsored multiple amendments to appropriations bills and budget resolutions that would fully fund No Child Left Behind so that school districts could implement the education reforms included in this law. In addition, Senator Corzine worked to prevent cuts in Title I funding, which provides assistance to improve the teaching and learning of children in high-poverty schools to enable those children to meet challenging state academic content and performance standards.

New Jersey has had thirty years of school finance reform litigation. The Education Law Center continues to represent the Abbott plaintiffs. With the election of a new governor, it will be interesting to see what relationship the Center will have with a new chief executive. Mr. Corzine promised during the campaign to deal with tax rebates but the underlying problem of reforming the state's antiquated tax structure is to deal with the complex challenge of the encrusted politics of the Statehouse to the fragmentation of county and municipal governments. Mr. Corzine "will need all of the strengths of his Wall Street track record to deal with Trenton's precarious finances on both the revenue and spending sides" (Kocienewski & Holl, 2005).

Jon Corzine won the gubernatorial election with 53 percent to Republican Douglas Forrester's 43 percent of the vote. Jeffrey Pawlowksi, the Libertarian candidate, and Hector Castillo, the Independent candidate, split 4 percent of the vote. There are 21 counties in New Jersey and all but Sussex, Morris, Somerset, Hunterdon, Monmouth, Ocean, and Cape May went for Jon Corzine. Sussex, Morris, Hunterdon, Ocean, and Cape May do not have Abbott school districts. Monmouth County has 3 Abbott districts (Long Branch, Asbury Park, and Neptune).

The governorship of New Jersey is generally considered to be the nation's most powerful governor's job, with vast appointment responsibilities and line-item veto power over the budget. However, the state's finances are troubled, and voters are expecting an overhaul of the burdensome property tax system. In addition, public confidence in government has been eroded by corruption scandals. The key element in education financing, programming, assessment, and accountability is the leadership that extends from the governor's mansion to the classroom.

The state has never had a Lieutenant Governor position but is now contemplating creating this position. When James McGreevey resigned his position in November 2004, the governorship transferred to Senate President Richard Codey, a seasoned and well-respected veteran legislator, to serve 14 months of his term. Governor McGreevey's resignation marked the second time in four years that the reins of the nation's most powerful governorship passed to a replacement for a protracted length of time. A similar power shift previously occurred in 2001, when former Governor Whitman left her office to join the Bush administration, enabling then Senate President Donald T. DiFrancesco to simultaneously serve in the executive and legislative branches for 11 months.

The state constitution was crafted in 1947 to designate the Senate President as the individual first in line to fill gubernatorial vacancies. This anomaly allows a "replacement" governor to assume powers that he or she was not duly elected to fulfill. Not only must the state have a reckoning with the disparities between Abbott and non-Abbott districts, it must resolve the issue of not having a Lieutenant Governor position.

Community, Heal Thyself

In 1996, John McKnight wrote *The Careless Society: Community and Its Counterfeits* (McKnight, 1996). Dr. McKnight is the director of the Community Studies Program at the Center for Urban Affairs and Policy Research at Northwestern University. The treatise of his book is the ability of neighborhoods to heal themselves from within. He writes that competent communities have been invaded and colonized by professionalized services—with often devastating results. Communities are overwhelmed by these social services, and the spirit of community falters: families collapse, schools fail, violence spreads, and medical systems spiral out of control. Instead of more or better services, the basis for resolving many of America's social problems is the capacity of the local citizens.

At some point, residents of any community have to take their destiny into their own hands. While children cannot be expected to provide housing, food, and a social structure that is conducive to them growing into productive adults, it is incumbent upon adults in a community to provide an environment for children to grow and flourish. That said, it is incumbent upon the failing school districts in the largest urban school districts in New Jersey to begin to heal themselves. All of the social and educational supports from any government cannot heal what goes on in a child's home. This has been my greatest lesson and an underlying outcome of my examination of the Abbott districts.

Over the course of the thirty years of *Robinson* and *Abbott*, I have gone through my own personal journey. While it was instructive for me to study school districts in the United States in the abstract by a review of the literature, it was beneficial for me to go inside public schools in not only New Jersey but in Colorado, New York, Pennsylvania, Texas, Virginia, Wisconsin, and Illinois. What I have seen is not always indicative of the public schools we want to project to the country. But my greatest criticism is not directed at the state government or educational establishment that allows mediocrity or failure to find a place, but with parents who allow their children to attend failing schools.

The 1966 Coleman Report, the landmark study also called Equality of Educational Opportunity lead by James S. Coleman (Coleman & others, 1966), was instrumental in promoting racial balance between schools. The report presented to the U.S. Congress found that poor black children did better academically in integrated, middle-class schools. This study helped to usher in the policy of busing school children to schools outside their neighborhoods. The aim was to achieve racial balance between schools by preventing black enrollment from exceeding 60 percent. A child must come to school prepared to learn without the constraints of negative family conditions. This is true whether a child attends a school in a racially mixed environment or one that is racially homogeneous.

Researchers who have studied highly effective schools across the nation pinpoint some common underlying principles. The most consistent feature of these schools is that all adults work as a team to improve education, including the teachers, parents, school board, principal, and community agencies (Moore, 2005; Bryk, 1999; Burke, 1990; Wong, 1999). Designs for Change, an education research reform organization in Chicago, Illinois, has organized the common practices of effective schools around Five Essential Supports for Student Learning. They are effective school leadership; social supports for learning (school culture); family and community partnerships support learning; adults collaborate and learn; and quality learning activities.

Jonathan Kozol's book, *The Shame of the Nation: The Restoration of Apartheid Schooling in America,* looks at the resegregation of public schools (Kozol, 2005). In an ideal world, we want children to be exposed to people from diverse backgrounds. But it is the neighborhoods that parents purchase homes or choose to rent in that produce our public schools. No one wants their child to grow up in an environment that is crime infested or has poor housing, so people who can afford it choose to purchase a home or rent housing in a safe environment. Essentially, the Tiebout treatise that people "will vote with their feet" plays out in every neighborhood in this country (Tiebout, 1956).

There is a circular argument that researchers participate in when they discuss the education system in the United States. This argument is working itself out in a microcosm in New Jersey through the establishment of Abbott districts. Does money buy better schools, or does a child's home life play a larger role in the education of a child?

A Final Look at the Research Questions: Financial, Political, and Social Outcomes

Rebell and Wardenski (2004), Wenglinsky (1997), and Laine, Greenwald, and Hedges (1994) write that money does matter in improving the nation's most disadvantaged schools. Since the 1960s and after the Coleman Report raised the issue of whether money made a difference in improving public schools for poor and minority students, substantial academic research and judicial analysis has overwhelmingly debunked the methodology of Hanushek (1996, 1998), one of the major proponents of the money is immaterial to student learning. The resultant studies and court holdings have strongly concluded that money spent on qualified teachers, smaller class sizes, pre-school initiatives, and academic intervention programs does make a substantial difference in student achievement—especially for poor and minority students.

The Education Law Center represented 20 public school children in their quest to obtain greater parity in school funding. After considerable judicial and legislative wrangling, 31 special needs districts were created. The special needs districts received additional funding, increased programming, significant ancillary programs that allowed for placing tutors, nurses, social workers, and school aids in schools. The most significant developments were state funding for new facilities and repairs to existent facilities; and the introduction of mandatory pre-school for all 3- and 4-year-old children in these districts. The increased funding, services, and facilities were tied to a new and more stringent accountability system to ensure education improvement at the classroom, school, and district levels.

Veteran educator and reformer Deborah Meier, best known for founding innovative, successful alternative public schools, indicates that the accountability systems that many policymakers rely on place too much emphasis on test taking and test scores. She remarks:

Once you think test scores are the achievement measure you can start proving that 'money doesn't matter.' At the high school I ran in New York, 90 percent of the kids graduated from high school and went on to college and did well in college. But their test scores didn't change much. So when people say to me, "Well, more money doesn't help test scores," I say that's not the only measure. You didn't send your kid to a private school just because their test scores would go up. You sent them because they had wonderful art programs, because they pushed your kid to think more deeply. None of which are picked up in the test. The extra measures that money offers kids—such as smaller class sizes—are not sensitive to test scores. (Paulson, 2002)

The City of Camden, New Jersey, was recently named the most dangerous city in America by Morgan Quintno Press (a publishing and research company) for the second year in a row (Morgan & Morgan, 2004). The distinction is based on crime data for murder, rape, robbery, aggravated assault, burglary, and motor vehicle theft (Rosenburg, 2005). Camden, New Jersey, is the former home of Raymond Abbott, the lead plaintiff in *Abbott v. Burke*, and one of the larger Abbott districts. All of the economic development and master plans for Camden, and the well-intentioned support from the city and state government cannot do for Camden what its residents need to do to remove this shameful distinction from the home of Walt Whitman.

Raymond Abbott is the product of middle-class parents who happened to attend an under-funded school system. When his parents realized the education he was receiving was inadequate, they and 19 other children with their parents joined forces with the Education Law Center. With the courageous support and legal acumen of Paul Tractenberg, Marilyn Morheuser, and David Sciarra, the Abbott districts came into existence and have received more financial support and services. It is incumbent upon the families who are the recipients of the financial largess of the state to do their part in providing the home environment where education is valued and nurtured.

Abbott v. Burke is the most closely watched legal decision in the annals of school finance reform because researchers are determined to use this case and others like it to answer the question, does money matter? The courts have decisively rejected Hanushek's approach to understanding the magnitude and effect of class size on student achievement and how additional funding equates into student achievement.

The New Jersey Supreme Court concluded that money mattered and used the research performed by national school finance and curriculum experts to enhance the academic achievement in both early and later school years. Extensive research is being conducted by the New Jersey Department of Education and external evaluators to ensure that the taxpayers of New Jersey and other stakeholders are getting their monies worth. For those of us who care about the education of children in urban public-school districts, we can only hope that the most important stakeholders, the children in the Abbott districts receive the "thorough and efficient" education that is guaranteed to them by the state constitution.

The Abbott districts undoubtedly received considerable funding and attention from the state, however, there continues to be a need sustain funding for a "thorough and efficient" education for *all* the children of New Jersey. As Ritter and Lauver reported, there are unintended consequences for singling out special needs districts when middle districts are losing ground financially and need similar supports that have been afforded the Abbott districts (Ritter & Lauyer, 2003).

The Abbott v Burke Aftermath: Using Federal Spending Power to Secure State Funding Reform

The Education Law Center in Newark, New Jersey filed the original *Abbott* lawsuit and represented the children and their families through twenty-seven iterations. In their subsequent report, *Making the Grade 2021,* the authors Farrie and Sciarra document the prevalence and persistence of unfair school funding practices across the country (Farrie & Sciarra, 2021). Under Democratic Presidents and Governors there are changes to Title 1 Funding that improves school funding for historically marginalized groups that are overrepresented I the lowest funded and/or least progressive states.

There is an urgent need to build political support in state capitols so that lawmakers and governors commit to school funding reform and greater investments in education. Finally, Farrie and Sciarra draw a strong parallel to the Medicaid Expansion lessons and education reform. The states that expanded Medicaid also have better school finance systems. Constituents of equitable treatment in healthcare can teach all education constituents a lesson. Healthcare advocates led successful ballot initiatives for expansion in six red states (Maine, Idaho, Nebraska, Utah, Oklahoma, and Missouri), and three more are expected in 2022 (Florida, Mississippi, and South Dakota). As Farrie and Sciarra end their report with the admonition, these success stories give hope that effective advocacy and the democratic process can prevail over misguided politics.

REFERENCES

21st Century School Fund. (2002). *For Generations to Come: A Leadership Guide to Renewing Public School Buildings*. 21st Century School Fund.

Aaron, H. J. (1975). *Who Pays the Property Tax? A New View*. Brookings Institution Press.

Abbott v. Burke, 100 N.J. 269, 495 A. 2D 376 (New Jersey 1985).

Abbott v. Burke, 119 N.J. 287, 575 A. 2d 359 (New Jersey 1990).

Abbott v. Burke, 136 N.J. 444, 643 A.2d 575 (New Jersey 1994).

Abbott v. Burke, 149 N.J. 119 (New Jersey 1997).

Abbott v. Burke, 153 N.J. 480, 710 A.2d 450 (New Jersey 1998).

Abbott v. Burke, 163 N.J. 95, 748 A. 2d 82 (New Jersey 2000).

Abbott v. Burke, 170 N.J. 537, 790 A. 2d 842 (New Jersey 2002).

Abbott v. Burke, 172 N.J. 294, 798 A. 2d 602 (New Jersey 2002).

Abbott v. Burke, 177 N.J. 578, 832 A. 2d 891 (New Jersey 2003).

Abbott v. Burke, 177 N.J. 596, 83 A. 2d 906 (New Jersey 2003).

Anvon, J. (1997). *Ghetto Schooling: A POlitical Economy of Urban Education Reform*. Teachers College Press.

Anvon, J. (2005). *Radical Possibilities: Public Policy, Urgan Education, and a New Social Movement*. Routledge, Taylor and Francis Group.

Augenblick, W. (2001). *Recommendations to the National Center for Education Statistics to Improve Its Role Regarding School Finance Data: The Perspective of State Policymakers*. U.S. Department of Education, National Center for Education Statistics.

Baker, B., & Green, P. (2002). Commentary: Can Minority Plaintiffs Use the Department of Education Implementing Regulations to Challenge School Finance Disparieis. *Texas Forum on Civiil Liberties and Civil Rights*, *7*(2), 141–165.

Barro, S. (1992). *What Does the Education Dollar Buy? Relationships of Staffing, Staff Characteristics, and Staff Salaries to State Per-Pupil Spending*. The Finance Center of CPRE.

Beck, M. (1958). Government Finance in New Jersey. In The Economy of New Jersey: A Report Prepared for the Department of Conservation and Economic Development of the State of New Jersey, (p. 560). Rutgers University Press.

Berne, R., & Stiefel, L. (1984). *The Measurement of Equity in School Finance: Conceptual, Methodological and Empirical Dimensions*. The Johns Hopkins University Press.

Berne, R., & Stiefel, L. (1999). Concepts of School Finance Equity: 1970 to Present. In H. F. Ladd (Ed.), *Equity and Adequacy in Education Finance: Issues and Perspectives,* (pp. 7–33). National Academy Press.

Blanchard, L. A., & Duncombe, W. (1999). Tax Policy and Public School Finance. In J. Hildreth & W. B. Richardson (Eds.), *Handbook on Taxation* (pp. 345–400). Marcel Dekker, Inc.

Bordentown Register News. (2005, August 22). Budget-Making Process Ruins Our Appetite. *Bordentown Register News*.

Braun, R. (1990, October 26). School Chiefs Say Funding Law Threatens the Best. *Neward Star-Ledger*, p. 1.

Brogan, D. W. (1943). *The American People, Impressions and Observations*. Knopf.

Brown v. Board of Education, 347 U.S. 483 (U.S. 1954).

Bryk, A. S. (1999). *Improving School-Community Connections: Ideas for Moving Toward a System of Community Schools*. Annie E. Casey Foundation.

Bryson, J., & Crosby, B. (1992). *Leadership for the Common Good*. Jossey-Bass Publishers.

Burke, F. G. (1990). *Public Education: Who's in Charge?* Praeger Publishers.

Burr, N. R. (1942). *Education in New Jersey: 1630-1871*. Princeton University Press.

Burtless, G. (1996). *Does Money Matter? The Effect of School Resources on Student Achievement and Adult Success*. Brookings Institute.

Byrne, B. T. (2004, November 2). *Interview on New Jersey News (NJN)*. http://www.directactions.net/ActivistKit.txt

Card, D., & Krueger, A. B. (1992, February). Does School Quality Matter? Returns to Education and the Characteristics of Public Schools in the United States. *Journal of Political Economy, 100*(1), 1–40.

Carnoy, M. (1982). *Economics and Education. In Encyclopedia of Educational Research,* (5th ed., Vol. 2). Macmillan Press.

Carr, M. C., & Fuhrman, S. H. (2003). The Politics of School Finance in the 1990s. In H. F. Ladd, R. Chalk, & J. S. Hansen (Eds.), *Equity and Adequacy in Education Finance: Issues and Perspectives*. National Academy of Sciences.

Carter, K. B. (1990, January 30). Two Judges Reprimanded for Attending Florio Ball. *New Star-Ledger*, p. 1.

Coleman, J. (1966). *Equality of Educational Opportunity*. Department of Health, Education, and Welfare.

Coons, J. E., Clune, W. H., & Sugarman, S. D. (1970). *Private Wealth and Public Education*. Harvard University Press.

Council on State Governments. (1987). *The Book of States, 1986-87*. Council of State Governments.

Cubberly, E. P. (1947). *Public Education in the United States*. Riverside Press.

Davis, M. (2003, June 23). Student Scores Show Progress but Critics Question Price. *The Newark Star-Ledger*, p. 1.

Duncombe, W., Ruggiero, J., & Yinger, J. (1996). Alternative Approaches to Measuring the Cost of Education. In H. F. Ladd (Ed.), *Holding Schools Accountable: Performance Based Reform in Education,* (pp. 327–356). Brookings Institution Press.

Education Law Center. (2002-2022). *EdLawCenter*. EdLawCenter.org: https://edlawcenter.org

Education Week. (2001). *Quality Counts 2001: A Better Balance--Standards, Tests, and the Tools to Succeed.* Education Week.

Education Week. (2005). *Quality Counts 2005: No Small Change--A Level Playing Field.* Education Week.

Education Week. (2006). *Quality Counts 2006: Quality Counts at 10--A Decade of Standards-Based Education.* Education Week.

Enrich, P. (1995). Leaving Equality Behind: New Directions in School Finance Reform. *Vanderbilt Law Review*, *48*, 101–194.

Evans, W., Murray, S., & Schwab, R. (1997). State Education Finance Policy After Court Mandated Reform: The Legacy of Serrano. In *1996 Proceedings of the Eighty-Ninth Annual Conference on Taxation.* National Tax Association-Tax Institute of America.

Farrie, D., & Sciarra, D. G. (2021). *Making the Grade: How Fair Is School Funding in Your State.* Education Law Center.

Felzenberg, A. S. (1978). *The Impact of Guernatorial Style on Policy Outcomes*. Princeton University.

Fennimore, B. S. (1996). Equity Is Not an Option in Public Education. *Educational Leadership*, *54*(2), 53–55.

Fennimore, B. S. (2005, September). Brown and the Failure of Civic Responsibility. *Teachers College Record*, *107*(9), 1905–1932.

Fino, S. (1987). *The Role of State Supreme Courts in the New Judicial Federalism*. Greenwood Press.

Firestone, W. A., Goertz, M. E., & Natriello, G. (1997). *From Cashbox to Classroom*. Teachers College Press.

Fischel, W. A. (1998). School Finance Litigation and Property Tax Revolts: How Undermining Local Control turns Voters Away from Public Education. Lincoln Institute of Land Policy. Dartmouth College.

Friedman, L., & Wiseman, M. (1978). Understanding the Equity Consequences of School Finance Reform. *Harvard Educational Review*, *48*, 193–226.

Froojian, J. (1991, April 29). Report: Property Tax Bad for New Jersey. *Atlantic City Press*.

Gettleman, J. (2005, August 26). As School Building Plan Fails, New Jersey Is Left with Slums. *New York Times*, p. 1.

Gewertz, C. (2005). *A Level Playing Field. Quality Counts 2005*. Education Week.

Glick, H. (1979). The Judicial Ten: America's Greatest Judges. *Southern Illinois University Law Journal. Southern Illinois University at Carbondale. School of Law*, *405*, 432.

Goertz, M. E. (1979). *Money and Education: How far have we come? Financing New Jersey Education in 1979*. Educational Policy Research Institute, Educational Testing Service.

Goertz, M. E. (1992). School Finance Reform in New Jersey: The Saga Continues. *Journal of Education Finance, 18*(4), 346–365.

Goldman, C. A. (1988). *Tax Disparites*. Council for New Jersey Affairs, New Jersey Issues.

Hanushek, E. A. (1996). School Resources and Student Performance. In Does Money Matter? The Effect of School Resources on Student Achievement and Adult Success, (pp. 43-73). Brookings Institution Press.

Hanushek, E. A. (1998). *Conclusions and Controversies about the Effectiveness of School Resources*. Economic Policy Reviews.

Harrington, M. (1962). *The Other America: Poverty in the United States*. Collier Books.

Hedges, L. V., Laine, R., & Greenwald, R. (1994). Does Money Matter? A Meta-Analysis of Studies of the Effects of Differential School Inputs on Student Outcomes. *Educational Researcher, 23*, 5–14.

Kilbourne, C. (1994). *Former Nun Fighting for New Jersey Schools--and Her Life*. Bicoastal.com: https://www.bicoastal.com/home/xlip11.html

Kladko, B. (1997, May 22). Abbot vs. Burke: Not Just Names on a Suit. *Asbury Park News*, p. 1.

Kocienewski, D., & Holl, J. (2005, November 10). Corzine Prepares to Assume New Title, and the Problems that Go with It. *New York Times*.

Kozol, J. (1991). *Savage Inequalities: Children in America's Schools*. Harper Perennial.

Kozol, J. (2005). *The Shame of the Nation: The Restoration of Apartheid Schooling in America*. Crown Publishers.

Ladd, H. (1975). Local Education Expenditures, Fiscal Capacity and the Composition of the Property Tax Base. *National Tax Journal, 28*(2), 145–158.

Ladd, H., & Yinger, J. (1994). The Case for Equalizing Aid. *National Tax Journal, 47*(1), 211–224.

Lee, V. E., & Burkam, D. T. (2002). *Inequality at the Starting Gate: Social Background Differences in Achievement as Children Begin School*. Economic Policy Institute.

Lehne, R. (1978). *The Quest for Justice: The Politics of School Finance Reform*. Longman.

Lehne, R., & Rosenthal, A. (1979). *Politics in New Jersey*. Eagle Institute of Politics, Rutgers University.

Levine, G. (1991). Meeting the Third Wave: Legislative Approaches to Recent Judicial School Finance Rulings. *Harvard Journal on Legislation, 28*, 506–542.

Lukemeyer, A. (2002). Financing a Constitutional Educaton: Views from the Bench. *Conference on State Aid to Education, sponsored by the Educational Finance and Accountability Project*.

Lukemeyer, A. (2003). *Courts as POlicymakers: School Finance Reform Litigation*. LFB Scholarly Publishing LLC.

Mackey, P. E. (2002). *Using Naitonal Best Practices to Improve New Jersey's Management of Education Data*. Rutgers University School of Law.

Mansnerus, L. (2002, April 5). Big Increase in Local Taxes Is Expected in New Jersey. *New York Times*.

Massell, D., & Fuhrman, S. H. (1994). *Ten Years of State Education Reform, 1983-1993*. Consortium for Policy Research in Education.

McKnight, J. (1996). *The Careless Society: Community and Its Counterfeits*. Basic Books.

Minorini, P. A., & Sugarman, S. (1999). Educational Adequacy and the Courts: The Promise and Problems of Moving to a New Paradigm. In H. F. Ladd, R. Chalk, & J. S. Hansen (Eds.), *Equity and Adequacy in Education Finance: Issues and Perspectives*. National Academy Press.

Minorini, P. A., & Sugarman, S. D. (1999). School Finance Litigation in the Name of Educational Equity: Its Evolution, Impact, and Future. In H. F. Ladd, R. Chalk, & J. S. Hansen (Eds.), *Equity and Adequacy in Educational Finance: Issues and Perspectives*. National Academy Press.

Monk, D. H., & Brent, B. O. (1997). *Raising Money for Education: A Guide to the Property Tax*. Corwin Press, Inc.

Moore, D. R. (2005). *The Big Picture: School-Initiated Reforms, Centrally Initiated Reforms, and Elementary School Achievement in Chicago (1990 to 2005)*. Designs for Change.

Morgan, S., & Morgan, K. (2004). *Crime State Rankings*. Morgan Quitno Press.

Moser, M., & Rubenstein, R. (2002). The Equality of Public School District Funding in the United States: A Natioal Status Report. *Public Administration Review*, *62*(1), 63–72.

National Conference of State Legislatures. (2005, May 29). *NCSL NCEF*. NCSL.org: https://www.ncls.org/programs/edu/NCEF.htm

Netzer, D. (1966). *Economics of the Property Tax*. Brookings Institution Press.

New Jersey Department of Education. (2001). *Public Education in New Jersey*. State.NJ.US: https://www.state.nj.us/education/genfo/penj.pdf

Odden, A. R. (1992). School Finance and Education Reform: An Overview. In A. R. Odden (Ed.), *Rethinking School Finance*. Jossey-Bass.

Odden, A. R., & Picus, L. O. (2004). *School Finance: A Policy Perspective*. Mc-Graw-Hill, Inc.

Paulson, A. (2002, September 17). *A Plea to Trust Schools--Not Just Tests*. CSMonitor.com. https://www.csmonitor.com/2002/0917/p14s01-lepr.html

Peterson, I. (2004, October 21). Two Ex-Governors Support a Tax Convention. *New York Times*.

Ponessa, J. (2004). *Breaking Ground: Rebuilding New Jersey's Urban Schools: The Abbott School Constrution Program*. Education Law Center.

Ravitch, D. (1987). *The Schools We Deserve*. Harper Collins.

Ravitch, D., & Finn, C. Jr. (1987). *What Do Our 17-Year-Olds Know?* Harper Collins.

Rebell, M. A. (2002). Education Adequacy, Democracy and the Courts. In T. Ready & C. Edley, C. E. Snow (Eds.), Achieving High Educational Standards for All: Conference Summary. National Research Council and National Academy Press.

Rebell, M. A. (2004). *Commentary: Why Adequacy Lawsuits Matter*. Education Week.

Rebell, M. A., & Wardenski, J. J. (2004). *Of Course Money Matters: Why the Arguments to the Contrary Never Added Up*. Campaign for Fiscal Equity.

Reed, D. S. (1996). Court-Ordered School Finance Equalization: Judicial Activism and Democratic Opposition. In W. J. Fowler (Ed.), *Developments in School Finance, 1996,* (pp. 91–120). National Center for Education Statistics.

Reed, D. S. (1998). Twenty-Five Years after Rodriguez: School Finance Litigation and the Impact of the New Judicial Federalism. *Law & Society Review*, *32*(1), 175–220.

Reed, D. S. (2001). *On Equal Terms: The Constitutional Politics of Educational Opportunity*. Princeton University Press.

Reschovsky, A. (1994). Fiscal Equalization and School Finance. *National Tax Journal*, *47*, 185–187.

Reschovsky, A., & Imazeki, J. (1998). The Development of School Finance Formulas to Guarantee the Provision of an Adequate Education to Low INcome Students. In *Developments in School Finance 1997: Does Money Matter?* (pp. 121–148). U.S. Department of Education, National Center for Education Statistics.

Rich, B. (1957). *The Government and Politics of New Jersey*. Crowell Press.

Ritter, G. W., & Lauyer, S. C. (2003). School Finance Reform in New Jersey: A Piecemeal Response to a Systemic Problem. *Journal of Education Finance*, *28*, 575–598.

Robinson v. Cahill, 62 N.J. 473, 303 A. 2d 273 (New Jersey 1972).

Rodriguez v. San Antonio Independent School District 337, 337 F. Supp. 280 (W.D. Tex. 1971).

Salmore, B. G., & Salmore, S. A. (1998). *New Jersey Politics and Government*. University of Nebraska Press.

Schneider, M. (2002). *Do School Facilities Affect Academic Outcomes?* National Clearinghouse for Educational Facilities.

Schrag, P. (2003). *Final Test: The Battle for Adequacy in America's Schools*. The New Press.

Serrano v. Priest, 5 Cal. 3d 584, 487 P.2d 1241, 96 Cal Rptr. 601 (California 1971).

Shank, A. (1969). *New Jersey Reapportionment Politics*. Associated University Presses.

Sheil, J. C. (2000). The Just-Do-It Decision: School-Funding Litigation Tests the Limits of Judicial Deference. *Seton Hall Law Review*, *28*, 620.

Smith, A. (1993). *An Inquiry into the Nature and Causes of the Wealth of Nations*. Oxford University Press.

Swanson, A. D., & King, R. (1997). *School Finance: Its Economics and Politics,* (2nd ed.). Longman Publishers.

Tarr, G. A., & Porter, C. A. (1988). *State Supreme Courts in State and Nation*. Yale University Press.

Thro, W. (1993). The Role of Language of the State Education Clauses in School Finance Litigation. *Education Law Report*, *79*(19), 277–289.

Tiebout, C. (1956). A Pure Theory of Local Expenditures. *Journal of Political Economy*, *54*, 416–424.

Wenglinsky, D. (1997). *When Money Matters: How Educational Expenditures Improve Student Performance and How They Don't*. Educational Testing Service.

Williams, R. F. (1997). *The New Jersey State Constitution: A Reference Guide*. Rutgers University Press.

Winter, G. (2004, October 6). Financial Gap Is Widening for Rich and Poor Schools. *New York Times*, p. A.23.

Wise, A. (1983). Educational Adequacy: A Concept in Search of Meaning. *Journal of Education Finance*, *8*(3), 300–316.

Wise, A. E. (1968). *Rich Schools, Poor Schools: A Promise of Equal Opportunity*. University of Chicago Press.

Wong, K. K. (1999). *Funding Public Schools: Politics and Policies*. University Press of Kansas.

ENDNOTE

1 www.corzine.senate.gov/priorities/education.html

Chapter 18
A Comparative Analysis of American and Dutch Primary Public Education and Teacher Training:
Essential Institutional Factors for Success

Lauren Joyce Hensel
Launch Education Advisors, The Netherlands

ABSTRACT

This chapter provides a comparative analysis of the Dutch versus American primary public education systems within the framework of Donald Moore's Five Essential Supports. In addition, it analyzes and explores the importance of professional capacity/quality and its connection to standardized test scores on the TIMSS, PIRLS, and PISA. It starts with an overview of the state of the American public education system and moves into a comparative analysis in two separate parts: (1) within the macro, meso, and micro levels and (2) within the Five Essential Supports. Special focus is given to the professional capacity/quality of pre-service teacher training programs to better understand the interconnectedness of this support within the framework and its effects on test outcomes. By analyzing test score data, the authors explore if and how improved practicum teacher-training may improve standardized test scores and explore ways in which policy can change to improve teacher-training at the university level.

INTRODUCTION

Why Study Public Schools in America and The Netherlands?

The author is an adamant and enthusiastic supporter of progressive and innovative public education, but the United States of America's (America, or US) public education system continually leaves the greater public feeling somber and dismayed—a sentiment calculated by *Education Next* (Education Next,

DOI: 10.4018/978-1-6684-2314-1.ch018

2016). In their 2016 poll, 53% of the public gave public schools nationally a C-grade. With the decrease in the arts and physical activity programs, the loss of child-centered environments, a growing funding disparity, and the pervasive overuse of standardized testing (add ref for standardized testing?), America's public education system continues to leave people seeking better opportunities for their children, teachers struggling to find joy in their profession, and school leadership being overworked and undertrained.

America's public education policies continually pressure minorities, special needs parents, teachers and educators, and scholars to develop an animosity towards American politicians, lobbyists, and policy makers who often do not understand the educational system or acknowledge its gross inequalities.[1] NPR's Cory Turner reported on a list of recommendations from the U.S. Commission on Civil Rights in which their 150-page report details the vast inequities plaguing the American system.

To this day, though, states are all over the map when it comes to how equitably they spend their own money in schools. The problem was baked into the system from the beginning, with local property taxes being an important driver of both school funding and of inequities in school funding. (Turner, 2018)

The lack of constitutional protection for equal education for all provides a foundation for confusion, varying and conflicting curriculum guidelines, and regulations which reduce teacher autonomy, satisfaction, and productivity. Instead, American public education tends to cultivate a competitive silo culture amongst teachers, which forces teachers to work alone thus discouraging teacher collaboration and innovation, reducing child-centered learning, and impeding teacher autonomy. Furthermore, schools continually fail to integrate with the communities they serve consequently straining trust between students, parents, and educators. The combination of these factors lead many parents to feel dissatisfied with their public school options and lead them to pursue alternatives in independent, private, or charter schools. Many parents seek schools where students can learn in a more progressive educational environment that fosters community, provides quality instruction, and presents a consistent curriculum.

While doing research on how to create progressive and pragmatic public schools, the author came across a 2013 study by UNICEF entitled *Child Well-being in Rich Countries: A comparative overview* (Adamson, 2013). Within this study, out of 29 countries studied, the United States of America ranked low at 26 and its education system at 27. To better understand this ranking, the author looked to the highest ranked country, the Netherlands (NL), to see what the American public schools could do differently. The study mentions, "The Netherlands retains its position as the clear leader and is the only country ranked among the top five countries in all dimensions of child well-being." To better understand the rankings, the author explored what factors were taken into account for these rankings, particularly in the education field.

These factors are listed in Table 1.

Table 1. UNICEF Child Well-being Analysis

Dimension 3 **Education** Figure 3.0	Participation	Participation rate: early childhood education	3.1a
		Participation rate: further education, age 15–19	3.1b
		NEET rate (% age 15–19 not in education, employment, or training)	3.1c
	Achievement	Average PISA scores in reading, maths, and science	3.2

Source: Adamson (2013).

While these are all great factors, they do not tell a complete picture of the educational system in America nor The Netherlands, which provided the basis for this paper. Although the two starkly different societies—in terms of values, government structure, constitutional rights, etc.—present a challenge, analyzing both countries from a broad public administration perspective and Donald Moore's Five Essential Supports for educational success will reveal ways in which the American public education system can be improved without additional funding or restructuring the current funding structure. To understand and develop solutions to America's public education struggle, this paper steps outside the American educational construct and looks internationally to identify institutional context where children are ranked happiest in the world—the Netherlands (Holland).

What Is the Comparability of the Two Countries?

Despite America and Holland both being rich, developed, first-world countries, they differ immensely in their cultural beliefs, which are evident in their constitutions, educational funding structures, and public policy initiatives. While identifying similarities may be difficult due to vastly differing cultural norms, constitutional rights, funding schemes, and population size, the Dutch continually value innovation and work to develop progressive, pragmatic educational policies to better all children. This differs drastically from the educational system in America, which according to Dr. Geoffrey Canada's TED talk,[2] is failing children.

Those of us in education have held onto a business plan that we don't care how many millions of young people fail, we are going to continue to do the same thing that didn't work. And nobody, nobody is getting crazy about it to say enough is enough. So here is a business plan that simply does not make any sense. Why haven't we allowed innovation to happen? (Canada, 2013)

On the contrary, the Dutch "somehow see that path forward to greater teacher control of schools" (Butrymowicz, 2015).

It is important to compare the two countries on basic information such as gross domestic product (GDP), percentage of GDP allocated for education, amount spent per student on education, total population, total student-age population, and each country's place within multiple global rankings with differing perspectives. By their rankings,[3] we are able to see global differences within the two countries through larger, well-funded studies. These multiple-year rankings help to visualize and understand key differences within each society. The rankings come from:

1. Global Competitiveness Index (Sala-i-Martin, et al., 2012)
2. The Economist's Democracy Index (Economist Intelligence Unit, 2006-2017)
3. Reporters without Borders Press Freedom Index (Reporters Sans Frontieres, 2015-2017)
4. Global Innovation Index (Dutta, Lanvin, Rivera Leon, & Wunsch-Vincent, 2012)
5. Legatum Prosperity Index (Legatum Institute, 2007-2016)

Table 2 and Chart 1 (NL vs US Global Ranking Comparison) provide a visual of the average outcomes per country for each ranking revealing the strengths and weakness overall as a nation and in regards to education. The further out the data point, the higher the rank. Overall, the Dutch, through a variety of pragmatic policies in numerous areas have fostered overall a balanced society compared to America, who displays weaknesses in education, press freedom, and prosperity.

Table 2. NL vs US Global Ranking Comparison

Global Ranking	NL Avg	US Avg
GCI Overall	6	4
GCI Primary Education	8	33
Democracy Index	9.1	8.1
Press Freedom Index	4	44
Global Innovation Index (GII) Overall	6	7
GII Gov't Expen Edu	36	45
GII Education Overall	17	33
Prosperity Index Overall	5	17
Prosperity Index Edu	1	5

Figure 1. NL vs US Global Ranking Comparison

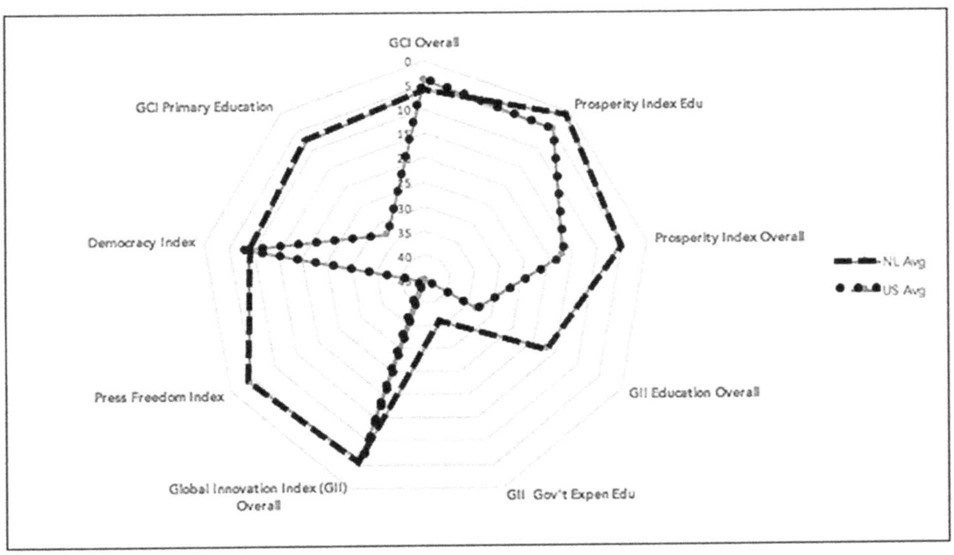

Despite having a much smaller population, the ratio of students to the entire population is similar to that of America. However, the Dutch spend 33% less per student and 20.9% less of their GDP (Chart 2) while achieving better outcomes on PISA during the high school years and similar scores during the primary year tests—TIMSS and PIRLS, which is the foundation upon which we are able to grade the quality of teachers in this paper. The PISA exam describes primary education from a long-term outcome

Figure 2. Percent of GDP Spent on Primary Education

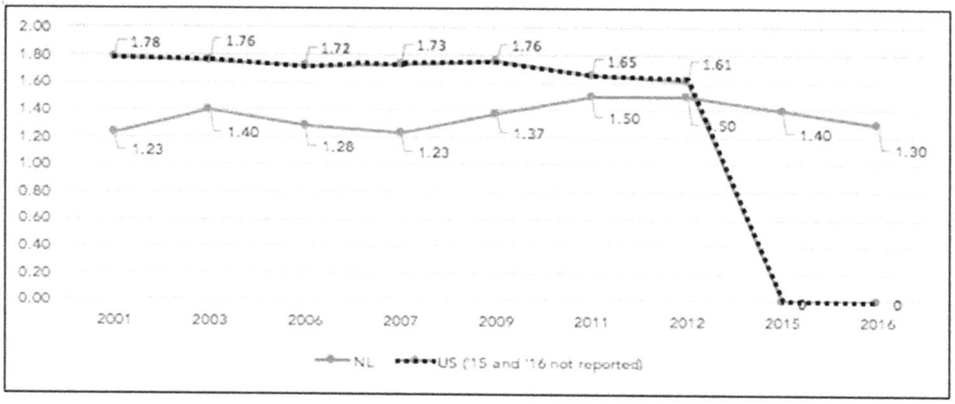

perspective because students take the PISA at 15 years old, which proves what is learned in earlier years contributes to these drastically different outcomes as the test takers have not finished their second year of high school/secondary school. The primary school exams—TIMSS and PIRLS—allow one to understand the state of education and correlations between the Five Essential Supports implementation during the primary years and the outcomes on PISA in later years.

What Points Are Comparable?

To improve public education in America, it is essential to compare and study institutional differences within the context of Donald Moore's Five Essential Supports and pinpoint structural and implementation differences contributing to better outcomes in Holland. Moore's Five Essential Supports are

1. School leadership
2. Parent-community ties
3. Professional capacity/quality
4. Student-centered learning environment
5. Ambitious instruction.

By comparing these two differing countries within the Five Essential Supports context, this study focusses on identifying institutional aspects within the Dutch public education system that could benefit American public schools while accounting for differences in population size, funding structures, and governmental support of education.

Depending on perspective, the priority of the Five Essential Supports could be arranged in a variety of ways. However, to help narrow this paper's scope to a manageable size, the main focus is on school leadership and professional capacity/quality as those frequently set a strong foundation and consequently influence the other three supports. The layered perspective taken in this paper is visible in Figure 1.

Figure 3. Layered Perspective of Five Essential Supports

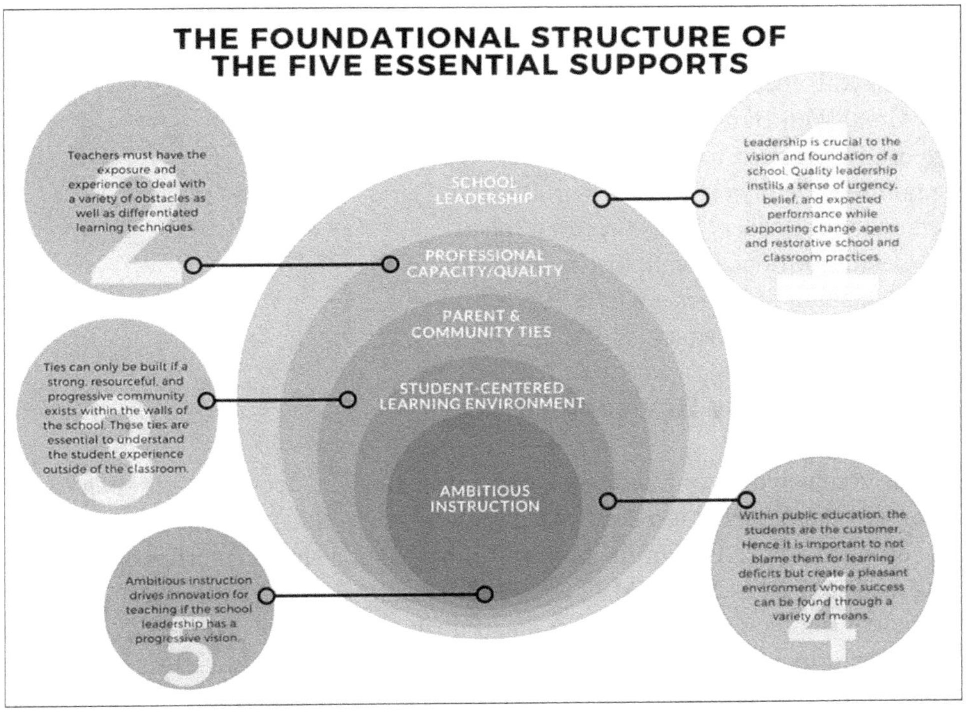

Methods for Data Collection

Data collection for this comparative study was cumbersome and time consuming as there is not one single database available for all data collected. The data falls into three separate categories for this study: (1) country global rankings to give a better idea of each country's overall wellness in multiple sectors, (2) educational data—demographics, total enrolled students, percent of funding from GDP, percentage of population who are students younger than 12, unfilled teacher vacancies, and (3) standardized test scores from TIMSS, PIRLS, and PISA over four years, average number of weeks for teacher training per country, and average years teaching per country. The data collected in the first and second categories help provide a robust picture of the educational landscape and are not intended for data analysis. The third set of data collected is where data analysis occurs. This analysis seeks to understand the relationship between the amount of time spent in teacher training programs (in weeks) and any correlation to better test scores on TIMSS, PIRLS, and PISA. Data were collected through the following websites and organizations:

- Organisation for Economic Co-operation and Development (OECD)
- Central Bureau voor de Statistiek (Netherlands)
- TIMSS testing results PDFs
- PIRLS testing results PDFs
- PISA testing results PDFs

- World Bank website
- Dienst Uitvoering Onderwijs: Ministerie van Onderwijs, Cultuur, en Wetenschap (Netherlands)
- Global Innovation Index
- Global Competitiveness Index
- UNICEF Child Well Being
- Hertiage.org Economic Freedom Index
- The Economist's Democracy Index
- Reporters without Borders Press Freedom Index
- National Center for Education Statistics (USA)
- Digest of Education Statistics—NCES (USA)
- UNESCO Institute of Statistics

Data Analysis and Policy Review Methods

The data analysis conducted is a simple t-test to discover if differences exist between the Netherlands and America on the standardized tests. By comparing scores in this manner, we can understand if the score differences are statistically significant scores throughout a student's primary educational career. The data being analyzed is Grade 4 TIMSS and PIRLS results as well as PISA results.

Two independent sample t-tests help determine if the means of US vs NL test scores are statistically significant and to determine if teacher pre-service programs may positively affect scores and the rest of the Five Essential Supports. An independent sample t-test is important due to the small sample sizes, availability of scores, and lack of data pre- and post-test. Had the scores gone beyond five to ten years or had the research been testing policy implementation, a different method of analysis would be employed.

The biggest questions through this simple analysis are: If the country were to change the number of teacher training hours, would the outcomes on standardized tests improve? How do teacher hours influence the other Five Essential Supports? Although the null hypothesis (H_0) for all t-tests is the mean difference of test scores will be 0, an alternative hypothesis (H_1) states the Dutch test scores will be better than the US scores. From here, this paper hopes to conclude increased pre-service practical teaching training results in higher test scores for Dutch public schools than American public schools or the international average.

For policy review methods, it is important to employ an APGAR analysis of the teacher training programs in American universities, which is available in the Recommendations section. Knowing the training available to Dutch teachers and the policies in place at the teacher training institutions, one can provide alternatives for America to better the teacher pre-service training programs. A final analysis (see section on Recommendations) will review the concluding recommendations and their effects on the other Five Essential Supports. Furthermore, this paper seeks to prove the improved effectiveness of teacher training is a viable change to the education institutional context. Beside teacher training, the other Five Essential Supports provide additional institutional contexts for student success and positive outcomes.

Limitations

As with any study, limitations exist, and it is important to acknowledge their existence and influence on the study.

1. Lack of consistent year-over-year reporting thus resulting in some years not being included in the data analysis, which could yield skewed averages.
2. Inability to secure classroom observations in Dutch public schools due to the author's non-affiliation with a Dutch university such as University of Amsterdam, Leiden, or Utrecht. This resulted in a lack of data regarding recess times, amount of times students are sitting versus standing, and tracking the types of instruction employed by teachers.
3. Cultural differences leading to differing educational expectations, funding structures, organizational autonomy, and educational structures.
4. Lack of parental participation in an initial parental happiness survey, which has been excluded from consideration and analysis.
5. Varying numbers reported to different agencies in regards to GDP, amount spent per pupil, total public school enrollment.
6. Lack of consistent reporting on number of weeks spent in practicum leading to utilizing an assumed average based on research.

The biggest limitation, the inability to secure observations within Dutch public schools, necessitated a different approach to the hypothesis that better primary school teacher training at the university level leads to better student outcomes on the TIMSS, PIRLS, and PISA standardized tests. Initially, although the author wanted to explore all Five Essential Supports, without access to Dutch schools, it is difficult to witness them in practice without observation ability. However, through in-depth research, the author gathered quality information that helped to explain how Dutch teacher and administration training effect the other essential supports.

THE STATE OF AMERICAN PUBLIC EDUCATION

Over the past 50 years, researchers, administrators, and educators continually discuss the same problems plaguing the American public education system and putting it in crisis—lack of Constitutional clarity on the availability of equal and fair (financial) public education for all, pervasive over testing, a decentralized instructional guidance system, subpar teacher training, loss of community ties and teacher autonomy, and a shift from student-centered learning. Combined, these issues are some of the reasons America continues to fall behind many countries on the Program for International Student Assessment (PISA).

Overspend but Underdeliver: Diminishing Global Test Scores

Despite being a first-world country, a global superpower, and spending an average of $12,000 USD per student (Organisation for Economic Co-operation and Development, 2016), the American public education system continues to fail children and expose structural weaknesses namely in student outcomes and teacher preparation. These two outputs often go hand-in-hand as teacher preparation and ability directly relates to student outcomes. While global research continues to show the importance of differentiated learning, 21st century experiential learning, and immense teacher autonomy, the American system (with some exceptions) continues to scoff at innovation (Canada, 2013), thus harming the future of America—the children.

Admittedly, American public schools are not failing given that they educate everyone as a right. But the author does disagree with education advocates such as Steven Singer (Singer, 2017), who states, "America's public schools are *not* failing. They are among the best in the world...Here's why: the United States educates everyone. Most other countries do not." While he acknowledges America's public education problems, he states US schools have not worsened since the first TIMSS in 1995. His article does shed light on some integral social and economic issues that may lead to failing test scores such as the US' high child poverty rate in the western world, the broad spectrum of children who take the tests, a high amount of special needs education accessibility, and more. However, he fails to mention the misappropriation of funds, the pervasive over-testing issue, and loss of teacher autonomy, which hinders teachers' abilities to make progress with students from diverse backgrounds.

In McKinsey & Company's study, *The Economic Impact of the Achievement Gap in America's Schools*, it was found "...despite large educational expenditures, school spending in the United States is among the least cost-effective in the world" (McKinsey & Company, 2009, p. 9). McKinsey later mentions how America spends $165 USD to get a point on the PISA exam, which is about 60% more than other OECD countries and 37% more than the Netherlands, who only spends $103 USD. Although education advocates such as Singer will state educating fewer students is easier, it does not explain how the Dutch can allocate 20.9% less of their GDP (on average), as seen in Chart 3, to primary education and achieve similar if not better results.

Figure 4. Average % of GDP Spent on Primary Education

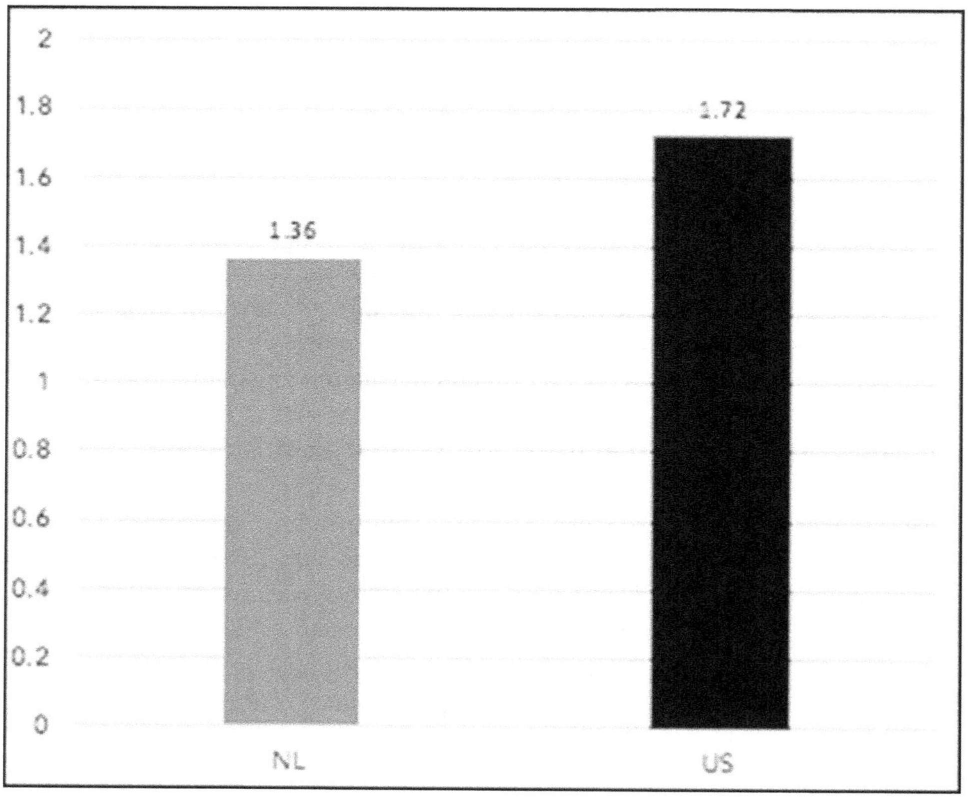

Less Innovation, More Testing

According to Valerie Strauss at the *Washington Post* (Strauss, 2015), reporting on a study by the Council of the Great City Schools, "The average student in America's big-city public schools takes some 112 mandatory standardized tests between pre-kindergarten and the end of 12th grade—an average of about eight a year, the study says." This amount of student testing decreases the amount of time teachers can put into student-centered learning, which puts strain on school leadership and negates instructional guidance systems. By increasing the amount of standardized tests in classes, teachers must build test preparation into their lesson plans, reducing the amount of time allowed to teacher innovatively and creatively.

As American politicians, lobbyists, and policy makers continue to focus on standardized testing as a method to spur reform, they seem to have forgotten the negative outcomes of utilizing this method as the reform. "A reliance on testing as the reform, rather than a component of a comprehensive improvement agenda, is particularly problematic when these reforms are layered on a starkly unequal educational system" (Darling-Hammond, 2006). Juxtaposed to the Dutch, students in America must suffer through a seemingly inescapable school funding disparity that is tied to, through value-added modeling, testing outcomes. Hence, teaching salaries and additional resources are often determined by test scores, which would leave those in economically disadvantaged areas at a loss.

Lack of Vocational Training

Sala-i-Martin et al. state in *The Global Competitiveness Index 2012-2013: Strengthening recovery by raising productivity*, "basic education increases the efficiency of each individual worker" (Sala-i-Martin, et al., 2012). America finds itself at a crossroads with its education and teacher training. As we continued to push for advanced education and degrees and viewed vocational training as a dumping ground for "less fortunate students" (Foroohar, 2017), the skills gap for workers continued to widen. With the increased need of knowledge-based workers after the internet boom, not only did the U.S. cultural belief about education change, but the education system itself began to phase out the training programs to provide students skills to succeed post-graduation as the country pushed to become the strongest knowledge-based economy in the world.

However, Porter, Sachs, and McArthur state in their executive summary of the *Global Competitiveness Report* say, "old strategies become the new weakness" (Porter, Sachs, & McArthur, 2002) Ironically, this is the current situation within America. Nearly two-thirds of those jobs will require some post-secondary education. But the majority of the fastest-growing categories will be those in the "sub-BA" market, which do not necessarily require a degree" (Foroohar, 2017). American public education is failing to address this need within the primary, secondary, and tertiary education avenues, resulting in institutional system failure. Hence, it is imperative America solves its education problem to prepare for future economic growth to avoid constraints on business development and the federal budget.

Who Is to Blame?

As American parents continually lose faith in their public education choices, they seek school alternatives (charter, private, and independent schools), often sacrificing future savings to better their child's chances at receiving a quality, innovative, education. However, a vast majority of Americans do not have access to a school of their choice, thus forcing some of the most vulnerable communities to tolerate their failing school system. Dr. Geoffrey Canada spoke candidly about the omnipresent failure of American schools in May 2013 stating, "You know, I grew up in the inner city, and there were kids who were failing in schools 56 years ago when I first went to school, and those schools are still lousy today, 56 years later" (Canada, 2013). His quote points to several long-standing overarching problems within the American public education system at all levels (macro, meso, and micro):

1. Lack of equitable education funding and access at the macro level.
2. Disparities in curriculum creation, alignment, and standards across the meso level due to macro level centralization failure.
3. Inadequate teachers and administrator training at the meso and micro levels.
4. Lack of autonomy protection at the meso and micro level.
5. Lack of school choice at the meso and micro level.

These five problems fall within the framework of this paper. For America to thrive in the future, it is imperative that culture demands change at all levels to ensure future workers are able to "adapt rapidly to their changing environment and the evolving needs of the economy" (Sala-i-Martin, et al., 2012). The power to combat the overarching problems, to change the future, and to prepare future workers lies in providing better preparation pre-service teacher training at university.

THE DUTCH VS AMERICAN PUBLIC EDUCATION STRUCTURE

The Dutch viewpoint on education is well-stated in the Coalition Agreement of 2017-2021[4] entitled *Confidence in the Future* released in October 2017 (People's Party for Freedom and Democracy (VVD), Christian Democratic Alliance (CDA), Democrats '66 (D66), and Christian Union (CU), 2017). As the Dutch are an egalitarian society, there is an immense focus on allowing all citizens and members of society to be equal and helping them achieve their own personal greatness. Being cognizant of the *whole* society is fundamentally important to the Dutch culture and a cornerstone of their values.

When too many people are left behind, the entire society suffers. Social divisions turn into social tensions, which can quickly grow, especially now that international instability and unrest are contributing to the sense of discontent and alienation in the US (People's Party for Freedom and Democracy (VVD), Christian Democratic Alliance (CDA), Democrats '66 (D66), and Christian Union (CU), 2017, p. 3). Consequently, the recent coalition documents how the kingdom will move forward in developing productive public policy solutions within the education realm. Good education brings out the best in people, reduces and prevents learning disadvantage and enables talent to flourish. Good education lays the foundations for a healthy and successful society. The government will therefore continue to invest in further improvements to education and research, and in the people working in this field (People's Party for Freedom and Democracy (VVD), Christian Democratic Alliance (CDA), Democrats '66 (D66), and Christian Union (CU), 2017, p. 12).

Resulting from their cultural beliefs, the Dutch public education structure as seen in Figure 2 (Netherlands Ministry of Education, Culture, and Science, 2016)[5] is vast, dynamic, and full of opportunity for all Dutch residents. This system provides access to quality educational opportunities at all levels, thus increasing the employability and economic contributions of their society.

The American public education system as shown in Figure 3 (Institute of Education Sciences, U.S. Department of Education, 2009), though strong in its own regard, segregates communities and increases achievement gaps due to limited or out-of-reach choice. This structure is based on the meritocracy belief of people moving forward and upward based on doing something well, but this belief only delivers results in theory. The increasing competition between public and private schools for students results in the wealthy typically receiving a better education from not only a financial perspective, but teacher perspective as well. Although the American public education system is vast, the disparities within it and lack of choice should be apparent. Nevertheless, American residents seem to believe the American public education has stuck closely to its founding values of personal freedom, individuality, and diversity (within limits)[6]; however, those on the receiving end of disparities would argue against this belief.

Figure 5. Dutch Education System
Source: Ministry of Education, Culture, and Science. (2016). Key Figures: Education. p. 3.

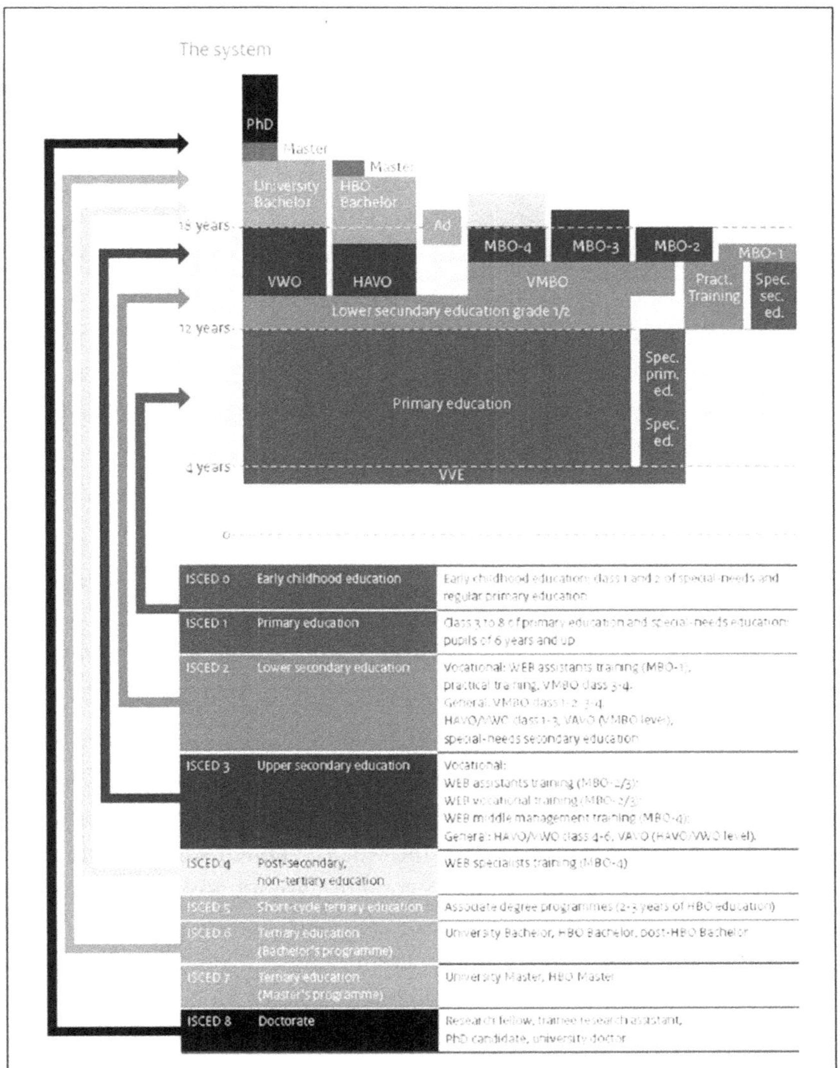

Figure 6. American Education System
Source: Wikipedia. (2017). Diagram of education in the United States.

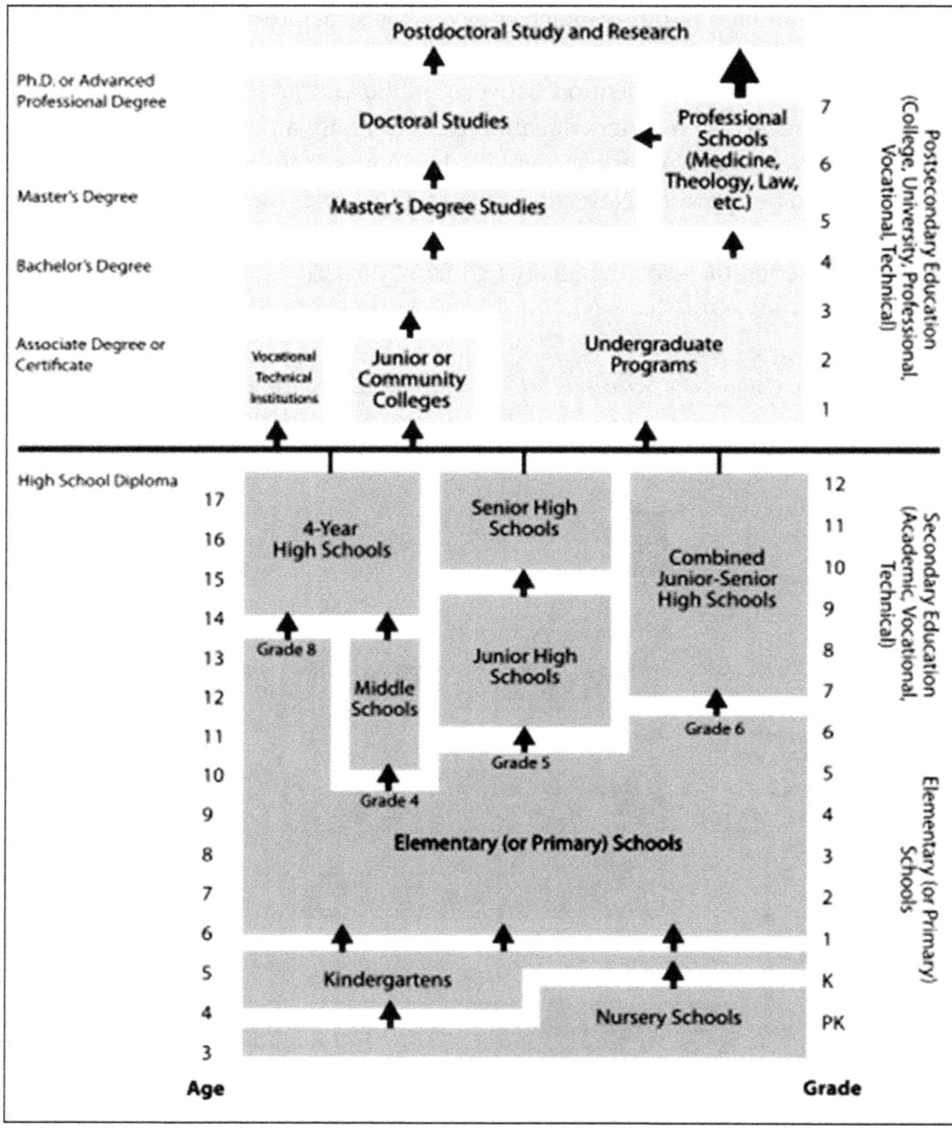

American culture influences the education system (Lynch, 2016). Essentially, American culture and education are mutually inclusive just like the Five Essential Supports. America tends to value personal freedom, individuality, and meritocracy, but not in the way the Dutch value freedom of choice. Americans believe you can do what you want and be who you are without government constraint. Unlike the Dutch, Americans devalue the importance of government intervention and often support deregulation in many sectors. This is evident in the vague statement on the U.S. Department of Education's website, "Our mission is to promote student achievement and preparation for global competitiveness by fostering educational excellence and ensuring equal access" (U.S. Department of Education, 2017).

In addition, America was founded on political and social equality, which in theory sounds amazing, but has been difficult to upkeep throughout the years due to segregation, racism, and biases which contribute to disparate impact and disadvantages for many minority groups. Despite the Department of Education's mission, little is done at the federal level to centralize standards and improve the quality of state and local education with true reform and embodiment of the Five Essential Supports. Lastly, because American government is centered around two political parties, bipartisan efforts are difficult and reform efforts divided and often paradoxical to societal improvement. The Dutch, being egalitarian, strive for compromise and coalition and creating reform movements producing the most good for the most people.

Macro, Meso, Micro Organizational Framework

To gain a better understanding of the Dutch and American public education structures, it is best to view both countries comparatively through the macro, meso, and micro perspectives. By comparing the countries on these levels, it becomes easier to understand how each level interacts and consequently improves or impairs teacher outcomes.

The American and Dutch public education systems differ greatly at the macro level. The stark difference on the macro level appears in how Dutch politicians and residents embrace education egalitarianism and centralization within their constitution.

One of the key features of the Dutch education system, the freedom of education, is safeguarded by Article 23 of the Constitution. It covers the freedom to set up schools, organise teaching systems at schools and determine the founding principles. Any citizen has the right to set up a school and provide education based on religious, ideological or educational beliefs. (Netherlands Ministry of Education, Culture, and Science, 2016)

The protection afforded by the Dutch constitution provides a safeguard for quality within freedom of choice, and improves the competitiveness of schools by ensuring all are receiving the macro-level support needed to succeed. Despite this freedom, there are limitations which both public and private schools must adhere to regarding quality standards set forth by the Ministry of Education, Culture, and Science.

These standards prescribe the subjects to be studied, the attainment levels or examination syllabuses and the content of national examinations, the number of teaching periods per year, which qualifications teachers must have, giving parents and pupils a say in school matters, planning and reporting obligations. (Netherlands Ministry of Education, Culture, and Science, 2016)

Simply from the constitution, we can understand how Dutch schools provide parents freedom of choice and educators a high level of autonomy through a highly centralized national standard and complimentary decentralized implementation structure at the meso and micro levels.

American public education equality is only protected (not stated) through the First and Fourteenth Amendments. As a result, instructional guidance is left to the states, districts, and municipalities to carry out how they would like" (Joyce, 2017 August). This complete decentralization of power allows for the macro level to avoid additional work and places significant stress on the meso level, which inadvertently effects the micro level structure. In America, despite the intent of the federal government to implement national standards, this simply cannot happen at the macro level without a constitutional change, which given the current state of politics in America seems like a distant hope. The US Department of Education website states:

Education is primarily a State and local responsibility in the United States. It is States and communities, as well as public and private organizations of all kinds, that establish schools and colleges, develop curricula, and determine requirements for enrollment and graduation. (U.S. Department of Education, 2017)

This statement by the federal government reaffirms decentralization at the macro level and centralization at the meso and micro levels, which are opposite of the Dutch system.

Due to the conflicts between centralization and decentralization of standards and curriculum goals in America, teachers and therefore students, are faced to uphold more standards than their Dutch counterparts due to the macro, meso, and micro level standards being implemented simultaneously. Furthermore, the centralization-decentralization conflict produces a culture of pervasive overtesting resulting in loss of teacher autonomy. As Laguardia and Pearl state, "Education decisions in state capitals and in Washington do not reflect the thinking of ordinary people; student input is nonexistent and as a result burning issues are never addressed in classrooms" (Laguardia & Pearl, 2009).

The two countries also differ on the meso and micro levels due to the structure at the macro level. Since the Dutch guaranteed citizens equal education and freedom of choice, there is a vast array of school choice within all regions of The Netherlands. In the 2009 report *Inclusive Education in the Netherlands*, author Annette Thijs states,

National curriculum policy in the Netherlands has increasingly shifted from a belief in the necessity of solid steering at macro level to a belief in the power at meso level, the level of school policy. The central curriculum policy has turned into processes of decentralisation and an increase in local autonomy. (Thijs, van Leeuwen, & Zandbergen, 2009, p. 14)

This statement illustrates the importance the Dutch place on the meso and micro level autonomy to achieve their outcomes and how much power is given to regions/school boards. Unfortunately, America has attempted to transfer authority to the meso level, meaning the states, but with overall failure as disparate outcomes are more apparent between America and other OECD nations. Although the meso level works well within the Dutch system, the American system would need to bypass the meso level moreso and instill autonomy on the micro level (individual schools and teachers) to improve outcomes and success.

The Dutch system provides parents the opportunity to attend any numbers of schools within their district, improving opportunities for success at the micro level. Although students may live in the Centrum (Central) district of Hilversum, the child may attend a school in Zuidwest (Southwest) if the school has a seat for them. Consequently, this freedom of choice allows parents to achieve optimum school fit without having to pay exuberant tuition fees like their American counterparts.

At the micro level, American public schools attempt to balance the requests and standards of the meso and macro levels. However, parents are left with relatively few opportunities consisting of varying standards, imbalanced availability funds/resources (which we be discussed in section 2.2), and lack of autonomy. Therefore, schools struggle to meet the needs of their students and community. As a result, students from low-income and disadvantaged backgrounds are the ones who suffer most with this funding structure. Because Dutch and American public schools can vary on teaching methods, vision, mission, etc. at the micro level, drastic differences may not be seen as frequently. Furthermore, parents usually only have one or two options within their district (meso/micro) resulting in limited school choice. This may produce situations of poor choice and lack of faith in public schools for many families.

Funding Structure

Dutch private and public schools, under the Constitution, are guaranteed equal public funding (Ministry of Education, Culture, and Science, 2016). In addition, private schools[7] receive equal national funding as public schools, and although they are subject to private law, must adhere to national curriculum standards set forth by the Ministry of Education, Culture, and Science. Currently, The Netherlands employs a type of equitable and pragmatic funding scheme allowing for a reduction in funding inequalities.

Contrary to America's tax-base structure, Dutch public schools introduced a grant-block funding scheme, where nearly 100% of funding is received from the federal government (macro level) as seen in Figure 4.

Figure 7. Dutch Primary Education Funding Structure

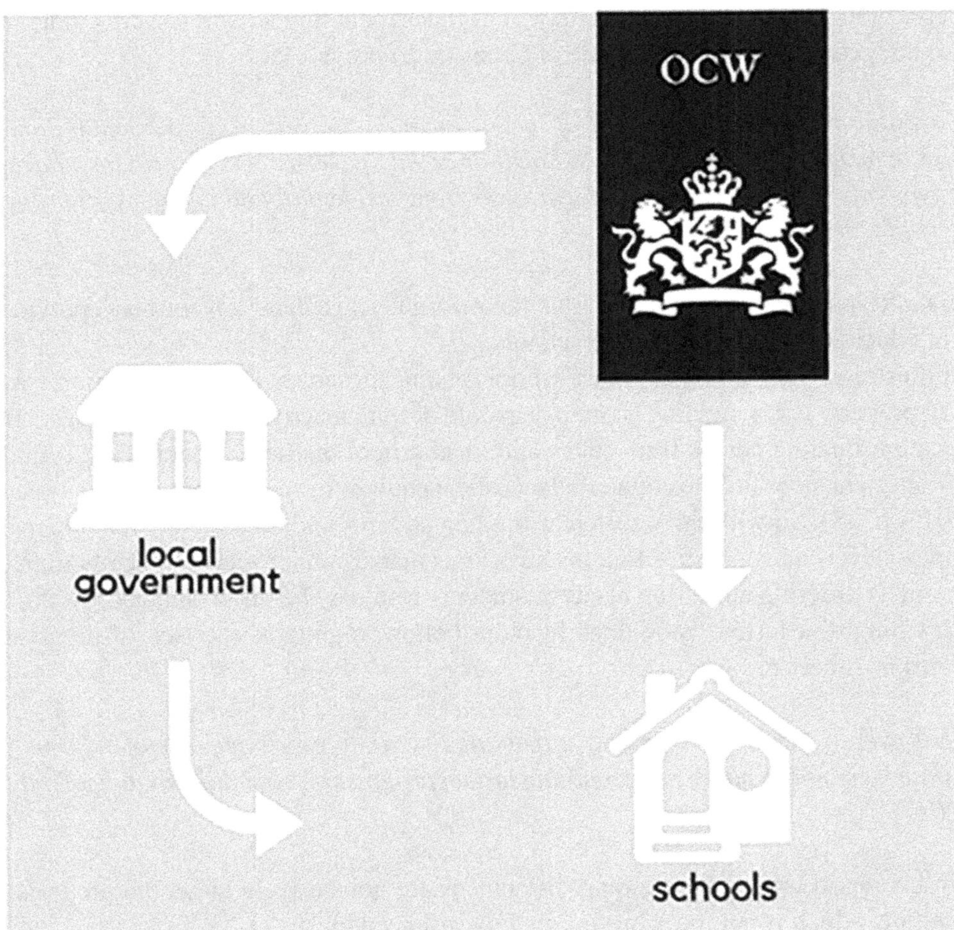

Although all schools receive equal initial amounts of funding, the government—out of grave concern for students from disadvantaged backgrounds—developed calculations to allocate additional funds for students coming from two major categories: (1) pupils who parents have low education attainment (lvo/vbo) and (2) pupils with one parent with primary level education and the other with no more than lbo/vbo attainment. Although there is some private contribution to education, it is quite low and statistically insignificant at .3% (Ministry of Education, Culture, and Science, 2016, p. 2). While the Dutch public education system struggles with lack of funding for teachers' salaries, school leaders have freedom at the micro level to distribute their funds as they see fit because of the progressive policies in place to help achieve an equitable balance for all students. Although the block grant funds are distributed to school boards (micro), the boards have a better idea of how much money is in their budget due to the equitable release of funds and transparent weight structure.

Although the American government spends, on average, 20% of more of its GDP on primary education, the method in which those funds are distributed differ greatly from the Dutch system. The average expenditure between 2001 and 2016 for Dutch and America is 1.36% and 1.72% respectively. As seen earlier in Chart 2, the percentage of GDP distributed for education between the Dutch government and American government during testing years 2001-2016 shows a minimal difference. American public schools receive their funding through a variety of avenues including federal (macro), state (meso), and local (micro) budgets. The National League of Cities (n.d.) provides a

...national average of around 49 percent of their education budgets using a combination of income taxes, corporate taxes, sales taxes and fees. Local or county governments contribute on average about 43 percent, typically using revenue from local taxes from residential and commercial properties. (National League of Cities, n.d.)

From this information, one can deduce that the macro level (federal government) provides approximately 8% of education funding overall to schools.

Figure 8 illustrates the American public school funding structure. Due to the multiple avenues and fluctuation in property taxes, funding is often disparate despite macro-level contributions. "Because the bulk of education funding comes from states and local school districts, federal Title I funding, while helpful and important, does little to counterbalance the inequities of state school finance systems" (Coley & Baker, 2013, p. 38). So with three different funding streams and the macro stream being the weakest, states (meso level) must produce funding structures that account for economically impaired school districts as well as differing education needs of students who may be disadvantaged.[8] A 2017 report by Matthew M. Chingos, a former Brookings Institute Fellow, highlights the lack of progressiveness in funding reform in America:

...the fact that overall funding progressivity remains low despite two decades of reforms enacted by courts and state legislatures suggests a troubling lack of progress on equitable funding of public schools. (Chingos, 2017)

Although his report admits the funding differences are not savagely huge, the progress to provide equitable funding, which is not the same as equal, is still needed.

Figure 8. American public school Funding Structure

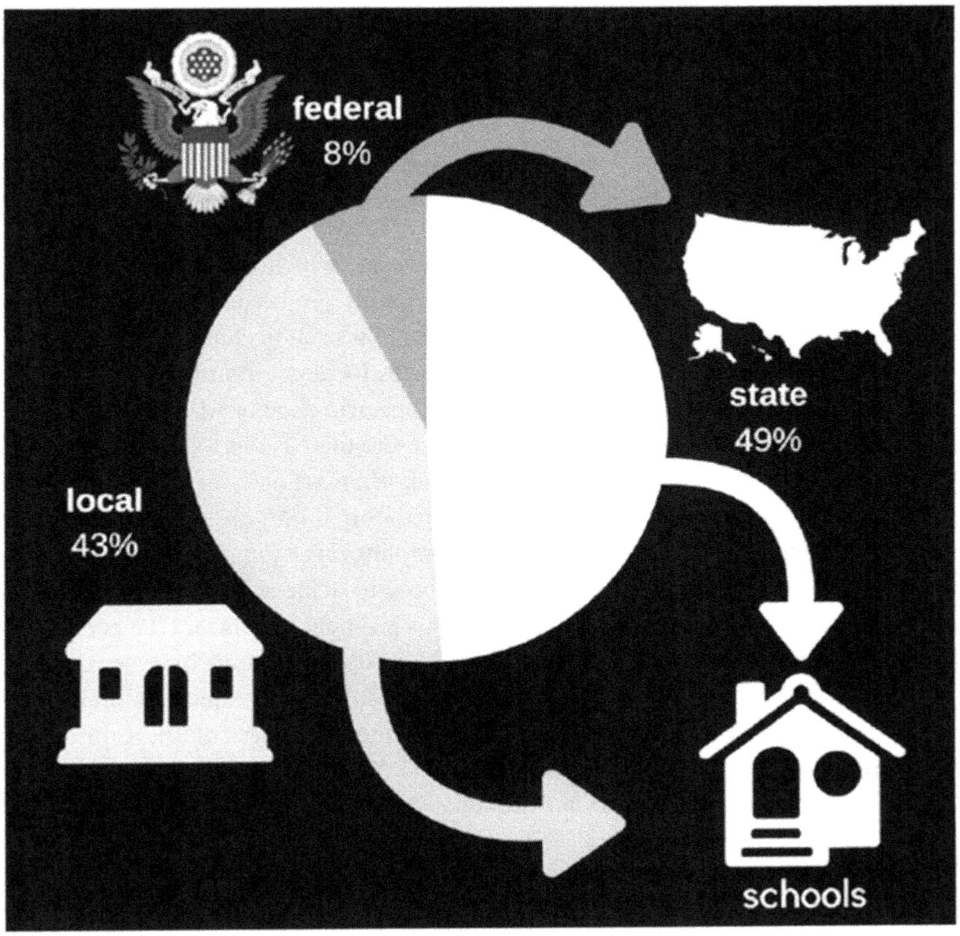

Accountability Standards

Organizational accountability is important in any business and large organization. Public education is one of the largest businesses governments operate, and it is important the schools within these systems are held to standards at the macro, meso, and micro levels. The Dutch government's centralization of standards help ensure all schools are held accountable to same the curriculum outcomes, thus ensuring all students have access to a high standard of education. Several measures exist within the Dutch public education system which help keep schools accountable:

1. Level-specific education acts
2. Common outcome standards (7 total)
3. Core objectives (58 total)
4. Prescribed curriculum hours
5. Inspectorate monitoring

Primary education is overseen by the *Primary Education Act (WPO) of 1998*[9] which insists the following subjects must appear in the curriculum, where possible in an integrated form: (i) sensory coordination and physical education; (ii) Dutch; (iii) arithmetic and mathematics; (iv) English; (v) a number of factual subjects, including geography, history, science (including biology), (vi) social structures (including political studies) and religious and ideological movements; (vii) expressive activities, including use of language, drawing, music, handicrafts, and play and movement; (viii) social and life skills, including road safety, and (ix) healthy living (Thijs, van Leeuwen, & Zandbergen, 2009, p. 13).

By communicating subject curriculum goals precisely, school leaders, school boards, and teachers know what they are working towards daily in the classroom, which can help increase transparency, school partnerships, and positive culture within the community. To better guide implementation at the micro level, the government includes core objectives within these subject areas all while leaving implementation completely up to the micro level which increases local autonomy. "Schools are given more scope for the development of education in line with the specific needs and local environment of their pupils" (Thijs, van Leeuwen, & Zandbergen, 2009). With the increase in local autonomy and freedom to differentiate education for individual learners, it is important schools meet these common, national standards to ensure and protect implementation decentralization. If they are not upholding the standards, it will be found out through the Education Inspectorate monitoring system.

In America, there seems to be a struggle amongst how to achieve accountability standards at the three levels with the American system due to dichotomous political beliefs and the pervasive overuse of standardized tests. "The assessments are ''high stakes'' because test scores have serious consequences for students and schools" (Laguardia & Pearl, 2009, p. 355). The consequences include reduction of funds, job loss, reorganization, transfer students, and rewriting their curriculum. Riddled with a variety of accountability standards centered around tests, America's public education system needs a vast reform, not just bandaids. Currently, school leaders and administrators must meet accountability standards from:

1. Local school district
2. State department of education
3. US Department of Education

Although it appears to be less standards than the Dutch system, the creation of the federal *Every Student Succeeds Act (ESSA)* gives perceived increased autonomy at the state level as states must create individualized accountability plans, which are then approved or rejected by the US Department of Education. This strive towards increased state accountability does not direct states in a clear and transparent manner, thus leaving much up to interpretation resulting in a wide array of plans, ideas, goals, and actions.

The accountability standards are not equitable across the country, leading to additional school disparities especially among disenfranchised communities. For example, the State of Illinois' accountability plan under the *ESSA* plans to start measuring school quality in 2018-2019 through

standardized tests, alternative assessments, academic growth, English language proficiency, science scores, success on college entrance tests, and graduation rates, as well as factors such as chronic absenteeism and school climate surveys. (Krishnamurthy, 2017, para. 6)

Once the results of these accountability systems are in, schools will receive a grade and categorized into one of four tiers (1 being the best and 4 being the worst). Although the notion behind allowing states to create customized accountability plans falls into increased meso-level autonomy, it does not guarantee outcomes or accountability. Instead the increased pressure placed on testing and rates increases administrator and teacher pressure to create lessons geared towards improving those factors in the value-added model. With the lack of equitable funding, schools, despite making growth and strides with students who start the school year behind, will be ranked lower than other schools where the school received high funding. With these muddled, test-focused accountability standards, it is no wonder the curriculum and testing structure is drastically different between the Dutch and American systems.

Curriculum/Testing Structure

Dutch schools limit the amount of standardized testing their students encounter with students sitting for the CITO exam during their last year of primary school to help guide their placement into secondary school. The test is not the only factor reviewed, but helps administrators and teachers provide families guidance when choosing a secondary school. The Dutch believe in being proactive and pragmatic in their approach to education while mandated to adhere to a national curriculum standard.

Successful schools are also more effective at adjusting the curriculum to suit the pupil population. This ensures that the subject matter and level match the pupils' opportunities and the curriculum is meaningful, stimulating and challenging. Often, teams collectively design and arrange the classes, scheduling and organisation as well as monitoring learning success and tackling problems. We also see that moments of success for individual pupils often have an intrinsically motivational effect on their learning. (Education Inspectorate: Ministry of Education, Culture, and Science, 2017A)

While Dutch students must take the CITO exam to help determine their placement at the secondary school level, students are not exposed to the stress of learning for a test. Instead, they can learn for the sake of learning.

In addition to limited standardized testing, schools and teachers are able to structure their lessons however they choose so long as it helps students reach the national core objectives within the subject areas mentioned in section 2.3 at the end of the year. Since the Ministry of Education, Science, and Culture is responsible for setting the curriculum standards, implementation is left to the meso and micro levels, which improves freedom of choice for parents and autonomy for school leaders and educators.

The Education Inspectorate says teachers work together frequently in groups to strategize and create lesson plans, design classes, and organize the schools. This results in increased teacher autonomy and motivation, something sorely lacking in American public schools. The intentional effort by administrators to increase teamwork in Dutch public schools ensures teachers are not working in silos and continually developing their craft. The one aspect the curriculum has not addressed is the decreased motivation among Dutch students to exceed standards. Often, it is culturally acceptable to meet and not exceed standards, which causes scores to fall on global, standardized tests such as TIMSS, PIRLS, and PISA. Overall, it appears the curriculum standards set by the government are met and exceeded due to autonomy at the micro level.

In America, students are tested frequently to ensure they are proficient in curriculum standards at the local, state, and national level (micro, meso, and macro). However, there are multiple standardized tests these students take, and they change throughout the years. The Iowa Test of Basic Skills was replaced by the ISATs, until currently states utilize any number of the following:

- National Assessment for Education Progress (NAEP)
- Stanford Achievement Test (SAT-9, SAT-10)
- TerraNova
- Standardized Testing and Reporting (STAR)
- Partnership for Assessment of Readiness for College and Careers (PARCC)

In addition, the website Time4Learning.com lists out the numerous and varied state standardized tests each state utilizes, which helps visualize just how individualized and varied American public education standards are. The combination of varied standardized testing and lack of national curriculum alignment leads to unaligned standards, which. Dr. Linda Darling-Hammond states in her 2006 policy report *Standards, Assessment, and Educational Policy: In Pursuit of Genuine Accountability:*

Furthermore, where a comprehensive reform is not pursued, assessments are often unaligned to the standards. And in many states, the standards and curriculum are aimed more at superficial coverage of topics than mastery of content. For example, international assessments such as the Trends in International Mathematics and Science Study (TIMSS) have shown that students in the United States are typically asked to cover many more topics in fields such as mathematics as students in other countries that have higher levels of achievement (Darling-Hammond, 1996; Lapointe, Mead, & Phillips, 1989; McKnight et al., 1987). (Darling-Hammond, 2006)

Pervasive overtesting to measure proficiency and growth are the norm in American public schools. Contrary to their private counterparts, public school students see upwards of eight standardized tests per year. According to Valerie Strauss at the *Washington Post* (2015), "The average student in America's big-city public schools takes some 112 mandatory standardized tests between pre-kindergarten and the end of 12th grade — an average of about eight a year, the study says" (Council of the Great City Schools, 2015). By increasing the amount of standardized tests in classes, teachers must build test preparation into their lesson plans, reducing the amount of time allowed to teacher innovatively and creatively.

This type of pervasive and varied testing without a doubt affects teachers in the classroom, but another study should explore those[10]. However, this paper acknowledges, "The reform undermines teacher morale and teacher initiative, both of which are fundamental for a positive educational experience" (Laguardia & Pearl, 2009).

Enrollment Demographics

While the total population of Holland and the United States differs drastically as see in Chart 4, the proportion (in percentage form) of primary age students enrolled in primary (NL) or elementary school (US) within the total population is similar as seen in Chart 5. The interesting aspect to gain from these simple enrollment demographics helps negate arguments that since America is a larger country, it is harder to implement standards for that many students.

However, if you look at the proportion of primary students to the total population, achieving national standards through centralization is possible as the Dutch public education system has achieved. Although other factors must be accounted for such as constitutional rights, cultural values, and funding structure, the proportion illustrates the possibility of education reform.

Figure 9. Total Population NL vs US

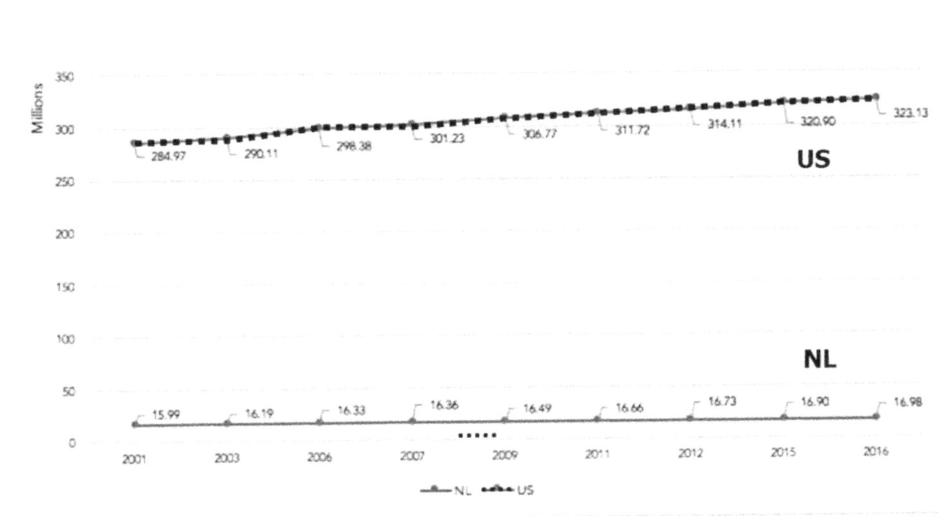

Figure 10. Primary Population as % of Total Population

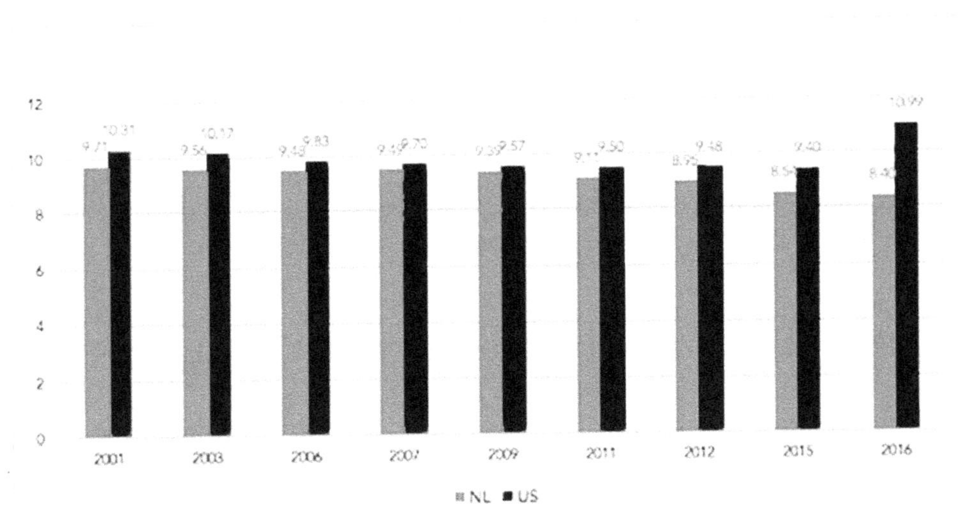

Further research into native-born versus foreign-born residents could be crucial to understanding the importance of pre-service teacher training and its interaction within the Five Essential Supports.

The Dutch Faults

The Dutch public education system is not without its faults, which are important to address to ensure an unbiased research approach. In *The State of Education 2015-2016,* published by the Education Inspectorate within the Ministry of Education, Culture, and Science (2017), the following were found to be faults within the Dutch public education system. Although this report by the government focuses on the entire education system from early childhood education to tertiary education, this paper focuses on the Dutch primary public education system, which displays the following shortfalls:

1. The Dutch number of high performing students decreased from 50% to 37%, a much greater rate compared to fellow nations (p. 6).
2. International studies continually and recently show Dutch students are "less motivated than pupils in other countries" (p. 6).
3. Dutch primary school pupils displayed a significant decline in science performance
4. "Fewer primary-school children achieve the reference level for arithmetic." The percentage of students failing to achieve increased from 9% to 13% between 2011 and 2015 (p. 6).
5. Despite the freedom of choice, there is growing inequality in the education system mainly between students with less-educated parents and those with highly-educated parents, which is "particularly evident in the recommendations issued to primary-school leavers" (p. 13).
6. The Dutch schools experience differences in quality at the primary level "as has been observed by inspectors visiting the schools" (p. 22).
7. "The significant drop in the intake levels of teacher training (PABO) programmes is a worrying development. In addition, there is little diversity in the group of entrants: few men, few students with a migrant background and few graduates of natural sciences and/or technical subjects" (p. 30).
8. "It therefore appears that the teachers that need professionalisation the most are the ones that do not participate in such activities" (p. 31).

This paper could continue to identify faults within the Dutch public education system, but that can be done with any education system in the world, even the best ones. That is outside the scope of this paper, but it is important to note the areas needing improvement in the Dutch system to limit bias.

A COMPARATIVE REVIEW WITHIN THE FIVE ESSENTIAL SUPPORTS

As previously mentioned, this comparative study focuses on the American versus Dutch public education system's institutional differences within the framework of Moore's Five Essential Supports for schools. It is fundamentally imperative to understand the basic requirements for each pillar of support to gain a better understanding of the Dutch public education system and its operability potential within this American-based framework.

By understanding the implementation of each support, we can better understand the interrelatedness between dynamic teacher training (both in and out of university) and improvement within the rest of the supports. Furthermore, by understanding this interconnectedness, we can logically identify (through a logic model and APGAR analysis) potential positive outcomes in economics, civic engagement, innovation, human development, and prosperity amongst other global identifiers of societal health.

School Leadership

Within this essential support, “improving students’ learning and performance requires leadership from the faculty, the parents, and the community” (Sebring, Allensworth, Bryk, & Easton, 2006, p. 9). The authors point to the ability of every stakeholder at the micro-level is capable of displaying and acting upon their leadership abilities to better the organization. In theory this is a perfect way to run any organization because it allows for flexibility and improves the use of human talent; however, not every school in the US employs this mindset due to the macro structure of education. However, this type of mindset is more prevalent in Dutch schools, which is attributed to the increased meso- and micro-level autonomy.

While not every Dutch education administrator is original and groundbreaking, the realistic outlook and down-to-earth cultural attitudes of the Dutch produce contemporary leaders. The combination of culture with the immense amount of micro-level leadership autonomy allows leaders to create team-based environments, which are key to improved professional capacity/quality, community partnerships, and ambitious instruction.

“Successful schools are more likely to have a higher level of teamwork amongst the staff” (Education Inspectorate: Ministry of Education, Culture, and Science, 2017A). This statement was verified in earlier OECD studies. The Inspectorate of Education also finds that in many schools, teachers, school leaders and school board members are working hard to improve the quality of education (Education Inspectorate: Ministry of Education, Culture, and Science, 2017B). Although there are clear areas for further improvement, the quality and dedication of teachers is one of the key reasons for the success of the Dutch school system (OECD, 2016, p. 40). School leaders and local school boards are able to have more control over the vision and direction of the school since they can choose how to implement training programs that will benefit their community and focus on inclusive leadership that considers all stakeholders (parents, teachers, administrators, parents, community). Decentralization allows autonomy to occur at the micro-level, which is highly uncommon in America. However, it does not leave the Dutch system without struggles for school leadership.

Amidst a teacher shortage, school leadership realizes “...teachers looking for a job are more likely to choose schools with an easier pupil population, so vacancies at schools with a more challenging pupil population are harder to fill” (Education Inspectorate: Ministry of Education, Culture, and Science, 2017A, p. 23). This gap means there is a variance in the amount of qualified teachers available at the primary school level, which could be a reason for lower test scores. However, school leaders can counteract this variance with autonomy to hire or restructure the day-to-day workings of the school to maximize the abilities of the staff.

School leadership in America differs drastically between schools with some believing in a very heavy top-down structure and others with a bottom-up or flattened approach to leadership. The type of leadership is the most important of the Five Supports as it is the driver for change. While top-down policies stifle comprehensive and inclusive leadership in American public schools, innovative administrators such as Hamish Brewer, who made national news in 2017, reveal the possibilities for innovative leadership. Noted for having an “unconventional style”, tattoos, and riding around school on a skateboard, Brewer’s former and now current employee (she followed him to his new school) Nicole Sweezy stated in an interview with the *Washington Post*, “I wanted to make sure I kept *[sic]* in a workplace where that passion continued” (Hunley, 2017).

Brewer is one of the most innovative leaders in school and dedicates his time to turning around some of the worst performing schools. His innate ability to connect with faculty, students, and parents, while balancing the demands at the local, state, and federal level are worthy of additional research. Some examples of innovative thinking and leadership employed by Brewer include turning a meeting room off the main hallway into his office instead of utilizing a regular principal's office "so he can be in the middle of the action and quickly build relationships with students" (Hunley, 2017 July). It's the absence of these out-of-the box solutions from American public schools that reduces the efficiency and capabilities of the school community.

"Schooling is a human-resource-intensive enterprise. Schools are only as good as the quality of faculty, the professional development that supports their learning, and the faculty's capacity to work together to improve instruction" (Bryk, Bender Sebring, Allensworth, Luppescu, & Easton, 2010). While the US must acknowledge the vast inequalities facing different school districts, teachers, and educators, there school leadership must believe their teachers and students are worthy of success. When this type of belief is present and instilled in the culture of the school through in-service training, increased support of teacher autonomy, and willingness to step outside comfort zones, the faculty will proceed to work together to improve instruction, the school community, and the school's community partnerships.

Overall, this essential support is of the utmost importance as it spurs positive, organizational change in all other supports. Just as teachers can change the beliefs of children, it is leadership that changes the beliefs of the community surrounding them.

Parent-Community Ties

"Schools, children and teenagers flourish when parents are involved in education. To this end, the government wants to strengthen collaboration between parents and schools" (People's Party for Freedom and Democracy (VVD), Christian Democratic Alliance (CDA), Democrats '66 (D66), and Christian Union (CU), 2017). This statement reaffirms the government's belief in building a long-lasting partnerships for the betterment of their society and that education is a key responsibility of government. Contrastingly, we do not have this belief in America, resulting in disparities and lack of restorative school communities by and large.

There is a huge rise in the amount of Dutch community schools. The Nederlands Juegd Instituut published a fact sheet on its community schools and state,

In the community school concept a large number of community-based activities and services are integrated. It is a practical implementation of the integrated youth policy in which the school has a central role. The community school links education to various important children and parents' services like parenting support, child day care, health centres, etc. By combining services in a network or in a shared building, they become more accessible. Also, the various services can join forces and adjust their services to match and complement each other as well as meet the needs of the children and parents. (Netherlands Youth Institute, 2017, para. 2)

By affording citizens the opportunity to attend community schools, the Dutch government is providing better freedom of choice and support for the disadvantaged communities who typically need more support than the advantaged. Although some studies show the importance of the community school's concept, others show little is to be gained from these types of situations. Hence, critical further research is needed in this area and lies outside the scope of this paper. However, research for this paper indicates most Dutch schools provide resource avenues for parents in terms of before and after school care and certain after-school activities. By integrating themselves into the lives of working parents on this level, Dutch public schools show they care and empathize with parents.

A school's utilization of their social capital to improve the community's and school's outcomes is often overlooked by American public school leadership and teachers resulting in top-down policies and reduction in the ability for a school environment to confront brutal facts about the out-of-school environments of students. Consequently, disadvantaged neighborhoods are left with staff who are lacking the cultural understanding of their community leading to isolation and further degradation of a potential support system. Furthermore, by placing extreme emphasis on standardized tests, teachers lose their initiative to connect as education becomes more of a business. "The reform undermines teacher morale and teacher initiative, both of which are fundamental for a positive educational experience" (Laguardia & Pearl, 2009, p. 357). And while public schools are a business, *every* student is a customer and deserves the best customer service. When teachers feel disconnected, they do not want to utilize social capital to improve the community.

US public school district diversity allows for some of the best schools to shine, but those schools typically only sit in the wealthy district, where parents are highly educated, provide support for their children, and are inherently motivated to help build their community. This is not the case with poorly-funded school districts, where parents are used to being in survival mode, operating in silos, having to work multiple jobs to earn a living, or having little faith in a public education system that failed them. These factors reduce available time to dedicate to school community improvement. Thus, social capital is of utmost importance when building parent/community ties especially in areas of need. Social capital helps re-establish citizenship preparation, inclusion, and a student-centered learning environment while easing problems such as "minimal trust and palpable discomfort" (Sebring, Allensworth, Bryk, & Easton, 2006).

The key to this community building in US public schools is the teacher, which will of course be inspired and encouraged by traditional school leadership. While many American public schools believe they do enough with internal communication, schools fail to acknowledge and engage the influential community stakeholders, such as church groups, after school programs, and libraries. Teachers must be trained and inspired to utilize these resources to improve the outcomes for their students. "Teachers have a crucial role in our vision of educational change" (Laguardia & Pearl, 2009, p. 359). As teachers build community partnerships with parents, they gain a better understanding of community problems, possible solutions, and increase parental participation in student outcomes, which improves a student's internal attitude towards learning. And in a digital age, when students encounter more and more "external locus of control," personal relationships within the community are evermore important because external factors directly connect to internal beliefs (Goodwin, 2016, p. 84). However, teachers will continue to struggle to build community and parent partnerships without the autonomy to do so.

Professional Capacity/Quality

When talking about the quality of teachers, it is important to understand the factors used to measure quality. Often within America, standardized tests are utilized as the main measure for teacher quality. "The surge in standardized student testing has fulfilled this gap by providing an accountability measure to stakeholders—commonly termed as the 'value-added' approach" (van Ruijven, 2016, p. 8). While standardized tests provide some insight, they do not successfully indicate all factors required for quality and capable educators. What is known is that higher quality teachers improve the outcomes of students in the long term. Ron Chetty and John Friedman published a paper entitled *The Long Term Impacts of Teachers: Teacher Value-Added and Student Outcomes in Adulthood*, where they found "...that teacher VA has substantial impacts on a broad range of outcomes" (Chetty, Friedman, & Rockoff, 2014):

- raises the probability of college attendance
- raises the quality of the colleges that students attend
- elevates earnings trajectories, with significantly higher earnings growth rates in their 20s
- significantly reduces the probability of having a child while being a teenager
- increases the quality of the neighborhood in which the student lives
- raises 401(k) retirement savings rates (2014, p. 3)

Although Chetty and Friedman's paper does an excellent job of pinpointing the tangible effects of quality teachers, the question remains, "what constitutes a quality teacher?"

Through the research done for this paper and the current knowledge about the American and Dutch education systems, this comparative analysis pinpoints four overarching factors as pinpointed within the Five Essential Supports (Sebring, Allensworth, Bryk, & Easton, 2006, p. 16): (1) content knowledge coupled with pedagogical skills and their ability to engage in teamwork, (2) beliefs and values that teachers and educators are responsible for change, (3) focus on local improvement efforts, and (4) ability to work cohesively in a professional community. By measuring teacher quality within the structure of these four qualities, one can see differences between the American and Dutch systems, which as Chety and Friedman admit, cause changes to student outcomes thus resulting in a causal relationship presence. It is important to note standardized tests, while able to measure content knowledge, cannot measure the other three factors as all are mutually inclusive. Despite being able to exclusively pinpoint each factor as measurable, additional research must be done to understand and measure the relationship of these four factors on teacher quality at both the pre-service and in-service level. We can pinpoint differences between the Dutch and American teachers with the four factors. It is important to note the Dutch are increasingly critical of their education system, but this paper looks at it in comparison to the American system[11]. The biggest differences between the Dutch and American professional capacity/quality lies in aforementioned factors 1 and 3.

For factor 1, Dutch student-teachers attend Hogeschools or universities and enroll in a PABO program where students spend approximately 60% of their time on theory and pedagogy with approximately 40% of their time in practicum. This division of time allows student-teachers to develop a strong understanding of pedagogy and improve their didactic quality due to the leaning and practice feedback circle created within their first year of PABO. By being able to practice what they learn through mentorship or lessons, students are able to receive continual feedback, which improves their content knowledge and interpersonal skills, which are crucial to improving teacher success. In addition, the training institutions provide clearcut standards of what is acceptable for teachers in terms of the four factors by expanding professional quality to seven capacities as seen in Figure 6, taken from the Study Guide at Hogeschool Utrecht for their Teacher Training Program in English and established by the national government.

While teacher education institutions have great flexibility, minimum competency requirements are set out in seven domains in the Education Professions Act (2006), which covers competencies such as: in-

terpersonal, pedagogical, subject-specific and didactical, organisational competencies, competencies to co-operate with colleagues and with the environment, and self-reflective and developmental competencies. (OECD, 2015a; OECD, 2016)

This centralized mandate coupled with the decentralized implementation provides autonomy for teacher education programs to improve their student teachers based on the population and maintain a national level of excellence.

Figure 11. Primary Teacher Competency Requirements
Source: Hogeschool Utrecht. (2017). Primary Teacher Competencies.

Professional situation: / Professional roles:	With pupils	With colleagues	With the community	With oneself
Interpersonal	1. competent in interpersonal relations	5. competent in cooperating with colleagues	6. competent in cooperating with the community	7. competent in reflection and development
Pedagogical	2. pedagogically competent			
Subject-related and didactic competency	3. competent in the subject and didactic competency			
Organizational	4. organizationally competent			

The key to Factor 3's success is the high level of autonomy due to decentralization of implementation standards. While standards are set at a national level for teacher training and curriculum, every teacher training program and local school can choose how they want to improve the structure of their programs without having to worry about meeting micro and meso level standards, which is very prevalent in American public schools. Training and growth at the local (micro) level is essential to a strong school community and productive student outcomes. "Dutch teachers work on professionalisation as much as their colleagues in other countries, although a notable factor is that the professionalisation activities are often informal" (Education Inspectorate: Ministry of Education, Culture, and Science, 2017A). By increasing the availability of informal professional development activities, teachers can grow their skills and craft in relaxed environments and allow them to step outside their teaching silos, which are often present in American culture.

Furthermore, new and underqualified teachers receive more professional development opportunities than experienced teachers to help improve their quality. "New teachers and teachers who are not yet qualified participate in more professionalisation activities than more experienced teachers" (Education Inspectorate: Ministry of Education, Culture, and Science, 2017A). By being able to funnel resources towards new teachers, Dutch public schools can maintain a level of excellence for new teachers without fully compromising the development of their experienced teachers whose classroom often receive more visits from colleagues. A report by the Education Inspectorate also notes successful schools provide lessons of high pedagogic *[sic]* and didactic quality. They also monitor the quality of the lessons and teachers, often via intervision, supervision, guidance, training, and a supportive personnel policy. This is regularly combined with school-wide discussions regarding the educational focus of the school. A vision is created and implemented into concrete agreements and the school leader ensures a firm basis for this vision. (Education Inspectorate, 2017A, p. 28)

Hence, Dutch schools place an emphasis on continual feedback in a variety of methods depending on what is best suited for the local school itself. Not only does this method ensure professional capacity/quality, it creates a positive feedback loop to ensure a student-centered learning environment discussed earlier.

American public schools encounter a variance in teacher quality first and foremost because of the array of post-secondary teacher training institutions available and will be discussed in section 4.2. However, a list of competencies varies depending on the state in which a teacher is studying and practicing. This variance affects factor 1. In addition, what is deemed a competent teacher is often times solely restricted to content knowledge on national reviews. For example, a review of the US Department of Education's Highly Qualified Teachers Revised State Plans website (2013) showed an immense focus on highly qualified teachers having "(1) a bachelor's degree, (2) full state certification or licensure, and (3) prove that they know each subject they teach" (U.S. Department of Education, 2017). These requirements do not encompass all soft skills necessary to display professional competence and quality, which improve a school and its ability to connect with its community and provide ambitious instruction.

The current teacher training in America prepares students to meet these minimalist standards, but does not prepare students to develop into well-rounded educators who learn from master teachers and improve their retention of content knowledge. Nowhere in the state reports were teachers reviewed on their interpersonal ability, beliefs and values, or local improvement efforts. Thus a teacher in America could be deemed highly qualified and capable simply by having a degree and high level of content knowledge with only 16 weeks of practical training. If this teacher is paired with high achieving students, they will be credited with being the reason for high test scores. If paired with disadvantaged students, the students will take the blame if they do not make the minimum test scores. Hence, it appears the American public school measurement system focuses more on test scores and content than a well-rounded teacher with an ability to change the local community and cohesively become a member of a team.

Since an immense amount of power is given to the states (meso-level) in the American public school system, teachers often do not feel motivated to create a vision and strive for local community improvement. This lack of belief in local impact and reduction in utilization of social capital means teachers cannot actively contribute to Factor 3 although they have the innate vision to improve society. Laguardia and Pearl state,

The only way education can move to be more democratic is through bottom-up change with teachers demonstrating and documenting the impact that democracy has on education and education has on democracy. (Laguardia & Pearl, 2009, p. 359)

While this is a good thought in practice, its implementation is almost nonexistent at schools within America. However, there are outliers who seem to improve the abilities of their staff and community despite varying state perspectives on teacher quality. These outliers are accounted for in Hale and Rollins article (Hale & Rollins, 2006, p. 5) where breakthrough high school principals stated using a mixture of the following strategies to improve their teacher capacity/quality:

- creating a supportive environment for learning in public;
- establishing non-negotiables, such as goals and standards;
- holding teachers accountable; and
- using a mix of leadership actions which can best be categorized as "intangibles."

While lacking of micro-level autonomy, some principals find creative ways to circumnavigate standards that hinder the progress teachers can make and want to make to improve their professional development and capacity, which ultimately reduces the overall quality of a teacher and their school community. Hence, it is important to note the working relationship between School Leadership and Professional Capacity and how if implemented properly, they contribute immensely to a positive student-centered environment.

Student-Centered Learning Environment

In a study conducted by sociologist James Coleman more than half a century ago, he found the most powerful barrier to success: "A single 'student attitude factor' (or lack thereof) showed a 'stronger relationship to achievement than . . . all the 'school' factors together'..." (Goodwin, 2016). Coleman's study reveals something that officials responsible for making educational decisions fail to take into account—the tie between external locus of control and internal locus of control. The Dutch have a more pragmatic approach to solution-based policy creation than the US. With the most basic factor of the student-centered learning environment being safety, the Dutch will continually be ahead of US public schools. These policies and education structure/funding help produce student-centered learning environments more conducive to positive student outcomes.

School safety is important to student success because unless students feel safe, they are unable to effectively focus and produce quality work. The Dutch government has some of the strictest gun laws in the country making it virtually impossible for anyone but hunters, target shooters, and police to carry weapons. Combine these laws with Constitutionally guaranteed health care and equal education and the Dutch public education system helps provide students a safe and healthy environment in which to study. Culturally, the directness of the Dutch allows schools to set clear expectations and help parents and students understand how to achieve those goals. Currently, there is much debate about inclusionary education in the Dutch public education system, and the government is actively taking steps to ensure a more balanced educational approach for special needs students and gifted students.

And despite the criticisms present in their State of Education reports, the Dutch are doing things better than America. The Education Inspectorate acknowledges the importance of "collective adjustment of the curriculum" (Education Inspectorate: Ministry of Education, Culture, and Science, 2017B) based on the needs of a student population. Hence, the federal government encourages schools at the local level to adjust curriculum and pedagogic methods to ensure students can meet the national standards, objectives, and goals. By placing power in the hands of the educators, the government increases the chances of better student-centered learning environments. These environments require educators to possess content expertise and didactic skills, pupil understanding at the socioemotional development, the ability to include student thoughts in a lesson, and to seek professional help and guidance for challenging students (Education Inspectorate: Ministry of Education, Culture, and Science, 2017B). Combined together, these freedoms improve the quality of a student-centered environment not just in the classroom but within the school community. This is often not the case in America.

Unlike the Dutch society, the US constitution supports the right to bear arms while not constitutionally guaranteeing healthcare and education resulting in dangerous school communities in some areas. In this context, communities do not only include the school itself, but also the walking/bus routes to school, homes, and after-school facilities. By increasing danger in each of these areas and not providing proper health care and education overall, American public school students may face perilous environments daily which hinder their ability to achieve academic success.

Within the school, an American student-centered learning environment realistically consists of classroom management requiring all students to do the same exact thing, listen to instruction, and to fit within a box to ensure not a minute of instruction is wasted for the sake of "the test". However, this is not possible for all students and is an antiquated thought process. Today, students receive less and less movement time, yet studies prove over and over again students requirement movement to learn about the world around them and process information. In essence, the American public school chase for higher scores on standardized tests leads to loss of teacher autonomy and innovation, less opportunities for exploration, and the stifling of students' natural and scientifically-proven tendencies. If teachers are unable to expand the use of their social capital for fear of lower test scores, they are doing students, particularly those in low-income or minority areas an injustice. "Hence, schools where teachers have been able to engage students in the learning process and where the school community has been able to shape a strong ethic for academic achievement are much more likely to achieve growth in student learning" (Sebring, Allensworth, Bryk, & Easton, 2006, p. 13). Better teacher training, increased autonomy, and a reduction in standardized testing would allow this type of student-centered environment to flourish within the American public education system.

Ambitious Instruction

Ambitious instruction is the "single most direct factor that affects student learning" (Sebring, Allensworth, Bryk, & Easton, 2006, p. 14). While ambitious instruction includes a teacher's ability to have broad content knowledge, it must also include the ability to motivate students to meet and exceed standards through differentiated learning, material organization, and purposeful assignments. Lastly, school leadership and teachers must ensure they fully understand and address macro-, meso-, and micro-level standards to guarantee an aligned curriculum across the school community. If these steps are not taken, curriculum is misaligned, student outcomes are varied, and teacher cohesiveness is erratic.

As previously mentioned, the structure of the Dutch accountability system coupled with micro-level autonomy allows teachers to achieve ambitious instruction overall. Recently, the Education Inspectorate's Search and Compare ranked 6,857 Dutch primary schools as Sufficient to Good and only 108 as Inadequate, Weak, or Very Weak (2017).

Knowing the structure of the school system within the previously discussed Five Essential Supports, those factors allow teachers to pursue ambitious instruction without fear of value-added modeling, standardized testing, loss of autonomy, or cumbersome top-down leadership. The Education Inspectorate also hints to the quality of teacher training programs as a reason for student success in their 2017 report.

Compared to teachers in other European countries, Dutch teachers are very skilled in a number of areas. They plan the lessons well, the content of the lessons is good and the teachers clearly explain to pupils what is expected of them and what the goals of the lesson are. (Education Inspectorate: Ministry of Education, Culture, and Science, 2017A, p. 30)

By preparing teachers with immense practical training and exposing them to a variety of different learning environments, Dutch teachers are more prepared to challenge a wide array of students including those coming from low education backgrounds[12]. Furthermore, schools are able to meet the same centralized education standards, objectives, and goals as mentioned previously.

Providing teachers more time through centralization of standards and reduction of standardized tests, Dutch public schools can improve the abilities of their teachers and instruction by providing feedback from other teachers as well as school leaders.

Approximately 80% of primary school teachers "have at least one of their lessons observed by the school leader each year" (Education Inspectorate, 2017, p. 32). By having these types of feedback loops present in combination with a team-based and strong vision, Dutch public schools will consistently outperform their American counterparts on the PISA.

On the contrary, American public schools vary greatly in their attempt for ambitious instruction especially in disadvantaged areas, where often children are not thought be capable of greatness. "In America ambitious instruction is disparate for a variety of reasons. because unless a school believes in the abilities of their students, not all children are held to high expectations or viewed capable of handling ambitious instruction.

There will be no serious elimination of the achievement gap until deficit thinking is eradicated. And deficit thinking cannot be eradicated until all students are equally encouraged to succeed. For students to be equally encouraged to succeed all students must have access to an optimum learning environment in which teachers can make a conscientious effort to include all students as valuable members of a learning community. (Laguardia & Pearl, 2009)

The absence of egalitarianism in American culture contributes to deficit thinking.

Furthermore, if teachers do not receive the exposure to a variety of school atmospheres, they will not understand the vast disparity present in American public schools and may miss their true calling of inspiring those in the most need of ambitious instruction.

By improving the amount of time in practicum, teachers can learn from mentors how to engage disadvantaged students, which is pointed out in Goodwin's article. "...providing students with 'proximal' personal learning goals...helped them achieve at higher levels than did having students set 'distal' goals or no goals at all" (Goodwin, 2016, p. 84). When teachers are given opportunities to implement these theories and sciences in a realistic setting before becoming in-service teachers, they are better equipped to create ambitious instruction plans for their students, thus broadening opportunities for success with the student, standardized tests, and the school as a whole.

TEACHER TRAINING PROGRAMS AND ANALYSIS

Teacher Training in the Netherlands

Dutch primary teacher training (known as Lerarenopleiding Basisonderwijs or PABO) differs dramatically from American primary teacher training although both societies share one big similarity—the perception and stigma of the teaching profession in society. According to a 2013 study by the Varkey Foundation, "In the Netherlands the status of teachers was seen as most comparable with social workers, as was common across most European countries" (Varkey GEMS Foundation, 2018, p. 40).

Teaching is not considered a "high status profession" thus resulting in a reduction of talented teaching candidates. This stigma must be addressed to account for test scores not being as high as they could be if the Dutch could attract higher quality candidates with intrinsic motivation to inspire students to strive higher than the standard. Although over 90% of teachers are satisfied with their jobs, only 40% believe society views them as essential (OECD, 2016, p. 96). Despite this obstacle, teacher training in The Netherlands is comprehensive, engaging, and demanding with policy changes continually evolving.[13] "Some of the policy changes came about due to the, what the Dutch perceived, falling test scores of primary school students" (van Ruijven, 2016, p. 5). However, the robust training teachers receive improve the professional capacity of Dutch public schools over American public schools.

Through extensive research of applied science universities (over 40) offering PABO programs, there are a few apparent differentiating aspects to the education including the following.

Total Time of Practical Experience Including Applied Research

The total amount of practical training Dutch teachers receive is far above that of their American counterparts. While Dutch teachers receive on average 51.2 weeks of practical training, American teachers receive an average of 16 weeks leading to a 27.5% difference in time teachers have to learn from mentors, understand different learning environments, and receive exposure to all subjects and grade levels. Although this extra time does not change a student's socioeconomic status, it does allow teachers to develop a deeper understanding of teaching pedagogy and its real life implementation resulting in better student-centered learning environments to support disadvantaged students.

Figure 12. NL vs US Pre-Service Training Time

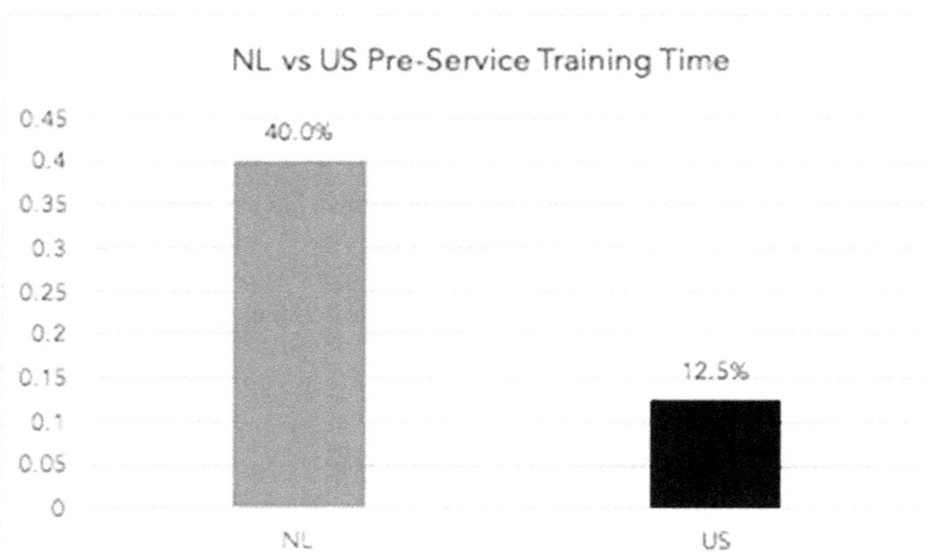

Accountability Testing

Currently, the PABO program is still seen as a higher vocational level program (HBO), which is a deterrent for high achieving students. All students who complete higher level secondary school may apply to PABO programs. To improve the capabilities of their teachers, the Dutch PABO system implemented quality enhancements starting in 2006 and have continued to improve upon them as seen in the van Ruijven's table in Appendix C. Starting in 2007, the tests—although always existent—were directly tied to the academic dismissal policy at PABO. "In case the student has still not successfully, completed either one of the tests after the first year, an academic dismissal (i.e. negatief bindend studieadvies) is given to the student, implying it is obliged to leave the PABO" (van Ruijven, 2016, pp. 7-8). By tying the continuation of a student's teaching career to these accountability tests, PABO and the inspectorate are attempting to improve the legitimacy of the teaching profession while simultaneously improving the quality of the teachers who come out of the PABO programs.

Although there is currently a labor shortage of teachers within The Netherlands, it should not come as a surprise to the Dutch who predicted the shortage in as early as 2002.[14] The result of this shortage is drastically apparent as the year 2016 faced 5600 teacher vacancies. The growth in teacher vacancies can be seen below in Chart 7.

Figure 13. NL Teacher Vacancies (Unfilled)

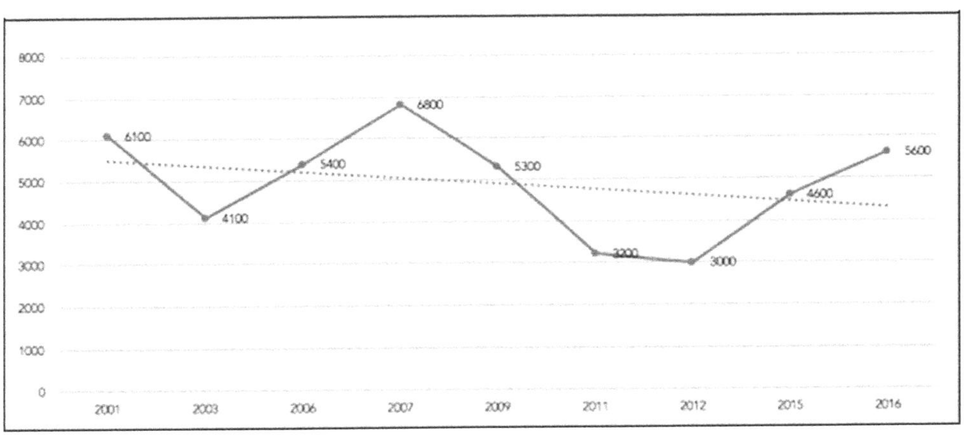

These shortages can be compared to the policy changes in PABO education requirements in Appendix C. Despite the shortage, the government believes it will lead to big changes in the long run. Simply put, " the government, [Sander] Dekker told us, has refused to compromise on quality" (Tucker, 2017). While the amount of students who are admitted to and complete the PABO program decreased, in the long term, the quality control tests should function more so like medical school exams to produce high quality teachers, which improve the outcomes for students.

Exchange Program Affordability

Since Dutch higher education is more affordable than that in America, Dutch students can travel globally to increase their exposure to progressive and innovative education pedagogy and practice. Global exposure is crucial to innovation development and the production of enlightened teachers and educators with reformist mindsets. Although there are options available through the American education programs, students cannot take advantage of exchange programs due to the cost of international travel and living. So, despite the existence of the option, the cost deters students from seizing the opportunity.

Availability of Dual Degrees in Educational Sciences for Advanced Students

Although the compensation of teachers continues to be a sticking point in negotiations, and this year alone teachers have had at least three strike days, Sander Dekker, State Secretary for Education, Culture and Science, knows something must change for the profession to continually improve student results. In an interview with *Education Week* in April 2017, Dekker states,

[he] saw that getting teachers from the upper ranges of graduating high school classes would depend not just on improving teachers' compensation, but also on restructuring teachers' careers so that they look more like the careers of high-status professionals. (Tucker, 2017)

While money certainly helps, it is not the only component essential to better teacher outcomes, and this is something many American politicians do not understand. The Dutch are effective at being innovative with their solutions, and America must do the same to improve the quality of teachers.

In order to motivate students with academic ambitions to enter the teaching force and to raise the academic potential of the force, initiatives have been taken to start a teacher training course for primary school teachers at academic[15] level. For example, the University of Utrecht offers a combined course of teacher training for primary education and educational science for VWO graduates (European Agency for Special Needs and Inclusive Education, 2017). The elevation of training programs and the ability to combine a teaching degree with one in educational sciences could be moderately to extensively attractive to high achieving students, which should increase the quality of teachers. Furthermore, this course of action should help draw in more potential, quality teaching candidates who possess the ability to complete their studies and reduce the self-inflicted Dutch teacher shortage.

Teacher Training in America—Pre-Service

Just as the Netherlands suffers from the downplayed importance of teachers and their contributions to society, teachers in America suffer a similar fate. The Varkey Foundation confirmed this notion in 2013, "People in the US were most likely to compare a teacher to a librarian, and were twice as likely to compare teachers to librarians as any other profession" (p. 49). By the public not understanding the role of teachers, those choosing to enter the profession are already guaranteed to encounter stigmas and reduced support throughout their career. However, there are two aspects unique to the American teacher training system:

1. Over 1,300 teacher training programs for student-teachers leading to preparation variance.

2. Focus on theory and pedagogy instead of practical training with scientific foundations.

Although America is home to some of the best institutions of higher learning in the world, not all teacher programs are on the same level. In fact, despite the rigor of top programs, many teacher training programs do not attract top quality candidates resulting in lower quality teachers. In addition, many of the teacher training programs continually operate in the manner they did over 50 years ago, with little practical experience and a greater focus on theory. The result are unprepared teachers and a modest societal view of a teacher's importance in society.

Programs that do not prepare teachers to deal with globalization and teachers who are unwilling to find ways to encourage discussion, research, and analysis of it are not prepared to deal with the educational issues of the 21st century. (Laguardia & Pearl, 2009)

While this and previous statements are not meant to detract from or discredit the quality of American teacher training programs in existence, we must admit overall the system is struggling to provide teachers opportunities to become the most dynamic, well-rounded, and forward-thinking educators they can.

A quick view of teaching programs available to American students uncovers stark disparities. For example, at Vanderbilt University's Peabody School of Education, the university promises "Students whom we recommend for licensing must complete practicum placements throughout their program of studies, culminating with the 15-week student teaching experience" (Vanderbilt University, 2017A). Vanderbilt is ranked #1 according to Niche.com; Western Illinois University (WIU) is ranked #368. WIU's website states "...students begin observing children early in the program and begin working with them as tutors and classroom aides in their junior year. During the comprehensive pre-student teaching field experience in the first semester of their senior year, students teach lessons in mathematics, science, reading, language arts and social studies. The program culminates in a 12-week student teaching experience" (Western Illinois University, 2017). Even with practicums present in the curriculum, these requirements[16] are different resulting in teacher quality variance. When students do not receive the same instruction, requirements, and practicum time, quality will differ. Similar to PABO, students in America must pass competency tests; however, these tests depend on the state requirements which result in varied teacher quality. To use the previous example between Vanderbilt and WIU, see Table 3. While Table 3 shows the steps in place to ensure teachers meet basic requirements, they are varied, and undoubtedly the practicum experience is drastically different.

This small sample of over 1,300 universities offering elementary education programs, provides a glimpse of varying teacher training requirements. The National Council on Teacher Quality[17] determined a vast amount of training institutions were not adequately preparing graduates leading to an uproar in education circles across America (2013).

However, this mass deficiency was revealed half a decade before. According to Emily Richmond from *The Atlantic,*

Arthur Levin, ...former president of Columbia University's Teachers College, who sounded the alarm in a landmark report in 2006. The overall findings are consistent with his own research, that there are "some strong ed schools and a fair number of weak ed schools and that preparation for teachers is inadequate." (Richmond, 2013)

Table 3. US Teacher Training Program Comparison Example

	Vanderbilt (#1)	WIU (#550)
PRAXIS	x	
edTPA	x	x
Content Area Test	x	x
Test of Academic Proficiency		x
SAT or ACT Minimums	x	x
CPR/First Aid Certification	x	

Teacher training programs in America must understand the impact their trainings have on the ability of educators to influence not only their students but educational policy. Furthermore, macro-level reforms must occur to hold all teachers to the same standard in an effort to level the playing field.

In addition, the number of hours US teachers encounter in pre-service practicum is drastically below the Dutch teacher preparation. While students in Dutch teacher training programs encounter hands-on experience in all grades within their Primary school system, the US student teachers merely participate in observations until they get to their student-teaching semester, where they spend anywhere from 12-16 weeks on site. The lack of practical training adversely impacts not only teachers, but also students, school leaders, and communities connected to the schools. Why? Simply because the change agents—the teachers—are ill prepared to deal with the obstacles and shocking external factors[18] their students must encounter daily.

This practicum time difference produces ill-prepared educators especially those graduating from weak education preparation schools. The large amount of ill-equipped teacher training programs in American society is negatively affecting students because, if anyone can enroll in an education, then are standards really guaranteeing the best teachers for the future? The suggestions to improve America's teacher training programs are covered in the Recommendations section.

Data Analysis

The null hypothesis (H_0) of this paper states there are no differences between the countries on their performance. The alternative hypothesis (H_1) states increased practical teacher training improves test scores (NL (M_1)> US(M_2)) . A total of seven t-tests were run with this assumption:

1. NL vs US four-year average (with PISA)
2. NL vs US (with PISA)
3. NL vs INT'L (with PISA)
4. US vs INT'L (with PISA)
5. NL vs US (without PISA)
6. NL vs INT'L (without PISA)
7. US vs INT'L (without PISA)
8. NL vs US (PISA only)

Initially, the results in Chart 7 looked promising for the Dutch public education system before running analysis and plotting scores of PISA (Chart 8) separate from TIMSS, and PIRLS (Chart 9) looked promising when viewed from a four-year perspective before running tests 1, 2, and 5.

Chart 8 shows us the Dutch have an advantage over the Americans particularly on the PISA, but differences are miniscule at the TIMSS and PIRLS level. Chart 9's trendline for each country shows the Dutch system is on an upward trend, but this includes the PISA scores. Chart 10 displays a downward trend for test scores on the TIMSS and PIRLS, which is accounted for in this paper due to lack of high achieving students in Dutch culture.

Figure 14. Dutch, American, and International Test Results: Four-Year Test Averages

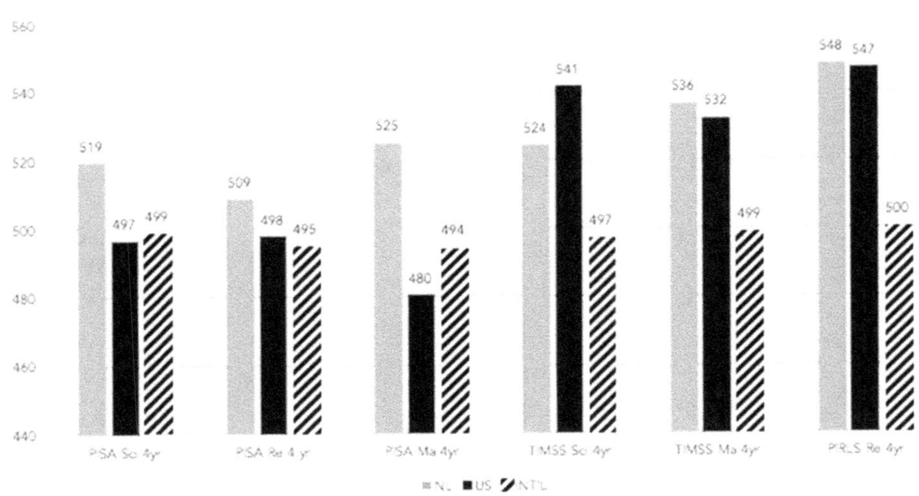

Despite national alarm about falling American test scores, the score comparison revealed interesting results during the t-test analysis.

The t-test results for test one through seven displayed some predictable and some surprising results. While it was tempting to increase the alpha to .1, it was kept at .05 to ensure the analysis did not display bias towards Dutch public schools. The results highlighted in light gray mean no significance while those in dark gray convey a strong significance.

Figure 15. NL vs US Test Scores (with PISA)

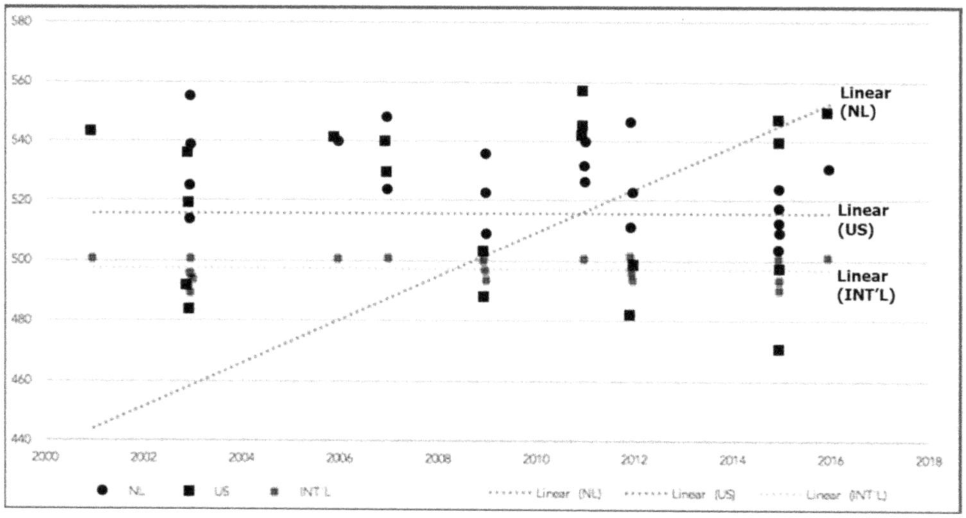

Figure 16. NL vs US Test Scores (without PISA)

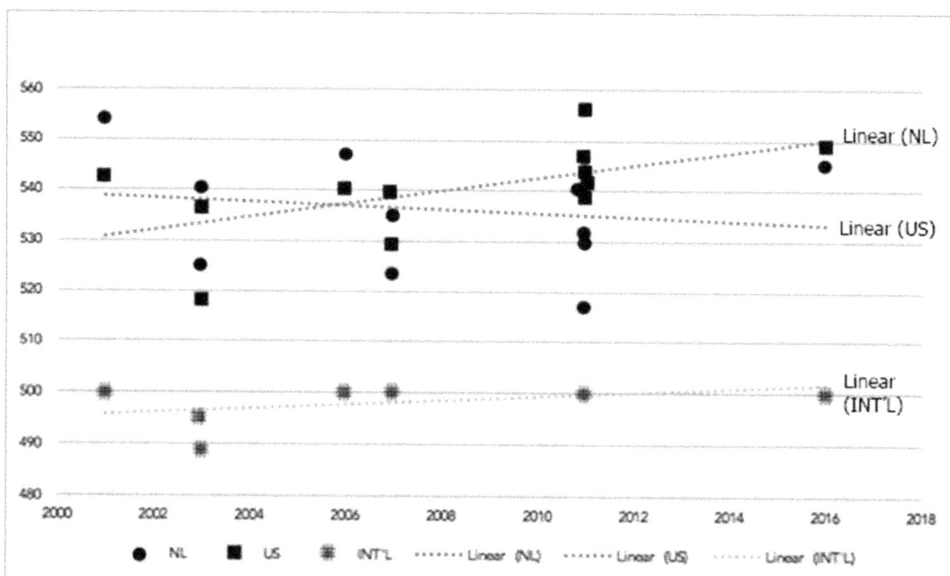

Overall, it is important to look at the on-tailed p-value for each of the tests as we are always saying value one (first country listed) is higher/better than value two (second country listed). While Test 1 reveals little significance between the two systems in a four-year average scenario (Table 4), when each score within each year is accounted for, the Dutch system proves significant in the one-tail test. Since having the same mean is overall unimportant for this paper, we really want to see if there is an advantage to the Dutch system over the American system. Table 5 proves this.

Table 4. Test 1 Results

t-Test: Two-Sample Assuming Unequal Variances
US vs NL Four-Year Average

	NL	US
Mean	526.833333	515.666667
Variance	186.716667	766.216667
Observations	6	6
Hypothesized Mean Di	0	
df	7	
t Stat	0.88606977	
P(T<=t) one-tail	0.20249495	
t Critical one-tail	1.89457861	
P(T<=t) two-tail	0.40498991	
t Critical two-tail	2.36462425	

Table 5. Test 2 Results

t-Test: Two-Sample Assuming Unequal Variances
NL vs US (all scores)

	NL	US
Mean	526.833333	515.666667
Variance	195.449275	700.57971
Observations	24	24
Hypothesized Meai	0	
df	35	
t Stat	1.82754527	
P(T<=t) one-tail	**0.03807693**	
t Critical one-tail	1.68957246	
P(T<=t) two-tail	0.07615387	
t Critical two-tail	2.03010793	

Table 6. Test 3 Results

t-Test: Two-Sample Assuming Unequal Variances
NL vs INT'L

	NL	INT'L
Mean	526.833333	497.291667
Variance	195.449275	14.0416667
Observations	24	24
Hypothesized Meai	0	
df	26	
t Stat	9.99903272	
P(T<=t) one-tail	**1.0622E-10**	
t Critical one-tail	1.70561792	
P(T<=t) two-tail	**2.1243E-10**	
t Critical two-tail	2.05552944	

Table 7. Test 4 Results

t-Test: Two-Sample Assuming Unequal Variances
US vs INT'L

	US	INT'L
Mean	516.73913	497.173913
Variance	703.565217	14.3320158
Observations	23	23
Hypothesized Mean Di	0	
df	23	
t Stat	3.5020106	
P(T<=t) one-tail	0.00095932	
t Critical one-tail	1.71387153	
P(T<=t) two-tail	0.00191863	
t Critical two-tail	2.06865761	

Table 8. Test 5 Results

t-Test: Two-Sample Assuming Unequal Variances
NL vs US NO PISA

	NL	US
Mean	536.0833333	539.916667
Variance	124.6287879	92.4469697
Observations	12	12
Hypothesized Mean	0	
df	22	
t Stat	-0.901283761	
P(T<=t) one-tail	0.188599428	
t Critical one-tail	1.717144374	
P(T<=t) two-tail	0.377198857	
t Critical two-tail	2.073873068	

Table 9. Test 6 Results

t-Test: Two-Sample Assuming Unequal Variances
NL vs INT'L NO PISA

	Variable 1	Variable 2
Mean	536.0833333	498.666667
Variance	124.6287879	11.3333333
Observations	12	12
Hypothesized Mean	0	
df	13	
t Stat	11.11595429	
P(T<=t) one-tail	2.60167E-08	
t Critical one-tail	1.770933396	
P(T<=t) two-tail	5.20335E-08	
t Critical two-tail	2.160368656	

Table 10. Test 7 Results

t-Test: Two-Sample Assuming Unequal Variances
US vs INT'L NO PISA

	Variable 1	*Variable 2*
Mean	539.916667	498.666667
Variance	92.4469697	11.3333333
Observation:	12	12
Hypothesize	0	
df	14	
t Stat	14.0267517	
P(T<=t) one-t	6.1608E-10	
t Critical one	1.76131014	
P(T<=t) two-t	1.2322E-09	
t Critical two	2.14478669	

Table 11. Test 8 Results

t-Test: Two-Sample Assuming Unequal Variances
NL vs US PISA

	NL	*US*
Mean	517.5833333	491.416667
Variance	97.35606061	89.3560606
Observations	12	12
Hypothesized Mean	0	
df	22	
t Stat	6.63365328	
P(T<=t) one-tail	5.69414E-07	
t Critical one-tail	1.717144374	
P(T<=t) two-tail	1.13883E-06	
t Critical two-tail	2.073873068	

Tables 6, 7, 9, and 10 prove both countries are significantly better at public education than many countries as both score above the international average. Tables 6 and 7 show all scores, and although both countries show some significance over the international average, the Dutch public education system displays a great difference with a one-tailed p-value of 1.06217279008376E-10—essentially equating to 0. The American system produces a one-tailed p-value of 0.000959317241334518. We can take analysis a step further and compare the p-values in the two-tail test, which put the Dutch outcome at 2.12434558016752E-10 and the American outcome at 0.00191863448266904. Again from a purely mathematical standpoint, although they show no significance against each other, the Dutch come out ahead as their significance amongst the international community is larger.

Although there is little significance between the Dutch and American public education results on the TIMSS and PIRLS as determined in Test 5 (Table 8), this paper attributes the lack of significance to the

American acceptance of pervasive testing culture coupled with the push for high achieving students from an early age. The Dutch education system does not favor standardized testing the same as America. In addition, Dutch students are given time to appropriately develop their love of learning instead of focusing on being the best. These two factors alone can account for the lack of significance between test scores, and this does not affect this paper's call for teacher training reform.

However, when you remove the PISA scores and compare TIMSS and PIRLS to the international scores, both the Dutch and American systems display one-tailed significance at the one-tailed p-values of 2.60167250986124E-08 and 6.16080190642783E-10 respectively meaning the American system has a slight edge over the Dutch system. These factors attributing to this difference were mentioned above. When the PISA test scores are isolated, the Dutch public education system show significant strength over the American system with both the one-tailed and two-tailed tests displaying significant statistical variance (Table 11).

The data, while not showing direct correlation between increasing teacher training time and improved test scores, provides insight for future research on how cultural differences can negate improved teacher training and countrywide success on standardized tests. This analysis and research also lays the groundwork for further research on teacher training reform and its effects on the Five Essential Supports. In regards to the Dutch public education system, the data analysis helps conclude correlation does not exist between increased student-teacher training practicum hours and improved test scores. Instead, the integration and interconnectedness of the Five Essential Supports is important to future growth on standardized tests. This paper concludes, due to cultural differences in education attitude, the Five Essential Supports are ever more crucial to improve the Dutch mindset towards education but also improve the American public school system.

RECOMMENDATIONS

While there is always room for improvement and each system has its strengths, it is best to find fiscally feasible/conservative changes/reforms America can make to improve its public education system and outcomes for students. This section will explore the recommendations for both the American and Dutch systems, but details will only be given for the American system given the scope of the paper.

For America

Despite the presence of many high performing primary schools and school districts, the American public education system struggles with equity, opportunity, funding, and teacher quality. Together, these factors drastically affect the Five Essential Supports. Consequently, policy experts, educational experts, and politicians must explore fiscally conservative changes to improve the functioning of existing institutional contexts and bring about reform.

Revolutionize and Transform Teacher Training at the University Level

A revamp to the teacher training programs nationally is essential to increase teacher and student outcomes. The varied requirements within teaching programs does not effectively prepare students to teach in diverse environments, provide inclusive and differentiated education, or overcome situational obstacles out of their control. As the Dutch PABO programs offer 27.5% (or an additional 362 hours) more pre-service training than

America teacher preparation programs and statistical analysis shows a significance in Dutch scores over American scores on TIMSS, PIRLS, and PISA. This factor and change must be explored, researched, created, and implemented in the early education years to improve the American education system. This study suggests three main improvements to the American teaching training programs:

1. *Increased practicum time/training rotation*—based on prior research in PA 581, eliminating 24 credits of general education would mean prospective teachers gain 50% more practical time through training rotations. (Joyce, 2017 August).
2. *Centralize university admission and licensure standards*—through centralization at the federal level, states and local standards would decrease as would reliance on standardized testing results.
3. *Provide more affordable exchange programs or offer affordable alternatives*—better exchange programs provide prospective teachers the opportunity to study with the best and brightest mentors and educators in their specialization/subject area. A creative solution would be to work on tuition-exchange partnerships that include the cost of flights for US students. In addition, creating nationwide exchange programs would make studying in different environments and with different educators more affordable for American students. Although the economics are not explored in this paper, this is an important element needing further research.

Provide Standardized Test Feedback Earlier So Teachers Can Alter Lesson Plans and Work Toward Educational Betterment for All Students

Much like entrance exams utilized for high schools and universities, it is important America starts proactively providing test scores earlier in the year to assist teachers in knowing where their students are struggling as well as excelling. Currently, many teachers receive results at the end of the school year, when it is too late to implement curriculum changes within their own classroom. As Dr. Canada states in his TED Talk, "Teachers need real information right now about what's happening to their kids." Without this valuable feedback, real education reform is out of the question. Teachers cannot actively engage in bettering their teaching and working with their mentors to improve their teaching and accessibility.

Centralization of Educational Standards and From a Federal Level, Which would Require a Grassroots Movement from Politicians on a Meso and Micro Level

One of the best methods of improvement within Dutch schools came from centralizing education standards at the federal (macro) level and leaving the implementation to the meso and micro levels. In America's case, it would be the states (meso) and local districts/schools (micro). It is imperative American public schools all have the same accountability standards but the autonomy to structure schools and teach in ways that would most benefit their customers (the students within their districts). Additional research and ideas could be generated through the use of social capital and restorative justice research.

Reduction of Standards and Their Variance at the State Level, Which Would Require a Grassroots Movement from Politicians at the Micro Level

While research would be required from a budgetary perspective and collaboration among policy-makers, politicians, and lobbyists, the reduction in standard variance through a centralized federal standard would help schools create programs aimed at restorative justice through education. This policy change could be achieved through a slow, steady state-by-state movement fueled by the grassroot efforts of parents, teachers, students, administrators, and educational reform advocates gathering support from local politicians and encouraging state representatives to vote in a more socialist manner. While costs are not known for the short, mid, and long term, further research is required to determine the overall fiscal conservativeness and its effects on healthcare and the economy.

Constitutionally Revamp Funding Structure to Ensure Equitable Funding to Increase Positive Outcomes for Society as a Whole

Undoubtedly, the hardest and most costly change is changing the American constitution to guarantee equitable, uniform, and high-quality education for all just as was done in the Constitution of the Kingdom of the Netherlands. This is also the suggestion least likely to occur due to the huge cultural differences within the societies' beliefs of socialism versus capitalism, egalitarian versus meritocracy. A change of this magnitude would demand tax reform and increases, which many Americans would protest. However, through careful use of social capital, community building, and grassroots initiatives, this could be done over a long course of time. Although many Americans will end up paying more in taxes, it would improve the intellectual quality of society and provide people avenues to exit the poverty cycle, thus reducing economic and social issues that result from extreme poverty.

For the Netherlands

Although the Dutch public education system is supported by a realistic foundation seeking utmost efficiency and justice for all, some students and families suffer due to weakened supports within the realms of student-centered learning and the unchecked power of school boards. These weaknesses result in the Dutch government's resolve to push and further support inclusive education, a reduction in teacher workload, and a realignment of expectations on the meso level. While there are complaints about the multiple expectations from the Ministry, boards, and management, the Dutch talk freely and openly about these issues to develop a solution and encourage teachers to inquire why they are expected to do something and to say no (Corre & Van der Kaaden, 2017). The following are priority areas of improvement for the Dutch, though this proposal will require additional research and is outside the scope of this paper.

1. Provide increased pay for teachers while including their feedback in the future of the school.
2. Reduce the decision-making capabilities of the school boards to ensure monopolies of power do not occur.
3. Increase the amount of Centrale opvang basis onderwijs (COBO) programs available to students entering primary school with Dutch as as second language.
4. Increase integration within communities through embracing community and parent partnerships.
5. Provide additional inclusive education for both special education and gifted education candidates.

6. Increase differentiated-learning techniques to benefit all children and increase the amount of high achievers for Holland.

What Has Been Learned

Through this long, comparative paper, while acknowledging the cultural differences between The Netherlands the United States of America, we have discovered the vast differences between the two countries within the Five Essential Supports. Overall, this paper offers four main areas of improvement that are fiscally conservative to help overhaul and reform the American public education system. Although these changes would take time and effort up front, the long-term effects could be extremely productive for not only US teachers and schools but for the country and its residents by improving the abilities of schools and restoring autonomy and school access. More research is needed to determine the exact economic impacts of each of the four suggestions, and it would be beneficial to develop studies in conjunction with economists, educational scientists, and education policy makers.

ACKNOWLEDGMENT

This chapter is an edited version of a Master's thesis presented by the author to the Stuart School of Business, Illinois Institute of Technology.

REFERENCES

Adamson, P. (2013). *Child Well-being in Rich Countries: A comparative overview.* Retrieved from UNICEF Office of Research: https://www.unicef-irc.org/publications/683-child-well-being-in-rich-countries-a-comparative-overview.html

BobboSphere. (2012, November 12). *Don Moore 1942-2012: A lion who roared on behalf of public education.* Retrieved from Daily Kos: https://www.dailykos.com/stories/2012/11/12/1160687/-Don-Moore-1942-2012-A-l%20ion-who-roared-on-behalf-of-public-educat
ion

Brown Hamilton, T. (2015, June 18). *Solving the Problem of Amsterdam's 'Black' and 'White' Schools.* Retrieved from The Atlantic: https://www.theatlantic.com/education/archive/2015/06/amsterdam-school-racial-segregation/396176/

Bryk, A. S., Bender Sebring, P., Allensworth, E., Luppescu, S., & Easton, J. Q. (2010). *Organizing Schools for Improvement: Lessons from Chicago.* University of Chicago Press.

Butrymowicz, S. (2015, January). *In Dutch Schools, More Time in School and More Educator Control.* Retrieved from The Hetchinger Report: http://hechingerreport.org/in-dutch-schools-more-time-in-school-and-more-educat or-control/

Canada, G. (2013, May). *Our Failing Schools. Enough Is Enough!* Retrieved from TED: https://www.ted.com/talks/geoffrey_canada_our_failing_schools_enough_is_enough?language=en

Centralbureau voor de statistiek. (2017). *Total Number of Primary Pupils: Selected Years 2001 Through 2016.* Retrieved from Statline.CBS.NL: http://statline.cbs.nl/Statweb/publication/?DM=SLEN&PA=03753ENG&D1=1&D2=1&D3=0&D4=a&D5=11-21&LA=EN&VW=T

Chetty, R., Friedman, J. N., & Rockoff, J. E. (2014). Measuring the Impacts of Teachers I: Evaluating Bias in Teacher Value-Added Estimates. *The American Economic Review, 104*(9), 2593–2632. doi:10.1257/aer.104.9.2593

Chingos, M. M. (2017). *How progressive is school funding in the United States?* The Brookings Institution.

Coley, R. J., & Baker, B. (2013). Poverty and Education: Finding the Way Forward. Princeton, NJ: Report of the ETS Center for Research on Human Capital and Education.

Compareyourcountry.org. (n.d.). *PISA Scores.* Retrieved from Compareyourcountry.org: https://www.compareyourcountry.org/pisa/country/NLD?lg=3n

Corre, A., & Van der Kaaden, A. (2017, April 21). *De meester/juf heeft het te druk om les te geven.* Retrieved from NRS.NL: https://www.nrc.nl/nieuws/2017/04/21/de-meesterjuf-heeft-het-te-druk-om-les-tegeven-8336254-a1555503

Darling-Hammond, L. (2006). Standards, Assessment, and Educational Policy: In pursuit of genuine accountability (Eighth Annual WilliamH. Agnoff Memorial Lecture). Princeton, NJ: Educational Testing Service.

Dutta, S., Lanvin, B., Rivera Leon, L., & Wunsch-Vincent, S. (2012). *The Global Innovation Index 2012: Stronger Innovation Linkages for Global Growth.* Retrieved from INSEAD and World Intellectual Property Organization Global Innovation Index: https://www.globalinnovationindex.org/userfiles/file/GII-2012-Report.pdf

Economist Intelligence Unit. (2006-2017). *Democracy Index 2006-2017.* Retrieved from The Economist: https://www.eiu.com/topic/democracy-index

Education Inspectorate: Ministry of Education, Culture, and Science. (2017a, November 23). *Search and Compare Schools.* Retrieved from https://zoekscholen.onderwijsinspectie.nl: https://zoekscholen.onderwijsinspectie.nl/zoek-en-vergelijk?redir

Education Inspectorate: Ministry of Education, Culture, and Science. (2017b, April). *The State of Education 2015-2016.* Retrieved from https://english.onderwijsinspectie.nl: https://english.onderwijsinspectie.nl/binaries/onderwijsinspectie_eng/documents/ann ual-reports/2017/04/12/the-state-of-education-in-the-netherlands-2015-2016/state+o f+education+2015+2016+web.pdf

Education Next. (2016). *Program on Education Policy and Governance—Survey 2016*. Retrieved from Education Next: http://educationnext.org/2016-ednext-poll-interactive/

European Agency for Special Needs and Inclusive Education. (2017). *Netherlands - Financing*. Retrieved February 5, 2018, from European-agency.org: https://www.european-agency.org/country-information/netherlands/national-overview/financing

Foroohar, R. (2017, June 15). *U.S. workforce: paying young Americans to learn the right skills*. Retrieved from Financial Times: https://www.ft.com/content/b5ceec2a-50e4-11e7-a1f2-db19572361bb

Goodwin, B. (2016). Flip the Script on Fate Control. *Educational Leadership*, *74*(3), 83–84.

Hale, E., & Rollins, K. (2006). What those "breakthrough" high schools broke through to discover. *Education Digest*, *72*(1), 4–9.

Hogeschool Utrecht. (2017). *Teacher Education in English Study Guide 2017-2018*. Retrieved from International.hu.nl: https://www.international.hu.nl/~/media/LLL/Docs/Studiegidsen/FE/2017/TeacherEducation-in-English-vt.pdf?la=en

Hunley, J. (2017, July 23). Replicating a Schools Turnaround. *The Washington Post*. Retrieved February 12, 2018, from http://www.highbeam.com/doc/1P4-1922260701.html?refid=easy_hf

INSEAD and the World Intellectual Property Organization. (2010-2017). *Global Innovation index*. Retrieved January 9, 2018, from Globalinnovationindex.org: https://www.globalinnovationindex.org

Institute of Education Sciences, U.S. Department of Education. (2009, July 17). *Diagram of Education in the United States*. Retrieved from Wikipedia: https://en.wikipedia.org/wiki/Education_in_the_United_States#/media/File:Education_in_the_United_States.svg

Krishnamurthy, M. (2017, April 5). State education board develops new accountability plan for schools. *Daily Herald*. Retrieved February 13, 2018, from https://www.dailyherald.com/article/20170405/news/170409431/

Laguardia, A., & Pearl, A. (2009). Necessary Educational Reform for the 21st Century: The Future of Public Schools in Our Democracy. *The Urban Review*, *41*(4), 352–368. doi:10.100711256-008-0115-9

Legatum Institute. (2007-2016). *Prosperity Index 2007-2016*. Retrieved January 9, 2018, from Prosperity.com: https://www.prosperity.com/about/resources

Lynch, M. (2016, September 19). *3 Important Themes of American Culture that Influence Our Schools*. Retrieved from The Edvocate: https://www.theedadvocate.org/3-important-themes-of-american-culture-that-influence-our-schools/

McKinsey & Company. (2009, April). *The economic impact of the achievement gap in America's schools*. Retrieved from National Dropout Prevention Center: http://dropoutprevention.org/wp-content/uploads/2015/07/ACHIEVEMENT_GAP_ REPORT_20090512.pdf

Ministry of Education, Culture, and Science. (2016). *Key Figures: Education*. Retrieved from Ocwincijfer.nl: https://www.ocwincijfers.nl/binaries/ocwincijfers/documenten/publicaties/2016/05/31/key-figures-education/keyfigures-education-2016.pdf

National center for Education Statistics. (2018). *Digest of Education Statistics*. Retrieved from NCES.ed.gov: https://nces.ed.gov/programs/digest/2016menu_tables.asp

National Center for Education Statistics Institute of Education Sciences. (2012, July). *Growth Models: Issues and Advice from the States*. Retrieved from NCES.ed.gov: https://nces.ed.gov/programs/slds/pdf/guide_growth-model.pdf

National League of Cities. (n.d.). *Financing Public Education*. Retrieved February 5, 2018, from NLC.org: https://www.nlc.org/financing-public-education

Netherlands Ministry of Education, Culture, and Science. (2016). *Key Figures: Education*. Retrieved from OCW in cijfers (OCW in figures): https://www.ocwincijfers.nl/binaries/ocwincijfers/documenten/publicaties/2016/05/31/key-figures-education/keyfigures-education-2016.pdf

Netherlands Youth Institute. (2017). *Community Schools*. Retrieved from NJI.nl: https://www.nji.nl/nl/Download-NJi/Publicatie-NJi/Community_schools_Netherlan ds_2010.pdf

OECD. (2014, October). *Educational Policy Outlook: The Netherlands*. Retrieved from OECD.

OECD. (2015). *Programme for International Student Assessment: Selected Years 2003, 2009, 2012, 2015*. Retrieved from OECD.org: https://www.oecd.org/pisa

OECD. (2016). *Netherlands 2016: Foundations for the future, reviews of national policies for education*. Paris: OECD Publishing. doi:10.1787/9789264257658-en

OECD. (2017). *Education Policy Outlook*. Retrieved from OECD iLibrary: https://data.oecd.org/education.htm

Organisation for Economic Co-operation and Development. (2016). *OECD Data*. doi:10.1787/9789264257658-en

People's Party for Freedom and Democracy (VVD), Christian Democratic Alliance (CDA), Democrats '66 (D66), & Christian Union (CU). (2017). *Confidence in the Future*. Retrieved from government.nl: https://www.government.nl/binaries/government/documents/publications/2017/10/1 0/coalition-agreement-confidence-in-the-future/coalition-agreement-2017-confide nce-in-the-future.pdf

Porter, M. E., Sachs, J. D., & Mcarthur, J. W. (2002). *Executive Summary: Competitivenesws and States of economic Development. The Global Competitiveness Report 2001-2002*. Retrieved from Sustainable Development Networking Programme. https://citeseerx.ist.psu.edu/viewdoc/download?doi=10.1.1.476.4940&rep=rep1&type=pdf

Reporters Sans Frontieres. (2015-2017). *Index RSF*. Retrieved from RSF.org: https://rsf.org/en/index?year=2021

Richmond, E. (2013, June 18). *America's Teacher-Training Programs Aren't Good Enough*. Retrieved February 9, 2018, from The Atlantic: https://www.theatlantic.com/national/archive/2013/06/americas-teacher-training-pro grams-arent-good-enough/276993/

Sala-i-Martin, X., Bilbao-Osorio, B., Blanke, J., Crotti, R., Drzeniek Hanouz, M., Geiger, T., & Ko, C. (2012). The Global Competitiveness Index 2012–2013: Strengthening Recovery by Raising Productivity. *The Global Competitiveness Report 2012-2013*, 3-48.

Sebring, P. B., Allensworth, E., Bryk, A. S., & Easton, J. Q. (2006). *The Essential Supports for School Improvement*. Consortium on Chicago School Research, University of Chicago.

Singer, S. (2017, February 13). *U.S. Public Schools Are Not Failing. They're Among the Best in the World*. Retrieved from Huffington Post: https://www.huffingtonpost.com/entry/us-public-schools-are-not-failing-theyre-am ong_us_5894e819e4b061551b3dfe51

Strauss, V. (2015, October 24). *Confirmed: Standardized testing has taken over our schools. But who's to blame?* Retrieved from Washington Post: https://www.washingtonpost.com/news/answer-sheet/wp/2015/10/24/confirmed-standardized-testing-has-taken-over-our-schools
-but-whos-to-blame/

Thijs, A., van Leeuwen, B., & Zandbergen, M. (2009). Inclusive Education in the Netherlands. *International Journal of Inclusive Education*, *1*, 1–61.

Time4Learning, Inc. (n.d.). *Standardized Testing by State*. Retrieved January 25, 2018, from Time4Learning.com: https://www.time4learning.com/testprep/

TIMSS and PIRLS International Study Center, Lynch School of Education, Boston College. (2015). *PIRLS Reading Results (Selected years 2001 through 2016)*. Retrieved from TIMSS and PIRLS International Study Center: https://timssandpirls.bc.edu

TIMSS and PIRLS International Study Center, Lynch School of Education, Boston College. (2015). *TIMSS Mathematics and Science Results (Selected years 2001 through 2016)*. Retrieved from TIMSS and PIRLS International Study Center: https://timssandpirls.bc.edu

Tucker, M. (2017, April 6). *The Netherlands: Top-Performing School System Looking to Get Better*. Retrieved February 9, 2018, from blogs.edweek.org: https://blogs.edweek.org/edweek/top_performers/2017/04/the_netherlands_top_performer_in_motion.html

Turner, C. (2018). *Report on Recommendations from the U.S. Commission on Civil Rights* [Recorded by N. P. Radio]. Academic Press.

U.S. Department of Education. (2017). *About ED: Overview and Mission Statement*. Retrieved from U.S. Department of Education: https://www2.ed.gov/about/landing.jhtml

van Ruijven, K. (2016, October). *The effects ofentry-tests during primary-school teacher education in the Netherlands*. Retrieved from Thesis.eur.nl: https://thesis.eur.nl/pub/36746/Ruijven.pdf

Vanderbilt University. (2017A). *2017-2018 Peabody Undergraduate Handbook*. Retrieved from Vanderbilt.edu: https://peabody.vanderbilt.edu/admin-offices/oas/2017-2018_Peabody_Undergraduate_Handbook_final-8.11.2017.pdf

Vanderbilt University. (2017B). *Elementary Program*. Retrieved from Vanderbilt.edu: https://peabody.vanderbilt.edu/departments/tl/undergraduate_program/elementary_program.php

Varkey GEMS Foundation. (2018, February 10). *Global Teacher Index (Rep.)*. Retrieved from Varkeyfoundation.org: https://www.varkeyfoundation.org/teacherindex

Western Illinois University. (2017). *Elementary Education*. Retrieved from WIU.edu: http://www.wiu.edu/academics/majors/education_and_human_services/elementary-e ducation.php

World Bank Group. (2017). *Population, total - Netherlands (selected years, 2001 through 2016)*. Retrieved from World Bank Data: https://data.worldbank.org/indicator/SP.POP.TOTL?locations=NL

World Bank Group. (2017). *United States Population Total (Selected years, 2001 through 2016)*. Retrieved from World Bank Data: https://data.worldbank.org/indicator/SP.POP.TOTL?locations-US

ENDNOTES

1 It is important to note The Netherlands is not without its own disparities. The Netherlands, due to large influxes of Syrian, Turkish, and Moroccan refugees are experiencing strains on their system and increasing amounts of segregation. More about the disparities and inequalities are available in "Solving the Problem of Amsterdam's 'Black' and 'White' Schools" (Brown Hamilton, 2015).

2 While not specifically addressing teacher training, Dr. Canada points to vast systematic changes within the innovation realm which must take place in American public education for it to become better (Canada, 2013).

3 These rankings provide a broad basis to understand the overall wellness of a country. Some rankings were left off due to lack of historical data including *US News & World Report*, IMF Income Per Capita, and OECD Better Life Index.

4 Education is one of the many topics covered within the agreement, which is agreed upon by four differing political parties—People's Party for Freedom and Democracy (VVD), Christian Democratic Alliance (CDA), Democrats '66 (D66), and Christian Union (CU).

5 OECD's representation of education structure is available in Appendix B.

6 There are still groups who are not protected and given the same rights under the US Constitution. Diversity is all relative for the purpose of this discussion.

7 Privately-run, denominational schools in Holland may deny admission to students who do not subscribe to their belief or ideology.

8 These needs usually include socioeconomically disadvantaged, special education, and rural communities.

9 This act was recently updated and requires schools to stimulate active citizenship and social integration.

10 Given the scope of this paper, additional analysis cannot be completed on the effects of pervasive standardized testing on teacher morale, initiative, and training. However, is is important to acknowledge the importance of this factor in American public education.

11 A full report is available through the OECD titled "Reviews of national policies for education: The Netherlands, foundations for the future."

12 To gain a better idea from students' perspectives of Dutch teachers, see the Figure 8 in Appendix B.

13 To see the evolution of policy changes succinctly, review Table 12 in Appendix B by Koen van Ruijven from Erasmus University, Erasmus School of Economics.

14 For more information, read the following story: https://www.expatica.com/nl/news/country-news/New-Dutch-teachers-face-jobs-drought_117257.html.

15 Academic here means the equivalent of a research university in America.

16 Requirements include practical learning time, licensure requirements, standardized tests, safety/first aid, etc.

17 NCTQ is a bipartisan, non-profit organization focused on improving education in America through research, evaluation, recommendation, and guidance. For more information, visit https://www.nctq.org/.

18 Home life, poverty, hunger, homelessness, abuse, mental illness, etc.

APPENDIX A: TEACHER TRAINING APGAR ANALYSIS AND LOGIC MODEL

How will the results of your analysis be used, and by whom? How will you involve them? The results of this analysis could be utilized by research in the arenas of educational economics, educational sciences, and curriculum/educational leadership. Furthermore, this analysis could be utilized by educational reform activists to gain a better understanding of how each country operates within the Five Essential Supports and how increased pre-service teacher training can improve outcomes within the supports due to their interconnectedness.

APGAR Outline

A - This is a societal, institutional, and governmental agenda as education is deeply connected to the society at large through institutions and guided by the government at the macro-, meso-, and micro-levels. The results of teacher training reform can be seen in short, medium, and long term. The importance of this is medium as America continues to sort out their politics, immigration, gun control, and healthcare reform. Although the current urgency is low for teacher training reform as it does not draw significant attention, it should be a medium to high priority as teachers have the best opportunity to impact students and their character, internal locus of control, and more.

P - The problem pre-service teacher training reform addresses is the visible disparity amongst America's public school teachers ability to successfully impact a wide array of students from a variety of economic and education backgrounds. *The problem that may arise from improved teacher training is higher taxes at the national level if standards are centralized.*

G - By improving pre-service teacher training programs with more robust practical training, public schools should see an increase in teacher retention, innovative teaching, and student outcomes as teachers are more prepared for different atmospheres.

A - Alternatives

Alt 1 - Current teacher training system (12-16 weeks of practical training)

Alt 2 - Increased teacher training hours by 50%
Alt 3 - Required teacher rotation program starting first year
Alt 4 - Develop more school partnerships to provide students more site options

R - How does the new policy affect teacher training enrollment? Do teachers feel more prepared for their teaching environments post-training? Are their students reaching better outcomes than previous teachers?

Figure 17. Logic Model

What new and existing resources will be used to support the project?	What are the main things the project will do?	What products will be created? (typically, things that can be directly observed and that will continue to exist after the project ends)	What will occur as a direct result of the activities and outputs? (typically, changes in knowledge, skills, attitudes)	What results should follow from the initial outcomes? (typically, changes in behavior, policies, practice)	What results should follow from the initial outcomes? (typically, changes in broader conditions)
Inputs	**Activities**	**Outputs**	**Short-Term Outcomes**	**Mid-Term Outcomes**	**Long-Term Outcomes**
University teacher training institutions and educational researchers	Establish school partnerships. Increase practicum time by 50%. Develop rotation program.	Lower teacher attrition. Increased teacher retention. Greater placement in high-need schools.	Possible teacher shortage. Reduced enrollment at subpar schools.	Subpar teacher-training programs close. More teachers enroll in competant programs. Improved student-teaching	Teachers produce improved student outcomes. Improve test results by 10% after 4 years of program.
Public schools and their stakeholders: parents, students, faculty, administration	Establish university partnerships. Conduct student-teacher workshops. Build community relations.	Parent activities once per month. Staff volunteer work every other month. 3-5% increase in comm. part.	Increased community trust. Increased avilability of resources.	Measurable increase in community/parent involvement.	Measurable improved student outcomes.
Politicians, government officials, administrators, policy makers	Create macro-level policy, which universities must follow. Push towards central standards.	Step program for universities to follow. Reduce standardized tests by 50%.	Unhappy constituents. Politicians lose elections. Strong political opposition to decreased accountability efforts.	Increase in parental and student happiness.	Equitable education outcomes and reduction in state-by-state variance.
Federal, state, and local government structures and education departments	Provide small, government grants to improve teacher-training programs.	Set aside 5-10% of funding earmarked for PD.	Increased PD opportunities and teacher-training improvement. More dynamic teaching environments.	Increase in the amount of breakthrough schools and innovative educators.	Stronger community with better outcomes. More school trust. Implementation of Five Essential Supports successful.

APPENDIX B: ADDITIONAL INFORMATION FOR CONTEXT

Table 12. Evolution Policy Changes PABO

Entrance cohort	Admission Changes	Required Level
2006-07	Implementation of mathematics entry-test for first-year pabo students, in combination with an academic dismissal policy (BSA). Relatedly, the language entry-test was also implemented, however here only an advisable standard was set.	Minimum required math skills of at least the 20 percent best –scoring pupils of the eight primary-school grade. Maximum of three opportunities. Anyone with at least a MBO-4 certificate is able to subscribe to the pabo.
2007-08	The language entry-test for first-year pabo students also mandatory, in combination with an academic dismissal (BSA).	Minimum required language skills of at least havo-4 level Maximum of three opportunities. Anyone with at least a MBO-4 certificate is able to subscribe to the pabo.
2008-09	Establishment of academic pabo's, comprising a combination of the pabo education itself and either an university bachelor of pedagogic sciences or a pre-master pedagogic science. Possible increased attractiveness of pabo's for VWO'ers	VWO
2011-12	Implementation of 14 mandatory 'knowledge-bases'; these consists of required end-levels of specific-pabo subjects. These have to be mastered by the student in order to guarantee each graduated pabo-student has sufficient capabilities to succeed as a teacher. Partially initiated by pabo's themselves.	In practice, students have to successfully complete numeracy and literacy tests during the third-year of their study. Pabo's themselves develop these tests.
2012-13	Implementation of mandatory entry-tests of 'Mens & Wereld' for first-year pabo-students, in combination with an academic dismissal (BSA). These concern three subjects; history, geography and natuur&techniek.	Minimum required geography, history and natuur & techniek skills of at least the 20 percent best–scoring pupils of the eight primary-school grade. Maximum of three opportunities. Anyone with at least a MBO-4 certificate is able to subscribe to the pabo, independent of the pre-educational background.
2015-16	Concerns about the difficulty and quality-content of HBO teacher education studies remain[8]. The objective was, once and for all, to increase the quality of outflowing pabo-students by selecting students before they start the pabo. In this way, pabo's can guarantee a similar quality-level of outflowing pabo-students[9] and do not have to adhere their curricula to the quality of inflowing students. All prospective students have to show -either due to satisfactory secondary school grades or by passed test tailored for prospective pabo-students- that their cognitive abilities for the subjects English, history, geography and natuur&techniek are sufficient to enroll at the pabo.	Selection before the gate as constituted within Dutch law; minimum required entry level in the subjects geography history and natuur&techniek of at least havo-3/vmbo-4 level. There are two ways the student can show it has sufficient cognitive capabilities (i) by showing satisfactory secondary school grades (vmbo and havo) within the subjects. An unsatisfactory grade is allowed in only one of the subjects. A sufficient grade for the secondary-school subjects of either physics, biology or NLT can be used for the subject natuur&techniek or (ii) by passing test specifically tailored for prospective pabo students in these subjects. If the student fails in only one of these test it can still be provided with an assessment to enter. The math entry-tests during the first year of the pabo remain. The standardized language tests will end after the cohort 2015-2016.

Source: van Ruijven, K. (2016 October). The effects of entry-tests during primary-school teacher education in the Netherlands.

Figure 18. Dutch Student Beliefs
Source: Education Inspectorate, Ministry of Education, Culture, and Science. (April 2017). State of Education 2015-2016, p. 33

Chapter 19

Application of Social Cognitive Theory in the Mentoring of African American Males

Regina D. Berry
Roosevelt University, USA

Joanne Howard
Illinois Institute of Technology, USA

ABSTRACT

The primary purpose of this qualitative review was to examine the benefits of the Sigma Beta Club mentoring program on the educational experiences of African American male participants and to explore the perceptions and challenges mentors incurred while working with young men of color in the Sigma Beta Club mentoring program. The secondary purpose was to provide understanding regarding the utilization of SCT by the Sigma Beta Club mentoring program. The effects of systemic racism and discrimination have resulted in African American young men developing a distrust for lawmakers and their agents. A reconnection and an establishment of trust needs to take place.

INTRODUCTION

In America, there is a desperate need for intervention to positively influence the lives of young men of color. African American males are reared in concentrated poverty and are systematically discriminated against at a disproportionate rate. Despite multiple advances, young men of color in the aggregate still face several roadblocks to success. Significant disparities in living conditions, access to education, and due process in the criminal justice system persist between African American young men and Caucasian young men.

Education in its purest form is a gateway to knowledge and understanding. It is the building block to inform society of its rights and responsibilities, as well as an igniter of dreams and abilities. However, inadequate education primarily exists in communities that suffer from socioeconomic deprivation or

DOI: 10.4018/978-1-6684-2314-1.ch019

concentrated poverty (Annie E. Casey, 2017). When concentrated poverty and inadequate education combine, it often impairs academic completion and ultimately leads students to drop out.

Concentrated poverty is defined as a neighborhood where the poverty rate exceeds 30% (Annie E. Casey, 2017). More African American young men reside in areas of concentrated poverty than their Caucasian counterparts. According to the U.S. Census Bureau (2017), 40% of African American young men live in areas of concentrated poverty, compared to 14% of Caucasian young men. The U.S. currently has 48.8 million people below the poverty line; of that number, 30.8% of them are high school dropouts (Annie E. Casey, 2017). According to the National Center of Education Statistics (NCES; 2017), every year, 3 million high school students withdraw from the educational arena; that equates to a little more than 8,000 per day or 1 student every second. The NCES reports the dropout rate for African American young men in grades 7 through 12 is 13.9%, while Caucasians of the same grades total 5.0%. It is important to identify the factors that influence dropping out, considering that the lack of high school completion limits economic growth and reduces access to higher education and financial opportunity. The Annie E. Casey Foundation, using U.S. Census Bureau (2015) data, projects an individual who graduates from high school can potentially earn $260,000 more during his or her lifetime than someone who drops out. The condition of poverty combined with inadequate education alone does not cause the dropout occurrence. However, it is the base of the culminating dynamics in the process. The rest can be attributed to systemic racism in legal policies that ultimately seal the fate of education.

In 1994, a major piece of legislation had negative consequences on young men attempting to pursue an education while residing in poverty. The legislative act was the Gunfree Schools Act (1994), which came to be the Zero-Tolerance Policy (H.R. 987). African American young men from impoverished communities suffered de facto discrimination with the Zero-Tolerance Policy. The escalation of poverty has become the burden of those forced to live in it, despite not being the cause of it. The Zero-Tolerance Policy was intended for students whose immediate behavior caused impending concern about the probability of gun violence on the school's premises. Zero tolerance was to demonstrate that such gateway behaviors were unacceptable and would be dealt with severely. Unfortunately, young men of color suffered the greatest consequences despite having the lowest record of gun incidents on school premises (Civil Rights Data Collection, 2012). The students most often criminalized using the Zero-Tolerance Policy were minority students from disadvantaged communities, which often caused them to fall behind and be at risk of failing.

African American students have suffered academic injury due to the misappropriation of legislative policies, especially African American young men. In 2013, only 18% of all African American fourth-graders were proficient in reading, and only 19% of that same group demonstrated proficiency in mathematics. In that same year, only 16% of African American eighth-graders scored proficiently in reading and 13% in mathematics (National Center for Education Statistics, 2014). The effects of systemic racism and discrimination have resulted in African American young men developing a distrust for lawmakers and their agents. A reconnection and an establishment of trust needed to take place.

My Brother's Keeper Program

In 2014, President Barack Obama launched the My Brother's Keeper (MBK) initiative and commissioned a task force (Obama, 2014; U.S. White House, 2014). The purpose of the initiative was to address opportunity gaps impeding young men of color. The president's goal was to help these young men reach their maximum potential. A focal point of the MBK initiative was to operate with a sense of urgency and courage to call out and tear down discrimination in every system and policy.

The MBK task force compiled a report that outlined persistent barriers that have prevented young men of color from accomplishing academic and career success. The barriers included severe poverty, significant dropout rates, chronic crime, high unemployment, negative self-perceptions, and a greater likelihood of incarceration (Obama, 2014; U.S. White House, 2014). The task force identified six key milestones that predict success for young men of color from cradle to career (Obama, 2014; U.S. White House, 2014). The milestones were that young men of color: enter school ready to learn; read at grade level by the third grade; graduate from high school ready for college and career; complete post-secondary education or training; successfully enter the workforce; and reduce exposure to violence and provide a second chance to those involved in the criminal justice system.

President Obama issued a "call to action" for individuals and organizations to engage in transformative relationships with young men of color (Obama, 2014; U.S. White House, 2014). He challenged communities and public officials to formulate a cradle to college and career strategy to improve the futures of young men. Since the ultimate goal was to move young men through the obstacles that could negatively impact academic success, mentors who completed high school and pursued higher education were sought. Therefore, the president called upon Black Greek letter fraternal organizations.

Phi Beta Sigma, Inc.

Phi Beta Sigma, Inc. (Sigma) is a historically African American fraternity with ties to the African American community at large for over 100 years. Sigma has demonstrated a commitment to the academic success and empowerment of young men of color through its Education Scholarship Program and the Sigma Beta Club (SBC) youth mentoring program. Among Black Greek letter fraternal organizations, Sigma was the first to start a youth mentoring program (Phi Beta Sigma, n.d.). At a meeting between the task force and Sigma, the task force requested that Sigma collaborate formally with the president's MBK initiative. Subsequently, Sigma enhanced its SBC youth mentoring program aligned with the MBK initiative (U.S. Newswire, 2014).

Sigma Beta Club

SBC is a national youth mentoring organization that works primarily with African American young men aged 8 to 18. Currently, more than 150,000 young men have been mentored through the SBC on a national level. The mentors are primarily African American men reared in poverty who learned to avoid negative influences. They are African American men who have had to overcome multiple policy obstacles to achieve academic success (Sigma Beta Club, 2015).

Problem Statement

There are several definitions for mentoring. For this research, it is defined as a process where one individual positively influences the life of another. Mentoring builds confidence, develops resilience and character, raises aspirations, and develops skills or knowledge (Merriam Webster, 2018). Research shows that young people who participate in mentoring are more likely to finish high school and pursue higher education. They are less likely to join a gang, abuse drugs, or have an active role in the juvenile justice system (Jarjoura, 2013). Mentoring relationships influence a mentee's positive socioemotional cognitive identity and ability to achieve the desired goal.

There is literature on the impact mentoring has on positive youth development and some specific to the need for mentoring of African American males. However, there is no literature specific to African American male mentees targeted for high school completion being deliberately paired with African American male mentors.

The relationship of African American mentees and African American mentors can help to instill racial pride and a positive socioemotional cognitive identity. The perpetual negative debasing of African American young men in society contributes to negative perceptions of self and others. Negative portrayals of African Americans in movies and television roles, news reports, or even video games reinforce the image of African Americans as untrustworthy and criminal (McCrae & Galen, 2000). The deliberate pairing of African American male mentors to African American male mentees who were reared in poverty yet managed to successfully complete high school and college, and transition into a career, debunks the stereotypical perceptions.

THEORETICAL FRAMEWORK

The theoretical framework for this study was social cognitive theory (SCT), a triadic causation model concerned with changes in psychosocial development functioning (Bandura, 1989). SCT is a reciprocating determinism encompassing three essential components: sociocultural influences, environment, and behavior. SCT includes four self-systems: self-observation, self-evaluation, self-reaction, and self-efficacy. Each self-system is interrelated and affects motivation and goal achievement. The practical application of SCT is through cognitive behavioral therapy (CBT) in counseling settings. CBT is used to treat individuals who suffer from psychological conditions, such as posttraumatic stress disorder. Therefore, SCT provides a useful framework when mentoring African American males from severely challenged socioeconomic communities.

During mentoring sessions, Sigma Beta Club uses the four SCT subsets, aligning with President Obama's call to action for young men to take ownership of their lives and actions. The SCT subsets are self-observation, self-evaluation, self-reaction, and self-efficacy. Mentees are taught to look in retrospect at their actions and behaviors relative to a situation that lacked a favorable outcome. In self-observation, individuals look at how their behavior or the behavior of others contributed to an outcome. Mentees reflect on how the situation could have been handled differently. Self-evaluation requires individuals to weigh the worthiness of a possible behavior change. The mentees discuss alternative behaviors and likely outcomes, which constitute self-reaction. The last subset is self-efficacy, which is a very critical element. Self-efficacy is one's belief in the ability to succeed at a goal. The SBC mentors help mentees believe in their ability to set a goal and accomplish it, despite the obstacles.

Mentoring programs must be deliberate and focused. SBC deliberately focuses on young African American men and teams them with African American adult male role models who have shared life experiences. The primary focus is to help young men finish high school and transition into college or career. The use of the four subsets of SCT teaches goal-setting and accomplishment for academic success and life. The ultimate accomplishment is when the role models inspire mentees to become educated, law-abiding adults that avail themselves to healthy relationships and environments. The value associated with these deliberate mentoring relationships is not limited to academia.

Purpose of Study

The primary purpose of this qualitative review was to examine the benefits of the Sigma Beta Club mentoring program on the educational experiences of African American male participants and explore the perceptions and challenges mentors incurred while working with young men of color in the Sigma Beta Club mentoring program. The secondary purpose was to provide understanding regarding the utilization of SCT by the Sigma Beta Club mentoring program.

Research Questions

The following are the research questions in this study:

- What are the perspectives of African American male students who completed the Sigma Beta Club mentoring program on the factors that influence academic success?
- What do the African American male students perceive was the impact of the SBC mentoring program on their educational experience?
- What are the perspectives of Sigma Beta Club mentors on the factors that influence the academic success of African American male high school students?
- What do the mentors perceive was the impact of SBC's mentoring practices on the educational experiences of their African American male students?
- How did SBC apply components of SCT in their mentoring of African American male students?
- What is the efficacy of SCT application in the SBC mentoring of African American male students?

Significance of the Study

As discussed earlier, there is a desperate need for intervention to positively influence the lives of young men of color. This study adds to the existing body of literature on African American males by focusing on using SCT in mentoring African American males to achieve academic success. It helps address the question: "What can we do to improve the academic success of African American males?" This work also enriches the existing body of literature on African American male academic success and the body of research on mentoring African American males. The literature shows, in the mentor-mentee relationship, young people, especially African American males, desired expressive, supportive relationships. They appreciated the opportunity to be heard and to make their own decisions. The young men desired to have some ownership of their mentoring relationships (Larson, 2006). Research also shows that young people who participate in mentoring are more likely to finish high school and pursue higher education. However, there is no literature specific to African American male mentees targeted for academic completion deliberately paired with African American male mentors. The literature also does not address African American male mentors applying SCT in mentoring African American males for academic completion. The relationship of African American mentees and African American mentors can help to instill racial pride and a positive social-emotional cognitive identity.

This research documented the lived experiences and interventions of seven African American male mentees and the lived experiences of their mentors. Through reporting on their stories, other students, faculty, staff, policymakers, and stakeholders can gain a deeper understanding of the role of mentoring on African American male students' academic achievement. This information made it possible to draw implications for practice when exploring interventions to assist this population achieve academic success. Study findings have the potential to inform the design and implementation of strategies for mentoring African American males from communities of concentrated poverty.

Methodological Process

This qualitative study is based on a phenomenological research design to explore the lived experiences of the SBC mentees and mentors. The participants for this study were randomly assigned by the Sigma Beta Club mentoring program. The research consisted of two individual semi-structured interviews of seven high school graduates who participated in the SBC mentoring program during their high school years. The research also included two individual semi-structured interviews of three Sigma Beta Club mentors. Additionally, the researcher participated as an observer of a group session to examine the dynamics between mentees and mentors.

ORGANIZATION OF THE STUDY

This study is organized into five chapters. Chapter one includes an introduction that sets the framework for the necessity of mentoring and an overview of the structure of the study. Chapter one identifies some systemic factors that act as impediments to academic achievement for African American young men. It also provides a brief description of the My Brother's Keeper program, Phi Beta Sigma, and the Sigma Beta Club mentoring program. Additionally, Chapter one introduces the theoretical framework and research questions. Chapter one concludes by highlighting the purpose of the study, the significance of this research, and discusses the relevancy of the topic. Chapter two consists of a review of literature for trisecting themes identified in the MBK program. The first theme is a key piece of legislation that negatively impacted the academic success of African American young men. The second theme is the value of mentoring to challenge the barriers of systemic discrimination and negative propaganda that often derails the academic futures of African American young men. The third theme is the use of the principal subsets of SCT. The third chapter describes the methods of gathering the research data for this study. The fourth chapter includes a presentation and analysis of the data related to each research question. Subsequently, the fifth chapter includes a discussion of the overall topic, limitations of the study, recommendations for future research, and implications.

Literature Review

The chapter provides a review of the literature, which is divided into three main sections: The first section explores a key federal education legislative act that negatively impacted the academic achievement of young men of color. The federal legislative act was the Zero-Tolerance Policy (formally the Gun-free Schools Act of 1994) (GFSA) (Gun-free Schools Act, 1994). The second section provides an overview of the history and development of elementary and secondary school mentoring in the United States. The components of this section include the early history of mentoring, mentoring defined, models of mentoring, and essential components (cultural relevance) related to mentoring African American young men. The third section provides an overview of SCT and its utilization in mentoring young men of color.

A Key Federal Legislative Act

As previously mentioned in Chapter one, according to the U.S. Census Bureau (2017), 40% of African American young men live in areas of concentrated poverty, compared to 14% of Caucasian young men. The United States currently has 48.8 million people below the poverty line; of that number, 30.8% are high school dropouts (AEC, 2017). According to the NCES (2017), every year, 3 million high school students withdraw from the educational arena; that equates to just over 8,000 per day or one student every second. The NCES reports the dropout rate for African American young men in grades 7 through 12 is 13.9%, while Caucasians of the same grades total 5.0%. Some of these statistics could be attributed partly to the Zero-Tolerance Policy.

In 1983, the National Commission on Excellence in Education submitted a report to President Ronald Reagan titled *A Nation at Risk*. The report stated that the U.S. educational institutions were failing to adequately educate their students (Gardner, 1983). It also stated that disciplined efforts were needed to provide order that would return the education system to its original purpose.

Also, during the time of the National Commission's report, an increasing concern for school safety was taking place. According to the National Center for Education Statistics (2017), between 1980 and 1983, there was a combined total of 10 elementary and high school shootings. The rising concern for school safety, together with the National Commission's report on the lack of school excellence, prompted legislators to explore corrective action policies. As a solution, the Zero-Tolerance Policy, formally the GFSA, was implemented to set some disciplinary criteria for weapon violations

Zero-Tolerance (Gun-free Schools Act of 1994)

The Zero-Tolerance Policy began as the GFSA (American Psychological Association, 2008; Gun-free Schools Act, 1994). The GFSA required each state that received federal funds for its elementary and secondary education to adhere to a strict set of guidelines, including a predetermined consequence for student gun possession. The predetermined consequence was a minimum suspension of one year for any student found possessing a firearm.

The GFSA (1994) was meant to be tough on crime for young people to discourage their participation in the escalating violence in schools (American Psychological Association, 2008; Chu, 2013). Federal funding in education incentivized state rules that required school districts to expel students (Chu, 2013; Gun-free Schools Act, 1994; Kang-Brown et al., 2013). The GFSA (1994) provided additional funding for in-school police officers, security guards, metal detectors, school safety courses, as well as drug and alcohol prevention courses (American Psychological Association, 2008). In addition to expulsion, the GFSA mandated that students possessing a firearm automatically be referred to the juvenile justice system. As a further requirement, states or school districts had to develop their own policies dealing with students susceptible to particular risk factors. The risk factors included alcohol, tobacco, or illegal drugs, in addition to violent behavior by youth in schools or their community. States and school districts were allowed the discretionary latitude to determine other risk factors and define disruptive behavior that could ultimately influence a student to take a gun to school. However, the GFSA only applied to state-funded schools, could be altered for individuals with disabilities, and the expulsion requirement could be modified on a case-by-case basis (Gun-free Schools Act, 1994; U.S. Department of Education, 1994).

Due to the severity of GFSA (1994) and the latitude of schools to include other behaviors, it was eventually labeled the Zero-Tolerance Policy (American Psychological Association, 2008). The American

Psychological Association (2008) described the Zero-Tolerance Policy as a "philosophy or policy that mandated the application of predetermined consequences, most often severe and punitive in nature, that are intended to be applied regardless of the gravity of behavior, mitigating circumstances, or situational context" (p. 1). Although this policy was initially meant to deal with severe violations, such as guns and drugs, some school districts made their local policies inclusive of pocket knives and fingernail clippers (Skiba, 2000).

The American Bar Association (2001) described the Zero-Tolerance Policy as a one-size-fits-all nondiscretionary policy that redefined students as criminals. Critics argued that the policy was often misappropriated to incorporate minor infractions, such as talking back and attendance. The policy was also applied to infractions as insignificant as hairstyles or clothing (American Bar Association, 2001; Skiba et al., 2006). The one-year expulsion rule applicable to guns and drugs was applied to such insignificant infractions as well. Additionally, in-school police officers and security guards were involved in the disciplinary process. Subsequently, in accordance with the policy, the student's disciplinary reason and record were turned over to the juvenile justice system. Christle, Jolivette, and Nelson (2005) determined that by the early 2000s, school discipline was identical to the juvenile prison system and criminalized young people.

Studies have concluded that the suspension or expulsion of students using zero-tolerance policies contributed to lower academic achievement and higher dropout rates. Moreover, zero-tolerance policies have adversely affected young men of color more than other demographic populations of students (Skiba et al., 2006). Research corroborates that African American youths are suspended or expelled almost four times higher than their Caucasian counterparts (Bradley & Renzulli, 2011; Kang-Brown et al., 2013; Neely & Griffin-Williams, 2013; Suh & Suh, 2007). Additionally, male students are more likely to be suspended or expelled than female students (Bowers, Sprott, & Taff, 2013; Kokko, Tremblay, Lacourse, Nagin, & Vitaro, 2006). These statistics have been verified through the U.S. Department of Education, National Center for Education Statistics (2006, 2010, 2012).

The purpose of the Zero-Tolerance Policy was to make schools safer. However, safety has not been the result. According to the American Psychological Association's Zero-Tolerance Task Force (2008) and Skiba et al. (2006), removing a disruptive student from school failed to dissuade others and did not create a safer environment. While the Zero-Tolerance Policy had no impact on disruptive behavior (Skiba, 2000; Skiba et al., 2006), removing a disruptive student from school failed to dissuade others and did not create a safer environment. Christle et al. (2005) revealed that it exponentially increased the school-to-prison pipeline. As stated, in accordance with the GFSA (1994), the Zero Tolerance policies resulted in legal authority involvement in minor school-related matters (American Bar Association, 2001; American Psychological Association, 2008). Thus, the excessive profiling of youths of color increased, despite no minority student ever being involved in any massive or random school shootings (American Psychologist, 2008). The American Bar Association (2001) and Christle et al. (2005) agreed that students should be disciplined in a developmentally appropriate manner. Kang et al. validated the findings of the American Bar Association and Christle et al. and further stated that suspensions or expulsions increased the risk of a student not being promoted to a higher grade. Thus, successful completion of school becomes obstructed, which exacerbates the poverty level in communities of color.

Relevance

This key piece of federal legislation is relevant to the present study in that it negatively impacted the academic success of African American young men. The Zero-Tolerance Policy was constructed to curtail behaviors that would lead to guns and drugs on school premises. However, the broad misappropriation of use for age-appropriate actions in adolescent development morphed into an educational hindrance. The literature clearly demonstrates that young men of color were severely victimized by the broad application (Kang-Brown et al., 2013). They were penalized with either expulsion or suspension, which led to falling behind and, for some, dropping out. This is an education policy barrier that MBK saw and that the SBC mentoring program stepped up to address. This study sought to understand the impact of the SBC mentoring program on the educational experiences of African American male participants.

Mentoring

This section provides a review of the applicable literature on mentoring from the last 30 years as the subject matter has evolved. A research study conducted by Wyche and Frierson (1990) stated that mentoring "is a process by which an individual of superior rank, special achievement, and prestige, instructs, counsels, guides and facilitates the intellectual and/or career development of individuals identified as protégé" (p. 30). Subsequently, Jacobi (1991) conducted an extensive literature review to determine whether there was a standard definition of mentoring. She concluded that no comprehensive definition existed in the literature. Crisp and Cruz (2009) found multiple quasi-definitions and ultimately agreed with Jacobi (1991). They realized that some researchers used the term mentoring in describing a specific set of activities. However, other researchers used the term to define a concept or process. For this research, mentoring was defined as a process where one individual positively impacted the life of another, with the impact not isolated to one area. It can influence the mentee's choices, behaviors, confidence level, perseverance, and academic performance.

Function of a Mentor

Henderson's (1985) research identified the primary function of a mentor was to provide guidance, instruction, advice, counsel, and operate as a role model that motivated and protected the mentee. Alleman (1986) stated that mentors not only taught and provided guidance, but they also challenged the mentee in their choices, refined their talents, and highlighted their accomplishments. Wyche and Frierson (1990) believed the mentor should provide counseling, guidance, and tutoring. However, they believed mentoring should start in the early adolescent years. Ardery (1990) agreed with Wyche and Frierson (1990) that mentoring needed to start early to be truly effective. She stated that the mentor should provide wisdom and sound judgment to the mentee. Moreover, Galbraith (2003) stated, "the primary goal of mentoring is directed toward enhancing personal and professional growth through the development of the learner's self-concept and self-efficacy efforts" (p. 16).

Is mentoring a one-directional or reciprocal relationship? Alleman (1986), Henderson (1985), and Wyche and Frierson (1990) agreed that a traditional mentoring relationship was one-directional, where the mentee learned and benefited from the knowledge and expertise of the mentor. Within this relationship, Galbraith and Cohen (1995) contended that a hierarchical, one-directional relationship must exist to enable the mentor to provide guidance to the mentee. In contrast, Ardery (1990) found that mentoring is an exchange of knowledge and learning supported by Gunn's (1995) description of a mentoring relationship being a partnership or a two-way transfer of skills and expertise. Prior to Gunn's findings, Jacobi's (1991) literature review found a preponderance of the literature revealed that mentoring relationships were reciprocal, meaning that there was a mutual benefit to the mentor and mentee. Haensly and Parsons (1993) concurred with the aforementioned researchers, explaining that effective mentoring happened when the mentor and mentee influenced one another. Effective mentoring was described as "a multi-dimensional, dynamic, reciprocal relationship between a more advanced practitioner and a novice" (Girves, Gwathmey, & Zepeda, 2005, p. 453). More recently, Crisp and Cruz (2009) concluded that mentoring was a mutually beneficial, necessary exchange between parties, whether that relationship existed as hierarchical or as an equal partnership. Since this research focuses on the impact that SBC mentors have on mentees, it is important to understand the dynamics of the relationship and how this contributes to the program's effectiveness.

Mentoring Types

McHale (2000) asserted that there were nine types of mentoring: mentoring from the business community; career mentoring with specific groups; mentoring situations that demanded specialized training; mentoring within educational settings; mentoring based on language, culture, gender, or ethnicity; specific needs or focused programs mentoring; group mentoring; youth to youth or peer mentoring; and cross-age or intergenerational mentoring (p. 13). McHale's nine types of mentoring correspond to several components of the My Brother's Keeper program. MBK's call to action for mentoring includes mentoring from the business community. The business community was asked to focus its efforts on young men of color. Also, MBK asked mentors to programmatically focus on education to career mentoring in groups.

After McHale's (2000) research, the *Mentor: National Mentoring Partnership* (2015) focused their research on youth mentoring and concluded there were five types of youth mentoring: traditional one-to-one mentoring, group mentoring, team mentoring, peer mentoring, and e-mentoring. Traditional one-to-one mentoring is a type in which one adult is assigned to establish a relationship with one youth. One-to-one mentoring is found in both formal and informal models. The pair determines their settings, activities, and outcomes.

Group mentoring is a type in which one adult forms a relationship with a group of up to four young people. Team mentoring involves several adults working with small groups of young people, with an adult-to-youth ratio not greater than one to four. In group mentoring and team mentoring models, the mentor assumes the role of a leader and makes a commitment to meet regularly with the group over a long period. Most interaction is guided by the session structure, which includes time for personal sharing. If the mentoring program has a sponsoring organization, it may specify certain activities in which the group must participate. In some cases, the mentor may choose or design appropriate activities. Some group mentoring activities may be intended as teaching exercises, while others may simply be for fun.

Peer mentoring involves an older youth developing a guiding, teaching relationship with a slightly younger individual. Peer mentoring usually encompasses specified curriculum-based activities. In addition, peer mentoring programs often resemble a mentor in a training program. Therefore, these relationships are closely monitored. The youth mentors serve as positive role models to mentees while providing ongoing support. Usually, in a peer mentoring relationship, the mentor and the mentee meet frequently over the course of a semester or an entire school year.

The most recent type, e-mentoring (also known as online mentoring or telementoring), involves connecting one adult with one youth through an internet-based communication tool. In e-mentoring, the mentor and a mentee primarily communicate using internet-based software at least once per week over a period of six months to a year. This type, like peer mentoring, has to be closely supervised and is typically arranged through a formal youth sponsoring organization. Some organizations arrange two or three face-to-face meetings between the mentors and mentees, one being an introductory session. Often, the mentor will serve as a guide or advisor in school or career-related areas. Understanding the types of mentoring helps to identify and define the type of mentoring structure SBC operates within.

The Effects of Mentoring Programs

Several research studies confirm youth development mentoring programs provide necessary social and educational experiences for young men of color. Galbraith (2003) posited that if a mentor engaged in some specific behaviors while working with the mentee, it would result in academic achievement. His behaviors were to challenge, advise, encourage, motivate, and foster a trusting relationship with the mentee. Gordon, Iwamoto, Ward, Potts, and Boyd (2009) conducted a study to ascertain whether youth mentoring impacted mentee academic achievement. The results showed that mentees demonstrated significantly greater academic success than their non-mentored peers.

Eby, Allen, Evans, Ng, and Dubose's (2007) study findings also rendered favorable outcomes for mentored youths in multiple areas, including behavior, attitude, motivation, and career decisions. Woodland, Martin, Hill, and Worrell (2009) stated that the influence of mentoring achieved positive results in their youth development research. The positive results were not limited to improved academic outcomes. The mentees reported experiencing increased self-confidence and a greater sense of personal accountability.

Although Dubois et al. (2002), in their meta-analysis of research study on mentoring, insisted that much more research was required to give concrete validity to the claim that mentoring programs deter young people from committing crime, they attested to the positive in academics. Their study contended that mentoring programs provided the support needed by young people to make positive decisions. Larson (2006) found that having mentors interacting with young people motivated a desire to please and immolate their adult mentors. Raposa et al. (2019) affirmed that youth mentoring programs provided positive interventions psychosocially and academically. However, they caution that a one-size-fits-all approach to mentoring youths is ineffective. The research demonstrates that mentoring programs focused on academic success, such as SBC, have a likelihood of success. Therefore, there is validity to SBC's programmatic thrust.

Essential Components of Mentoring Young Men of Color

Time

There are three primary mentoring components: time, relationship, and cultural relevance (Woodland et al., 2009). Several research studies found that the more time in terms of duration of the relationship that a young person has invested in a mentoring program, the less likely he is to depart from that relationship or its lessons (Grossman & Rhodes, 2002; Jarjoura, 2013). Research findings also indicated that mentor and mentee relationships that were less than six months in duration had no real impact on the mentee's life in terms of academic improvement (Grossman & Rhodes, 2002). Grossman, Chan, Schwartz, and

Rhodes (2011) concurred with the earlier findings by Grossman and Rhodes (2002) that early departure of the mentor showed no improvements in the academic performance of the mentee. However, the impact was very different for the mental and emotional stability of the mentee. Grossman et al. (2011) found that when an early departure from a mentoring relationship happens, the mentee is more inclined to make poor choices (e.g., alcohol, substance abuse, promiscuity) based on the perceived rejection, even when they are rematched with a replacement mentor. Psychologically, the mentee may process the mentor's departure negatively and interpret it as his or her fault. In contrast, relationships that lasted a year or more had a significant impact on helping mentees make more positive choices due to the time invested in establishing a positive relationship with the mentor (Grossman & Rhodes, 2002; Jarjoura, 2013).

Relationship

Researchers agreed that the quality of relationships between mentors and youth mentees significantly impacted the mentees' decision-making and commitment to the mentoring arrangement (Grossman & Rhodes, 2002; Jarjoura, 2013). Larson's (2006) study showed that in the mentor-mentee relationship, young people, especially African American males, desired expressive, supportive relationships. They appreciated the opportunity to be heard and to make their own decisions. The young men desired to have some ownership of their mentoring relationships. African American young men reported being most involved in programs that promoted ownership (Gordon et al., 2009). The mentors and mentees expressed that the ability of mentees to own and control their actions and outcomes improved their leadership abilities (Gordon et al., 2009; Grossman & Rhodes, 2002; Larson, 2006; Rhodes, 2011).

Cultural Relevance

The findings of Gordon et al. (2009) coincided with Woodland et al.'s (2009) findings regarding the importance of cultural relevance to African American young men. In particular, Gordon et al. (2009) noted that highlighting cultural history gave some African American young men a sense of racial identity and pride. A study conducted on the Benjamin E. Mays Institute revealed a rise in the academic achievement of the control group that employed a self-identity component (Gordon et al., 2009). The Benjamin E. Mays Institute is a mentoring organization designed to assist African American young men academically, whose principles are based on an Afro-centric framework. The study showed that using positive self-identification concepts, such as Sankofa (go back and fetch), resulted in positive intrinsic motivations of responsibility and self-discipline (Gordon et al., 2009).

Mentors help African American mentees process images around them and the positive or negative impact of those images. Researchers (Burrell, 2010; Mastro, 2015; Yancy, 2008) agreed that some of the images shown in multiple streams of media perpetuated negative stereotypes of African Americans and influenced societal views. The effects of the negative stereotypes caused Caucasians to operate with attributional biases and unfavorably view African Americans and apply unsympathetic policy decisions (Martin, 2008; Yancy, 2008). The negative images and stereotypes had a direct impact on adolescent development and racial identity. Martin (2008) stated that youth identity is overwrought with continual stress and anxiety. However, African American youths had the additional burden of learning to navigate the challenge of being Black in America. That challenge was inundated with negative racial stereotypes. She indicated that the use of positive images in media, especially on television, as well as social support, subverted the stereotypical images in society and personally.

Tukachinsky, Mastro, and Yarchi (2017) conducted a longitudinal study exploring the intragroup effects of Latino and African American depictions on television from 1987 to 2008. The study was restricted to primetime shows with recurring characters. The depictions of African Americans were primarily in African American sitcoms and crime dramas. The study found that before the 1980s, African Americans almost always appeared in negative roles (e.g., slaves, servants, pimps, prostitutes, drug dealers). During the 1980s, African Americans transitioned to respectable, professional roles. However, the 1990s reflected an increase in the less respectable roles once again. In the 2000s, the increase in negative roles persisted. The representations of African Americans showed them more likely to be unemployed or in blue-collar positions, even in reality television programs. Latinos had very few roles and primarily were depicted in a sexual nature or as blue-collar workers and often as objects of ridicule or criminals.

The effects of Tukachinsky et al.'s (2017) research showed that often Caucasians believed the negative propaganda regarding minorities. The members of those devalued ethnic groups displayed negative psychological impacts, such as lowered self-esteem and group esteem. The study also revealed that some members would dissociate themselves and display a strong affinity for the majority group. Therefore, they began to justify the oppressive treatment and negative connotations suffered by their minority group. Adams-Bass, Stevenson, and Kotzin (2014) examined how African American youths interpreted and responded to negative images. Their research indicated that racial identity and socialization of African American youths in their study were adversely affected. However, the research found that African American youths who received positive affirmations and those knowledgeable about African American history were less likely to be influenced by the negative stereotypes.

Topos Partnership (2011) reviewed the social science literature regarding the psychological ramifications of the unfavorable portrayal of African American men in the media. The study examined public attitudes and the perceptions African American men developed regarding themselves. The review found that the negative reflections bred negative perceptions by the public about African American men. Martin (2008) posited that promoting positive racial images would create positive self-identity in African American youths. The development of a positive self-identity will counteract the negative effects of racial discrimination the youths will eventually encounter. Given the bombardment of negative images and misappropriation of laws plaguing people of color, it is imperative that mentors provide positive cultural reinforcements to people of color, especially young African American men.

The value of African American young men having the benefit of mentorship from African American men who have faced the same academic and societal challenges is invaluable. The mentees can observe or visualize the lived experiences of the mentors and mimic the behavior. The pressure to meet or debunk a stereotype at such a critical time of development directly affects the trajectory of African American male academic and career success. African American men from similar backgrounds are able to provide fundamental guidance to navigate the various systems that would otherwise impede success. As with President Obama's call to young men of color to take responsibility for their lives and actions, mentors help facilitate the ability. Given the multiple barriers most young men must overcome, from societal hate to sometimes even self-hate because of systemic conditioning, a mentor is imperative. It is clear that the history of African Americans in the United States, in addition to the current racial climate, dictates that young African American men desperately need the positive input of African American men committed to a consistent relationship of dedicated time.

On a programmatic level, African American male mentoring programs must instill personal responsibility through the lens of self-observation, evaluation, reaction, and efficacy. Programs must teach young men to examine their role in all situations and to define how they want to see themselves in the future. Young men must be taught to weigh their actions and determine appropriate and inappropriate responses. Most importantly, young African American men must be given permission to believe in themselves, their abilities, and their self-worth.

Those techniques are the components of Bandura's SCT self-system.

Social Cognitive Theory

SCT is a process of human development focused on alterations in psychosocial functioning (Bandura, 1978). SCT was founded by psychologist and behavioral theorist Albert Bandura. The foundation of the SCT was based on four principles of observational learning: attention, retention, reproduction, and motivation (Bandura, 1978). Attention is when an observer notices the behavior of another. Retention is the ability of the observer to remember the behavior that was previously demonstrated by another. Reproduction is an observer's ability to mimic the behavior previously demonstrated. Motivation is the reason an observer notices, remembers, and mimics the behavior of another. The motivation portion of Bandura's theory states that observers only mimic the behavior of someone relatable, admired, or rewarded. Those four principles are the root of Bandura's theory of observational learning based upon modeled behavior.

SCT is described as the triadic reciprocal determinism model of behavior, cognition, and environment (Bandura, 1978; Williams & Williams, 2010). Bandura (1978, 2001) posited that each component reciprocally influences the others, though not all equally. Bandura (1978) stated that the reciprocating determinism of behavior, cognition, and environment creates the human experience. Bandura found that people are agentic, meaning they are both producers and products of a social system (2001). Bandura (2001) and Nevid (2009) agreed that individuals function as respondents and influencers of their environment through their own motivation and behavior.

SCT is concerned with changes in psychosocial development functioning to help individuals understand and modify their behavior (Bandura, 1989). Bandura defined reciprocal determinism as an individual's behavior being shaped by his or her environment while also affecting the environment, consequently shaping that individual's cognition (1978). Bandura (1978, 2001) found a person's environment can be more influential on his or her behavior than genetics. Therefore, with proper interventions, people can reprogram their cognition to change their behavior and positively influence their environment.

Bandura (1982) found that people ultimately desire to feel a sense of control over their own lives and behavior. Therefore, they subconsciously implement proactive and reactive strategies to move toward self-regulation. He believed there are four self-systems directing an individual's behavior (Bandura, 1978, 1982). Each self-system is interrelated and affects an individual's motivation and goal achievement. The four self-systems are self-observation, self-evaluation, self-reaction, and self-efficacy. The exploration of the use of SCT in mentoring at SBC should reveal the degree of use in relation to the self-systems. Understanding the extent of use can inform the research regarding the SBC overall effectiveness of African American adult men mentoring young African American men.

Self-Observation

Self-observation is an introspection of one's own thoughts, feelings, and behaviors that includes observing self and others (Bandura, 1978). Bandura considered self-observation to be a catalyst for change. He said it enhances cognitive processes, which are needed for deliberate self-regulation. Bandura described behavioral learning as acquired by observation of the environment. However, he expanded upon the concept of behavioral learning to add that mediating processes are happening between the stimuli and the response (Bandura, 2001). The mediating processes analyze the behavior observed, whether from self or a model. Self-observation is a therapeutic form involving an individual becoming aware of his or her actions and understanding his or her reasoning.

Bandura (1978) stated that children watch people in their environment behaving in a particular way and unconsciously establish those individuals as models. He clarified that models are not limited to relatives or those close in a child's inner circle. However, Bandura posited that children are likely to imitate those they perceive to be similar to them. Bandura's research found that the characteristics of any model must be relevant to the observer. The ability of the observer to relate is critical in observational learning. Albeit, models can be television characters, sports stars, media personalities, or even fictional characters from books (Williams & Williams, 2010). Models become examples of behavior that is observed and imitated. Bandura (1978) stated that when children watch the behavior of models, they encode these observed behaviors for later use.

Bandura's (1978) research of modeled behavior is based upon his Bobo doll experiment of 1961. The experiment was used to evaluate aggressive behavior by subjects toward a model. The behavior included hitting and kicking the doll as well as using aggressive language. Each child was given an opportunity to play with the doll. The children in the control group behaved the same way as the model, demonstrating extremely aggressive behavior. When given the opportunity to play with the doll normally or even play with other toys, they continued the aggressive behavior on the doll. Although weapons were not used in the demonstration, the children began progressively utilizing various weapons, including a toy gun. This was measured against another group of children who had not seen the aggressive behavior modeled. Those children normally played with the doll without displaying any aggression.

Therefore, Bandura (1978) concluded that children imitate modeled behavior and may eventually take the behavior to another level. He further stated that individuals around the child provide either a reinforcing or punitive response to the imitated behavior. If the imitated behavior was met with some form of reward, the behavior was likely to occur again. However, children considered the consequences of the model, which determined whether the behavior should be copied.

Fireman and Kose (2002) supported Bandura's (1989) use of self-observation as a behavioral learning tool. However, Fireman and Kose disagreed that self-observation should be used as a tool for comprehensive learning and development. Their research showed that a limited amount of learning takes place when an individual imitates modeled behavior. They believed that modeled behavior does not teach children to interpret, only to imitate.

Consequently, children only develop a system of emulation instead of developing their problem-solving abilities through cause and effect. Therefore, Fireman and Kose concluded that modeled behavior was an effective means of promoting performance. However, it was limited in cognizant problem-solving. Albright and Malloy's (1999) research agreed with Fireman and Kose. They found that adolescents became problem solvers when they were able to observe themselves attempting to resolve an issue, as opposed to when it is demonstrated by someone else.

Foster, Laverty-Finch, Gizzo, and Osantowski (1999) reviewed the use of self-observation in mentoring. They found it to be a useful way to help adolescents better understand themselves. However, they did not address Fireman and Kose's (2002) findings regarding the link between self-observation and problem-solving. Foster et al. (1999) affirmed Bandura's (1989) conclusion that self-observation is an effective tool, albeit they stated that its use must be limited to specific, targeted behaviors. Foster et al.

(1999) found that when several behaviors are tackled at once, it becomes too cumbersome and intrusive to the participant. The present research revealed that the SBC mentees' observations of the mentors inspired the mentees to replicate the modeled academic success of the mentors.

Self-Evaluation

Self-evaluation is an internal comparative standard by which performance motivation is gauged and enhanced (Bandura & Cervone, 1983). Expanding upon the theory, Chang, Ferris, Johnson, Rosen, and Tan (2012) described self-evaluation as an assessment made by an individual regarding his or her abilities and self-worth. It can also be described as a process of systematically observing, analyzing, and weighing one's own actions for stability or improvement (Lewis, 1991). Chang et al. proposed that self-evaluations are the most fundamental evaluations a person can make. It reflects a baseline appraisal that is reflected in all other beliefs and evaluations. Bandura (1989) considered self-evaluations as a judgmental process. He indicated that these judgments are impacted by the value placed on a task or skill. Those values function as determinism in how and where efforts are placed.

Self-evaluation is not limited to a measurement of oneself. It can also involve measuring one's own abilities and skills against others (Lewis, 1991). The other person can be a member of the individual's peer group, a family member, or even a random stranger with whom the person has come in contact. Hofseth, Toering, Jordet, and Ivarsson (2017) cautioned that this type of comparative self-evaluation can lead to overestimating one's true skills. They determined that realistic views regarding a skill level or task help individuals reach their maximum potential.

Teasley and Lee (2006) considered the educational self-assessments of African American adolescents against their Caucasian counterparts. The study revealed that despite systemic discrimination, the African American subjects maintained high self-worth. In fact, Bem (1967) indicated that while African Americans recognized that their social and economic status was often lower than Caucasians, they remained resolved to continue pursuing their goals. Rosenberg (1965) stated that despite discrimination, which can hinder some African Americans from fully achieving their goals, they do not take it as their own failure. Krause (1983) supported Rosenberg's findings and concluded that African Americans do not truly compare themselves to Caucasians when assessing their self-worth in terms of strengths, weaknesses, and areas of improvement. African Americans use the attributes of those personally relevant to them.

Krause and Rosenberg's findings are aligned with Bandura (1978) that the social psychological perspective of an individual is often limited to his or her interpersonal environment. The idea that African Americans do not allow inequality to define their self-worth demonstrates their ability to distinguish between self and circumstance. Hughes and Demo (2017) hypothesized a different point of view. They initially thought the research would show that societal discrimination would be interpreted as a personal failure. Moreover, African Americans would believe they had no true control of their own lives (self-efficacy). This would complicate their ability to conduct a realistic self-evaluation. However, they found African Americans with self-perceived high self-worth were not negatively affected by systemic societal discrimination. Given the climate of overt discrimination African Americans encounter, this research explored the affirmations of self-worth SBC instills in mentees to enhance their academic motivation.

Self-Reaction

Self-reaction is the adjustment of one's behavior to achieve the desired outcome (Bandura, 1978, 1982). Contrary to the other components of Bandura's (1978, 1982) self-systems, self-reaction is not shaped as an independent theory. Self-reaction is often illustrated as a component of self-regulation theory. Schunk (1995) described self-reaction as an active process of behavioral learning. It is the adaptive behavior necessary for successful goal achievement. Self-reaction is activated by the belief that one can and is making progress toward a goal. Self-reaction relates to the adjustment made to fit the conditions and alter one's behavior to achieve the desired outcome. Bandura (1997) stated that self-reaction is consequential to social cognition for behavior modification.

Wonberg, Zhu, and Van Hooft (2010) defined self-reaction as a concept in which the individual addresses perceptions of success and failure in relation to the pursuit of a goal. Bandura (1991) explained that through self-reaction, the individual is able to assess current progress against desired outcomes. When individuals perceive progress is being achieved, their level of happiness (subjective well-being) was increased. In contrast, when failure is perceived, feelings of anxiety and discontentment were reported. It should be noted that the feelings of elation or sadness are only present in goals that hold significance. Bandura (1991) referred to the significance as a valuation of activities, meaning the value an individual places on a particular goal. The value of a goal dictates how an individual responds to obstacles. Wonberg et al. (2010) contributed to our understanding of Bandura's (1999) theory of efficacy. When progress is achieved, efficacy increases and the reaction is that the individual becomes less likely to quit or become demotivated. SBC assists mentees with goal-setting and encourages them to believe in the possibility of attainment. Mentees are taught to alter behaviors that would be a hindrance to their success.

Self-Efficacy

Self-efficacy is an individual's belief that despite environment or experiences, they possess the capacity to achieve their goals (Bandura, 1978). Bandura stated that self-efficacy is a belief an individual possesses the power and the ability to organize and execute his or her own course of action. He stated that when individuals believe they have control over their own lives, they set goals and pursue them. Snyder and Lopez (2007) corroborated Bandura's definition of self-efficacy as an individual's belief that he or she can accomplish a task with his or her own skills. Van der Bijl and Shortidge-Baggett (2002) and Gekas (2004) supported the concept of self-efficacy but described it as a self-fulfilling prophecy.

Bandura's research shows that task proficiency encourages and increases self-efficacy. Lunenburg (2011) posited that self-efficacy not only impacts an individual's actions but also his or her continued motivation and ability to learn. Williams and Williams (2010) concluded that individuals with a high level of self-efficacy continually challenge themselves with progressively more difficult tasks. In contrast, individuals with low self-efficacy are likely to avoid difficult tasks and view them as threats. Albeit Lunenburg (2011) and Bandura (1977, 2001) concurred that self-efficacy, like the other self-systems, must be limited to a specific task or goal.

Bandura's (1977) findings are that people differ in their levels of efficacy. Building upon Bandura's (1977) research, Williams and Williams (2010) explained that there are five cognitive sources of information an individual utilizes in the development of efficacy: performance experiences, vicarious experiences, imagined experiences, verbal persuasion, and physiological feedback. Performance experiences encompass both positive and negative experiences related to previous performance to determine the likelihood of success. Vicarious experiences draw from the performance of others and make a comparative analysis of one's own ability. Imagined experiences are mentally derived scenarios created in the psyche of an individual that are understood to be fictional. Verbal persuasion is the external encouragement or discouragement regarding performance and ability. Physiological feedback is emotional arousal or an internal sensation derived from the consideration of a task. This research demonstrates that people must believe in their ability to achieve a desired outcome to persevere through difficulty. As stated in self-reaction, the SBC program teaches mentees goal-setting. They start with small goals, and as those goals are achieved, they are replaced with more significant goals. The purpose is to build the mentees' self-efficacy belief that despite what happens externally, they internally possess the power to succeed.

In Summary

As stated in Chapter 1, young men of color need some positive intervention to help them achieve academic success. The available studies highlight trends in the literature: (a) the Zero-Tolerance Policy adversely affected African American male students through expulsions and suspensions, (b) mentoring has no specific definition, (c) mentors are useful to provide guidance, advice and be a role model, (c) mentoring programs provide necessary social and educational support, (d) time and relationship are essential elements of effectiveness in mentoring, (e) cultural relevance is necessary when mentoring African American males to develop self-love and self-worth, (f) cultural relevance helps to combat negative social stereotypes, and (g) mentoring programs for African American males benefit from the usage of the self-systems of the SCT. These trends unveil the discussions around the topic of mentoring, especially mentoring African American males who are pursuing academic completion.

This dissertation contributes to the study of mentoring. First, it adds to the subject by showing that mentoring can help young African American men navigate educational legislation using SCT. Second, this dissertation provides a perspective on the benefits of pairing African

American mentees with African American mentors to achieve academic success.

METHODS

The SBC mentoring program was selected by the MBK task force for participation in President Obama's initiative due to its longstanding devotion to mentoring young men of color.

Although not a restricted program, the SBC chapter reviewed for this research comprised all African American male mentors and mentees. This qualitative phenomenological study explored the impact mentoring had on the educational aspirations of a sample population of SBC mentor program participants. Yin (2014) explained that qualitative research intends to represent the participants' perspectives and covers the contextual conditions of people's lives. Its focus is to provide insight into human behavior through historic or new concepts, and it uses multiple sources of evidence to add credibility and trustworthiness. Creswell (2014) defined qualitative research as "a means of exploring and understanding the meaning individuals or groups ascribe to a social or human problem" (p. 4). He defined a phenomenological study as "a design of inquiry coming from philosophy and psychology in which the researcher describes the lived experiences of individuals about a phenomenon as described by participants" (p. 14).

The goal was to identify the use of SCT in the SBC mentoring program from the mentors' and mentees' perspectives. Using qualitative phenomenology was the most appropriate method because it allowed the researcher to gain an understanding from the African American male participants regarding their experiences with the SBC mentoring program. They had the opportunity to express the contributions SBC made to facilitate their academic success. For the purposes of this research, academic success was qualified as the completion of high school. Since qualitative research involves face-to-face meetings and observations, the researcher gained a clearer understanding of the contextual aspects of some words and expressions used by the participants. This qualitative phenomenological study allowed the participants to describe the richness of their experience by attributing meaning to it.

The research questions that guided this dissertation are:

1. What were the perspectives of African American male students who completed the Sigma Beta Club mentoring program on the factors that influence academic success?
2. What did the African American male students perceive was the impact of the Sigma Beta Club mentoring program on the educational experience?
3. What were the perspectives of Sigma Beta Club mentors on the factors that influenced the academic success of African American male high school students?
4. What did the mentors perceive was the impact of Sigma Beta Club's mentoring practices on the educational experiences of their African American male students?
5. How did Sigma Beta Club apply components of SCT in their mentoring of African American male students?
6. What was the efficacy of SCT application in the SBC mentoring of African American male students?

This chapter outlines the design of the study, the study's framework, procedures, data collection, and data analysis.

Design of the Study

This study consisted of seven former mentees (participants) of SBC and three mentors. The sample size was a nonprobability sample based upon availability. The availability was the young men who had remained in contact with the program post-graduation. The sample of seven participants provided enough to detect the emergence and pattern of themes. The study participants were assigned by the SBC. This study utilized mixed qualitative methods that included a group session and interviews. The phenomenon of the study was the impact of intentionally placing African American mentees with African American mentors to achieve academic success by applying the subsets of SCT. The criteria for participation were to be African American former mentees of the SBC while in high school. The participants needed to be 18 years old or more and recent high school graduates. Recent high school graduates were the focus because the study's goals were to explore the impact of SBC and its use of SCT in the programmatic format to help mentees achieve academic success.

The participants were from various neighborhoods, some cities, and some suburbs. There was also a mix of income levels and family structures. However, approximately 70% of the participants grew up in single-parent homes, in which the head of the household was female. The value of including participants from varying backgrounds was to explore whether mentoring with SCT was the commonality of academic success. Income and family structure were ruled out as being the commonality of success by the research. African Americans from affluent backgrounds have access to better resources. However, by virtue of being African American, they are also marginalized.

Theoretical Framework

The theoretical framework for this study was SCT. As mentioned in Chapter 2, SCT involves four subsets, known as the self-systems: self-observation, self-evaluation, self-reaction, and self-efficacy. They are useful for individuals interested in modifying their behavior to achieve a goal. The self-system of SCT aligns with the mentoring format of SBC. The curriculum of SBC requires the mentees to commit to a goal of high school completion and take an oath of individual accountability. Subsequently, the young men must make an honest assessment of their behaviors that has or could derail their goals. The mentees were given the assignment of analyzing the importance of the behavior to gain self-awareness of the value placed on the behavior and the consequences of failing to achieve their goals. They also outline the benefits associated with achieving the goal of finishing high school from a personal and global perspective. The mentees worked with the mentors in roleplay exercises and discussions to redirect their behavior to achieve a more positive outcome. Throughout the exercises and assessments, the most critical element of the SCT was utilized. The mentees recited positive affirmations, songs, and prayers, regarding their responsibility as young African American men to succeed, instilling the belief that success is possible.

The second prong of the MBK program's call to action was to young men. The young men were challenged to strive to do better and take responsibility for their actions and decisions. The self-system of SCT directly correlates with helping young men take responsibility and modify the behavior that impedes their success. Therefore, SCT was the most suitable theory for this study.

Procedure

All participants were assigned by the organization. The researcher and the participants went over the details of the verbal consents for the focus group observation and the individual interviews to ensure the participants were clear of their right to decline to answer any questions, their right to withdraw at any time, and their right for the researcher to be excused from the focus group at any time. The researcher met with the mentors individually and opened the conversation with introductions and consents. Once the mentors agreed, the interviews began. After the first round of mentor interviews, the group session took place. For the group session, the mentors reminded mentees of the researcher's participation and that participation was not mandatory. At the opening of the group session, the researcher was introduced to the mentees and placed in a breakout room. The researcher went over the consent for the observation with each participant as they were assigned to the room. Upon conferral each participant clicked to join the main room all the way until the last consent. Once all verbal consents were conferred, the researcher was granted the access to the focus group for observation. At the close of the session, the researcher thanked everyone for their time and gave her closing speech. Subsequently, the respective interviews with the mentees were conducted on their arranged dates and times. At the beginning of each interview, the researcher re-introduced herself and went over the verbal consent. All interviews (mentors and mentees) started with Pseudonyms being selected by each participant to protect their identity.

The research for this study consisted of one focus group and two individual semi-structured, informal interviews per participant. Fetterman (2009) stated that the informal interview was the most common type of interview technique in qualitative research. The focus group was held using the Zoom platform. Esterberg (2002) stated that focus groups help participants feel more comfortable and remove some of the perceived hierarchical power that emerges in one-on-one interviews. She pointed out that one of the advantages of a focus group is the ability to collect a large amount of data in a short period. The focus group approach allows the researcher to observe the group dynamics between the mentees and the mentors. Additionally, conducting the focus group allows the participants to relive some collective experiences and develop some familiarity with the researcher in advance of the one-on-one interviews.

The individual, one-on-one interviews were conducted using the Zoom virtual platform. The virtual platform allowed for a visual meeting providing most of the effects of an in-person, face-to-face meeting. However, due to the limitations of the screen, it was not possible to determine if a participant was fidgeting or rocking his lower body, which are gestures that inform researchers' interpretations (Drisko, 2016). Face-to-face meetings help the researcher observe and document all facial expressions and gestures associated with narrative statements. This information provided a deeper insight into the narrative. These interviews consisted of open-ended questions, allowing the participants to tell stories about their experiences.

Data Collection

As stated, the participants were assigned by the Sigma Beta Club. The criteria for participation were to be African American and a high school graduate who participated in the Sigma Beta Club mentoring program during his high school years. The local Sigma Beta Club administrator surveyed former mentees who remained in contact with the Sigma Beta Club, which provided various statuses. Some participants continued their academic endeavors to graduate school. Some graduated high school and went into trades or the workforce.

The data were collected by (a) observing a group meeting and (b) through informal interviews using a semi-structured interview method. The first interviews were with the mentors. The mentors provided information regarding the programmatic thrust and structure. The mentors gave their perspectives of the program and the mentees. Also, mentors provided their own mentoring backgrounds that may impact the service delivery. After conducting the first round of interviews with the mentors, there was a group session observation that consisted of the mentors and the former mentees. As stated, the group session provided insight into the group dynamics and interactions. Subsequently, the mentees were interviewed. The interviews with the mentees provided information regarding the benefits of participating in the Sigma Beta

Club and how it made a difference in the educational experience. The second round of interviews was used as needed to provide follow-up or clarification of a previously mentioned or observed item.

The interviews were flexible enough to allow for relevant storytelling. The group session lasted two hours, each initial interview lasted approximately 90 minutes, and the subsequent interviews lasted approximately 20 minutes. All interviews were audio-recorded with the permission of each participant. All initial interviews began with a reminder of the purpose of the study and the right to withdraw at any time. Field notes were taken by the researcher throughout the interviews. At the conclusion of each interview, recorded interviews were immediately transcribed into Microsoft Word using the Nuance Dragon Dictation Software. All notes and recordings were maintained in a locked file cabinet to protect the confidentiality of the participants. After three years, all files will be destroyed.

Data Analysis

After transcribing the participant interviews into Microsoft Word using the Nuance Dragon Dictation Program, the transcriptions were imported into NVivo software. The researcher then imported the data from the literature review for comparison. To analyze the data, the researcher used the NVivo software program to code the data and analyze the themes that trended in the interviews. The data were analyzed using an inductive approach based on the research questions and the theoretical framework used to guide the study. The next step for the researcher was to create nodes in the NVivo software system. Nodes act as containers that sort data by theme or relationship. There can be multiple levels to nodes, which are dependent upon the researcher's structure. It can be flatlined or hierarchical. The structure for this study was hierarchical. The nodes were created using the research questions as parent nodes. The data were sorted into the nodes, and emergent themes and subthemes were coded by frequency of use in the inductive coding process. The inductive approach is flexible and allowed findings to emerge (Creswell, 2014). The questions explored the participants' perspectives and determined the alignment with the varying subsets of the self-systems. The data were coded utilizing repeating themes that emerged from the individual interviews. The coded themes were examined using research sources to establish a coherent justification for those themes. This process, known as the triangulation of data, was used to add validity to the study.

Summary

The section has provided a detailed description of the overall research study design. The data collection and analysis processes were highlighted to provide the reader with a greater understanding of the study, the researcher, the setting, and the participants. The methods used to collect the data were identified, and the steps were laid out. This was all done to prepare the reader for the information appearing in the subsequent chapters.

DATA COLLECTION FINDINGS

The primary purpose of this study was to examine the benefits of the Sigma Beta Club mentoring program on the educational experiences of African American male participants and to explore the perceptions and challenges mentors encountered while working with young African American men in the Sigma Beta Club mentoring program. The secondary purpose was to provide understanding regarding the utilization of SCT by the Sigma Beta Club mentoring program. The research findings were based on data collection and analysis of 10 individual interviews and a focus group observation. The 10 individual interviews were comprised of seven former Sigma Beta Club mentees and three Sigma Beta Club mentors.

This chapter delineates the findings of the research and is laid out in six sections. The first section is an overview of the data collection process. The second section is the data analysis process. The third section is a description of the research participants. The fourth section reports the data germane to the research questions related to the mentees. The fifth section reports the data germane to the research questions related to the mentors. The sixth section reports the data germane to the theory. The seventh section reports the data relevant to the observation.

Data Collection

The data collection relevant to the mentees' perspectives involved seven former mentees of the SBC mentoring program. The mentees were selected to participate in this research by the SBC program. The selection was based on the time of the mentee's enrollment in SBC. The enrollment of the mentees coincided with the "call to action" and partnership with the My Brother's Keeper initiative. An additional requirement was that the mentees needed to have graduated from high school while participating in SBC.

The data collection was conducted using semi-structured, primarily open-ended interview questions. The researcher constructed an individual set of exploratory questions for each participant group. The groups consisted of three SBC mentors and seven former SBC mentees. The mentors' interviews were conducted using the Zoom communications video-calling platform. The interviews were recorded using a miniature voice recorder. Additionally, field notes were taken by the researcher to immediately capture pertinent points relative to the literature. After each interview, the recorded notes were transcribed using Nuance Dragon dictation software in Microsoft Word. The researcher reviewed each transcription in detail for accuracy. The process involved playing the recording while following along word-by-word. Using this method of review helped the researcher to enter the required punctuation for subsequent analysis. The mentors' initial interviews lasted approximately two hours and were all conducted in one day. There were follow-up interviews via Zoom with 2 mentors the following day that lasted approximately 30 minutes each.

A group observation was conducted between the interviews of the mentors and mentees. The purpose of the observation was to see the relationship dynamics between the mentors and mentees. The observation provided interpretive data for the researcher regarding phrases and body language. Due to the sensitive nature of some possible discussions, it was agreed that the researcher would not use the content of the observation. Also, if needed, at any time, the researcher could be asked to leave. The observation lasted about two hours.

The mentee interviews were conducted using the Zoom communications video-calling platform. The interviews were recorded using a miniature voice recorder and field notes by the researcher. The mentee interviews were conducted over a two-day consecutive period. The interviews lasted from an hour and a half to two hours. As with the mentors, the mentees' interviews were transcribed using Nuance Dragon dictation software in Microsoft Word. The same data validity reviews were implemented for the mentees as with the mentors. No follow-up interviews were needed for the mentees.

Data Analysis

The process for data analysis was through the use of NVivo software for computer-assisted qualitative data analysis. NVivo software takes a multi-layered approach to analyzing qualitative data for emergent themes. It conducts a thematic analysis to analyze word and sentence structures. Also, NVivo conducts a narrative analysis to help understand the underlying events and their effects on the overall outcome.

After transcribing all of the participant interviews into Microsoft Word, the transcriptions were imported into the NVivo software. The researcher then imported the data from the literature review for comparison. The next step for the researcher was to create nodes in the NVivo software system. Nodes act as containers that sort data by theme or relationship. There can be multiple levels to nodes, which are dependent upon the researcher's structure. It can be flatlined or hierarchical. The structure for this study was hierarchical. The nodes were created using the research questions as parent nodes. The data were sorted into the nodes, and emergent themes and subthemes were coded by frequency of use in the inductive coding process. In the next section, we review a description of the research participants by mentee and mentor categories. The descriptions comprised direct responses to the first few interview questions that did not lend themselves to much discussion.

Participants

The participants' real names were replaced with pseudonyms of their choosing.

Mentees

Lucius. Lucius was 14 years old when he began participating in SBC. He was raised in a two-parent household. The SBC mentoring program was his first mentoring program. At the time of this study, he was employed full-time. Lucius was also participating in upward mobility, continuing education program through his employer. The purpose of the program was to prepare him for a leadership role in the organization.

Blake. Blake was 12 years old when he began participating in SBC. He was raised in a two-parent household. SBC was his first mentoring program. Blake was enrolled in SBC by his mother. At the time of this study, he had recently completed an undergraduate degree and was set to start a graduate program in the fall.

Tahj. Tahj was 13 or 14 years old when he was enrolled in SBC. He was raised in a single-parent, female-headed household. The SBC was his first mentoring program. Tahj was enrolled by his aunt, who thought he needed some African American male guidance. At the time of the study, Tahj was completing a graduate program in clinical psychology.

Ezra. Ezra was 13 years old when he began participating in SBC. He was raised in a single-parent, female-headed home. Ezra was enrolled by his mother, who wanted to ensure that he had "positive African American male influencers" actively involved in his life. At the time of this study, Ezra was completing a Master of Public Administration Degree and started his own mentoring program.

Chad. Chad was enrolled into the SBC at 14 years old. At the point of enrollment, Chad resided in a two-parent household. By the time of completion, it was a single, male-headed household. The SBC was Chad's second mentoring program. He was previously involved in a school-based mentoring program. Chad was in medical school at the time of the study.

Isaiah. Isaiah was enrolled into the SBC at 14 years old. He resided in a two-parent household, where his mother was the most dominant. His father traveled for work very often. Therefore, his mother maintained the lead role. Though not the primary wage earner, she managed all of the household affairs, including the rearing of he and his brother. The SBC mentoring program was Isaiah's only mentoring involvement. Isaiah was completing a Master's of Business Administration at the time of the study.

Justice. Justice began participating in the SBC at the age of 13. He was raised in a single-parent, female-headed household. Justice was enrolled in a school-based mentoring program. However, he was never paired with a mentor. Therefore, he did not have an opportunity to actively participate. At the time of this study, Justice was entering law school.

Mentors

Dubi. Dubi worked with SBC for approximately 16 years. Dubi was originally screened and trained by another historic mentoring program. His interest in mentoring originated from the diminishing opportunities and lack of positive influences in his community. He believed that young African American men need advocates and role models. Dubi was raised in a two-parent household in a severely impoverished, disadvantaged community. Dubi participated in a mentoring program as a teen and was always interested in community engagement. He completed his bachelor's degree.

Kevin. Kevin worked with SBC for approximately 10 years. He was lovingly called the principal by the mentees. Kevin became a mentor at SBC out of a longing for his little brothers. He relocated and was not often able to return home. Becoming a mentor filled a longing for his family. Kevin was a mentee when he was younger. He was able to draw from that experience when he became a mentor. Kevin had a master's degree and was in the process of completing a doctorate degree.

Matthew. Matthew worked with SBC for 11 years. Being a mentor to young African American men was extremely important to Matthew. In his youth, he participated in a church mentoring program. Matthew's appreciation for his youthful mentoring experience inspired him to become a mentor with SBC. Matthew had completed a Master's in Social Work Degree.

Next, we examine the findings of the coded data arranged in the order of the research questions. The coded data represented the core themes of the phenomenon of SBC mentoring. The summary of the phenomenon revealed themes regarding how mentors and mentees perceived the factors and impacts of SBC on their lived experiences. The coded data also provided quality information regarding the application of SCT in the mentoring practices of SBC. The data demonstrated evidence of efficacy as a useful tool in the phenomenon of mentoring in the SBC. In the next section, we review the emergent themes regarding the perceived factors that influenced the academic success of the mentees from their perspectives.

What are the perspectives of African American male students who completed the SBC on the factors that influence academic success? The data provided several themes in response to this particular research question. They included academic support, a sense of belonging, a positive self-identity, and community responsibility.

Academic Support

Tutoring

Most of the mentees believed SBC had a very positive impact on their educational experiences. When asked what their grades were prior to SBC, Ezra and Chad explicitly stated that their grades were somewhat poor prior to their SBC enrollment. They said that academic support had a significant impact on their academic success. Ezra recalled:

My grades ranged from Bs to Ds. I failed a course in my freshman year of high school. The mentors tutored me over the summer to help me prepare to take the class again. Despite my fear, I took the class and got a "B." I participated in SBC to improve my grades and get out of the hood.

Chad reported having the greatest struggle. He stated, "My best grades were Ds. I was barely able to remain enrolled." Subsequently, while discussing what program components had the greatest impact, Chad added that tutoring helped him. He said, "The mentors saw I was trying, so they started helping me with my homework. They tutored me and even helped me make a rap to remember facts for my classes." Tutoring was an important component of the program. When asked the interview question, "What made you believe you could finish high school or college?," Justice also stated, "The tutoring" among other components. Though he never had to take advantage of the tutoring, knowing that it was available if he were to need it was helpful.

College Tours

A part of SBC's programming included college tours for high-school-level mentees. The mentees spoke about the influential experiences associated with participating in the college tours. Tahj referenced the importance of the college tours when discussing what made him believe he had the capacity to finish high school. He said, "Taking the college tours encouraged me to look beyond the moment of high school and begin to think about my next steps." Additionally, Chad and Blake mentioned the influence of the college tours when they were asked about the specific components of SBC that had the greatest impact on their academic success. Chad stated, "The college tours gave me exposure I never would have had." Blake added, "The college tours afforded me exposure to a world outside of my normal environment. They changed my life." The mentees expressed that the various mechanisms utilized by the SBC program in the academic realm helped to facilitate their academic success.

A Sense of Belonging

Accountability

The mentees expressed the impact of the relationship between them and the mentors. They believed that the mentors demonstrated a genuine interest that made them feel like a family. When asked, "What made you believe you had the capacity to finish high school or college?" Lucius credited the support of the mentors, "We were corrected when we needed to be, but still unconditionally supported." Chad also discussed the genuine interest of the mentors while responding to the impactful components of the program. He stated, "and cared about me. If I missed, they called or came to my home to check on me." Justice summed it up with his specific components that influenced him. He said, "It was belonging to something positive."

Brotherhood/Family

In fact, the mentees often addressed one another as brothers and the mentors as big brothers. When responding to the specific components of the program that had the greatest impact, Ezra mentioned "being tutored by mentors and brothers." In response to the same question, Chad stated, "My brothers challenged me." Justice's response included, "The brotherhood." Isaiah said, "The brothers and I would compete with one another for the highest grades. Additionally, regarding a sense of belonging, a portion of Lucius response to the specific components, he added:

The brotherhood of the other participants. We were from different backgrounds with the same goals. Learning from one another how to deal with what we encounter. We received lots of love and positive energy from the big brothers. Being a part of a brotherhood and a community.

Although the mentees have graduated from the SBC program, they all mentioned to some degree that the relationship with the mentors continues to be relevant in their lives to this day. Isaiah and Lucius even stated, "If my mentor called me for anything, I would come running. That is the kind of relationship we have." Though these statements were made at different times, they shared the same sentiment.

The young men also talked about their mentors getting to know their families. Lucius stated, "The big brothers had a relationship with my parents and my sibling. My parents would talk to them regarding their concerns and my behavior all of the time." Ezra said, "The mentors connected with my mom so well that she started the parent support committee." It meant a lot to the mentees that the mentoring relationship extended beyond the program facility. Justice reminisced on a lesson he and the other mentees received. He stated:

The mentors stressed the idea of the program being an extension of the family. The lesson was that family is interwoven like the threads that make up fabric. The thread independent of the rest is simply string. However, the thread woven in with the rest becomes fabric. A string can be easily broken by itself, but fabric cannot be easily destroyed. All of the threads support one another and reinforce one another. That is the *SBC program.* It is a family, supporting one another and accountable to one another. Justice said the lesson was also applicable to them as African American young men and who they were to their families and their communities.

Isaiah believed the SBC program and mentors saved him. He stated:

I would not have survived my teen years if not for SBC. I had started cutting school, hanging out, and not caring where my life ended up. I did not believe that I would live to see, even the age I am now. My mentor began started calling me and showing up at my home. He even started picking me up for our meetings and outings.

Commitment

Another resounding theme for the mentees was commitment. The mentees expressed that the mentors were extremely committed to them and their success. Tahj stated, "But I must add the mentor's commitment to us as mentees" when responding to the components of the program that had the greatest impact. He further stated, "The mentors gave us rides to and from program. They devoted extra time, which helped me feel comfortable to open up and develop trust." When asked, "What made you believe you could finish high school?"

Lucius also pointed to the mentor's commitment. He stated, "The support system and commitment got me through." Later in the conversation, Lucius laughingly stated, "The commitment is also attributed to making sure I kept going [to school] when I tried to quit. My mentor took me to school every day to make sure I didn't quit." The mentees stated that in addition to working with them at the SBC facility, the mentors displayed an interest in their personal lives and extracurricular activities. The mentors attended sports games, recitals, plays, church functions, birthday parties, etc. The young men talked about the dedication of time that the mentors showed. Justice believed, "The commitment of the mentors not only facilitated my success in school, it encouraged me holistically to become a more positive person." He mentioned it in reference to what made him believe he could finish high school or college.

Promoted Positive Self-identity

Role Models

The mentees talked about various factors of the SBC program that inspired their success, but the most impactful were their cultural and social identities and those of the mentors. All of the mentees talked about the value and importance of having African American male mentors from similar backgrounds. The mentees expressed that the educational and career accomplishments of the mentors made them believe it was possible for them. Chad stated: The mentors did not just tell us what we should do. They provided themselves as the example. They mirrored who we are and what is possible. Most importantly, these were men that looked just like me, that could relate to me and my experiences, that eliminated my excuses. If they could do it, so could I.

The positive self-identity theme also surfaced when the mentees were asked what made them believe they had the capacity to finish high school or college. Blake responded, "I saw that the mentors graduated and was doing great things. I wanted to do just as well or better." The mentees' observations of the mentors' success set a trajectory of possibilities in motion. Blake added, "The mentors talked about their college experiences, including pledging their fraternity and the support they received being a part of a brotherhood. I was excited for my chance to be a part of that!" Justice's response was a blend of both Chad and Blake. He stated, "It was a combination of the encouragement of the mentors, the tutoring, and because the mentors did it. I just believed if they did it and believed I could, then I can. So, I did." Tahj's belief in his ability to finish school was very similar to the others in terms of the mentor's belief in the mentee's ability. Additionally, Tahj stated, "It wasn't a matter of "Can we finish?" it was a matter of "Let's do that." Successfully finishing school wasn't a possibility. It was the expectation."

Self-worth

As the discussion turned to the importance of cultural relevance in their mentoring program, the mentees expressed being able to relate to the mentors' experiences. The relatability helped them to embrace their "badge of Blackness," as Blake called it. The mentees talked about the negative experiences of being African American males and the relief that the mentors understood their plight. Isaiah spoke about the challenges of being viewed as a threat,

"It's a hardship trying to prove that I am not harmful, that my Blackness does not make me a threat." He said the mentor reaffirmed his goodness and told him not to allow external forces to change him. Isaiah said, "He reminded me that our ancestors endured worse and still became great." Isaiah respected that his mentor challenged him to continue being his best.

When asked about the specific components of mentoring that contributed to academic success, the mentees attributed a great deal of their success to their relationship and ability to identify with their mentors. Tahj expressed:

There were several things that culturally relevant mentorship for education was a culture shock. I wasn't used to that. But that representation helped define my goals and helped shape my thinking. Seeing those Black male figures opened doors for my belief in myself. I was guided by the success and accomplishments of my mentor.

Table 1. Emergent themes of research question 1

Themes	Subthemes
Academic support	Tutoring College tours
A sense of belonging	Accountability Brotherhood Commitment
A positive self-identity	Role models Self-worth
Community responsibility	Community service

Community Responsibility

Community Service Projects

Last, the mentees expressed the importance of community service. They talked about the value of the community service projects they participated in, especially when responding to the specific components that contributed to their academic success. Lucius stated, "The community service was really important. It stopped me from being, so me focused and broadened my consideration of others." Most of the projects took place in the mentees' own communities. Therefore, the mentees understood that the service they gave directly contributed to a better living environment. Tahj described it as "communal responsibility." He stated, "It helped me to understand that everything I did either added to or took away from my community." Also, being an African American man, he had a responsibility to contribute to the vitality of his community. "I realized that my community service was not just beneficial externally. My family and friends were direct recipients. Once I began to look at it from that lens, my idea of myself and others improved." He stated, "SBC made me a better person, which helped me in my educational endeavors. Subsequently, SBC indirectly inspired my career {therapy}, because I realized that Black people in America have suffered so much trauma being Black, that therapy is greatly needed." Ezra also believed community service was important. He stated, "It helped me qualify for college, and it made me feel a sense of obligation to my community."

When the question of the specific components that had the greatest impact was discussed, Tahj stated, "The community service was really important. Making us take responsibility for the community helped us to see it as an extension of ourselves." The inputs from the mechanisms of this section act as a conduit of the outputs or results for the next section on impacts. The impacts are the outcomes of the programmatic structure of SBC.

In summary, several themes emerged from the mentees regarding the factors of SBC that influenced their academic success. The themes began with academic support, a sense of belonging, and promoted a positive self-identity. Those themes included subthemes of tutoring, college tours, brotherhood, accountability, and commitment. The mentees also included promoted a positive self-identity theme, which included subthemes of role models and self-worth. The final theme related to factors for the mentees was community responsibility in the form of community service projects. In the next section, we review the emergent themes regarding the SBC mentoring program's perceived impacts on the mentees' educational experience from their perspectives.

What do the African American male students perceive was the impact of the SBC mentoring program on their educational experience? Several themes surfaced regarding the impact of the SBC mentoring program on the educational experience. The themes included academic support, promoted a positive self-identity, community responsibility, and self-efficacy.

Academic Support and Promoted a Positive Self-identity

HBCUs, Role Models, and Self-worth

As previously stated, a part of SBC's programming included college tours for high-school-level mentees. The tours included HBCUs, which the mentees identified as having a significant influence on their self-worth. When asked about the importance of cultural relevance in the mentoring program, Justice pointed to the tours of the HBCUs as an important part. He said, "The HBCU tours exposed us to African American men of high intelligence."

Subsequently, Tahj, Blake, and Chad reflected on their tours to HBCUs as they responded to what specific components of the SBC program had the greatest impact on their academic success. As they learned the history of HBCUs, they knew it would be their destiny. Each of them completed undergraduate degrees from an HBCU. They talked about the inherent pride they felt as they identified with the institutions. Chad stated, "The HBCUs did it for me! To see my brothers and sisters there. They were looking good! I was going, whatever it took." The tour of Morehouse College was especially life-changing for the mentees because they walked on the soil where the Rev. Dr. Martin Luther King Jr. once stood. Lucius stated, "Even though I didn't go to college, going to Morehouse had an effect on me. I was in the place of legends, who changed the world. I was reminded that I have a purpose in this world." Tahj reflected:

Visiting to the HBCUs was a culture shock. Living in my community, I didn't see the most positive figures. The media continues to inundate the public with negative images of Black people. It becomes easy to believe the stereotypes are true. But the representation at the HBCUs, especially Morehouse, helped to define my goals and reshape my thinking regarding Black male figures. It opened doors for my belief in myself. The mentors were extremely positive role models, but, at first, to me as a kid, they were an anomaly. The HBCUs provided a broader, more informed perspective.

Additionally, Blake recalled:

When I got to Morehouse, I was emotionally moved. Do you know all of the greats that passed through there? I was honored to stand where they stood. We saw African American sororities and fraternities. They talked to us about changing our narrative. In that moment, I knew I was going to college, and I was going to try my best to go there.

My life changed forever that day!

It was obvious that going on the college tours and the incorporation of HBCUs was extremely impactful on the mentees. As they discussed that particular aspect of the program, the young men were smiling and laughing. Their responses were generally conversational throughout the data collection phase. However, the HBCU discussion evoked a more poignant reaction. The sense of pride was apparent as they reminisced. At one point, Blake was walking outside. When he started talking about Morehouse College, he stopped and directed his full attention to that response. He smiled extremely wide, talking about his visit. It was apparent that he identified with that school and internalized the doctrine of Black positivity.

Throughout the interviews, the mentees talked about their admiration for their mentors. It was apparent that they viewed the mentors as role models. However, it became equally apparent that the African American male students of the HBCUs, Morehouse in particular, also became role models for them. Additionally, the mentees took pride in being able to identify with the HBCU students.

Academic Scholarship

Interestingly, the mentees believed a portion of the SBC program's effectiveness was attributed to the scholarship conferred upon graduation and college acceptance. When asked about the specific components of the SBC program that had the greatest impact on their academic success, the mentees included the scholarship. Tahj stated, "The scholarship was a great bonus." While listing the components that impacted him, Justice also said, "the scholarship."

The promise of the scholarship served as a reward for the mentee's hard work and dedication to their educational pursuits. Tahj added, "I was always pretty good in school, but it may not have resulted in going to college. My family couldn't afford it. Qualifying for the SBC scholarship inspired me to apply for others." During the mentoring program, mentees were encouraged to attend college after they completed high school. The SBC scholarship helped to mitigate the challenge of affordability.

Additionally, the mentees were encouraged to apply for other scholarships and participate in activities that would merit scholarship funds. Several of the mentees admitted that the knowledge of the scholarship inspired them to pursue academic excellence. Blake said, "The scholarship had a great impact. It was definitely an incentive." Blake was doing well in school but lacked guidance for how his grades could facilitate his academic success. He said:

My mentor always said I had the capacity to be and do anything. He said if I kept getting exemplary grades, organizations would pay me to go to college. He was right! I stopped settling for a "B" average. I graduated at the top of my class and received multiple scholarships.

Blake's mentor showed him the qualifications of various scholarships and helped him understand that higher education was an option. Blake continually credited the exposure that he received while participating at SBC for his academic success.

Promoted Positive Self-identity

Self-worth

When the mentees were asked, "How did your participation in SBC influence your perception of yourself and other African American males?" the subtheme was the value of self-worth. Isaiah stated:

It made me insist on representation and pay attention to messaging. I also gained an understanding of the detrimental effects of systemic racism. If I accept the negative messaging about us, I develop self-hate. I choose to love myself.

Chad stated:

That's a really good question. I learned respect for myself and others. It changed my vernacular. I used to say the "N" word all of the time. That's how I addressed everyone. SBC taught us the negative connotations associated with the word. I learned about the pain of the word.

Last, Justice replied:

I always felt like the world looked down on Blk people. The negative media representation, the historic victimization of Black people, society treated us like people had to be scared of us and that we had to fear one another. The mentor's interactions with us helped me see African American men without fear. Mentors did a lot of African American-related activities with us to build our self-confidence and self-worth. They made sure we understood that African American people made numerous contributions. So many that we don't even get credit for.

Community Responsibility

Leadership

Mentees agreed that SBC taught them to lead positively and avoid negative influences. Most of the mentees mentioned that an essential part of the mentoring program included leading to inspire. When asked how different the mentees thought their lives would be if they had not participated in SBC, some mentees talked about leadership. Lucius stated regarding the question, "I would not be where I am today with my job. The leadership skills I learned at SBC prepared me for the leadership program I'm in at work."

Isaiah laughingly shared his realization that he was a leader and the responsibility associated with it:

A younger mentee was somewhat disrespectful to a big brother. I tried to correct him, and he said that I had done the same thing earlier. Big brother [the mentor] reminded me that I have the power to influence and to use it wisely. Meaning people will follow what I do. I became very conscious of myself after that.

Mentees were often reminded of their responsibility to the younger mentees who also participate in the mentoring program. Therefore, every action they took was to be an example of what the younger mentees should imitate. The mentees understood the responsibility of leadership relative to graduating high school. However, they learned to embrace the responsibility to demonstrate positive leadership qualities at home and at school. Isaiah further stated, "When I learned that my behavior spoke for who I was, I became cognizant of my actions. SBC says our actions tell the story our mouths can't convey."

Mentees were taught that their representation and behavior had a direct impact on the program. Thus, if a mentee was known to participate in the SBC program, mentors impressed upon them that their behavior was a direct reflection regarding SBC. Understanding that poor behavior would negatively reflect the SBC program, mentees strived to be on their best behavior and eagerly pursued graduation. Ezra, who lost a family member to gun violence, had a younger brother entering the SBC program. The mentors worked with him extensively to help him embrace the responsibility of positive leadership at home. During our interview, he talked about his current desire to make his mother proud. Ezra said:

When I was younger, I didn't know how to tell my mom that I appreciated the sacrifice she made for me and my brother. I thought acknowledging her sacrifices meant I was soft. I thought leaders had to be arrogant and self-absorbed. Now, I talk to my mom every day. I end our calls with I love and appreciate you.

As previously mentioned, Ezra was completing an advanced degree and had started his own mentoring program.

Self-efficacy

Career

An important point the interviewees revealed when discussing how their lives would be different if they had not participated in SBC was career options and choices. Although the question leads to speculation, there is value. The young men knew the behavior they were engaged in and exposed to before and during their participation in the program. Additionally, this question allowed the mentees to draw conclusions that took their environment into account. One of the programmatic components of SBC involved business and entrepreneurialism. Some of the mentees discussed the revelations they gained due to their participation in that component.

Justice stated:

Who would've ever thought that I could be where I am? Thanks to SBC programming, I learned that I had endless possibilities. I recall being 14 years old with no clue of what I should do with my future.

Justice laughingly described his initial lack of direction. He asked his mentor, "What do you think I should be when I grow up?" The mentor told him to figure out what he loved doing.

Justice said, "At first, I was upset that the mentor didn't just tell me what to do. In hindsight, I'm very grateful that he didn't." The mentors challenged him to get to know himself and his passions; Justice discovered that he was creative. "I draw really well! I have a good eye for what looks good." That's when he knew he could be a designer. Justice attended sessions of the SBC focused on entrepreneurialism and was inspired. Without providing many details, Justice expressed that he started a part-time business redesigning shoes and clothes.

Chad had already determined that he wanted to go into medicine in his long-term career. However, he was also inspired to set a short-term goal of becoming an entrepreneur and making money in the immediate. Chad talked about his inspiration when he was asked what specific components of SBC had the greatest impact. Chad said:

During one of the entrepreneur sessions, a brother from the Phi Beta Sigma Fraternity discussed how to be an entrepreneurial . . . I could not get it out of my mind . . . in my senior year, I made a generic business plan. It wasn't that great, but it served the purpose . . . and my business was started.

He collected and restored furniture and some clothing (leather coats and jackets). "I was able to pay for prom and graduation. Then I did it in college and paid my way through school. I had minimal loan debt." As stated at the beginning of the chapter, Chad was in medical school. He continued to operate his business and was utilizing the funds as supplemental income for tuition.

Table 2. Emergent themes of research question 2

Themes	Subthemes
Academic support	HBCU Scholarships
Promoting a positive self-identity	Role models Self-worth
Community responsibility	Leadership
Self-efficacy	Careers

In summary, several themes emerged from the mentees regarding the impact of SBC on their educational experience. The themes began with academic support and positive self-identity. Those themes included subthemes of college tours to HBCUs, role models, and self-worth. The mentees also included a community responsibility theme in the form of leadership. The final theme related to impact for the mentees was self-efficacy in the form of career guidance and choices. In the next section, we review the emergent themes regarding the factors of the SBC program from the perspective of the mentors.

What are the perspectives of Sigma Beta Club mentors on the factors that influence the academic success of African American male high school students? The mentors and mentees shared a lot of the same thoughts on the influential factors. The themes that commonly emerged from the mentors were academic support, a sense of belonging, positive self-identity, self-efficacy, and community responsibility.

Academic Support

Tutoring and Partnerships with Schools

To ascertain whether the efforts made by the mentors through SBC aligned with the contributions the mentees felt were beneficial to them, the mentors were allowed to describe their inputs. When asked how SBC affected the academic success of African American males, a portion of the responses centered around tutoring, and there was some discussion involving partnerships. Matthew pointed out, "All participants of the SBC mentoring program are required to maintain a grade point average of 2.5 or above." Dubi explained, "At entry, approximately 85% to 90% of the mentees ranked below the required 2.5 GPA. However, SBC has a 98% high school graduation rate." Where mentees demonstrated difficulty acquiring or maintaining the required GPA, supportive services were provided.

Supportive services were administered in various forms, depending upon the mentee's needs. Kevin explained, "SBC partnered with schools and community tutoring programs, brought in reading and math specialists, worked with the school counselors, even met with the mentees' teachers to understand the mentees' needs." Matthew added, "Mentors were facilitators that helped mentees obtain the assistance they needed to achieve success. However, mentees were required to ask for the help they needed."

Matthew expressed that this was sometimes the most difficult requirement for most mentees. He stated:

Asking for help required a vulnerability that was not easy to show. Some mentees viewed vulnerability as a reflection of weakness. But it was really pride. We had to teach them to seek out help, so they could accomplish something to take pride in.

The mentors hoped the mentees understood that there will be a time in everyone's life where they would require assistance. Kevin said, "A sign of a good leader is one who knows when help is needed and seek it." Matthew concurred and added, "I told the mentees all of the time, asking for help is not and should never be viewed as a weakness. It is a definite sign of strength." The lesson was imperative for the mentees as they pursued higher education. "In total transparency," Kevin clarified, "Although we had established partnerships, some of the mentees experienced a difficulty accessing them. Unfortunately, they had to pass through neighborhoods that were inundated with gang activity. . . . Therefore, mentees were reluctant to take advantage of the services."

Tutoring (SBC)

In response to the lack of safety in acquiring external resources through the partnerships, SBC developed a plan to meet the tutoring needs in-house. Kevin stated, "SBC began intentionally recruiting mentors from the field of education to assist with tutoring at its location. Also, some of the parents got involved to host tutoring sessions." Matthew added, "Some of our fraternity brothers volunteered to provide tutoring and supplemental instruction for the mentees." In addition to working with them in general education subjects, they taught specialized areas, such as business and technology.

Scholarship

While still engaged in the discussion regarding how SBC affected the academic success of mentees, the mentors mentioned the added bonus of the SBC scholarship.

Kevin reaffirmed, "SBC is an academic program. Therefore, at graduation, each mentee that graduates high school and is accepted into college gets at least a $1000 scholarship." Matthew also stated, "We also pushed the scholarship as a means to encourage mentees to maintain at least the 2.5 GPA." Dubi added:

If they knew finances would not be a barrier, they were incentivized to get better grades. They began working to meet the required GPA for SBC, and from there, they soared. All they needed from us was support. In addition, to providing an SBC scholarship, we taught them how to acquire others.

A Sense of Belonging

Accountability

While discussing how SBC affected the academic success of the mentees, the subject of accountability also surfaced. Matthew stated, "As a condition of participation, mentees were periodically required to show their school progress reports to their mentor. Reviewing their progress reports helped us assess the mentee's academic progress and determine where they needed help." Kevin added, "Our reviewing their progress reports made them [the mentees] have to be honest about how they were doing and where they were struggling. We can't solve a problem if we don't know it exist."

Accountability also emerged when asked to describe what is involved in a mentoring session. Matthew included the check-ins:

Check-ins are a point in the rap sessions where the young men talk about what is happening with them. All of the young men are required to give a check-in. No one can say pass. Once the young man shares, the others are allowed to ask exploratory questions. Although the mentee cannot decline a check-in, he can decline providing exploratory details.

Matthew explained, "Check-ins help the group know where participants are at in their mental and emotional state. We are in this together [speaking of the mentoring program] and responsible, to and for, one another. This is our safe space. It's a no-judgment zone."

The rap sessions challenged the mentees to remove the guards and allow themselves to be vulnerable with one another. Matthew stated, "Initially, mentees were resistant. However, they slowly warmed up to the idea of sharing. The sessions helped the mentors and mentees develop an understanding of one another." Also, it contributed to future decision-making by the mentees.

Kevin stated, "The boys would come back talking about something they were tempted to do but changed their mind because of something we said at a check-in rap session." The mentees looked forward to the praises when sharing positive check-ins. However, they embraced a code of honesty and dealt with the consequences of negative behavior. Kevin stated, "You would think that the mentees would only share positive check-ins to avoid the consequences or feedback related to negative behavior. However, they were quite transparent in their disclosures and owned their behavior." The mentees knew they were expected to take accountability for their actions and not project the blame. Dubi said, "I talked to them about projecting all of the time. When they got a good grade or did well, they took credit. But when they got a low grade or had to be reprimanded, then the teacher gave them, or they said I did." He said, "I wanted them to understand that the things they practice now, they'll execute later. Therefore, it was imperative that they develop a habit of honesty and accountability."

Commitment

The mentors also mentioned the necessity of commitment when discussing how SBC affected the academic success of the mentees. The mentors indicated that mentoring is not a role of convenience. It requires commitment and dedication. Commitment builds trust. Kevin stated, "It's our commitment that helps the mentees succeed. We don't give up on them." He recounted a time when a mentee called him in distress and needed his intervention. Kevin said, "While going out with friends, I got the call. Hesitantly, I went. He [the mentee] confided in me. I realized that he trusted me." Kevin also added that authenticity was important. "Young people can tell when you truly care." Dubi expressed, "Mentoring is not for the faint of heart. Devotion is needed to strengthen the relationship. Sporadic involvement is harmful to the mentee. A lack of consistency can conjure up feelings of abandonment in mentees with absent fathers." Matthew added, "I found myself at several family gatherings. But I had to invest time to build bonds with the mentees."

The mentors specified that time was needed to build and strengthen the mentor/mentee relationship. Kevin stated:

Time is needed to build trust because, as African American men, so many negative stereotypes promulgate their daily lives. The boys need time to understand what we really think. That we aren't speaking positively to them to be nice. It's what we really see.

While discussing time as a factor of commitment, Matthew stated, "Mentors can't have a wandering spirit or mind," meaning they should not wander in and out of a mentee's life. The disappointment could have devastating consequences, such as a lack of trust or commitment from the mentee. Matthew believed, "The mentees experienced enough rejection, without having to encounter it in a program that is supposed to be dedicated to them." He said, "Some of these boys don't have fathers. We're all they got sometimes."

The mentors also spoke about authenticity in the mentoring relationship as a by-product of commitment. Kevin stated:

Young people can tell when someone truly cares versus when they are just going through the motions. As with any relationship, perfection may be desired, but it is not realistic from mentors or mentees. However, care and genuine concern overshadows any mistakes along the way. We all made mistakes. The key is to acknowledge the error and behave differently going forward. That's the lesson we gave the boys because that's the lesson we learned ourselves. They had so much respect for us as mentors because they knew we had a genuine interest in their well-being.

Authentic relationships between mentors and mentees have been developed over time due to the commitment of the mentors. Kevin shared, "In reflecting back, sometimes I may have been too strict. But my boys knew that I only wanted the best for them. Because I took the time to build a relationship with every one of them."

A Sense of Belonging and Promoting a Positive Self-identity

Role Models

The label of a role model was only mentioned twice by the mentors. First, during Matthew and Kevin's responses to the effects the SBC program had on the academic success of African American males, and second when Dubi was discussing his fondest mentoring memory. Otherwise, it appeared that the dynamic of the relationship was just understood. When addressing the necessity of commitment in the relationship, Matthew stated, "Yes, we want the mentees to bond with one another, but as role models, we need them to also bond with us." He explained, "It's those bonds that help them to trust our guidance."

Brotherhood, Rites of Passage, and Self-worth

The final collection of subthemes the mentors provided are intertwined. The subthemes are brotherhood and rites of passage. The rite of passage the mentors shared was a ritual of completion for the mentees. The rites of passage celebration was a highlight of the mentors as they responded to the question of their fondest mentoring memory. Kevin stated in describing the significance of the ceremony:

In SBC, the young men are elected to various offices by their peers (president, vice-president, treasurer, secretary, and sergeant-at-arms) during their junior and senior years of high school. As the officers are graduating from the mentoring program and high school, they pass the mantel. The mantel is represented by an SBC jacket the current officer gives to his successor. The jacket symbolizes a cloak of responsibility and ceremoniously imparting knowledge. Additionally, the mentors present a gift to the graduates and speak affirmations.

The ceremony represents a coming of age that an African village would host for boys entering adulthood. In this case, the rites of passage marked the stage of the mentees' lives to commemorate the celebration of passing to the next level. It is a time for the village (family and mentoring organization) to celebrate the growth of the mentees while also conveying the expectations and responsibilities of their next phase. It also reassures the mentees of their identity (the beauty and power of their Blackness) and reinforces a sense of belonging and tribal connection and responsibility. The mentors expressed looking forward to the "rites of passage" ceremony as much as the mentees. The mentors believe the ceremony provided a sense of empowerment for the mentees.

Kevin said, "It's hard to describe, but it's as though they transcend to manhood right before your eyes. They literally transfer from boys to men when they drape that jacket on their successor's shoulders." In Kevin's reflection, he said:

We acknowledge the mentees progress during the celebration. Mentees started SBC completely unqualified for leadership. However, they all worked together as brothers to develop one another. One time a very shy kid ran against a popular one. The popular kid told everyone to vote for the shy kid. That brought him out of his shell. He shared his appreciation for that support at the Rite-of-passage ceremony before he placed his jacket on the incoming officer. That was my fondest memory.

Similarly, Matthew stated:

We had the highest enrollment during that time. At the Rites of Passage, the mentees were standing there with tuxedo and Kente' bow ties, pocket squares, cummerbunds, and kufis. Our theme was Sankofa, meaning to go back a retrieve those left behind. All of the Sigma brothers were there. They draped Kente scarfs around the mentee's collars and welcomed them into manhood. The Rites of Passage is our traditional celebration that symbolizes our African village.

The factors the SBC mentors believed influenced academic success were relative to some of the factors the mentees mentioned. However, while the mentees' findings were from the lens of a recipient, the mentors' perspective was administrative.

Community Responsibility

Community Service

The young men of SBC were taught to develop a responsibility to their community and the global community through community service projects. The mentors mentioned the requirement of the community service projects when they were asked to describe the SBC mentoring program. As a result, Dubi stated:

We teach the young man leadership through the rise and the thunder curriculum. The young men are given the tools to embrace personal and community responsibility. Sigma Beta Club is very committed to the community at large. The mentees are required to fulfill community service hours which helps to develop community responsibility.

Kevin described a shift that happened with the program. He stated, "Prior focus of SBC was limited to the needs of the participants. Over time the club evolved to include the needs of society, which included leadership and community service."

Subsequently, when asked how SBC affects African American males' academic success, Kevin and Matthew discussed how community service contributed to the mentees' college qualifications. Kevin stated that a major contributing factor to academic success was the community service component. "Sometimes, people don't realize the importance of community service to academic success. College-bound mentees needed community service hours to impress higher education officials and scholarship awardees."

Matthew corroborated Kevin's belief in the value of community service to academic success. However, he further stated, "Community service was actually required for some of the mentees to graduate from high school. In SBC, we often used community service to teach leadership skills and responsibilities. It was also necessary for academic achievement."

Self-efficacy

The mentees of SBC were taught leadership through the Rise and the Thunder programmatic thrust. The young men were given the tools to develop their leadership skills. The Rise and Thunder programmatic thrust allowed mentees to exercise some control over their program delivery by selecting activities that suited their individual interests while accomplishing the overall objective. The activities included a balance of academic, personal, and community.

Programmatic Thrust

When asked to describe SBC's mentoring program, the mentors pointed to the mission and curriculum. Dubi explained:

All mentoring programs need a mission and a format to be able to measure its effectiveness. SBC's overall mission with the mentees is to equip them with the necessary tools to be leaders in their communities and possibly on a larger platform.

Kevin explained, "The goal is to prepare the mentees to be future leaders through education and service." Subsequently, when asked to describe a mentoring session, Dubi indicated that meetings open with a recitation of the motto:

The motto of SBC that the mentees recite at the start of each meeting is: The next generation of leaders accepting the responsibility and loving the challenge. The recitation of the motto is to instill in the mentees the expectation of who they are to become.

SBC's programmatic thrust, as explained by Dubi, was, "Rise and Thunder," which includes five components that help to develop self-efficacy in the mentees. "The Rise and Thunder curriculum is a set of measurable benchmarks gradually accomplished to achieve an ultimate crowning moment." The individual components and benchmarks can be found in Exhibit D.

The mentors found the curriculum most useful when working with mentees on goalsetting, which is directly linked to the self-efficacy portion of SCT. Individual goal-setting in the Rise and Thunder curriculum helped mentees tailor the SBC program to their distinctive needs.

Kevin stated:

The mentees appreciated the opportunity to choose which activities worked best for them and subsequently having a sense of accomplishment. They understood that the overarching goal was to develop leadership qualities through education that would help them make positive decisions, also known as transferable competencies. The opportunity to make decisions in their mentoring program contributed to their success.

Additionally, Kevin mentioned the programmatic thrust when asked to describe SBC's mentoring program. He stated, "We deal with issues unique to African American young men."

Resilience, Emotional Competence, and Cultural Relevance

Another subtheme that surfaced from the mentors regarding the factors that influenced the academic success of the mentees was emotional competence and cultural relevance. The mentors believed that emotional competence and cultural relevance were important factors when mentoring the young SBC men. The mentors taught the mentees that discriminatory treatment does happen, but it does not need to be counteracted with emotional outbursts. Kevin shared an experience of one of the mentees during a trip with his school's sports team:

The coach, a Caucasian male, allowed the team to stop at a convenience store. The mentee noticed that he was being followed by the store's security, also Caucasian. When the mentee confronted security, he was told that someone who resembled the him had shoplifted and escaped. The mentee was devastated at being racially profiled and felt the coach lacked regard for his predicament. . . . The rap session shifted to a "dealing with racism" training.

The mentors expressed times of talking individually with mentees about discriminatory practices. They also described several group sessions held over the years with the mentees about how to behave when stopped by the police, whether stopped and frisked or for traffic violations.

Dubi said, "It was heart-wrenching because we know it isn't a conversation Caucasian parents or mentors have to regularly address with Caucasian children." Matthew passionately described the anxiety he felt as he relived a moment where he was encountered by a police officer:

I'm a grown man, yet the police officer kept referring to me as "boy." I really believe that he was trying to cause me to react, to justify a use excessive force. In that moment, I had a choice, and I chose to stand in "my personal power," meaning I did not react to anything that was said. I respected myself enough not to allow anyone the power to make me be disrespectful. You always have a choice whether to respond or react.

Always choose to respond!

The lessons given on emotional competence, especially in the space of cultural relevance, were critical. Matthew described it as a "survival technique, given the various obstacles African American young men must face." Dubi further stated, "As Black men, we must learn to positively explore and understand our feelings."

Table 3. Emergent themes of research question 3

Themes	Subthemes
Academic Support	Tutoring Partnerships Scholarships
A sense of belonging	Accountability Commitment Brotherhood
Promoting a positive self-identity	Role models Rites of passage Self-worth
Community responsibility	Community service
Self-efficacy	Programmatic thrust Emotional competence Resilience

In summary, several themes emerged from the mentors regarding the factors of SBC on the academic success of African American male high school students. The themes began with academic support and a sense of belonging. The themes included subthemes such as tutoring, partnerships, scholarships, accountability, commitment, and brotherhood. The mentors also included the promotion of a positive identity theme in the form of brotherhood and rites of passage. The final theme related to impact for the mentees was self-efficacy in the form of programmatic thrust and emotional competence. In the next section, we review the emergent themes regarding the impacts of the SBC program from the perspective of the mentors.

What do the mentors perceive was the impact of SBC's mentoring practices on the educational experiences of their African American male students? The mentors and mentees shared a lot of the same thoughts on the influential factors. The themes that commonly emerged from the mentors were academic support, positive self-identity, self-efficacy, and community responsibility.

Academic Achievement

Improved GPAs

Improved GPAs were referenced by the mentors directly in some cases and implied in others. When asked to describe the SBC mentoring program, a part of Matthew's response was, "It's a program that assists young men to achieve the highest GPAs."

When providing responses to the question of how SBC affects the academic success of African American males, Matthew stated, "We helped them improve their grades so that they could qualify for graduation and college." He also stated:

Black boys have enough challenges in schools. With unfair policies and racist administration, they don't need to help the system by getting low grades . . . We helped them put in the work to get their grades up because most of them wanted to go to college.

They did it too!

Dubi alluded to the improved GPAs when he said, "85% to 90% came into the program below 2.5 GPA. However, SBC has a 98% graduation rate." In that discussion, he stated that the mentees' grades improved due to supportive services, etc. Additionally, Matthew alluded to improvement when he talked about the scholarships, when he said, "If mentees knew finances would not be a barrier, they were incentivized to get better grades. They began working to meet the required GPA, and from there, they soared." Another point regarding grade improvement, also linked to scholarships in which Kevin stated, "when mentees understood how much money could be . . . mediocrity was no longer an option. They quickly realized their academic potential and began to strive for better grades."

Scholarships

The mentors of SBC assisted the mentees in identifying and applying for various scholarships. Kevin stated, "The idea of free money for academic achievement was really encouraging." The mentors talked about mentees who previously acquired mediocre grades became inspired at the grants and higher education sessions of SBC. Dubi commented, "Often, when we talk about college, the mentees aren't initially engaged. College does not appear attainable to people struggling to meet their day-to-day needs. But when they saw the multiple streams of finances, they got excited." During the college readiness sessions of the program, mentors outlined the cost of a semester and deducted hypothetical scholarships. Kevin stated, "When the mentees understood how much money could be deducted from the cost of tuition, mediocrity was no longer an option."

Kevin said, "Sometimes, all you have to do is show them how something can be accomplished. They'll take it from there. Them boys got that money." Matthew stated: We pushed scholarships. There was money they could get that would help them. Some of these kids were the first in their families to go to college. We had to find a way. The money was there. They had some academics, some sports. There was even a music scholarship that came in.

Higher Education

The mentors expressed great pride that most of the mentees attended college. The comments were made while discussing how SBCs affect the academic success of African American males. Dubi stated, "We provided the roadmap, and they followed it. Most of the mentees went on to pursue higher education, and many of them finished. Some have gone into graduate programs." Kevin added, "My boys knew they had to go to college . . . But it's not enough to get them in. Just like high school, they were expected to graduate. A lot of them are in graduate programs." Matthew stated:

The main priority was to get them through high school because they can't do anything without a high school diploma. Then we needed to get them through college. The work didn't stop because they graduated the program. Most of them got undergrad degrees from some really prestigious schools.

Academic Achievement and Promoted a Positive Self-identity

College Tours and HBCUs

The mentors were asked to describe their fondest memory. None of the participants restricted the response to a single memory. They had several fond memories of working with the mentees. A particular memory was taking the mentees to tour various college campuses. The tours were not limited to HBCUs. However, they were the most significant. As Dubi pointed out, "College tours made the idea of college become a real option. HBCUs made college right for them [the mentees]." Matthew stated, "The mentees often developed a sense of urgency to get their grades up after attending a college tour." The mentors believed it was a combination of being physically present on a college campus and seeing other African American young men who made the possibility of college become a viable option.

"Unless they have family members who attended college, it's sometimes just a foreign object to the mentees. For some of them, we take them so they can see that it really does exist." The mentors arranged tours to multiple universities. However, as stated, the greatest value was placed on the visits to the HBCUs. Dubi said:

I knew when we were on the grounds of Morehouse, and they [the mentees] saw the sign that said, "We don't just educate students, we produce men of distinction." They would never think of themselves or college the same way. The college tours are always lifechanging for the mentees.

Matthew and Kevin believed that touring the HBCUs made an indelible impression on the mentees. They recalled seeing some of the mentees become emotional as they walked around the HBCU campuses. Kevin stated:

Some of our boys would be crying. We had boys that didn't even want to go back home. They wanted to stay on those campuses, especially Morehouse. The boys were so used to seeing the negative imagery that accompanies poverty. When they got a chance to be in a more positive environment of people that looked just like them, they didn't want to let it go.

Matthew said, "We never had to talk to them about doing better in school ever again. They returned from the tours focused on their grades." He also stated, "The HBCU's helped the mentees see the possibilities. They weren't relegated to a life of crime or degradation." Despite any obstacles, they knew that those mentees would not allow anything to derail their goal of reaching their maximum potential. Kevin referred to the HBCU visits as "life-changing experiences. Transformational." The mentors witnessed a shift in the attitudes of the mentees over time. "Dubi stated, "The HBCU visits was just one of the many ingredients to teaching the mentees to love themselves and to embrace education." When asked to describe SBC's mentoring program, while discussing the goal of teaching African American young men to disregard the stereotypical propaganda, Dubi talked about the purpose of taking mentees to HBCUs. He said, "In an effort to teach the mentees self-confidence, the program provides HBCU exposure. We don't just want them to go to school . . . we want them to embrace the beauty of their Blackness and learn to love themselves." The mentors described it as a transformation from the stereotypical, self-deprecating persona to community-conscious, self-appreciating men.

Self-Efficacy

Self-Worth and Resilience

Some of the areas of self-worth have already been touched upon, such as in the discussion of HBCUs. Albeit a primary focus of SBC is to promote resilience through self-worth among the mentees. The resilience through self-worth takes place with multiple streams of socialization. In response to the interviewer's request to describe SBC's mentoring program, Matthew said, "We offer social and cultural awareness skills in youth development." As part of his response, Kevin stated, "We enhance the social skills of the mentees and provide exposure to a world outside of the classroom."

There was a great deal of discussion around the topic of developing self-worth when the mentors were asked how SBC affects African American males' academic success. Dubi stated: Culturally relevant encouragement was useful as a positive reinforcement tool to develop self-worth. I would encourage them to reach their highest academic potential. I would tell them that academic success promotes Black excellence. I also reminded them that they could change the narrative by telling their own stories.

As part of the curriculum, the SBC mentors took the mentees to various historic venues that highlighted African American contributions to the world. Matthew pointed out, "We wanted to expose them to the strength of character of African Americans. We needed them to identify with our ingenuity as a people. To take pride in who they were." The trips were in response to mentees' expressions of shame for Black History Month. They believed that the framing of Black History Month made African Americans look weak and susceptible to chattel slavery. The mentees' way of thinking goes back to the relevance of Kevin's point:

We dealt with problems unique to African American males. We offered culturally relevant events and programming that was necessary for holistic African American development. We mentored them at a pivotal time. The adolescent years set the trajectory for who they would become.

The mentors strategized on methods to reframe the thinking and the narrative. Kevin stated:

Society would have African American young men believe they are worthless. We taught them the opposite. The most feared man is an educated Black man. He's born with strength and has an innate ability to persevere. He just needs to learn to channel it.

Matthew also stated:

We were intentional in our efforts. We took the boys on outings and dealt with topics that were significant to our race. . . . We went to formal restaurants to develop their social skills as well as historic museums and trips.

In reference to being intentional with the outings, Dubi mentioned, "We took them to the Dred Scott and DuSable Museums." In addition to field trips, the mentors created rewards for the most explorative research on African American ingenuity that cut the poignant satire. As the mentees learned extensively about the history and contributions of African Americans, Matthew reflected on the shift in their posture as well as their disposition. He stated:

They began to smile more. They started walking with their heads up and shoulders back. They were so proud to be Black men! Then we revisited the subject of slavery. The truth of history can be rewritten, but it can't be changed.

The mentors found that allowing the mentees to explore their history instead of using the usual popular figures provided greater understanding. Matthew stated, "Knowing the story of Dr. King is good, but knowing about Marcus Garvey, Mary McLeod-Bethune, Henry 'Box' Brown . . . is even better. We had

Table 4. Emergent themes of research question 4

Themes	Subthemes
Academic achievement	Improved GPAs Scholarships Higher education College tours
Promoted a positive self-identity	HBCUs Self-worth
Self-efficacy	Resilience
Community responsibility	Leadership

the responsibility of providing as broad a perspective as possible." They recalled the mentees referring to themselves as different African American historic figures. Dubi stated, "After exploring the historic contributions of our ancestors, I would hear mentees debating the philosophy they identified with." The mentors witnessed a shift in the attitudes of the mentees over time. The mentees embraced their history as African Americans.

While still discussing self-worth through resilience for the mentees, Kevin also added, "The SBC taught mentees self-determination. They learned to plan, persist and shift when needed, but never give up." His statement was in reference to the interviewer's question of how SBC's mentoring program affected the academic success of African American males. He further stated, when speaking of the resilience of an educated, African American man, "he can fall down and get back up, every time. Each time, he gets up stronger and more determined than when he fell."

Community Responsibility

Leadership

The topic of leadership emerged when Kevin, responding to the interviewer's request to describe SBC's mentoring program, stated, "SBC promotes self-efficacy and provides exposure to a world outside of the classroom. It is a training ground for leadership with the use of the Rise and Thunder program." He added, "In an effort to be attractive to the youth, the mentees helped to shape the programming while remaining focused on the objective of leadership and education."

Subsequently, when asked to describe a mentoring session, the affirmation of leaders and the demonstration of leadership were mentioned. Dubi said, "To set the tone for the expectations of the mentees, the mentoring sessions start with a recitation of the motto "The Next Generation of Leaders Accepting the Responsibility and Loving the Challenge." Dubi further stated, "In an effort to instill leadership skills in terms of handling the business of SBC and follow-up action items, elected officers present reports."

Additionally, as previously mentioned, when responding to how SBC affected the academic success of African American males, Matthew added, "In SBC we often used community service to teach leadership skills and responsibilities, it was also necessary for academic achievement."

In summary, the mentors expressed several themes regarding their beliefs of the SBC mentoring program's impact on the academic achievements of the African American male mentees. The initial theme of academic achievement emerged from the responses. The mentors observed an overall improvement in the GPAs of the mentees, which resulted in them qualifying for scholarships and higher education. The theme of promoting a positive self-identity emerged also. The mentors discussed in length the augmentation in reference to a sense of self-worth through the development of resilience in mentees. The sense of self-worth was enhanced using several vehicles, which included visits to HBCUs. Finally, the mentors' responses drew upon the theme of self-efficacy through resilience. As a final point in this section regarding the impact of the SBC program on the mentees, the mentors believed the mentees developed a community-conscious awareness through the enhancement of leadership roles. To affirm the consistent manifestation of leadership, mentees were required to open meetings with the recitation of the SBC motto. In the next section, we review the emergent themes regarding the application of SCT in the SBC program from the perspective of the mentors and the mentees.

How did SBC apply components of SCT in their mentoring of African American male students? As a reminder, SCT is a process of human development focused on alterations in psychosocial functioning (Bandura, 1978). It is based on four principles of observational learning: attention, retention, reproduction, and motivation. Attention is when an observer notices the behavior of another. Retention is the ability of the observer to remember the behavior. Reproduction is to mimic the behavior, and motivation is the reason the behavior is noticed. Motivation requires the observer to either relate to or admire the behavior or see that the behavior is rewarded in some way. SCT is a triadic reciprocal deterministic model of behavior, cognition, and environment (Bandura, 1978; Williams & Williams, 2010). It means that people are agentic. They function as respondents and influencers of their environment through their own motivation and behavior (Bandura, 2001; Nevid, 2009).

SCT is concerned with changes in psychosocial development functioning to help people understand and change their behavior (Bandura, 1989). A key finding in SCT is that people need to feel a sense of control over their own lives and behavior. Therefore, they subconsciously develop behaviors that move them to their goal of feeling in control. SCT encompasses four self-systems that direct behavior: self-observation, self-evaluation, self-reaction, and self-efficacy. If the self-systems can be positively impacted, positive behavior can be the result. The application of SCT should be task-oriented. An approach to apply it too broadly can be cumbersome. Sigma Beta Club unintentionally utilized the principles of SCT throughout various phases of the mentoring program to accomplish their mission (task). The task was to inspire mentees of the program to graduate high school with the hopes that the mentees would continue on into college.

Triadic Reciprocal Determinism Model

A simulation of the triadic reciprocal determinism model shows up twice in the interviews. In the mentee section of interviews, they discussed community service projects. A shift in how the mentees viewed the community service is their cognition. The shift in thinking influenced how they approached the task, which is their behavior. Subsequently, it led to a better environment. Tahj described it as "communal responsibility." He stated, "It helped me to understand that everything I did either added to or took away from my community." Also, being an African American man, he had a responsibility to contribute to the vitality of his community. "I realized that my community service was not just beneficial externally. My family and friends were direct recipients."

Additionally, in a more intimate scope, a change in how the mentees viewed education led to a change in the work they were willing to put in, which eventually led to a change in their environment, such as going to college. Matthew stated, "The mentees often developed a sense of urgency to get their grades up after attending a college tour."

Agentic

Agency represents being an influencer while also being influenced by a system. Some of the statements made by the mentees and mentors lend to the credit of the program and participants of this study being agentic. Lucius stated, "Learning from one another how to deal with what we encounter." Justice stated, "That is the SBC program. It's a family, supporting one another and accountable to one another." Talking about the mentor's impacts on the mentees, Matthew stated, "We learned just as much from them as they learned from us." Additionally, Kevin inadvertently talked about agency when reflecting on his most difficult memory. He said:

In hindsight, sometimes I wonder if I was too hard on the boys when we [he and the mentees] talk about some of the stuff they did and my reaction. I was the fun one, but I did not play with their futures.

Kevin's reflections caused him to go through the process of the self-systems. Seeing where the mentees are in their lives now has made him wonder whether, if he was not as tough on them, would they have the same results. Kevin did an introspection (self-observation), looking at his response to the situation at hand. He assessed (self-evaluation) how he responded to the situation at that time and weighed it against having a different response. He questioned whether a shift or behavior adjustment (self-reaction) was needed. Ultimately, Kevin persevered (self-efficacy). The mentees still reached out to him for guidance, and he continued to provide the support they needed. In the course of the discussion, the interviewer asked if any of the young men complained about Kevin's style? Admittedly, they had not, as witnessed during the research observation. Most of the memories and responses were humorous to the mentees, while Kevin still looked very serious.

Self-systems

Self-observation

Self-observation happens when an individual conducts an introspection and selects models whose behavior is motivational. The mentees expressed that the educational and career accomplishments of the mentors made them believe it was possible for them. Chad stated:

The mentors did not just tell us what we should do. They provided themselves as the example. They mirrored who we are and what is possible. Most importantly, these were men that looked just like me, that could relate to me and my experiences, that eliminated my excuses.

Blake responded, "I saw that the mentors graduated and was doing great things. I wanted to do just as well or better." The mentees' observation of the mentors' success set a trajectory of possibilities in motion. Blake added, "The mentors talked about their college experiences, including pledging their fraternity and the support they received being a part of a brotherhood."

When asked about the specific components of mentoring that contributed to academic success, the mentees attributed a great deal of their success to their relationship and ability to identify with their mentors. Tahj expressed:

There were several things that culturally relevant mentorship for education was a culture shock. I wasn't used to that. But that representation helped define my goals and helped shape my thinking. Seeing those Black male figures opened doors for my belief in myself. I was guided by the success and accomplishments of my mentor.

In addition to the mentors, the mentees' discussions regarding the HBCUs provided self-observation models, which took them through the rest of the self-systems to goal attainment.

Justice pointed to the tours of the HBCUs as an important part. He said, "The HBCU tours exposed us to African American men of high intelligence."

Subsequently, Tahj, Blake, and Chad reflected on their tours to HBCUs as they responded to what specific components of the SBC program had the greatest impact on their academic success. Each of them completed undergraduate degrees from an HBCU. They talked about the inherent pride they felt as they identified with the institutions. Chad stated, "The HBCUs did it for me! To see my brothers and sisters there. They were looking good! I was going, whatever it took." They walked on the soil where the Rev. Dr. Martin Luther King Jr. once stood. Lucius stated, "Even though I didn't go to college, going to Morehouse had an effect on me. I was in the place of legends, who changed the world. I was reminded that I have a purpose in this world." Tahj reflected:

Visiting to the HBCUs was a culture shock. Living in my community, I didn't see the most positive figures. The media continues to inundate the public with negative images of Black people. It becomes easy to believe the stereotypes are true. But the representation at the HBCUs, especially Morehouse, helped to define my goals and reshape my thinking regarding Black male figures. It opened doors for my belief in myself. The mentors were extremely positive role models, but, at first, to me as a kid, they were an anomaly. The HBCUs provided a broader, more informed perspective.

Self-evaluation

Self-evaluation takes place when an individual assesses his or her abilities and self-worth in comparison to the model. In reference to the mentors' academic and career success, Chad said, "If they could do it, so could I." Blake, assessing the mentor's college experience, stating, "I was excited for my chance to be a part of that!" Another example of self-evaluation was when Blake stated, "I saw that the mentors graduated and was doing great things. I wanted to do just as well or better."

Self-reaction

Self-reaction is the change in behavior that takes place. Isaiah believed the SBC program and mentors saved him. He stated:

I would not have survived my teen years if not for SBC. I had started cutting school, hanging out, and not caring where my life ended up. I did not believe that I would live to see, even the age I am now.

Lucius stated, "Even though I didn't go to college, going to Morehouse had an effect on me. I was in the place of legends, who changed the world. I was reminded that I have a purpose in this world." When talking about the impact of the HBCUs, Tahj reflected:

Visiting to the HBCUs was a culture shock. Living in my community, I didn't see the most positive figures. The media continues to inundate the public with negative images of Black people. It becomes easy to believe the stereotypes are true. But the representation at the HBCUs, especially Morehouse, helped to define my goals and reshape my thinking regarding Black male figures. It opened doors for my belief in myself. The mentors were extremely positive role models, but, at first, to me as a kid, they were an anomaly. The HBCUs provided a broader, more informed perspective.

Self-efficacy

Self-efficacy is an individual's belief that despite environment or experiences, they can achieve their goal. Ezra said, "I participated in SBC to improve my grades and get out of the hood." He believed his participation would make him successful. Additionally, during our interview, Ezra talked about his current desire to make his mother proud. He said:

When I was younger, I didn't know how to tell my mom that I appreciated the sacrifice she made for me and my brother. I thought acknowledging her sacrifices meant I was soft. I thought leaders had to be arrogant and self-absorbed. Now, I talk to my mom every day. I end our calls with I love and appreciate you.

As previously mentioned, Ezra was completing an advanced degree and had started his own mentoring program.

The application of the self-system is often situational. Generally, a specific situation generates a cognitive reflection, which results in an individual determining whether a shift in behavior or pursuit. There were several situations in the interviews where the self-systems emerged. When Blake recalled:

When I got to Morehouse, I was emotionally moved. Do you know all of the greats that passed through there? I was honored to stand where they stood. We saw African American sororities and fraternities. They talked to us about changing our narrative. In that moment, I knew I was going to college, and I was going to try my best to go there.

My life changed forever that day!

Another example of SCT was shared during Dubi's response to his fondest memory. One of Dubi's fondest memories was when the mentees began to take ownership of their mentoring experience and recommended some rap session topics. He said:

I was surprised by the forward-thinking in their choices. They asked for a risk management session on sexual behavior, domestic violence prevention and dating responsibility, financial planning, living on your own, as well as a resilience course on perseverance, goal-setting, and time management. They even wanted to learn parliamentary procedures (Robert's Rules of Order) for their executive board meetings. Dubi emphasized, "They wanted to emulate the behavior of the Sigmas. I was deeply moved by that. Clearly, we had made an impression."

In summary, these are only some of the examples of the application of SCT with the implications of the self-system. The mentors of the Sigma Beta Club inadvertently applied the theory of SCT while working with the mentees. The ultimate goal of SBC was to create community and career leaders through the use of education. The individual task was to assist their adolescent African American male mentees in navigating the educational system, conquering barriers, and graduating from high school. The mentors of SBC understood that mentoring cannot be effective utilizing a one-size-fits-all approach. Therefore, they utilized multiple tools to encourage and inspire the mentees (e.g., tutoring, college tours, scholarships, the bonds of brotherhood and relationship). In the next section, we review the emergent themes regarding the efficacy of the SBC program from the perspective of the mentors and the mentees. *What is the efficacy of SCT application in the SBC mentoring of African American male students?*

A key element of SBC was that African American young men obtain the education necessary to become leaders. Therefore, education was an essential goal of the mentoring program. The study participants highlighted the goal of education and the value associated with it. As such, the immediate task was the completion of high school accompanied by a future life plan. Efficacy is how well the desired result is achieved. The desired result of SBC was that mentees graduated high school and college and/or careers. The introduction of the participants at the beginning of this chapter reflects how well the result was achieved. Of the seven mentee participants in this research, all of them graduated from high school. Only one participant of this research did not go to college. He entered the workforce and as stated, is currently participating in a management training program. In order for these results to come into fruition, mentees had to develop problem-solving, goal-setting and conflict resolution skills. The development of these skills are critical elements for the application of SCT in the SBC program.

The mentors were asked to provide a few scenarios where they provided guidance that involved problem-solving, goal-setting, or conflict resolution. In Bandura's SCT, self-efficacy was imperative. It involved being able to set a goal and, despite the obstacles, being able to persevere. Bandura's SCT involved an individual developing the necessary skills to work through problems and the maturity to properly resolve conflicts. The mentors gave a few illustrations. The following were most relevant to the research. One of Dubi's examples included goal-setting for an unprepared mentee:

I had a mentee who was nearing graduation with no life plan. Developing realistic next steps is a requirement of the program. Despite his attitude, I worked with him to explore his interests. Instead of chastisement, I walked him through to empowerment.

The example Kevin shared included problem-solving and conflict resolution:

A lot of our boys come from high crime areas and could find themselves or a family member a victim at some point. I worked with the mentees on restorative justice in decision-making instead of retaliation. It gives the perpetrator a chance to take ownership of their actions and understand the impact. We did a restorative justice exercise look at some community issues. We determined the key players, did some deductive reasoning, weighed some escalation factors, and then looked for options—what could've been done differently. The point was to assess ownership of community help and responsibility.

Matthew provided an example that involved conflict resolution in a family. Matthew shared: A mentee was having problems at home with his mother. He believed his mother was being antagonistic and attempting to instigate an argument. The mentee was frustrated and wanted to leave the home. However, he had nowhere else to live.

Matthew worked with him on respectful communication. He said, "I taught him to understand things from his mother's perspective to avoid anger and frustration. Then he could respond to the situation and avoid an explosive reaction."

The mentors stressed that the hardest part of mentoring was developing efficacy in African American male mentees. Dubi stated:

Most of the mentees are from socio-economically disadvantaged communities that are plagued with crime and negativity. Additionally, they are experiencing a fear of law enforcement because of the multiple shootings of unarmed African American men and women.

Also, Kevin mentioned, "We try to equip our boys with the tools to do deductive reasoning and de-escalation. We want them to survive whatever situation they find themselves."

Relative to Kevin's point, Justice recalled a time he and a friend had a negative legal encounter. Justice stated, "I knew my rights were violated, but I also knew that the authorities wouldn't do anything if I reported it." Justice said he was now entering law school. Initially, he wanted to go into politics. However, while driving home one day, he saw two separate occurrences of young African American men sitting on the curb handcuffed while their cars were searched. Those incidents were pivotal moments for Justice. He understood that he needed to be an advocate in the courtroom for young men whose rights were routinely violated.

While further discussing efficacy, responding to the interviewer's question of how SBC affected the academic success of the mentees, Dubi stated, "Often the type of childhood you have, is the type of adult you become." Therefore, the SBC mentors strove to show patience and consistency in the lives of the mentees. During our discussion, Dubi mentioned SBC's policy that allowed mentees to be expelled for certain offenses. However, he could not recall a time when a mentee had been expelled from the program. The mentors chose to work through the problems with the mentees. Dubi stated:

If the pattern of a mentee's life is to be abandoned or thrown away, they go through life operating from a place of rejection. Sometimes when people operate from that mindset, they lack fortitude. If a situation gets hard, they'll quit to escape the possibility of being rejected.

Along the same thought process, responding to the same question, Kevin stated, "We want our young men to develop efficacy and resiliency. We continuously work with them in the development of self-determination. SBC mentors teach the mentees to plan and persist as well as to shift when needed." "As mentors, we offer social and cultural awareness skills in youth development," stated Matthew. "We teach conflict resolution and self-respect. If a mentee learns to respect himself, then he will respect others."

Responding to the question of his most difficult memory, Dubi replied that was when he had to talk to the mentees about marginalized Blackness. Dubi said:

I always started with telling them that they were kissed by the sun. I wanted them to embrace their Blackness and love themselves. We have to help our boys through acts of discrimination, past and present. My mentee had a negative interaction with a racist officer that scarred him. I was hurt because he was hurting. I believe he was at a fork in the road. The mentee said that being Black shouldn't have to be this hard.

Table 5. Emergent themes of research question 6

Themes	Subthemes
Community responsibility	Leadership
Self-efficacy	Goal-setting Resilience Emotional competence

Kevin's most difficult memory involved the discipline of mentees. He stated:

I was always the fun mentor. Some mentees required a tougher approach. So, we had to hold them accountable. A mentee was fighting at school, he had to be removed from his leadership position. I didn't want to do it, but his actions were a reflection on the program.

Matthew's most difficult mentoring memory was accompanying the mentees to the funeral of an SBC graduate. Matthew became slightly emotional, recalling, "The mentee was home for Christmas break during his freshman year of college and was shot. It was a case of mistaken identity. He was an awesome kid with so much potential." Matthew added, "His little brother was still in the program. He took it real hard, the other mentees supported him tremendously. I was really proud of them." Matthew and the other mentors talked with the mentees about the various emotions they were experiencing as a result. Some of the mentees had wished they could retaliate.

When asked how his life would be different, but for his participation in SBC, Tahj stated, "His trust in mentorship wouldn't have been as strong. The efficacy developed due to the influence of the program and the mentors positively impacted his decision-making." The effectiveness of the SBC program to develop the mentees' leadership abilities in their communities was demonstrative in the current statuses of the young men.

As Dubi stated, "The SBC mentoring program has a 95% success rate for mentees graduating high school and pursuing college degrees." For the mentees who chose to forego college and enter employment, the expectation of leadership was understood. As Lucius mentioned, "College wasn't for me. I was tired of school. So, I went to work. I still had to be a leader." As stated previously, Lucius was in a management training program job at the time of his interview. Grossman and Rhodes (2002) stated, "Young people will meet or even exceed the expectations of their mentors when those expectations are made known." The beginning of this chapter includes an introduction of the participants. Almost all of them were pursuing graduate degrees. The efficacy of SBC's application of SCT was evident in the fact that all of the participants graduated high school and continued into colleges or careers.

The essence of the SBC program is to effectively assist African American male mentees in development. It is influenced by the mission to raise positive leaders through education. The mentors devoted extensive time and effort to the mentees. Over the years, the mentees have been able to embrace the lessons of SBC, graduate from high school, and pursue college or careers. The success was attributed to five themes that individually encompassed a set of subthemes. The themes were academic support, a sense of belonging, promoted positive self-identity, community responsibility, and self-efficacy. These were the detectable themes that emerged during the data collection interviews and were accentuated during the observation. In the next section, we discuss the value added to the research study through the observation of the group dynamics as reflected by the mentors and mentees.

Observation

The observation demonstrated the relationship and camaraderie of the mentors and mentees as they relived shared experiences. There were a lot of laughs and jokes shared by everyone. As per the consent agreement, the specifics of the group observation discussion have not been reported. The purpose of the observation was to examine the relationship dynamics. At one point during the observation, an intense subject was raised. It was obvious by the initial reactions that the matter was still slightly uncomfortable for some of the mentees. However, one of the mentees joked about a response at the time of the incident. Subsequently, the mentors and mentees laughed and joked throughout the remainder. It was clear that although the mentees were adults, they still had an appreciation and hierarchical respect for their mentors. The mentees still addressed the mentors as big brothers and fondly spoke of the SBC program's impact on their lives.

Examining the group dynamics when the mentees were conversing with one another exemplified the resemblance of the brotherhood mentioned in the interviews. Additionally, a cohesive, supportive relationship was apparent among the mentors. Without going into detail, there was a particularly sad conversation that was mentioned. The individual became emotional, the other research participants were very encouraging and consoling. The support provided the strength needed to comfortably describe his feelings and put his vulnerability on display. The camaraderie was also evident as the mentors and mentees discussed their lived experiences.

The observation proved to be a useful tool in the subsequent interviews with the mentees. One of the mentees was in a public place during his interview, and therefore, had to wear a mask (due to the pandemic). During the observation, the researcher noticed that when the mentee thought something was funny, he would raise his eyebrows and say a particular phrase. While sharing his perspective on the SBC, he made the expression and remark, which provided context given the researcher was unable to see the mentee's mouth.

CONCLUSION

The essence of the SBC program is to effectively assist African American male mentees in development. It is influenced by the mission to raise positive leaders through education. The mentors devote extensive time and effort to the mentees. Over the years, the mentees have been able to embrace the lessons of SBC, graduate from high school, and pursue college or careers. The success was attributed to five themes that individually encompassed a set of subthemes. The themes were academic support, a sense of belonging, promoted positive self-identity, community responsibility, and self-efficacy. These were the detectable themes that emerged during the data collection interviews and were accentuated during the observation.

Discussion and Conclusion

Mentoring is a process where one individual positively impacts the life of another. The impact is not isolated to one area. It can influence the choices, behaviors, confidence, perseverance, and academic performance of the mentee. The SBC mentoring program utilizes a group mentoring forum. The effects of the mentoring program as reflected in the literature and the findings conclude that the SBC mentoring program has been influential on the academic success of the African American male mentees. In the next section, we discuss some of the main points of the research findings in comparison to the literature.

What are the perspectives of African American male students who completed the Sigma Beta Club mentoring program on the factors that influence academic success?

As the receivers of the mentoring services, it was important to know the factors mentees believed were influential to their academic success. The mentees believed the opportunity to receive tutoring and support from their African American mentors improved their outcomes and decision-making skills. Dubois et al. (2007) found that mentoring programs provide support to mentees to help them make positive decisions. The mentees also expressed that exposure to colleges and universities through the college tours afforded them a unique opportunity for success. Martin (2008) found that positive representation and social support helped to counteract the negativity. The college tours gave the mentees an opportunity to observe African American young men and women intellectuals embracing the higher education experience. The mentees admired the mentors' unconditional support and thought the overall experience provided them an opportunity to develop brotherly relationships with other mentees. Larson (2006) stated that young people, especially African American males, desire a supportive relationship. The commitment of the mentors to be present for activities outside of the program facility left an indelible mark. The mentees believed the program instilled a responsibility to the community and the chance to be positively impacted through community service projects. As a final important factor, mentees believed that holistically the program challenged them to be better by promoting a positive self-identity for them as African American males. Gordon et al. (2009) uncovered the importance of cultural relevance when mentoring young African American men.

In particular, Gordon et al. (2009) noted that highlighting cultural history gave some African American young men a sense of racial identity and pride.

The data collected from the mentees regarding the factors they perceived were influential to their academic success align with the literature. African American young men need positive support and affirmations to encourage them to make positive choices. Additionally, given the bombardment of negative images and representation, African American mentors' support is more impactful to help promote a healthy self-belief. African American male mentors set a positive example and diminish negative stereotypes. The last factor leads to the outcome or result of the inputs of the section. The next section speaks to the impact of their participation in the SBC program.

What do African American male students perceive was the impact of the SBC mentoring program on their educational experience?

The mentees perceived that the impact on their educational experience was that they developed positive self-worth. Their positive self-worth happened due to their exposure to positive role models at SBC and the HBCUs. Additionally, their educational opportunities were enhanced. Due to the academic support, especially the various avenues of tutoring, the mentees' grades improved. The improvement of their grades provided access to various scholarships. Mentees who otherwise would not have graduated from high school raised their GPAs and qualified for graduation. Subsequently, mentees became interested in college, either from grade improvements or exposure to higher education institutions. Woodland et al. (2009) found that mentoring improved academics, high self-confidence, and a greater sense of personal accountability.

The mentees also developed self-awareness regarding innate skills they possessed, which enabled them to explore positive opportunities to acquire short-term funds. Some of the mentees reported side businesses they started based on lessons learned during their time with SBC. The development of self-awareness also helped mentees establish long-range career goals they are currently pursuing. Eby et al. (2007) found that youth mentoring positively impacted behavior, attitude, motivation, and career outcomes. There was an overwhelming consensus among the mentees that they foster positive self-worth and academically thrived from their time at SBC.

The impact of SBC on the educational experiences of the mentees was critical. The mentees were at a pivotal point in their lives, where their decisions would define their futures.

The SBC program helped the mentees to make sound decisions that defined them as educated leaders. The SBC program also contributed to the mentees becoming community-conscious and career-minded. The supportive environment of SBC inspired the mentees to complete high school with grades high enough to gain access to college. Therefore, the attributes of SBC and its selection of mentors greatly contributed to the academic success of the mentees. In the next section, we discuss the perspectives of the mentors.

What are the perspectives of Sigma Beta Club mentors on the factors that influence the academic success of African American male high school students?

The mentors' perspective regarding the factors that influence the academic success of the mentees was similar to the mentees' perspective. The mentors believed that the academic support components in the form of tutoring were helpful. However, they did not attribute all of the credit to themselves. The mentors believed the tutoring success was a joint effort of the partnerships with schools, fraternity members, and parents.

The mentors also believed the financial investment in the form of scholarships also contributed to the mentees' success. Additionally, the provision of community service projects complemented college and scholarship applications. The mentors looked for opportunities to enlighten the minds of mentees regarding their heritage to develop fortitude, resilience, and self-pride. As previously stated, Gordon et al. (2009) uncovered the importance of cultural relevance when mentoring young African American men. In particular, Gordon et al. (2009) noted that highlighting cultural history gave some African American young men a sense of racial identity and pride.

Another component of the SBC program that facilitated academic success was the programmatic thrust of "Rise and Thunder," which allowed mentees input and selection to meet their individual needs. African American young men reported being most involved in programs that promoted ownership (Gordon et al., 2009). Raposa et al. (2019) found that a one-size-fits-all approach to mentoring is ineffective. It limits the mentees' opportunity to develop decision-making skills and fosters a sense of ownership. When given the opportunity to choose a "best fit" program application, it provides positive interventions psychosocially and academically. Additionally, the mentors believed authentic mentor and mentee relationships and the investment of time were key in the academic success of the mentees. Galbraith (2003) found that if mentors engaged in behaviors to challenge, advise, encourage, motivate, and foster a trusting relationship with mentees, it would result in academic achievement.

The input on behalf of SBC rendered by the mentors left an indelible mark on the mentees and contributed to their academic success. The mentors' care and support for the mentees truly enriched their academic experience. The commitment to the mentoring relationship the mentors displayed and genuine concern for the individual needs of each mentee were inspirational. The collective work of the SBC program mentors, facilitators, parents, and community was useful in helping mentees progress academically and socially. This research question was geared toward the useful inputs of mentors to guide mentees to successful completion of high school. The next research question examined the outcomes mentors observed due to the assistance they provided the mentees.

What do mentors perceive was the impact of SBC's mentoring practices on the educational experiences of their African American male students?

The impacts on the mentees as perceived by the mentors were academically and socially inclined. Galbraith (2003) found that if mentors engaged in behaviors to challenge, advise, encourage, motivate, and foster a trusting relationship with mentees, it would result in academic achievement. Woodland et al. (2009) agreed with Galbraith's findings. However, they added that a high self-confidence would be realized, which the data support. The more improvement the young men experienced in school, the more confident they became. Also, the more exposure they had to positive African American representation, the greater their awareness of the possibilities of success. The mentees learned to love themselves and developed a great respect for other young African American men. Additionally, the mentees completed high school, and most of them went on to college. Some even went to a HBCU. The mentees identified with HBCUs so strongly during the SBC college tour trip.

The positive imaging of SBC clearly helped the mentees visualize successful outcomes. The idea of SBC being a safe space to reveal vulnerabilities without judgment allowed a trusting relationship to flourish. As pointed out in St. John's (2011) research, mentors become confidants to whom their mentee could be open to receiving guidance, resulting in academic success. The academic success and culturally relevant exposure bolstered the self-confidence of the mentees. The mentors' positive belief in the mentees inspired the mentees to believe in themselves. The ability of the mentees to add to the programming and select their interests developed leadership abilities that the mentees have taken into their communities. This research question focused on the outputs mentors observed by the mentees. The next research question focuses on the observable traits of SCT in the mentoring program administered by SBC.

How did SBC apply components of SCT in their mentoring of African American male students?

The purpose of SCT is to change the psychosocial behavior of individuals and was found to be most useful for people who have endured or experienced traumatic situations. The behavior changes took place through the application of four self-systems. The self-systems were self-observation, which happens by introspection or studying to mimic the behavior of their role models; self-evaluation happens by making a comparison of one's skill and ability to that of another; self-reaction happens by implementing a shift or adjustment of behavior; and, self-efficacy, which is the belief that despite what happens externally, the mentees possess an internal, inherent ability to succeed, happens over time. The data in response to this research question were extrapolated from the responses throughout the interviews of the mentors and the mentees.

Bandura (1978, 2001) found that in self-observation, a person's environment can be more influential on their behavior than genetics. Therefore, with proper interventions, people can reprogram their cognition to change their behavior. Additionally, he found that children imitate the behavior of their role models and may even take it to another level. The mentees identified the mentors as role models and spoke of their desire to be like them or better. The mentees also related to the African American students at the HBCUs as people they admired. For self-evaluation, Bandura and Cervone (1983) described it as a comparative standard by which performance motivation is gauged. Fritscher (2017) found that it can be very useful for individuals striving for self-improvement. The mentees compared themselves and their ability to succeed with their mentors and the African Americans at the various HBCUs. Self-reaction, as defined by Bandura (1978), is consequential to social cognition for behavior modification. The mentees stated that admiration of their role models at SBC and the HBCUs inspired them to change their behavior academically, socially, or both to acquire the same achievements. The last component of the self-systems is self-efficacy. Lunenburg (2011) posited that self-efficacy not only impacts an individual's actions but also their continued motivation and ability to learn. Bandura (1978) further explained self-efficacy as one's belief that one possesses the power and ability to organize and execute one's own plan of action. The mentors worked with the mentees to accomplish various goals; the incremental successes encouraged mentees to strive for even greater successes. The actions of SBC to develop self-efficacy through goal-setting efforts were supported by the research of Williams and Williams. They found that individuals with high levels of self-efficacy would continually challenge themselves with progressively difficult tasks.

The Rise and Thunder program required mentees to gradually set and attain incremental goals. Additionally, with each accomplishment, greater resilience was developed.

The programming features of SBC incorporated the principles of SCT. Those principles include the agency and self-systems. The principles of SCT were evident in the influential aspects of the mentors as role models to the Rise and Thunder program. Components of SCT are identifiable. The SBC program did not shy away from the climate of discrimination that mentees are likely to encounter. Instead, much effort was made to teach mentees how to navigate it. The program taught mentees to face discrimination while also taking responsibility for their lives and being true to themselves. The mentees were taught to take responsibility for their goals and be intentional about their success. The SBC program inadvertently utilized the principles of SCT in their mentoring process. The SBC program provided replicable tools to enlighten the cognition of mentees, which inspired a commendatory behavior adjustment that produced a positive input to their environment. The next research question explores SBC's application of efficacy.

What is the efficacy of SCT application in the SBC mentoring of African American male students?

The responses of the mentors and mentees unveiled multiple instances of efficacy in direct correlation with the principles of SCT. Efficacy is how an individual handles a particular situation at a point in time. St. John (2011) stated that mentors function as reflectors to provide feedback to mentees. They provide situational guidance and serve as role models for social and emotional development. The mentors and mentees discussed the development of emotional competence. Emotional competence is the practice of properly assessing the situation and rendering the appropriate response. The goal was to help mentees learn to respond instead of emotionally reacting in their decision-making, which could have perilous consequences.

The mentors and mentees considered the historic plight of African American men in America and the negative stereotypes. The lack of humanity and empathy with law enforcement and the justice system served as a reminder that they must exercise great care to reduce the chances of negative encounters with either one. Martin (2008) stated that youth identity is overwrought with continual stress and anxiety. However, African American youths have the additional burden of learning to navigate the challenge of being Black in America. The challenge is inundated with negative racial stereotypes. If success and longevity were to be the mentees' end result, they had to learn to make sound decisions and develop a pattern of emotional competence.

The opportunity to take part in culturally relevant mentoring with a focus on academics and leadership led to the success of the research participants. They were taught endurance and resilience. Research showed that using positive self-identification concepts resulted in mentees drawing on positive intrinsic motivations of responsibility and self-discipline (Gordon et al., 2009). The mentors and mentees expressed the ability of mentees to own and control their actions and outcomes, improved their leadership abilities (Grossman & Rhodes, 2002; Rhodes, 2011). A research finding that surfaced during the data collection phase was the individual contributory niche of each mentor. All of the mentors were committed to effecting change and being role models as positive African American mentors to young African American mentees.

However, the individuality of each mentor added to the experience for the mentees. Dubi was devoted to providing the historical aspects of Blackness to help mentees embrace all they are in their skin to develop self-love and self-confidence. Kevin ensured that the practical aspects of learning and development were programmatically administered while teaching belief in self and others. He emphasized the concept of collaboration and the benefits associated with forming a lasting relationship. Finally, Matthew brought structure and enforcement. He firmly believed in the necessity of establishing a relationship that encompasses proper boundaries. Matthew clearly stated that within the mentor and mentee relationship, there is a hierarchy. "My role is not to be their friend. We can joke around. However, the mentees cannot become that comfortable or familiar that the lines of respect get blurred." Matthew's beliefs regarding the mentoring relationship of a mentor and mentee are supported by Galbraith and Cohen (1995), who contended that mentoring relationships must be hierarchical. The collaborative inputs of the mentors and their distinguished contributions worked well to support the success of the SBC mentoring program.

CONCLUSION

The work of the SBC program proved valuable to the participants of this study. They successfully completed high school and pursued college or careers. They have each experienced their share of trials along the way, in school, at home and societal. However, they learned to draw from the lessons of SBC. The mentees take responsibility for themselves, their families, and the community. They allow themselves some grace because the SBC program stressed that perfection is nonexistent. Subsequently, the mentees persisted through all obstacles to attain favorable outcomes. The mentees and mentors spoke with great pride regarding the SBC program. The mentors were honored to give such a labor of love. Additionally, the mentees delighted in having caring, supportive role models who taught them to pursue their dreams.

The findings related to the SBC program are directly aligned. The participants of SBC joined in their adolescent years, embraced the experience, and are now in graduate programs or careers. It is apparent that SBC has had a positive effect on the mentees. The mentees come from varying demographics and varying academic backgrounds. Albeit, they have all achieved the same result. All of the mentees that participated in this study graduated from high school and most completed undergraduate degrees. Subsequently, of the mentees that went to college, they have continued into graduate school. The possibility of other influences have been eliminated and the input of SBC has resounded.

Limitations of the Study

The sample size was sufficient to connect the application of SCT. However, a larger sample size may be useful to further evaluate the impact African American mentors have on the academic achievements of African American mentees. For this study, only seven former mentees and three former mentors participated. Therefore, the findings can only be generalized to the seven former mentees and three mentors.

Another limitation of the study was the selection of the former mentees. The former mentees were assigned by the program mentors in correlation with the period when they participated in SBC. The use of randomly selected mentees may render a different finding in relation to the application of SCT. Additionally, randomly selected former mentees may reflect adverse outcomes and effectiveness in deliberately pairing African American young men with African American mentors.

The interviews were unable to be conducted in person due to the COVID-19 global pandemic. The interviews were performed utilizing the Zoom video communications platform. During one interview, the video stalled while the audio continued to play. The technical issues restricted the researcher's ability to capture all of the expressions of the participant.

Additionally, at times the technology had glitches. Beyond the technical issues, using a video platform limited the researcher's ability to see the participants' body language.

Another limitation was the lack of a clear, concise definition of mentoring. The inability to have a succinct definition revealed gaps in the literature to ascertain the differences between mentoring and youth development. The description of youth development often mirrors the descriptors associated with youth mentoring. This research contributes to the literature to define mentoring.

A final limitation was that this study was limited to one local Sigma Beta Club chapter. Sigma Beta Club is a national program. The findings may change if other chapters are included. The inclusion of other chapters could either further support or contradict the findings of this study. Therefore, if this research is ever replicated, comparing more than one chapter could provide greater insights.

Recommendations for Future Research

The following recommendations for future research are based on the limitations of this study and the findings that emerged. The recommendations include sample size, additional SBC locations, a random sample of mentees, and parental impact. The first recommendation for future research is to replicate this study using additional former mentees and mentors of the program to ascertain the value of the additional perspectives. As stated, the research of this study was limited to seven former mentees and three mentors. A larger sample size could possibly alter the findings for the purpose of the study.

The second recommendation is to replicate the study using more than one Sigma Beta Club chapter. Expanding the research to include multiple chapters could help the researcher compare delivery methods to discover if the application of SCT is used in a broad spectrum. The use of SCT could possibly be limited to one club. Also, the results regarding educational attainment and career aspirations could shift. It would be important to consider the differences in experience regarding the mentors and how that may affect the outcome of findings in a comparative.

The third recommendation is to utilize a random sample size. The participants for this research were assigned by the mentors. In the essence of time and ease of access, working with the group of assigned mentees was conducive. However, the findings could vary if a random sample of former mentees were solicited for participation. Additionally, the success and impacts of the mentees and relationship reflections may not be the same.

The fourth recommendation is independent of the limitations above; however, it could further enlighten the findings. Building upon this study's research to determine the level of parental involvement and its effects, during the data collection portion of this study, some references to parental involvement and contact were mentioned. Therefore, it would be helpful to understand how that parental involvement influenced the SBC program outcomes.

Implications

When the My Brother's Keeper initiative was launched, mentors were asked to be active in the lives of African American mentees from cradle to college to career. Albeit there was a special emphasis placed on the adolescent years. The MBK task force acknowledged that the adolescent years were critical in making decisions that set the course for life. Therefore, being sure to mentor African American adolescents is imperative. Mentoring through the first few years of their career could be extremely beneficial.

The implications associated with this study are wide-reaching in the lives of African American males. First, this research is helpful for individuals interested in participating in one-to-one mentoring. This form of mentoring usually involves one adult mentor being assigned or selected to work with one mentee, as described in Chapter 2. The research contained in this study can equip a mentor with the tools to support a mentee successfully and independently.

Second, this study can also provide a framework for mentoring organizations with formal programs. The framework would be helpful to programs that are interested in enhancing their service delivery. Additionally, the research provides a structure and necessary elements for organizations interested in starting a mentoring program. If formal mentoring programs have a framework to start with, more time can be allocated to find mentors equipped with the qualifications described in the literature and findings.

Third, this study is useful in the education realm for high schools, colleges, and universities. If African American males are unable to successfully complete high school, it is impossible for them to gain access to higher education. This research equips schools with insight and encouragement to provide support for African American males in danger of failing. Included in this study are social and emotional support components that facilitate academic success.

Additionally, these components are useful for higher education institutions interested in developing programs to support African American male retainage. Despite numerous efforts, African American males seem challenged with completing higher education. This research, along with the literature, clarifies that a one-size-fits-all approach to mentoring does not work. The findings reveal that while a programmatic thrust exists, it needs to contain some flexibility to allow participants some customization. As higher education institutions implement programs to provide support, this research could serve as a guide.

Fourth, this research could be useful to employers that engage in career mentoring. The distinct elements of the SBC program are transferable. Understanding the need for support and exposure is helpful to all. Additionally, the components of the self-systems are applicable to adolescents and adults. If employers are engaging in mentoring to assist newer employees with getting acclimated and working toward growth, deliberately pairing African American mentees with mentors will help them navigate. Also, the deliberate pairing will help mentees avoid pitfalls that would otherwise be undetectable except with guidance from relatable figures.

These are just some areas where this research could be useful. It should be noted that while these examples are in the social arena, this research could be useful in a family setting. In some cases, mentors are representative of surrogate fathers. Therefore, this research could help fathers, especially those who grew up without fathers, realize their position as role models. Such a realization will help them be cognizant of their example so that the addition of a mentor could be a bonus, not a requirement.

REFERENCES

Adams-Bass, V. N., Stevenson, H. C., & Kotzin, D. (2014). Measuring the meaning of Black media stereotypes and their relationship to the racial identity: Black history knowledge and racial socialization of African American youth. *Journal of Black Studies*, *45*(5), 367–395. doi:10.1177/0021934714530396

Albright, L., & Malloy, T. (1999). Self-observation of social behavior in metaperception. *Journal of Personality and Social Psychology*, *77*(4), 726–734. doi:10.1037/0022-3514.77.4.726 PMID:10531669

Alleman, E. (1986). Measuring mentoring frequency, quality, and impact. In W. A. Gray & M. M. Gray (Eds.), *Mentoring: Aid to excellence in career development, business, and the professions* (pp. 44–51). The Xerox Reproduction Centre.

American Psychological Association Zero Tolerance Task Force. (2008). Zero tolerance policies effective in the schools? An evidentiary review and recommendations. *The American Psychologist*, *63*(9), 852–862. doi:10.1037/0003-066X.63.9.852 PMID:19086747

Anderson, K., & Jack, D. (1991). Learning to listen: Interview techniques and analyses. *Women's words: The feminist practice of oral history by Gluck,* 11-15.

Annie E. Casey Foundation. (2017). *Data snapshot on high poverty communities*. Kids count. Retrieved from http://www.aecf.org/~/media/Pubs/Initiatives/KIDSCOUNT/ Data SnapshotonPovertyCommunities.pdf

Ardery, G. (1990). Mentors and protégés: From ideology to knowledge. In J. Mccloskey & H. Grace (Eds.), *Current issues in nursing* (pp. 58–63). Mosby.

Bandura, A. (1977). Self-efficacy: Toward a unifying theory of behavioral change. *Psychological Review*. Retrieved from ProQuest database. (63957362)

Bandura, A. (1978). The self-system in reciprocal determinism. *American Psychologist, 33*(4), 344-358. http://dx.doi.org.ezproxy.roosevelt.edu:2048/10.1037/0003-06 6X.33.4.344

Bandura, A. (1982). Self-efficacy mechanism in human agency. *American Psychologist, 37*(2), 122-147. http://dx.doi.org.ezproxy.roosevelt.edu:2048/10.1037/0003-06 6X.37.2.122

Bandura, A. (2001). Social cognitive theory: An agentic perspective. *Annual Review of Psychology*, 52, 1-26. http://dx.doi.org.ezproxy.roosevelt.edu:2048/ 10.1146/annure v.psych.52.1

Bandura, A., Barbaranelli, C., Capara, G. V., & Pastorelli, C. (2001). Self-efficacy beliefs as shapers of children's aspirations and career trajectories. *Child Development*, *72*(1), 187–206. doi:10.1111/1467-8624.00273 PMID:11280478

Bandura, A., & Cervone, D. (1983). Self-evaluative and self-efficacy mechanisms governing the motivational effects of goal systems. *Journal of Personality and Social Psychology, 45*(5), 1017-1028. http://dx.doi.org.ezproxy.roosevelt.edu:2048/10.1037/0022-35 14.45.5.1017

Bem, D. J. (1967). Self-perception: An alternative interpretation of cognitive dissonance phenomena. *Psychological Review*, *74*(3), 183–200. doi:10.1037/h0024835 PMID:5342882

Benight, C. C., & Bandura, A. (2004). Social cognitive theory of posttraumatic recovery: The role of perceived self-efficacy. *Behaviour Research and Therapy*, *42*(10), 1129–1148. doi:10.1016/j.brat.2003.08.008 PMID:15350854

Burrell, T. (2010). *Brainwashed: Challenging the myth of black inferiority*. Smiley Books.

Centers for Disease Control. (2014). Preventing youth violence: Opportunities for action. Injury Prevention and Control: Division of Violence Prevention. National Center of Injury Prevention and Control.

Centers for Disease Control. (2018). Injuries deaths on the rise among American youth. *National Vital Statistics Reports*, *67*(4).

Chang, C. H., Ferris, D. L., Johnson, R. E., Rosen, C. C., & Tan, J. A. (2012). Core self-evaluations: A review and evaluation of the literature. *Journal of Management*, *38*(1), 81–128. doi:10.1177/0149206311419661

Christle, C., Jolivette, K., & Nelson, C. M. (2005). Breaking the school to prison pipeline: Identifying school risk and protective factors for youth delinquency. *Exceptionality*, *13*(2), 69–88. doi:10.120715327035ex1302_2

Chu, V. (2013). *Congressional authority to regulate firearms: A legal overview*. Congressional Research Service.

Creswell, J. W. (2014). *Research design: Qualitative, quantitative, and mixed methods approaches*. SAGE.

Crisp, G., & Cruz, I. (2009). Mentoring college students: A critical review of the literature between 1990 and 2007. *Research in Higher Education*, *50*(6), 525–545. doi:10.100711162-009-9130-2

Department of Education. (2015). *Civil rights data collection: 2011-12 discipline estimations by disability status*. Author.

Dillberti, M., Jackson, M., Kemp, J., & Hansen, K. (2017). *Crime, violence, discipline, and safety in U.S. public schools: Findings from the school survey on crime and safety*. U.S. Department of Education. National Center for Education Statistics.

Drisko, J. W. (2016). Teaching qualitative research: Key content, course structures, and recommendations. *Qualitative Social Work: Research and Practice*, *15*(3), 307–321. doi:10.1177/1473325015617522

DuBois, D. L., Holoway, B., Valentine, J., & Cooper, H. (2002). Effectiveness of mentoring programs for youth: A meta-analytic review. *American Journal of Community Psychology*, *30*(2), 157–197. doi:10.1023/A:1014628810714 PMID:12002242

Dubois, D. L., Portillo, N., Rhodes, J. E., Silverthorn, N., & Valentine, J. C. (2011). How effective are mentoring programs for youth? A systematic assessment of the evidence. *Psychological Science in the Public Interest*, *12*(2), 57–91. doi:10.1177/1529100611414806 PMID:26167708

Ebony. (1992). Black sororities and fraternities: Phi Beta Sigma. *Ebony*.

Esterberg, K. G. (2002). *Qualitative methods in social research*. McGraw-Hill.

Fetterman, D. M. (1998). Applied social research methods: Vol. 17. *Ethnography: Step by step* (2nd ed.). SAGE.

Fireman, G., & Kose, G. (2002). The effect of self-observation on children's problem-solving. *The Journal of Genetic Psychology*, *163*(4), 410–423. doi:10.1080/00221320209598693 PMID:12495228

Foster, S. L., Laverty-Finch, C., Gizzo, D. P., & Osantowski, J. (1999). Practical issues in self-observation. *Psychological Assessment*, *11*(4), 426–438. doi:10.1037/1040-3590.11.4.426

Fujioka, Y. (2005). Black media images as a perceived threat to African American ethnic identity: Coping responses, perceived public perception, and attitudes towards affirmative action. *Journal of Broadcasting & Electronic Media*, *49*(4), 450–467. doi:10.120715506878jobem4904_6

Galbraith, M. W. (2003). The adult education as mentor: A means to enhance teaching and learning. Perspectives. *The New York Journal of Adult Learning*, *1*(1), 9–20. doi:10.1177/104515950301400403

Galbraith, M. W., & Cohen, N. H. (1995). *Mentoring: New strategies and challenges. New directions for adult and continuing education*. Jossey-Bass.

Gardner, D. P. (1983). A nation at risk: The imperative for educational reform: A report to the nation and the Secretary of Education. United States Department of Education. Washington, DC: The Commission.

Girves, J., Gwathmey, J. K., & Zepeda, Y. (2005). Mentoring in a post-affirmative action world. *The Journal of Social Issues*, *61*(3), 449–479. doi:10.1111/j.1540-4560.2005.00416.x

Gordon, D., Iwamoto, D., Ward, N., Potts, R., & Boyd, E. (2009). Mentoring urban Black middle school male students: Implications for academic achievement. *The Journal of Negro Education*, *78*(3), 277–289. PMID:20379371

Grossman, J., & Rhodes, J. (2002). The test of time: Predictors and effects of duration in youth mentoring relationships. *American Journal of Community Psychology*, *30*(2), 199–219. doi:10.1023/A:1014680827552 PMID:12002243

Gun-free Schools Act of. 1994, H.R. 987, 103rd Cong. (1994).

Gunn, E. (1995). Mentoring: The Democratic version. *Training (New York, N.Y.)*, *32*(8), 64–67.

Haensly, P. A., & Parsons, J. L. (1993). Creative, intellectual, and psychosocial development through mentorship: Relationships and stages. *Youth & Society*, *25*(2), 202–221. doi:10.1177/0044118X93025002002

Henderson, D. (1985). Enlightened mentoring: A characteristic of public management professionalism. *Public Administration Review*, *45*(November/December), 857–863. doi:10.2307/975361

Herrera, C., Dubois, D., & Grossman, J. B. (2013). *The role of risk: Mentoring experiences and outcomes for youth with varying risk profiles*. Manpower Demonstration Research Corporation.

Higginbotham, B., MacArthur, S., & Dart, P. C. (2010, June 30). 4-H Mentoring: Youth and families with promise—adult engagement and the development of strengths in youths. *Journal of Prevention & Intervention in the Community*, *38*(3), 229–243. Advance online publication. doi:10.1080/10852352.2010.486300 PMID:20603759

Hofseth, E., Toering, T., Jordet, G., & Ivarsson, A. (2017). Self-evaluation of skills and performance level in youth elite soccer: Are positive self-evaluations always positive? *Sport, Exercise, and Performance Psychology*, *6*(4), 370–383. doi:10.1037py0000094

Hughes, M., & Demo, D. H. (1989). Self-perceptions of Black Americans: Self-esteem and personal efficacy. *American Journal of Sociology*, *95*(1), 132–159. doi:10.1086/229216

Inzer, L. D., & Crawford, C. B. (2005). A review of formal and informal mentoring: Processes, problems, and design. *Journal of Leadership Education*, *4*(1), 31–51. doi:10.12806/V4/I1/TF2

Jacobi, M. (1991). Mentoring and undergraduate academic success: A literature review. *Review of Educational Research*, *61*(4), 501–532. doi:10.3102/00346543061004505

Jarjoura, G. R. (2013). Effective strategies for mentoring African American boys. American Institute for Research.

Kang-Brown, J., Trone, J., Fratello, J., & Daftary-Kapur, T. (2013). *A generation later: What we've learned about zero tolerance in schools*. Vera Institute of Justice.

Klopf, G., & Harrison, J. (1981). Moving up the career ladder: A case for mentors. *Principal*, *2*(3), 41–43.

Kokko, K., Tremblay, R. E., Lacourse, E., Nagin, D. S., & Vitaro, F. (2006). Trajectories of Staff, J. & Kreager, D. (2008). Too cool for school? Violence, peer status, and high school dropout. *Social Forces*, *87*(1), 445–471.

Krause, N. (1983). The racial context of Black self-esteem. *Social Psychology Quarterly*, 46.

Larson, R. (2006). Positive youth development, willful adolescents, and mentoring. *Journal of Community Psychology*, *34*(6), 677–689. doi:10.1002/jcop.20123

Leary, M. R., Tate, E. B., Allen, A. B., Adams, C. E., & Hancock, J. (2007). Self-compassion and reactions to unpleasant self-relevant events: The implications of treating oneself kindly. *Journal of Personality and Social Psychology*, *92*(5), 887–904. doi:10.1037/0022-3514.92.5.887 PMID:17484611

Lewis, M. (1991). Ways of knowing: Objective self-awareness or consciousness. *Developmental Review*, *11*(3), 231–243. doi:10.1016/0273-2297(91)90011-C

Luna, G., & Cullen, D. L. (1995). Empowering the faculty: Mentoring redirected and renewed. *ASHE-ERIC Higher Education Report*, *3*, 1–87.

Lunenburg, F. (2011). Self-efficacy in the workplace: Implications for motivation and performance. *International Journal of Management. Business Administration (London)*, *14*(1).

Martin, A. (2008). Television media as a potential negative factor in the racial identity development of African American youth. *Academic Psychiatry*, *32*(4), 338–342. doi:10.1176/appi.ap.32.4.338 PMID:18695037

Mastro, D. (2015). Why the media's role in issues of race and ethnicity should be in the spotlight. *The Journal of Social Issues*, *71*(1), 1–16. doi:10.1111/josi.12093

McCrae, C. N., & Galen, V. B. (2000). Social cognition: Thinking categorically about others. *Annual Review of Psychology*, *51*, 27. PMID:10751966

McHale, G. (2000). Turning points: A white paper on the course of mentoring. In *Proceedings of the National Mentoring Conference of Project Literacy*. Washington, DC: National Educational Association.

Mentor: National Mentoring Partnership. (2015). *Mentor in real life.* National Mentoring Resource Center. http://nationalmentoringresourcenter.org

Musu-Gillette, L., de Brey, C., McFarland, J., Hussar, W., Sonnenberg, W., & Wilkinson-Flicker, S. (2017). *Status and trends in the education of racial and ethnic groups 2017.* U.S. Department of Education. National Center for Education Statistics.

National Association for the Advancement of Colored People. (2017). *Criminal justice fact sheet.* Retrieved from www.naacp.org/criminal-justice-fact-sheet

Nevid, J. S. (2009). *Psychology: Concepts and applications* (3rd ed.). Houghton Mifflin Company.

U.S. Newswire. (2014). *Phi Beta Sigma announces centennial week activities, July 16-20.* Author.

Obama, B. (2014). My brother's keeper. *Reclaiming Children and Youth Journal, 23*(1), 5–8.

Phi Beta Sigma. (n.d.a). *About.* Retrieved from https://phibetasigma1914.org/index.php/about/ history

Phi Beta Sigma. (n.d.b). *Programs.* Retrieved from https://phibetasigma1914.org/index.php/ programs

Punyanunt-Carter, N. (2008). The perceived realism of African American portrayals on television. *The Howard Journal of Communications, 19*(3), 241–257. doi:10.1080/10646170802218263

Rhodes, J. (2011). Ethical principles for youth mentoring relationships. Mentor: National Mentoring Partnership, 1-6.

Rosenberg, M. (1965). *Society and the adolescent self-image.* Princeton University Press. doi:10.1515/9781400876136

Salinitri, G. (2005). The effects of formal mentoring on the retention rates for first-year, low achieving students. *Canadian Journal of Education, 28*(4), 853–873. doi:10.2307/4126458

Schunk, D. (1995). Self-efficacy, motivation, and performance. *Journal of Applied Sport Psychology, 7*(2), 109–134. doi:10.1080/10413209508406961

Sigma Beta Club. (2015a). *News and updates.* Retrieved from https://sigmabetaclub.org/ newsupdates

Sigma Beta Club. (2015b). *Our story.* Retrieved: https://sigmabetaclub.org/our-story

Snyder, C. R., & Lopez, S. J. (2007). *Positive psychology: The scientific and practical explorations of human strengths.* SAGE.

Steele, C. M. (1997). A threat in the air: How stereotypes shape intellectual identity and performance. *American Psychologist, 52*(6), 613-629. Retrieved from ProQuest database (839058469).

Stillwell, R., & Sable, J. (2013). *Public school graduates and dropouts from the common core of data: School year 2009-10.* National Center for Education Statistics. U.S. Department of Education.

Suh, S., & Suh, J. (2007). Risk factors and levels of risk for high school dropouts. *Professional School Counseling, 10*(3), 297–306. doi:10.5330/prsc.10.3.w26024vvw6541gv7

Teasley, M. L., & Lee, E. (2006). Examining the association between academic achievement and self-esteem in African American male youth in a community after-school program. *School Social Work Journal*, *30*, 64–81.

Topos Partnership. (2011). *Social science literature review: Media representation and impact on the lives of Black men and boys*. The Opportunity Agenda.

Tukachinsky, R., Mastro, D., & Yarchi, M. (2017). The effect of primetime television ethnic/racial stereotypes on Latino and Black American: A longitudinal national study. *Journal of Broadcasting & Electronic Media*, *61*(3), 538–556. doi:10.1080/08838151.2017.1344669

United States National Commission on Excellence in Education. (1983). *A nation at risk*. https://www2.ed.gov/pubs/NatAtRisk/index.html

U.S. Department of Education. (2014). *Policy statement on expulsion and suspension policies in early childhood settings*. Retrieved from https://www2.ed.gov/policy/gen/guid/ schooldiscipline/policy-statement-ece-expulsions-suspensions.pdf

U.S. White House. (2014). *My brother's keeper task force report to the president*. Retrieved from https://www.whitehouse.gov/my-brothers-keeper

U.S. White House. (2015). *My brother's keeper task force: One-year progress report to the president*. Retrieved: https://www.whitehouse.gov/my-brothers-keeper

U.S. White House. (2016). *My brother's keeper 2016 progress report: Two years of expanding opportunity and creating pathways to success*. Retrieved from https://www.wh.gov/mbk

Whaley, A. L. (1993). Self-esteem, cultural identity, and psychosocial adjustment in African American children. *The Journal of Black Psychology*, *19*(4), 406–422. doi:10.1177/00957984930194003

Williams, T., & Williams, K. (2010). Self-efficacy and performance in mathematics: Reciprocal determinism in 33 nations. *Journal of Educational Psychology, 102*(2), 453. Retrieved from ProQuest database (336826006).

Wonberg, C. R., Zhu, J., & Van Hooft, E. A. J. (2010). The job search grind: Perceived progress, self-reactions, and self-regulation of search effort. *Academy of Management Journal*, *53*(10), 788–807. doi:10.5465/amj.2010.52814599

Woodland, M., Martin, J., Hill, R., & Worrell, F. (2009). The most blessed room in the city: The influence of a youth development program on three young black males. *The Journal of Negro Education*, *78*(3), 233–245.

Wyche, J. H., & Frierson, H. T. Jr. (1990). Minorities at majority institutions. *American Association for the Advancement of Science*, *249*(4972), 989–991. doi:10.1126cience.2396103 PMID:2396103

Yancy, G. (2008). *Black bodies, white gazes: The continuing significance of race*. Rowman & Littlefield Publishers.

Yin, R. (2014). *Case study research: Design and methods* (5th ed.). SAGE.

Chapter 20
The Cost of Success for BRMI Leaders

Helen Ezenwa
DePaul University, USA

ABSTRACT

Black, racialized minorities, and Indigenous leaders (BrmI) in higher education are part of an elite group of educators. Less than 5% of full professors are Black and Hispanic, and it is typically from this pool that academic leaders (e.g., Provost, Dean) are selected. This research aims to understand one potential reason for lack of ascension into positions of power for academic leaders of color: the cost of that success. This study hypothesizes that academic BrmI leaders consider the interpersonal and intrapersonal time-based cost of their career success to be greater than their white counterparts. It also anticipates the support that BrmI academic leaders accumulate—social, capital, and institutional support—may be perceived to lessen that overall cost. Over 100 tenured-track BrmI leaders in higher education were surveyed to evaluate their perception of the cost of success, and 26 completed the survey. The results can assist in encouraging interventions to these costs to increase the number of BrmI leadership roles in higher education.

INTRODUCTION

Character cannot be developed in ease and quiet. Only through experience of trial and suffering can the soul be strengthened, ambition inspired, and success achieved.

—Helen Keller

Success reflects the accomplishment of a goal or purpose. Leaders are often considered pillars of professional success given the tournament-style competition to achieve promotions at work (Connelly et al., 2014). That said, "winning" this competition to transcend into a leadership position is a costly pursuit as cognitive and emotional resources are exhausted to obtain and retain a level of success (Yukl, 2012). For example, leadership in the corporate space has its own challenges, including things such as being

DOI: 10.4018/978-1-6684-2314-1.ch020

beholden to a Board of Directors, as well as meeting the demands of the clients, employees, and organizational operations. These demands are magnified for leaders in higher education, where leadership can be particularly personally costly due to the human capital demands and expectations, such as responsibilities for student learning outcomes relative to shifting job market demands, coordinating complex curricula, and management and evaluation of a highly specialized, empowered personnel, such as faculty (O*NET, n.d.). In addition to the financial demands in the business of higher education, there is also great pressure on leaders to create and deliver a customized educational product that meets the needs of the consumer in a context where consumers are highly attuned to return on investment (Blaschke et al., 2014).

Given the intricacies of these demands, many have said that there is a cost to successful accession into and through leadership roles in a professional space (Baez, 2000). When you intersect race and professional leadership, there are new layers of demands that BrmI in leadership positions must bear, especially in a context where, in large part, organizations are playing catch-up with respect to creating progressive, inclusive policies to combat racism (Trenerry & Paradies, 2012), and where effective strategies to counteract bias and restriction of economic opportunities for BrmI are hard to come by (Dovidio & Gaertner, 2004; Gaertner & Dovidio, 2000). More pointedly, the cost of ascending to leadership positions for BrmI may be greater than for white counterparts, considering the adage that a Black person must work "twice as hard for half as much" (DeSante, 2013) (This adage is often shared by Black parents to their children.) Research evidence offers some initial support for this idea: research from a recent National Bureau of Economic research shows that Black employees received laser-like surveillance from supervisors, which negatively impacted performance reviews and wages, which, over time lead to larger racial gaps in the workforce (Cavounidis & Lang, 2015).

Applying an evidence-based lens to the "twice as hard for half as much" adage within the context of higher education leadership, this research study will first establish if the time-based cost of professional success for BrmI leaders in higher education is, in fact, perceived to be greater when compared to white counterparts. For instance, this research study will examine if the additional effort required of a BrmI, who strove to attain a top academic leadership position may come at the sacrifice of time spent on their interpersonal and intrapersonal relationships (Social Sciences Feminist Network Research Interest Group, 2017), such as family time, health, community investment, and the like. A second aim of this research is to evaluate attributes that predict the relative time-based costs of success for BrmI leaders in higher education. Stress occurs when you overtax personal resources, and that overtaxing of resources is a direct personal cost. Conservation of Resources Theory suggests that the costliness of leadership ascension for BrmI may be mitigated by having enough resources to devote to the mobility's challenges (Hobfoll, 1989). Specifically, social support (Cohen & Wills, 1985), capital support, and institutional support are three forms of resources that may mitigate that costliness by replenishing a BrmI's resource coffers. *Social support* reflects interpersonal support, such as mental, spiritual or sponsor/mentor support. *Capital support* reflects the political skill that a BrmI leader may have deployed to navigate their upward leadership trajectory more efficiently. Finally *institutional support* reflects the climate of inclusion that a BrmI worked in during their ascendency, and includes the dimensions of equitable employment practices, integration of differences and inclusion in decision-making. In examining each of these forms of support, this research will examine the extent to which BrmI leaders in higher education perceive that the time-based cost of their career to their intrapersonal and interpersonal relationships was less, equal, or more costly when directly compared to their white counterparts, relative to the capital they accumulated. Because of extensive research on the stigma and discrimination costs incurred by the BrmI (Mekawi et

Figure 1. Hypothesized Relationships

al., 2021), I anticipate the costs to be *greater* and therefore also want to understand if various forms of support (social, capital, and institutional) mitigate some of the cost. Please see Figure 1.

This research is important for several reasons. First, the evaluation of the time-based cost of leadership ascension will be examined in a higher education context. Typically, such contexts lean more liberal and whiter, espousing many commitments to equality and justice. Yet we know a pernicious form of racism, *aversive racism,* thrives in such environments (Dovidio & Gaertner, 2004; Gaertner & Dovidio, 2000). Aversive racism is non-blatant racism, and instead is the neglect of or the turning of a blind-eye through policies, practices, and cultural pressures that allow white people to keep power (e.g., deciding to not engage in blind resume review) (Gaertner & Dovidio, 2000; Roberts & Rizzo, 2020). The present research will provide some portion of evidence of the costs of success for the BrmI relative to their white counterparts—which reflects a form of aversive racism—in institutions that historically support more egalitarian values. Description of additional costs for BrmI leaders in higher education will provide a clear mandate for an improved ethnically and racially diverse leadership promotion and retention strategy in this industry.

A related reason that this research is important includes the *meaning* of a cost discrepancy. If there are greater costs associated with leadership accession for BrmI, it alerts institutions that they need to (a) work harder to minimize these costs for the sake of true equity, and (b) work harder to minimize these costs for the sake of not burning out their BrmI leaders (Haberman, 2005). Further, if there are cost differences between BrmI and their white counterparts that are minimized by certain resources, this should activate sponsorship networks that are rife with the most impactful resources, as when senior level leaders provide more support to those more junior (Stanton-Salazar, 2011). In other words, this research's results will also give clearer direction about *what types* of support reduce the costs of leadership ascension for BrmI academics. Further, university administrators and human resource policy makers who are aware of this research's findings can provide more visibility around the problem of unequal costs so that allies and advocates can be confronted with these costs and begin to address the inequities (Melaku et al., 2020).

Finally, this research is important because quite clearly North America struggles with placement of BrmI in positions of power at historically majority institutions. A recent article in *The New York Times* article identified 992 people who represent the faces of power in the United States (Lu, D., Huang, J.,

Seshagiri, A., Park, H. & Griggs, T., 2020) . While 40% of the U.S. population identify as Black, Hispanic, Asian, Native American or multi-racial, only 20% of the 992, comprise the top academic leadership jobs. Of the presidencies of the 25 highest ranked institutions of higher education listed in *U.S. News and World Report,* only Massachusetts Institute of Technology has a Hispanic president. Research that investigates impediments to upward mobility at work can add to the narrative about what can clear the path for BrmI to ascend into more senior positions.

To evaluate the proposed research, this study focuses on a select sample of BrmI leaders in higher education. Due to the limited number of participants that exist in this elite group of professional educators and administrators, the survey distribution will be limited to those in the president, provost, chancellor and dean, chair and program director positions. Research shows that Blacks and Hispanics represent less than 5% of full professors (Perna, 2001), which is a job title typically required for advanced academic leadership roles, further limiting the sample. Responses from these most senior roles in higher education will inform the attributes of success relative to the cost of success.

THEORY AND HYPOTHESES

In this section, I review why being a BrmI in a professional space may be costly to a BrmI: stigmatization, discrimination and bias, and disinterest to social relationships. Each of these reasons for costliness hinges on the consistent, unfair devaluation of racial identify, largely based on attributes that signal membership in a racial group, such as skin color, language used, and styling choices. These reasons for time-based costliness are each discussed next.

Stigma's Cost to the Black, Racialized Minority and Indigenous People

Stigma occurs when a perceiver attaches negative meaning to a benign attribute or aspect of a person (Goffman, 1959; Major & O'Brien, 2005). Stigmatization harms the recipient because an unfair judgment (and subsequent reaction) is made about them simply because they possess some defining characteristic, such as an accent, a wheelchair, or, pertinent here, attributes that signal racial identity. This harm accrues because of how a person from a stigmatized group is made to feel (typically: different; negative) and the outcome or results of that feeling (Major et al., 2003). As such, being stigmatized is connected to a decline in mental and physical health as well as social status (Major & O'Brien, 2005). When the stress of coping with stigma is unabated, research demonstrates this causes trauma in the body (Hatzenbuehler et al., 2013; McEwen & Stellar, 1993). The health-impacting role of stigma-induced stress has presented itself in several models that depict the stigma process. One such model is Minority Stress Theory, which examines how social position (and social power) influence racialized minority individual's daily lived experience and highlights how both external stigmatizing pressures and internal stress-based responses erode well-being (Hatzenbuehler et al., 2013).

Stigma also impacts the BrmI people through intangible thoughts allocated to them. The cost as it relates to stigma and BrmI is the energy spent on navigating the traffic of associations or assumptions made based on the group(s) others assign you to due to your physical features (Zhang et al., 2020). For example, academics have been found to second guess their placements due to comments made regarding their ethnic backgrounds rather than their academic acumen (Niemann, 2003). This navigation causes rumination when thoughts could otherwise be professional or personal in meaning. This navigation also causes stress because the person being stigmatized is consistently feeling uncertain about how any interpersonal interaction will go. When resources are allocated to coping with uncertainty and anxiety, the stigmatized person may feel less focused on core job responsibilities, with the consequence being that they must spend more time on their work to complete it—let alone trying to advance into leadership positions.

Bias and Discrimination's Cost to the Brml

In addition to stigma, bias and discrimination also increase the cost of career progress for BrmI. If stigma reflects thoughts and stereotypes made about an attribute, *bias* reflects the summarizing negative attitude—specifically the prejudice—that develops toward a particular group as a result of internalizing those stigmatizing thoughts. From bias (an attitude), people act discriminatorily (a behavior) (Ajzen, 1991). In the context of the BrmI people, *bias* is prejudice towards BrmI, manifesting often as discriminatory behavior that is unjust, exclusionary, or otherwise detrimental toward that group. Discrimination toward BrmI *at work* manifests through both macro decision making (e.g., who is interviewed; who is hired) to micro decision-making (e.g., who receives credit for performance), in addition to its non-work applications (e.g., housing) (Pager & Shepherd, 2008). Examples and details of bias and discrimination are covered next.

Through self-reported data, research finds that racial bias in the workplace towards Black women strongly exists (Hughes & Dodge, 1997). Regular encounters with racial bias depletes energy needed to do one's job well. Many BrmI have found that there is a time-based cost to storing up or regularly replenishing this energy to continue to perform at an optimal level (Deitch et al., 2003). As an illustrative example, in responding to a question about racialized minority women in science and the experience of bias in academia during a recent podcast, Dr. Suzet McKinney described how she has seen minorities in STEM academic positions experience more bias than whites. She recalled how previous faculty discouraged racialized minorities from selecting certain complex research topics and rigorous academic courses (Adil & Negron, n.d.), presumably because of the bias that minorities did not have appropriate cognitive research ability for such challenging work. She elaborated that: " unfortunately I think that women experience bias much more than men and I also think that minorities experience bias much more than our white counterparts and my life and my career has certainly been no exception to that" (Adil & Negron, n.d.). For Dr. McKinney, establishing and building her reputation as an academic was made that much more difficult because her peers held the attitude that she did not "fit" with challenging work assignments. Her thesis chair questioned her topic and referred to it as a fad. Other professors prescribed that she take the most difficult science courses first or stack them with challenging non-STEM core requirements as a strategy to weed her out. Dr. McKinney still succeeded in her studies and career, but her path was not easy given the prevailing attitude of "doubt" about her abilities; she had to rely on her will and drive to push through, essentially devoting more time to building herself up, re-focusing on her values, and fending off the persistent doubt levied on her by those meant to manage her doctoral education. Her journey embodies the fact that inherently there is, then, a cost to doing worthy work—in this case, taking time to fight for the space to do that work—that will earn a BrmI merit and acclaim. It is easy to see why the next career step—from establishing a professional research stream (in the case described above) to management of other faculty—may feel particularly costly.

In addition to racial bias, another obstacle that BrmI are faced with in the workplace is discrimination, which is the unjust treatment of certain categories of people. This discrimination manifests at work as unfair pay, promotion, performance evaluation, and recruitment and selection practices. Even though Title VII of the 1964 Civil Rights Act made discrimination in the workplace based on race illegal, the most experience with discrimination in the workplace is reported by African Americans and the least by their white counterparts (Hirsh & Lyons, 2010). Another damning experience relates to the *rate* of discrimination at work: Around 80,000 claims are filed annually regarding discrimination in the workplace with the EEOC and other civil rights agencies, which reflect the prevalence of discrimination and its impact (Bielby, 2000). (Only about 15% of those cases result in relief—that is, compensation—for the aggrieved party (Jameel, 2019).). Outside of reported filings, a recent survey of Americans indicated that more than half of Blacks have said they still feel discrimination due to the color of their skin. They have experienced discrimination in the way of job promotion, hiring, and by not being seen as intelligent or capable (Horowitz et al., 2019). Stereotypes have also played a role in inhibiting opportunities—that is, activating discrimination. Stereotypes that have existed for Blacks in the United States, for example, are vast, and at their core show up as perceptions of incompetence (and resulting behavior toward this group) in the workplace (Carton & Rosette, 2011).

When leadership and race meet, it can intensify discriminatory behavior. BrmI women have reported feeling stereotyped due to management or co-workers' discomfort with their skin color, which contribute to lost opportunities in promotion to leadership roles. This has been most apparent for BrmI women (Sanchez-Hucles & Davis, 2010). Unfortunately, these stereotypes could sometimes play out in the hiring process, which is a barrier of entry for diverse faculty and leadership in higher education (Hughes & Dodge, 1997), with the unfortunate consequence of BrmI professionals having to spend more time within the hiring process (e.g., apply to more positions; dealing with unexpected barriers to entry). In aggregate, the cost of discrimination is unrewarded work, unoffered job opportunities, and unacknowledged effort, all of which time for the BrmI professional to counteract if they wish to ascend into positions of leadership in the workplace.

Contextual cues highlight why discrimination at work (in all its forms) exists.

Discrimination is commonly experienced by employees whose superiors feel that it is condoned in the workplace by management (Trentham & Larwood, 1998), which indicates that attitudes of permissiveness can increase tolerance for discrimination. Further, organizations that do not invest in just, fair, and transparent systems for hiring, training, and performance evaluations create environments where demographic features become a basis for decision-making (Nishii, 2012). Finally "taste-based" racial discrimination (that is, discrimination rooted in stigma and bias specifically related to race) persists even when disconfirming evidence is presented, which suggests that the enormity and embeddedness of cultural/social attitudes toward race do not easily shift in professional environments that historically purport to rely on data.

Even though blatant discrimination in the workplace may be declining (at a rate of about 8%; Dovidio & Gaertner, 2004), the narrative does not appear to be improving overall because, increasingly, racialized minorities report experiencing covert microaggressions (Basford et al., 2014; Williams, 2019a, 2019b). In the workplace, microaggressions are comments or actions that are made by a BrmI person's colleagues that are meant to undermine and belittle BrmI. An example microaggression would be to tell a BrmI colleague that their presentation was "articulate"—while culturally "articulate" is a compliment with a history of being derogatory because it is implied that what is actually meant is "articulate, *for a Black person.*" Frustratingly, researchers have even found that microaggressive behavior has a negative (physical, psychological) impact on other BrmI people that *witness* these microaggressions, not just the victims themselves, because it implies a culture permissive of stereotyping (Basford et al., 2014).

For the BrmI person experiencing a microaggression, the impact is just as profound: it undermines the person's sense of confidence and well-being, and can interrupt a person's sense of efficacy around their work (Williams, 2019a, 2019b). The BrmI professional must, therefore, invest time in coping with this aggression. As such, clearly for the BrmI it is costly (in many senses, but here, specifically, in terms of time-based cost) to psychologically cope with microaggressions at work as they progress in their career. In addition to combating discrimination that impacts the psyche, racial discrimination can also manifest itself in physical health polarity for BrmI (Deitch et al., 2003). The cost of discrimination and bias experienced by the BrmI spans to a BrmI people's financial health, too. Financial costs can arise through the lens of tournament theory, which is an organizational environment where resources, rewards, and promotions are finite and allocated according to who is best performing (Connelly et al., 2014). For the BrmI person, performing at a level required to achieve rewards is made that much harder by (a) the automatic downgrading of performance and abilities inherently in the stereotyping process, and (b) the emotional and energetic expenses of operating in an environment where one must cope with microaggression, discrimination, bias, and stigma. The BrmI loses finite, valuable time addressing and coping with these discriminatory processes.

Disinterest in Social Relationship's Cost to the Black, Racialized Minority, and Indigenous People

This section will outline the costliness of advancement for BrmI because of their comparatively weak (to white) social networks. This perspective is derived from an analysis of the consequences of stereotyping at work; the consequences of being seen as someone who is treated consistently unfairly; and the challenges of pushing those in one's network to suppress prejudicial thoughts.

As described above, BrmI are less likely to thrive at work because of stigma, bias, and discrimination—they may be denied promotions, training opportunities, or even jobs. This reduces their social capital because, consequently, they have less social status given their comparative deficit in career success. For this reason, they may be less likely to develop a strong social network, and must—to counteract this—spend more of their time building their network. Because most academic leadership positions require using one's network to advance objectives (e.g., a tenured professor can tell their Dean "No" with little job security repercussions, so a Dean may instead rely on the strength of their relationship with a faculty member when making a request), this makes the difficulties of leadership in an academic unit that much harder.

Bearing witness to (or even participating in the occurrences of) discrimination and bias can deter whites from meaningful and supportive relationships with their Black and Brown colleagues (Kulik et al., 2008; Pryor et al., 2004). In an effort to rationalize the outcome and avoid their own discomfort at seeing an unfair process, a majority employee may view a BrmI who was treated unfairly during an organizational decision as toxic, tacitly undeserving, or even pity the person (Trentham & Larwood, 1998). These reasons further weaken a BrmI's social network, making it increasingly challenging to lead others through softer means of influence at work.

BrmI must, consequently, spend more time proactively making professional connections, and must work harder to form bonds through the morass of stereotyping. In effect, they must engage in activities or behaviors that *suppress* prejudicial behavior of others (Crandall & Eshleman, 2003). Justification-suppression theory (Crandall & Eshleman, 2003) describes how overt attempts to undermine stereotypes can jolt an observer into reducing their own prejudice against an actor. As a non-race-related example, a fat-bodied secret shopper drinking a milkshake (which aligns with the stereotype that fat people over-indulge) were treated more poorly than a fat-bodied secret shopper drinking a Diet Coke (which aligns with the stereotype that fat-bodied people must be trying to reduce their weight by controlling calories) (King et al., 2006). Relevant to race-based prejudice, Black workers are perceived as more "professional" when they engage in code-switching behaviors, such as adjusting their speech or styling to reflect white norms (McCluney et al., 2021). Black workers, then, must *actively work* to manage their fit with white professional standards, which again takes from their finite, valuable time (to monitor the environment for opportunities to switch and to actually multi-task and switch). In essence, to suppress the stereotype levied by white professional culture, there is a notable time-based cost to Black employees.

Prior research has revealed the systemic discrimination within organizations that stem from a cycle of discouraging BrmI to seek opportunities of growth and lower their expectations for opportunities of power or advancement by inundating them with remedial tasks and blocking access to social networks, which leave BrmI at a loss when advocating for their own career (Greenhaus et al., 1990). Research from an EEOC African American workgroup report highlighted a disadvantage in the labor market for Blacks due to having weaker social networks than other groups (EEOC, n.d.) And the duty to make up for this weaker social network falls squarely on the shoulders of the BrmI: rates of advocacy, coaching, mentorship, and sponsorship is lower for BrmI than for majority workers (Greenhaus et al., 1990). As such, to counteract all these effects of systematic discrimination—that is, to suppress the prejudicial stereotypes, BrmI employees are placed in the position to go above and beyond to be rewarded. Going above and beyond means, at its core, spending more time on work. For instance, for an BrmI professional's work to be seen and to make their talents known since they are not afforded the social networks held by their white counterparts, BrmI must invest far more time in self-advocacy, which is a very real cost with respect to time, energy, and emotional resources, to name only a few. BrmI must spend more time attempting to find opportunities to take on challenging, growth-oriented work, must be very intentional and vocal about their contributions, and must continually, proactively grow their network because it will not contain the same pace of organic growth as their white counterparts.

TALLYING THE PERSONAL COSTS TO BLACK, RACIALIZED MINORITY, AND INDIGENOUS PEOPLE

As a clear example of this, consider the case highlighted in a recent Chronicle of Higher Education article reviewing the Nikole Hannah-Jones tenure case. Ms. Hannah- Jones was initially denied tenure at North Carolina Chapel Hill School of Journalism over controversy of her research. Her research was focused on the origins of slavery in the United States and its connection to systemic racism. She advocated clearly for the need for critical racial theory. A board member that felt that this is not something he wanted the school to be associated with exhibited his influence with the schools' Dean in an attempt to discourage hiring Nikole Hannah-Jones (with tenure). Historically board members have not gotten involved with the tenure process, but clearly BrmI person Ms. Hannah-Jones received all-too-common hyper-monitoring of her work (Cavounidis & Lang, 2015). Witnessing the aftermath of the situation, a chairperson of the North Carolina Black Caucus commented on the fact that these types of things happen because there is not (diverse) representation when decisions are being made. This results in missed opportunities for BrmI people (Stripling, 2021).

For academic BrmI leaders, considering the costs of leadership ascension, a plethora of resources are needed to succeed at work. The resources include but are not limited to time, money, patience, persistence, and coping (Pryor et al., 2004). Importantly and quite obviously, these resources are finite. As such, because BrmI people are challenged with attempting to shed being stereotyped and discriminated against even after achieving success (Pinel, 1999), expending additional time-based resources at work to counteract stigma, bias, and discrimination, to advocate for one's work product and achievements when otherwise they would be overlooked, and to build one's professional network, as required by leadership roles, can easily and naturally pull resources from other life domains. Specifically, I argue that the time-based resources that the BrmI must invest beyond their majority counterparts must be taken from other domains (given the finite nature of time), including the personal relationships they develop with others (i.e., family, community, friendships), and personal relationships they have with themselves (i.e., their time spent on activities that support their health; their own stress regulation; their own self-care; their own leisure time). Importantly, I must note a distinctive use of "health" second hypothesis: here health reflects investment in health-promotion behaviors (which functions as a resource, much like time spent on self-care functions as a resource), rather than health as an eventual dependent variable (e.g., blood pressure, as been evaluated in Minority Stress Theory models). As such, I hypothesize that academic BrmI leaders will perceive that they have spent less time on interpersonal and intrapersonal relationships as they moved into leadership roles than their majority counterparts.[1]

Hypothesis 1: BrmI people will report spending less time (a) with their family, (b) on their community, and (c) on their friendships than their white counterparts.

Hypothesis 2: BrmI people will report spending less time (a) on their health, (b) on stress management, (c) on self-care, and (d) on leisure than their white counterparts.

Resources that Mitigate the Cost of BrmI Career Success

I anticipate that the time-based cost of success for academic BrmI leaders to be both interpersonally and intrapersonally high. Understanding this, there are factors that can reduce those costs. The main way that these costs are reduced is by offsetting resource loss (e.g., more time, energy spent on developing one's professional network) with resource gain, which is one of the central tenants of Conservation of Resources theory (Hobfoll, 1989; Hobfoll et al., 2017). When resources are gained (or off-set), BrmI may feel less stressed about their resource usage because the total "cost" is reduced (Hobfoll, 1989), which incidentally can also stall the effect of stress on cognition (which is required for work performance) (Lupien et al., 2007). (It is true that actually acquiring the resources to offset resource loss associated with succeeding at work as a BrmI person can, on its own, be costly.) This off-setting effect is echoed by the Stress Buffering Hypothesis, which states in particular that social support ameliorates the intensity of stressors (Cohen & Wills, 1985). Through an appraisal of the stressor process, resources that help offset costs make stress feel more manageable, like the prospects of success feel less hopeless or doubtful in the face of the stressor, or that the focal person has specific aid to cope with the stressor (Cohen & Wills, 1985; Lazarus & Folkman, 1987). This is true specifically for more intense social stressors (Wilcox, 1981) and those coping with not being rewarded equitably for their efforts (Ducharme & Martin, 2000), such as the recurrent pressure on a BrmI person to invest in their work to get ahead. Moreover, these sources of support can be essential in coping with the stressful demands found in leadership positions. There are many different types of support, but in general support for work-related endeavors can be seen as a tool or network to cope, grow, and/or excel. The three that I will focus on in this dissertation are social support, capital support, and institutional support.

Social support. Social support is defined as the feeling of being cared for, and/or provided with the resources to cope with stressors of any kind by another person. Social support can, therefore, manifest as the belief that you are being looked after by someone in your trusted social network (Cobb, 1976). Another manifestation of social support involves the perception of having access to a community that can be relied on for intel, and other concrete assistance (Viswesvaran et al., 1999). Social support is an important element of being successful and productive in the workplace because it implies that people help you, tend to your needs, and proactively ensure that you receive the resources that you need (Cohen & Wills, 1985; Kossek et al., 2012). When faculty, BrmI staff and students experience the availability of supportive relationships and social network of peers there is a positive influence on growth and retention at the organization (Greenhaus et al., 1990). With social support, academic BrmI leaders offset the cost of hyper investment in their own professional network because the fruits of their own social network give them the material support they need to offset the time-based costliness of contending with leadership ascension as a BrmI professional. They may also reap the benefit of personal sponsorship, such as when someone helps the BrmI academic leader navigate organizational politics or promote career growth through the work of "forging connections" by the mentors for their academic leader mentees (Zambrana et al., 2015). Four forms of social support will be explored: personal social support, mental health support, spiritual support, and sponsor/coach/mentor support.

Capital support. Capital support for our purposes is support that directly advances or advocates for the goals of an individual (Seibert et al., 2001). Leaders of color are put at a disadvantage due to systemic racism and discrimination in the workplace as reviewed earlier. That disadvantage lends itself to a drive for capital support in the organization to assist with mitigating stress and advocating advancement—or put another way, BrmI academic leaders may directly attempt to build their own capital support. One particular form of capital support will be evaluated here: the political skill of the BrmI academic leader. Political skill is a resource that reflects an academic leader's strength and quality of political network, as well as their adeptness and authenticity at navigating critical network-based relationship (Ferris et al., 2005). When a BrmI leader builds their own political capital, leadership influence occurs more frequently, productivity (efficiency) increases, and their ability to manage a team improves (Ahearn et al., 2004; Brouer et al., 2013; Harris et al., 2007; Munyon et al., 2013), which both reduce the overall time-based costs of these leadership activities. In essence, a politically skilled BrmI professional will offset some time-based costs of working while being a BrmI person with efficient network building.

Institutional support. The final area type of support is institutional support which, in the context of this dissertation, is considered a level of assistance provided by the organization in order to accomplish the demands of one's role. As documented above, leaders of color are faced with racism and other forms of discrimination on a daily basis. Support from the institution helps in coping with those challenges and it helps to maintain a path to success. This support can come in many forms, but, as Nishii (2012) describes support that increases *fairness and equity* in the organization best supports historically disadvantaged groups. She describes three institutional support elements to this end: equitable employment practices (e.g., just decision-making procedures as it relates to pay, promotions, etc…); integration of differences (e.g., respect, honor, and voice for *all* employees); and inclusion in decision-making (e.g., transparency and voice given to *all* employees). How might such practices play out to reduce the costliness of success for BrmI people? BrmI Faculty are disproportionately asked to serve the needs of people from their own ethnic backgrounds, which is coined "cultural taxation" and reflects additional time-based resources a BrmI professional must invest at work (Baez, 2000). Further, research shows how women and BrmI people routinely engage in more "care" work, such as serving on committees, task forces, groups that concern themselves with building culture, all at the expense of progress toward "objective" career success (unless they commit additional time compared to their majority peers) (Social Sciences Feminist Network Research Interest Group, 2017). University policies that clearly state how this service work is distributed and rewarded, that clearly give BrmI faculty a voice in *how* the work is carried out, and that gives BrmI a voice in how the workload is allocated would reflect a university that provides its BrmI faculty institutional support. The forms of institutional support described here should provide BrmI with supplementary resources that reduce the total time investment a BrmI person is expected to make beyond their white peers, or even stem the loss of resources related to discrimination, bias, and stigma less likely given this form of support's commitment to developing a more equitable workplace culture, which together means that the time-based cost of success on other domains is reduced for BrmI working in environments of greater institutional support.

Hypothesis 3a: (a) Social support, (b) mental health support, (c) spiritual support, and (d) sponsor/coach/mentor support will be negatively related to loss of time spent with *family* relative to white counterparts.

Hypothesis 3b: (a) Social support, (b) mental health support, (c) spiritual support, and (d) sponsor/coach/mentor support will be negatively related to loss of time spent with *community* relative to white counterparts.

Hypothesis 3c: (a) Social support, (b) mental health support, (c) spiritual support, and (d) sponsor/coach/mentor support will be negatively related to loss of time spent with *friendships* relative to white counterparts.

Hypothesis 3d: (a) Social support, (b) mental health support, (c) spiritual support, and (d) sponsor/coach/mentor support will be negatively related to loss of time spent with *health* relative to white counterparts.

Hypothesis 3e: (a) Social support, (b) mental health support, (c) spiritual support, and (d) sponsor/coach/mentor support will be negatively related to loss of time spent with *stress management* relative to white counterparts.

Hypothesis 3f: (a) Social support, (b) mental health support, (c) spiritual support, and (d) sponsor/coach/mentor support will be negatively related to loss of time spent with *self-care* relative to white counterparts.

Hypothesis 3g: (a) Social support, (b) mental health support, (c) spiritual support, and (d) sponsor/coach/mentor support will be negatively related to loss of time spent with *leisure* relative to white counterparts.

Hypothesis 4a: Political skill will be negatively related to loss of time spent with *family* relative to white counterparts.

Hypothesis 4b: Political skill will be negatively related to loss of time spent with *community* relative to white counterparts.

Hypothesis 4c: Political skill will be negatively related to loss of time spent with *friendships* relative to white counterparts.

Hypothesis 4d: Political skill will be negatively related to loss of time spent with *health* relative to white counterparts.

Hypothesis 4e: Political skill will be negatively related to loss of time spent with *stress management* relative to white counterparts.

Hypothesis 4f: Political skill will be negatively related to loss of time spent with *self-care* relative to white counterparts.

Hypothesis 4g: Political skill will be negatively related to loss of time spent with leisure relative to white counterparts.

Hypothesis 5a: (a) Equitable employment practices, (b) integration of differences, and (c) inclusion in decision-making will be negatively related to loss of time spent with *family* relative to white counterparts.

Hypothesis 5b: (a) Equitable employment practices, (b) integration of differences, and (c) inclusion in decision-making will be negatively related to loss of time spent on *community* relative to white counterparts.

Hypothesis 5c: (a) Equitable employment practices, (b) integration of differences, and (c) inclusion in decision-making will be negatively related to loss of time spent on *friendships* relative to white counterparts.

Hypothesis 5d: (a) Equitable employment practices, (b) integration of differences, and (c) inclusion in decision-making will be negatively related to loss of time spent on *health* relative to white counterparts.

Hypothesis 5e: (a) Equitable employment practices, (b) integration of differences, and (c) inclusion in decision-making will be negatively related to loss of time spent on *stress_management* relative to white counterparts.

Hypothesis 5f: (a) Equitable employment practices, (b) integration of differences, and (c) inclusion in decision-making will be negatively related to loss of time spent on *self-care* relative to white counterparts.

Hypothesis 5g: (a) Equitable employment practices, (b) integration of differences, and (c) inclusion in decision-making will be negatively related to loss of time spent on *leisure* relative to white counterparts.

METHOD

Participants

The total sample size goal for hypothesis testing was 43, based upon a power analysis computed using G*Power (multiple regression, moderate effect size, one-tailed test, alpha error rate of .05, and six total predictors). A Qualtrics survey was distributed to a total of 85 participants through a recruitment email. The link to the survey was embedded in the email. The email explains the purpose of the survey and addresses why the individual was selected to receive the email. The participants are BrmI leaders in higher education in North America and hold the positions of president, provost, chancellor, dean, chair, or program director. Given the limited number of these leaders in the highest rank of president, provost, chancellor and dean, the pool was expanded to included program director and chair. All genders were selected for the survey. The initially recruited participant was asked to forward the survey to anyone in their network who also met the study's inclusion criteria, for an increase of 28 additional respondents (i.e., the snowball technique). Participants are informed of the length of time anticipated to complete the survey, and that the data collected will be anonymous and confidential. The survey utilizes mixed method survey questions that include a Likert scale and open-ended questions.

Procedure

After an information sheet that outlined the study's purpose and requirements, participants who elected to participate in the research were shown a survey. The first set of questions asked inclusion criteria questions. The inclusion criteria questions asked if participants were 18 years of age or older, identified as a BrmI people, if they were tenured or tenured track professor in higher education, if they held a leadership position at their university and the name of the leadership position at the university. They were asked not to include the name of the university in their response. After answering questions verifying that they met the inclusion criteria, participants were told they would be asked to complete a survey containing multiple choice and short-answer questions about their experiences with success in higher education, their personality, and demographic information, such as age, race, gender, income, and years of service with their current/most recent organization, and within their career overall. The survey includes questions related to how costly they believe their career success has been relative to their white counterparts, as well as questions related to what forms of support were received during their career ascendancy. Several quality checks are embedded in the survey, and participants not meeting quality checks are not included in the final sample.

Measures

Below is a summary of the measures used in the survey instrument.

Interpersonal costs. These variables describe the relative costs of success regarding interpersonal costs of family, community involvement and friendships relative to whites (alpha reliability = .90, .96, .96, respectively). The items were derived from Keeney and colleagues (2013) measure of domain-based conflict; modifications include a stem that asked respondents to compare themselves to their white counterparts and a shift in referent from where work drew resources. An example item is *Throughout my career, compared to my white counterparts the time I spent on work cut into the time I spent on my family*. To tap different domains from which work could draw resources, "family" was replaced by community and relationships in subsequent questions. Three items were used for each referent (family, community, relationships). The response options ranged from 1 = much less time compared to my white counterparts to 5 = much more time compared to my white counterparts.

Intrapersonal costs. These variables describe the relative costs of success regarding interpersonal costs of health, self-care, stress management and leisure relative to whites (alpha reliability =.97, .99, .98, .97, respectively). The items were derived again from the Keeney and colleagues (2013) measure, with the same modifications except the domains included: health, stress management, self-care, and leisure. Three items were used for each referent. An example item is *Throughout my career, compared to my white counterparts my work keeps me from leisure more than I would have liked to*. The response options ranged from 1 = much less time compared to my white counterparts to 5 = much more time compared to my white counterparts.

Support. Three forms of support were evaluated. The directions for all forms of support read: You indicated you currently hold an academic leadership position. For these questions, consider the time in your career when you actively sought to advance into a leadership role(s). **Social support** is support provided by one's personal network. A single item was used to evaluate, separately, social support, mental health support, and spiritual support. An example item is: *I engage in social self-care (for example, engagement with a friend, family member, or message board) if I am upset*. These items were written for this survey, but the referent (social self-care, mental health support, spiritual support) were taken from Richards et al. (2010). Mentor/coach/sponsor support was evaluated using a single item (*I have a career mentor/coach/sponsor.*) from Riskin (1979).

Capital support was evaluated using Ferris and colleagues (2005) 18-item political skill measure (alpha reliability = .83). An example item is: *I am able to communicate easily and effectively with others*. Finally, **institutional support** was evaluated using Nishii's (2012) three-dimensional scale. Items were modified to reflect a referent of *university*. The first dimension, equitable employment practices, was measured by four items, with an example item being: *My university has a fair promotion process.* Unfortunately, the alpha reliability for this scale was below the acceptable threshold of significant, and "dropping" item(s) did not improve it. No subsequent analyses were performed with this variable. The second dimension, integration of differences, was measured by seven items, with an example item being: *My university provides safe ways for employees to voice their grievances* (alpha reliability = .86). The final dimension, inclusion in decision-making, was evaluated using four items, with an example item being: *In my university, employee input is actively sought* (alpha reliability = .87).

Control variables. This study controls for conscientiousness and resiliency. For BrmI to transcend into academic leadership positions, they must, as outlined, combat discrimination and bias. A particular level of conscientiousness and resiliency is needed for them to succeed, and we wanted to control for these influences relative to support. Conscientiousness was evaluated using Saucier's (1994) five-item scale, with an example item being: *Please rate the extent to which you think each statement describes you: organized* (alpha reliability = .93). Resiliency was evaluated using Smith's six-item scale (2008), with an example item being: *I tend to bounce back quickly after hard times* (alpha reliability = .73).

Qualitative questions. These questions were written only for background information only; no hypothesis testing will be derived from participant's answers to these questions. See Appendix A for a complete copy of the survey, including qualitative questions.

Demographics. This section controls for and allows the participant to self-identify the following: age, ethnicity, gender, marital status and sexual orientation. Table 1 includes a summation of these characteristics.

RESULTS

Means, standard deviations, and correlations are provided in Table 2. Hypotheses 1 and 2 will be assessed by evaluating the mean scores for the various "costs." Mean scores above 3 (neutral point) indicate greater cost perceptions by BrmI academic leaders, when comparing their experiences to white counterparts. Hierarchical regression was used to evaluate Hypotheses 3-5 (separately), with the control variables of conscientiousness and resiliency included in each model. For example, consider Hypothesis 3a: (a) social support, (b) mental health support, (c) spiritual support, and (d) sponsor/coach/mentor support will be negatively related to loss of time spent with *family* relative to white counterparts. In a hierarchical regression model, Step 1 will include conscientiousness and resiliency, and Step 2 will include the four forms of support.

Table 1. Descriptive Statistics of Demographic Variables

Minimum Age	*37*		
	Maximum Age	*68*	
	Mean Age	*50*	
Gender		*N*	*%*
	M	*11*	*46*
	F	*13*	*54*
	Total	*24*	*100*
Age		*N*	*%*
	30-40	*2*	*9*
	41-50	*8*	*35*
	51-60	*9*	*39*
	61-70	*4*	*17*
	Total	*23*	*100*
Marital Status		*N*	*%*
	M	*18*	*75*
	S	*6*	*25*
	Total	*24*	*100*
Ethnicity		*N*	*%*
	Black/African American	*20*	*83*
	Hispanic	*1*	*4*
	Asian	*3*	*13*
	Total	*24*	*100*
Sexual Orientation		*N*	*%*
	Heterosexual	*20*	*91*
	LGBTQ	*2*	*9*
	Total	*22*	*100*

Note: Not all participants provided demographic information.

Hypothesis Testing

H1a was supported: the interpersonal cost to family was greater than 3 (3.78), as was H1b (interpersonal cost to community; mean = 3.72) and H1c (interpersonal cost to friendships, 3.49). H2a was also sup-

Table 2. Means, Standard Deviations, and Correlations

	M	*SD*	1	2	3	4	5	6	7
1. Interpersonal cost: Family	3.782	0.736	.902[a]						
2. Interpersonal cost: Community Involvement	3.718	0.798	.761**	.955					
3. Interpersonal cost: Friendships	3.487	0.963	.633**	.545**	.957				
4. Intrapersonal cost: Health	3.731	0.975	.776**	.721**	.500**	.974			
5. Intrapersonal cost: Stress	3.692	0.859	.832**	.666**	.614**	.815**	.988		
6. Intrapersonal cost: Self-Care	3.744	0.850	.731**	.603**	.523**	.766**	.807**	.976	
7. Intrapersonal cost: Leisure	3.769	0.868	.753**	.717**	.443*	.695**	.617**	.669**	.971
8. Social support	4.040	1.248	0.068	0.078	-0.038	0.315	0.173	0.273	0.193
9. Mental health support	3.350	1.599	0.339	0.163	0.033	0.353	0.314	.470*	0.233
10. Spiritual support	3.810	1.497	-0.052	-0.192	-0.247	-0.165	-0.12	-0.093	0.159
11. Sponsor/coach/mentor support	3.270	1.402	-0.238	-.466*	-0.338	-0.081	-0.05	0.083	-0.287
12. Political skill	4.013	0.458	-0.128	-0.206	-0.065	0.161	-0.035	-0.003	-0.236
13. Integration of differences	3.269	0.683	-.436*	-0.313	-.413*	-0.339	-0.341	-0.303	-0.328
14. Inclusion in decision-making	3.308	0.779	-.390*	-.418*	-0.324	-0.352	-0.321	-0.168	-0.265
15. Conscientiousness	4.477	0.763	.416*	0.09	0.292	0.301	.440*	0.36	0.161
16. Resiliency	3.795	0.647	-0.168	-0.323	-0.154	-0.172	-0.262	-0.209	-0.206
17. Predominantly diverse university (0 = No, 1 = Yes)	0.385	0.496	-0.09	-0.22	-0.213	0.002	-0.181	-0.105	-0.033

	8	9	10	11	12	13	14	15	16	17
1. Interpersonal cost: Family										
2. Interpersonal cost: Community Involvement										
3. Interpersonal cost: Friendships										
4. Intrapersonal cost: Health										
5. Intrapersonal cost: Stress										
6. Intrapersonal cost: Self-Care										
7. Intrapersonal cost: Leisure										
8. Social support	--									
9. Mental health support	.474*	--								
10. Spiritual support	0.368	0.079	--							
11. Sponsor/coach/mentor support	0.337	0.207	0.197	--						
12. Political skill	0.185	0.012	-0.027	.414*	.826					
13. Integration of differences	0.256	-0.11	0.209	-0.001	0.012	.861				
14. Inclusion in decision-making	-0.218	-0.322	0.053	0.168	-0.054	.553**	.869			
15. Conscientiousness	-0.062	0.233	0.055	.399*	0.037	-0.346	-0.136	.931		
16. Resiliency	-0.204	-0.283	0.219	0.159	0.216	.395*	0.362	0.155	.733	
17. Predominantly diverse university (0 = No, 1 = Yes)	0.04	-0.074	0.157	0.248	0.247	0.036	0.096	0.151	0.11	--

Note. *N* = 26

* *p* < .05. ***p* < .01

[a] alpha reliabilities appear in the diagonal

ported: the intrapersonal cost to health was greater than 3 (3.73), as was H2b (intrapersonal cost to stress; mean = 3.69), H2c (intrapersonal cost to self-care, 3.74), and H2d (intrapersonal cost to leisure, 3.77).

H3a received mixed support (F = 3.02, p = .03; r2 = .48). Social support (H3a.a; B = .12, p = .37), mental health support (H3a.b; B = .11, p = .25), and spiritual support (H3a.c; B = -.02, p = .84) did not relate to loss of time spent with family relative to white counterparts. However, sponsor/coach/mentor support did, indicating that those BrmI individuals with greater sponsor/coach/mentor support perceived *less* loss of time with family relative to white counterparts (H3a.d, B = -.29, p = .01). These relationships persisted after controlling for conscientiousness (B = .58, p = .01) and resiliency (B = -.06, p = .79). That said, H3b also received mixed support (F = 2.30, p = .08; r2 = .41). Social support (H3b.a; B = .22, p = .16), mental health support (H3b.b; B = .04, p = .74), and spiritual support (H3b.c; B = -.08, p = .46) did not relate to loss of time spent with community involvement relative to white counterparts. However, sponsor/coach/mentor support did, indicating that those BrmI individuals with greater sponsor/coach/mentor support perceived *less* loss of time with community involvement relative to white counterparts (H3b.d, B = -.36, p = .01). These relationships persisted after controlling for conscientiousness (B = .39, p = .09) and resiliency (B = -.17, p = .49). H3c also received mixed support (F = 2.30, p = .11; r2 = .38). Social support (H3c.a; B = .26, p = .18), mental health support (H3b.b; B = -.05, p = .69), and spiritual support (H3c.c; B = -.15, p = .25) did not relate to loss of time spent with friendships relative to white counterparts. However, again sponsor/coach/mentor support did, indicating that those BrmI individuals with greater sponsor/coach/mentor support perceived *less* loss of time with friendships relative to white counterparts (H3c.d, B = -.37, p = .02). These relationships persisted after controlling for conscientiousness (B = .71, p = .01) and resiliency (B = -.06, p = .83). H3d received mixed2support (F = 2.50, p = .05; r2 = .45). Mental health support (H3d.b; B = .05, p = .69) and spiritual support (H3d.c; B = -.22, p = .09) did not relate to loss of time spent with health relative to white counterparts. However, social support (H3d.a; B = .46, p = .02) and sponsor/coach/mentor support did (H3d.d, B = -.30, p = .05) were significant. For those BrmI individuals with greater sponsor/coach/mentor support perceived *less* loss of time with health relative to white counterparts, but those with more social support experienced greater cost to health relative to white counterparts. This contrary finding will be discussed later. These relationships persisted after controlling for conscientiousness (B = .65, p = .21) and resiliency (B = .06, p = .85). H3e received no support (F = 2.48, p = 06; r2 = .44). Social support (H3e.a; B = .24, p = .16), mental health support (H3e.b; B = .03, p = .85), spiritual support (H3e.c; B = -.10, p = .39) and sponsor/coach/mentor support) H3e.d; B = -.22, p = .10) did not relate to loss of time spent on stress management relative to white counterparts. Also, H3f received no support (F = 1.87, p = 014; r2 = .37). Social support (H3f.a; B = .20, p = .26), mental health support (H3f.b; B = .15, p = .24), spiritual support (H3f.c; B = -.11, p = .36) and sponsor/coach/mentor support) H3f.d; B = -.11, p = .41) did not relate to loss of time spent on self-care relative to white counterparts. Finally, H3g received mixed support (F = 1/73, p = .17; r2 = .35). Social support (H3g.a; B = .20, p = .27), mental health support (H3g.b; B = .04, p = .77), and spiritual support (H3g.c; B = .10, p = .43) did not relate to loss of time spent on leisure relative to white counterparts. However, sponsor/coach/mentor support did, indicating that those BrmI individuals with greater sponsor/coach/mentor support perceived *less* loss of time on leisure relative to white counterparts (H3g.d, B = -.35, p = .02). These relationships persisted after controlling for conscientiousness (B = .46, p = .08) and resiliency (B = -.18, p = .52).

H4a did not receive support (F = 2.26, p = .11, r2 = .13) in that political skill did not negatively relate to loss of time spent with family relative to white counterparts (B = -.10, p = .73), nor did H4b: (F = 1.04, p = .39, r2 = .12) in that political skill did not negatively relate to loss of time spent with community relative to white counterparts (B = -.13, p = .70). H4c did not receive support (F = 1.04, p = .39, r2 = .12) in that political skill did not negatively relate to loss of time spent on friendships relative to white counterparts (B = .01, p = .97), nor did H4d (F = 1.62, p = .22, r2 = .18) in that political skill did not negatively relate to loss of time spent on health relative to white counterparts (B = .44, p = .31). H4e did not receive support (F = 3.24, p = .04, r2 = .31) in that political skill did not negatively relate to loss of time spent on stress management relative to white counterparts (B = .04, p = .91). Further, H4f did not receive support (F = 1.87, p = .16, r2 = .20) in that political skill did not negatively relate to loss of time spent on self-care relative to white counterparts (B = .08, p = .83). And finally,

H4g did not receive support (F = .99, p = .42, r2 = .12) in that political skill did not negatively relate to loss of time spent on leisure relative to white counterparts (B = -.38, p = .34).

H5a.b and H5a.c did not receive support (F = 2.48, p = .07, r2 = .31). Integration of differences (B = -.13, p = .58) and inclusion in decision making (B = -.21, p = .32) did not relate to loss of time spent with family relative to white counterparts, nor did H5b.b and H5b.c: (F = 1.65, p = .20, r2 = .23). Integration of differences (B = -.07, p = .81) and inclusion in decision making (B = -.33, p = .18) did not relate to loss of time spent with community relative to white counterparts. H5c.b and H5c.c did not receive support (F = 1.54, p = .23, r2 = .22). Integration of differences (B = -.32, p = .34) and inclusion in decision making (B = -.17, p = .55) did not relate to loss of time spent with friendships relative to white counterparts. H5d.b and H5d.c did not receive support (F = 1.35, p = .29, r2 = .20). Integration of differences (B = -.12, p = .76) and inclusion in decision making (B = -.30, p = .33) did not relate to loss of time spent on health relative to white counterparts. H5e.b and H5e.c did not receive support (F = 2.55, p = .07, r2 = .33). Integration of differences (B = .04, p = .90) and inclusion in decision making (B = -.19, p = .44) did not relate to loss of time spent on stress management relative to white counterparts. H5f.b and H5f.c did not receive support (F = 1.37, p = .28, r2 = .31). Integration of differences (B = -.12, p = .73) and inclusion in decision making (B = .02, p = .94) did not relate to loss of time spent on self-care relative to white counterparts. And finally, H5g.b and H5g.c did not receive support (F = .78, p = .55, r2 = .13). Integration of differences (B = -.25, p = .49) and inclusion in decision making (B = -.12, p = .67) did not relate to loss of time spent on leisure relative to white counterparts.

Supplemental Analyses

With respect to hours worked, those in the sample reported working about 41-50 hours per week as part of their professional obligations. On average, they reported working *more* hours than their white counterparts (mean = 3.93 on a scale from 1 = much less to 5 = much more). Ultimately, we did not control for the school type (predominantly diverse over not) because of concerns about sample size relative to number of variables in the model.

Discussion

Summary of Results

The first two hypotheses were fully supported by the data, which indicates that the BrmI participants in the sample perceived that their work requirements kept them from spending time with family, community, and friendships at a greater rate than their white counterparts. BrmI participants also reported that, because of their work, compared to their white counterparts, they spent less time investing in their health, stress management, self-care, and leisure. These results are striking because they indicate that BrmI participants felt they had less time for social activities that play a role in fundamental well-being, including ability to rebound, cope, or otherwise recover from acute stressors (Cohen & Wills, 1985; DuPont et al., 2020).

From this research's exploratory hypotheses that evaluated antecedents of BrmI participant's reduced time for social and physical caretaking of themselves, key influential variables were identified: sponsor/coach/mentor support reduced the *relative* perceived costs of the BrmI participants' work to their family time, community involvement, investment in friendships, time spent tending to physical health, and time spent enjoying leisure. BrmI participants are therefore suggesting that some parity in work investment relative to the opportunity cost of that investment with white counterparts, only when sponsor/coach/mentor support is provided. Institutional support—namely the robustness with which the participant's institution attempted to integrate trans-demographic differences and include underrepresented voices in decision-making—did not, in regression models, reduce the perception of interpersonal or intrapersonal costs. That said, examining the zero-order correlations between these variables revealed that further exploration in a more robust sample size may allow a statistically relevant relationship to be ascertained. Social capital (namely, political capital) also did not relate to perceptions of reduced costs relative to white counterparts, but this may indicate a small silver-lining: the onus of political skill is on the enactor to develop, hone, and practice this skill; these results *do not* suggest adding this skill practice to the already-full plate of BrmI university administrators.

Theoretical Implications

The fact that BrmI participants reported widespread relative costliness of success to their personal lives indicate that theories of career success must factor in that cost. Ascension to university administrative ranks clearly requires *more* investment by BrmI individuals relative to white counterparts. On a basic level, this pushes models of career success to "balance the equation"—if BrmI people are not ascending at the same rates as their white counterparts, bias, discrimination, and stigmatization clearly play an established role (e.g., which we already know with respect to gender) (Eddleston et al., 2004). But, also, what is the role of basic feelings of exhaustion or burnout given the amount of energy (relative to white peers) BrmI people must invest, especially that investment's opportunity cost to home, persona, leisure, and other health-physical and mental health-oriented areas of life? Setting aside aptitude, educational attainment, personality, and bias (Judge et al., 1995, 1999), what of the basic human factor (energy) in these models? Revisiting the adage that BrmI people must *work twice as hard for half as much*: of course mental fatigue accrues due to stigmatization and the need to approach or avoid such detrimental perceptions (Major & O'Brien, 2005; Pryor et al., 2004). However, based on this study's results, a deeper understand of the scope of this *work* needs investigation. This *work* must include the cost of work investment at the expense of personal growth and nurturance.

This research also provides some direction as to what types of support reduces the cost of ascension in the workplace for BrmI leaders. The data showed social support outweighed capital or institutional support for reducing that cost, and in particular having a sponsor/coach/mentor helped defray some relative personal life costs for BrmI leaders. The data supported the Stress Buffering Hypothesis (Cohen & Wills, 1985), which emphasizes that social networks play a key role in reducing the toll of stress by providing individuals with psychological resources, otherwise lost due to challenging events or chronic stressors. Why might this be? A sponsor, coach, and/or mentor has specific responsibility for providing the space needed for an individual to grow and thrive. Further, a sponsor is an influential advocate for a BrmI person that may not have access to those in decision making positions or certain social networks (Fu et al., 2014; Reskin, 1979). A coach focuses on enhancing skills or positioning leaders for the next opportunity, and a mentor is a confidant and guide for a leader in understanding and learning workplace experiences. Those BrmI participants with a sponsor/coach/mentor reported less perceived loss of time with family, community, friendships, health, and leisure relative to white peers. Yet this finding resurfaces the preceding question: if finding a sponsor/coach/mentor will ultimately reduce the mental burden of work investment for BrmI workers, what about the costs associated with *finding, nurturing,* and *collaborating* with that sponsor/coach/mentor? Mentoring is more effective when contact is frequent and involved (Scandura & Williams, 2001), and further race-matched mentor-proteges (and sponsor-sponsee) report more successful relationships (Ensher & Murphy, 1997; Ortiz-Walters & Gilson, 2005; Randel et al., 2021). The mentorship process itself, then, requires *more* investment (recruitment, selection, maintenance), adding to the prior definition of *work*. While we certainly do not downplay the significance of a BrmI leader having an invested sponsor/coach/mentor to making work investment feel more equitable compared to white counterparts; I do want to ask, theoretically, what is the true cost/benefit of that relationship?

There was no support for the fourth hypotheses. With respect to political skill, it appears that interpersonal savvy does not reduce the efforts required of BrmI individuals at work relative to their white peers, when considering those efforts cost on one's personal life. This could be attributed to the limited opportunities and positioning for political skill deployed by a BrmI person. These skills are, after all, groomed over years, even beginning outside of the office. Seen another way, through halo effects and snowballing privilege, the political skill of white counterparts may simply heed more benefit than their BrmI peers, making political skill a less potent tool for BrmI leaders to use to manage workload relative to white counterparts. (Of note: the results do not suggest that BrmI respondents use less political skill than their white counterparts. It says, instead, that it is not an effective means to reduce the cost of work to one's personal life relative to white peers.)

With respect to Hypotheses 5a-5g, research has also shown that at many times when BrmI leaders have ascended to roles of increased responsibility, they have still been historically left out of the decision-making process or been less exposed to the process. This may result in feeling that organizational efforts to integrate differences or include them in decision-making is too little (or too little too late), and therefore BrmI people may not see such institutional supports as assisting in the management of workload, relative to white peers. Further, white peers also benefit from these organizational efforts, meaning that—for example—inclusion of more voices in decision making means *all* voices are louder rather than just BrmI voices, negating the advantage to BrmI people. Further work is needed to tease apart if, why, and how political support and institutional support has less positive impact for BrmI leaders than anticipated, when considering these support's effects on offsetting the personal cost of work efforts.

Practical Implications

The results of this research can be applied to hiring and retention plans for senior leaders in higher education. The research suggests that establishing a structure of support that includes access to a sponsor/mentor/coach could assist with managing the basic workload (and consequently burnout) of BrmI leaders. This research also supports the growing movement towards inclusive leadership. Taking a closer look at the systems in place and the results that it has been producing can significantly shift BrmI representation that currently exists in higher education. This may be an opportunity to apply management expert's Deming's principle of transformation (Deming, 1986), specifically principle 7, which focus on leadership removing barriers to success such as the costs for success that were supported in this research. A clear barrier identified by this research is astoundingly simple **and** important: time. BrmI leaders perceive greater time investment in their career (at the expense of time spent in personal domains) for the same outcomes as white counterparts, creating a recipe for burnout and disengagement (Alarcon, 2011).

Strengths

This research included a rarified sample: tenured senior underrepresented leaders of color in higher education institutions. The most common job post in this sample was Dean, indicating that people of power, influence, and great achievement compose this sample. A glimpse into their perceptions of the work environment, especially on such a sensitive topic, makes this research meaningful because their voices are so rarely heard in academic research. Another strength of this research is the manifold ways in which support was evaluated. Investigated forms of support included the intrapersonal (in the form of personality), interpersonal (social support, political support), and intergroup (institutional support). This array of support gives a broader picture on what does (and does not) assist BrmI leaders with regulating their work input relative to white peers.

Limitations

Given the nature of the study, it was predicted that there will be a small sample size. In total, there were 40 attempts to complete the survey, but only 26 completed the survey. Interestingly, the drop-off occurred as soon as sensitive questions appeared, specifically when efforts *relative to white counterparts* were inquired about. As such, I believe the sensitivity of the questions with a very elite group of professionals resulted in a lower completion rate.

The survey was distributed to 100 plus individuals within the BrmI community, as well as allies. The majority of those that completed the survey were Black with a few Asian and one self-identified Hispanic. No one identified themselves as Indigenous, and as such, racial representation of the sample is not at its most effective. There were also a fairly even split between male and female respondents. Given there were fewer respondents at the highest senior levels in higher education (specifically the president, provost and chancellor level), separate future research on this cadre of people may be needed. Being in such a senior, elite position, it is possible the limited completions were related to not wanting to impact their representation of their institutions by completing the survey, capacity to take time to complete the survey given their multiple demands and responsibilities, or even (the lack of) interest in the subject matter after living the experience denoted in the survey questions. So, in sum, the representativeness of BrmI people was a limitation.

Future Research

One area ripe for future exploration is between-hierarchy differences in resources. While my sample size prevented such further research, it would be interesting to evaluate if, for example, political skill *did* have an impact at the highest echelon of a university (where more outward-facing jobs appear) because of this skill's emphasis on diverse social network development. Or, alternatively, if institutional supports provided to Deans (who are often the *beneficiaries* rather than the *creators* of such supports) provide more benefit than to the most senior leaders. Analyzing how resources help (or hinder) at different levels of leadership may expose, for BrmI leaders, escalating or deescalating costs to their personal lives

Another area for future research relates to intersectionality, specifically as it relates to gender. Given the lagging number of women in senior leadership positions (Samuelson et al., 2019), is there a compounding effect of reduced forms of support for BrmI academic leaders? Female BrmIs may experience increased stigmatization and stereotyping, leaving open questions of if higher thresholds of resources are needed to assist this group? (And returning to the question proposed in the theoretical implications, is there, then, a greater cost to BrmI *women*?). Of course, intersectional questions related to age, sexual orientation, colorism, and other demographic characteristics provide a great opportunity to investigate the equality of benefit of supports to those identifying as BrmI.

A final area for future research is conducting more in-depth interviews about the subject matters of this dissertation. These interviews could give us a better idea about more senior-level BrmI leader's unique costs given their greater leadership ascendency. For example, do the costs of leadership grow linearly, or exponentially—that is, are the costs from going from a faculty member to Associate Dean proportionate from going from the level of Dean to Provost? I may also learn if there are unique domains in which costs accrue, such as a disproportionate cost to family or community involvement, given the spread of emotional resources required to ascend into senior leadership positions.

CONCLUSION

This research hopes to advance the dialogue around inclusion of BrmI leaders that hold senior level positions in higher education. Even though there was mixed support for the types of support that make work investments by BrmI leaders feel more equitable to their white counterparts, we do know that (a) BrmI leaders feel, frankly, that they are doing more work for the same career success (and *more* personal life sacrifice) than their white counterparts, and (b) sponsor/mentor/coach support solely appears to, only in part, stem this cost. Universities looking to attract and retain BrmI leaders must attune to this inequity if they have hopes of increasing the proportion of BrmI leaders beyond the less than 10% that currently exist at predominantly white-serving institutions, let alone arriving at concrete standards of workload fairness.

REFERENCES

Adil, A., & Negron, A. (n.d.). Revolutionizing Chicago ft. Dr. Suzet McKinney. Academic Press.

Ahearn, K. K., Ferris, G. R., Hochwarter, W. A., Douglas, C., & Ammeter, A. P. (2004). Leader Political Skill and Team Performance. *Journal of Management*, *30*(3), 309–327. doi:10.1016/j.jm.2003.01.004

Ajzen, I. (1991). The theory of planned behavior. *Organizational Behavior and Human Decision Processes*, *50*(2), 179–211. doi:10.1016/0749-5978(91)90020-T

Alarcon, G. M. (2011). A meta-analysis of burnout with job demands, resources, and attitudes. *Journal of Vocational Behavior*, *79*(2), 549–562. doi:10.1016/j.jvb.2011.03.007

Baez, B. (2000). Race-Related Service and Faculty of Color: Conceptualizing Critical Agency in Academe. *Higher Education*, *39*(3), 363–391. doi:10.1023/A:1003972214943

Basford, T. E., Offermann, L. R., & Behrend, T. S. (2014). Do you see what I see? Perceptions of gender microaggressions in the workplace. *Psychology of Women Quarterly*, *38*(3), 340–349. doi:10.1177/0361684313511420

Bielby, W. T. (2000). Minimizing Workplace Gender and Racial Bias. *Contemporary Sociology*, *29*(1), 120. doi:10.2307/2654937

Blaschke, S., Frost, J., & Hattke, F. (2014). Towards a micro foundation of leadership, governance, and management in universities. *Higher Education*, *68*(5), 711–732. doi:10.100710734-014-9740-2

Brouer, R. L., Douglas, C., Treadway, D. C., & Ferris, G. R. (2013). Leader Political Skill, Relationship Quality, and Leadership Effectiveness: A Two-Study Model Test and Constructive Replication. *Journal of Leadership & Organizational Studies*, *20*(2), 185–198. doi:10.1177/1548051812460099

Carton, A., & Rosette, A. (2011). Explaining Bias against Black Leaders: Integrating Theory on Information Processing and Goal-Based Stereotyping. *Academy of Management Journal*, *54*(6), 1141–1158. doi:10.5465/amj.2009.0745

Cavounidis, C., & Lang, K. (2015). *Discrimination and Worker Evaluation*. Social Science Research Network. https://papers.ssrn.com/abstract=2669801

Cobb, S. (1976). Social support as a moderator of life stress. *Psychosomatic Medicine*, *38*(5), 300–314. doi:10.1097/00006842-197609000-00003 PMID:981490

Cohen, S., & Wills, T. A. (1985). Stress, Social Support, and the Buffering Hypothesis. *Psychological Bulletin*, *98*(2), 310–357. doi:10.1037/0033-2909.98.2.310 PMID:3901065

Connelly, B. L., Tihanyi, L., Crook, T. R., & Gangloff, K. A. (2014). Tournament Theory: Thirty Years of Contests and Competitions. *Journal of Management*, *40*(1), 16–47. doi:10.1177/0149206313498902

Crandall, C. S., & Eshleman, A. (2003). A justification-suppression of the expression and experience of prejudice. *Psychological Bulletin*, *129*(3), 414–446. doi:10.1037/0033-2909.129.3.414 PMID:12784937

Deitch, E., Barsky, A., Butz, R., Chan, S., Brief, A., & Bradley, J. (2003). Subtle Yet Significant: The Existence and Impact of Everyday Racial Discrimination in the Workplace. *Human Relations*, *56*(11), 1299–1324. doi:10.1177/00187267035611002

Deming, W. E. (1986). *Out of the crisis*. Massachusetts Institute of Technology, Center for Advanced Engineering Study.

DeSante, C. (2013). Working Twice as Hard to Get Half as Far: Race, Work Ethic, and America's Deserving Poor. *American Journal of Political Science*, *57*(2), 342–356. Advance online publication. doi:10.1111/ajps.12006

Dovidio, J. F., & Gaertner, S. L. (2004). Aversive racism. In *Advances in experimental social psychology* (Vol. 36, pp. 1–52). Elsevier Academic Press., doi:10.1016/S0065-2601(04)36001-6

Ducharme, L., & Martin, J. K. (2000). Unrewarding Work, Coworker Support, and Job Satisfaction: A Test of the Buffering Hypothesis. *Work and Occupations*, *27*(2), 223–243. doi:10.1177/0730888400027002005

DuPont, C. M., Weis, T. M., Manuck, S. B., Marsland, A. L., Matthews, K. A., & Gianaros, P. J. (2020). Does well-being associate with stress physiology? A systematic review and meta-analysis. *Health Psychology*, *39*(10), 879–890. Advance online publication. doi:10.1037/hea0000979 PMID:32686951

Eddleston, K. A., Baldridge, D. C., & Veiga, J. F. (2004). Toward modeling the predictors of managerial career success: Does gender matter? *Journal of Managerial Psychology*, *19*(4), 360–385. doi:10.1108/02683940410537936

Ensher, E. A., & Murphy, S. E. (1997). Effects of Race, Gender, Perceived Similarity, and Contact on Mentor Relationships. *Journal of Vocational Behavior*, *50*(3), 460–481. doi:10.1006/jvbe.1996.1547

Ferris, G. R., Treadway, D. C., Kolodinsky, R. W., Hochwarter, W. A., Kacmar, C. J., Douglas, C., & Frink, D. D. (2005). Development and Validation of the Political Skill Inventory. *Journal of Management*, *31*(1), 126–152. doi:10.1177/0149206304271386

Fu, T. Z. J., Song, Q., & Chiu, D. M. (2014). The academic social network. *Scientometrics*, *101*(1), 203–239. doi:10.100711192-014-1356-x

Gaertner, S. L., & Dovidio, J. F. (2000). The aversive form of racism. In *Stereotypes and prejudice: Essential readings* (pp. 289–304). Psychology Press.

Goffman, E. (1959). *The presentation of self in everyday life*. Doubleday.

Greenhaus, J., Parasuraman, S., & Wormley, W. (1990). Effects of Race on Organizational Experiences, Job Performance Evaluations, and Career Outcomes. *Academy of Management Journal*, *33*(1), 64–86. doi:10.2307/256352

Gurchiek, K. (2020). *SHRM Research Finds Need for More Awareness, Understanding of Racial Inequality* (HR News). SHRM. https://www.shrm.org/hr-today/news/hr-news/pages/shrm-research-finds-need-for-more-awareness-understanding-of-racial-inequality.aspx

Haberman, M. (2005). Teacher Burnout in Black and White. *New Educator*, *1*(3), 153–175. doi:10.1080/15476880590966303

Harris, K., Kacmar, K., Zivnuska, S., & Shaw, J. (2007). The impact of political skill on effectiveness. *The Journal of Applied Psychology*, *92*, 278–285. doi:10.1037/0021-9010.92.1.278 PMID:17227169

Hatzenbuehler, M. L., Phelan, J. C., & Link, B. G. (2013). Stigma as a Fundamental Cause of Population Health Inequalities. *American Journal of Public Health*, *103*(5), 813–821. doi:10.2105/AJPH.2012.301069 PMID:23488505

Henry, F., Dua, E., Kobayashi, A., James, C., Li, P., Ramos, H., & Smith, M. S. (2017). Race, racialization and Indigeneity in Canadian universities. *Race, Ethnicity and Education*, *20*(3), 300–314. doi:10.1080/13613324.2016.1260226

Hirsh, E., & Lyons, C. J. (2010). Perceiving Discrimination on the Job: Legal Consciousness, Workplace Context, and the Construction of Race Discrimination. *Law & Society Review*, *44*(2), 269–298. doi:10.1111/j.1540-5893.2010.00403.x

Hobfoll, S. E. (1989). Conservation of resources: A new attempt at conceptualizing stress. *The American Psychologist*, *44*(3), 513–524. doi:10.1037/0003-066X.44.3.513 PMID:2648906

Hobfoll, S. E., Halbesleben, J., Neveu, J.-P., & Westman, M. (2017). *Conservation of Resources in the Organizational Context: The Reality of Resources and Their Consequences*. Academic Press.

Horowitz, J. M., Brown, A., & Cox, K. (2019, April 9). *Views on Race in America 2019*. Pew Research Center's Social & Demographic Trends Project. https://www.pewresearch.org/social-trends/2019/04/09/race-in-america-2019/

Hughes, D., & Dodge, M. A. (1997). African American women in the workplace: Relationships between job conditions, racial bias at work, and perceived job quality. *American Journal of Community Psychology*, *25*(5), 581–599. doi:10.1023/A:1024630816168 PMID:9485575

Jameel, M. (2019, February 28). *Workplace discrimination is illegal. But our data shows it's still a huge problem*. Vox. https://www.vox.com/policy-and-politics/2019/2/28/18241973/workplace-discrimination-cpi-investigation-eeoc

Judge, T. A., Cable, D. M., Boudreau, J. W., & Bretz, R. D. (1995). An empirical investigation of predictors of executive career success. *Personnel Psychology*, *48*(3), 485–519. doi:10.1111/j.1744-6570.1995.tb01767.x

Judge, T. A., Higgins, C. A., Thoresen, C. J., & Barrick, M. R. (1999). The Big Five Personality Traits, General Mental Ability, and Career Success Across the Life Span. *Personnel Psychology*, *52*(3), 621–652. doi:10.1111/j.1744-6570.1999.tb00174.x

Keeney, J., Boyd, E. M., Sinha, R., Westring, A. F., & Ryan, A. M. (2013). From "work–family" to "work–life": Broadening our conceptualization and measurement. *Journal of Vocational Behavior*, *82*(3), 221–237. doi:10.1016/j.jvb.2013.01.005

King, E. B., Shapiro, J. R., Hebl, M. R., Singletary, S. L., & Turner, S. (2006). The stigma of obesity in customer service: A mechanism for remediation and bottom-line consequences of interpersonal discrimination. *The Journal of Applied Psychology*, *91*(3), 579–593. doi:10.1037/0021-9010.91.3.579 PMID:16737356

Kossek, E. E., Ruderman, M. N., Braddy, P. W., & Hannum, K. M. (2012). Work–nonwork boundary management profiles: A person-centered approach. *Journal of Vocational Behavior*, *81*(1), 112–128. doi:10.1016/j.jvb.2012.04.003

Kulik, C. T., Bainbridge, H. T. J., & Cregan, C. (2008). Known by the company we keep: Stigma-by-association effects in the workplace. *Academy of Management Review*, *33*(1), 216–230. doi:10.5465/amr.2008.27752765

Lazarus, R. S., & Folkman, S. (1987). Transactional theory and research on emotions and coping. *European Journal of Personality*, *1*(3), 141–169. doi:10.1002/per.2410010304

Lu, D., Huang, J., Seshagiri, A., Park, H., & Griggs, T. (2020, September 9). *Faces of power: 80% are White even as US becomes more diverse*. https://www.nytimes.com/interactive/2020/09/09/us/powerful-people-race-us.html

Lupien, S. J., Maheu, F., Tu, M., Fiocco, A., & Schramek, T. E. (2007). The effects of stress and stress hormones on human cognition: Implications for the field of brain and cognition. *Brain and Cognition*, *65*(3), 209–237. doi:10.1016/j.bandc.2007.02.007 PMID:17466428

Major, B., Kaiser, C. R., & McCoy, S. K. (2003). It's Not My Fault: When and Why Attributions to Prejudice Protect Self-Esteem. *Personality and Social Psychology Bulletin*, *29*(6), 772–781. doi:10.1177/0146167203029006009 PMID:15189632

Major, B., & O'Brien, L. T. (2005). The Social Psychology of Stigma. *Annual Review of Psychology*, *56*(1), 393–421. doi:10.1146/annurev.psych.56.091103.070137 PMID:15709941

McCluney, C. L., Durkee, M. I., Smith, R. E. II, Robotham, K. J., & Lee, S. S.-L. (2021). To be, or not to be…Black: The effects of racial codeswitching on perceived professionalism in the workplace. *Journal of Experimental Social Psychology*, *97*, 104199. doi:10.1016/j.jesp.2021.104199

McEwen, B. S., & Stellar, E. (1993). Stress and the individual. Mechanisms leading to disease. *Archives of Internal Medicine*, *153*(18), 2093–2101. doi:10.1001/archinte.1993.00410180039004 PMID:8379800

Mekawi, Y., Hyatt, C. S., Maples-Keller, J., Carter, S., Michopoulos, V., & Powers, A. (2021). Racial Discrimination Predicts Mental Health Outcomes Beyond the Role of Personality Traits in a Community Sample of African Americans. *Clinical Psychological Science*, *9*(2), 183–196. doi:10.1177/2167702620957318

Melaku, T. M., Beeman, A., Smith, D. G., & Johnson, W. B. (2020, November 1). Be a Better Ally. *Harvard Business Review*. https://hbr.org/2020/11/be-a-better-ally

Miller, S. (2020). *Black Workers Still Earn Less than Their White Counterparts* (Compensation). SHRM. https://www.shrm.org/resourcesandtools/hr-topics/compensation/pages/racial-wage-gaps-persistence-poses-challenge.aspx

Munyon, T., Summers, J., Thompson, T., & Ferris, G. (2013). Political Skill and Work Outcomes: A Theoretical Extension, Meta-Analytic Investigation, and Agenda for the Future. *Personnel Psychology*, *68*(1), 143–184. Advance online publication. doi:10.1111/peps.12066

Niemann, Y. F. (2003). The psychology of tokenism: Psychosocial realities of faculty of color. doi:10.4135/9781412976008.n5

Nishii, L. H. (2012). The Benefits of Climate for Inclusion for Gender-Diverse Groups. *Academy of Management Journal*, *56*(6), 1754–1774. doi:10.5465/amj.2009.0823

O*NET. (n.d.). *11-9033.00—Education Administrators, Postsecondary*. Retrieved July 26, 2021, from https://www.onetonline.org/link/summary/11-9033.00

Ortiz-Walters, R., & Gilson, L. L. (2005). Mentoring in academia: An examination of the experiences of protégés of color. *Journal of Vocational Behavior*, *67*(3), 459–475. doi:10.1016/j.jvb.2004.09.004

Pager, D., & Shepherd, H. (2008). The Sociology of Discrimination: Racial Discrimination in Employment, Housing, Credit, and Consumer Markets. *Annual Review of Sociology*, *34*(1), 181–209. doi:10.1146/annurev.soc.33.040406.131740 PMID:20689680

Patten, E. (2016). *Racial, gender wage gaps persist in U.S. despite some progress*. Pew Research Center. https://www.pewresearch.org/fact-tank/2016/07/01/racial-gender-wage-gaps-persist-in-u-s-despite-some-progress/

Perna, L. W. (2001). Sex and Race Differences in Faculty Tenure and Promotion. *Research in Higher Education*, *42*(5), 541–567. doi:10.1023/A:1011050226672

Pinel, E. C. (1999). Stigma consciousness: The psychological legacy of social stereotypes. *Journal of Personality and Social Psychology*, *76*(1), 114–128. doi:10.1037/0022-3514.76.1.114 PMID:9972557

Pryor, J. B., Reeder, G. D., Yeadon, C., & Hesson-McLnnis, M. (2004). A dual-process model of reactions to perceived stigma. *Journal of Personality and Social Psychology*, *87*(4), 436–452. doi:10.1037/0022-3514.87.4.436 PMID:15491270

Randel, A. E., Galvin, B. M., Gibson, C. B., & Batts, S. I. (2021). Increasing Career Advancement Opportunities Through Sponsorship: An Identity-Based Model With Illustrative Application to Cross-Race Mentorship of African Americans. *Group & Organization Management*, *46*(1), 105–142. doi:10.1177/1059601120978003

Reskin, B. (1979). Academic Sponsorship and Scientists' Careers. *Sociology of Education*, *52*(3), 129–146. doi:10.2307/2112319

Richards, K. C., Campenni, C. E., & Muse-Burke, J. L. (2010). Self-care and well-being in mental health professionals: The mediating effects of self-awareness and mindfulness. *Journal of Mental Health Counseling*, *32*(3), 247–264. doi:10.17744/mehc.32.3.0n31v88304423806

Roberts, S. O., & Rizzo, M. T. (2020). The psychology of American racism. *The American Psychologist*. Advance online publication. doi:10.1037/amp0000642 PMID:32584061

Roepe, L. R. (2021). *Barriers for Black Professionals* (All Things Work). SHRM. https://www.shrm.org/hr-today/news/all-things-work/pages/racism-corporate-america.aspx

Samuelson, H. L., Levine, B. R., Barth, S. E., Wessel, J. L., & Grand, J. A. (2019). Exploring women's leadership labyrinth: Effects of hiring and developmental opportunities on gender stratification. *The Leadership Quarterly*, *30*(6), 101314. doi:10.1016/j.leaqua.2019.101314

Sanchez-Hucles, J. V., & Davis, D. D. (2010). Women and women of color in leadership: Complexity, identity, and intersectionality. *The American Psychologist*, *65*(3), 171–181. doi:10.1037/a0017459 PMID:20350016

Saucier, G. (1994). Mini-Markers: A brief version of Goldberg's unipolar Big-Five markers. *Journal of Personality Assessment*, *63*(3), 506–516. doi:10.120715327752jpa6303_8 PMID:7844738

Scandura, T. A., & Williams, E. A. (2001). An Investigation of the Moderating Effects of Gender on the Relationships between Mentorship Initiation and Protégé Perceptions of Mentoring Functions. *Journal of Vocational Behavior*, *59*(3), 342–363. doi:10.1006/jvbe.2001.1809

Seibert, S., Kraimer, M., & Liden, R. (2001). A Social Capital Theory of Career Success. *Academy of Management Journal*, *44*(2), 219–237. Advance online publication. doi:10.2307/3069452

Smith, B. W., Dalen, J., Wiggins, K., Tooley, E., Christopher, P., & Bernard, J. (2008). The brief resilience scale: Assessing the ability to bounce back. *International Journal of Behavioral Medicine*, *15*(3), 194–200. doi:10.1080/10705500802222972 PMID:18696313

Social Sciences Feminist Network Research Interest Group. (2017). The Burden of Invisible Work in Academia: Social Inequalities and Time Use in Five University Departments. *Humboldt Journal of Social Relations*, *39*, 228–245.

Stanton-Salazar, R. D. (2011). A Social Capital Framework for the Study of Institutional Agents and Their Role in the Empowerment of Low-Status Students and Youth. *Youth & Society*, *43*(3), 1066–1109. doi:10.1177/0044118X10382877

Stripling, J. (2021, June 11). 'What the Hell Happened?' Inside the Nikole Hannah-Jones Tenure Case. *The Chronicle of Higher Education*. https://www.chronicle.com/article/what-the-hell-happened

Taylor, M., Turk, J. M., Chessman, H., & Espinosa, L. L. (2020). *Race and ethnicity in higher education*. American Council on Higher Education. https://devacerehe.wpengine.com/wp-content/uploads/2020/11/REHE-2020-final.pdf

Trenerry, B., & Paradies, Y. (2012). Organizational Assessment. *An Overlooked Approach To Managing Diversity And Addressing Racism In The Workplace.*, *7*(1), 16.

Trentham, S., & Larwood, L. (1998). Gender Discrimination and the Workplace: An Examination of Rational Bias Theory. *Sex Roles*, *38*(1), 1–28. doi:10.1023/A:1018782226876

Viswesvaran, C., Sanchez, J. I., & Fisher, J. (1999). The Role of Social Support in the Process of Work Stress: A Meta-Analysis. *Journal of Vocational Behavior*, *54*(2), 314–334. doi:10.1006/jvbe.1998.1661

Wilcox, B. L. (1981). Social support, life stress, and psychological adjustment: A test of the buffering hypothesis. *American Journal of Community Psychology*, *9*(4), 371–386. doi:10.1007/BF00918169 PMID:7282647

Williams, M. T. (2019a). Microaggressions: Clarification, Evidence, and Impact. *Perspectives on Psychological Science*. Advance online publication. doi:10.1177/1745691619827499 PMID:31418642

Williams, M. T. (2019b). Psychology Cannot Afford to Ignore the Many Harms Caused by Microaggressions. *Perspectives on Psychological Science*. Advance online publication. doi:10.1177/1745691619893362 PMID:31801042

Wilson, V., & Jones, J. (2018). *Working harder or finding it harder to work: Demographic trends in annual work hours show an increasingly fractured workforce*. Economic Policy Institute. https://www.epi.org/publication/trends-in-work-hours-and-labor-market-disconnection/

Yukl, G. (2012). Effective Leadership Behavior: What We Know and What Questions Need More Attention. *The Academy of Management Perspectives*, *26*(4), 66–85. doi:10.5465/amp.2012.0088

Zambrana, R. E., Ray, R., Espino, M. M., Castro, C., Douthirt Cohen, B., & Eliason, J. (2015). "Don't Leave Us Behind": The Importance of Mentoring for Underrepresented Minority Faculty. *American Educational Research Journal*, *52*(1), 40–72. doi:10.3102/0002831214563063

Zhang, R., Wang, M. S., Toubiana, M., & Greenwood, R. (2020). Stigma Beyond Levels: Advancing Research on Stigmatization. *The Academy of Management Annals*, *15*(1), 188–222. doi:10.5465/annals.2019.0031

ENDNOTE

1 Studies on how white versus BrmI professionals spend their work time, on the surface, tell a contrary story: White people tend to work more hours (Wilson & Jones, 2018). These studies, however, do not capture specifically professionals ascending into leadership positions (let alone leadership in academia), nor do they catalogue the increased hours devoted to countering and proactively fending off bias, prejudice, discrimination, and the like at work, which the BrmI professional must engage in as argued here and in other professional reports (Gurchiek, 2020; Roepe, 2021). Instead these stories talk about how the hours available to BrnI individuals are using at less desirable, lower-wage (for same amount of effort as whites) jobs (Miller, 2020; Patten, 2016).

APPENDIX A

Information Sheet for Participation in Research Study

The Cost of Leadership for People of Color

You may print this information for your records. By completing the survey you are indicating your agreement to be in the research. Please click the “>>” below to continue.

18_plus

Are you 18 years of age or older?

Yes (1)

No (2)

person_of_color

Do you identify as a person of color?

Yes (1)

No (2)

tenure_status

Are you a tenured or tenure-track professor in a higher education institution?

Tenured (1)

Tenure-track (2)

Neither of these options (3)

leadership_yn

Do you hold a leadership position (e.g., Program Director; Department Chair; Dean; Provost; President) at your university?

Yes (1)

No (2)

job_title

What is the name of your leadership position (e.g., Program Director; Department Chair; Dean; Provost; President)? You should not include the name of your university.

social_support

You indicated you currently hold an academic leadership position. For these questions, consider the time in your career when you actively sought to advance into a leadership role(s). Please rate the extent to which you agree or disagree with each statement.

Strongly disagree (1)

Somewhat disagree (2)

Neither agree nor disagree (3)

Somewhat agree (4)

Strongly agree (5)

I engage in social self-care (for example, engagement with a friend, family member, or message board) if I am upset). (social_sup)

I engage in psychological self-care (for example, meditation; journaling; therapy). (mental_health_sup)

I engage in spiritual self-care (for example, religion-affiliated group activities). (spiritual_sup)

I have a career mentor/coach/sponsor. (sponsor_sup)

capital_support

You indicated you currently hold an academic leadership position. For these questions, consider the time in your career when you actively sought to advance into a leadership role(s). Please rate the extent to which you agree or disagree with each statement.

Strongly disagree (1)

Somewhat disagree (2)

Neither agree nor disagree (3)

Somewhat agree (4)

Strongly agree (5)

I spend a lot of time and effort at work networking with others. (na_1)

I am good at building relationships with influential people at work. (na_2)

I have developed a large network of colleagues and associates at work whom I can call on for support when I really need to get things done. (na_3)

At work, I know a lot of important people and am well connected. (na_4)

I spend a lot of time at work developing connections with others. (na_5)

I am good at using my connections and network to make things happen at work. (na_6)

I am able to make most people feel comfortable and at ease around me. (ii_1)

I am able to communicate easily and effectively with others. (ii_2)

It is easy for me to develop good rapport with most people. (ii_3)

I am good at getting people to like me. (ii_4)

I understand people very well. (sa_1)

I am particularly good at sensing the motivations and hidden agendas of others. (sa_2)

I have good intuition or savvy about how to present myself to others. (sa_3)

I always seem to instinctively know the right things to say or do to influence others. (sa_4)

I pay close attention to people's facial expressions. (sa_5)

When communicating with others, I try to be genuine in what I say and do. (as_1)

It is important that people believe I am sincere in what I say and do. (as_2)

I try to show a genuine interest in other people. (as_3)

institutional_support

You indicated you currently hold an academic leadership position. For these questions, consider the time in your career when you actively sought to advance into a leadership role(s). Please rate the extent to which you agree or disagree with each statement.

Strongly disagree (1)

Somewhat disagree (2)

Neither agree nor disagree (3)

Somewhat agree (4)

Strongly agree (5)

My university has a fair promotion process. (eep_1)

The performance review process is fair in my university. (eep_2)

My university invests in the development of all of its employees. (eep_3)

Employees in my university receive "equal pay for equal work." (eep_4)

My university provides safe ways for employees to voice their grievances. (id_1)

My university is characterized by a non-threatening environment in which people can reveal their "true" selves. (id_2)

My university values work-life balance. (id_3)

My university commits resources to ensuring that employees are able to resolve conflicts effectively. (id_4)

Employees of my university are valued for who they are as people, not just for the jobs that they fill. (id_5)

In this my university, people often share and learn about one another as people. (id_6)

My university has a culture in which employees appreciate the differences that people bring to the workplace. (id_7)

In my university, employee input is actively sought. (idm_1)

In my university, everyone's ideas for how to do things better are given serious consideration. (idm_2)

In my university, employees' insights are used to rethink or redefine work practices. (idm_3)

Top management exercises the belief that problem-solving is improved when input from different roles, ranks, and functions is considered. (idm_4)

conscientiousness

Please rate the extent to which you think each statement describes you.

Strongly disagree (1)

Somewhat disagree (2)

Neither agree nor disagree (3)

Somewhat agree (4)

Strongly agree (5)

Organized (cons_1)

Systematic (cons_2)

Efficient (cons_3)

Practical (cons_4)

Careful (cons_5)

resiliency

Please rate the extent to which you agree or disagree with each statement about yourself.

Strongly disagree (1)

Somewhat disagree (2)

Neither agree nor disagree (3)

Somewhat agree (4)

Strongly agree (5)

I tend to bounce back quickly after hard times. (resil_1)

I do not have a hard time making it through stressful events. (resil_2)

It does not take me long to recover from a stressful event. (resil_3)

I do not have difficulty snapping back when something bad happens. (resil_4)

I usually come through difficult times with little trouble. (resil_5)

I tend to take a short time to get over set-backs in life. (resil_6)

interpersonal_costs

Please rate the extent to which you agree or disagree with each statement.
Much less (1)
Less (2)
About the same (3)
More (4)
Much more (5)

Throughout my career, compared to my white counterparts the time I spent on work cut into the time I spent on my **family**. (ic_family_1)

Throughout my career, compared to my white counterparts the amount of time my work takes up made it difficult to find enough time for my **family**. (ic_family_2)

Throughout my career, compared to my white counterparts my work keeps me from my **family** more than I would have liked to. (ic_family_3)

Throughout my career, compared to my white counterparts the time I spent on work cut into the time I spent on **community involvement.** (ic_ci_1)

Throughout my career, compared to my white counterparts the amount of time my work takes up made it difficult to find enough time for **community involvement.** (ic_ci_2)

Throughout my career, compared to my white counterparts my work keeps me from **community involvement** more than I would have liked to. (ic_ci_3)

Throughout my career, compared to my white counterparts the time I spent on work cut into the time I spent on **friendships**. (ic_friend_1)

Throughout my career, compared to my white counterparts the amount of time my work takes up made it difficult to find enough time for **friendships.** (ic_friend_2)

Throughout my career, compared to my white counterparts my work keeps me from **friendships** more than I would have liked to. (ic_friend_3)

Q18

Please rate the extent to which you agree or disagree with each statement.
Much less (1)
Less (2)
About the same (3)
More (4)
Much more (5)

Throughout my career, compared to my white counterparts the time I spent on work cut into the time I spent on my **health**. (ic_health_1)

Throughout my career, compared to my white counterparts the amount of time my work takes up made it difficult to find enough time for my **health**. (ic_health_2)

Throughout my career, compared to my white counterparts my work keeps me from taking care of my **health** more than I would have liked to. (ic_health_3)

Throughout my career, compared to my white counterparts the time I spent on work cut into the time I spent on **stress management.** (ic_stress_1)

Throughout my career, compared to my white counterparts the amount of time my work takes up made it difficult to find enough time for **stress management.** (ic_stress_2)

Throughout my career, compared to my white counterparts my work keeps me from **stress management** more than I would have liked to. (ic_stress_3)

Throughout my career, compared to my white counterparts the time I spent on work cut into the time I spent on **self-care.** (ic_selfcare_1)

Throughout my career, compared to my white counterparts the amount of time my work takes up made it difficult to find enough time for **self-care.** (ic_selfcare_2)

Throughout my career, compared to my white counterparts my work keeps me from **self-care** more than I would have liked to. (ic_selfcare_3)

Throughout my career, compared to my white counterparts the time I spent on work cut into the time I spent on **leisure**. (ic_leisure_1)

Throughout my career, compared to my white counterparts the amount of time my work takes up made it difficult to find enough time for **leisure**. (ic_leisure_2)

Throughout my career, compared to my white counterparts my work keeps me from **leisure** more than I would have liked to. (ic_leisure_3)

edu_journey

Would you share your educational journey (area of doctoral study, how graduate program was selected, work experience prior to doctoral study)?

learn_early_career

What did you learn from your early career academic jobs that led you to your current position?

notable_circum

Were there any notable circumstances that occurred throughout your career that led you to your current position?

resilience

Being in an academic leadership position involves considerable sacrifice personally and professionally. Is there anything that you encountered throughout your academic journey that has provided you with resilience to perform your current job?

awards

Without giving identifying information, have you earned any academic professional awards?

age

What is your current age?

0 10 20 30 40 50 60 70 80 90 100

gender

What is your gender?

marital_status

What is your marital status?

Single (1)

Committed Relationship (2)

ethnicity

What is your ethnicity?

sexual_orientation

What is your sexual orientation?

Chapter 21
Educational Democracy:
Calling for a New Phase in Progressive Education

Leodis Scott
DePaul University, USA

Joanne Howard
Illinois Institute of Technology, USA

ABSTRACT

This chapter will review the productive phases of the progressive education movement. It will detail several practices for educational democracy rooted from adult continuing education theory and practice. Educational historians know that education was broader than only education for children in formal public schools. In the past, many progressive educators have discounted adult continuing education, but in this new phase and age, the education and environment for children and adults are one-and-the-same. Some educators and historians may view the progressive movement as dead or out-of-date, but they miscalculate its continuing broader connection to society for addressing cultural, political, civic, academic, and economic matters. This new phase and age of progressivism makes it reasonable to bring the progressive education movement back-to-life and keep it in-style. The need for a new progressive movement to address current concerns about threats to democracy is paramount.

INTRODUCTION

Since the time of educator and philosopher John Dewey, there has been a progressive education movement. From Dewey's seminal book, *Democracy and Education* (1916), numerous radical-to-moderate educational views have emerged for reforming schools and/or changing society. Dewey is applauded for stimulating a range of progressive, educational, and democratic ideals, yet Dewey was not the first to connect education to democracy in America. Booker T. Washington (1896) spoke years before Dewey's work in a speech in New York actually entitled, "Education and Democracy," where Washington gives his

DOI: 10.4018/978-1-6684-2314-1.ch021

views on race, democracy, and education in the United States (BlackPast, 2010). As Washington explains: "The time may not be far off when...we shall have to decide the course of our democratic institutions..."

Washington points out the inequality and disparity of money spent for education between the races: "And yet," Washington exclaims, "each citizen of this country is expected to share the burdens and privileges of our democratic form of government...intelligently and conscientiously."

Washington further makes the connections between American education, democracy, and citizenship. As Washington states,

When a great national calamity stares us in the face, we are, I fear, too much given to depending on a short campaign of education to do on the hustings what should have been accomplished in the school-room...let us examine with more care the work to be done...before all classes will be fit for the highest duties of citizenship.

Thus, Washington concludes,

Education, whether [for a] black man or white man, that gives one physical courage to stand in front of the cannon and fails to give him moral courage to stand up in defense of right and justice is a failure (BlackPast, 2010).

Both Washington and Dewey, at this time in America, knew that the union or duality of education and democracy had not been realized. Unfortunately, over a century later, democracy and education still have not been fully implemented, nor reimagined for a new period in America.

Metaphorically, while democracy seems to have grown up and matured a bit (i.e., politically, socially, and economically), education, on the other hand, has seemed to remain in its infancy—stunted in growth (i.e., philosophically, intelligently, and morally). For Dewey (1916) explains philosophy as "the general theory of education" (p. 328); where education "is the laboratory in which philosophic distinctions become concrete and are tested" (p. 329). For Washington (1896) education should give its citizens both 'physical' and 'moral courage.' Both educational thinkers envision an inextricable role of education to complement democracy. Without coming together, democracy is bankrupt of philosophy, intelligence, and courage. Likewise, education is void of political, social, and economic value.

However, the history of the dis-union between education and democracy would have been told for centuries; and we would have continued to accept this un-equal relationship until the end of time. This analogy where democracy has reached some level of maturity, while education inchoate still supports Dewey's intentional message of democracy and education being inextricably tied together, as to what Adler (1982) calls "revolutionary." Adler (1988) further explains in another work, *Reforming Education: The Opening of the American Mind,* that the education, which still exists in the United States, has been "thoroughly antidemocratic" (p. xxv).

Then something happened: The pandemic came; the world changed, and our existing American democratic system had severely shifted-and-split into extremes. Now, in this new time and century, the once grown-up democracy is in distress: in real trouble of ending altogether. Meanwhile, education is still there, under-developed and under-utilized, yet able to contribute to democracy whereby their union can address the political, social, and economic problems of today, or what Washington describes as the "great national calamity" [that] stares us in the face.

Optimistically, those familiar with the Ancient Greek myth of Pandora's Box (*Works and Days* by Hesiod) are aware in the story that despite all of the world's ills, including both physical and emotional curses of humankind being released (e.g., sickness, death, and unspecified evils); it was suggested that when Pandora finally closed the box (or jar), the one-and-only thing that remained was *Hope*.

In the story of this chapter, hope rests in education that was left behind. It may be too soon to develop education enough to become as equal to democracy, as Dewey or Washington had conceived, but the next best step is to integrate the practices of education *into* democracy, which will be described as "educational democracy." During the past century, political and social issues have distorted the face of democracy where now democracy is almost unrecognizable. Politics and social activists have dominated the debate about democracy, while educators reluctantly remained in the distance. The progressive education movement itself is not blameless, and clearly lost its way as well. But instead of rehashing old arguments and old debates about the demise of progressivism, this chapter offers a new path, which begins with a call for educational democracy in ushering a new age of progressive educators.

Nevertheless, this chapter will explore some of the productive phases and guiding principles along with historical views about the progressive education movement. It will detail several practices for educational democracy rooted from adult continuing education theory and practice. The field of adult continuing education has also been in the distance from traditional education, which is restricted to only formal schools of elementary and secondary instruction. Educational historians such as Lawrence Cremin (1961) always knew that education was broader than only education for children in formal public schools. In the past, many progressive educators have discounted adult continuing education, but in this new phase and age, the education and environment for children and adults are one-and-the-same.

Some educators and historians may view the progressive movement as dead or out-of-date, but they miscalculate its continuing broader connection to society for addressing cultural, political, civic, academic, and economic matters. This new phase and age of progressivism makes it reasonable to bring the progressive education movement back-to-life and keep it in-style. Although other historical phases of progressivism may have passed away also, the need for a new progressive movement to address current concerns about threats to democracy is absolutely paramount. Again, this chapter calls for a new phase in progressive education called educational democracy, and a new age of progressive educators. Such educators will practice inside-and-outside of schools, colleges, and universities, and within-and-across all aspects of society, especially in neighborhoods, communities, vicinities, and localities for actively participating as learning cities for an American democracy (Scott, 2015).

DEWEY'S INFLUENCE ON THE PROGRESSIVE EDUCATION MOVEMENT

James Scott Johnston, *Inquiry and Education,* encourages and reinforces similar inferences by educators "who give more than a passing glance" of Dewey's writings. For example, Johnston (2006) takes as sharper focus on *inquiry*, as a specific concept, emphasizing that for inquiry to function in schools, these schools would be context-based, open-ended, and self-correcting. Johnston explains that such schools would be "amenable to transformation" depending on the context and circumstances (p. 195). In addition, Johnston provides a very strong explanation concerning inquiry, and its connection to other concepts such as *growth*, *community*, *democracy*, and education itself. Johnston's account of inquiry and these other related concepts provides some details as to how an educational democracy can function, in what Johnston depicts as "educating democracy" (p. 192). Compared to the proposal of educational democracy, educating democracy serves a similar purpose in aiding democracy; however, simply educating democracy is not enough. Educational democracy takes a step further in putting in place an overall practice. Many people may come up with ways to educate democracy, but ultimately these ways must be collected, measured, and evaluated as a practice: a practice of educational democracy.

Still, it should be immediately noted that Johnston's work graciously help to advance Dewey's devoted reliance on inquiry and the scientific method in schools of education. This does not suggest that Johnston was an ardent Deweyan apologist, quite the contrary, given that Johnston points out sharply how *Dewey's Laboratory School* was at its weakest in not having students with different cultures and opinions, but rather Dewey's school "drew children from predominantly white, upper-middle-class professorial families, and paid less than deserving attention to social problems in the larger community" (p. 194). Johnston's contribution offers a clear-eyed view about how to consider Dewey's practice of democracy, about what should count as a democracy, and about why such a democracy is needed, even now.

What this chapter attempts to contribute is to offer a similar clear view about how to consider Dewey's notion of democracy *and* education, about what practices enable an *educational democracy*, and about how an educational democracy is not only needed now, but whose time has finally come. The unfortunate fate of progressivism and progressive education is that may have come a generation and century too soon. The progressive movement had formed by the turn of the twentieth century, when the United States was undergoing great social, economic, and political changes, along with other related problems and issues of its day, such as rapid urbanization, mass immigration, industrialization, and civil rights among others (Elias & Merriam, 2005; Fallace, 2011; Kett, 1994).

Fallace (2011) focuses on Dewey's influence during the formative years of progressive education (1903-1951) with conclusions he describes as "merely suggestive," still Fallace provides three essential assertions:

1. Dewey was often used by contemporaries to reconcile positivistic social science with pragmatic philosophy;
2. Numerous Dewey texts are cited without reference to any other text, most notable, *Democracy and Education*.
3. Dewey's philosophy was used to support competing reform agendas aimed at not only social control and social adjustment; but also social reconstruction and social justice (Fallace, 2011, p. 464).

This third assertion explains the diverse and often conflicting views and actions of the progressive era and the progressive education movement. But, this assertion provides an opportunity to revisit some of Dewey's writings in a more targeted educational agenda, such as a new practice of educational democracy that goes beyond merely childhood school curriculum as Fallace (2011) considered. Likewise, more than solely examining Dewey's writings for educational theory schools of progressive, civic, and social education, there is a long overdue approach that targets Dewey's writings in the practice of educating both children and adults for educational democracy.

PHASES, GUIDING PRINCIPLES, & HISTORICAL VIEWS OF THE PROGRESSIVE EDUCATION MOVEMENT

The origins of progressive education that developed in Europe and advanced in the United States relied upon reason and rational thought, scientific and empirical methods, also feeling and experience (Elias & Merriam, 2005). While Dewey's influence on progressivism and progressive education is undeniable, there are many earlier thinkers that attribute to progressive educational thought, starting with Charles Darwin (1859) and his inductive methods of science that challenged the traditional deductive approaches in philosophy and theology. The inductive approach placed a greater inference on empirical knowledge instead of the authority of the scriptures and the written word (Elias & Merriam, 2005). In the course of reviewing the central tenets of progressivism and progressive education there have been identified phases and guiding principles of the movement as well as an historical view that places Dewey and others in proper context.

Three Phases

Some authors describe three phases of the progressive movement: 1) student-centered/learner potential; 2) social reform/reconstruction; and 3) experimentalism (Elias & Merriam, 2005). Again, one of the dominant voices for the progressive movement in education through his voluminous writings and philosophical advancement of pragmatism is John Dewey, but Dewey was not the only one. However, specifically in Dewey's writings, there are supportive statements that defend these three phases. Yet other authors have also provided description about the progressive education movement that will be explored as well.

Guiding Principles

Alberty (1929) identifies three guiding principles about the progressive education movement in schools: 1) Children are creative by nature; 2) Children need freedom; and 3) Activities ought to be self-initiated by each individual child, where curriculum centers on each child's present needs and interests.

The first guiding principle that children are creative by nature supports the notion of natural creativeness as an "unknown mysterious hidden force" which appears only when left to itself (Alberty, 1929). Many educators refer to Rousseau's work *Emile* for guidance regarding Rousseau's views about nature and natural selection. One of Rousseau most famous quotes, "[t]he world of reality has its limits; the world of imagination is boundless," positions the real world as a certain opponent against a child's imagination and creativity. Alberty (1929) actually challenges this position.

The second guiding principle that children need freedom aligns to the first guiding principle for children to be creative. This freedom also relates to the environment which should be free from restraint and coercion where the child's innate abilities can grow and develop. Thus, this freedom is both physical and individual. Physical in the sense of the configuration of the classroom. As Alberty describes,

[T]he traditional classroom with its straight rows of seats and desks, screwed to the floor, all arranged in such a matter as to give the despot her position of vantage on the rostrum a clear view of every one of the "young barbarians" she is to subdue must be banished forever (p.166).

Alberty further describes how progressive educators expect the classroom to be configured,

In its place is a pleasant room with gay curtains and hangings, with tables and comfortable chairs arranged quite informally, with attractive book shelves from which the children may select such books as please their fancies without the permission of the teacher (p. 166).

The physical and aesthetic freedom demonstrated in the change in the classroom positions the teacher as a participant along with the students. The teacher serves as a guide without oppressive authority or superiority.

Individual freedom relates to allowing the child to discover knowledge unencumbered. The concept of freedom and autonomy is central to the tenets of democracy. Such freedom suggest that children will continue to be creative as well as be able to pursue activities according to their creativity, which aligns to the third principle.

The third guiding principle supports child-initiated activities based upon each child's present needs and interests. Alberty (1929) believes that this third principle is the most significant and dominant as a practice within progressive schools. This third principle points to another conflict between the "self-initiated" activity and the "teacher-imposed" instruction. This principle argues for the curriculum being centered on the needs and interests of the child rather than the "remote and vague needs of an adult society" (Alberty, 1929, p. 167). While Alberty does not appear to be on the side of the firm critics of the progressive education movement, he does challenge many of the strong held beliefs that supports these principles.

Alberty (1929) raises concerns that guide the reader to consider some of the more confusing aspects of the progressive education movement. For instance, the mingling together opposing agenda between the teacher and child. While the child is to be free to be creative, at the same time, the teacher must be removed from the creative environment, however, if progressive education is a means for democracy, then the adult also serves as a means in introducing the practice of democracy to the child, unless progressive educators wrongheadedly believe that the child is naturally democratic (which Rousseau, a reported champion to the progressive movement, would clearly reject.)

Likewise, rejecting the third principle of the child-initiated activity in concern for teacher-imposed instruction and curriculum being from the "remote and vague needs of an adult society." Arguably, such a view undermines the role of progressive education in educating for democracy as a need in society. Not many educators in America, progressive or otherwise, would consider any critical need or interest in democracy to be merely remote or vague. However, democracy to a child would initially be distant and unclear without the guidance, instruction, and direction from the teacher or the adult. Moreover, it appears that many of the criticisms of the progressive education movement are worth noting; thus signaling for a fresher perspective with rationally-aligned ideas. To start, there is a need to consider the historical views of progressive education to discover where it lost its way.

HISTORICAL VIEWS

Lawrence Cremin (1961) provides a definitive account about the history of the Progressive education movement. Cremin chronicles that the progressive education movement began in 1867 and ended in 1957, two years after the death of the Progressive Education Association and its journal *Progressive*

Education. Cremin explains the beginnings of progressive education as being part of a "vast [many-sided] humanitarian effort to apply the promise of American life" through using "schools to improve the lives of individuals" (p. viii). With the ideal of an American government by, of, and for the people, progressive education had attempted to practice humanitarian efforts with an American ideal to confront the "puzzling new urban-industrial civilization" during the latter half of the nineteenth century (Cremin, 1961, p. viii).

Among the many-sided efforts, Cremin (1961) describes four general meanings to the progressive education movement. These meanings include 1) broadening the school, its program and functions, to include direct concern for health, vocation, and family/community life; 2) applying classroom pedagogical principles from new scientific research derived in psychology and social sciences; 3) tailoring instruction to different kinds and classes of students; and 4) placing faith that everyone can benefit from culture and the pursuit of the arts in addition to the new sciences (p. viii).

Kett (1994) offers an alternative view and meaning of the progressive education movement that keenly focuses on "educating the public." This meant teaching citizens "to think more rationally and scientifically about their jobs, their health, the raising of their children, and community issues" (Kett, 1994, p. 293). Kett's view of progressive education reinforces the notion that Progressives did not restrict education to only schooling, but rather to a broader educating-the-public crusade through the practice of "popular self-education." Kett prefers to use popular-self education versus adult education, continuing education, or even lifelong learning, given that the term "adult education" was not commonly used until the 1920s.

The progressive education movement that Kett (1994) describes involved Progressives becoming "educational innovators by necessity" (p. 294). Progressives wanted to convince the public about their commitment to make changes for the good of society, and receive support not only in garnering votes at the ballot box, but also for the public to yearn for their advice and ideas. In this regard, the progressive movement emerged from the field of sociology, most notable Lester Frank Ward and George Edward Vincent, who helped to describe the "social intellect" of society. This means that society is not simply physical or mechanical, but rather a mental system and psychic organism (Kett, 1994). In short, the society itself would have its own individual, single consciousness, with its own progressive intellect and will (Kett, 1994; Ward, 1893).

Historical writings of the progressive era and the progressive education movement beginning in 1876 became after more than a decade of Reconstruction (1863-1876), which Eric Foner described as "America's unfinished revolution." There are important efforts in education during Reconstruction including in the 1860s where hundreds of men and women went to the south to teach "the freedmen" eventually under the auspices of the Freedmen's Bureau (Cremin, 1961). Du Bois, *Of the Dawn of Freedom*, describes the greatest success of the Freedmen's Bureau being planting free schools with idea of free elementary education among all people.

The Freedmen Bureau, formerly the Bureau of Refugees, Freedmen, and Abandon Lands was an agency from 1865 to 1872 during the Reconstruction. Parker (1954) describes the educational activities of the Freedmen's Bureau. As Parker explains that in the total educational program of the Freedmen's Bureau, special attention was given to higher education. It was the responsibility of the Bureau to teach the freedmen the following duties and obligations:

1. The duties and privileges of freedom.
2. To work to support themselves and their families;

3. To observe necessary habits of cleanliness for community and personal health and for the control of communicable diseases;
4. To enter into contracts which they had made;
5. The obligation of husband and wife to each other; and
6. The political obligations of being informed on issues and candidates to vote wisely (Parker, 1954, p. 16).

As Parker explains:

Because the socialization of the individual, in its broadest concept, is not complete with the education of the intellect, but involves also the refinement of feelings, and the discipline of the will in the achievement of such self-control that the individual consciously modifies his behavior, these activities were probably as powerful a force for social change as were the activities traditionally termed "educational" (p. 16-17).

What Parker gets to is a broader understanding about the role of education in a supposed democracy. Reading, writing, and arithmetic would be strictly considered educational, but Parker reveals a broad sense of education that includes the socialization of the individual that requires not only the education of the intellect but also the emotional, moral, ethical, and social concepts of education, and their related educational activities. Also Parker's view of the education that took place at the Freedmen's Bureau further supports the impact of education for social change, especially social change in an American democracy.

Many of the early sociologists and social scientists had individual/family connections with the Protestant ministry (Kett, 1994). As Kett (1994) further points out, their religious backgrounds would inspire them to believe that scholars, just as ministers, had public responsibilities; and as Progressive sociologists, had a serious interest in social change, even social engineering and social control. For example, Edward Alsworth Ross, *Social Control* (1901), would describe social scientists and sociologists as social engineers, and prescribe their task for being influential to those who wield the instruments of control, politically and morally. The so-called, political instruments of society would include national, regional, and local political leaders to initiate legislation. The moral instruments would be those who administer the moral capacity of society, namely clergy, editors, lawmakers, judges, and also teachers (Kett, 1994).

Herbert Spencer: Education for Complete Living

The beginnings of the progressive education movement is attributed to the philosophy of Herbert Spencer, especially his work on education that at the peak of in 1882 was the most widely read in America (Cremin, 1961). Spencer's works such as *Social Statics* (1850), *Education: Intellectual, Moral and Physical* and early volumes of the *Synthetic Philosophy*, advance a comprehensive theory of evolution and educational thought. Often described as an hypothesis of Social Darwinism, Spencer considers the progressive development of the mind, culture, society, and most notably education. Spencer's conclusions about education draws from this larger hypothesis of Social Darwinism relating to the development and evolutionary progress of the mind, body, and laws of nature.

In applying Darwin's ideas within a social context, Herbert Spencer (1861) had the most far-reaching influence on teacher and teacher training alongside the progressive movement (Batho, 2001; Elias & Merriam, 2005). A popular example of Spencer's (1861) progressive educational ideas states that:

Children should be led to make their own investigations, and to draw their own inferences. They should be told as little as possible, and induced to discover as much as possible (p. 94).

Although the phrase "induced to discover" Spencer attributes to children, it clearly can also be applied to adult learners and social life. Spencer considers education even broader than for children but an overall preparation for complete living for all humans. For example, Spencer explains that:

To prepare us for complete living…is the function which education has to discharge; and the only rational mode of judging of any educational course is, to judge in what degree it discharges such function (p. 31)

Again, Spencer's writings consider the broader function of education to prepare everyone, children and adults, for "complete living" and also that education should address parenthood and citizenship. Similarly, Spencer advocates for training children not by fear but by freedom (Batho, 2001), which is equally applicable to how adults, as citizens, should function in a democracy–not by fear, but by freedom.

According to Cremin (1961), Spencer classifies the ideal education for complete preparation of living into five divisions or activities that: 1) minister to self-preservation; 2) secure the necessaries of life; 3) rearing and disciplining of offspring; 4) maintain proper social and political relations; and 5) devotion to the gratification of tastes and feelings (Cremin, 1961, p. 92). These five divisions serve as an instructive guide to the broad landscape of progressive education and the progressive education movement. Immediately, we see that education, for children only, is not expressed in Spencer's view on an ideal education. In fact, Spencer found children schooling to be deficient, and relied more on the promise of science in all its forms of intellectual, moral, and religious life; thus science would be the most efficient and economical study for maintaining health, for earning a living, for parenting, for civic duty, and even for the highest expression of the arts (Cremin, 1961).

Spencer's five divisions still provides a productive framework for a new age and era of progressive education. These divisions prescribes a comprehensive approach that includes both the self and the society, as well as properly placing the education of children alongside the fulfillment of adult life and complete living.

Pragmatism as the Philosophy for Progressive Education

This ideal of freedom and liberation is central to progressive education and America. Many American thinkers believe that education can solve social, economic, and political problems (Perkinson, 1977; Elias & Merriam, 2005). Such a belief and knowledge in solving human problems underscore a distinctive American philosophy called Pragmatism, which is the philosophical basis of progressivism and progressive education. Pragmatism views knowledge as a practical activity, or what the pragmatist philosopher, Charles Sanders Peirce (pronounced as, 'purse'), explains as "to do is to know" (Magee, 1998). Besides Peirce, other widely-known philosophers and thinkers of pragmatism include William James and John Dewey. While Peirce's view of pragmatism describes a theory of meaning, William James, on the other hand, explains pragmatism as a theory of truth, stating that truth has a "cash value," meaning that truth's worth is depended upon our specific or relevant environment and experience. Unfortunately, James' view has been misunderstood as suggesting that truth is only relative or whatever works.

Finally, John Dewey further advances the philosophy of pragmatism through the importance of the scientific method and acquiring knowledge as "learning by doing." Perhaps the most salient qualities that progressive education adopts from pragmatism is the emphasis on learning by doing, or hands-on training. Other related qualities include problem solving, critical thinking, and lifelong learning. Thus, through the works of Peirce, James, and Dewey, pragmatism provides the progressive education movement with meaning, truth, and method.

Yet, the uppermost agenda for progressive education is the education for democracy. Dewey (1916) defines democracy as "primarily a form of associated living, a conjoint communicated experience" (p. 93). There are two important terms (and their related description) to consider in Dewey's definition of democracy. These are 1) *living* (i.e., associated living); and 2) *experience* (i.e., conjoint communicated experience). In simple terms, according to Dewey, democracy is about the living that involves our shared experience. Given that pragmatism seeks meaning, truth, and method related to practice, experience, and even action, then progressive education has a vital task in helping persons acquire knowledge from practice, learning from experience, and truth from action.

The philosophy of pragmatism and its connection to progressivism and progressive education is vital for the practice of an educational democracy. The central tenets of pragmatism and its approach to gaining meaning, truth, and methods from shared experience takes on broader tasks such as education for a democracy.

Besides Peirce, James, and Dewey, there are other contemporary American philosophers of pragmatism that further provide perspectives for considering the new practice of educational democracy. While the latter part of Dewey's academic career was at Columbia University and Teachers College in New York, Dewey previously was appointed at the University of Chicago to head a combined department of philosophy, psychology, and pedagogy (Diner, 1980). Dewey and the Chicago pragmatist philosophers, such as George Herbert Mead and James Hayden Tufts, argued for both mind and matter, as a duality, in viewing the world and society as a dynamic, changing process (Diner, 1980).

George Herbert Mead and his work became better recognized after his death where his books where compiled by former students; and his work profoundly influence the development of social psychology within sociology. James Hayden Tufts specialized in ethics and considering the moral and ethical dimensions of social problems for reform (Diner, 1980).

Other pragmatists beyond the classical pragmatists of Peirce, James, and Dewey (including F.C.S. Schiller), are best described as neo-pragmatists or extenders of pragmatism, which some include C.I. Lewis, W.V.O. Quine, C. Wright Mills, and Richard Rorty. The neo-pragmatists both converge and diverge from the classical pragmatists, but offer important insights into the evolution of pragmatism and its effects on the social sciences, public administration, and education.

Another less-acknowledged pragmatist philosopher, W.E.B. DuBois, who was actually a student of William James at Harvard, has applied pragmatism and pragmatist principles to his work and writings. In a book called, the Color of Democracy, DuBois provides further context to what Booker T. Washington explained in his 1896 speech. While many try to place both Washington and DuBois against each other, especially given their ideas about what is the best course of action for Black people in America, truly both held similar views about the role of democracy and its important relationship to education. When Parker (1954) describes the educational activities of the Freedmen's Bureau, Parker notes a quote from DuBois in *Black Reconstruction* (1935):

An individual's estimate of the events of reconstruction depends upon whether he believes that the Negro in America and in general is an average and ordinary human being who under a given environment develops like other human beings, or regards him as a distinctly inferior creation who can never take part in modern civilization and whose emancipation and enfranchisement were gestures against nature.

The distinctive perspective of pragmatism from DuBois features the role of persons and equality among all human beings. This is a critical and vital starting point in terms of the education that occurs in the Reconstruction and even now. What we can begin to see is that the activities or practices that are labelled as 'educational' means more than course subjects and academic disciplines. It involves the entire cultivation of the individual and diverse persons as human in concert with and in contribution to the ultimate progression and evolution of society.

Still, there are those you argue that progressivism and progressive education is a bygone movement. The aims of this movement was never realized. From the moderate view of progressivism, such as Dewey, to the more radical view, such as George Counts, progressivism never really transformed education from the traditional liberal and behavioral approaches. For example, liberal learning still dominates our schools, colleges, and universities; and course objectives still are measures for changes in learning and behavior. Schools, colleges, and universities that promote problem-solving, critical thinking, and social responsibility are scarce in American education.

Antidemocratic System of Schooling

In a democracy, especially an American democracy, it would seem reasonable to believe that education, and all its institutions, levels, and stages, would prepare all persons, as citizens, to participate within a democracy. So what happened?

Actually, Adler (1988) blames Thomas Jefferson, who in 1817 called upon the Virginia legislature to give three years of common schooling to all the children of the state, then after three years, Jefferson advocated for dividing the children into groups of those either destined for labor or destined for leisure and learning. The latter group of children would be sent to college in preparation for citizenship and public office (Adler, 1988, p. xxv). In American education, there still exist a division between college-bound and non-college-bound students, which Adler argues neither quality of education has prepared children for citizenship. About democracy and education, Adler concludes:

It is still a fundamentally antidemocratic system of schooling with a sharp differentiation between two tracks, one for those of inferior ability and one for their betters...[t]he real departure from Jefferson's antidemocratic policy...occurred this century with startling pronouncements by John Dewey and Robert Hutchins...[because] of their commitment to a democratic system of education (p. xxv).

Adler mentions another American educational philosopher, Robert Maynard Hutchins, former University of Chicago president (1929-1945) for his commitment to democracy and education. Hutchins has been widely attributed for saying "the best education for the best was the best education for all."

The key point here is that these educational philosophers and thinkers, namely Dewey, Hutchins, and Adler envision the same education for all children in a democratic society, where our children would become intelligent citizens of our republic and lead full and enriched lives. While these educational philosophers and thinkers prescribed a democratic proposal for all education, they still restricted such an education for children only. This child-only education restriction has inhibited the growth of education to fully complement democracy.

The reasons to explain the underdevelopment of education are clearly complex and complicated, but this chapter identifies at least one specific misstep. Simply, the national narrative that restricts the term education to mean almost entirely the formal schooling of children and adolescents. Included in the broader landscape of education are informal ways of education beyond-the-school and the inclusion of adults as fellow learners.

In assessment, it appears that the Dewey's influence on progressivism and progressive education rests on Dewey's philosophical synthesis of pragmatism leading to conclusions upon education. While Dewey's writings have been often difficult to discern, placing his works with a broader philosophical lens has further led to needless ambiguity and abstraction. The salient contribution of Dewey is what Adler points out is to conceptualize an education for democracy. How progressive educators have interpreted what constitutes such an education for democracy must rather rely on distinguishable principles and practices. In other words, the development of an educational democracy would put such practices into immediate action.

ADULT EDUCATION AS LIFEBLOOD OF DEMOCRACY

Paul Bergevin (1967), an advocate for adult education, underscores this child-only restriction of American education and schooling. Bergevin's argument is that in every society, adults make the decisions, thus the quality of any society will depend upon the educational level of its adults. Bergevin presents the analogy of children's formal schooling as an "educational meal," suggesting that while children's education is important, adults believe that the education they received (the educational meal) as children was enough to carry them through the "vicissitudes of adult life," and as Bergevin continues, "[t]he one big, or maybe not so big, educational meal taken as children can hardly be expected to sustain us through a lifetime full of challenge and change and adjustment" (p. v). The Bergevin argument for a broader view of education that includes adults is more than formal schooling at one-moment-in-time, but rather a continuous feeding of education that sustains throughout the span of our lifetime. If we consider what it might take for education to meet the challenge and change and adjustment of a democracy, then, at present, we are citizens, who are uneducated to participate, in other words, in our democracy, we are educationally malnourished.

The kind of education, or to borrow Bergevin words, the 'educational meal' that is required to prepare both children and adults to continually live, experience, and participate in a democracy requires a newer movement. Some of the infrastructure of progressivism and the progressive education movement are functioning and intact, but still requires remodeling that changes the structure of progressive education through both demolition and a finished reconstruction that will bring into existence a new phase of education that is broader and more inclusive in every way.

Eduard Lindeman, a leader in adult education, considers the role of democracy and its relationship to not only adult education but education for both children and adults. Best known for the book entitled, *The Meaning of Adult Education* (1926), Lindeman would write many relevant works from the span of 1915-1953, during the same timeframe of many of John Dewey's most significant works. Lindeman derives many of his ideas from Dewey and like Dewey, Lindeman considers himself to be a pragmatist and "social philosopher," who extend epistemology and logic of philosophy into the social problems of society and humankind (Stewart, 1987).

A Lindeman biographer, David Wood Stewart (1987), noted how many sentences in Dewey's writings, in fact assures Dewey "a place among the important forebears of adult education in the United States" (p. 137). Sentences that Stewart selects from Dewey's *Democracy and Education* (1916) to support this point includes how Dewey sees education as "continuous process of growth, having as its aim at every stage an added capacity of growth" (Dewey, 1916, p. 63), and "education means the enterprise of supplying the conditions which insure growth, or adequacy of life, irrespective of age" (Dewey, 1916, p. 61).

Although such sentences and passages in Dewey's writings show genuine concern for the education of adults, Stewart (1987) points how Dewey had little time for adult education, and "busied himself with other interests," most notably education in the childhood years, for the development and advancement of what would eventually be called "progressive education" (p.137). Thus, Lindeman seized upon Dewey's ideas, and would "integrate them with freshets coming from other philosophical sources, and apply them with potency to the field of adult education" (p. 137).

Lindeman challenges some Deweyian terms to explain the concept of adult education, such as "maturity," which is a concept used in psychology, and perhaps a vestige of William James' views within pragmatism. Lindeman rejects the term maturity and prefers to explain the concept of adult education as a continuing process of evaluating experiences, and that adult education was not merely for the preparation of life, but rather is a process that is "coterminous" with life itself (Stewart, 1987, p.138).

Because Lindeman has written indiscriminately in books, journals, periodicals and others, Stewart makes a valuable contribution in identifying four central assumptions about adult education in Lindeman's writings, especially from *The Meaning of Adult Education* (1926). Lindeman (1926) frames adult education in a universal context through the "categories of experience," showing how education provides experiences in the continuous relationship of the adult (as learner) to society, and to life itself. Stewart (1987) lists four key revised assumptions that can be drawn from Lindeman views of adult education:

1. Education is *a process coterminous with all of* life–not a mere preparation for an unknown kind of future living;
2. Adult education revolves around non-vocational and nonacademic ideals;
3. The approach to adult education will be via the route of situations, not subjects; and
4. The resource of highest value in adult education is the learner's experience (p. 111-112, italics emphasized in the original).

Lindeman's four assumptions about adult education would also be applied to his values of democracy. As Stewart (1987) explains, Lindeman held that democracy was fragile, and that the future of democracy would depend upon the intelligent use of adult education as the "chief instrument of the democratic process," or in other words, adult education, in Lindeman's view would serve as the "lifeblood of democracy" (p. 171).

Lindeman's writings serve as a catalyst into the practice of educational democracy for this new century. Another misstep in the history of progressive education, was its limited focus on the childhood years of education, especially as it had related to democracy, which was a central focus of progressive education. Thus, in the practice of educational democracy, education across the years of childhood, adolescence, and adulthood are required.

Bergevin (1967) presents a framework of beliefs concerning a philosophy of adult education that many of them not only advances Lindeman's notion of adult education for the future of democracy, but also as an additional outline of principles for a new era of progressive education. Among the twenty-two beliefs that Bergevin presents, there are five that are essential to considering the means by which adults contribute to education and democracy:

1. Adults must be offered and helped to use the opportunity to act responsibly in several facets of their lives: political, vocational, cultural, spiritual, and physical;
2. Adults should assume the obligation to learn to become more productive citizens;
3. Vital concepts as freedom, discipline, and responsibility can be comprehended by experiences them through a variety of inspired learning experiences in a host of subjects;
4. What is called a free or democratic society must strongly emphasize lifelong learning for all its citizens, if they propose to remain free and to use their freedom effectively; and
5. The democratic idea fits the nature of man and also of adult education (Bergevin, 1967, p. 5-6)

These five Bergevin beliefs gets at the focal point in the practice of educational democracy, where the lives of adults and children are continuously developed in a free and democratic society. In comparing Lindeman's assumptions and Bergevin's beliefs, there are some details worth highlighting. Lindeman takes a more restricted view about adult education, demarcating clear lines between adult education and vocational education also formal academic schooling. Also Lindeman assumes that situations and not course subjects is the right approach toward adult education. These distinctions make clear Lindeman's concern about education being viewed as a preparation for future living, rather than education being a process "coterminous" with all of life that treats the learner's experience as the highest value of education.

Bergevin's beliefs are broader, including both formal schooling and vocational education under the aegis of adult education. Also, Bergevin sees all facets of life (namely, political, vocational, cultural, spiritual, and physical) alongside large-scale concepts such as freedom, discipline, and responsibility. Yet the most important feature of Bergevin's belief summons all adults to be "productive citizens" in a free and democratic society through the use of lifelong learning, which basically comes down to one essential duty: our "obligation to learn." It is the obligation to learn that pulls it altogether; it will serve as the first practice of educational democracy.

The Practices of Educational Democracy

This chapter explores the progressive era and the progressive education movement according to its historical views, phases, and guiding principles. Also this chapter explores several foundations and disciplines of progressivism; from the sociology of Darwinism to the philosophy of Pragmatism. The embodiment of the progressive era and the progressive education movement rests upon the social philosopher, John Dewey, who among his voluminous writings and words (especially from Democracy and Education) provide a definitive foundation for any past and future progressive movement. This chapter calls for a new movement in progressive education not bounded by the actions of its past but for its applicability for its urgency in cultivating a democracy.

Such cultivation requires a new way at looking at the same-old problems. In America, educators from the past progressive movement, at the start of the twentieth century, were facing some the same social, economic, and political challenges that we still face today—decades into the twenty-first century. They faced rapid urbanization, mass immigration, and industrialization, and today we face economic gentrification, immigration/citizenship, and far-reaching technological advances. In a democracy, there will always be challenges, but how we face those challenges through an effective means of education can keep our republic intact.

The practice of educational democracy is an effective means to address the problems, challenges, and changes in America. One inescapable problem that has existed since its founding, is the race problem in the United States. Many American leaders throughout history have spoken to this persistent problem: Frederick Douglass, Booker T. Washington, W.E.B. DuBois, Alexander Crummell, Martin Luther King Jr., and also Malcolm X, Stokely Carmichael, James Baldwin, Ida B. Wells, Cornell West, and Eddie Glaude Jr. As you read this list of leaders, they are often described as political, maybe philosophical, social, even radical, but never *educational*.

One of the practices of educational democracy is open communication and dialogue among everyone. For no comprehensive solution can be achieved, if no communication is given to all aspects of the problem. Even the race problem requires communication; even more than the voices from the leaders aforementioned, but from every person, Black or White (or any other race or ethnicity), to gain the full scope and depth of the problem. If education is to help democracy with such problems, open communication must occur. To be clear, open communication and dialogue should not be confused with debate and divisive argument. Debate seeks a winner and loser (a remnant of political bantering); however, communication and dialogue seeks truth and understanding.

Another practice of educational democracy is the reconstruction of schools, colleges, and universities, as well as neighborhoods, communities, and cities being relational than transactional. At present, schools are not only seen as limited to children, but they look at scores, grades, and examinations as the only measures of achievement. Schools should be for both children and adults, not according to grade, but according to the degree of interest in learning throughout one's lifetime.

A third practice of educational democracy that would rebuild our democracy is the "obligation to learn." An obligation has a binding characteristic that compels us physically, morally, intelligently, culturally, and philosophically. The educational democracy practice that obligates us to learn, would achieve a freedom and unity through our binding together, our sense of duty, responsibility, and promise to one another, as fellow learners, as fellow citizens, as one people.

Final Thoughts

The premise of this chapter assumed an unequal relationship between democracy and education; which confronts Dewey's description about their duality. Both as an educator and philosopher, the author subscribes to Dewey's intention, but confirm that education in its present sense, is still inadequate to be on par with democracy. For education to meet the challenge, change, and adjustment of democracy, the practice of educational democracy must be implemented. Before education can reach its rightful place as an equal to democracy, education must grow and develop. Such growth and development not only includes access to both children and adults, but also includes changing curriculum and instruction, as well as transforming its assessment and evaluation. One of the central tenets of the progressive educator is to adopt a clear understanding of what progress means. Darwin's evolution began an entire body of scholarship that began on the premise that society could evolve as well, in a continuing state of evolution and progress. Thus, the historical progressive movement believed in "Social Darwinism."

However the practice of educational democracy begins a new experiment that proves education's worth and value to democracy and society as a whole. Even labeling Education with a capital "E" is not enough. At the time of this writing, the author began to consider what is called, "Educationality," as a more creative and aspirational term that expresses when education has reached its fullest potential—in union with Democracy. Perhaps in the future progressive educators may tell an innovative new story of Educationality and Democracy, not as disrespect to Dewey, but rather as a momentous milestone for progressive educators' hopeful aims.

REFERENCES

Alberty, H. B. (1929). The progressive education movement. *Educational Research Bulletin, 8*(8), 163–169.

Apple, M. W., & Teitelbaum, K. (2001). John Dewey 1859-1952. In J. A. Palmer (Ed.), *Fifty Major Thinkers on Education: From Confucius to Dewey* (pp. 177–182). Routledge.

Batho, G. R. (2001). Herbert Spencer 1820-1903. In J. A. Palmer (Ed.), *Fifty Major Thinkers on Education: From Confucius to Dewey* (pp. 120–123). Routledge.

Bellah, R. N., Madsen, R., Sullivan, W. M., Swidler, A., & Tipton, S. M. (1991). *The good society.* Alfred A. Knopf.

Benne, K. D. (1967). *Education for tragedy: Essays in disenchanted hope for modern man.* University of Kentucky Press.

Bergevin, P. (1967). *A philosophy for adult education.* The Seabury Press.

BlackPast. (2010, July 13). *(1896) Booker T. Washington, "Democracy and Education."* Retrieved from BlackPast.org: https://www.blackpast.org/african-american-history/speeches-african-american-history/1896-booker-t-washington-democracy-and-education/

Cremin, L. A. (1961). *The transformation of the school: Progressivism in the American education 1876-1957.* Vintage.

Cremin, L. A. (1988). *American education: The metropolitan experience 1876-1980.* Harper & Row Publishers.

Cuban, L. (2015). Federal education policy and democracy. *Teachers College Record, 177*, 1–7.

Dewey, J. (1916). *Democracy and education: An introduction to the philosophy of education.* The Free Press.

Elias, J. L., & Merriam, S. B. (2001). *Philosophical foundations of adult education* (3rd ed.). Krieger.

Fallace, T. D. (2011). Tracing John Dewey's influence on progressive education, 1903-1951: Toward a received Dewey. *Teachers College Record, 113*(3), 463–492. doi:10.1177/016146811111300307

Foner, E. (1988). *Reconstruction: America's unfinished revolution 1863-1877.* Harper & Row Publishers.

Goodlad, J. I. (1994). *What schools are for* (2nd ed.). Phi Delta Kappa Educational Foundation.

Goodlad, J. I. (1997). *In praise of education.* Teachers College Press.

Goodlad, J. I., Mantle-Bromley, C., & Goodlad, S. J. (2004). *Education for everyone: Agenda for education in a democracy*. Jossey-Bass.

Gruber, F. C. (1973). *Historical and contemporary philosophies of education*. Thomas Y. Crowell.

Howard, D. M., Howard, J., & Scott, L. (2017). From the classroom to the workforce: Empowering students to find their career passion. *The Journal of Health Administration Education*, *34*(3), 395–405.

Johnston, J. S. (2006). *Inquiry and education: John Dewey and the quest for democracy*. SUNY Press.

Kett, J. F. (1994). *The pursuit of knowledge under difficulties: From self-improvement to adult education in America, 1750-1990*. Stanford University Press.

Osborn, H. F. (2021). *Huxley on education: Address at the opening of the college year, Columbia University, September 28, 1910*. Mt. San Antonio College.

Perkinson, H. (1977). *The imperfect panacea: American faith in education 1865-1976*. Random House.

Pope Leo, X. I. I. I. (2021). *Catholicism and Socialism: Encyclicals of Pope Leo XIII: Rerum Novarum (1878), Quaod Apostolici Muneris (1891), Gravis de Communi Re (1901)*. Claritas Publications.

Ross, E. A. (1901). *Social control: A survey of the foundations of order*. The Macmillan Company.

Schneider, H. W. (1963). *A history of American philosophy* (2nd ed.). Columbia University Press.

Scott, L. (2015). Learning cities for adult learners. New Directions for Adult and Continuing Education. San Francisco, CA: Jossey-Bass.

Scott, L. (2017). Learning cities. In A. Knox, S. Conceicao, & L. Martin (Eds.), Mapping the Field of Adult and Continuing Education: An International Compendium (Vol. 4). Sterling, VA: Stylus.

Scott, L. (2021). Learning cities as smart cities: Connecting lifelong learning and technology. In F. Annansingh (Ed.), *Examining the Socio-Technical Impact of Smart Cities* (pp. 68–90). IGI Global. doi:10.4018/978-1-7998-5326-8.ch003

Scott, L., Mizzi, R. C., & Merriweather, L. R. (2020). Philosophical foundations of adult continuing education. In *2020 Handbook of Adult and Continuing Education. Sterling* (pp. 11–21). Stylus.

Severson, D. (2009). *John Dewey's Essentials for Democracy and Education*. Proficiency Publishers.

Ward, L. F. (1893). *The psychic factors of civilization*. Ginn & Company.

Westbrook, R. B. (1991). *John Dewey and American democracy*. Cornell University Press.

Compilation of References

21st Century School Fund. (2002). *For Generations to Come: A Leadership Guide to Renewing Public School Buildings.* 21st Century School Fund.

Aaron, H. J. (1975). *Who Pays the Property Tax? A New View*. Brookings Institution Press.

AARP. (2022). *List of Coronavirus-Related Restrictions in Every State.* Retrieved March 22, 2022, from https://www.aarp.org/politics-society/government-elections/info-2020/coronavirus-state-restrictions.html

Abbott v. Burke, 100 N.J. 269, 495 A. 2D 376 (New Jersey 1985).

Abbott v. Burke, 119 N.J. 287, 575 A. 2d 359 (New Jersey 1990).

Abbott v. Burke, 136 N.J. 444, 643 A.2d 575 (New Jersey 1994).

Abbott v. Burke, 149 N.J. 119 (New Jersey 1997).

Abbott v. Burke, 153 N.J. 480, 710 A.2d 450 (New Jersey 1998).

Abbott v. Burke, 163 N.J. 95, 748 A. 2d 82 (New Jersey 2000).

Abbott v. Burke, 170 N.J. 537, 790 A. 2d 842 (New Jersey 2002).

Abbott v. Burke, 172 N.J. 294, 798 A. 2d 602 (New Jersey 2002).

Abbott v. Burke, 177 N.J. 578, 832 A. 2d 891 (New Jersey 2003).

Abbott v. Burke, 177 N.J. 596, 83 A. 2d 906 (New Jersey 2003).

Abbott, K. W., Genschel, P., Snidal, D., & Zangl, B. (2010) *IOs as Orchestrators*. Paper presented at the 7th Pan-European Conference on International Relations, Stockholm, Sweden.

Abdallah-Pretceille, M. (2006). Socio-interculturalism as a paradigm for thinking about diversity. *Socio-intercultural Education, 17*(5), 475–483. doi:10.1080/14675980601065764

Adams-Bass, V. N., Stevenson, H. C., & Kotzin, D. (2014). Measuring the meaning of Black media stereotypes and their relationship to the racial identity: Black history knowledge and racial socialization of African American youth. *Journal of Black Studies, 45*(5), 367–395. doi:10.1177/0021934714530396

Adamson, P. (2013). *Child Well-being in Rich Countries: A comparative overview.* Retrieved from UNICEF Office of Research: https://www.unicef-irc.org/publications/683-child-well-being-in-rich-countries-a-comparative-overview.html

Adil, A., & Negron, A. (n.d.). Revolutionizing Chicago ft. Dr. Suzet McKinney. Academic Press.

Age Discrimination in Employment Act, 29 U.S.C. § 621 (1967).

AHA. (2021, May 26). *Fact Sheet: Strengthening the Health Care Workforce*. American Hospital Association. https://www.aha.org/fact-sheets/2021-05-26-fact-sheet-strengthening-health-care-workforce

Ahearn, K. K., Ferris, G. R., Hochwarter, W. A., Douglas, C., & Ammeter, A. P. (2004). Leader Political Skill and Team Performance. *Journal of Management*, *30*(3), 309–327. doi:10.1016/j.jm.2003.01.004

Ahmed, S. M., & Palermo, A. (2010). Community engagement in research: Frameworks for education and peer review. *American Journal of Public Health*, *100*(8), 1380–1387. doi:10.2105/AJPH.2009.178137 PMID:20558798

Ahuja, G., & Lampert, C. (2016). Entrepreneurship in the large corporation: A longitudinal study of how established firms create breakthrough inventions. *Strategic Management Journal*, (22), 521–543.

Ajzen, I. (1991). The theory of planned behavior. *Organizational Behavior and Human Decision Processes*, *50*(2), 179–211. doi:10.1016/0749-5978(91)90020-T

Alarcon, G. M. (2011). A meta-analysis of burnout with job demands, resources, and attitudes. *Journal of Vocational Behavior*, *79*(2), 549–562. doi:10.1016/j.jvb.2011.03.007

Alberty, H. B. (1929). The progressive education movement. *Educational Research Bulletin*, *8*(8), 163–169.

Albright, L., & Malloy, T. (1999). Self-observation of social behavior in metaperception. *Journal of Personality and Social Psychology*, *77*(4), 726–734. doi:10.1037/0022-3514.77.4.726 PMID:10531669

Alesina, A., Campante, F. R., & Tabellini, G. (2008, September). Why is Fiscal Policy Procyclical? *Journal of the European Economic Association*, 1–2.

Alexander, E. R. (1995). *How Organizations Act Together: Interorganizational Coordination in Theory and Practice*. Gordon & Breach.

Alleman, E. (1986). Measuring mentoring frequency, quality, and impact. In W. A. Gray & M. M. Gray (Eds.), *Mentoring: Aid to excellence in career development, business, and the professions* (pp. 44–51). The Xerox Reproduction Centre.

Alliance, D. P. (2018). *Women, prison, and the drug war*. Academic Press.

Almeida, T., Heitor, M., Santos, O., Costa, A., Virgolino, A., Rasga, C., & Vicente, A. (2020). *Relatório final: SM-COVID19 – Saúde mental em tempos de pandemia*. Instituto Nacional de Saúde Doutor Ricardo Jorge.

Alsan, M., Garrick, O., & Graziani, G. (2019). Does diversity matter for health? Experimental evidence from Oakland. *The American Economic Review*, *109*(12), 4071–4111. doi:10.1257/aer.20181446

Altibi, A. M., Pallavi, B., Liaqat, H., Slota, A. A., Sheth, R., Al Jebbawi, L., George, M. E., LeDuc, A., Abdallah, E., Russell, L. R., Jain, S., Shirvanian, N., Masri, A., & Kak, V. (2021). Characteristics and comparative clinical outcomes of prisoner versus non-prisoner populations hospitalized with COVID-19. *Scientific Reports*, *11*(1), 1–9. doi:10.103841598-021-85916-w PMID:33753786

Amalgamated Transit Union, Local 900 v. Suburban Bus Div. of Regional Transp. Authority, 262 Ill.App.3d 334, 341 (1st Dist. 1994).

American Psychological Association Zero Tolerance Task Force. (2008). Zero tolerance policies effective in the schools? An evidentiary review and recommendations. *The American Psychologist*, *63*(9), 852–862. doi:10.1037/0003-066X.63.9.852 PMID:19086747

ANA. (n.d.). *Nurses, ethics, and the response to the covid 19 pandemic*. American Nurses Association. https://www.nursingworld.org/~495c6c/globalassets/practiceandpolicy/work-environment/health--safety/coronavirus/nurses-ethics-and-the-response-to-the-covid-19-pandemic.pdf

Anderson, K., & Jack, D. (1991). Learning to listen: Interview techniques and analyses. *Women's words: The feminist practice of oral history by Gluck,* 11-15.

Anderson, M. (2019). US airline orders first passenger electric plane: The battery-powered nine-seater aircraft will enter service in 2022. *IEEE Spectrum*, *56*(09), 10–11. doi:10.1109/MSPEC.2019.8818579

Angelis, J. D., & Kupchik, A. (2009). Ethnicity, trust, and acceptance of authority among police officers. *Journal of Criminal Justice*, *37*(3), 273–279. doi:10.1016/j.jcrimjus.2009.04.007

Ang, S., & Inkpen, A. C. (2008). Cultural intelligence and offshore outsourcing success: A framework of organization-level socio-intercultural capability. *Decision Sciences*, *2008*(39), 337–358. doi:10.1111/j.1540-5915.2008.00195.x

Annie E. Casey Foundation. (2017). *Data snapshot on high poverty communities*. Kids count. Retrieved from http://www.aecf.org/~/media/Pubs/Initiatives/KIDSCOUNT/ Data SnapshotonPovertyCommunities.pdf

Anonymous. (1984). Collective Bargaining in the Public Sector. *Harv. Law Review*, *97*(1676), 1680–1681.

Antcliff, K., Borer, N., Sartorius, S., Saleh, P., Rose, R., Gariel, M., . . . Oullette, R. (2021). *Regional Air Mobility: Leveraging Our National Investments to Energize the American Travel Experience*. Retrieved from NASA: https://sacd.larc.nasa.gov/sacd/wp-content/uploads/sites/102/2021/04/2021-04-20-RAM.pdf

Anvon, J. (1997). *Ghetto Schooling: A POlitical Economy of Urban Education Reform*. Teachers College Press.

Anvon, J. (2005). *Radical Possibilities: Public Policy, Urgan Education, and a New Social Movement*. Routledge, Taylor and Francis Group.

Apple, M. W., & Teitelbaum, K. (2001). John Dewey 1859-1952. In J. A. Palmer (Ed.), *Fifty Major Thinkers on Education: From Confucius to Dewey* (pp. 177–182). Routledge.

Arabena, K. (2005). *Not fit for modern Australian society. Aboriginal and Torres Strait Island people and the new arrangements for the administration of Indigenous Affairs.* Research Discussion Paper No. 16. AIATSIS.

Ardery, G. (1990). Mentors and protégés: From ideology to knowledge. In J. Mccloskey & H. Grace (Eds.), *Current issues in nursing* (pp. 58–63). Mosby.

Armstrong, L. (2003). *Financial management and business systems: the backbone of an effectively resourced capacity for governance*. Paper presented to the Building Effective Indigenous Governance Conference. http://www.nt.gov.au/cdsca/indigenous conference/web/html/papers.html

Armstrong, L. (2007). Finding Australia's soul: rebuilding our Indigenous communities. *The Circle*, *1*, 74–6. https://www.socialventures.com.au/files/pdf/TC%20mag%20Leah%20Armstrong.pdf

Association of American Medical Colleges. (2019). *Diversity in medicine: Facts and figures 2019*. Association of American Medical Colleges.

AT&T Technologies v. Communications Workers, 475 U.S. 643 (1986).

Atkins, P., Enard, K. R., Griffin-Hunter, K., & Howard, D. (2021, July 22). *Amplifying Black Voices: What health care organizations can do to advance diversity, equity, and inclusion in the workforce*. Retrieved from Deloite.com: https://www2.deloitte.com/us/en/insights/industry/health-care/diversity-in-healthcare-workforce.html

Augenblick, W. (2001). *Recommendations to the National Center for Education Statistics to Improve Its Role Regarding School Finance Data: The Perspective of State Policymakers*. U.S. Department of Education, National Center for Education Statistics.

Baez, B. (2000). Race-Related Service and Faculty of Color: Conceptualizing Critical Agency in Academe. *Higher Education*, *39*(3), 363–391. doi:10.1023/A:1003972214943

Bagshaw, G. (1977). *Analysis of Local Government in a Multi-Clan Community* [BA (Hons) Dissertation]. Department of Anthropology, The University of Adelaide.

Bagwell, S., & Evans, G. (2012). *Public Space Management, report to the socio-intercultural cities programme*. Council of Europe Publishing. www.coe.int/socio-interculturaLcitiezs

Baker Machinery Co., 184 NLRB 358 (1970).

Baker, B., & Green, P. (2002). Commentary: Can Minority Plaintiffs Use the Department of Education Implementing Regulations to Challenge School Finance Disparieis. *Texas Forum on Civiil Liberties and Civil Rights*, *7*(2), 141–165.

Bakker, A., & Demerouti, E. (2007). The Job Demands-Resources model: State of the art. *Journal of Managerial Psychology*, *22*(3), 309–328. doi:10.1108/02683940710733115

Bakker, A., Demerouti, E., & Euwema, M. (2005). ob Resources Buffer the Impact of Job Demands on Burnout. *Journal of Occupational Health Psychology*, *10*(2), 170–180. doi:10.1037/1076-8998.10.2.170 PMID:15826226

Balch, R. W. (1972). The police personality: Fact or fiction? *The Journal of Criminal Law, Criminology, and Police Science*, *63*(1), 106. doi:10.2307/1142281

Baldacci, E., Gupta, S., & Mulas-Granados, C. (2012). *How Effective Is Fiscal Policy Response in Financial Crises?* Retrieved from International Monetary Fund: https://www.imf.org/external/np/seminars/eng2012/fincrises/pdf/ch14.pdf

Bambra, C., Riordan, R., Ford, J., & Matthews, F. (2020). The COVID-19 pandemic and health inequalitites. *Journal of Epidemiology and Community Health*, *74*(11), 964–968. PMID:32535550

Bandura, A. (1977). Self-efficacy: Toward a unifying theory of behavioral change. *Psychological Review.* Retrieved from ProQuest database. (63957362)

Bandura, A. (1978). The self-system in reciprocal determinism. *American Psychologist, 33*(4), 344-358. http://dx.doi.org.ezproxy.roosevelt.edu:2048/10.1037/0003-066X.33.4.344

Bandura, A. (1982). Self-efficacy mechanism in human agency. *American Psychologist, 37*(2), 122-147. http://dx.doi.org.ezproxy.roosevelt.edu:2048/10.1037/0003-066X.37.2.122

Bandura, A. (2001). Social cognitive theory: An agentic perspective. *Annual Review of Psychology*, 52, 1-26. http://dx.doi.org.ezproxy.roosevelt.edu:2048/ 10.1146/annurev.psych.52.1

Bandura, A., & Cervone, D. (1983). Self-evaluative and self-efficacy mechanisms governing the motivational effects of goal systems. *Journal of Personality and Social Psychology, 45*(5), 1017-1028. http://dx.doi.org.ezproxy.roosevelt.edu:2048/10.1037/0022-3514.45.5.1017

Bandura, A., Barbaranelli, C., Capara, G. V., & Pastorelli, C. (2001). Self-efficacy beliefs as shapers of children's aspirations and career trajectories. *Child Development, 72*(1), 187–206. doi:10.1111/1467-8624.00273 PMID:11280478

Banilower, E. R., Smith, P. S., Malzahn, K. A., Plumley, C. L., Gordon, E. M., & Hayes, M. L. (2018). *Report of the 2018 NSSME*. Horizon Research, Inc.

Bansal, M. (2020). Cardiovascular disease and COVID-19. *Diabetes & Metabolic Syndrome, 14*(3), 247–250. doi:10.1016/j.dsx.2020.03.013 PMID:32247212

Baron, C. (2003). La gouvernance: Débats autour d'un concept polysémique. *Droit Social*, (54), 329–351. doi:10.3917/drs.054.0329

Barreto, C. (2020). Prevalência de burnout é maior em médicos que atuam na linha de frente da Covid-19. *PedMed, 8*(6), 1781–1790.

Barro, S. (1992). *What Does the Education Dollar Buy? Relationships of Staffing, Staff Characteristics, and Staff Salaries to State Per-Pupil Spending*. The Finance Center of CPRE.

Basford, T. E., Offermann, L. R., & Behrend, T. S. (2014). Do you see what I see? Perceptions of gender microaggressions in the workplace. *Psychology of Women Quarterly, 38*(3), 340–349. doi:10.1177/0361684313511420

Batho, G. R. (2001). Herbert Spencer 1820-1903. In J. A. Palmer (Ed.), *Fifty Major Thinkers on Education: From Confucius to Dewey* (pp. 120–123). Routledge.

Baumeister, S., Leung, A., & Ryley, T. (2020). The emission reduction potentials of first generation electric aircraft (FGEA) in Finland. *Journal of Transport Geography, 85*(C), 102730. doi:10.1016/j.jtrangeo.2020.102730

Beck, M. (1958). Government Finance in New Jersey. In The Economy of New Jersey: A Report Prepared for the Department of Conservation and Economic Development of the State of New Jersey, (p. 560). Rutgers University Press.

Behrendt, L., McCausland, R., Williams, G., Reilly, A., & McMillan, M. (2007). The promise of regional governance for Aboriginal and Torres Strait Islander communities. *Ngiya: Talk the Law. Governance in Indigenous Communities, 1*, 126–166.

Bellah, R. N., Madsen, R., Sullivan, W. M., Swidler, A., & Tipton, S. M. (1991). *The good society*. Alfred A. Knopf.

Bem, D. J. (1967). Self-perception: An alternative interpretation of cognitive dissonance phenomena. *Psychological Review, 74*(3), 183–200. doi:10.1037/h0024835 PMID:5342882

Benevides-Pereira, A. (2002). *Burnout: quando o trabalho ameaça o bem estar do trabalhador*. Casa do Psicólogo.

Benevides-Pereira, A. (2002). *Burnout: quando o trabalho ameaça o bem-estar do trabalhador*. Casa do Psicólogo.

Benight, C. C., & Bandura, A. (2004). Social cognitive theory of posttraumatic recovery: The role of perceived self-efficacy. *Behaviour Research and Therapy, 42*(10), 1129–1148. doi:10.1016/j.brat.2003.08.008 PMID:15350854

Benne, K. D. (1967). *Education for tragedy: Essays in disenchanted hope for modern man*. University of Kentucky Press.

Bennet, H. (2003). Humour in medicine. *Scientific Medical Journal, 96*(12), 1257–1261.

Berger, J., Polivka, B., Smoot, E. A., & Owens, H. (2015). Compassion fatigue in pediatric nurses. *Journal of Pediatric Nursing*, *30*(6), e11–e17. doi:10.1016/j.pedn.2015.02.005 PMID:25800590

Bergevin, P. (1967). *A philosophy for adult education*. The Seabury Press.

Berkhout, S. G., & Richardson, L. (2020). Identity, politics, and the pandemic: Why is COVID-19 a disaster for feminism(s)? *History and Philosophy of the Life Sciences*, *42*(4), 1–6. doi:10.100740656-020-00346-7 PMID:33048278

Berne, R., & Stiefel, L. (1984). *The Measurement of Equity in School Finance: Conceptual, Methodological and Empirical Dimensions*. The Johns Hopkins University Press.

Berne, R., & Stiefel, L. (1999). Concepts of School Finance Equity: 1970 to Present. In H. F. Ladd (Ed.), *Equity and Adequacy in Education Finance: Issues and Perspectives,* (pp. 7–33). National Academy Press.

Bernier v. Morningstar, Inc., 495 F.3d 369 (7th Cir. 2007).

Bernstein, S., & Cashore, B. (2007). Can Non-State Global Governance be Legitimate? *Regulation & Governance*, *1*(4), 347–371. doi:10.1111/j.1748-5991.2007.00021.x

Bertsch, L., Simons, D. G., & Snellen, M. (2015). Aircraft Noise: The major sources, modelling capabilities, and reduction possibilities (IB 224-2015 A 110 ed.) DLR.

Beyer, J., & Hassel, A. (2002). The market for corporate control and financial internationalization of German firms. *Economy and Society*, 31.

Bibeau, G., Dussault, G., Larouche, M., Lippel, K., Saucier, F., Véniza, M., & Vidal, M. (1989). *Certaine aspects culturels, diagnostiques et juridiques de burnout*. Condefération de Syndicats Nationaux.

Bidarian, S., & Jafari, P. (2012). The relationship between organizational justice and organizational trust. *Procedia: Social and Behavioral Sciences*, *47*, 1622–1626. doi:10.1016/j.sbspro.2012.06.873

Bielby, W. T. (2000). Minimizing Workplace Gender and Racial Bias. *Contemporary Sociology*, *29*(1), 120. doi:10.2307/2654937

BlackPast. (2010, July 13). *(1896) Booker T. Washington, "Democracy and Education."* Retrieved from BlackPast.org: https://www.blackpast.org/african-american-history/speeches-african-american-history/1896-booker-t-washington-democracy-and-education/

Blanchard, L. A., & Duncombe, W. (1999). Tax Policy and Public School Finance. In J. Hildreth & W. B. Richardson (Eds.), *Handbook on Taxation* (pp. 345–400). Marcel Dekker, Inc.

Blaschke, S., Frost, J., & Hattke, F. (2014). Towards a micro foundation of leadership, governance, and management in universities. *Higher Education*, *68*(5), 711–732. doi:10.100710734-014-9740-2

BobboSphere. (2012, November 12). *Don Moore 1942-2012: A lion who roared on behalf of public education*. Retrieved from Daily Kos: https://www.dailykos.com/stories/2012/11/12/1160687/-Don-Moore-1942-2012-A-l%20ion-who-roared-on-behalf-of-public-education

Bordentown Register News. (2005, August 22). Budget-Making Process Ruins Our Appetite. *Bordentown Register News*.

Borges, F., Aragão, D., Borges, F., Borges, F., Sousa, A., & Machado, A. (2021). atores de risco para a Síndrome de Burnout em profissionais da saúde durante a pandemia de COVID-19. *Revista Enfermagem Atual In Derme*, *95*(33), 1–15. doi:10.31011/reaid-2020-v.94-n.32-art.835

Börzel, T., & Risse, T. (2010). Governance without a state: can it work? *Regulation and Governance, 4*(2), 113–34.

Bostock v. Clayton County, Georgia, 140 S. Ct. 1731 (2020).

Bragard, I., Dupuis, G., & Fleet, G. (2015). Quality of work life, burnout, and stress in emergency department physicians: a qualitative review. *European journal of emergency medicine: official journal of the European Society for Emergency Medicine, 22(4)*, 227-234.

Brand, N., & Biren, M. H. (2008). *Discipline and Discharge in Arbitration* (2nd ed.). American Bar Association Section of Labor and Employment Law.

Braun, R. (1990, October 26). School Chiefs Say Funding Law Threatens the Best. *Neward Star-Ledger*, p. 1.

Bremen High School District 228, 37 PERI ¶ 94 (ISLRB 2021).

Brennan Center. (2022). *Fact Sheet: The Impact of Voter Suppression on Communities of Color.* Retrieved from Brennan Center: https://www.brennancenter.org/our-work/research-reports/impact-voter-suppression-communities-color

Bresser, R., & Millonig, K. (2003). Institutional capital: Competitive advantage considering the new institutionalism in organisational theory. *Schmalenbach Business Review, 55*(3), 220–241. doi:10.1007/BF03396675

Brogan, D. W. (1943). *The American People, Impressions and Observations*. Knopf.

Brouer, R. L., Douglas, C., Treadway, D. C., & Ferris, G. R. (2013). Leader Political Skill, Relationship Quality, and Leadership Effectiveness: A Two-Study Model Test and Constructive Replication. *Journal of Leadership & Organizational Studies, 20*(2), 185–198. doi:10.1177/1548051812460099

Brown Hamilton, T. (2015, June 18). *Solving the Problem of Amsterdam's 'Black' and 'White' Schools.* Retrieved from The Atlantic: https://www.theatlantic.com/education/archive/2015/06/amsterdam-school-racial-segregation/396176/

Brown v. Board of Education, 347 U.S. 483 (U.S. 1954).

Bryk, A. S. (1999). *Improving School-Community Connections: Ideas for Moving Toward a System of Community Schools.* Annie E. Casey Foundation.

Bryk, A. S., Bender Sebring, P., Allensworth, E., Luppescu, S., & Easton, J. Q. (2010). *Organizing Schools for Improvement: Lessons from Chicago*. University of Chicago Press.

Bryson, J., & Crosby, B. (1992). *Leadership for the Common Good.* Jossey-Bass Publishers.

Burke, F. G. (1990). *Public Education: Who's in Charge?* Praeger Publishers.

Burrell, T. (2010). *Brainwashed: Challenging the myth of black inferiority.* Smiley Books.

Burr, N. R. (1942). *Education in New Jersey: 1630-1871.* Princeton University Press.

Burtless, G. (1996). *Does Money Matter? The Effect of School Resources on Student Achievement and Adult Success.* Brookings Institute.

Buse, K., Bernstein, R. S., & Bilimoria, D. (2016). The Influence of Board Diversity, Board Diversity Policies and Practices, and Board Inclusion Behaviors on Nonprofit Governance Practices. *Journal of Business Ethics, 133*(1), 179–191. doi:10.100710551-014-2352-z

Butrymowicz, S. (2015, January). *In Dutch Schools, More Time in School and More Educator Control.* Retrieved from The Hetchinger Report: http://hechingerreport.org/in-dutch-schools-more-time-in-sch ool-and-more-educat or-control/

Byrne, B. T. (2004, November 2). *Interview on New Jersey News (NJN).* http://www.directactions.net/ActivistKit.txt

Cabello, I., Echavez, J., Ripoll, M., Navarro, D., Roque, M., Moreno, G., & Bradley, D. (2020). Impact of viral epidemic outbreaks on mental health of healthcare workers: a rapid systematic review. MedRxiv, 1-92

Callahan, J., Ito, M., Campbell, R. S., & Wortman, A. (2019). *Influences on Occupational Identity in Adolescence: A Review of Research Programs.* Connected Learning Alliance.

Canada, G. (2013, May). *Our Failing Schools. Enough Is Enough!* Retrieved from TED: https://www.ted.com/talks/geoffrey_canada_our_failing_school s_enough_is_enough?language=en

Cantor, N., Cooper, T., Brown, M., & Englot, P. (2019). *Tackling "The Two Americas" with City-wide Collaboration in Newark.* Rutgers University.

Card, D., & Krueger, A. B. (1992, February). Does School Quality Matter? Returns to Education and the Characteristics of Public Schools in the United States. *Journal of Political Economy, 100*(1), 1–40.

Carden, D. (2018, February 5). *Indiana house advances South Shore line financing plan to senate.* Retrieved from NWITimes.com: https://www.nwitimes.com/news/local/govt-and-politics/articl e_f9bd402b-ab51-5450-be9d-083578868e3a.html

Carlotto, M. (2002). A Síndrome de Burnout e o Trabalho Docente. *Psicologia em Estudo, 7*(1), 21–29. doi:10.1590/S1413-73722002000100005

Carlotto, M. (2012). *Síndrome de Burnout em Professores Avaliação, fatores associados e intervenção.* LivPsic.

Carlotto, M., & Câmara, S. (2008). Análise da produção científica sobre a Síndrome de Burnout no Brasi. *PSICO, 39*(2), 142–158.

Carnoy, M. (1982). *Economics and Education. In Encyclopedia of Educational Research,* (5th ed., Vol. 2). Macmillan Press.

Carr, M. C., & Fuhrman, S. H. (2003). The Politics of School Finance in the 1990s. In H. F. Ladd, R. Chalk, & J. S. Hansen (Eds.), *Equity and Adequacy in Education Finance: Issues and Perspectives.* National Academy of Sciences.

Carter, K. B. (1990, January 30). Two Judges Reprimanded for Attending Florio Ball. *New Star-Ledger,* p. 1.

Carton, A., & Rosette, A. (2011). Explaining Bias against Black Leaders: Integrating Theory on Information Processing and Goal-Based Stereotyping. *Academy of Management Journal, 54*(6), 1141–1158. doi:10.5465/amj.2009.0745

Cashore, B., Auld, G., Bernstein, S. and McDermott, C. (2007). Can non-state governance "ratchet up" global environmental standards? Lessons from the forest sector. *Review of European Community, and International Environmental Law, 16*(2), 158–72.

Cavanagh, N., Cockett, G., Heinrich, C., Doig, L., Fiest, K., Guichon, J. R., Page, S., Mitchell, I., & Doig, C. J. (2020). Compassion fatigue in healthcare providers: A systematic review and meta-analysis. *Nursing Ethics, 27*(3), 639–665. doi:10.1177/0969733019889400 PMID:31829113

Cavounidis, C., & Lang, K. (2015). *Discrimination and Worker Evaluation.* Social Science Research Network. https://papers.ssrn.com/abstract=2669801

CDC. (2022). *Covid-19 Vaccines for Children and Teens*. Retrieved March 5, 2022, from CDC: https://www.cdc.gov/coronavirus/2019-ncov/vaccines/recommendations/children-teens.html

Center on Budget and Policy Priorities. (2020, March 26). *How Much Each State will Receive from the Coronavirus Relief Fund in the CARES Act*. Retrieved from cbpp.org: https://www.cbpp.org/research/how-much-each-state-will-receive-from-the-coronavirus-relief-fund-in-the-cares-act

Centers for Disease Control. (2014). Preventing youth violence: Opportunities for action. Injury Prevention and Control: Division of Violence Prevention. National Center of Injury Prevention and Control.

Centers for Disease Control. (2018). Injuries deaths on the rise among American youth. *National Vital Statistics Reports*, *67*(4).

Central bureau voor de statistiek. (2017). *Total Number of Primary Pupils: Selected Years 2001 Through 2016*. Retrieved from Statline.CBS.NL: http://statline.cbs.nl/Statweb/publication/?DM=SLEN&PA=03753ENG&D1=1&D2=1&D3=0&D4=a&D5=11-21&LA=EN&VW=T

Central City Educ. Ass'n v. Illinois Educational Labor Relations Bd., 149 Ill.2d 496 (1992).

Cerros v. Steel Technologies, Inc., 398 F.3d 944, 951-52 (7th Cir. 2005).

Chagnon, N. A. (1968). *Yąnomamö: The fierce people*. Holt, Rinehart and Winston.

Chang, C. H., Ferris, D. L., Johnson, R. E., Rosen, C. C., & Tan, J. A. (2012). Core self-evaluations: A review and evaluation of the literature. *Journal of Management*, *38*(1), 81–128. doi:10.1177/0149206311419661

Chemali, Z., Ezzeddine, F., Dosset, M., Salameh, J., Bizri, M., Dubale, B., & Fricchione, G. (2019). Burnout among healthcare providers in the complex environment of the Middle East: A systematic review. *BMC Public Health*, *19*(1), 19. doi:10.118612889-019-7713-1 PMID:31640650

Cheng, K. (2006). Characteristics and Application of Structural Equation Model. *Statistics & Decisions*, (10), 22–25.

Cheng, W., & Ge, H. (2012). Application of Structural Equation in Management Research. *Statistics & Decisions*, (22), 90–92.

Chetty, R., Friedman, J. N., Hendren, N., Jones, M. R., & Porter, S. R. (2018). *The Opportunity Atlas: Mapping the Childhood Roots of Social Mobility*. National Bureau of Economic Research. doi:10.3386/w25147

Chetty, R., Friedman, J. N., & Rockoff, J. E. (2014). Measuring the Impacts of Teachers I: Evaluating Bias in Teacher Value-Added Estimates. *The American Economic Review*, *104*(9), 2593–2632. doi:10.1257/aer.104.9.2593

Chicago Department of Public Health. (2016). *City of Chicago*. Retrieved from CityofChicago.org: https://data.cityofchicago.org

Chingos, M. M. (2017). *How progressive is school funding in the United States?* The Brookings Institution.

Chou, L.-P., Li, C.-Y., & Hu, S. (2014). Job stress and burnout in hospital employees: Comparisons of different medical professions in a regional hospital in Taiwan. *BMJ Open*, *4*(2), 1–7. doi:10.1136/bmjopen-2013-004185 PMID:24568961

Christie, M. (2007). Knowledge management and natural resource management. In M. K. Luckert, B. Campbell, & J. T. Gorman (Eds.), *Investing in indigenous natural resource management* (pp. 86–90). Charles Darwin University Press.

Christle, C., Jolivette, K., & Nelson, C. M. (2005). Breaking the school to prison pipeline: Identifying school risk and protective factors for youth delinquency. *Exceptionality*, *13*(2), 69–88. doi:10.120715327035ex1302_2

Chung, H. T., Fallick, B., Nekarda, C. J., & Ratner, D. D. (2014). Assessing the Change in Labor Market Conditions. *Finance and Economics Discussion Series*. Washington, DC: Divisions of Research & Statistics and Monetary Affairs, Federal Reserve Board.

Chu, V. (2013). *Congressional authority to regulate firearms: A legal overview*. Congressional Research Service.

City of Chicago. (2021a, September 20). *Chicago Recovery Plan*. Retrieved from chicago.gov: https://www.chicago.gov/content/dam/city/depts/obm/supp_info/2022Budget/ChicagoRecoveryPlan.pdf

City of Chicago. (2021b). *2022 Budget Overview*. Retrieved from chicago.gov: https://www.chicago.gov/content/dam/city/depts/obm/supp_info/2022Budget/2022OverviewFINAL.pdf

Civic Federation. (2019, February 8). *Measuring the State of Illinois' Bill Backlog*. Retrieved from civicfed.org: https://www.civicfed.org/iifs/blog/measuring-state-illinois-bill-backlog

Civic Federation. (2020, April 15). *How Will CARES Act Funding Be Divided Among Illinois and Its Local Governments?* Retrieved from civicfed.org: https://www.civicfed.org/iifs/blog/how-will-cares-act-funding-be-divided-among-illinois-and-its-local-governments

Civic Federation. (2021a, March 5). *Final Cook County Coronavirus Relief Fund Allocations*. Retrieved from civicfed.org: https://www.civicfed.org/blog/final-cook-county-coronavirus-relief-fund-allocations

Civic Federation. (2021b, October 1). *City of Chicago Fy2022 Proposed Budget: Analysis and Recommendations*. Retrieved from civicfed.org: https://www.civicfed.org/ChicagoState

Civil Rights Act, 42 U.S.C. § 2000e, *et. seq.* (1964).

Clapp, J. R. & Ad Hoc Advisory Group on Diversity Leadership. (2007). *Becoming a Better Organization: Promoting Diversity as a Part of the Culture at Rush University Medical Center*. Chicago: Rush University Medical Center.

Clarke, J. G., & Simon, R. E. (2013). Shackling and separation: Motherhood in prison. *AMA Journal of Ethics*, *15*(9), 779–785. doi:10.1001/virtualmentor.2013.15.9.pfor2-1309 PMID:24021108

Clifford, J. (1997). *Routes: Travel and Translation in the Twentieth Century*. Harvard University Press.

Cobb, S. (1976). Social support as a moderator of life stress. *Psychosomatic Medicine*, *38*(5), 300–314. doi:10.1097/00006842-197609000-00003 PMID:981490

Cocker, F., & Joss, N. (2016). Compassion fatigue among healthcare, emergency and community service workers: A systematic review. *International Journal of Environmental Research and Public Health*, *13*(6), 618. doi:10.3390/ijerph13060618 PMID:27338436

Cohen, S., & Wills, T. A. (1985). Stress, Social Support, and the Buffering Hypothesis. *Psychological Bulletin*, *98*(2), 310–357. doi:10.1037/0033-2909.98.2.310 PMID:3901065

Coleman, A., Palmer, S. R., Rippner, J., & Riley, R. W. (2009). *A 21st Century Imperative: Promoting Access and Diversity in higher education: A Policy Paper on Major Developments and Trends*. www.collegeboard.com/access

Coleman, J. (1966). *Equality of Educational Opportunity*. Department of Health, Education, and Welfare.

Coley, R. J., & Baker, B. (2013). Poverty and Education: Finding the Way Forward. Princeton, NJ: Report of the ETS Center for Research on Human Capital and Education.

Coll, A. C. (2004). *The socio-intercultural challenge*. Pipal Tree.

Collaborative fro Academic, Social, and Emotional Learning. (2015). *Fundamentals of SEL*. https://casel.org/fundamentals-of-sel

Compareyourcountry.org. (n.d.). *PISA Scores*. Retrieved from Compareyourcountry.org: https://www.compareyourcountry.org/pisa/country/NLD?lg=3n

Connelly, B. L., Tihanyi, L., Crook, T. R., & Gangloff, K. A. (2014). Tournament Theory: Thirty Years of Contests and Competitions. *Journal of Management*, *40*(1), 16–47. doi:10.1177/0149206313498902

Cook County. (2018, November 14). *Policy Roadmap*. Retrieved from cookcountyil.gov: https://www.cookcountyil.gov/service/policy-roadmap

Cook County. (2021, October 7). *Executive Budget Recommendation, Fiscal Year 2022*. Author.

Cook County. (n.d.). *Roadmap to Recovery: Cook County's American Rescue Plan*. Retrieved from cookcountyil.gov: https://www.cookcountyil.gov/ARPA

Coons, J. E., Clune, W. H., & Sugarman, S. D. (1970). *Private Wealth and Public Education*. Harvard University Press.

Cordes, C., & Dougherty, T. (1993). A review and an integration of research on job burnout. *Academy of Management Review*, *18*(4), 621–656. doi:10.2307/258593

Cornell, S., & Begay, M. (2004). *What is cultural match and why is it so important? Lessons from 14 years of the Harvard Project*. Paper presented at the Building Effective Governance Conference, Jabiru.

Cornell, S., & Kalt, J. P. (2000). Where's the glue? Institutional and cultural foundations of American Indian economic development. *Journal of Socio-Economics*, *29*(5), 443–470. doi:10.1016/S1053-5357(00)00080-9

Corre, A., & Van der Kaaden, A. (2017, April 21). *De meester/juf heeft het te druk om les te geven*. Retrieved from NRS.NL: https://www.nrc.nl/nieuws/2017/04/21/de-meesterjuf-heeft-het-te-druk-om-les-tegeven-8336254-a1555503

Council on State Governments. (1987). *The Book of States, 1986-87*. Council of State Governments.

Courtesy Bus Co., Inc., 354 NLRB No. 66 (2009).

COW. (2022). *New Mayo Clinic Report Sheds Light on Healthcare Professional Well-Being*. Champions of Wellness. https://www.championsofwellness.com/new-mayo-clinic-report-sheds-light-on-healthcare-professional-well-being/

Crandall, C. S., & Eshleman, A. (2003). A justification-suppression of the expression and experience of prejudice. *Psychological Bulletin*, *129*(3), 414–446. doi:10.1037/0033-2909.129.3.414 PMID:12784937

Crank, J. P. (2003). Institutional theory of police: A review of the state of the art. *Policing*, *26*(2), 186–207. doi:10.1108/13639510310475723

Cremin, L. A. (1961). *The transformation of the school: Progressivism in the American education 1876-1957*. Vintage.

Cremin, L. A. (1988). *American education: The metropolitan experience 1876-1980*. Harper & Row Publishers.

Creswell, J. W. (2014). *Research design: Qualitative, quantitative, and mixed methods approaches*. SAGE.

Crisp, G., & Cruz, I. (2009). Mentoring college students: A critical review of the literature between 1990 and 2007. *Research in Higher Education*, *50*(6), 525–545. doi:10.100711162-009-9130-2

Cross, S. (2008) *The Scale Politics of Reconciliation* [PhD. Dissertation]. Department of Human Geography, Macquarie University.

Cruz, R., Andrade, J., Moscon, D., Micheletto, R., Esteves, G., Delben, P., & Carlotto, P. (2020). COVID-19: Emergência e impactos na saúde e no trabalho. *Revista Psicologia Organizações e Trabalho*, *20*(2), 1–3.

Cuban, L. (2015). Federal education policy and democracy. *Teachers College Record*, *177*, 1–7.

Cubberly, E. P. (1947). *Public Education in the United States*. Riverside Press.

Curtis, C. (2012, May). Delivering the 'D' in transit-oriented development: Examining the town planning challenge. *Journal of Transport and Land Use*, *5*(3), 83–99. doi:10.5198/jtlu.v5i3.292

Dallacosta, F. (2019). Estresse e Síndrome de Burnout: quando a saúde do trabalhador pede socorro. Saúde (Santa Maria), 45(2).

Darling-Hammond, L. (2006). Standards, Assessment, and Educational Policy: In pursuit of genuine accountability (Eighth Annual WilliamH. Agnoff Memorial Lecture). Princeton, NJ: Educational Testing Service.

Davidson, J., & Stratford, E. (2000). *Building the knowledge base of the social and institutional dimensions of natural resource management*. Land and Water Resources Research and Development Corporation.

Davis, G., & Rhodes, R. A. W. (2000). From hierarchy to contracts and back again: reforming the Australian public service. In M. Keating, J. Wann, & P. Weller (Eds.), Institutions on the Edge? Capacity for Governance. Allen & Unwin.

Davis, M. (2003, June 23). Student Scores Show Progress but Critics Question Price. *The Newark Star-Ledger*, p. 1.

de Alcantara, C. H. (1998). Uses and abuses of the concept of governance. *International Social Science Journal*, *155*(155), 105–113. doi:10.1111/1468-2451.00113

Deane, C., Dine, K. C., Dolan, H. P., Gainer, T. W., Hudson, S., White, S., & Ramsey, C. (2013). *"Work of Policing" A 10th Peelian Principle? Creating Partnerships and Trust within Police Organizations*. Retrieved from http://www.bjaexecutivesessiononpoliceleadership.org/movie/04_A_10th_Peel_Principle.html

Deitch, E., Barsky, A., Butz, R., Chan, S., Brief, A., & Bradley, J. (2003). Subtle Yet Significant: The Existence and Impact of Everyday Racial Discrimination in the Workplace. *Human Relations*, *56*(11), 1299–1324. doi:10.1177/00187267035611002

Del Bo, C., Ferraris, M., & Florio, M. (2017). Governments in the market for corporate control: Evidence from M&A deals involving state-owned enterprises. *Journal of Comparative Economics*, *45*(1), 89–109. doi:10.1016/j.jce.2016.11.006

Deloitte Insights. (2021). *CHS Health Care D&I Workforce NAHSE*. Retrieved from NAHSE.org: https://www.nahse.org/wp-content/uploads/2021/08/Deloitte-and-NAHSE-Amplifying-Black-Voices-7-22-21.pdf

Deming, W. E. (1986). *Out of the crisis*. Massachusetts Institute of Technology, Center for Advanced Engineering Study.

Dentico, N. (2020). Editorial: The Vital Pedagogy of the New Coronavirus. *Development*, *63*(2-4), 145–149. doi:10.105741301-020-00279-5 PMID:33311953

Department of Education. (2015). *Civil rights data collection: 2011-12 discipline estimations by disability status*. Author.

Department of Transportation. (2017). *Essential Air Service*. Retrieved from transportation.gov: https://www.transportation.gov/policy/aviation-policy/small-community-rural-air-service/essential-air-service

Department of Transportation. (2021). *Subsidized Essential Air Service communities (48 Contiguous States, Hawaii, and Puerto Rico)*. Retrieved from transportation.gov: https://www.transportation.gov/office-policy/aviation-policy/subsidized-essential-air-service-communities-48-contiguous-states

Department of Transportation. (2022). *US DOT Innovation Principles*. Retrieved from transportation.gov: https://www.transportation.gov/priorities/innovation/us-dot-innovation-principles

DeSante, C. (2013). Working Twice as Hard to Get Half as Far: Race, Work Ethic, and America's Deserving Poor. *American Journal of Political Science*, *57*(2), 342–356. Advance online publication. doi:10.1111/ajps.12006

Dewa, C., Loong, D., Bonato, S., Thanh, N., & Jacobs, P. (2014). How does burnout affect physician productivity? A systematic literature review. *BMC Health Services Research*, *14*(325), 1–10. doi:10.1186/1472-6963-14-325 PMID:25066375

Dewey, J. (1916). *Democracy and education: An introduction to the philosophy of education*. The Free Press.

Dillberti, M., Jackson, M., Kemp, J., & Hansen, K. (2017). *Crime, violence, discipline, and safety in U.S. public schools: Findings from the school survey on crime and safety*. U.S. Department of Education. National Center for Education Statistics.

Dingwerth, K., & Pattberg, P. (2009). World Politics and Organizational Fields: The Case of Transnational Sustainability Governance. *European Journal of International Relations*, *15*(4), 707–743. doi:10.1177/1354066109345056

Dirks, K. T. (2000). Trust in leadership and team performance: Evidence from NCAA basketball. *The Journal of Applied Psychology*, *85*(6), 1004–1012. doi:10.1037/0021-9010.85.6.1004 PMID:11125648

Diversity Leadership Council. (2014). Diversity Leadership Informational Handbook. Rush University Medical Center.

Diversity Leadership Council. (2020). Diversity Leadership Informational Strategy PPT. Rush University Medical Center.

Domone, J. (2018). *The challenges and benefits of the electrification of aircraft*. SNC Lavalin.

Donald, H. M. (2017). *The war on cops: How the new attack on law and order makes everyone less safe*. Encounter Books.

Dovidio, J. F., & Gaertner, S. L. (2004). Aversive racism. In *Advances in experimental social psychology* (Vol. 36, pp. 1–52). Elsevier Academic Press., doi:10.1016/S0065-2601(04)36001-6

Dragicevic, N. (2015). *Anchor Institutions*. Mowat Publications.

Drennan, M. P., & Brecher, C. (2012, May). Does public transit use enhance the economic efficiency of urban areas? *Journal of Transport and Land Use*, *5*(3), 53–67. doi:10.5198/jtlu.v5i3.247

Drisko, J. W. (2016). Teaching qualitative research: Key content, course structures, and recommendations. *Qualitative Social Work: Research and Practice*, *15*(3), 307–321. doi:10.1177/1473325015617522

Drydakis, N. (2015). The effect of unemployment on self-reported health and mental health in Greece from 2008 to 2013: A longitudinal study before and during the financial crisis. *Social Science & Medicine*, *128*, 43–51. doi:10.1016/j.socscimed.2014.12.025 PMID:25589031

Duarte, I., Teixeira, A., Castro, L., Marina, S., Ribeiro, C., Cristina, J., & Nunes, R. (2020). Burnout among Portuguese healthcare workers during the COVID-19 pandemic. *Research Square*, *1*, 1–16. doi:10.21203/rs.3.rs-87357/v1

Duarte, I., Teixeira, A., Castro, L., Marina, S., Ribeiro, C., Jácome, C., & Nunes, R. (2020). Burnout among Portuguese healthcare workers during the COVID-19 pandemic. *BMC Public Health*, *20*(1), 1–10. doi:10.118612889-020-09980-z PMID:33287794

DuBois, D. L., Holoway, B., Valentine, J., & Cooper, H. (2002). Effectiveness of mentoring programs for youth: A meta-analytic review. *American Journal of Community Psychology*, *30*(2), 157–197. doi:10.1023/A:1014628810714 PMID:12002242

Dubois, D. L., Portillo, N., Rhodes, J. E., Silverthorn, N., & Valentine, J. C. (2011). How effective are mentoring programs for youth? A systematic assessment of the evidence. *Psychological Science in the Public Interest*, *12*(2), 57–91. doi:10.1177/1529100611414806 PMID:26167708

Ducharme, L., & Martin, J. K. (2000). Unrewarding Work, Coworker Support, and Job Satisfaction: A Test of the Buffering Hypothesis. *Work and Occupations*, *27*(2), 223–243. doi:10.1177/0730888400027002005

Duncombe, W., Ruggiero, J., & Yinger, J. (1996). Alternative Approaches to Measuring the Cost of Education. In H. F. Ladd (Ed.), *Holding Schools Accountable: Performance Based Reform in Education,* (pp. 327–356). Brookings Institution Press.

DuPont, C. M., Weis, T. M., Manuck, S. B., Marsland, A. L., Matthews, K. A., & Gianaros, P. J. (2020). Does well-being associate with stress physiology? A systematic review and meta-analysis. *Health Psychology*, *39*(10), 879–890. Advance online publication. doi:10.1037/hea0000979 PMID:32686951

Dutta, S., Lanvin, B., Rivera Leon, L., & Wunsch-Vincent, S. (2012). *The Global Innovation Index 2012: Stronger Innovation Linkages for Global Growth.* Retrieved from INSEAD and World Intellectual Property Organization Global Innovation Index: https://www.globalinnovationindex.org/userfiles/file/GII-2012-Report.pdf

Dyncorp, 343 NLRB 1197, 1998 (2004), *affd.* Fed. Appx. 419 (6th Cir. 2007).

Ebony. (1992). Black sororities and fraternities: Phi Beta Sigma. *Ebony.*

Economic Innovation Group. (2016, February). *The 2016 Distressed Communities Index: An Analysis of Community Well-Being Across the United State.* Retrieved from EIG.org: https://eig.org/wp-content/uploads/2016/02/2016-Distressed-Communities-Index-Report.pdf

Economist Intelligence Unit. (2006-2017). *Democracy Index 2006-2017.* Retrieved from The Economist: https://www.eiu.com/topic/democracy-index

Eddleston, K. A., Baldridge, D. C., & Veiga, J. F. (2004). Toward modeling the predictors of managerial career success: Does gender matter? *Journal of Managerial Psychology*, *19*(4), 360–385. doi:10.1108/02683940410537936

Eddy, J. M., & Poehlmann-Tynan, J. (Eds.). (2019). *Handbook on children with incarcerated parents: Research, policy, and practice.* Springer Nature. doi:10.1007/978-3-030-16707-3

Education Inspectorate: Ministry of Education, Culture, and Science. (2017a, November 23). *Search and Compare Schools.* Retrieved from https://zoekscholen.onderwijsinspectie.nl: https://zoekscholen.onderwijsinspectie.nl/zoek-en-vergelijk?redir

Education Inspectorate: Ministry of Education, Culture, and Science. (2017b, April). *The State of Education 2015-2016*. Retrieved from https://english.onderwijsinspectie.nl: https://english.onderwijsinspectie.nl/binaries/onderwijsinspectie_eng/documents/annual-reports/2017/04/12/the-state-of-education-in-the-netherlands-2015-2016/state+of+education+2015+2016+web.pdf

Education Law Center. (2002-2022). *EdLawCenter*. EdLawCenter.org: https://edlawcenter.org

Education Next. (2016). *Program on Education Policy and Governance—Survey 2016*. Retrieved from Education Next: http://educationnext.org/2016-ednext-poll-interactive/

Education Week. (2001). *Quality Counts 2001: A Better Balance--Standards, Tests, and the Tools to Succeed*. Education Week.

Education Week. (2005). *Quality Counts 2005: No Small Change--A Level Playing Field*. Education Week.

Education Week. (2006). *Quality Counts 2006: Quality Counts at 10--A Decade of Standards-Based Education*. Education Week.

Elias, J. L., & Merriam, S. B. (2001). *Philosophical foundations of adult education* (3rd ed.). Krieger.

Enrich, P. (1995). Leaving Equality Behind: New Directions in School Finance Reform. *Vanderbilt Law Review*, *48*, 101–194.

Ensher, E. A., & Murphy, S. E. (1997). Effects of Race, Gender, Perceived Similarity, and Contact on Mentor Relationships. *Journal of Vocational Behavior*, *50*(3), 460–481. doi:10.1006/jvbe.1996.1547

Eojina, K., Liang, T., & Bosselman, R. (2018). Measuring customer perceptions of restaurant innovativeness: Developing and validating a scale. *International Journal of Hospitality Management*, *74*, 85–98. doi:10.1016/j.ijhm.2018.02.018

Escola Nacional de Saúde Pública. (2020). *Escola Nacional de Saúde Pública*. Obtido de Resultados do Questionário 3: Profissionais de saúde exaustos, para além de um número pouco aceitável de infetados?: https://barometro-covid-19.ensp.unl.pt/resultados-do-questionario-3-profissionais-de-saude-exaustos-para-alem-de-um-numero-pouco-aceitavel-de-infetados/

Esque, A., Riedel, R., & Riefer, D. (2021). *Reducing aviation emissions over the long and short haul*. McKinsey & Company. Retrieved from https://www.mckinsey.com/industries/aerospace-and-defense/our-insights/future-air-mobility-blog/reducing-aviation-emissions-over-the-long-and-short-haul

Esterberg, K. G. (2002). *Qualitative methods in social research*. McGraw-Hill.

European Agency for Special Needs and Inclusive Education. (2017). *Netherlands - Financing*. Retrieved February 5, 2018, from European-agency.org: https://www.european-agency.org/country-information/netherlands/national-overview/financing

Evans, W., Murray, S., & Schwab, R. (1997). State Education Finance Policy After Court Mandated Reform: The Legacy of Serrano. In *1996 Proceedings of the Eighty-Ninth Annual Conference on Taxation*. National Tax Association-Tax Institute of America.

Eyster, L., & Gebrekristos, S. (2018). *Fulfilling the Promise of Career Pathways*. Urban Institute.

Fair Labor Standards Act, 29 U.S.C. § 201, *et. seq.* (1938).

Fallace, T. D. (2011). Tracing John Dewey's influence on progressive education, 1903-1951: Toward a received Dewey. *Teachers College Record*, *113*(3), 463–492. doi:10.1177/016146811111300307

Family Medical Leave Act, 29 U.S.C. § 2601, *et. seq.* (1993).

Fanelli, R. M. (2021). Barriers to adopting new technologies within rural small and medium enterprises (SMEs). *Social Sciences*, *10*(11), 430. doi:10.3390ocsci10110430

Faragher v. City of Boca Raton, 524 U.S. 775 (1998).

Faro, A., Bahiano, M., Nakano, T., Reis, C., Silva, B., & Vitti, L. (2020). COVID-19 e saúde mental: A emergência do cuidado. *Estudo Psicologia*, *37*, 1–29. doi:10.1590/1982-0275202037e200074

Farrie, D., & Sciarra, D. G. (2021). *Making the Grade: How Fair Is School Funding in Your State*. Education Law Center.

Federal Reserve Bank of Chicago. (2020, October 20). *The Federal Reserve's Dual Mandate*. Retrieved from Chicagofed.org: https://www.chicagofed.org/research/dual-mandate/dual-mandate

Federal Reserve Bank of Chicago. (2021, January 26). *Statement on Longer-Run Goals and Monetary Policy Strategy*. Retrieved from Federalreserve.gov: https://www.chicagofed.org/monetarypolicy/files/FOMC_LongerRunGoals.pdf

Federal Service Labor-Management Relations Statute, 5 U.S.C. § 7101, *et. seq.* (1970).

Felzenberg, A. S. (1978). *The Impact of Guernatorial Style on Policy Outcomes*. Princeton University.

Fennimore, B. S. (1996). Equity Is Not an Option in Public Education. *Educational Leadership*, *54*(2), 53–55.

Fennimore, B. S. (2005, September). Brown and the Failure of Civic Responsibility. *Teachers College Record*, *107*(9), 1905–1932.

Ferreira, N., & Lucca, S. (2015). Síndrome de burnout em técnicos de enfermagem de um hospital público do Estado de São Paulo. *Revista Brasileira de Epidemiologia*, *18*(1), 68–79. doi:10.1590/1980-5497201500010006 PMID:25651012

Ferris, G. R., Treadway, D. C., Kolodinsky, R. W., Hochwarter, W. A., Kacmar, C. J., Douglas, C., & Frink, D. D. (2005). Development and Validation of the Political Skill Inventory. *Journal of Management*, *31*(1), 126–152. doi:10.1177/0149206304271386

Fetterman, D. M. (1998). Applied social research methods: Vol. 17. *Ethnography: Step by step* (2nd ed.). SAGE.

Fino, S. (1987). *The Role of State Supreme Courts in the New Judicial Federalism*. Greenwood Press.

Fireman, G., & Kose, G. (2002). The effect of self-observation on children's problem-solving. *The Journal of Genetic Psychology*, *163*(4), 410–423. doi:10.1080/00221320209598693 PMID:12495228

Firestone, W. A., Goertz, M. E., & Natriello, G. (1997). *From Cashbox to Classroom*. Teachers College Press.

Fischel, W. A. (1998). School Finance Litigation and Property Tax Revolts: How Undermining Local Control turns Voters Away from Public Education. Lincoln Institute of Land Policy. Dartmouth College.

Fitzgerald, J. (2004). Moving the workforce intermediary agenda forward. *Economic Development Quarterly*, *18*(1), 3–9. doi:10.1177/0891242403259992

FLA. STAT. § 447.403 (1974).

FLA. STAT. § 447.505 (1974).

Fleissig, W. K. (2011, February 7). Reframing Transit & Development to TOD 3.0. In *TransACT, APTA CEO Seminar*. American Public Transportation Association.

Flex Frac Logistics, LLC, 358 NLRB 1131 (2012).

Foner, E. (1988). *Reconstruction: America's unfinished revolution 1863-1877*. Harper & Row Publishers.

Foroohar, R. (2017, June 15). *U.S. workforce: paying young Americans to learn the right skills*. Retrieved from Financial Times: https://www.ft.com/content/b5ceec2a-50e4-11e7-a1f2-db19572361bb

Foster, S. L., Laverty-Finch, C., Gizzo, D. P., & Osantowski, J. (1999). Practical issues in self-observation. *Psychological Assessment*, *11*(4), 426–438. doi:10.1037/1040-3590.11.4.426

Frasquilho, M. (2003). Eu sou actor do meu stress. *Segurança*, *154*, 28–30.

Freide, R. (2020). Uma reflexão sobre as medidas iniciais adotadas no combate à Covid-19 no Brasil. *Revista Augustus*, *25*(51), 15–30. doi:10.15202/1981896.2020v25n51p15

Freudenberger, H. (1974). Staff Burn-Out. *The Journal of Social Issues*, *30*(1), 159–165. doi:10.1111/j.1540-4560.1974.tb00706.x

Friedman, L., & Wiseman, M. (1978). Understanding the Equity Consequences of School Finance Reform. *Harvard Educational Review*, *48*, 193–226.

Friedman, S. H., Kaempf, A., & Kauffman, S. (2020). The realities of pregnancy and mothering while incarcerated. *The Journal of the American Academy of Psychiatry and the Law*, *48*(3), 365–375. PMID:32404363

Froojian, J. (1991, April 29). Report: Property Tax Bad for New Jersey. *Atlantic City Press*.

Fuellhart, K., Dai, L., Grubesic, T., & Derudder, B. (2021). The US Essential Air Service Program and SARS C0V-2, 2019–2020. *Journal of Transport Geography*, 96.

Fujioka, Y. (2005). Black media images as a perceived threat to African American ethnic identity: Coping responses, perceived public perception, and attitudes towards affirmative action. *Journal of Broadcasting & Electronic Media*, *49*(4), 450–467. doi:10.120715506878jobem4904_6

Funk, C., & Parker, K. (2018). *Women and men in STEM often at odds over workplace equity*. Pew Research.

Fu, T. Z. J., Song, Q., & Chiu, D. M. (2014). The academic social network. *Scientometrics*, *101*(1), 203–239. doi:10.100711192-014-1356-x

Gaertner, S. L., & Dovidio, J. F. (2000). The aversive form of racism. In *Stereotypes and prejudice: Essential readings* (pp. 289–304). Psychology Press.

Galanis, P., Vraka, I., Fragkou, D., Bilali, A., & Kaitelidou, D. (2021). Nurses' burnout and associated risk factors during the COVID-19 pandemic: A systematic review and meta-analysis. *Journal of Advanced Nursing*, *77*(8), 3286–3302. doi:10.1111/jan.14839 PMID:33764561

Galbraith, M. W. (2003). The adult education as mentor: A means to enhance teaching and learning. Perspectives. *The New York Journal of Adult Learning*, *1*(1), 9–20. doi:10.1177/104515950301400403

Galbraith, M. W., & Cohen, N. H. (1995). *Mentoring: New strategies and challenges. New directions for adult and continuing education*. Jossey-Bass.

Gallego, A., & Rios, F. (1991). El síndrome de "burnout" o el desgaste profesional. *Revista de la Asociación Española de Neuropsiquiatría, 11*(39), 257–265.

Garcia v. San Antonio Metropolitan Transit Authority, 469 U.S. 528 (1985).

Garcia-Perez-de-Lema, D., Madrid-Guijarro, A., & Philippe Martin, D. (2017). Influence of university-firm governance on SMEs innovation and performance levels. *Technological Forecasting and Social Change, 123*, 250–261. doi:10.1016/j.techfore.2016.04.003

Gardner, D. P. (1983). A nation at risk: The imperative for educational reform: A report to the nation and the Secretary of Education. United States Department of Education. Washington, DC: The Commission.

Garrity v. State of N.J., 385 U.S. 493 (1967).

Gaudin, J.-P. (2002). *Pourquoi la gouvernance?* Presses de Sciences Po. doi:10.3917cpo.gaudi.2002.01

Gauss, J. W., & Jessamy, H. T. (2007). *The Board's Role in Developing a Diverse Leadership Team. American Hospital Association Trustee Magazine.*

Gent, E. (2022). *Eviation's Maiden Flight Could Usher in Electric Aviation Era.* Retrieved from IEEE.org: https://spectrum.ieee.org/eviations-maiden-flight-to-usher-in-era-of-electric-aviation

Georgia Pacific Corporation, 275 NLRB No. 17 (1985).

Gettleman, J. (2005, August 26). As School Building Plan Fails, New Jersey Is Left with Slums. *New York Times*, p. 1.

Gewertz, C. (2005). *A Level Playing Field. Quality Counts 2005.* Education Week.

Gies, H. (2019). A Blow But Not Fatal: 9 Months After Janus, AFSCME Reports 94% Retention. *In These Times*. https://inthesetimes.com/article/janus-afscme-supreme-court-union-labor-agency-fees

Giloth, R. P. (2004). Introduction: A case for workforce intermediaries. In Workforce Intermediaries for the Twenty-first Century, (pp. 3-30). Temple University Press.

Girves, J., Gwathmey, J. K., & Zepeda, Y. (2005). Mentoring in a post-affirmative action world. *The Journal of Social Issues, 61*(3), 449–479. doi:10.1111/j.1540-4560.2005.00416.x

Givoni, M., & Rietveld, P. (2010). The environmental implications of airlines' choice of aircraft size. *Journal of Air Transport Management, 16*(3), 159–167. doi:10.1016/j.jairtraman.2009.07.010

Gkypali, A., & Trianni, A. (2015). Evaluating the barriers to specific industrial energy efficience measures: An exploratory study in small and medium-sized enterprises. *Journal of Cleaner Production*, (82), 70–83.

Glick, H. (1979). The Judicial Ten: America's Greatest Judges. *Southern Illinois University Law Journal. Southern Illinois University at Carbondale. School of Law, 405*, 432.

Gluckman, M. (1968). The utility of the equilibrium model in the study of social change. *American Anthropologist, 70*(2), 219–237. doi:10.1525/aa.1968.70.2.02a00010

Goertz, M. E. (1979). *Money and Education: How far have we come? Financing New Jersey Education in 1979.* Educational Policy Research Institute, Educational Testing Service.

Goertz, M. E. (1992). School Finance Reform in New Jersey: The Saga Continues. *Journal of Education Finance, 18*(4), 346–365.

Goffman, E. (1959). *The presentation of self in everyday life*. Doubleday.

Goldman, C. A. (1988). *Tax Disparites*. Council for New Jersey Affairs, New Jersey Issues.

Gomes, R., & Cruz, F. (2009). Occupational stress in health professionals a study with Portuguese nurses. *Psicologia: Teoria e Pesquisa (Brasília)*, *25*(3), 307–318. doi:10.1590/S0102-37722009000300004

Gonçalves, M., Fontes, L., Simães, C., & Gomes, R. (2019). Stress and burnout in health professionals. In P. Arezes (Ed.), *Occupational and environmental safety and health,* (pp. 563–571). doi:10.1007/978-3-030-14730-3_60

Goodlad, J. I. (1994). *What schools are for* (2nd ed.). Phi Delta Kappa Educational Foundation.

Goodlad, J. I. (1997). *In praise of education*. Teachers College Press.

Goodlad, J. I., Mantle-Bromley, C., & Goodlad, S. J. (2004). *Education for everyone: Agenda for education in a democracy*. Jossey-Bass.

Goodwin, B. (2016). Flip the Script on Fate Control. *Educational Leadership*, *74*(3), 83–84.

Gordon, D., Iwamoto, D., Ward, N., Potts, R., & Boyd, E. (2009). Mentoring urban Black middle school male students: Implications for academic achievement. *The Journal of Negro Education*, *78*(3), 277–289. PMID:20379371

Gössling, S., & Lyle, C. (2021). Transition policies for climatically sustainable aviation. *Transport Reviews*, *41*(5), 643–658. doi:10.1080/01441647.2021.1938284

Gould, W. (2019). How Five Young Men Channeled Nine Old Men: Janus and the High Court's Anti-Labor Policymaking. *U.S.F. L. Rev.*, *43*(209), 218–219.

Government Finance Officers Association. (2021, May 5). *American Rescue Plan Spending: Recommended Guiding Principles*. Retrieved from www.gfoa.org: https://www.gfoa.org/american-rescue-plan-spending-guiding-principles

Graham, J. A., & Harris, Y. R. (2013). Children of color and parental incarceration: Implications for research, theory, and practice. *Journal of Multicultural Counseling and Development*, *41*(2), 66–81. doi:10.1002/j.2161-1912.2013.00028.x

Graham, J., Amos, B., & Plumptre, T. (2003). *Governance principles for protected areas in the 21st century*. Institute on Governance, Parks Canada, and the Canadian International Development Agency.

Greene, S., Turner, M. A., & Gourevitch, R. (2017). *Racial residential segregation and neighborhood disparities*. US Partnership on Mobility from Poverty.

Greenhaus, J., Parasuraman, S., & Wormley, W. (1990). Effects of Race on Organizational Experiences, Job Performance Evaluations, and Career Outcomes. *Academy of Management Journal*, *33*(1), 64–86. doi:10.2307/256352

Grigg, N. S. (2010). *Economics and finance for engineers and planners*. American Society of Civil Engineers.

Grossman, J., & Rhodes, J. (2002). The test of time: Predictors and effects of duration in youth mentoring relationships. *American Journal of Community Psychology*, *30*(2), 199–219. doi:10.1023/A:1014680827552 PMID:12002243

Gruber, F. C. (1973). *Historical and contemporary philosophies of education*. Thomas Y. Crowell.

Guan, Z., Wu, H., Tao, J., Cao, Z., Yang, J., & Wang, F. (2014). An Exploratory Study on the Role of Government Support and Success Factors in Industry University Research Cooperation: Based on the Survey Data of Enterprises and Universities/Scientific Research Institutions in Liaoning Province. *Science & Technology Progress and Policy*, (11), 43–48.

Guedes, D. (2009). Estresse ocupacional e produtividade: um estudo exploratório em torno da síndrome de burnout com docentes do ensino superior. *XXIX Encontro Nacional de Engenharia de Produção*, 1-12.

Gun-free Schools Act of. 1994, H.R. 987, 103rd Cong. (1994).

Gunn, E. (1995). Mentoring: The Democratic version. *Training (New York, N.Y.)*, *32*(8), 64–67.

Guo, Z., He, W., & Xiao, X. (2011). Government Subsidies, Extra Behaviors and Changes of R & D Activities in Strategic Emerging Industries. *Macroeconomics*, (11), 63–69.

Gurchiek, K. (2020). *SHRM Research Finds Need for More Awareness, Understanding of Racial Inequality* (HR News). SHRM. https://www.shrm.org/hr-today/news/hr-news/pages/shrm-research-finds-need-for-more-awareness-understanding-of-racial-inequality.aspx

Haberman, M. (2005). Teacher Burnout in Black and White. *New Educator*, *1*(3), 153–175. doi:10.1080/15476880590966303

Habermas, J. (1981). *The theory of communicative action: Reason and the rationalization of society*. Beacon Press.

Habib, D., Luo, J., & Zhong, J. (2018). A literature survey of financial reporting in private firms. *Research in Accounting Regulation*, *15*(4), 1–7. doi:10.1016/j.racreg.2018.03.005

Haensly, P. A., & Parsons, J. L. (1993). Creative, intellectual, and psychosocial development through mentorship: Relationships and stages. *Youth & Society*, *25*(2), 202–221. doi:10.1177/0044118X93025002002

Hair, J. F. J., Black, W. C., Babin, B. J., & Anderson, R. E. (2010). *Multivariate Data Analysis* (7th ed.). Prentice Hall.

Halbusi, H. A., Tehseen, S., Hamid, F., & Afthanorhan, A. (2018). A study of organizational justice on the trust in organization under the mediating role of ethical leadership. *Business Ethics and Leadership*, *2*(4), 89–98. doi:10.21272/bel.2(4).89-98.2018

Hale, E., & Rollins, K. (2006). What those "breakthrough" high schools broke through to discover. *Education Digest*, *72*(1), 4–9.

Handley, S. M., & Angst, C. M. (2015). The impact of culture on the relationship between governance and opportunism in outsourcing relationships. *Strategic Management Journal*, *2015*(36), 1412–1434. doi:10.1002mj.2300

Hansell, A. L., Blangiardo, M., Fortunato, L., Floud, S., De Hoogh, K., Fecht, D., . . . Elliott, P. (2013). *Aircraft noise and cardiovascular disease near Heathrow airport in London: Small area study*. Retrieved from bmj.com: https://www.bmj.com/content/347/bmj.f5432

Hanushek, E. A. (1996). School Resources and Student Performance. In Does Money Matter? The Effect of School Resources on Student Achievement and Adult Success, (pp. 43-73). Brookings Institution Press.

Hanushek, E. A. (1998). *Conclusions and Controversies about the Effectiveness of School Resources*. Economic Policy Reviews.

Han, Y., Luo, J., & Zhong, J. (2016). Research on the Influence of Dual Leadership on Team Innovation Performance: Based on the Perspective of Convention. *Chinese Journal of Management Science*, (1), 70–85.

Harrington, M. (1962). *The Other America: Poverty in the United States*. Collier Books.

Harris v. Forklift Systems, Inc., 510 U.S. 17 (1993).

Harris, K., Kacmar, K., Zivnuska, S., & Shaw, J. (2007). The impact of political skill on effectiveness. *The Journal of Applied Psychology*, *92*, 278–285. doi:10.1037/0021-9010.92.1.278 PMID:17227169

Harvard Gazette. (2020). *This is What a scientist looks like*. Harvard. https://news.harvard.edu/gazette/story/2020/07/i-am-a-scientist/

Hasenclever, A., Mayer, P., & Rittberger, V. (1997). *Theories of International Regimes*. Cambridge University Press. doi:10.1017/CBO9780511521720

Hatzenbuehler, M. L., Phelan, J. C., & Link, B. G. (2013). Stigma as a Fundamental Cause of Population Health Inequalities. *American Journal of Public Health, 103*(5), 813–821. doi:10.2105/AJPH.2012.301069 PMID:23488505

Hedges, L. V., Laine, R., & Greenwald, R. (1994). Does Money Matter? A Meta-Analysis of Studies of the Effects of Differential School Inputs on Student Outcomes. *Educational Researcher*, *23*, 5–14.

Heiman, H. J., & Artiga, S. (2015). *Beyond health care: The role of social determinants in promoting health and health equity*. Kaiser Family Foundation.

Heinsz, T. J., Nolan, D. R., & Bales, R. A. (2009). *Labor Law Collective Bargaining in a Free Society*. Thomson/West.

Henderson, D. (1985). Enlightened mentoring: A characteristic of public management professionalism. *Public Administration Review*, *45*(November/December), 857–863. doi:10.2307/975361

Henry, F., Dua, E., Kobayashi, A., James, C., Li, P., Ramos, H., & Smith, M. S. (2017). Race, racialization and Indigeneity in Canadian universities. *Race, Ethnicity and Education*, *20*(3), 300–314. doi:10.1080/13613324.2016.1260226

Hernandez, M., Barilla, D., & Bass, K. H. (2022). *Boards Must Address Equity Competencies: Health leaders' attention, connection and empathy will help guide difficult conversations*. American Hospital Association Trustee. https://trustees.aha.org/boards-must-address-equity-competencies

Herrera, C., Dubois, D., & Grossman, J. B. (2013). *The role of risk: Mentoring experiences and outcomes for youth with varying risk profiles*. Manpower Demonstration Research Corporation.

Herr, R. M., Bosch, J. A., Loerbroks, A., Genser, B., Almer, C., Vianen, A. E., & Fischer, J. E. (2018). Organizational justice, justice climate, and somatic complaints: A multilevel investigation. *Journal of Psychosomatic Research*, *111*, 15–21. doi:10.1016/j.jpsychores.2018.05.003 PMID:29935749

Higginbotham, B., MacArthur, S., & Dart, P. C. (2010, June 30). 4-H Mentoring: Youth and families with promise—adult engagement and the development of strengths in youths. *Journal of Prevention & Intervention in the Community*, *38*(3), 229–243. Advance online publication. doi:10.1080/10852352.2010.486300 PMID:20603759

Hillcourt, W. (1988). *Official Boy Scout handbook*. Boy Scouts of America.

Hirsh, E., & Lyons, C. J. (2010). Perceiving Discrimination on the Job: Legal Consciousness, Workplace Context, and the Construction of Race Discrimination. *Law & Society Review*, *44*(2), 269–298. doi:10.1111/j.1540-5893.2010.00403.x

Hobfoll, S. E., Halbesleben, J., Neveu, J.-P., & Westman, M. (2017). *Conservation of Resources in the Organizational Context: The Reality of Resources and Their Consequences*. Academic Press.

Hobfoll, S. E. (1989). Conservation of resources: A new attempt at conceptualizing stress. *The American Psychologist*, *44*(3), 513–524. doi:10.1037/0003-066X.44.3.513 PMID:2648906

Hodges, A. C. (2012). Maintaining Union Resources in an Era of Public-Sector Bargaining Retrenchment. *Employee Rts. & Emp. Pol'y J.*, *16*(599).

Hoepner, M. (2001). *Corporate governance in transition: ten empirical findings on shareholder value and industrial relations.* Discussion Paper 01/5. Max-Planck-Institut für Gesellschaftsforschung.

Hoepner, M., & Jackson, G. (2001). *An emergent market for corporate control? The Mannesmann takeover and German corporate governance.* MPIfG Discussion Paper 01/4. MPIf.G.

Hofseth, E., Toering, T., Jordet, G., & Ivarsson, A. (2017). Self-evaluation of skills and performance level in youth elite soccer: Are positive self-evaluations always positive? *Sport, Exercise, and Performance Psychology*, *6*(4), 370–383. doi:10.1037py0000094

Hogeschool Utrecht. (2017). *Teacher Education in English Study Guide 2017-2018.* Retrieved from International.hu.nl: https://www.international.hu.nl/~/media/LLL/Docs/Studiegidsen/FE/2017/TeacherEducation-in-English-vt.pdf?la=en

Holland, B. (2016). Both sides now: Toward the dual customer approach under the Workforce Innovation and Opportunity Act in the Untied States. *Local Economy*, *31*(3), 424–441. doi:10.1177/0269094216640476

Horowitz, J. M., Brown, A., & Cox, K. (2019, April 9). *Views on Race in America 2019.* Pew Research Center's Social & Demographic Trends Project. https://www.pewresearch.org/social-trends/2019/04/09/race-in-america-2019/

Hou, Y., & Moynihan, D. P. (2008, January). The Case for Countercyclical Fiscal Capacity. *Journal of Public Administration Research and Theory, 18*(1), 141. doi:10.1093/jopart/mum006

House, S., & Havens, D. (2017). Nurses' and physicians' perceptions of nurse-physician collaboration: A systematic review. *JONA: The Journal of Nursing Administration*, *47*(3), 165–171. doi:10.1097/NNA.0000000000000460 PMID:28157818

Howard, D. (2018). Demographic Profile of NAHSE Members. In D. Howard (Ed.), *Celebrating our Future by Remembering our Past: NAHSE at 50* (pp. 353–359). NAHSE.

Howard, D. (2018). Demographic Profile of NAHSE Members. In D. Howard (Ed.), *Celebrating Our Future by Remembering Our Past: NAHSE at 50* (pp. 353–359). NAHSE.

Howard, D. M., Howard, J., & Scott, L. (2017). From the classroom to the workforce: Empowering students to find their career passion. *The Journal of Health Administration Education*, *34*(3), 395–405.

Howitt, R. (2001). *Rethinking resource management: Justice, sustainability, and indigenous peoples*. Routledge.

Howlett, M., & Rayner, J. (2006). Convergence and divergence in 'new governance' arrangements: Evidence from European integrated natural resource strategies. *Journal of Public Policy*, *26*(2), 167–189. doi:10.1017/S0143814X06000511

Huang, Y., & Li, H. (2015). Research on Industry Characteristics, Government Support and Industry Innovation Performance. *Review of International Economics*, (9), 43–56.

Huang, Y., & Zhao, N. (2020). Generalized anxiety disorder, depressive symptoms and sleep quality during COVID-19 outbreak in China: A web-based cross-sectional survey. *Psychiatry Research*, *288*, 288. doi:10.1016/j.psychres.2020.112954 PMID:32325383

Hughes, D., & Dodge, M. A. (1997). African American women in the workplace: Relationships between job conditions, racial bias at work, and perceived job quality. *American Journal of Community Psychology*, *25*(5), 581–599. doi:10.1023/A:1024630816168 PMID:9485575

Hughes, M., & Demo, D. H. (1989). Self-perceptions of Black Americans: Self-esteem and personal efficacy. *American Journal of Sociology*, *95*(1), 132–159. doi:10.1086/229216

Hulme, M. (2010). Moving beyond climate change. *Environment, 52*(3), 15–19.

Hunley, J. (2017, July 23). Replicating a Schools Turnaround. *The Washington Post*. Retrieved February 12, 2018, from http://www.highbeam.com/doc/1P4-1922260701.html?refid=easy_hf

Hunt, J., & Smith, D. (2006). *Building Indigenous community governance in Australia: preliminary research findings.* CAEPR Working Paper No. 31. CAEPR, ANU.

Hunt, J., & Smith, D. E. (2007). *Indigenous Community Governance Project: Year two research findings.* CAEPR Working Paper No. 36. CAEPR, CASS, ANU.

Hyppolite, M. (2017A). Examining Four Major Vulnerabilities Faced by Families. *Community Mental Health: Challenges for the 21st Century*, 159.

Hyppolite, M. L. (2017B). Understanding child outcomes within a multiple risk model: Examining parental incarceration. *Social Sciences*, *6*(3), 82. doi:10.3390ocsci6030082

Illinois Comptroller. (2022, February 9). *COVID-19 Response and Resources*. Retrieved from Illinois Comptroller: https://illinoiscomptroller.gov/covid19-information

Illinois Comptroller. (n.d.). *Backlog Voucher Report*. Retrieved from Illinois Comptroller: https://illinoiscomptroller.gov/financial-data/backlog-voucher-report-bvr

Illinois Educational Labor Relations Act, 115 ILCS 5/1, *et. seq.* (1984).

Illinois General Assembly. (2004, February 2). Illinois Public Act 93-660.

Illinois General Assembly. (2021, February 17). *FY2022 State Budget*. Retrieved from illinois.gov: https://www2.illinois.gov/sites/budget/Documents/Budget%20Book/FY2022-Budget-Book/Fiscal-Year-2022-Operating-Budget.pdf

Illinois Governor's Office of Management and Budget. (2021, June 21). *FY22 Federal ARPA Funding Budget Summary*. Retrieved from illinois.gov: https://www2.illinois.gov/sites/budget/Documents/Budget%20Book/FY2022-Budget-Book/FY22_Enacted_ARPA_Summary_6.21.21.pdf

Illinois Human Rights Act. 775 ILCS 5/2, *et. seq.* (1980).

Illinois Minimum Wage Law, 820 ILCS 105/12(a) (1971).

Illinois Public Labor Relations Act, 5 ILCS 315/1, *et. seq.* (1984).

Illinois Uniform Arbitration Act, 710 ILCS 5/2 (1991).

Illlinois Institute of Technology. (2022, May 1). *History of Bronzeville*. Retrieved from IIT.edu: https://www.iit.edu/community-affairs/about/history-bronzeville

Industrial Wire Products, Inc., 317 NLRB 190 (1995).

INSEAD and the World Intellectual Property Organization. (2010-2017). *Global Innovation index.* Retrieved January 9, 2018, from Globalinnovationindex.org: https://www.globalinnovationindex.org

Institute for Illinois' Fiscal Stability. (2019, February 13). *State of Illinois FY2020 Budget Roadmap: State of Illinois Budget Overview, Projections and Recommendations for the Governor and the Illinois General Assembly*. Retrieved from civicfed.org: https://www.civicfed.org/sites/default/files/illinoisroadmap fy2020.pdf

Institute of Education Sciences, U.S. Department of Education. (2009, July 17). *Diagram of Education in the United States*. Retrieved from Wikipedia: https://en.wikipedia.org/wiki/Education_in_the_United_States #/media/File:Education_in_the_United_States.svg

International Brotherhood of Teamsters Local 700 v. Illinois Labor Relations Board, 2017 IL App (1st) 152993.

Investopedia. (2021a, August 29). *Monetary Policy*. Retrieved from Investopedia.com: https://www.investopedia.com/terms/m/monetarypolicy.asp

Investopedia. (2021b, October 10). *The Roots of Fiscal Policy*. Retrieved from Investopedia.com: https://www.investopedia.com/terms/f/fiscalpolicy.asp

Inzer, L. D., & Crawford, C. B. (2005). A review of formal and informal mentoring: Processes, problems, and design. *Journal of Leadership Education*, *4*(1), 31–51. doi:10.12806/V4/I1/TF2

Jackson, D. B., Testa, A., & Turney, K. (2022). Unpacking the connection between parental incarceration and parenting stress: The mediating role of child health and health care strains. *Journal of Criminal Justice*, 81.

Jackson, N. (2019). *Organizational justice in mergers and acquisitions: Antecedents and outcomes*. Palgrave Macmillan. doi:10.1007/978-3-319-92636-0

Jacobi, M. (1991). Mentoring and undergraduate academic success: A literature review. *Review of Educational Research*, *61*(4), 501–532. doi:10.3102/00346543061004505

Jacobson, J., & Forsyth, A. (2008). Seven American TODs: Good practices for urban design in transit oriented projects. *Journal of Transport and Land Use*, *1*(2), 51–88. doi:10.5198/jtlu.v1i2.67

Jameel, M. (2019, February 28). *Workplace discrimination is illegal. But our data shows it's still a huge problem*. Vox. https://www.vox.com/policy-and-politics/2019/2/28/18241973/workplace-discrimination-cpi-investigation-eeoc

Janssen, S. A., Vos, H., van Kempen, E. E., Breugelmans, O. R., & Miedema, H. M. (2011). Trends in aircraft noise annoyance: The role of study and sample characteristics. *The Journal of the Acoustical Society of America*, *129*(4), 1953–1962. doi:10.1121/1.3533739 PMID:21476651

Janus v. Am. Fed. Of State, Cnty., and Mun. Employees, Council 31, 138 S. Ct. 2448 (2018).

Jarjoura, G. R. (2013). Effective strategies for mentoring African American boys. American Institute for Research.

Jia, X., & Heng, L. (2016). On the Construction Paradigm of Chinese Local Management Theory Based on "Grounded Spirit". *Chinese Journal of Management*, (3), 336–346.

Jia, Z. (2015). The Application of Grounded Theory in Public Management Research: Method and Practice. *Chinese Public Administration*, (3), 90–96.

Jing, Z., & Aydm, O. (2014). Structure of Small and Medium-Sized Enterprises in Turkey and Global Competitiveness Strategies. *Procedia: Social and Behavioral Sciences*, (150), 212–220.

Johnston, J. S. (2006). *Inquiry and education: John Dewey and the quest for democracy*. SUNY Press.

Jones, L., Norris, K., Meade, B., & Koegel, P. (2009). The vision, valley, and victory of community engagement. *Ethnicity & Disease*, *19*(4), S6. PMID:20088076

Judge, T. A., Cable, D. M., Boudreau, J. W., & Bretz, R. D. (1995). An empirical investigation of predictors of executive career success. *Personnel Psychology*, *48*(3), 485–519. doi:10.1111/j.1744-6570.1995.tb01767.x

Judge, T. A., Higgins, C. A., Thoresen, C. J., & Barrick, M. R. (1999). The Big Five Personality Traits, General Mental Ability, and Career Success Across the Life Span. *Personnel Psychology*, *52*(3), 621–652. doi:10.1111/j.1744-6570.1999.tb00174.x

Kallman, M. E., Clark, T. N., Woo, C., & Lin, J. (2016). *The Third Sector: Community Organizations, NGOs, and Non-Profits*. University of Illinois Press. doi:10.5406/illinois/9780252040436.001.0001

Kang-Brown, J., Trone, J., Fratello, J., & Daftary-Kapur, T. (2013). *A generation later: What we've learned about zero tolerance in schools*. Vera Institute of Justice.

Katzenstein, P. J. (1996). Introduction: Alternative Perspectives on National Security. In P. J. Katzenstein (Ed.), *The Culture of National Security* (pp. 1–32). Columbia University Press.

Kean, K., & Gettinger, A. (2020, April 20). Now recovering from COVID-19, ICU nurse describes work at UCMC through a pandemic. *Hyde Park Herald*. https://www.hpherald.com/news/local/now-recovering-from-covid-19-icu-nurse-at-describes-work-at-ucmc-through-a-pandemic/article_50ff7e90-834a-11ea-a6e7-83e59cf618be.html

Keeney, J., Boyd, E. M., Sinha, R., Westring, A. F., & Ryan, A. M. (2013). From "work–family" to "work–life": Broadening our conceptualization and measurement. *Journal of Vocational Behavior*, *82*(3), 221–237. doi:10.1016/j.jvb.2013.01.005

Kelly, L., Runge, J., & Spencer, C. (2015). Predictors of compassion fatigue and compassion satisfaction in acute care nurses. *Journal of Nursing Scholarship*, *47*(6), 522–528. doi:10.1111/jnu.12162 PMID:26287741

Kelman, B. (2022, March 24). *At nurse RaDonda Vaught's trial, testimony points to Vanderbilt's responsibility: Shots—Health News*. NPR. https://www.npr.org/sections/health-shots/2022/03/24/1088397359/in-nurses-trial-witness-says-hospital-bears-heavy-responsibility-for-patient-dea

Keohane, R.O., & Victor, D. (2011). The regime complex for climate change. *Perspectives on Politics, 9*(1), 7–23.

Kesteven, S., & Smith, D. E. (1984). Contemporary Land-Tenure in Western Arnhem Land: An Investigation of Traditional Ownership, Resource Development and Royalties. Report to the Australian Institute of Aboriginal Studies and the Northern Land Council.

Kett, J. F. (1994). *The pursuit of knowledge under difficulties: From self-improvement to adult education in America, 1750-1990*. Stanford University Press.

Khan, M. (1964). Survey of Arbitration in 1962. In *Labor Arbitration – Perspectives and Problems 304*. National Academy of Arbitrators.

Kilbourne, C. (1994). *Former Nun Fighting for New Jersey Schools--and Her Life*. Bicoastal.com: https://www.bicoastal.com/home/xlip11.html

Kim, B., Kim, E., Miller, D. J., & Mahoney, J. T. (2016). The impact of the timing of patents on innovation performance. *Research Policy*, *45*(4), 914–928. doi:10.1016/j.respol.2016.01.017

Kim, K. Y., Eisenberger, R., & Baik, K. (2016). Perceived organizational support and effective organizational commitment: Moderating influence of perceived organizational competence. *Journal of Organizational Behavior, 37*(4), 558–583. doi:10.1002/job.2081

Kinder-Care Learning Centers, 299 NLRB 1171 (1990).

King, E. B., Shapiro, J. R., Hebl, M. R., Singletary, S. L., & Turner, S. (2006). The stigma of obesity in customer service: A mechanism for remediation and bottom-line consequences of interpersonal discrimination. *The Journal of Applied Psychology, 91*(3), 579–593. doi:10.1037/0021-9010.91.3.579 PMID:16737356

Kinner, S. A., Alati, R., Najman, J. M., & Williams, G. M. (2007). Do paternal arrest and imprisonment lead to child behaviour problems and substance use? A longitudinal analysis. *Journal of Child Psychology and Psychiatry, and Allied Disciplines, 48*(11), 1148–1156. doi:10.1111/j.1469-7610.2007.01785.x PMID:17995491

Kladko, B. (1997, May 22). Abbot vs. Burke: Not Just Names on a Suit. *Asbury Park News*, p. 1.

Kliewer, B. W., & Priest, K. L. (2019). Building collective leadership capacity: Lessons learned from a university-community partnership. *Collaboration: A Journal of Community-Based Research and Practice, 2*(1), 16. doi:10.33596/coll.42

Klopf, G., & Harrison, J. (1981). Moving up the career ladder: A case for mentors. *Principal, 2*(3), 41–43.

Kocienewski, D., & Holl, J. (2005, November 10). Corzine Prepares to Assume New Title, and the Problems that Go with It. *New York Times*.

Kokko, K., Tremblay, R. E., Lacourse, E., Nagin, D. S., & Vitaro, F. (2006). Trajectories of Staff, J. & Kreager, D. (2008). Too cool for school? Violence, peer status, and high school dropout. *Social Forces, 87*(1), 445–471.

Kollmann, T., & Stockmann, C. (2014). Filling the entrepreneurial orientation-performance gap: The mediating effects of exploratory and exploitative innovations. *Entrepreneurship Theory and Practice, 38*(5), 1001–1026. doi:10.1111/j.1540-6520.2012.00530.x

Kooiman, J. (2003). *Governing as Governance*. Sage Publications. doi:10.4135/9781446215012

Kossek, E. E., Ruderman, M. N., Braddy, P. W., & Hannum, K. M. (2012). Work–nonwork boundary management profiles: A person-centered approach. *Journal of Vocational Behavior, 81*(1), 112–128. doi:10.1016/j.jvb.2012.04.003

Kozol, J. (1991). *Savage Inequalities: Children in America's Schools*. Harper Perennial.

Kozol, J. (2005). *The Shame of the Nation: The Restoration of Apartheid Schooling in America*. Crown Publishers.

Krause, N. (1983). The racial context of Black self-esteem. *Social Psychology Quarterly*, 46.

Krishnamurthy, M. (2017, April 5). State education board develops new accountability plan for schools. *Daily Herald*. Retrieved February 13, 2018, from https://www.dailyherald.com/article/20170405/news/170409431/

Kulik, C. T., Bainbridge, H. T. J., & Cregan, C. (2008). Known by the company we keep: Stigma-by-association effects in the workplace. *Academy of Management Review, 33*(1), 216–230. doi:10.5465/amr.2008.27752765

La Vigne, N. G., Davies, E., & Brazzell, D. (2016). *Broken bonds: Understanding and addressing the needs of children with incarcerated parents*. Academic Press.

Labor-Management Relations Act, 29 U.S.C. 173 (1947).

Lacey, T. A., Toossi, M., Dubina, K. S., & Gensler, A. B. (2017). Projections overview and highlights, 2016-26. Monthly Labor Review. doi:10.21916/mlr.2017.29

Lacey, T. A., Dieppe, P., & Medina-Lara, A. (2016). Review of 99 self-report measures for assessing well-being in adults: Exploring dimensions of well-being and developments over time. *BMJ Open*, *6*(7), e010641. doi:10.1136/bmjopen-2015-010641 PMID:27388349

Ladd, H. (1975). Local Education Expenditures, Fiscal Capacity and the Composition of the Property Tax Base. *National Tax Journal*, *28*(2), 145–158.

Ladd, H., & Yinger, J. (1994). The Case for Equalizing Aid. *National Tax Journal*, *47*(1), 211–224.

Laguardia, A., & Pearl, A. (2009). Necessary Educational Reform for the 21st Century: The Future of Public Schools in Our Democracy. *The Urban Review*, *41*(4), 352–368. doi:10.100711256-008-0115-9

Lai, J., Ma, S., Wang, Y., Cai, Z., Hu, J., Wei, N., Wu, J., Du, H., Chen, T., Li, R., Tan, H., Kang, L., Yao, L., Huang, M., Wang, H., Wang, G., Liu, Z., & Hu, S. (2020). Factors Associated With Mental Health Outcomes Among Health Care Workers Exposed to Coronavirus Disease 2019. *JAMA Network Open*, *3*(3), e203976. doi:10.1001/jamanetworkopen.2020.3976 PMID:32202646

Lana, R., Coelho, F., Gomes, M., Cruz, O., Bastos, L., Villela, D., & Codeço, C. (2020). Emergência do novo coronavírus (SARS-CoV-2) e o papel de uma vigilância nacional em saúde oportuna e efetiva. *Cadernos de Saude Publica*, *36*(3), 1–5. doi:10.1590/0102-311x00019620 PMID:32187288

Lancet, T. (2020). COVID-19: protecting health-care workers. *PubMed Central* .

Lane, C. (2004). *Institutional transformation and system change: changes in corporate governance of Germancorporations* (Reihe Soziologie / Institut für Höhere Studien, Abt. Soziologie, 65). Wien: Institut für Höhere Studien (IHS). https://nbn-resolving.org/urn:nbn:de:0168-ssoar-220637

Larson, R. (2006). Positive youth development, willful adolescents, and mentoring. *Journal of Community Psychology*, *34*(6), 677–689. doi:10.1002/jcop.20123

Lazarescu, I., Dubray, B., Joulakian, M. B., Blanchard, P., Chauvet, B., Mahé, M. A., & Thureau, S. (2018). Prevalence of burnout, depression and job satisfaction among French senior and resident radiation oncologists. *Cancer radiotherapie: journal de la Societe francaise de radiotherapie oncologique, 22*(8), 784-789.

Lazarus, R. S., & Folkman, S. (1987). Transactional theory and research on emotions and coping. *European Journal of Personality, 1*(3), 141–169. doi:10.1002/per.2410010304

Leary, M. R., Tate, E. B., Allen, A. B., Adams, C. E., & Hancock, J. (2007). Self-compassion and reactions to unpleasant self-relevant events: The implications of treating oneself kindly. *Journal of Personality and Social Psychology*, *92*(5), 887–904. doi:10.1037/0022-3514.92.5.887 PMID:17484611

Ledoux, K. (2015). Understanding compassion fatigue: Understanding compassion. *Journal of Advanced Nursing*, *71*(9), 2041–2050. doi:10.1111/jan.12686 PMID:25981240

Lee, S. G., Hickman, M., & Tong, D. (2013, June). Development of a temporal and spatial linkage between transit demand and land-use patterns. *Journal of Transport and Land Use*, *6*(2), 33–46. doi:10.5198/jtlu.v6i2.268

Lee, V. E., & Burkam, D. T. (2002). *Inequality at the Starting Gate: Social Background Differences in Achievement as Children Begin School*. Economic Policy Institute.

Legatum Institute. (2007-2016). *Prosperity Index 2007-2016*. Retrieved January 9, 2018, from Prosperity.com: https://www.prosperity.com/about/resources

Lehne, R. (1978). *The Quest for Justice: The Politics of School Finance Reform*. Longman.

Lehne, R., & Rosenthal, A. (1979). *Politics in New Jersey*. Eagle Institute of Politics, Rutgers University.

Lehrer, P., & Woolfolk, R. (2021). *Principles and Practice of Stress Management,* (4th ed.). The Guildford Press.

LeRoy, G. (2005). *The Great American Jobs Scam: Corporate Tax Dodgingand the Myth of Job Creation*. Berrett-Koehler Publishers.

Levine, G. (1991). Meeting the Third Wave: Legislative Approaches to Recent Judicial School Finance Rulings. *Harvard Journal on Legislation*, *28*, 506–542.

Lewis, M. (1991). Ways of knowing: Objective self-awareness or consciousness. *Developmental Review*, *11*(3), 231–243. doi:10.1016/0273-2297(91)90011-C

Lima, C., Carvalho, P., Lima, I., Nunes, J., Saraiva, J., Souza, R., & Neto, M. (2020). The emotional impact of Coronavirus 2019-nCoV (new Coronavirus disease). *Psychiatry Research*, *287*, 287. doi:10.1016/j.psychres.2020.112915 PMID:32199182

Link, S. S., & Linder, C. (2014). Business Model Prototyping—Using the Morphological Analysis to Develop New Business Models. *Procedia: Social and Behavioral Sciences*, *148*, 1–9.

Litam, S. D. A., & Balkin, R. S. (2021). Moral injury in health-care workers during COVID-19 pandemic. *Traumatology*, *27*(1), 14–19. doi:10.1037/trm0000290

Liu, X., Shao, L., Zhang, R., Wei, Y., Li, J., Wang, C., & Zhou, F. (2020). Perceived Social Support and Its Impact on Psychological Status and Quality of Life of Medical Staffs After Outbreak of SARS-CoV-2 Pneumonia: A Cross-Sectional Study. *Lancet*, 1–21.

Li, X., Zhong, L., Wang, J., & Wang, W. (2018). The Influence of Open Innovation and Absorption capacity in Innovation Performance—Based on the Empirical Analysis of Auto Industry in China. *Science. Research Management*, (1), 45–52.

Loughran, C. S. (2006). *How to Prepare and Present a Labor Arbitration Case* (2nd ed.). BNA Books.

Lu, D., Huang, J., Seshagiri, A., Park, H., & Griggs, T. (2020, September 9). *Faces of power: 80% are White even as US becomes more diverse*. https://www.nytimes.com/interactive/2020/09/09/us/powerful-people-race-us.html

Lukemeyer, A. (2002). Financing a Constitutional Educaton: Views from the Bench. *Conference on State Aid to Education, sponsored by the Educational Finance and Accountability Project.*

Lukemeyer, A. (2003). *Courts as POlicymakers: School Finance Reform Litigation*. LFB Scholarly Publishing LLC.

Luna, G., & Cullen, D. L. (1995). Empowering the faculty: Mentoring redirected and renewed. *ASHE-ERIC Higher Education Report*, *3*, 1–87.

Lund, S., Madgavkar, A., Manyika, J., & Smit, S. (2020). *What's Next for Remote Work: An Analysis of 2,000 Tasks, 800 Jobs, and nine Countries*. Retrieved November 23, 2020, from https://www.mckinsey.com/featured-insights/future-of-work/whats-next-for-remote-work-an-analysis-of-2000-tasks-800-jobs-and-nine-countries

Lunenburg, F. (2011). Self-efficacy in the workplace: Implications for motivation and performance. *International Journal of Management. Business Administration (London)*, *14*(1).

Lupien, S. J., Maheu, F., Tu, M., Fiocco, A., & Schramek, T. E. (2007). The effects of stress and stress hormones on human cognition: Implications for the field of brain and cognition. *Brain and Cognition*, *65*(3), 209–237. doi:10.1016/j.bandc.2007.02.007 PMID:17466428

Lynch, M. (2016, September 19). *3 Important Themes of American Culture that Influence Our Schools.* Retrieved from The Edvocate: https://www.theedadvocate.org/3-important-themes-of-american-culture-that-influence-our-schools/

Mackey, P. E. (2002). *Using Naitonal Best Practices to Improve New Jersey's Management of Education Data.* Rutgers University School of Law.

Major, B., Kaiser, C. R., & McCoy, S. K. (2003). It's Not My Fault: When and Why Attributions to Prejudice Protect Self-Esteem. *Personality and Social Psychology Bulletin, 29*(6), 772–781. doi:10.1177/0146167203029006009 PMID:15189632

Major, B., & O'Brien, L. T. (2005). The Social Psychology of Stigma. *Annual Review of Psychology, 56*(1), 393–421. doi:10.1146/annurev.psych.56.091103.070137 PMID:15709941

Management & Training Corp., 366 NLRB No. 134 (2018).

Mansnerus, L. (2002, April 5). Big Increase in Local Taxes Is Expected in New Jersey. *New York Times.*

Manuel, L. (2012). Network Governance of Innovation Policies: The Technological Plan in Portugal. *Science & Public Policy, 39*(5), 655–668. doi:10.1093cipolcs043

Marika, R., Ngurruwutthun, D., & White, L. (1992). Always together, yaka gäna: Participatory research at Yirrkala as part of the development of a Yolngu education. *Convergence (Toronto), 25*, 23–39.

Marjanovic, Z., Greenglass, E., & Coffey, S. (2007). The relevance of psychosocial variables and working conditions in predicting nurses' coping strategies during the SARS crisis: An online questionnaire survey. *International Journal of Nursing Studies, 44*(6), 991–998. doi:10.1016/j.ijnurstu.2006.02.012 PMID:16618485

Marôco, J., & Marôco, A., Leite, Ema, Bastos, C., Vazão, M., & Campos, J. (2016). Burnout in Portuguese Healthcare Professionals: An Analysis at the National Level. *Acta Medica Portuguesa, 26*(1), 24–30. PMID:26926895

Marques, M., Alves, E., Queirós, C., Norton, C., & Henriques, A. (2018). The effect of profession on burnout in hospital staff. *Occupational Medicine (Oxford, England), 68*(3), 207–2010. doi:10.1093/occmed/kqy039 PMID:29546385

Marsh, E. E., Kappelman, M. D., Kost, R. G., Mudd-Martin, G., Shannon, J., Stark, L. A., & Carrasquillo, O. (2021). Community engagement during COVID: A field report from seven CTSAs. *Journal of Clinical and Translational Science, 5*(1), e104. doi:10.1017/cts.2021.785 PMID:34192058

Marte, J. (2022). *The Evolving Post-COVID U.S. Job Market in five Charts.* Retrieved March 16, 2022, from Reuters: https://www.reuters.com/world/us/evolving-post-covid-us-job-market-five-charts-2022-03-04/

Martin, A. (2008). Television media as a potential negative factor in the racial identity development of African American youth. *Academic Psychiatry, 32*(4), 338–342. doi:10.1176/appi.ap.32.4.338 PMID:18695037

Maslach, C. (2006). Stress and Quality of Working Life: Current Perspectives in Occupational Health. Information Age Publishing.

Maslach, C., & Wilmar, S. (1993). Historical and conceptual development of burnout. *Professional burnout: Recent developments in theory and research*, 1-16.

Maslach, C. (2003). Job Burnout: New Directions in Research and Intervention. *Current Directions in Psychological Science, 12*(5), 189–192. doi:10.1111/1467-8721.01258

Maslach, C., & Jackson, S. (1981). The measurement of experienced burnout. *Journal of Organizational Behavior, 2*(2), 99–113. doi:10.1002/job.4030020205

Maslach, C., Jackson, S., & Leiter, M. (1996). *Maslach Burnout Inventory Manual,* (3rd ed.). CPP, Inc.

Maslach, C., & Leiter, M. (2008). Early predictors of job burnout and engagement. *The Journal of Applied Psychology, 93*(3), 498–512. doi:10.1037/0021-9010.93.3.498 PMID:18457483

Maslach, C., Schaufeli, W., & Leiter, M. (2001). Job Burnout. *Annual Review of Psychology, 52*(1), 397–422. doi:10.1146/annurev.psych.52.1.397 PMID:11148311

Massell, D., & Fuhrman, S. H. (1994). *Ten Years of State Education Reform, 1983-1993.* Consortium for Policy Research in Education.

Mastro, D. (2015). Why the media's role in issues of race and ethnicity should be in the spotlight. *The Journal of Social Issues, 71*(1), 1–16. doi:10.1111/josi.12093

Mattingly, C. (2006). Pocahontas goes to the clinic: Popular culture as lingua franca in a cultural borderland. *American Anthropologist, 108*(3), 494–501. doi:10.1525/aa.2006.108.3.494 PMID:20706562

Matziou, V., Vlahioti, E., Perdikaris, P., Matziou, T., Megapanou, E., & Petsios, K. (2014). Physician and nursing perceptions concerning interprofessional communication and collaboration. *Journal of Interprofessional Care, 28*(6), 526–533. doi:10.3109/13561820.2014.934338 PMID:25003547

Maunder, R., Lancee, W., Balderson, K., Bennett, J., Borgundvaag, B., Evans, S., & Veldhorst, G. (2006). Long-term psychological and occupational effects of providing hospital healthcare during SARS outbreak. *Emerging Infectious Diseases, 12*(12), 1924–1932. doi:10.3201/eid1212.060584 PMID:17326946

Mazza, C., Ricci, E., Biondi, S., Colasanti, M., Ferracuti, S., Napoli, C., & Roma, P. (2020). A Nationwide Survey of Psychological Distress among Italian People during the COVID-19 Pandemic: Immediate Psychological Responses and Associated Factors. *International Journal of Environmental Research and Public Health, 17*(9), 3165. doi:10.3390/ijerph17093165 PMID:32370116

McCluney, C. L., Durkee, M. I., Smith, R. E. II, Robotham, K. J., & Lee, S. S.-L. (2021). To be, or not to be...Black: The effects of racial codeswitching on perceived professionalism in the workplace. *Journal of Experimental Social Psychology, 97*, 104199. doi:10.1016/j.jesp.2021.104199

McCombs, J. S., Whitake, A., & Yoo, P. (2017). *The Value of Out-of-School Time Programs.* Rand Corporation. doi:10.7249/PE267

McCrae, C. N., & Galen, V. B. (2000). Social cognition: Thinking categorically about others. *Annual Review of Psychology, 51*, 27. PMID:10751966

McDevitt, J., Posick, C., Zschoche, R., Rosenbaum, D. P., Buslic, M., & Fridell, L. L. (2011, February). National Police Research Platform. *Police integrity, responsibility, and discipline.* Retrieved from http://uicclj.squarespace.com/police-integrity-responsibili/

McEwen, B. S., & Stellar, E. (1993). Stress and the individual. Mechanisms leading to disease. *Archives of Internal Medicine, 153*(18), 2093–2101. doi:10.1001/archinte.1993.00410180039004 PMID:8379800

McHale, G. (2000). Turning points: A white paper on the course of mentoring. In *Proceedings of the National Mentoring Conference of Project Literacy.* Washington, DC: National Educational Association.

McKinsey & Company. (2009, April). *The economic impact of the achievement gap in America's schools.* Retrieved from National Dropout Prevention Center: http://dropoutprevention.org/wp-content/uploads/2015/07/ACHIEVEMENT_GAP_ REPORT_20090512.pdf

McKnight, J. (1996). *The Careless Society: Community and Its Counterfeits*. Basic Books.

Mekawi, Y., Hyatt, C. S., Maples-Keller, J., Carter, S., Michopoulos, V., & Powers, A. (2021). Racial Discrimination Predicts Mental Health Outcomes Beyond the Role of Personality Traits in a Community Sample of African Americans. *Clinical Psychological Science*, *9*(2), 183–196. doi:10.1177/2167702620957318

Melaku, T. M., Beeman, A., Smith, D. G., & Johnson, W. B. (2020, November 1). Be a Better Ally. *Harvard Business Review*. https://hbr.org/2020/11/be-a-better-ally

Melo, S., Strobel, A., Soares, B., Bastos, B., Silva, I., Silveira, L., & Reis, B. (2021). Síndrome de Burnout nos profissionais de saúde durante a pandemia da COVID-19: Uma revisão narrativa. *Revista Eletrônica Acervo Saúde*, *13*(11), 1–7. doi:10.25248/reas.e9225.2021

Mentor: National Mentoring Partnership. (2015). *Mentor in real life*. National Mentoring Resource Center. http://nationalmentoringresourcenter.org

Mercy Health Partners, 358 NLRB No. 69 (2012).

Mikesell, J. L. (2018). *Fiscal Administration* (10th ed.). Cengage Learning.

Miller, S. (2020). *Black Workers Still Earn Less than Their White Counterparts* (Compensation). SHRM. https://www.shrm.org/resourcesandtools/hr-topics/compensation/pages/racial-wage-gaps-persistence-poses-challenge.aspx

Mills, A. (2019, January 15). *Great Leadership Requires Humility*. Retrieved from https://www.policemag.com/501943/great-leadership-requires-humility

Ministry of Education, Culture, and Science. (2016). *Key Figures: Education*. Retrieved from Ocwincijfer.nl: https://www.ocwincijfers.nl/binaries/ocwincijfers/documenten/publicaties/2016/05/31/key-figures-education/keyfigures-education-2016.pdf

Minorini, P. A., & Sugarman, S. (1999). Educational Adequacy and the Courts: The Promise and Problems of Moving to a New Paradigm. In H. F. Ladd, R. Chalk, & J. S. Hansen (Eds.), *Equity and Adequacy in Education Finance: Issues and Perspectives*. National Academy Press.

Minorini, P. A., & Sugarman, S. D. (1999). School Finance Litigation in the Name of Educational Equity: Its Evolution, Impact, and Future. In H. F. Ladd, R. Chalk, & J. S. Hansen (Eds.), *Equity and Adequacy in Educational Finance: Issues and Perspectives*. National Academy Press.

Monk, D. H., & Brent, B. O. (1997). *Raising Money for Education: A Guide to the Property Tax*. Corwin Press, Inc.

Montemurro, N. (2020). The emotional impact of COVID-19: From medical staff to common people. *Brain, Behavior, and Immunity*, *87*, 23–14. doi:10.1016/j.bbi.2020.03.032 PMID:32240766

Moore, D. R. (2005). *The Big Picture: School-Initiated Reforms, Centrally Initiated Reforms, and Elementary School Achievement in Chicago (1990 to 2005)*. Designs for Change.

Morgan, G., Rocha, G., & Poynting, S. (2005). Grafting Cultures: Longing and Belonging in Immigrants' Ottaviano G.I.P., G. Peri (2005), Cities and cultures. *Journal of Urban Economics*, *58*, 304–337.

Morgan, S., & Morgan, K. (2004). *Crime State Rankings*. Morgan Quitno Press.

Morgantini, L., Naha, U., Wang, H., Francavilla, S., Acar, O., Flores, J., Crivellaro, S., Moreira, D., Abern, M., Eklund, M., Vigneswaran, H. T., & Weine, S. (2020). Factors contributing to healthcare professional burnout during the COVID-19 pandemic: A rapid turnaround global survey. *PLoS One*, *15*(9), e0238217. doi:10.1371/journal.pone.0238217 PMID:32881887

Morin, R., Parker, K., Stepler, R., Mercer, A., Morin, R., Parker, K., & Mercer, A. (2018, October 15). *What Police Think About Their Jobs*. Retrieved from https://www.pewsocialtrends.org/2017/01/11/behind-the-badge/

Morphy, H. (2007). *Becoming Art: Exploring Cross-Cultural Categories*. Berg.

Moser, M., & Rubenstein, R. (2002). The Equality of Public School District Funding in the United States: A Natioal Status Report. *Public Administration Review*, *62*(1), 63–72.

Moss, M., Good, S., Gozal, D., Kleinpell, R., & Sessler, N. (2016). An official critical care societies collaborative statement: burnout syndrome in critical care healthcare professionals: a call for action. *American Journal of Critical Care*, *44*(7), 1414–1421. PMID:27309157

Mosteiro, M., Almeida, M., Baptista, P., Zaballos, M., Diaz, F., & Diaz, M. (2019). Síndrome de burnout em trabalhadores de enfermagem brasileiros e espanhóis. *Revista Latino-Americana de Enfermagem*, 1–9.

Moua, L., Roa, J., Xie, Y., & Maxwell, D. (2020, August). Critical Review of Advancements and Challenges of All-Electric Aviation. In *International Conference on Transportation and Development 2020*. American Society of Civil Engineers. 10.1061/9780784483138.005

Muller, S. (2008). Accountability constructions, contestations, and implications: Insights from working in a yolngu cross-cultural institution, Australia. *Geography Compass*, *2*(2), 1–19. doi:10.1111/j.1749-8198.2007.00087.x

Munyon, T., Summers, J., Thompson, T., & Ferris, G. (2013). Political Skill and Work Outcomes: A Theoretical Extension, Meta-Analytic Investigation, and Agenda for the Future. *Personnel Psychology*, *68*(1), 143–184. Advance online publication. doi:10.1111/peps.12066

Murphy, K., & Tyler, T. (2008). Procedural justice and compliance behavior: The mediating role of emotions. *European Journal of Social Psychology*, *38*(4), 652–668. doi:10.1002/ejsp.502

Musu-Gillette, L., de Brey, C., McFarland, J., Hussar, W., Sonnenberg, W., & Wilkinson-Flicker, S. (2017). *Status and trends in the education of racial and ethnic groups 2017*. U.S. Department of Education. National Center for Education Statistics.

NAHSE Research Committee. (2021). *Election 20200: NAHSE Member Survey of Political Leadership in the United States*. Retrieved April 21, 2022, from http://www.nahsechicago.com/uploads/1/2/0/2/120299982/nahse_survey-members_020_presidential_election_2-5-21.pdf

Natinoal Academics of Sciences, Engineering, and Medicine. (2017). *Communities in Action: Pathways to Health Equity*. National Academies of Sciences, Engineering, and Medicine.

National Association for the Advancement of Colored People. (2017). *Criminal justice fact sheet*. Retrieved from www.naacp.org/criminal-justice-fact-sheet

National Association of State Budget Officers. (2019). *The Fiscal Survey of States*. NASBO.

National Center for Education Statistics Institute of Education Sciences. (2012, July). *Growth Models: Issues and Advice from the States*. Retrieved from NCES.ed.gov: https://nces.ed.gov/programs/slds/pdf/guide_growth-model.pdf

National center for Education Statistics. (2018). *Digest of Education Statistics*. Retrieved from NCES.ed.gov: https://nces.ed.gov/programs/digest/2016menu_tables.asp

National Conference of State Legislatures. (2005, May 29). *NCSL NCEF*. NCSL.org: https://www.ncls.org/programs/edu/NCEF.htm

National Conference of State Legislatures. (2010, October). *Fiscal Brief: State Balanced Budget Provisions*. Retrieved from ncsl.org: https://www.ncsl.org/research/fiscal-policy/state-balanced-budget-requirements-provisions-and.aspx

National Labor Relations Act of 1935, 29 U.S.C. § 151, *et. seq* (1935).

National Labor Relations Board v. J. Weingarten, Inc., 420 U.S. 251 (1975).

National Labor Relations Board v. Washington Aluminum Co., 370 U.S. 9 (1962).

National League of Cities. (n.d.). *Financing Public Education*. Retrieved February 5, 2018, from NLC.org: https://www.nlc.org/financing-public-education

National League of Cities. (n.d.). *Local Allocations in the American Rescue Plan*. Retrieved from nlc.org: https://www.nlc.org/resource/local-allocations-in-the-american-rescue-plan/

Nelson, A. H., Jenkins, D., Zanti, S., Katz, M. F., Berkowitz, E., Burnett, T. C., & Culhane, D. P. (2020). *A toolkit for centering racial equity throughout data integration*. Actionable Intelligence for Social Policy, University of Pennsylvania.

Netherlands Ministry of Education, Culture, and Science. (2016). *Key Figures: Education*. Retrieved from OCW in cijfers (OCW in figures): https://www.ocwincijfers.nl/binaries/ocwincijfers/documenten/publicaties/2016/05/31/key-figures-education/keyfigures-education-2016.pdf

Netherlands Youth Institute. (2017). *Community Schools*. Retrieved from NJI.nl: https://www.nji.nl/nl/Download-NJi/Publicatie-NJi/Community_schools_Netherlan ds_2010.pdf

Netzer, D. (1966). *Economics of the Property Tax*. Brookings Institution Press.

Nevid, J. S. (2009). *Psychology: Concepts and applications* (3rd ed.). Houghton Mifflin Company.

New Jersey Department of Education. (2001). *Public Education in New Jersey*. State.NJ.US: https://www.state.nj.us/education/genfo/penj.pdf

New York Times. (2022). Retrieved March 22, 2022. https://www.nytimes.com/interactive/2021/us/covid-cases.html

Newman, J., Barnes, M., Sullivan, H., & Knops, A. (2004). Public participation and collaborative governance. *Journal of Social Policy*, *33*(2), 203–223. doi:10.1017/S0047279403007499

Niemann, Y. F. (2003). The psychology of tokenism: Psychosocial realities of faculty of color. doi:10.4135/9781412976008.n5

Nightingale, C. H. (2012). *Segregation: A Global History of Divided Cities*. The University of Chicago Press. doi:10.7208/chicago/9780226580777.001.0001

Niles Co., Inc., 328 NLRB 411, 414 (1999).

Nishii, L. H. (2012). The Benefits of Climate for Inclusion for Gender-Diverse Groups. *Academy of Management Journal*, *56*(6), 1754–1774. doi:10.5465/amj.2009.0823

NLRB v. American National Insurance Co., 343 U.S. 395 (1952).

NLRB v. Fansteel Metallurgical Corp., 306 U.S. 240 (1939).

NLRB v. Local Union No. 1229, 346 U.S. 464 (1953).

NLRB v. Truitt Mfg. Co., 351 U.S. 149 (1956).

NLRB v. Wooster Div. of Borg-Warner Corp., 356 U.S. 342 (1958).

Noland, R. B., & DiPetrillo, S. (2015, February). Transit-oriented development and the frequency of modal use. *Journal of Transport and Land Use*, *8*(2), 21–44. doi:10.5198/jtlu.2015.517

O*NET. (n.d.). *11-9033.00—Education Administrators, Postsecondary*. Retrieved July 26, 2021, from https://www.onetonline.org/link/summary/11-9033.00

O'Donnell, G. (1999). Horizontal accountability in new democracies. In A. Schedler, L. Diamond, & M. F. Plattner (Eds.), *The Self-Restraining State: Power and Accountability in the New Democracies*. Lynne Rienner Publishers. doi:10.1515/9781685854133-004

O'Malley, P. (1998). Indigenous governances. In M. Dean & B. Hindess (Eds.), *Governing Australia: Studies in contemporary rationalities of government* (pp. 156–172). Cambridge University Press.

O'Sullivan, M. A. (2000). *Contests for Corporate Control. Corporate governance and economic performance in the United States and Germany*. Oxford University Press.

Obama, B. (2014). My brother's keeper. *Reclaiming Children and Youth Journal*, *23*(1), 5–8.

Odden, A. R. (1992). School Finance and Education Reform: An Overview. In A. R. Odden (Ed.), *Rethinking School Finance*. Jossey-Bass.

Odden, A. R., & Picus, L. O. (2004). *School Finance: A Policy Perspective*. Mc-Graw-Hill, Inc.

OECD. (2014, October). *Educational Policy Outlook: The Netherlands*. Retrieved from OECD.

OECD. (2015). *Programme for International Student Assessment: Selected Years 2003, 2009, 2012, 2015*. Retrieved from OECD.org: https://www.oecd.org/pisa

OECD. (2016). *Netherlands 2016: Foundations for the future, reviews of national policies for education*. Paris: OECD Publishing. doi:10.1787/9789264257658-en

OECD. (2017). *Education Policy Outlook*. Retrieved from OECD iLibrary: https://data.oecd.org/education.htm

Oliveira, T., Silva, K., Floriano, L., Xavier, P., & Righi, L. (2021). Possíveis estratégias de enfrentamento do Burnout entre profissionais de saúde durante a pandemia do coronavírus. *Revista de Medicina (São Paulo)*, *100*(6), 586–592. doi:10.11606/issn.1679-9836.v100i6p586-592

Oliver, C. (1997). Sustainable competitive advantage: Combining institutional and resource-based views. *Strategic Management Journal*, *18*(9), 697–713. doi:10.1002/(SICI)1097-0266(199710)18:9<697::AID-SMJ909>3.0.CO;2-C

Olshansky, S. J., Antonucci, T., Berkman, L., Binstock, R. H., Boersch-Supan, A., Cacioppo, J. T., & Jackson, J. (2012). Differences in life expectancy due to race and educational differences are widening, and many may not catch up. *Health Affairs*, *31*(8), 1803–1813. doi:10.1377/hlthaff.2011.0746 PMID:22869659

Organizing Committee for Assessing Meaningful Community Engagement in Health & Health Care Programs & Policies. (2022). Assessing Meaningful Community Engagement: A Conceptual Model to Advance Health Equity through Transformed Systems for Health. NAM Perspectives, National Academy of Medicine. doi:10.31478/202202c

Ortega-Campos, E., Vargas-Román, K., Velando-Soriano, A., Suleiman-Martos, N., Cañadas-de la Fuente, G. A., Albendín-García, L., & Gómez-Urquiza, J. L. (2020). Compassion fatigue, compassion satisfaction, and burnout in oncology nurses: A systematic review and meta-analysis. *Sustainability*, *12*(1), 72. doi:10.3390u12010072

Ortiz, J., Quintero, D., Córdoba, C., Ceballos, F., & Córdoba, F. (2020). Consecuencias de la pandemia de la COVID-19 en la salud mental asociadas al aislamiento social. *Colombian Journal of Anesthesiology*, *48*(4), 1–8.

Ortiz-Walters, R., & Gilson, L. L. (2005). Mentoring in academia: An examination of the experiences of protégés of color. *Journal of Vocational Behavior*, *67*(3), 459–475. doi:10.1016/j.jvb.2004.09.004

Osborn, H. F. (2021). *Huxley on education: Address at the opening of the college year, Columbia University, September 28, 1910*. Mt. San Antonio College.

Ostrower, F., & Stone, M. M. (2006). Governance: Research trends, gaps, and future prospects. In R. Steinberg & W. W. Powell (Eds.), *The Nonprofit Sector: A Research Handbook* (pp. 612–628). Yale University Press.

Özcan, İ. Ç. (2014). Economic contribution of essential air service flights on small and remote communities. *Journal of Air Transport Management*, *34*, 24–29. doi:10.1016/j.jairtraman.2013.07.005

Pager, D., & Shepherd, H. (2008). The Sociology of Discrimination: Racial Discrimination in Employment, Housing, Credit, and Consumer Markets. *Annual Review of Sociology*, *34*(1), 181–209. doi:10.1146/annurev.soc.33.040406.131740 PMID:20689680

Pappa, S., Ntella, V., Giannakas, T., Giannakoulis, V., Papoutsi, E., & Katsaounou, P. (2020). Prevalence of depression, anxiety, and insomnia among healthcare workers during the COVID-19 pandemic: A systematic review and meta-analysis. *Brain, Behavior, and Immunity*, *80*, 901–907. doi:10.1016/j.bbi.2020.05.026 PMID:32437915

Park, Y., & O'Kelly, M. E. (2017). Exploring accessibility from spatial interaction data: An evaluation of the Essential Air Service (EAS) program in the contiguous US air transport system. *Environment & Planning A*, *49*(4), 930–951. doi:10.1177/0308518X16680816

Pattberg, P., & Stripple, J. (2008). Beyond the public and private divide: remapping transnational climate governance in the 21st century. *International Environmental Agreements: Politics, Law, and Economics*, *84*(4), 367–88.

Patten, E. (2016). *Racial, gender wage gaps persist in U.S. despite some progress*. Pew Research Center. https://www.pewresearch.org/fact-tank/2016/07/01/racial-gender-wage-gaps-persist-in-u-s-despite-some-progress/

Paulson, A. (2002, September 17). *A Plea to Trust Schools--Not Just Tests*. CSMonitor.com. https://www.csmonitor.com/2002/0917/p14s01-lepr.html

People's Party for Freedom and Democracy (VVD), Christian Democratic Alliance (CDA), Democrats '66 (D66), & Christian Union (CU). (2017). *Confidence in the Future*. Retrieved from government.nl: https://www.government.nl/binaries/government/documents/publications/2017/10/1 0/coalition-agreement-confidence-in-the-future/coalition-agreement-2017-confide nce-in-the-future.pdf

Pereira, M., Torres, E., Pereira, M., Antunes, P., & Costa, C. (2020). Sofrimento emocional dos Enfermeiros no contexto hospitalar frente à pandemia de COVID-19. *Research. Social Development*, *9*(8), 1–21.

Perkinson, H. (1977). *The imperfect panacea: American faith in education 1865-1976*. Random House.

Perna, L. W. (2001). Sex and Race Differences in Faculty Tenure and Promotion. *Research in Higher Education*, *42*(5), 541–567. doi:10.1023/A:1011050226672

Perniciotti, P., Júnior, C., Guarita, R., Morales, R., & Romano, B. (2020). Síndrome de Burnout nos profissionais de saúde: Atualização sobre definições, fatores de risco e estratégias de prevenção. *Revista da SBPH (Belo Horizonte)*, *23*(1), 35–52.

Perry, B. L., Aronson, B., & Pescosolido, B. A. (2021, February 5). Pandemic precarity: COVID-19 is exposing and exacerbating inequalities in the American heartland. *Proceedings of the National Academy of Sciences of the United States of America*, *118*(8), e2020685118. doi:10.1073/pnas.2020685118 PMID:33547252

Peters, E. (2018, October). Compassion fatigue in nursing: A concept analysis. *Nursing Forum*, *53*(4), 466–480. doi:10.1111/nuf.12274 PMID:29962010

Peterson, E., Reichert, J., & Konefal, K. (2017, November 7). *Procedural Justice in Policing: How the Process of Justice Impacts Public Attitudes and Law Enforcement Outcomes*. Retrieved from http://www.icjia.state.il.us/articles/procedural-justice-in-policing-how-the-process-of-justiceimpacts-public-attitudes-and-law-enforcement-outcomes

Peterson, I. (2004, October 21). Two Ex-Governors Support a Tax Convention. *New York Times*.

Pew Foundation. (2021, December 22). *Fiscal 50: State Trends and Analysis*. Retrieved from pewtrusts.org: https://www.pewtrusts.org/en/research-and-analysis/data-visualizations/2014/fiscal-50#ind5

Pew Research Center. (2020). *Most Americans Say There Is Too Much Economic Inequality in the U.S., but Fewer Than Half Call It a Top Priority*. Pew Research Center.

Phi Beta Sigma. (n.d.a). *About*. Retrieved from https://phibetasigma1914.org/index.php/about/ history

Phi Beta Sigma. (n.d.b). *Programs*. Retrieved from https://phibetasigma1914.org/index.php/ programs

Piattoni, S. (2001). *Clientelism, Interests, and Democratic Representation: The European Experience in Historical and Comparative Perspective*. Cambridge University Press. doi:10.1017/CBO9781139175340

Pinel, E. C. (1999). Stigma consciousness: The psychological legacy of social stereotypes. *Journal of Personality and Social Psychology*, *76*(1), 114–128. doi:10.1037/0022-3514.76.1.114 PMID:9972557

Pines, A., & Aronson, E. (1983). Combattinhg burnout. *Children and Youth Services Review*, *5*(3), 263–275. doi:10.1016/0190-7409(83)90031-2

Piperopoulos, P., Jie, W., & Chengqi, W. (2018). Outward FDI, location choices and innovation performance of emerging marke enterprises. *Research Policy*, *47*(1), 232–240. doi:10.1016/j.respol.2017.11.001

Plumptre, T., & Graham, J. (1999). *Governance and Good Governance: International and Aboriginal Perspectives*. Institute on Governance.

Poehlmann, J. (2005). Representations of attachment relationships in children of incarcerated mothers. *Child Development*, *76*(3), 679–696. doi:10.1111/j.1467-8624.2005.00871.x PMID:15892786

Policemen's Benevolent and Protective Association, Unit #5, 36 PERI ¶ 113 (ILRB 2020).

Ponessa, J. (2004). *Breaking Ground: Rebuilding New Jersey's Urban Schools: The Abbott School Constrution Program*. Education Law Center.

Pope Leo, X. I. I. I. (2021). *Catholicism and Socialism: Encyclicals of Pope Leo XIII: Rerum Novarum (1878), Quaod Apostolici Muneris (1891), Gravis de Communi Re (1901)*. Claritas Publications.

Porter, M. E., Sachs, J. D., & Mcarthur, J. W. (2002). *Executive Summary: Competitivenesws and States of economic Development. The Global Competitiveness Report 2001-2002*. Retrieved from Sustainable Development Networking Programme. https://citeseerx.ist.psu.edu/viewdoc/download?doi=10.1.1.476.4940&rep=rep1&type=pdf

Porter, T. (2009). Global governance as configurations of state/non-state activity. In J. Whitman (Ed.), *Palgrave advances in global governance*. Palgrave Macmillan. doi:10.1057/9780230245310_5

Prapotnik Brdnik, A., Kamnik, R., Marksel, M., & Božičnik, S. (2019). Market and technological perspectives for the new generation of regional passenger aircraft. *Energies*, *12*(10), 1864. doi:10.3390/en12101864

Pratt, G., & Byrne, J. (2020, April 9). *City expects federal coronavirus stimulus package to give $1.5 billion to Chicago government, CPS and CTA*. Retrieved from Chicago Tribune: https://www.chicagotribune.com/coronavirus/ct-coronavirus-chicago-stimulus-lightfoot-trump-20200409-e2rwavkp5rg2zpejape6
args4i-story.html

Pryor, J. B., Reeder, G. D., Yeadon, C., & Hesson-McLnnis, M. (2004). A dual-process model of reactions to perceived stigma. *Journal of Personality and Social Psychology*, *87*(4), 436–452. doi:10.1037/0022-3514.87.4.436 PMID:15491270

Punyanunt-Carter, N. (2008). The perceived realism of African American portrayals on television. *The Howard Journal of Communications*, *19*(3), 241–257. doi:10.1080/10646170802218263

Quinn, D., & Polikoff, M. (2017). *Summer learning loss: What is it, and what can we do about it*. Brookings Institution.

Rakove, M. L. (1979). *We Don't Want Nobody Nobody Sent*. Indiana University Press.

Randel, A. E., Galvin, B. M., Gibson, C. B., & Batts, S. I. (2021). Increasing Career Advancement Opportunities Through Sponsorship: An Identity-Based Model With Illustrative Application to Cross-Race Mentorship of African Americans. *Group & Organization Management*, *46*(1), 105–142. doi:10.1177/1059601120978003

Ravitch, D. (1987). *The Schools We Deserve*. Harper Collins.

Ravitch, D., & Finn, C. Jr. (1987). *What Do Our 17-Year-Olds Know?* Harper Collins.

Reagan, B. (1990). The war on drugs: A war against women. *Berkeley Women's Law Journal*, *6*, 203.

Rebell, M. A. (2002). Education Adequacy, Democracy and the Courts. In T. Ready & C. Edley, C. E. Snow (Eds.), Achieving High Educational Standards for All: Conference Summary. National Research Council and National Academy Press.

Rebell, M. A. (2004). *Commentary: Why Adequacy Lawsuits Matter*. Education Week.

Rebell, M. A., & Wardenski, J. J. (2004). *Of Course Money Matters: Why the Arguments to the Contrary Never Added Up*. Campaign for Fiscal Equity.

Reed, D. S. (1996). Court-Ordered School Finance Equalization: Judicial Activism and Democratic Opposition. In W. J. Fowler (Ed.), *Developments in School Finance, 1996,* (pp. 91–120). National Center for Education Statistics.

Reed, D. S. (1998). Twenty-Five Years after Rodriguez: School Finance Litigation and the Impact of the New Judicial Federalism. *Law & Society Review*, *32*(1), 175–220.

Reed, D. S. (2001). *On Equal Terms: The Constitutional Politics of Educational Opportunity*. Princeton University Press.

Reeves, S., Kuper, A., & Hodges, B. D. (2008, August 7). Qualitative research methodologies: Ethnography. *BMJ (Clinical Research Ed.), 337*(a3), a1020. Advance online publication. doi:10.1136/bmj.a1020 PMID:18687725

Reith, T. (2018). Burnout in United States Healthcare Professionals: A Narrative Review. *PubMed Central, 10*(12).

Renz, D. O. (2004). Leadership, Governance, and the Work of the Board. In D. O. Rend (Ed.), *The Jossey-Bass Handbook of Nonprofit Leadership and Management*. John Wiley and Sons, Inc.

Renz, D. O. (2010). *The Jossey-Bass Handbook of Nonprofit Leadership and Management*. John Wiley and Sons, Inc.

Reporters Sans Frontieres. (2015-2017). *Index RSF*. Retrieved from RSF.org: https://rsf.org/en/index?year=2021

Republic Aviation Corp. v. National Labor Relations Board, 324 U.S. 793 (1945).

Reschovsky, A. (1994). Fiscal Equalization and School Finance. *National Tax Journal, 47*, 185–187.

Reschovsky, A., & Imazeki, J. (1998). The Development of School Finance Formulas to Guarantee the Provision of an Adequate Education to Low INcome Students. In *Developments in School Finance 1997: Does Money Matter?* (pp. 121–148). U.S. Department of Education, National Center for Education Statistics.

Reskin, B. (1979). Academic Sponsorship and Scientists' Careers. *Sociology of Education, 52*(3), 129–146. doi:10.2307/2112319

Reuben, K., & Randall, M. (2017). Debt Limits: How States Restrict Borrowing. Urban Institute.

Rhodes, J. (2011). Ethical principles for youth mentoring relationships. Mentor: National Mentoring Partnership, 1-6.

Rhodes, R. (2005). The unholy trinity of governance. The Blake Dawson Waldron Lecture, National Museum of Australia, Canberra.

Ribeiro, L., Vieira, T., & Sousa, K. (2020). Síndrome de burnout em profissionais de saúde antes e durante a pandemia da COVID-19. *Revista Eletrônica Acervo Saúde, 12*(11), 1–10. doi:10.25248/reas.e5021.2020

Ribot, J. C. (2002). *Democratic decentralization of natural resources: Institutionalizing popular participation*. World Resources Institute.

Richards, K. C., Campenni, C. E., & Muse-Burke, J. L. (2010). Self-care and well-being in mental health professionals: The mediating effects of self-awareness and mindfulness. *Journal of Mental Health Counseling, 32*(3), 247–264. doi:10.17744/mehc.32.3.0n31v88304423806

Rich, B. (1957). *The Government and Politics of New Jersey*. Crowell Press.

Richfield Hospitality, Inc., 369 NLRB No. 111 (2020).

Richmond, E. (2013, June 18). *America's Teacher-Training Programs Aren't Good Enough*. Retrieved February 9, 2018, from The Atlantic: https://www.theatlantic.com/national/archive/2013/06/america s-teacher-training-pro grams-arent-good-enough/276993/

Ritter, G. W., & Lauyer, S. C. (2003). School Finance Reform in New Jersey: A Piecemeal Response to a Systemic Problem. *Journal of Education Finance, 28*, 575–598.

Roberts, S. O., & Rizzo, M. T. (2020). The psychology of American racism. *The American Psychologist*. Advance online publication. doi:10.1037/amp0000642 PMID:32584061

Robinson v. Cahill, 62 N.J. 473, 303 A. 2d 273 (New Jersey 1972).

Rodriguez v. San Antonio Independent School District 337, 337 F. Supp. 280 (W.D. Tex. 1971).

Roepe, L. R. (2021). *Barriers for Black Professionals* (All Things Work). SHRM. https://www.shrm.org/hr-today/news/all-things-work/pages/racism-corporate-america.aspx

Romano, S. D., Blackstock, A. J., Taylor, E. V., Felix, S., Adjei, S., Singleton, C. M., & Boehmer, T. K. (2021). Trends in racial and ethnic disparities in COVID-19 hospitalizations, by region—United States, March-December 2020. *Morbidity and Mortality Weekly Report*, *70*(15), 560–565. doi:10.15585/mmwr.mm7015e2 PMID:33857068

Rosenau, J. N. (2000). Change, complexity, and governance in globalizing space. In J. Pierre (Ed.), *Debating governance* (pp. 167–200). Oxford University Press.

Rosenbaum, D. (2014, April 21). *Building Trust Inside and Out: Challenges Facing Police Leaders*. Retrieved from https://www.nij.gov/multimedia/presenter/presenterrosenbaum2/pages/presenter-rosenbaum2-transcript.aspx

Rosenberg, M. (1965). *Society and the adolescent self-image*. Princeton University Press. doi:10.1515/9781400876136

Ross, E. A. (1901). *Social control: A survey of the foundations of order*. The Macmillan Company.

Rush University System for Health. (2022). *Recognitions and Accreditations*. Rush University System for Health.

Ruviaro, M., & Bardagi, M. (2011). Síndrome de Burnout e satisfação no trabalho em profissionais da área de enfermagem do interior do RS. *BarBaroi*, 194–216.

Sala-i-Martin, X., Bilbao-Osorio, B., Blanke, J., Crotti, R., Drzeniek Hanouz, M., Geiger, T., & Ko, C. (2012). The Global Competitiveness Index 2012–2013: Strengthening Recovery by Raising Productivity. *The Global Competitiveness Report 2012-2013*, 3-48.

Salinitri, G. (2005). The effects of formal mentoring on the retention rates for first-year, low achieving students. *Canadian Journal of Education*, *28*(4), 853–873. doi:10.2307/4126458

Salmore, B. G., & Salmore, S. A. (1998). *New Jersey Politics and Government*. University of Nebraska Press.

Salucci, F., Trainelli, L., Bruglieri, M., Riboldi, C. E., Rolando, A. L., & García González, G. (2021). Capturing the Demand for an Electric-Powered Short-Haul Air Transportation Network. *AIAA SciTech 2021 Forum*. 10.2514/6.2021-0869

Samuelson, H. L., Levine, B. R., Barth, S. E., Wessel, J. L., & Grand, J. A. (2019). Exploring women's leadership labyrinth: Effects of hiring and developmental opportunities on gender stratification. *The Leadership Quarterly*, *30*(6), 101314. doi:10.1016/j.leaqua.2019.101314

Sanchez-Hucles, J. V., & Davis, D. D. (2010). Women and women of color in leadership: Complexity, identity, and intersectionality. *The American Psychologist*, *65*(3), 171–181. doi:10.1037/a0017459 PMID:20350016

Sanders, W. (2003). *Participation and representation in the 2002 ATSIC elections*. CAEPR Discussion Paper No. 252. CAEPR, ANU.

Sanders, W. (2004). *Thinking about Indigenous community governance*. CAEPR Discussion Paper No. 262. CAEPR, ANU.

Sangamon Cnty. Sheriff's Dept. v. Illinois Human Rights Comm'n, 233 Ill.2d 125 (2009).

Sanghera, J., Pattani, N., Hashmi, Y., Varley, K., Cheruvu, M., Bradley, A., & Burke, J. (2020). The impact of SARS-CoV-2 on the mental health of healthcare workers in a hospital setting—A Systematic Review. *Journal of Occupational Health*, *62*(1). doi:10.1002/1348-9585.12175 PMID:33131192

Sargeant, E., Antrobus, E., & Platz, D. (2017). Promoting a culture of fairness: Police training, procedural justice, and compliance. *Journal of Experimental Criminology*, *13*(3), 347–365. doi:10.100711292-017-9296-0

Saucier, G. (1994). Mini-Markers: A brief version of Goldberg's unipolar Big-Five markers. *Journal of Personality Assessment*, *63*(3), 506–516. doi:10.120715327752jpa6303_8 PMID:7844738

Scales, P. C., Boat, A., & Pekel, K. (2020). *Defining and measuring social capital for young people: A practical review of the literature on resource-full relationships*. Search Institute.

Scandura, T. A., & Williams, E. A. (2001). An Investigation of the Moderating Effects of Gender on the Relationships between Mentorship Initiation and Protégé Perceptions of Mentoring Functions. *Journal of Vocational Behavior*, *59*(3), 342–363. doi:10.1006/jvbe.2001.1809

Schacter, M. (2000). *When accountability fails: a framework for diagnosis and action. Policy Brief No. 9*. Institute on Governance.

Schaufeli, W., & Enzmann, D. (1998). *The burnout companion to study and practice: A critical analysis*. Taylor & Francis.

Schaufeli, W., & Greenglass, E. (2001). Introduction to special issue on burnout and health. *Psychology & Health*, *16*(5), 501–510. doi:10.1080/08870440108405523 PMID:22804495

Schedler, A. (1999). Restraining the state: conflicts and agents of accountability. In A. Schedler, L. Diamond, & M. F. Plattner (Eds.), *The Self-Restraining State: Power and Accountability in the New Democracies*. Lynne Rienner Publishers. doi:10.1515/9781685854133-021

Schneider, H. W. (1963). *A history of American philosophy* (2nd ed.). Columbia University Press.

Schneider, M. (2002). *Do School Facilities Affect Academic Outcomes?* National Clearinghouse for Educational Facilities.

Schrag, P. (2003). *Final Test: The Battle for Adequacy in America's Schools*. The New Press.

Schulhofer, S. J., Tyler, T. R., & Huq, A. Z. (2012). American policing at a crossroads: Unsustainable policies and the procedural justice alternative. *Policing*, *35*(3). Advance online publication. doi:10.1108/pijpsm.2012.18135caa.003

Schunk, D. (1995). Self-efficacy, motivation, and performance. *Journal of Applied Sport Psychology*, *7*(2), 109–134. doi:10.1080/10413209508406961

Schwab, A., Thomas, A., Bennett, J., Robertson, E., & Cary, S. (2021). *Electrification of Aircraft: Challenges, Barriers, and Potential Impacts (No. NREL/TP-6A20-80220). National Renewable Energy Lab*. NREL. doi:10.2172/1827628

Scott, L. (2015). Learning cities for adult learners. New Directions for Adult and Continuing Education. San Francisco, CA: Jossey-Bass.

Scott, L. (2017). Learning cities. In A. Knox, S. Conceicao, & L. Martin (Eds.), Mapping the Field of Adult and Continuing Education: An International Compendium (Vol. 4). Sterling, VA: Stylus.

Scott, J. C. (1998). *Seeing Like a State: How Certain Schemes to Improve the Human Condition Have Failed*. Yale University Press.

Scott, L. (2021). Learning cities as smart cities: Connecting lifelong learning and technology. In F. Annansingh (Ed.), *Examining the Socio-Technical Impact of Smart Cities* (pp. 68–90). IGI Global. doi:10.4018/978-1-7998-5326-8.ch003

Scott, L., Mizzi, R. C., & Merriweather, L. R. (2020). Philosophical foundations of adult continuing education. In *2020 Handbook of Adult and Continuing Education. Sterling* (pp. 11–21). Stylus.

Sebring, P. B., Allensworth, E., Bryk, A. S., & Easton, J. Q. (2006). *The Essential Supports for School Improvement*. Consortium on Chicago School Research, University of Chicago.

Secretariat, I. C. A. O. (2019). Electric, hybrid, and hydrogen aircraft-state of play. *Climate Change Mitigation: Technology and Operations*, 124-130.

Seibert, S., Kraimer, M., & Liden, R. (2001). A Social Capital Theory of Career Success. *Academy of Management Journal*, *44*(2), 219–237. Advance online publication. doi:10.2307/3069452

Selman, P. (2001). Social capital, sustainability, and environmental planning. *Planning Theory & Practice*, *2*(1), 13–30. doi:10.1080/14649350122850

Serin, G. (2022). *Gov. Newsom Lifts All, but 5% of COVID-19 Executive Actions. Here's What Remains*. Retrieved March 22, 2022, from KCRA: https://www.kcra.com/article/gov-newsom-lifts-all-but-5-covid-executive-actions-heres-what-remains/39233442#

Serrano v. Priest, 5 Cal. 3d 584, 487 P.2d 1241, 96 Cal Rptr. 601 (California 1971).

Serrano-Bedia, A. M., López-Fernández, C., & García-Piqueres, G. (2018). Complementarity between innovation knowledge sources: Does the innovation performance measure matter. *Business Research Quarterly*, *21*(1), 53–67. doi:10.1016/j.brq.2017.09.001

Serrano-Bedia, A. M., Piva, E., & Rossi-Lamastra, C. (2014). Open innovation and within-industry diversification in small and medium enterprises: The case of open source software firms. *Research Policy*, (43), 891–902.

Severson, D. (2009). *John Dewey's Essentials for Democracy and Education*. Proficiency Publishers.

Shah, K., Chaudhari, G., Kamrai, D., Lail, A., & Patel, R. (2020). How Essential Is to Focus on Physician's Health and Burnout in Coronavirus (COVID-19) Pandemic? *Cureus*, *12*(4). doi:10.7759/cureus.7538 PMID:32377486

Shang, H., & Huang, X. (2018). Dynamic Interaction Effects of Government Subsidies, R & D investment and Innovation Performance. *Studies in Science of Science*, (3), 446–455.

Shank, A. (1969). *New Jersey Reapportionment Politics*. Associated University Presses.

Sharp, S. F., & Eriksen, M. E. (2003). Imprisoned mothers and their children. *Women in prison: Gender and social control*, 119-136.

Sheet, F. (2015). *Trends in US corrections*. The Sentencing Project.

Sheil, J. C. (2000). The Just-Do-It Decision: School-Funding Litigation Tests the Limits of Judicial Deference. *Seton Hall Law Review*, *28*, 620.

Shjarback, J. A., Pyrooz, D. C., Wolfe, S. E., & Decker, S. H. (2017). De-policing and crime in the wake of Ferguson: Racialized changes in the quantity and quality of policing among Missouri police departments. *Journal of Criminal Justice*, *50*, 42–52. doi:10.1016/j.jcrimjus.2017.04.003

Shou, K., Wei, J., & Liu, Y. (2018). Portfolio Diversity Framework of Latecomer Alliances: A Qualitative Comparative Analysis. *Studies in Science of Science*, (7), 1254–1263.

Shu, C. L., Wang, Q., Gao, S. X., & Liu, C. (2015). Firm Patenting, Innovations and Government Institutional Support as a Double-Edged Sword. *Journal of Product Innovation Management*, *32*(2), 290–305. doi:10.1111/jpim.12230

Siewart, R. (2007). *Ministerial powers to seize assets of service providers in prescribed areas within the Northern Territory.* Background Briefing, Parliament House, Canberra. http://www.rachelsiewert.org.au/files/campaigns/extras/Brief ing_on_NT_seizure_powers.pdf

Sigma Beta Club. (2015a). *News and updates.* Retrieved from https://sigmabetaclub.org/ newsupdates

Sigma Beta Club. (2015b). *Our story.* Retrieved: https://sigmabetaclub.org/our-story

Simoulin, V. (2003). La gouvernance et l'action publique: Le succès d'une forme simmélienne. *Droit Social*, (54), 307–328. doi:10.3917/drs.054.0307

Singer, S. (2017, February 13). *U.S. Public Schools Are Not Failing. They're Among the Best in the World.* Retrieved from Huffington Post: https://www.huffingtonpost.com/entry/us-public-schools-are-n ot-failing-theyre-am ong_us_5894e819e4b061551b3dfe51

Sklarz, M., & Miller, N. (2018). *The Impact of Noise on Residential Property Value.* Collateral Analytics Research. Retrieved from https://www.collateralanalytics.com/wp-content/uploads/2018/ 10/CA-RESEARCH-The-Impact-of-Noise-on-Residential-Property-V alues.pdf

Smith, D. E. (1995). Representative politics and the new wave of native title organisations. In J. Finlayson & D. E. Smith (Eds.), Native Title: Emerging Issues for Research, Policy and Practice. CAEPR Research Monograph No. 10. CAEPR, ANU.

Smith, D. E. (1996). From cultural diversity to regionalism: The political culture of difference in ATSIC. In P. Sullivan (Ed.), Shooting the Banker: Essays on ATSIC and Self-determination. North Australia Research Unit, ANU.

Smith, D. E. (2004). *From Gove to governance: Reshaping Indigenous governance in the Northern Territory.* CAEPR Discussion Paper No. 265. CAEPR, ANU.

Smith, A. (1993). *An Inquiry into the Nature and Causes of the Wealth of Nations.* Oxford University Press.

Smith, B. W., Dalen, J., Wiggins, K., Tooley, E., Christopher, P., & Bernard, J. (2008). The brief resilience scale: Assessing the ability to bounce back. *International Journal of Behavioral Medicine*, *15*(3), 194–200. doi:10.1080/10705500802222972 PMID:18696313

Smith, D. E. (2007). Networked governance: Issues of process, policy, and power in a West Arnhem Land regional initiative. *Ngiya: Talk the Law. Governance in Indigenous Communities*, *1*, 24–52.

Smith, E., & Reeves, R. V. (2020). *SAT math scores mirror and maintain racial inequity.* Brookings Institute.

Smylie, S. (2022). *Chicago principals are again trying to unionize. Will new momentum help?* Chalkbeat Chicago. https://chicago.chalkbeat.org/2022/3/2/22958917/chicago-principals-unionize-illinois-legislature

Smyth, A., Christodoulou, G., Dennis, N., Marwan, A. A., & Campbell, J. (2012). Is air transport a necessity for social inclusion and economic development? *Journal of Air Transport Management*, *22*, 53–59. doi:10.1016/j.jairtraman.2012.01.009

SNS. (2019). *Serviço Nacional de Saúde.* https://www.inem.pt/2019/05/29/oms-inclui-burnout-na-lista-d e-doencas/

Snyder, C. R., & Lopez, S. J. (2007). *Positive psychology: The scientific and practical explorations of human strengths.* SAGE.

Social Sciences Feminist Network Research Interest Group. (2017). The Burden of Invisible Work in Academia: Social Inequalities and Time Use in Five University Departments. *Humboldt Journal of Social Relations*, *39*, 228–245.

Spokane International Airport. (2014). *Aircraft Noise Analysis. Spokane International Airport Master Plan*. Retrieved from http://business.zlcms.com/core/files/business/uploads/files/Master%20Plan/Chapter%206.pdf

Stadler, C., & Nobes, C. W. (2018). Accounting for government grants: Standard-setting and accounting choice. *Journal of Accounting and Public Policy*, *21*(5), 101–119. doi:10.1016/j.jaccpubpol.2018.02.004

Stanton-Salazar, R. D. (2011). A Social Capital Framework for the Study of Institutional Agents and Their Role in the Empowerment of Low-Status Students and Youth. *Youth & Society*, *43*(3), 1066–1109. doi:10.1177/0044118X10382877

Steele, A. (2018, February 4). *South Shore line capital plan total $1.2 billion over five years*. Retrieved from NWITimes.com: https://www.nwitimes.com/business/local/article_4186062c-7472-5e8c-af29-68caf4d3fb0c.html

Steele, C. M. (1997). A threat in the air: How stereotypes shape intellectual identity and performance. *American Psychologist, 52*(6), 613-629. Retrieved from ProQuest database (839058469).

Stevenson, A., & Chien, A. C. (2022). *Covid Live Updates: As Asia grapples with omicron, cases rise again in Europe*. Retrieved March 16, 2022, from The New York Times: https://www.nytimes.com/live/2022/03/16/world/covid-19-mandates-cases-vaccine

Stillwell, R., & Sable, J. (2013). *Public school graduates and dropouts from the common core of data: School year 2009-10*. National Center for Education Statistics. U.S. Department of Education.

Stoker, G. (1998). Governance as theory: Five propositions. *International Social Science Journal*, *155*(155), 17–28. doi:10.1111/1468-2451.00106

Stone, C. (2017, July 28). *What's the Fed to Do? The central bank is navigating through uncharted waters*. Retrieved from US News and World Report: https://www.usnews.com/opinion/economic-intelligence/articles/2017-07-28/the-fed-struggles-with-the-unemployment-inflati
on-trade-off

Stratford, E., & Davidson, J. (2002). Capital assets and intercultural borderlands: Socio-cultural challenges for natural resource management. *Journal of Environmental Management*, *66*(4), 429–440. doi:10.1006/jema.2002.0597 PMID:12503497

Strauss, V. (2015, October 24). *Confirmed: Standardized testing has taken over our schools. But who's to blame?* Retrieved from Washington Post: https://www.washingtonpost.com/news/answer-sheet/wp/2015/10/24/confirmed-standardized-testing-has-taken-over-our-schools
-but-whos-to-blame/

Strauss, V. (2019, November 1). The common mistake Betsy DeVos made aboutn new NAEP scores—and other problems with her "sky is falling" narrative. *The Washington Post*, pp. 1-19.

Streeck, W. (2001). *The transformation of corporate organization in Europe: an overview*. MPIfG Working Paper 01/8. MPIfG.

Stripling, J. (2021, June 11). 'What the Hell Happened?' Inside the Nikole Hannah-Jones Tenure Case. *The Chronicle of Higher Education*. https://www.chronicle.com/article/what-the-hell-happened

Struksnes Constr. Co., 165 NLRB 1062 (1967).

Sufrin, C., Beal, L., Clarke, J., Jones, R., & Mosher, W. D. (2019). Pregnancy outcomes in US prisons, 2016–2017. *American Journal of Public Health*, *109*(5), 799–805. doi:10.2105/AJPH.2019.305006 PMID:30897003

Suh, S., & Suh, J. (2007). Risk factors and levels of risk for high school dropouts. *Professional School Counseling*, *10*(3), 297–306. doi:10.5330/prsc.10.3.w26024vvw6541gv7

Su, J., & Liu, C. (2019). An Analysis of the Paradoxical Relationship between political Embeddedness and Independent Innovation Performance. *Studies in Science of Science*, *2*, 375–384.

Sullivan, P. (2005). Searching for the socio-intercultural, searching for the culture, in The Independent Commission for Good Governance in Public Services (TICGG). *The good governance standard for public services*. http://www.opm.co.uk/icggps/download_upload/Standard.pdf

Sun, Z., & Song, W. (2012). The Influence of R & D Investment on the Performance of Industrial Innovation: Empirical Evidence from Chinese Manufacturing Industry. *Shuliang Jingji Jishu Jingji Yanjiu*, *4*, 49–63.

Swanson, A. D., & King, R. (1997). *School Finance: Its Economics and Politics,* (2nd ed.). Longman Publishers.

Swavola, E., Riley, K., & Subramanian, R. (2016). *Overlooked: Women and jails in an era of reform*. Vera Institute of Justice.

Sweileh, W. M. (2020). Research trends and scientific analysis of publications on burnout and compassion fatigue among healthcare providers. *Journal of Occupational Medicine and Toxicology (London, England)*, *15*(1), 1–10. doi:10.118612995-020-00274-z PMID:32684943

Tachtsoglou, K., Lera, M., Iliadis, C., Frantzana, A., & Kourkouta, L. (2018). Occupational Burnout of Health Care Professionals in Hospitals. *Journal of Healthcare Communications*, *3*(38), 1–7.

Tapper, T. (2021, December 10). *Why Is Inflation rising Right Now?* Retrieved from Forbes.com: https://www.forbes.com/advisor/investing/why-is-inflation-rising-right-now

Tariq, M., Maswood, A. I., Gajanayake, C. J., & Gupta, A. K. (2017). Aircraft batteries: Current trend towards more electric aircraft. *IET Electrical Systems in Transportation*, *7*(2), 93–103. doi:10.1049/iet-est.2016.0019

Tarr, G. A., & Porter, C. A. (1988). *State Supreme Courts in State and Nation*. Yale University Press.

Taylor, M., Turk, J. M., Chessman, H., & Espinosa, L. L. (2020). *Race and ethnicity in higher education*. American Council on Higher Education. https://devacerehe.wpengine.com/wp-content/uploads/2020/11/REHE-2020-final.pdf

Taylor, S. (2019). The psychology of pandemics: Preparing for the next global outbreak of infectious disease. In Cambridge Scholars Publishing (Ed.). Cambridge, Scholars Publishing.

Teasley, M. L., & Lee, E. (2006). Examining the association between academic achievement and self-esteem in African American male youth in a community after-school program. *School Social Work Journal*, *30*, 64–81.

The New York Times. (2020, November 3). Presidential Election Results: Biden Wins. *The New York Times*. Retrieved April 8, 2022, from https://www.nytimes.com/interactive/2020/11/03/us/elections/results-president.html

The White House. (2021). *The Biden-Harris Administration Immediate Priorities (2021)*. Retrieved April 21, 2022, from https://www.whitehouse.gov/priorities/

Thelen, K. (2000). Timing and temporality in the analysis of institutional evolution and change. *Studies in American Political Development*, *14*(1), 101–108. doi:10.1017/S0898588X00213035

Thijs, A., van Leeuwen, B., & Zandbergen, M. (2009). Inclusive Education in the Netherlands. *International Journal of Inclusive Education*, *1*, 1–61.

Thomas v. Collins, 323 U.S. 516 (1945).

Thomas, R., & Bertolini, L. (2017, October). Defining critical success factors in TOD implementation using rough set analysis. *Journal of Transport and Land Use*, *10*(1), 139–154.

Thro, W. (1993). The Role of Language of the State Education Clauses in School Finance Litigation. *Education Law Report*, *79*(19), 277–289.

Tiebout, C. (1956). A Pure Theory of Local Expenditures. *Journal of Political Economy*, *54*, 416–424.

Time4Learning, Inc. (n.d.). *Standardized Testing by State*. Retrieved January 25, 2018, from Time4Learning.com: https://www.time4learning.com/testprep/

TIMSS and PIRLS International Study Center, Lynch School of Education, Boston College. (2015). *PIRLS Reading Results (Selected years 2001 through 2016)*. Retrieved from TIMSS and PIRLS International Study Center: https://timssandpirls.bc.edu

TIMSS and PIRLS International Study Center, Lynch School of Education, Boston College. (2015). *TIMSS Mathematics and Science Results (Selected years 2001 through 2016)*. Retrieved from TIMSS and PIRLS International Study Center: https://timssandpirls.bc.edu

Topos Partnership. (2011). *Social science literature review: Media representation and impact on the lives of Black men and boys*. The Opportunity Agenda.

Trenerry, B., & Paradies, Y. (2012). Organizational Assessment. *An Overlooked Approach To Managing Diversity And Addressing Racism In The Workplace.*, *7*(1), 16.

Trentham, S., & Larwood, L. (1998). Gender Discrimination and the Workplace: An Examination of Rational Bias Theory. *Sex Roles*, *38*(1), 1–28. doi:10.1023/A:1018782226876

Trigo, T., Teng, C., & Hallak, C. (2007). Síndrome de burnout ou estafa profissional e os transtornos psiquiátricos. *Rev Psiq Clín*, *34*(5), 223–233. doi:10.1590/S0101-60832007000500004

Tucker, E., Alonso, M., & Johnston, C. (2022). *Growing Number of States, Major Cities Lift COVID-19 Restrictions*. Retrieved March 6, 2022, from CNN: https://www.cnn.com/2022/02/19/us/covid-mandates-vaccine-indoor-dining/index.html

Tucker, M. (2017, April 6). *The Netherlands: Top-Performing School System Looking to Get Better*. Retrieved February 9, 2018, from blogs.edweek.org: https://blogs.edweek.org/edweek/top_performers/2017/04/the_netherlands_top_performer_in_motion.html

Tukachinsky, R., Mastro, D., & Yarchi, M. (2017). The effect of primetime television ethnic/racial stereotypes on Latino and Black American: A longitudinal national study. *Journal of Broadcasting & Electronic Media*, *61*(3), 538–556. doi:10.1080/08838151.2017.1344669

Turnbull, W. (2005). *Evaluation of current governance arrangements to support regional investment under the NHT and NAP*. Departments of Environment and Heritage and Agriculture, Fisheries and Forestry.

Turner, C. (2018). *Report on Recommendations from the U.S. Commission on Civil Rights* [Recorded by N. P. Radio]. Academic Press.

Tweedy, D. (2015). *Black man in a white coat: A doctor's reflections on race and medicine*. Picador/Macmillan.

Twersky-Glasner, A. (2005, March). Police personality: What is it and why are they like that? *Journal of Police and Criminal Psychology*, *20*(1), 56–67. doi:10.1007/BF02806707

Tyler, T. R. (2007/2008). Procedural Justice and the Courts. *Court Review: The Journal of the American Judges Association, 44*(1-2), 26-31. Retrieved from http://aja.ncsc.dni.us/publications/courtrv/cr44-1/CR44-1-2.pdf

Tyler, T. (2017). Procedural Justice and Policing: A Rush to Judgment? *Annual Review of Law and Social Science*, *13*(1), 29–53. doi:10.1146/annurev-lawsocsci-110316-113318

U.S. Congress. (2020, March 27). *H.R. 748 CARES Act*. Retrieved from congress.gov: https://www.congress.gov/bill/116th-congress/house-bill/748

U.S. Congress. (2021). *American Rescue Plan Act of 2021, sec. 9901, Public Law 117-2, codified at 42 U.S.C. 802.* https://www.congress.gov/bill/117th-congress/house-bill/1319

U.S. CONST. amend. V.

U.S. Department of Education. (2014). *Policy statement on expulsion and suspension policies in early childhood settings*. Retrieved from https://www2.ed.gov/policy/gen/guid/ schooldiscipline/policy-statement-ece-expulsions-suspensions.pdf

U.S. Department of Education. (2017). *About ED: Overview and Mission Statement*. Retrieved from U.S. Department of Education: https://www2.ed.gov/about/landing.jhtml

U.S. Department of Justice, Bureau of Justice Assistance. (2014). *Legitimacy and procedural justice: A new element of police leadership. A report by the Police Executive Research Forum (PERF)*. Author.

U.S. Department of the Treasury. (2021, March 18). *Fact Sheet: The American Rescue Plan Will Deliver Immediate Economic Relief to Families*. https://home.treasury.gov/news/featured-stories/fact-sheet-the-american-rescue-plan-will-deliver-immediate-economic-reli
ef-to-families

U.S. ex rel. Sanney v. Montanye, 500 F.2d 411, 416 (2d Cir. 1974).

U.S. Newswire. (2014). *Phi Beta Sigma announces centennial week activities, July 16-20*. Author.

U.S. White House. (2014). *My brother's keeper task force report to the president*. Retrieved from https://www.whitehouse.gov/my-brothers-keeper

U.S. White House. (2015). *My brother's keeper task force: One-year progress report to the president*. Retrieved: https://www.whitehouse.gov/my-brothers-keeper

U.S. White House. (2016). *My brother's keeper 2016 progress report: Two years of expanding opportunity and creating pathways to success*. Retrieved from https://www.wh.gov/mbk

Ubhayakar, S., Capeless, M., Owens, R., Snorrason, K., & Zuckerman, D. (2017). *Anchor Mission Playbook*. Rush University Medical Center and The Democracy Collaborative.

United Nations Educational, Scientific and Cultural Organization (UNESCO). (2008a). Background Note. A Review of Education for Sustainable Development (ESD) Policies from a Cultural Diversity and socio-intercultural Dialogue Perspective. Unpublished document. UNESCO/CLT/CPD/CPO20/11/2008. Paris: UNESCO.

United Nations Educational, Scientific and Cultural Organization (UNESCO). (2008b). UNESCO Concept Note. Towards a New Cultural Policy Profile. UNESCO/CLT/CPD 01/08/2008. Paris: UNESCO.

United Nations Educational, Scientific and Cultural Organization (UNESCO). (2008c). ESD Lens, version 2, draft 1: Comments from a cultural diversity perspective. Unpublished document. Paris: UNESCO.

United Paperworkers Intern. Union v. Misco, Inc., 484 U.S. 29 (1987).

United States National Commission on Excellence in Education. (1983). *A nation at risk*. https://www2.ed.gov/pubs/NatAtRisk/index.html

United States Postal Service v. National Labor Relations Board, 969 F.2d 1064, 1071 (D.C. Cir. 1992).

Vaca v. Sipes, 386 U.S. 171 (1967).

Van Mol, M. M., Kompanje, E. J., Benoit, D. D., Bakker, J., & Nijkamp, M. D. (2015). The prevalence of compassion fatigue and burnout among healthcare professionals in intensive care units: A systematic review. *PLoS One*, *10*(8), e0136955. doi:10.1371/journal.pone.0136955 PMID:26322644

van Ruijven, K. (2016, October). *The effects ofentry-tests during primary-school teacher education in the Netherlands.* Retrieved from Thesis.eur.nl: https://thesis.eur.nl/pub/36746/Ruijven.pdf

Vanderbilt University. (2017A). *2017-2018 Peabody Undergraduate Handbook*. Retrieved from Vanderbilt.edu: https://peabody.vanderbilt.edu/admin-offices/oas/2017-2018_Peabody_Undergraduate_Handbook_final-8.11.2017.pdf

Vanderbilt University. (2017B). *Elementary Program*. Retrieved from Vanderbilt.edu: https://peabody.vanderbilt.edu/departments/tl/undergraduate_program/elementary_program.php

Varkey GEMS Foundation. (2018, February 10). *Global Teacher Index (Rep.)*. Retrieved from Varkeyfoundation.org: https://www.varkeyfoundation.org/teacherindex

Vieira, I. (2010). Conceito(s) de burnout: Questões atuais da pesquisa e a contribuição da clínica. *Revista Brasileira de Saúde Ocupacional*, *35*(122), 269–276. doi:10.1590/S0303-76572010000200009

Vindegaard, N., & Benros, M. (2020). COVID-19 pandemic and mental health consequences: Systematic review of the current evidence. *Brain, Behavior, and Immunity*, *89*, 531–542. doi:10.1016/j.bbi.2020.05.048 PMID:32485289

Viswesvaran, C., Sanchez, J. I., & Fisher, J. (1999). The Role of Social Support in the Process of Work Stress: A Meta-Analysis. *Journal of Vocational Behavior*, *54*(2), 314–334. doi:10.1006/jvbe.1998.1661

Walczak, J. (2021, May 27). *State Aid in American Rescue Plan Act Is 116 Times States' revenue Losses*. Retrieved from Tax Foundation: https://taxfoundation.org/state-and-local-aid-american-rescue-plan

Wallerstein, N., Minkler, M., Carter-Edwards, L., Avila, M., & Sanchez, V. (2015). Improving health through community engagement, community organizations, and community building. *Health Behaviro: Theory, Research and Practice, 5*.

Wang, K., & Zhou, X. (2017). The Nonlinear Effect of R & D Investment on Technological Innovation Performance: An Empirical Analysis Based on Micro Data. *Statistics and Information Forum, 12*, 86-93.

Wang, T. (2012). *2012 Election Lessons Learned: How Voters Stood Up Against Suppression, ID, and Intimidation*. Demos. Retrieved from https://www.demos.org/policy-briefs/2012-election-lessons-learned

Wang, C., & Zhao, H. (2020). The Impact of COVID-19 on Anxiety in Chinese University Students. *Frontiers in Psychology*, *11*, 1–8. doi:10.3389/fpsyg.2020.01168 PMID:32574244

Wang, L., & Hu, Y. (2017). Does Venture Fund Promote Innovation Performance? An Empirical Test based on Panel Data of Chinese Enterprises. *Journal of Financial Research*, *1*, 177–190.

Ward, L. F. (1893). *The psychic factors of civilization*. Ginn & Company.

Ware, S. J. (2021). Labor Grievance Arbitration's Differences. *Cumb. L. Rev., 51*(275).

Waring, S., & Giles, S. (2020). Rapid Evidence Assessment of Mental Health Outcomes of Pandemics for Health Care Workers: Implications for the Covid-19 Pandemic. *Frontiers Public Health* .

Waterman, A., Garbutt, J., Hazel, E., Dunagan, C., Levinson, F., & Gallagher, T. (2007). The emotional impact of medical errors on practicing physicians in the United States and Canada. *Joint Commission Journal on Quality and Patient Safety*, *33*(8), 467–476. doi:10.1016/S1553-7250(07)33050-X PMID:17724943

Waters, J. (2022). Denver Air Connection and Boutique Air seek Alamosa air route. *Alamosa News*. Retrieved from https://alamosanews.com/article/denver-air-connection-and-boutique-air-seek-alamosa-air-route

Weiss, L. (2004). *Therapist' s guide to self-care*. Routledge. doi:10.4324/9780203340110

Welling, A. (2016). The paradox effects of uncertainty and flexibility on investment in renewables under governmental support. *European Journal of Operational Research*, *251*(3), 1016–1028. doi:10.1016/j.ejor.2015.12.027

Wenglinsky, D. (1997). *When Money Matters: How Educational Expenditures Improve Student Performance and How They Don't*. Educational Testing Service.

Westbrook, R. B. (1991). *John Dewey and American democracy*. Cornell University Press.

Western Illinois University. (2017). *Elementary Education*. Retrieved from WIU.edu: http://www.wiu.edu/academics/majors/education_and_human_services/elementary-e ducation.php

Whaley, A. L. (1993). Self-esteem, cultural identity, and psychosocial adjustment in African American children. *The Journal of Black Psychology*, *19*(4), 406–422. doi:10.1177/00957984930194003

WHO. (2021). *Obtido de Comprehensive mental health action plan 2013-2030*. World Health Organization. https://www.who.int/teams/mental-health-andsubstance- use

Wilcox, B. L. (1981). Social support, life stress, and psychological adjustment: A test of the buffering hypothesis. *American Journal of Community Psychology*, *9*(4), 371–386. doi:10.1007/BF00918169 PMID:7282647

Wilds, M. (2016, November 2). *South Shore extension meeting draws crowd in Dyer*. Retrieved from NWITimes.com: https://www.nwitimes.com/business/local/article_00f08ae9-8de8-5b8b-ba3e-352c67082490.html

Wilensky, H. L. (1964). The Professionalization of Everyone? *American Journal of Sociology*, *70*(2), 137–158. doi:10.1086/223790

Williams, T., & Williams, K. (2010). Self-efficacy and performance in mathematics: Reciprocal determinism in 33 nations. *Journal of Educational Psychology, 102*(2), 453. Retrieved from ProQuest database (336826006).

Williams, M. T. (2019a). Microaggressions: Clarification, Evidence, and Impact. *Perspectives on Psychological Science*. Advance online publication. doi:10.1177/1745691619827499 PMID:31418642

Williams, M. T. (2019b). Psychology Cannot Afford to Ignore the Many Harms Caused by Microaggressions. *Perspectives on Psychological Science*. Advance online publication. doi:10.1177/1745691619893362 PMID:31801042

Williams, N. M. (1982). A boundary is to cross observations on Yolngu boundaries and permission. In N. M. Williams & E. S. Hunn (Eds.), *Resource Managers: North American and Australian Hunter-Gatherers*. Australian Institute of Aboriginal Studies Press.

Williamson, O. E. (1991). Comparative economic organization: The analysis of discrete structural alternatives. *Administrative Science Quarterly*, *1991*(2), 269–296. doi:10.2307/2393356

Williamson, O. E. (1996). *The Mechanisms of Governance*. Oxford University Press.

Williamson, O. E. (2008). Outsourcing: Transaction cost economics and supply chain management. *The Journal of Supply Chain Management*, *2008*(44), 5–16. doi:10.1111/j.1745-493X.2008.00051.x

Williams, R. F. (1997). *The New Jersey State Constitution: A Reference Guide*. Rutgers University Press.

Wilson, V., & Jones, J. (2018). *Working harder or finding it harder to work: Demographic trends in annual work hours show an increasingly fractured workforce*. Economic Policy Institute. https://www.epi.org/publication/trends-in-work-hours-and-labor-market-disconnection/

Wilson, N., Ravaldi, C., Scoullar, L., Vogel, P., Szabo, A., Fisher, W., & Homer, E. (2020). Caring for the carers: Ensuring the provision of quality 48 maternity care during a global pandemic. *Women and Birth; Journal of the Australian College of Midwives*, *33*(3), 205–308. PMID:32241720

Winter, G. (2004, October 6). Financial Gap Is Widening for Rich and Poor Schools. *New York Times*, p. A.23.

Wise, A. (1983). Educational Adequacy: A Concept in Search of Meaning. *Journal of Education Finance*, *8*(3), 300–316.

Wise, A. E. (1968). *Rich Schools, Poor Schools: A Promise of Equal Opportunity*. University of Chicago Press.

Wolfe, S. E., Rojek, J., Manjarrez, V. M. Jr, & Rojek, A. (2018). Why does organizational justice matter? Uncertainty management among law enforcement officers. *Journal of Criminal Justice*, *54*, 20–29. doi:10.1016/j.jcrimjus.2017.11.003

Women, I. (2020). *Girls*. The Sentencing Project.

Wonberg, C. R., Zhu, J., & Van Hooft, E. A. J. (2010). The job search grind: Perceived progress, self-reactions, and self-regulation of search effort. *Academy of Management Journal*, *53*(10), 788–807. doi:10.5465/amj.2010.52814599

Wong, K. K. (1999). *Funding Public Schools: Politics and Policies*. University Press of Kansas.

Woodland, M., Martin, J., Hill, R., & Worrell, F. (2009). The most blessed room in the city: The influence of a youth development program on three young black males. *The Journal of Negro Education*, *78*(3), 233–245.

Worden, R. E., & McLean, S. J. (2017). *Mirage of police reform: Procedural justice and police legitimacy*. doi:10.1525/luminos.30

World Bank Group. (2017). *Population, total - Netherlands (selected years, 2001 through 2016)*. Retrieved from World Bank Data: https://data.worldbank.org/indicator/SP.POP.TOTL?locations=NL

World Bank Group. (2017). *United States Population Total (Selected years, 2001 through 2016)*. Retrieved from World Bank Data: https://data.worldbank.org/indicator/SP.POP.TOTL?locations-US

World Health Organization. (2020). *Preparedness, prevention and control of COVID-19 in prisons and other places of detention: interim guidance 15 March 2020* (No. WHO/EURO: 2020-1405-41155-55954). World Health Organization. Regional Office for Europe.

World Health Organization. (2022). *Health in prisons-COVID-19. Minimum dataset: summary of data reported from May 2020 to October 2021* (No. WHO/EURO: 2022-4752-44515-63010). World Health Organization. Regional Office for Europe.

Wu, H., & Chen, J. (2018). The Innovation Effect of Enterprises' Dual Strategy of internationalization: With the Adjustment of Competition Intensity. *Studies in Science of Science*, (2), 334–341.

Wyche, J. H., & Frierson, H. T. Jr. (1990). Minorities at majority institutions. *American Association for the Advancement of Science*, *249*(4972), 989–991. doi:10.1126cience.2396103 PMID:2396103

Xin, S., Chen, Y., & Zhang, C. (2014). Review on the Application of Structural Equation Modeling. *Journal of Industrial Technological Economics*, (5), 67–71.

Yan, T. (2014). The Motivation, Ways and Approaches of Government Supporting Scientific and Technological Innovation. *Economy Forum,* (10), 151-155.

Yancy, G. (2008). *Black bodies, white gazes: The continuing significance of race*. Rowman & Littlefield Publishers.

Yin, A. (2020, July 15). *Cook County crafts formula for CARES Act funding distribution with emphasis on struggling areas, aims to right inequities among suburbs during COVID-19 pandemic*. Retrieved from chicagotribune.com: https://www.chicagotribune.com/news/breaking/ct-cook-county-cares-act-equitable-funding-formula-20200715-5aaoc6zrcng5xc6
uqj6ps7mfoy-htmlstory.html

Yin, R. (2014). *Case study research: Design and methods* (5th ed.). SAGE.

Yukl, G. (2012). Effective Leadership Behavior: What We Know and What Questions Need More Attention. *The Academy of Management Perspectives*, *26*(4), 66–85. doi:10.5465/amp.2012.0088

Yun, J., Ma, W., & Chen, L. (2012). Research on the Interaction between Openness and Network Capability on Innovation Performance. *Science Research Management*, (7), 8–15.

Zambrana, R. E., Ray, R., Espino, M. M., Castro, C., Douthirt Cohen, B., & Eliason, J. (2015). "Don't Leave Us Behind": The Importance of Mentoring for Underrepresented Minority Faculty. *American Educational Research Journal*, *52*(1), 40–72. doi:10.3102/0002831214563063

Zelek, M. E. (1989). Labor Grievance Arbitration in the United States. *U. Miami Inter-Am. Law Review*, *21*(197), 202.

Zeng, M., Ly, S., & Wu, Q. (2014). Research on the Relationship between Government Support, Trust and External Integration of Supply Chain. *Chinese Journal of Management Science*, (12), 48–55.

Zeng, P., Liu, Y., & Wu, X. (2016). The Impact of Government Support on Technological Innovation of Enterprises—From the Perspective of integration of Resource Based View and System Based View. *Economic Management*, (2), 12–26.

Zhan, Z. (2018). The Mechanism of Channel Network Embeddedness on Cooperative Innovation Performance. *Economic Survey: With the Mediating Variables of Relational Learning and Dual Ability*, 115-122.

Zhang, R., Wang, M. S., Toubiana, M., & Greenwood, R. (2020). Stigma Beyond Levels: Advancing Research on Stigmatization. *The Academy of Management Annals*, *15*(1), 188–222. doi:10.5465/annals.2019.0031

Zhang, Y., Wang, C., Pan, W., Zheng, J., Gao, J., Huang, X., Cai, S., Zhai, Y., Latour, J. M., & Zhu, C. (2020). Stress, Burnout, and Coping Strategies of Frontline Nurses During the COVID-19 Epidemic in Wuhan and Shanghai, China. *Frontiers in Psychiatry*, *11*, 1–9. doi:10.3389/fpsyt.2020.565520 PMID:33192686

Zhao, Y., Xu, G., Liu, Z., & Xie, M. (2017). Research on the Innovation Performance of Chinese Enterprises from the Perspective of Government Support. *Science Research Management*, (4), 412–418.

Zhao, Z. J., Vardhan Das, K., & Larson, K. (2012, May). Joint development as a value capture strategy for public transit finance. *Journal of Transport and Land Use*, *5*(1), 5–17. doi:10.5198/jtlu.v5i1.142

Zheng, Y., & Wang, H. (2017). Government Support for SMEs Innovation: Theoretical Basis, Policy Representation and Function Path. *Modern Economic Research*, (10), 126–133.

Zhou, X., Snoswell, C., Harding, L., Bambling, M., Edirippulige, S., Bai, X., & Smith, A. (2020). he Role of Telehealth in Reducing the Mental Health Burden form COVID-19. *Telemedicine Journal and E-Health: The Official Journal of the American Telemedicine Association, 26*(4), 377-379.

Zhu, Q., Sarkis, J., & Lai, K.-H. (2012). Examining the effects of green supply chain management practices and their mediations on performance improvements. *International Journal of Production Research*, *2012*(50), 1377–1394. doi:10.1080/00207543.2011.571937

Zhu, Z., Xu, S., Wang, H., Liu, Z., Wu, J., Li, G., & Wang, W. (2020). *COVID-19 in Wuhan: Immediate Psychological Impact on 5062 Health Workers*. MedRxiv., doi:10.1101/2020.02.20.20025338

Zilberman, A., & Ice, L. (2021). Why computer occupations are behind strong STEM employment growth in the 2019–29 decade. *Computer, 4*(5), 11-15.

Zuckerman, D., Ansell, D., & Davis, M. (2019). Rethinking the Mission of Health Systems: Improving Community Health as Anchor Institutions. In J. L. Michener, B. C. Castrucci, D. W. Bradley, E. L. Hunter, & C. W. Thomas (Eds.), *The Practical Playbook II: Building Multisector Partnerships that Work.* Oxford University Press.

About the Contributors

, **Joanne E. Howard** Ph.D., is a Clinical Assistant Professor of Public Administration, Stuart School of Business, Illinois Institute of Technology.

***

Rhonda BeLue is Professor and Associate Dean at University of Texas at San Antonio.

Oscar Bernardes holds a Ph.D. in management, since 2013. He worked as management consultant for several years, in several organizations (social, profitable, and governmental). He is Invited Professor at Polytechnic Institute of Porto (P.Porto), Portugal, where he has been lecturing courses in the following areas: entrepreneurship, innovation, marketing, and general management. His research interests include entrepreneurship, gamification, innovation, and marketing.

Cynthia E. Boyd, MD, MBA is Professor of Medicine in the Department of Internal Medicine at Rush University Medical Center. She is Senior Associate Dean for Diversity and Inclusion and Associate Dean for Admissions and Recruitment at Rush University Medical College. Dr. Boyd's passion and efforts in medical education expands over two decades. She has been successful in increasing the diversity of the medical school class for over a decade by aligning and integrating Rush's institutional mission and strategic goals for diversity into all aspects of the medical school admissions processes. Dr. Boyd was instrumental in introducing and implementing holistic review in admissions to increase the diversity of the medical school and physician workforce. Dr. Boyd also serves as Senior Vice President and Interim Chief Compliance Officer for the Rush University System for Health. In this role she provides oversight of all aspects of Rush's Corporate Compliance Program.

Roland Calia is an Associate Dean at the Illinois Tech Stuart School of Business. Dr. Calia is also Director of the Master of Public Policy and Administration and the Master of Environmental Management and Sustainability Management programs. His research interests are state and local governance and fiscal policy. He previously served as a Senior Manager in the Research and Consulting Center of the Government Finance Officers Association (GFOA).Prior to his work at GFOA, Mr. Calia served as Director of Research for The Civic Federation, a governmental research organization in Chicago, where his research focused on state and local public policy and governmental taxes and budgeting. He has served as a member of the Governmental Accounting Standards Advisory Council (GASAC), the standard setting body for governmental accounting in the U.S. and as a trustee of the Governmental Research Association (GRA).

Rukiya Curvey Johnson serves as executive director of REACH and vice president, community health equity & engagement for Rush University Medical Center, where she collaborates with internal and external stakeholders to reduce inequities caused by the social, economic and structural determinants of health. Rukiya previously served as executive director of STEM and strategic initiatives at Chicago Public Schools, where she led the development and execution of the district's K-12 STEM strategy and the design of the CPS STEM Standards for Success. As champion and architect of a strategy to increase success for underrepresented students in STEM-related fields, she also led the district's Early College STEM initiative to successfully graduate its first students with dual high school diplomas and associate degrees in information technology. Rukiya is a member of the Chicagoland Healthcare Workforce Collaborative Steering Committee, the West Side United Executive Leadership Council, the Alliance for Health Equity and the ISBE CTE advisory group. She is also a board member of the Chicago Children's Advocacy Center. With a commitment and passion for providing equitable access to high-quality education and career opportunities, Curvey-Johnson believes in the power of collective action to make a difference for our youth and the communities we serve. Rukiya earned her MBA from the University of Michigan's Ross School of Business and her undergraduate degree from the University of Virginia.

Kathryn Dominguez currently holds a Senior Manager, Deployment position in Metra's IT department. Metra is one of the largest commuter rail agencies under the Federal Railroad Administration in the US. Kathryn's experience includes project, change and supply chain management with over 30 years of experience. Kathryn has a Masters of Arts in Communication and a Masters of Science in Technology from Purdue University and completed a Masters of Policy & Public Administration from IIT May 2022. Outside of work and studies, Kathryn is the married to her loving husband, Ricardo and they have three brilliant children. Kathryn also is the Minister of her Secular Franciscan Fraternity and edits their newsletter.

Ebbin Dotson is Assistant Professor of Health Management and Policy in the School of Public Health and serves as the Director of the Health Equity Leadership Pipeline Collaborative and the Faculty Director of the University Of Michigan Summer Enrichment Program.

Sheila A. Dugan MD, PT, is Professor and Interim Chair of the Department of PM&R at Rush University Medical Center. She teaches allied health and medical students in musculoskeletal & pelvic health and health equity. She mentors research and capstone projects.. She is a co-founder of the Rush Program for Abdominal and Pelvic Health. She has published numerous book chapters and articles, and lectures nationally. Prior to medical school, she was a PT in both orthopedic and neurological rehabilitation. Her research includes Community Based physical activity interventions, chronic conditions and health inequity, pelvic floor dysfunction and midlife women's health.

Keith Elder is Provost and Executive Vice President and Professor at Mississippi College.

Kimberly Enard is Program Director of the Health Policy & Management Department at St. Louis University.

Angel Evans is Assistant Professor in Health Policy and Management at Governors State University.

Rupert Evans is Professor and former Chair of the Health Policy and Management Department at Governors State University

Helen Ezenwa is the assistant dean for External Relations and Career Management at Illinois Tech Stuart School of Business. She cochairs the University DEI Committee and is the Presidential Fellow for Equity and Belonging. She came to the Stuart School of Business in 2013 with 18 years of experience in the private sector and higher education. She is also adjunct faculty at DePaul University and Illinois Tech and serves on a number of community and health care boards.

Angela Freeman works with REACH leadership and external partners to develop tools and gather data to inform operational and strategic outcomes. She also leads and supports a wide array of projects, including informing a continuous improvement strategy for new programs and building tools that measure implementation and impact. Before joining REACH, Angela served as a project manager in the Department of Health Systems Management in Rush University's College of Health Sciences, where she holds an adjunct faculty appointment. She oversaw the Building Healthy Urban Communities initiative to improve education, employment and health outcomes on Chicago's West and South sides through strategic partnerships with the Medical Home Network and City Colleges of Chicago. Angela earned a bachelor's degree in fine arts from Purdue University and a master's of public health in community health sciences from the University of Illinois Chicago School of Public Health; she's currently a doctoral student in health sciences at Northwestern University Feinberg School of Medicine. Her research interests center on using social and spatial epidemiological methods to understand the role of structural determinants in shaping health and racial/ethnic health inequities among historically marginalized communities.

Natalia Gallegos is REACH's program manager of strategic initiatives. As such, Natalia works to expand programs, build relationships and develop tools that increase educational attainment and support a cradle-to-career pipeline to STEM and health care fields. Her REACH portfolio includes overseeing the expansion of the mentoring program and establishing an approach for evaluating the ongoing effectiveness of programs. She also supports the development of innovative ideas for high-quality implementation and execution of the REACH Strategic Plan. Before joining Rush in 2018, Natalia was the manager of community engagement at MacNeal Hospital in Berwyn, Ill., where she was responsible for leading and coordinating all public relations, community wellness and education initiatives. She also managed more than 150 hospital volunteers of diverse ages and ethnicities who contributed to community, hospital and support activities. Natalia earned a master's degree in public health from the University of Illinois at Chicago School of Public Health and a bachelor's degree in health care management from Southern Illinois University Carbondale.

Allyson Hall is Professor of Health Policy and Management at University of Alabama at Birmingham.

Sam Hensel is in-house counsel with Service Employees International Union, Local 73, which represents predominantly public sector employees throughout Illinois and in Northwest Indiana. Sam routinely practices before the National Labor Relations Board, the Illinois Labor Relations Board, and the Illinois Educational Labor Relations Board, and has brought numerous contractual and disciplinary disputes to arbitration. He also provides advice on union internal affairs, as well as trainings for union organizers and staff. He also has pursued unpaid contributions owed by employers to pension and health funds on behalf of union members and their families, and stolen wages and overtime pay for employees in federal court, and has represented and advised clients on other matters pertaining to employment law. He graduated from the John Marshall Law School in 2019, where he founded the Labor & Employment Law Student Group, competed in moot court, and published a comment in the school's Review of Intellectual Property Law before serving as an editor for the publication. Sam is admitted to practice in Illinois, Indiana, and the Federal Bar, and has served as a Chapter Editor for multiple publications on behalf of the American Bar Association. Prior to his legal career, Sam worked for five years on a variety of political campaigns across Illinois as a field organizer, regional field director, and campaign manager. He is a lifelong resident of the Chicagoland area.

Diane M. Howard, PhD., is Associate Professor and Chair, Health Systems Management, Rush University Medical Center, Chicago, IL. Prior to her academic appointment, she was a hospital, association, and insurance executive. Dr. Howard is a fellow in the American College of Healthcare Executives. She completed her Ph.D. at University of Illinois-Chicago; MPH at University of Pittsburgh, and BA at Hampton Institute.

Wrenetha Julion is the Inaugural Dean for Equity & Inclusion in the Rush University College of Nursing. In this capacity she is responsible for spearheading the strategic planning for diversity, equity, and inclusion for students, faculty, and staff. She and co-Principal Investigator Paul Florsheim are funded by the Department of Health and Human Services, Administration for Children and Families to test a Model of Father Inclusive Prenatal Care. Her career has focused on the wellbeing of fathers and families and the advancement of diversity and inclusion in the health professions.

Christopher Nolan served as the System Manager, Community Health and Benefit at Rush University System for Health as well as Instructor, Department of Health Systems Management at Rush University.

Dale Sanders is Associate Professor and Director of Healthcare Administration at Alma College.

Laurie Shanderson is Professor and Chancellor of Methodist College.

Omar Vargas-González is Professor and Head of Systems and Computing Department at Tecnologico Nacional de Mexico Campus Ciudad Guzman, professor at Telematic Engineering at Centro Universitario del Sur Universidad de Guadalajara with a master degree in Computer Systems. Has been trained in Innovation and Multidisciplinary Entrepreneurship at Arizona State University (2018) and a Generation of Ecosystems of Innovation, Entrepreneurship and Sustainability for Jalisco course by Harvard University T.H. Chan School of Health. At present conduct research on diverse fields such as Entrepreneurship, Economy, Statistics, Mathematics and Information and Computer Sciences. Has collaborated in the publication of over 15 scientific articles and conducted diverse Innovation and Technological Development projects.

José G. Vargas-Hernández is a research professor with an M.B.A.; Ph.D. Member of the National System of Researchers of Mexico and a research professor at Tecnológico Mario Molina Unidad Zapopan formerly at University Center for Economic and Managerial Sciences, University of Guadalajara. Professor Vargas-Hernández has a Ph. D. in Public Administration and a Ph.D. in Organizational Economics. He has undertaken studies in Organisational Behaviour and has a Master of Business Administration, published four books and more than 200 papers in international journals and reviews (some translated to English, French, German, Portuguese, Farsi, Chinese, etc.) and more than 300 essays in national journals and reviews. He has obtained several international Awards and recognition.

Jacqueline Wiltshire is a Visiting Associate Professor at the Fairbanks School of Public Health at Indiana University.

Index

E

F

G

H

I

J

K

L

M

N

P

R

S

T

U

W

www.ingramcontent.com/pod-product-compliance
Lightning Source LLC
LaVergne TN
LVHW080404011026
849161LV00009B/2343